Life of William Hickling Prescott
by George Ticknor

Copyright © 2019 by HardPress

Address:
HardPress
8345 NW 66TH ST #2561
MIAMI FL 33166-2626
USA
Email: info@hardpress.net

LIFE

OF

WILLIAM HICKLING PRESCOTT.

BY

GEORGE TICKNOR.

BOSTON:
TICKNOR AND FIELDS.
1864.

Entered according to Act of Congress, in the year 1863, by
GEORGE TICKNOR,
in the Clerk's Office of the District Court for the District of Massachusetts.

UNIVERSITY PRESS:
WELCH, BIGELOW, AND COMPANY,
CAMBRIDGE.

TO

WILLIAM HOWARD GARDINER

AND

WILLIAM AMORY.

We are more than once mentioned together in the last testamentary dispositions of our friend, as persons for whom he felt a true regard, and to whose affection and fidelity he, in some respects, intrusted the welfare of those who were dearest to him in life. Permit me, then, to associate your names with mine in this tribute to his memory.

GEORGE TICKNOR

PREFATORY NOTICE.

THE following Memoir has been written in part payment of a debt which has been accumulating for above half a century. But I think it right to add, that my friend counted upon me, in case I should survive him, to prepare such a slight sketch of his literary life as he supposed might be expected, — that, since his death, his family, and I believe the public, have desired a biographical account of him ampler than his own modesty had deemed appropriate, — and that the Massachusetts Historical Society, who early did me the honor of directing me to prepare a notice of their lamented associate such as it is customary to insert in their official proceedings, have been content to accept the present Memoir as a substitute. It is, therefore, on all accounts, offered to the public as a tribute to his memory, the preparation of which I should not have felt myself at liberty to refuse even if I had been less willing to undertake it.

But if, after all, this Memoir should fail to set the author of the "Ferdinand and Isabella" before those who had not the happiness to know him personally, as a man whose life for more than forty years was one of almost constant struggle, — of an almost constant sacrifice of impulse to duty, of the present to the future, — it will have failed to teach its true lesson, or to present my friend to others as he stood before the very few who knew him as he was.

PARK STREET, BOSTON, November, 1863.

CONTENTS.

CHAPTER I.

CHAPTER II.

CHAPTER III.

CHAPTER IV.

CHAPTER V.

CHAPTER VI.

CHAPTER VII.

CHAPTER VIII.

CHAPTER IX.

CHAPTER XV.

CHAPTER XVI.

CHAPTER XVII.

CHAPTER XVIII.

CHAPTER XIX.

CHAPTER XX.

CHAPTER XXI.

CHAPTER XXII.

CHAPTER XXIII.

CHAPTER XXIV.

CHAPTER XXV.

CHAPTER XXVI.

CHAPTER XXVII.

CHAPTER XXVIII.

CHAPTER XXIX.

APPENDIX.

THE LIFE

OF

WILLIAM HICKLING PRESCOTT.

CHAPTER I.

1796 – 1811.

BIRTH AND PARENTAGE. — EARLY TRAINING. — REMOVAL TO BOSTON. —
DR. GARDINER'S SCHOOL. — LIFE AT HOME. — LOVE OF BOOKS. — DIF-
FICULTY OF OBTAINING THEM. — BOSTON ATHENÆUM. — WILLIAM S.
SHAW. — FAVORITE BOOKS. — STUDIES. — EARLY FRIENDSHIP. — AMUSE-
MENTS. — ENTERS COLLEGE.

WILLIAM HICKLING PRESCOTT was born in
Salem, New England, on the fourth day of May,
seventeen hundred and ninety-six.[1]

His father, then thirty-four years old, — a person of remarkable manly beauty, and great dignity and gentleness of character, — was already in the flush of his early success at the
bar, where he subsequently rose to much eminence and honor.
His mother, five years younger, was a woman of great energy,
who seemed to have been born to do good, and who had from
her youth those unfailing spirits which belong to the original
temperament of the very few who have the happiness to possess them, and which, in her case, were controlled by a good
sense and by religious convictions, that made her presence like
a benediction in the scenes of sorrow and suffering, which,
during her long life, it was her chosen vocation to frequent.
They had been married between two and three years when
William was born to them, inheriting not a few of the prominent characteristics of each. He was their second child; the
first, also a son, having died in very early infancy.

[1] For an account of the Prescott Family, see Appendix (A).

1   A

The family of Mr. and Mrs. Prescott was always a happy one, — respected and loved by those who came within the reach of its influence. Their pleasant, hospitable house in Salem is no longer standing; but the spot it occupied is well remembered, and is pointed out to strangers with pride, as the one where the future historian was born. Its site is now that of "Plummer Hall"; — a building erected for literary and scientific purposes, from funds bequeathed by the lady whose name it bears, and who was long a friend of the Prescott family.[*]

William's earliest education was naturally in the hands of his affectionate and active mother, his great obligations to whom he always loved to acknowledge, and from whom, with slight exceptions, it was his happiness never to be separated so long as they both lived. He felt, to the last, that her influence upon him had been one of the chief blessings of his life. On the afternoon of her death he spoke of it to me, as a guiding impulse for which he could not be too grateful.

But, like the children of most of the persons who constituted the society in Salem to which his family belonged, he was sent to a school for the very young, kept by Miss Mehitable Higginson, a true gentlewoman, descended from the venerable Francis Higginson, who emigrated to Salem in 1629, when there were only seven houses on the spot now covered by the whole city, and who, from his scholarship, eloquence, and piety, has sometimes been called the founder of the churches of New England. Miss Higginson understood, with an instinct for which experience affords no sufficient substitute, what belongs to childhood, and how best to direct and mould its opening faculties. It was her wont to call herself, not the school *mistress*, but the school *mother*, of her little flock; and a system of discipline which might be summed up in such a phrase could hardly fail of being effectual for good. Certainly it succeeded to a remark-

---

[*] Only a year before his death, the historian was invited to be present at the dedication of "Plummer Hall." He was not able to attend; but, in reply to the invitation, he said: "I need not assure you that I take a sincere interest in the ceremonies of the day, and I have a particular interest in the spot which is to be covered by the new edifice, from its having been that on which I first saw the light. It is a pleasant thought to me, that, through the enlightened liberality of my deceased friend, Miss Plummer, it is now to be consecrated to so noble a purpose."

able degree with her many pupils, during the half-century in which she devoted herself with truth and love to her calling. Of her more favored children, William was one.

From the tender and faithful hands of Miss Higginson, he passed to the school of Mr. Jacob Newman Knapp, long known in Salem as "Master Knapp," — a person who, as the best teacher to be obtained, had been procured by Mr. Prescott and a few of his more intimate friends, all of whom were anxious, as he was, to spare neither pains nor expense in the education of their children. Under Mr. Knapp's care William was placed at New-Year, 1803, when he was less than seven years old; and he continued there until the midsummer of 1808, when his father removed to Boston.

The recollections of him during these four or five years are distinct in the minds of his teacher, who still survives (1862) at a venerable old age, and of a few schoolmates, now no longer young. He was a bright, merry boy, with an inquisitive mind, quick perceptions, and a ready, retentive memory. His lessons were generally well learned; but he loved play better than books, and was too busy with other thoughts than those that belonged to the school-room to become one of Master Knapp's best pupils. He was, though large for his years, not very vigorous in his person. He never fancied rude or athletic sports, but amused himself with such boys of his own age as preferred games requiring no great physical strength; or else he made himself happy at home with such light reading as is most attractive to all children, and especially to those whose opening tastes and tendencies are quiet, if not intellectual. In the latter part of his life he used to say, that he recollected no period of his childhood when he did not love books; adding, that often, when he was a very little boy, he was so excited by stories appealing strongly to his imagination, that, when his mother left the room, he used to take hold of her gown, and follow her as she moved about the house, rather than be left alone. But in school he did not love work, and made no remarkable progress in his studies.

Neither was he so universally liked by the boys with whom he was associated in Salem, as he was afterwards by the boys in other schools. He had indeed his favorites, to whom he

was much attached and who were much attached to him, and
he never faltered in his kindness to them subsequently, however humble or unfortunate their condition became; but at
home he had been encouraged to speak his mind with a boldness that was sometimes rude; partly from parental indulgence, and partly as a means of detecting easily any tendencies
in his character that his conscientious father might think it
needful to restrain. The consequence was, that a similar habit
of very free speaking at school, joined to his great natural
vivacity and excessive animal spirits, made him more confident
in the expression of his opinions and feelings than was agreeable, and prevented him from becoming a favorite with a portion of his schoolmates. It laid, however, I doubt not, the
foundation for that attractive simplicity and openness which
constituted prominent traits in his character through life.

His conscience was sensitive and tender from the first, and
never ceased to be so. A sermon to children produced a striking effect upon him when he was still a child. It was a very
simple, direct one, by Dr. Channing; and William's mother
told him to read it to her one evening when his conduct had
required some slight censure, and she thought this the best
way to administer it. He obeyed her reluctantly. But soon
his lips began to quiver, and his voice to choke. He stopped,
and with tears said, "Mother, if I am ever a bad boy again,
won't you set me to reading that sermon?"

His temperament was very gay, like his mother's, and his
eager and sometimes turbulent spirits led him into faults of
conduct oftener, perhaps, than anything else. Like most school-
boys, he was fond of practical jokes, and ventured them, not
only in a spirit of idle mischief, but even rudely. Once he
badly frightened a servant-girl in the family, by springing unexpectedly upon her from behind a door. But his father, busy
and anxious as he was with the interests of others, and occupying himself less with the material concerns and affairs of his
household than almost any person I ever knew, had yet an eye
of unceasing vigilance for whatever related to the training of
his children, and did not suffer even a fault so slight to pass
without rebuke. After this, although William was always a
boy full of life and mischief, he gave no more trouble by such
rudeness at home.

No doubt, therefore, his early education, and the circumstances most nearly connected with it, were, on the whole, favorable to the formation of a character suited to the position in the world that he was likely to occupy; — a character, I mean, that would not easily yield to the temptations of prosperity, nor be easily broken down by adverse fortune, if such fortune should come upon it. It was, in fact, a condition of things that directly tended to develop those manly qualities which in our New-England society have always most surely contributed to progress and success.

Nor was there anything in the circle with which his family was most connected to counteract these influences. Life in those days was a very simple thing in Salem, compared with what it is now. It was the period when Mr. Gray and Mr. Peabody, the Pickmans and the Derbys, were too busy with their widely extended commerce to think often of anything else; when Mr. Justice Putnam was a young lawyer struggling up to eminence; when Mr. Story, afterwards the distinguished jurist and judge, was only beginning to be heard of; and when the mathematical genius of Dr. Bowditch, and the classical studies of Mr. Pickering, which were destined later to have so wide an effect on our community, were hardly known beyond the limits of their personal acquaintance.

In those active, earnest days, the modest luxury of hackney-coaches and hired waiters had not come to be deemed needful in Salem, even among those who were already prosperous and rich. When, therefore, Mrs. Prescott had invited friends to dine, — a form of social intercourse which she and her husband always liked, and which they practised more freely than most persons then did, — if the weather proved unfavorable, she sent her own chaise to bring her lady guests to her house, and carried them safely home in the same way when the hospitable evening was ended. Or, if the company were larger than her usual arrangements would permit to be well served, she borrowed the servants of her friends, and lent her own in return. But the days of such unpretending simplicity are gone by, and a tasteful luxury has naturally and gracefully taken its place. They were days, however, on which my friend always looked back with satisfaction, and I doubt not, nor did he doubt, that it was well for him that his character received something of its early direction under their influence.　He was always grateful that his first years were passed neither in a luxurious home nor in a luxurious state of society.[*]

Mr. Prescott the elder removed with his family to Boston in the summer of 1808, and established himself in a house on Tremont Street.　But although he had come to a larger town, and one where those of his own condition indulged in somewhat more free habits of expense, the manner of life that he preferred and followed in his new home was not different from the one to which he had been accustomed in Salem.　It was a life of cordial, open hospitality, but without show or pretension of any sort.　And so it continued to the last.

The promising son was sent in the early autumn to the best classical school then known in New England; for his father, bred at Dummer Academy by "Master Moody," who in his time was without an equal among us as a teacher of Latin and Greek, always valued such training more than any other. And it was fortunate for William that he did so; for his early classical discipline was undoubtedly a chief element in his subsequent success.

The school to which he was sent — if school it could properly be called — was one kept with few of the attributes of such an institution, but in its true spirit, by the Rev. Dr. Gardiner,[4] Rector of Trinity Church, Boston.　Dr. Gardiner was

[*] For this sketch of society as it existed in Salem at the end of the last century I am indebted to the venerable Mrs. Putnam, widow of Mr. Justice Putnam, whose family, early connected with that of the elder Mr. Prescott by bonds of friendship and affection, has, in the third generation, been yet more intimately and happily united to it by the marriage of the oldest son of the historian with a granddaughter of the jurist.

[4] Dr. Gardiner had earlier kept a regular school in Boston, with no small success; but, at the time referred to, he received in his own library, with little form, about a dozen youths, — some who were to be prepared for college, and some who, having been already graduated, sought, by his assistance, to increase their knowledge of the Greek and Latin classics.　It was excellent, direct, personal teaching; — the more effective because the number of pupils was so small.　It was, too, of a sort peculiarly adapted to make an impression on a mind and temperament like young Prescott's.　Indeed, it became the foundation of an attachment between him and his instructor, which was severed only by death, and of which a touching proof was afforded during the last, long-protracted illness of Dr. Gardiner, who, as his infirmities increased, directed his servant to admit nobody, beyond the limits of his

a good scholar, bred in England under Dr. Parr, who, some years afterwards, at Hatton, spoke of him to me with much regard and respect. But, besides his scholarship, Dr. Gardiner was a generous, warm-hearted man, who took a sincere interest in his pupils, and sympathized with them in their pursuits to a degree which, however desirable, is very rare. A great deal of his teaching was oral; some of it, no doubt, traditional, and brought from his English school; all of it was excellent. For, although recitations of careful exactness were required, and punishments not slight inflicted for negligence and breaches of discipline, still much knowledge was communicated by an easy conversational commentary, the best part of which could not readily have been found in books, while the whole of it gave a life and interest to the lessons that could have been given by nothing else.

It was in this school, as soon as he became a member of it, that I first knew William, as a bright boy a little more than twelve years old. I had then been under Dr. Gardiner's instruction some months, not as a regular member of any class, but at private hours, with one or two others, to obtain a knowledge of the higher Greek and Latin classics, not elsewhere to be had among us. Very soon the young stranger was brought by his rapid advancement to recite with us, and before long we two were left to pursue a part of our studies quite by ourselves. From this time, of course, I knew him well, and, becoming acquainted in his father's family, saw him not only daily at school, but often at home. It was a most agreeable, cheerful house, where the manners were so frank and sincere, that the son's position in it was easily understood. He was evidently loved — much loved — of all; his mother showing her fondness without an attempt at disguise, — his father not without

family connections, except Mr. Prescott. It is needless to add, that, after this, his old pupil was almost daily at his door. Nor did he ever afterwards forget his early kind teacher. Dr. Gardiner died in 1830, in England, where he had gone with the hope of recovery; and on receiving the intelligence of his death, Mr. Prescott published, in one of our newspapers, an interesting obituary of him. Subsequently, too, in 1848, he wrote to Dr. Sprague, in Albany, an affectionate letter (to be found in that gentleman's "Annals of the American Pulpit," Vol. V. p. 365, 1859) on Dr. Gardiner's character, and in the very last year of his life he was occupied with fresh interest about its publication.

anxiety concerning his son's spirits and the peculiar temptations of his age and position. Probably he was too much indulged. Certainly, in his fine, open nature there were great inducements to this parental infirmity; and a spirit of boyish mischief in his relations with those of his own age, and a certain degree of presumption in his manners toward those who were older, were not wanting to justify the suspicion. That he was much trusted to himself there was no doubt.

But he loved books of the lighter sort, and was kept by his taste for them from many irregular indulgences. Books, however, were by no means so accessible in those days as they are now. Few, comparatively, were published in the United States, and, as it was the dreary period of the commercial restrictions that preceded the war of 1812 with England, still fewer were imported. Even good school-books were not easily obtained. A copy of Euripides in the original could not be bought at any bookseller's shop in New England, and was with difficulty borrowed. A German instructor, or means for learning the German language, were not to be had either in Boston or Cambridge. The best publications that appeared in Great Britain came to us slowly, and were seldom reprinted. New books from the Continent hardly reached us at all. Men felt poor and anxious in those dark days, and literary indulgences, which have now become almost as necessary to us as our daily food, were luxuries enjoyed by few.

There was, however, a respectable, but very miscellaneous collection of books just beginning to be made by the proprietors of the Boston Athenæum; an institution imitated chiefly from the Athenæum of Liverpool, and established in an unpretending building not far from the house of the Prescott family in Tremont Street. Its real founder was Mr. William S. Shaw, who, by a sort of common consent, exercised over it a control all but unlimited, acting for many years gratuitously as its librarian. He was a near connection of the two Presidents Adams, the first of whom he had served as private secretary during his administration of the government; and in consequence of this relationship, when Mr. John Quincy Adams was sent as Minister of the United States to Russia, he deposited his library, consisting of eight or ten thousand volumes, in the Athenæum, and thus materially increased its resources during his absence abroad. The young sons of its proprietors had then, by the rules of the institution, no real right to frequent its rooms; but Mr. Shaw, with all his passion for books, and his anxiety to keep safely and strictly those instrusted to him, was a kind-hearted man, who loved bright boys, and often gave them privileges in his Athenæum to which they had no regular claim. William was one of those who were most favored, and who most gladly availed themselves of the opportunity which was thus given them. He resorted to the Athenæum, and to the part of it containing Mr. Adams's library, as few boys cared to do, and spent many of his play-hours there in a sort of idle reading, which probably did little to nourish his mind, but which, as he afterwards loved to acknowledge, had a decided influence in forming his literary tendencies and tastes.[5]

Of course such reading was not very select. He chiefly fancied extravagant romances and books of wild adventure. How completely he was carried away by the "Amadis de Gaula" in Southey's translation he recorded long afterwards, when he looked back upon his boyish admiration, not only with surprise, but with a natural regret that all such feelings belonged to the remote past. The age of chivalry, he said sadly, was gone by for him.[6]

But, whatever may have been his general reading at this early period, he certainly did not, in the years immediately preceding his college life, affect careful study, or serious intellectual cultivation of any kind. His lessons he learned easily, but he made a characteristic distinction between such as were indispensable for his admission to the University, and such as were prescribed merely to increase his classical knowledge and accomplishments. He was always careful to learn the first well, but equally careful to do no more, or at least not to seem willing to do it, lest yet further claims should be made upon him. I remember well his cheerful and happy recitations of the "Œdipus Tyrannus"; but he was very fretful at being required to read the more difficult "Prometheus Vinctus" of

[5] Letter of W. H. Gardiner, Esq. to T. G Cary, Esq., MS.
[6] North American Review, January, 1850.

1 *

Æschylus, because it was not a part of the course of study which all must pass through. Horace, too, of which we read some parts together, interested and excited him beyond his years, but Juvenal he disliked, and Persius he could not be made to read at all. He was, in short, neither more nor less than a thoroughly natural, bright boy, who loved play better than work, but who could work well under sufficient inducements and penalties.

During the whole of his school days in Boston, although he was a general favorite among the boys, his friend and *fidus Achates* was a son of his teacher, Dr. Gardiner, of just about his own age ; and, if not naturally of a more staid and sober character, kept by a wise parental discipline under more restraint. It was a happy intimacy, and one that was never broken or disturbed. Their paths in life diverged, indeed, somewhat later, and they necessarily saw each other less as they became engrossed by pursuits so different ; — the one as a severe, retired student ; the other as an active, eminent lawyer, much too busy with the affairs of others to be seen often out of his own office and family. But their attachment always rested on the old foundation, and the friend of his boyhood became in time Mr. Prescott's chief confidential adviser in his worldly affairs, and was left at last the sole executor of his considerable estate.

In the first few years of their acquaintance they were constantly together. Dr. Gardiner gave instruction only in Greek, Latin, and English. The two boys, therefore, took private lessons, as they were called, of other teachers in arithmetic and in writing ; but made small progress in either. They played, too, with French, Italian, and Spanish, but accomplished little ; for they cared nothing about these studies, which they accounted superfluous, and which they pursued only to please their friends. They managed, however, always to have the same instructors, and so were hardly separated at all. They learnt, indeed, the slight and easy lessons set them, but were careful to do no more, and so made no real progress.

Much of their free time they gave to amusements not altogether idle, but certainly not tending very directly to intellectual culture. Some of them were such as might have been readily expected from their age. Thus, after frequenting a circus, they imitated what they had seen, until their performances were brought to a disastrous conclusion by cruelly scorching a favorite family cat that was compelled to play a part in them. At another time they fired pistols till they disturbed the quiet neighborhood, and came near killing a horse in the Prescott stable. This was all natural enough, because it was boyish, though it was a little more adventurous, perhaps, than boys' sports commonly are. Of the same sort, too, was a good deal of mischief in which they indulged themselves, with little harm to anybody, in the streets as they went to their school exercises, especially in the evening, and then came home again, looking all the graver for their frolics. But two of their amusements were characteristic and peculiar, and were, perhaps, not without influence on the lives of each of them, and especially on the life of the historian.

They devised games of battles of all sorts, such as they had found in their school-books, among the Greeks and Romans, or such as filled the newspapers of the time during the contest between the English and the French in the Spanish Peninsula; carrying them out by an apparatus more than commonly ingenious for boys of their age. At first, it was merely bits of paper, arranged so as to indicate the different arms and commanders of the different squadrons; which were then thrown into heaps, and cut up at random with shears as ruthless as those of the Fates; quite severing many of the imaginary combatants so as to leave no hope of life, and curtailing others of their fair proportions in a way to indicate wounds more or less dangerous. But this did not last long. Soon they came to more personal and soldier-like encounters; dressing themselves up in portions of old armor which they found among the curiosities of the Athenæum, and which, I fear, they had little right to use as they did, albeit their value for any purpose was small indeed. What was peculiar about these amusements was, that there was always an idea of a contest in them, — generally of a battle, — whether in the plains of Latium with Æneas, or on Bunker Hill under William's grandfather, or in the fanciful combats of knights-errant in the " Amadis de Gaula"; and Prescott apparently cared more about them on this account than on any other.

The other especial amusement of the two friends was that of alternately telling stories invented as they went along. It was oftener their street-talk than anything else ; and, if the thread of the fiction in hand were broken off, by arriving at school or in any other way, they resumed it as soon as the interruption ceased, and so continued until the whole was finished ; each improvising a complete series of adventures for the entertainment of the other and of nobody else. Prescott's inventions were generally of the wildest ; for his imagination was lively, and his head was full of the romances that prevailed in our circulating libraries before Scott's time. But they both enjoyed this exercise of their faculties heartily, and each thought the other's stories admirable. The historian always remembered these favorite amusements of his boyish days with satisfaction ; and, only two or three years before his death, when he had one of his grandchildren on his knee, and was gratifying the boy's demand for a fairy tale, he cried out, as Mr. Gardiner entered the room : " Ah, there 's the man that could tell you stories. You know, William," he continued, addressing his friend, " I never had any inventive faculty in my life ; all I have done in the way of story-telling, in my later years, has been by diligent hard work." Such, near the close of his life, was his modest estimate of his own brilliant powers and performances.

How much these amusements may have influenced the character of the narrator of the Conquest of Mexico, it is not possible to determine. Probably not much. But one thing is certain. They were not amusements common with boys of his age ; and in his subsequent career his power of describing battles, and his power of relating a succession of adventures, are among his most remarkable attributes.[7]

But his boyish days were now over. In August, 1811, he was admitted to the Sophomore Class in Harvard College, having passed his examination with credit. The next day he wrote to his father, then attending the Supreme Court at Port-

---

[7] For the facts in this account of the school-boy days of Mr. Prescott, I am partly indebted, as I am for much else in this memoir, — especially what relates to his college career, — to Mr. William Howard Gardiner, the early friend referred to in the text.

land, in Maine, the following letter, characteristic of the easy relations which subsisted between them, but which, easy as they were, did not prevent the son, through his whole life, from looking on his admirable father with a sincere veneration.

TO THE HON. WILLIAM PRESCOTT.

BOSTON, Aug. 28, [1811].

DEAR FATHER,

I now write you a few lines to inform you of my fate. Yesterday at eight o'clock I was ordered to the President's, and there, together with a Carolinian, Middleton,[8] was examined for Sophomore. When we were first ushered into their presence, they looked like so many judges of the Inquisition. We were ordered down into the parlor, almost frightened out of our wits, to be examined by each separately; but we soon found them quite a pleasant sort of chaps. The President sent us down a good dish of pears, and treated us very much like gentlemen.[9] It was not ended in the morning; but we returned in the afternoon, when Professor Ware examined us in *Grotius de Veritate*.[10] We found him very good-natured, for I happened to ask him a question in theology, which made him laugh so that he was obliged to cover his face with his hands. At half past three our fate was decided, and we were declared 'Sophomores of Harvard University.'

As you would like to know how I appeared, I will give you the conversation, *verbatim*, with Mr. Frisbie, when I went to see him after the examination. I asked him, "Did I appear well in my examination?" Answer. "Yes." Question. "Did I appear *very* well, Sir?" Answer. "Why are you so particular, young man? Yes, you did yourself a great deal of credit."[11]

---

[8] This was, of course, his first knowledge of Mr. Arthur Middleton, with whom, as a classmate, he was afterwards much connected, and who, when he was Secretary of Legation and *Chargé d'Affaires* of the United States at Madrid, rendered his early friend important literary services, as we shall see when we reach that period of Mr. Prescott's life. Mr. Middleton died in 1853.

[9] President Kirkland, who had only a few months earlier become the head of the University, will always be remembered by those who knew him, not only for the richness and originality of his mind and for his great perspicacity, but for the kindliness of his nature. The days, however, in which a dish of pears followed an examination, were, I think, very few even in his time, — connected with no traditions of the past, and not suited to the state of discipline since. It was, I suspect, only a compliment to William's family, who had been parishioners of Dr. Kirkland, when he was a clergyman in Boston.

[10] Dr. Henry Ware was Hollis Professor of Divinity.

[11] Before this examination, William had, for a short time, been under the private and especial instruction of Mr. Frisbie, who was then a Tutor in Harvard College, and subsequently one of its favorite Professors, — too early taken away by death, in 1822.

I feel to-day twenty pounds lighter than I did yesterday. I shall dine at Mr. Gardiner's. Mr. and Mrs. Gardiner both say that on me depends William's going to college or not. If I behave well, he will go; if not, that he certainly shall not go. Mr. W. P. Mason has asked me to dine with him on Commencement Day, as he gives a dinner. I believe I shall go. As I had but little time, I thought it best to tell a long story, and write it badly, rather than a short one written well. I have been to see Mr. H—— this morning; — no news. Remember me to your fellow-travellers, C., & M., &c., &c. Love to mother, whose affectionate son I remain,

WM. HICKLING PRESCOTT.

CHAPTER II.

1811 — 1815.

COLLEGE LIFE. — GOOD RESOLUTIONS. — INJURY TO HIS SIGHT. — IMMEDIATE EFFECTS. — STATE OF HIS EYE. — RELATIONS WITH THE PERSON WHO INFLICTED THE INJURY. — STUDIES SUBSEQUENT TO THE INJURY. — MATHEMATICS. — LATIN AND GREEK. — PHI BETA KAPPA SOCIETY. — GRADUATED. — STUDIES. — SEVERE INFLAMMATION OF THE EYE. — HIS CHARACTER UNDER TRIAL. — ANXIETY ABOUT HIS HEALTH. — IS TO VISIT EUROPE.

AT the time William thus gayly entered on his collegiate career, he had, thanks to the excellent training he had received from Dr. Gardiner, a good taste formed and forming in English literature, and he probably knew more of Latin and Greek — not of Latin and Greek literature, but of the languages of Greece and Rome — than most of those who entered college with him knew when they were graduated. But, on the other hand, he had no liking for mathematics, and never acquired any; nor did he ever like metaphysical discussions and speculations. His position in his class was, of course, determined by these circumstances, and he was willing that it should be. But he did not like absolutely to fail of a respectable rank. It would not have been becoming the character of a cultivated gentleman, to which at that time he more earnestly aspired than to any other; nor would it have satisfied the just expectations of his family, which always had much influence with him. It was difficult for him, however, to make the efforts and the sacrifices indispensable to give him the position of a real scholar. He adopted, indeed, rules for the hours, and even the minutes, that he would devote to each particular study; but he was so careful never to exceed them, that it was plain his heart was not in the matter, and that he could not reasonably hope to succeed by such enforced and mechanical arrangements. Still, he had already a strong will concealed under a gay and light-hearted exterior. This saved him from many dangers.

He was always able to stop short of what he deemed flagrant excesses, and to keep within the limits, though rather loose ones, which he had prescribed to himself. His standard for the character of a gentleman varied, no doubt, at this period, and sometimes was not so high on the score of morals as it should have been; but he always acted up to it, and never passed the world's line of honor, or exposed himself to academical censures by passing the less flexible line drawn by college rules. He was, however, willing to run very near to both of them.

Among the modes he adopted at this time to regulate his conduct, was one which had much more influence with him later, than it had at first. It was that of making good resolutions; — a practice in which he persevered through life to an extraordinary extent, not always heeding whether he kept them with great exactness, but sure to repeat them as often as they were broken, until, at last, some of them took effect, and his ultimate purpose was, in part at least, accomplished. He pardoned himself, I suppose, too easily for his manifold neglects and breaches of the compacts he had thus made with his conscience; but there was repentance at the bottom of all, and his character was strengthened by the practice. The early part of his college career, however, when for the first time he left the too gentle restraints of his father's house, was less affected by this system of self-control, and was the most dangerous period of his life. Upon portions of it he afterwards looked back with regret.

"It was about this time,"—says Mr. Gardiner, in a very interesting paper concerning his acquaintance with Mr. Prescott, which he has been good enough to place at my disposition, — "it was about this time, that is, pretty early in his college life, when the first excitements of perfect liberty of action were a little abated, that he began to form good resolutions, — to form them, not to keep them. This was, so far as I remember, the feeble beginning of a process of frequent self-examination and moral self-control, which he afterwards cultivated and practised to a degree beyond all example that has come under my observation in cases of like constitutional tendency. It was, I conceive, the truly great point of his moral character, and the chief foundation of all he accomplished in after life as a literary man; a point which lay always concealed to transient observers under lightness and gayety of manner.

"This habit of forming distinct resolutions about all sorts of things, sometimes important, but often in themselves the merest trifles in the world, grew up rapidly to an extent that became rather ludicrous; especially as it was accompanied by another habit, that of thinking aloud, and, concealing nothing about himself, which led him to announce to the first friend he met his latest new resolution. The practice, I apprehend, must have reached its acme about the time when he informed me one day that he had just made a new resolution, which was, — since he found he could not keep those which he had made before, — that he would never make another resolution as long as he lived. It is needless to say that this was kept but a very short time.

"These resolutions, during college days, related often to the number of hours, nay, the number of minutes, per day to be appropriated to each particular exercise or study; the number of recitations and public prayers per week that he would not fail to attend; the number of times per week that he would not exceed in attending balls, theatrical entertainments in Boston, &c., &c. What was most observable in this sort of accounts that he used to keep with himself was, that the errors were all on one side. Casual temptations easily led him, at this time of life, to break through the severer restrictions of his rule, but it was matter of high conscience with him never to curtail the full quantity of indulgences which it allowed. He would be sure not to run one minute *over*, however he might sometimes fall *short* of the full time for learning a particular lesson, which he used to con over with his watch before him, lest by any inadvertence he might cheat himself into too much study.

"On the same principle, he was careful never to attend any *greater* number of college exercises, nor any *less* number of evening diversions in Boston, than he had bargained for with himself. Then, as he found out by experience the particular circumstances which served as good excuses for infractions of his rule, he would begin to complicate his accounts with himself by introducing sets of fixed exceptions, stringing on amendment, as it were, after amendment to the general law, until it became extremely difficult for himself to tell what his rule actually was in its application to the new cases which arose; and, at last, he would take the whole subject, so to speak, into a new draft, embodying it in a bran-new resolution. And what is particularly curious is, that all the casuistry attending this process was sure to be published, as it went along, to all his intimates.

"The manner in which he used to compound with his conscience in such matters is well illustrated by an anecdote, which properly belongs to a little later period, but which may well enough be inserted here. It is one which I was lately put in mind of by Mr. J. C. Gray, but which I had heard that gentleman tell long ago in Prescott's presence, who readily admitted it to be substantially true. The incident referred to occurred at the time he and Mr. Gray were travelling together in Europe. An oculist, or physician, whom he had consulted at Paris, had advised him, among other things, to live less freely, and when pushed by his patient, as was his wont, to fix a very precise limit to the quantity of wine he might take, his adviser told him that he ought never to exceed two glasses a day. This rule he forthwith announced his resolution to adhere to scrupulously. And he did. But his manner of observing it was peculiar. At every new house of entertainment they reached in their travels, one of the first things Prescott did was to require the waiter to show him specimens of all the wine-glasses the house afforded. He would then pick out from among

B

them the largest; and this, though it might contain two or three times the quantity of a common wine-glass, he would have set by his plate as his measure at dinner to observe the rule in."

But just at the period of his college history to which Mr. Gardiner chiefly refers, or a very little later, the painful accident befell him which, in its consequences, changed the whole aspect of the world to him, and tended, more than any single event in his life, to make him what he at last became. I refer, of course, to the accident which so fatally impaired his sight. It occurred in the Commons Hall, one day after dinner, in his Junior year. On this occasion there was some rude frolicking among the undergraduates, such as was not very rare when the college officers had left the tables, as they frequently did, a few minutes before the room was emptied. There was not, however, in this particular instance, any considerable disorder, and Prescott had no share in what there was. But when he was passing out of the door of the Hall, his attention was attracted by the disturbance going on behind him. He turned his head quickly to see what it was, and at the same instant received a blow from a large, hard piece of bread, thrown undoubtedly at random, and in mere thoughtlessness and gayety. It struck the *open* eye; — a rare occurrence in the case of that vigilant organ, which, on the approach of the slightest danger, is almost always protected by an instant and instinctive closing of the lids. But here there was no notice, — no warning. The missile, which must have been thrown with great force, struck the very disk of the eye itself. It was the left eye. He fell, — and was immediately brought to his father's house in town, where, in the course of two or three hours from the occurrence of the accident, he was in the hands of Dr. James Jackson, the kind friend, as well as the wise medical adviser, of his father's family.[1]

The first effects of the blow were remarkable. They were, in fact, such as commonly attend a concussion of the brain.

---

[1] There is a graceful tribute to Dr. Jackson in Prescott's Memoir of Mr. John Pickering, where, noticing the intimacy of these two distinguished men, he says, that in London Mr. Pickering was much with Dr. Jackson, who was then "acquiring the rudiments of the profession which he was to pursue through a long series of years with so much honor to himself and such widely extended benefit to the community." Collections of the Massachusetts Historical Society, Third Series, Vol. X. p. 208.

The strength of the patient was instantly and completely prostrated. Sickness at the stomach followed. His pulse was feeble. His face became pale and shrunken, and the whole tone of his system was reduced so low, that he could not sit up in bed. But his mind was calm and clear, and he was able to give a distinct account of the accident that had befallen him, and of what had preceded and followed it.

Under such circumstances no active treatment was deemed advisable. Quiet was strictly prescribed. Whatever could tend to the least excitement, physical or intellectual, was forbidden. And then nature was left to herself. This, no doubt, was the wisest course. At any rate, the system, which had at first yielded so alarmingly to the shock, gradually recovered its tone, and in a few weeks he returned to Cambridge, and pursued his studies as if nothing very serious had happened ; — a little more cautiously, perhaps, in some respects, but probably with no diminution of such very moderate diligence as he had previously practised.[*] But the eye that had been struck was gone. No external mark, either then or afterwards, indicated the injury that had been inflicted ; and, although a glimmering light was still perceptible through the ruined organ, there was none that could be made useful for any of the practical purposes of life. On a careful examination, such as I once made, with magnifying lenses, at his request, under the direction of a distinguished oculist, a difference could indeed be detected between the injured eye and the other, and sometimes, as I sat with him, I have thought that it seemed more dim; but to common observation, in society or in the streets, as in the well-known case of the author of the " Paradise Lost," no change was perceptible. It was, in fact, a case of obscure, deep paralysis of the retina, and as such was beyond the reach of the healing art from the moment the blow was given.

One circumstance, however, in relation to the calamity that thus fell on him in the freshness of his youth, should not be

[*] This account of the original injury to Mr. Prescott's eye, and the notices of his subsequent illnesses and death, in this Memoir, are abridged from an interesting and important medical letter, which Dr. Jackson was good enough to address to me in June, 1859, and which may be found entire in a little volume entitled, "Another Letter to a Young Physician," (Boston, 1861,) pp. 130 – 156.

overlooked, because it shows, even at this early period, the development of strong traits in his character, such as marked his subsequent life. I refer to the fact that he rarely mentioned the name of the young man who had thus inflicted on him an irreparable injury, and that he never mentioned it in a way which could have given pain either to him or to those nearest to him. Indeed, he so often spoke to me of the whole affair as a mere chance-medley, for which nobody could be to blame, and of which little could be distinctly known, that, for a time, I supposed he was really ignorant, and preferred to remain ignorant, from whose hand the fatal blow had come. But it was not so. He always knew who it was; and, years afterwards, when the burden of the injury he had received was much heavier on his thoughts than it had been at first, and when an opportunity occurred to do an important kindness to the unhappy person who had inflicted it, he did it promptly and cordially. It was a Christian act, — the more truly Christian, because, although the blow was certainly given by accident, he who inflicted it never expressed any sympathy with the terrible suffering he had occasioned. At least, the sufferer, to whom, if to anybody, he should have expressed it, never knew that he regretted what he had done.

When William returned to College, and resumed his studies he had, no doubt, somewhat different views and purposes in life from those which had most influenced him before his accident. The quiet and suffering of his dark room had done their work, at least in part. He was, compared with what he had been, a sobered man. Not that his spirits were seriously affected by it. They survived even this. But inducements and leisure for reflection had been afforded him such as he had never known before; and, whether the thoughts that followed his accident were the cause or not, he now determined to acquire a more respectable rank in his class as a scholar, than he had earlier deemed worth the trouble.

It was somewhat late to do it; but, having no little courage and very considerable knowledge in elegant literature, he in part succeeded. His remarkable memory enabled him to get on well with the English studies; even with those for which, as for the higher metaphysics, he had a hearty disrelish. But mathematics and geometry seemed to constitute an insurmountable obstacle. He had taken none of the preparatory steps to qualify himself for them, and it was impossible now to go back to the elements, and lay a sufficient foundation. He knew, in fact, nothing about them, and never did afterwards. He became desperate, therefore, and took to desperate remedies.

The first was to commit to memory, with perfect exactness, the whole mathematical demonstration required of his class on any given day, so as to be able to recite every syllable and letter of it as they stood in the book, without comprehending the demonstration at all, or attaching any meaning to the words and signs of which it was composed. It was, no doubt, a feat of memory of which few men would have been capable, but it was also one whose worthlessness a careful teacher would very soon detect, and one, in itself, so intolerably onerous, that no pupil could long practise it. Besides, it was a trick; and a fraud of any kind, except to cheat himself, was contrary to his very nature.

After trying it, therefore, a few times, and enjoying whatever amusement it could afford him and his friends, who were in the secret, he took another method more characteristic. He went to his Professor, and told him the truth; not only his ignorance of geometry, and his belief that he was incapable of understanding a word of it, but the mode by which he had seemed to comply with the requisitions of the recitation-room, while in fact he evaded them; adding, at the same time, that, as a proof of mere industry, he was willing to persevere in committing the lessons to memory, and reciting by rote what he did not and could not understand, if such recitations were required of him, but that he would rather be permitted to use his time more profitably. The Professor, struck with the honesty and sincerity of his pupil, as well as with the singularity of the case, and seeing no likelihood that a similar one would occur, merely exacted his attendance at the regular hours, from which, in fact, he had no power to excuse him; but gave him to understand that he should not be troubled further with the duty of reciting. The solemn farce, therefore, of going to the exercise, book in hand, for several months, without looking at the lesson, was continued, and Prescott was always grateful to the kindly Professor for his forbearance.

On another occasion, he was in danger of more serious trouble with one of the Professors. In this case it arose from the circumstance, that, at all periods of his life, Prescott was now and then affected with a nervous laugh, or fit of laughter, which, as it was always without adequate cause, sometimes broke out most inopportunely. In a very interesting sketch of some passages in his life, by his friend Gardiner, which I have received since this Memoir was prepared, there is an account of two such outbreaks, both of which I will give here, because they are connected, and belong to nearly the same period in his life, and because the last is strictly to be placed among his college adventures. Speaking of this involuntary merriment, Mr. Gardiner says : —

"How mirthful he was, — how fond of a merry laugh, — how overflowing with means to excite one on all admissible occasions, — I have already mentioned. But what I now speak of was something beyond this. He had a sense of the ludicrous so strong, that it seemed at times quite to overpower him. He would laugh on such occasions, — not vociferously indeed, but most inordinately, and for a long time together, as if possessed by the spirit of Momus himself. It seemed to be something perfectly uncontrollable, provoked often by the slightest apparent cause ; and sometimes, in his younger days, under circumstances that made its indulgence a positive impropriety. This seemed only to aggravate the disease. I call it a disease ; for it deprived him at the time of all self-control, and in one of the other sex would have been perhaps hysterical. But there was something irresistibly comic in it to the by-standers, accompanied, as it used to be, by imperfect efforts, through drolleries uttered in broken, half-intelligible sentences, to communicate the ludicrous idea. This original ludicrous idea he seldom succeeded in communicating ; but the infection of laughter would spread, by a sort of animal magnetism, from one to another, till I have seen a whole company perfectly convulsed with it, no one of whom could have told what in the world he was laughing at, unless it were at the sight of Prescott, so utterly overcome, and struggling in vain to express himself.

"To give a better idea of this, I may cite an instance that I witnessed in his younger days, either shortly before, or just after, his first European tour. A party of young gentlemen and ladies — he and I among them — undertook to entertain themselves and their friends with some private theatricals. After having performed one or two light pieces with some success, we attempted the more ambitious task of getting up Julius Cæsar. It proceeded only to two partial rehearsals ; but the manner in which they ended is to the present point. When all had sufficiently studied their parts, we met for a final rehearsal. The part of Mark Antony had been allotted to Prescott. He got through with it extremely well till he came to the speech in the third act which begins, 'O pardon me, thou bleeding piece of earth !' This was addressed to one of our company, extended on the floor, and enacting the part of Cæsar's murdered corpse, with becoming stillness and rigidity. At this point of the performance the ludicrous seized upon Prescott to such a degree, that he burst out into one of his grand fits of laughing, and laughed so immoderately and so infectiously, that the whole company, corpse and all, followed suit, and a scene of tumult ensued which put a stop to further rehearsal. Another evening we attempted it again, after a solemn assurance from Prescott that he should certainly command himself, and not give way to such a folly again. But he did, — in precisely the same place, and with the same result. After that we gave up Julius Cæsar.

"A more curious instance occurred while he was in college. I was not present at this, but have heard him tell it repeatedly in after life. On some occasion it happened that he went to the study of the Rhetorical Professor, for the purpose of receiving a private lesson in elocution. The Professor and his pupil were entirely alone. Prescott took his attitude as orator, and began to declaim the speech he had committed for the purpose; but, after proceeding through a sentence or two, something ludicrous suddenly came across him, and it was all over with him at once, — just as when he came to the 'bleeding piece of earth,' in the scene above narrated. He was seized with just such an uncontrollable fit of laughter. The Professor — no laughing man — looked grave, and tried to check him; but the more he tried to do so, the more Prescott was convulsed. The Professor began to think his pupil intended to insult him. His dark features grew darker, and he began to speak in a tone of severe reprimand. This only seemed to aggravate Prescott's paroxysm, while he endeavored, in vain, to beg pardon; for he could not utter an intelligible word. At last, the sense of the extreme ludicrousness of the situation, and the perception of Prescott's utter helplessness, seized hold of the Professor himself. He had caught the infection. His features suddenly relaxed, and he too began to laugh; and presently the two, Professor and pupil, the more they looked at each other the more they laughed, both absolutely holding on to their sides, and the tears rolling down their cheeks. Of course, there was an end of all reprimand, and equally an end of all declamation. The Professor, as became him, recovered himself first, but only enough to say: 'Well, Prescott, you may go. This will do for to-day.'"

Mathematics, by the indulgence of his teacher, being disposed of in the manner I have mentioned, and several other of the severer studies being made little more than exercises of memory, he was obliged to depend, for the distinction he desired to obtain at college, and which his family demanded from him, almost entirely on his progress in Latin and Greek, and on his proficiency in English literature. These, however, together with his zeal in pursuing them, were, by the kindness of those in academical authority, admitted to be sufficient. He received, in the latter part of his college career, some of the customary honors of successful scholarship, and at its close a

Latin poem was assigned to him as his exercise for Commencement.

No honor, however, that he received at college was valued so much by him, or had been so much an object of his ambition, as his admission to the Society of the Phi Beta Kappa, which was composed, in its theory and pretensions, and generally in its practice, of a moderate number of the best scholars in the two upper classes. As the selection was made by the undergraduates themselves, and as a single black-ball excluded the candidate, it was a real distinction; and Prescott always liked to stand well with his fellows, later in life no less than in youth. From his own experience, therefore, he regarded this old and peculiar society with great favor, and desired at all periods to maintain its privileges and influence in the University.[3]

The honor that he received on his graduation was felt to be appropriate to his tastes, and was not a little valued by him and by his father, as a proof of diligence in his classical studies. It is a pity that the poem cannot be found; but it seems to be irrecoverably lost. Only a few months before his death, his college classmate, Mr. S. D. Bradford, sent him one of a few copies, which he had privately printed for his children and friends, of his own scattered miscellanies, among which was a college exercise in Latin prose. Prescott then said, alluding to his own Latin poem: " I wish I had taken as good care of it as you have of your exercises. I have hunted for it in every quarter where I supposed I could have mislaid it, but in vain. If I should find it," he adds, with his accustomed kindliness, " I shall feel content if the Latin will pass muster as well as in your performance."

It was a pleasant little poem, on Hope, " Ad Spem," and, if

---

[3] The Φ B K, it should be remembered, was, at that period, a society of much more dignity and consequence than it is now. It had an annual public exhibition, largely attended by such graduates as were its members, and, indeed, by the more cultivated portion of the community generally. The undergraduates were in this way associated at once with the prominent and distinguished among their predecessors, who were themselves pleased thus to recall the rank, both as scholars and as gentlemen, which they had early gained, and which they still valued. Membership in such an association was precisely the sort of honor which a young man like Prescott would covet, and he always regretted that its influence among the undergraduates had not been sustained.

I remember rightly, it was in hexameters and pentameters. It was delivered in a hot, clear day of August, 1814, in the old meeting-house at Cambridge, to a crowded audience of the most distinguished people of Boston and the neighborhood, attracted in no small degree by an entertainment which Mr. and Mrs. Prescott were to give the same afternoon in honor of their son's success, — one of the very last of the many large entertainments formerly given at Cambridge on such occasions, and which, in their day, rendered Commencement a more brilliant festival than it is now. I was there to hear my friend. I could see, by his tremulous motions, that he was a good deal frightened when speaking before so large an assembly; but still his appearance was manly, and his verses were thought well of by those who had a right to judge of their merit. I have no doubt they would do credit to his Latinity if they could now be found, for at school he wrote such verses better than any boy there.

After the literary exercises of the day came, of course, the entertainment to the friends of the family. This was given as a reward to the cherished son, which he valued not a little, and the promise of which had much stimulated his efforts in the latter part of his college life. It was, in fact, a somewhat sumptuous dinner, under a marquee, at which above five hundred persons of both sexes sat down, and which was thoroughly enjoyed by all who took an interest in the occasion. His mother did not hesitate to express the pleasure her son's success had given her, and if his father, from the instincts of his nature, was more reserved, he was undoubtedly no less satisfied. William was very gay, as he always was in society, and perfectly natural; dancing and frolicking on the green with great spirit after the more formal part of the festivities was over. He was not sorry that his college life was ended, and said so; but he parted from a few of his friends with sincere pain, as they left Cambridge to go their several ways in the world, never to meet again as free and careless as they then were. Indeed, on such occasions, notwithstanding the vivacity of his nature, he was forced to yield a little to his feelings, as I have myself sometimes witnessed.[*]

[*] There are some remarks of Mr. Prescott on college life in his Memoir of

2

Immediately after leaving college, he entered as a student in his father's office; for the law was, in some sort, his natural inheritance, and — with his own talents already sufficiently developed to be recognized, and with the countenance and aid of a lawyer as eminent as his father was — the path to success at the bar seemed both tempting and sure. But his tastes were still for the pursuits which he had always most loved. He entertained, indeed, no doubt what would be his ultimate career in life; but still he lingered fondly over his Greek and Latin books, and was encouraged in an indulgence of his preference by his family and friends, who rightly regarded such studies as the safest means and foundations for forensic eminence. He talked with me about them occasionally, and I rejoiced to hear his accounts of himself; for, although I had then been myself admitted to the bar, my tastes were the same, and it was pleasant for me to have his sympathy, as he always had mine.

Four or five months were passed in this way, and then another dark and threatening cloud came over his happy life. In January, 1815, he called one day on his medical adviser,

Mr. Pickering, written in 1848, not without a recollection of his own early experiences, which may well be added here. " The four years of college life form, perhaps, the most critical epoch in the existence of the individual. This is especially the case in our country, where they occur at the transition period, — when the boy ripens into the man. The University, that little world of itself, shut out by a great barrier, as it were, from the past equally with the future, bounding the visible horizon of the student like the walls of a monastery, still leaves within them scope enough for all the sympathies and the passions of manhood. Taken from the searching eye of parental supervision, the youthful scholar finds the shackles of early discipline fall from him, as he is left to the disposal, in a great degree, of his own hours and the choice of his own associates. His powers are quickened by collision with various minds, and by the bolder range of studies now open to him. He finds the same incentives to ambition as in the wider world, and contends with the same zeal for honors which, to his eye, seem quite as real — and are they not so? — as those in later life. He meets, too, with the same obstacles to success as in the world, the same temptations to idleness, the same gilded seductions, but without the same power of resistance. For in this morning of life his passions are strongest; his animal nature is more sensible to enjoyment; his reasoning faculties less vigorous and mature. Happy the youth who, in this stage of his existence, is so strong in his principles that he can pass through the ordeal without faltering or failing; — on whom the contact of bad companionship has left no stain for future tears to wash away." Collections of the Massachusetts Historical Society, Third Series, Vol. X., (1849,) pp. 206, 207.

Dr. Jackson, and consulted him for an inconsiderable inflammation of his right eye.   It was his sole dependence for sight, and therefore, although it had served him tolerably well for above a year and a half since the accident to the other, the slightest affection of its powers inevitably excited anxiety. The inflammation was then wholly on the surface of the organ, but yet he complained of a degree of difficulty and pain in moving it, greater than is commonly noticed in a case of so little gravity as this otherwise seemed to be.   Leeches, therefore, were ordered for the temple, and a saturnine lotion, — simple remedies, no doubt, but such as were sufficient for the apparent affection, and quite as active in their nature as was deemed judicious.

But in the course of the night the pain was greatly increased, and on the following morning the inflammation, which at first had been trifling, was found to be excessive, — greater, indeed, than his physician, down to the present day, after a very wide practice of above sixty years, has, as he informs me, ever witnessed since.   The eye itself was much swollen, the cornea had become opaque, and the power of vision was completely lost. At the same time the patient's skin was found to be very hot, and his pulse hard and accelerated.   The whole system, in short, was much disturbed, and the case had evidently become one of unusual severity.

To his calm and wise father, therefore, — to his physician, who was not less his friend than his professional adviser, — and to himself, for he too was consulted, — it seemed that every risk, except that of life, should be run, to save him from the permanent and total blindness with which he was obviously threatened.   Copious bleedings and other depletions were consequently at once resorted to, and seemed, for a few hours, to have made an impression on the disease ; but the suffering returned again with great severity during the subsequent night, and the inflammation raged with such absolute fury for five days, as to resist every form of active treatment that could be devised by his anxious physician, and by Dr. John C. Warren, who had been summoned in consultation.   The gloomiest apprehensions, therefore, were necessarily entertained ; and even when, on the sixth day, the inflammation began to yield, and, on the morning of the seventh, had almost wholly subsided, little encouragement for a happy result could be felt; for the retina was found to be affected, and the powers of vision were obviously and seriously impaired.

But in the afternoon of the seventh day the case assumed a new phasis, and the father, much alarmed, hastened in person to Dr. Jackson, telling him that one of the patient's knees had become painful, and that the pain, accompanied with redness and swelling, was increasing fast. To his surprise, Dr. Jackson answered very emphatically that he was most happy to hear it.

The mystery which had hung over the disease, from the first intimation of a peculiar difficulty in moving the organ, was now dispelled. It was a case of acute rheumatism. This had not been foreseen. In fact, an instance in which the acute form of that disease — not the chronic — had seized on the eye was unknown to the books of the profession. Both of his medical attendants, it is true, thought they had, in their previous practice, noticed some evidence of such an affection; and therefore when the assault was made on the knee in the present case, they had no longer any doubt concerning the matter. As the event proved, they had no sufficient reason for any. In truth, the rheumatism, which had attacked their patient in this mysterious but fierce manner, was the disease which, in its direct and indirect forms, persecuted him during the whole of his life afterwards, and caused him most of the sufferings and privations that he underwent in so many different ways, but, above all, in the impaired vision of his remaining eye. Bad, however, as was this condition of things, it was yet a relief to his anxious advisers to be assured of its real character; — not, indeed, because they regarded acute rheumatism in the eye as a slight disease, but because they thought it less formidable in its nature, and less likely at last to destroy the structure of the organ, than a common inflammation so severe and so unmanageable as this must, in the supposed case, have been.

The disease now exhibited the usual appearances of acute rheumatism; affecting chiefly the large joints of the lower extremities, but occasionally showing itself in the neck, and in other parts of the person. Twice, in the course of the next three months after the first attack, it recurred in the eye, accompanied each time with total blindness; but, whenever it left the eye, it resorted again to the limbs, and so severe was it, even when least violent, that, until the beginning of May, a period of sixteen weeks, the patient was unable to walk a step.

But nothing was able permanently to affect the natural flow of his spirits, — neither pain, nor the sharp surgical remedies to which he was repeatedly subjected, nor the disheartening darkness in which he was kept, nor the gloomy vista that the future seemed to open before him. His equanimity and cheerfulness were invincible.

During nearly the whole of this trying period I did not see him; for I was absent on a journey to Virginia from the beginning of December to the end of March. But when I did see him, — if seeing it could be called, in a room from which the light was almost entirely excluded, — I found him quite unchanged, either in the tones of his voice or the animation of his manner. He was perfectly natural and very gay; talking unwillingly of his own troubles, but curious and interested concerning an absence of several years in Europe which at that time I was about to commence. I found him, in fact, just as his mother afterwards described him to Dr. Frothingham, when she said: "I never in a single instance, groped my way across the apartment, to take my place at his side, that he did not salute me with some expression of good cheer, — not a single instance, — as if we were the patients, and his place were to comfort us." [5]

The following summer wore slowly away; not without much anxiety on the part of his family, as to what might be the end of so much suffering, and whether the patient's infirmities would not be materially aggravated by one of our rigorous winters. Different plans were agitated. At last, in the early autumn, it was determined that he should pass the next six months with his grandfather Hickling, Consul of the United States at St. Michael's, and then that he should visit London and Paris for the benefit of such medical advice as he might find in either metropolis; travelling, perhaps, afterwards on the

[5] Proceedings of the Massachusetts Historical Society, (Boston, 1859,) p. 183.

Continent, to recruit the resources of his constitution, which by such long-continued illness had been somewhat impaired. It was a remedy which was not adopted without pain and misgiving on both sides; but it was evidently the best thing to be done, and all submitted to it with patience and hope.

CHAPTER III.

1815 — 1816.

VISIT TO ST. MICHAEL'S. — HIS LIFE THERE. — SUFFERING IN HIS EYE. — HIS LETTERS TO HIS FATHER AND MOTHER ; TO HIS SISTER ; AND TO W. H. GARDINER.

IN fulfilment of the plan for travel mentioned in the last chapter, he embarked at Boston, on the 26th of September, 1815, for the Azores. Besides the usual annoyances of a sea-voyage in one of the small vessels that then carried on our commerce with the Western Islands, he suffered from the especial troubles of his own case ; — sharp attacks of rheumatism and an inflammation of the eye, for which he had no remedies but the twilight of his miserable cabin, and a diet of rye pudding, with no sauce but coarse salt. The passage, too, was tediously long. He did not arrive until the twenty-second day. Before he landed, he wrote to his father and mother, with the freedom and affection which always marked his intercourse with them : —

"I have been treated," he said, "with every attention by the captain and crew, and my situation rendered as comfortable as possible. But this cabin was never designed for rheumatics. The companion-way opens immediately upon deck, and the patent binnacle illuminators, *vice* windows, are so ingeniously and impartially constructed, that for every ray of light we have half a dozen drops of water. The consequence is, that the orbit of my operations for days together has been very much restricted. I have banished *ennui*, however, by battling with Democrats and bed-bugs, both of which thrive on board this vessel, and in both of which contests I have been ably seconded by the cook, who has officiated as my *valet de chambre*, and in whom I find a great congeniality of sentiment."

An hour after writing this letter, October 18th, he landed. He was most kindly received by his grandfather, — a generous, open-handed, open-hearted gentleman, seventy-two years old, who had long before married a lady of the island as his second wife, and was surrounded by a family of interesting children, some of whom were so near the age of their young nephew of the half-blood, that they made him most agreeable companions and friends.   They were all then residing a few miles from Ponta Delgada, the capital of the island of St. Michael's, at a place called Rosto de Cão, from the supposed resemblance of its rocks to the head of a dog.   It was a country-house, in the midst of charming gardens and the gayest cultivation.   The young American, who had been little from home, and never beyond the influences of the rude climate in which he was born, enjoyed excessively the all but tropical vegetation with which he found himself thus suddenly surrounded ; the laurels and myrtles that everywhere sprang wild ; and the multitudinous orange-groves which had been cultivated and extended chiefly through his grandfather's spirit and energy, until their fruit had become the staple of the island, while, more than half the year, their flowers filled large portions of it with a delicious fragrance ; " Hesperian fables true, if true, here only."

But his pleasures of this sort were short-lived.   He had landed with a slight trouble in his eye, and a fortnight was hardly over before he was obliged to shut himself up with it. From November 1st to February 1st he was in a dark room ; — six weeks of the time in such total darkness, that the furniture could not be distinguished ; and all the time living on a spare vegetable diet, and applying blisters to keep down active inflammation.   But his spirits were proof alike against pain and abstinence.   He has often described to me the exercise he took in his large room, — hundreds of miles in all, — walking from corner to corner, and thrusting out his elbows so as to get warning through them of his approach to the angles of the wall, whose plastering he absolutely wore away by the constant blows he thus inflicted on it.   And all this time, he added, with the exception of a few days of acute suffering, he sang aloud in his darkness and solitude, with unabated cheer.   Later, when a little light could be admitted, he carefully covered his eyes, and listened to reading ; and, at the worst, he enjoyed much of the society of his affectionate aunts and cousins.

But he shall speak for himself, in two or three of the few letters which are preserved from the period of his residence in the Azores and his subsequent travels in Europe.

TO HIS FATHER AND MOTHER.

ROSTO DE CÃO, 18 Nov., 1815.

It is with heart-felt joy, my beloved parents, that I can address you from this blessed little isle.   I landed on Wednesday, October 18th, at 10 A. M., after a most tedious passage of twenty-two days, although I had made a fixed determination to arrive in ten.   I cannot be thankful enough to Heaven that it had not cased in these rheumatic shackles the navigating soul of a Cook or a Columbus, for I am very sure, if a fifth quarter of the globe depended upon me for its exposure, it would remain *terra incognita* forever. . . . . I was received on the quay by my Uncles Thomas and Ivers, and proceeded immediately to the house of the latter, where I disposed of a *nescio quantum* of bread and milk, to the no small astonishment of two or three young cousins, who thought it the usual American appetite.

The city of Ponta Delgada, as seen from the roads, presents an appearance extremely unique, and, to one who has never been beyond the smoke of his own hamlet, seems rather enchantment than reality.   The brilliant whiteness of the buildings, situated at the base of lofty hills, whose sides are clothed with fields of yellow corn, and the picturesque, admirably heightened by the turrets which rise from the numerous convents that disgrace and beautify the city, present a *coup d'œil* on which the genius of a Radcliffe, or indeed any one, much less an admirer of the beauties of nature than myself, might expend a folio of sentimentality and nonsense. After breakfast I proceeded to Rosto de Cão, where I have now the good fortune to be domesticated.   My dear grandfather is precisely the man I had imagined and wished him to be.   Frank and gentlemanly in his deportment, affectionate to his family, and liberal to excess in all his feelings, his hand serves as the conductor of his heart, and when he shakes yours, he communicates all the overflowings of his own benevolent disposition. His bodily virtues are no less inspiring than his mental.   He rises every morning at five, takes a remarkable interest in everything that is going forward, and is so alert in his motions, that, at a fair start, I would lay any odds he would distance the whole of his posterity.   He plumes himself not a little upon his constitution, and tells me that I am much more deserving of the title of " old boy " than himself.

I should give you a sort of biography of the whole family, but my aunt, who officiates as secretary, absolutely refuses to write any more encomiums on them, and, as I have nothing very ill to say of them at present, I shall postpone this until you can receive some official documents *sub mea manu*.   The truth is, I am so lately recovered from a slight inflammation, which the rain water, salt water, and other marine comforts are so well calculated to produce, that I do not care to exert my eyes at present, for which reason my ideas are communicated to you by the hand of my aunt.

We move into town this week, where I have been but seldom since my arrival, and have confined my curiosity to some equestrian excursions round the country.   Novelty of scenery is alone sufficient to interest one who has been accustomed to the productions of Northern climates.   It is very curious, my dear parents, to see those plants which one has been accustomed to see reared in a hot-house, flourishing beneath the open sky, and attaining a height and perfection which no artificial heat can command. When I wander amid the groves of boxwood, cypress, and myrtle, I feel myself transported back to the ages of Horace and Anacreon, who consecrated their shades to immortality.

The climate, though very temperate for winter, is much too frigid for summer, and before I could venture a flight of poesy, I should be obliged to thaw out my imagination over a good December fire. The weather is so capricious, that the inhabitants are absolutely amphibious; — if they are in sunshine one half of the day, they are sure to be in water the other half. . . . .

Give my best affection to Aunt A——'s charming family, and be particular respecting Mrs. H——'s health. Tell my friends, that, when my eyes are in trim, I shall not fail to fatigue their patience.

Remember me to our good people, and think often, my beloved parents, of your truly affectionate son,

WILLIAM.

TO HIS SISTER.

St. Michael's, Ponta Delgada, March 12, 1816.

I am happy, my darling sister, in an opportunity of declaring how much I love, and how often I think of you. . . . .

Since my recovery — to avail myself of a simile not exactly Homeric — I may be compared to bottled beer, which, when it has been imprisoned a long time, bursts forth with tremendous explosion, and evaporates in froth and smoke. Since my emancipation I have made more noise and rattled more nonsense than the ball-rooms of Boston ever witnessed. Two or three times a week we make excursions into the country on jacks, a very agreeable mode of riding, and visit the orangeries, which are now in their prime. What a prospect presents itself for the dead of winter! The country is everywhere in the bloom of vegetation; — the myrtles, the roses, and laurels are in full bloom, and the dark green of the orange groves is finely contrasted with "the golden apples" which glitter through their foliage. Amidst such a scene I feel like a being of another world, new lighted on this distant home. . . . .

The houses of this country are built of stone, covered with white lime. They are seldom more than two stories in height, and the lower floors are devoted to the cattle. They are most lavish of expense on their churches, which are profusely ornamented with gilding and carving, which, though poorly executed, produces a wonderful effect by candle-light. They are generally fortified with eight or ten bells, and when a great character walks off the carpet, they keep them in continual jingle, as they have great faith in ringing the soul through Purgatory. When a poor man loses his child, his friends congratulate him on so joyful an occasion; but if his pig dies, they condole with him. I know not but this may be a fair estimate of their relative worth. . . . .

The whole appearance of this country is volcanic. In the environs I have seen acres covered with lava, and incapable of culture, and most of the mountains still retain the vestiges of craters. Scarcely a year passes without an earthquake. I have been so fortunate as to witness the most tremendous of those convulsions within the memory of the present inhabitants. This was on the 1st of February, at midnight. So severe was the shock, that more than forty houses and many of the public edifices were overthrown or injured, and our house cracked in various places from top to bottom. The whole city was thrown into consternation. Our family assembled *en chemise* in the corridor. I was wise enough to keep quiet in bed, as I considered a cold more dangerous to me than an earthquake. But we were all excessively alarmed. There is no visitation more awful than this. From most dangers there is some refuge, but when nature is convulsed, where can we fly? An earthquake is commonly past before one has time to estimate the horrors of his situation; but this lasted three minutes and a half, and we had full leisure to summon up the ghosts of Lisbon and Herculaneum, and many other recollections equally soothing, and I confess the idea of terminating my career in this manner was not the most agreeable of my reflections.

A few weeks since, my dear sister, I visited some hot springs in Ribeira Grande, at the northern part of the island; but, as I have since been to "the Furnace," where I have seen what is much more wonderful and beautiful in nature, I shall content myself with a description of the latter excursion.

Our road lay through a mountainous country, abounding in wild and picturesque scenery. Our party consisted of about twenty, and we travelled upon jacks, which is the pleasantest conveyance in the world, both from its sociability, and the little fatigue which attends it. As we rode irregularly, our cavalcade had a very romantic appearance; for, while some of us were in the vale, others were on the heights of the mountains, or winding down the declivities, on the brink of precipices two hundred feet perpendicular.

As my imagination was entirely occupied with the volcanic phenomena for which the Furnace is so celebrated, I had formed no idea of any milder attractions. What was my surprise, then, when, descending the mountains at twilight, there burst upon our view a circular valley, ten miles in circumference, bounded on all sides by lofty hills, and in the richest state of cultivation. The evening bell was tolling, as we descended into the plain, to inform the inhabitants of sunset, — the Angelus, — and this, with the whistle of the herdsmen, which in this country is peculiarly plaintive, and the "sober gray" of evening, all combined to fill my bosom with sentiments of placid contentment. . . . . .

I consider it almost fruitless to attempt to describe the Caldeiras [the Caldrons], as can I convey no adequate idea of their terrible appearance. There are seven principal ones, the largest about twenty feet in diameter. They are generally circular, but differing both in form and dimensions. They boil with such fervor as to eject the water to the height of twenty feet, and make a noise like distant thunder. . . . . .

Grandfather's house is situated in the centre of this beautiful valley. It has undergone several alterations since mother was here. The entrance is through a long avenue of shady box-trees, and you ascend to it by a flight of fifty stone steps. Near the house is a grove which was not even in embryo when mother was here. In front of it is a pond, with a small island in the middle, connected with the main land by a stone bridge. In this delightful spot I had some of the happiest hours which I have spent since I quitted my native shores. At "Yankee Hall"[1] every one is *sans souci*. The air of the place is remarkably propitious both to good spirits and good appetites.[2]

In my walks I met with many villagers who recollected Donna Catherina,[3] and who testified their affection for her son in such hearty *embrassades* as I am not quite Portuguese enough to relish. . . . . .

Adieu, my darling sister. I know not how I shall be able to send you this letter. I shall probably take it with me to London, where opportunities will be much more frequent, and where your patience will be much oftener tried by your sincerely affectionate

W.

TO WILLIAM H. GARDINER.

PONTA DELGADA, St. Michael's, March, 1816.

I am fortunate, my dear Will, in an opportunity of addressing you from the orange bowers of St. Michael's, and of acknowledging the receipt of your Gazettes, with their budgets scandalous and philosophical. I must pronounce you, my friend, the *optimus editorum*, for, in the language of the commentators, you have not left a single *desideratum* ungratified. It is impossible to be too minute. To one absent from home trifles are of importance, and the most petty occurrences are the more acceptable, as they transport us into scenes of former happiness, and engage us in the occupations of those in whom we are the most interested. I was much distressed by the death of my two friends. R——'s I had anticipated, but the circumstances which attended it were peculiarly afflicting. Few I believe have spent so long a life in so short a period. He certainly had much benevolence of disposition; but there was something uncongenial in his temper, which made him unpopular with the mass of his acquaintance. If, however, the number of his enemies was great, that of his virtues exceeded them. Those of us who shared his friendship knew how to appreciate his worth.[4] P——, with less steadiness of principle, had many social qualities which endeared him to his friends. The sprightliness of his fancy has beguiled us of many an hour, and the vivacity of his wit, as you well know, has often set our table in a roar. . . . . .

Your letters contain a very alarming list of marriages and matches. If the mania continues much longer, I shall find at my return most of my fair companions converted into sober matrons. I believe I had better adopt your advice, and, to execute it with a little more *éclat*, persuade some kind nun to scale the walls of her convent with me.

Apropos of nunneries: the novelty of the thing has induced me to visit them frequently, but I find that they answer very feebly to those romantic notions of purity and simplicity which I had attached to them. Almost

---

[1] The name of the large house his grandfather had built at the "Caldeiras," remembering his own home.

[2] Elsewhere he calls this visit, "Elysium, four days."

[3] His mother's Christian name.

[4] A college friend of great promise who died in England in 1815.

every nun has a lover; that is, an innamorato who visits her every day, and swears as many oaths of constancy, and imprints as many kisses on the grates as ever Pyramus and Thisbe did on the unlucky chink which separated them. I was invited the other day to select one of these fair penitents, but, as I have no great relish for such a — correspondence, I declined the politeness, and content myself with a few ogles and sighs *en passant*.

It is an interesting employment for the inhabitants of a free country, flourishing under the influences of a benign religion, to contemplate the degradation to which human nature may be reduced when oppressed by arbitrary power and papal superstition. My observation of the Portuguese character has half inclined me to credit Monboddo's theory, and consider the inhabitants in that stage of the metamorphosis when, having lost the tails of monkeys, they have not yet acquired the brains of men. In mechanical improvements, and in the common arts and conveniences of life, the Portuguese are at least two centuries behind the English, and as to literary acquisitions, if, as some writers have pretended, "ignorance is bliss," they may safely claim to be the happiest people in the world.

But, if animated nature is so debased, the beauties of the inanimate creation cannot be surpassed. During the whole year we have the unruffled serenity of June. Such is the temperature of the climate, that, although but a few degrees south of Boston, most tropical plants will flourish; and such is the extreme salubrity, that nothing venomous can exist. These islands, however, abound in volcanic phenomena. I have seen whole fields covered with lava, and most of the mountains still retain the vestiges of craters. I have, too, had the pleasure of experiencing an earthquake, which shook down a good number of houses, and I hope I shall not soon be gratified with a similar exhibition.

But the most wonderful of the natural curiosities are the hot wells, which are very numerous, and of which it would be impossible to give you an adequate conception. The fertility of the soil is so great, that they generally obtain two crops in a year, and now, while you are looking wofully out of the window waiting for the last stroke of the bell before you encounter the terrific snow-banks which threaten you, with us the myrtle, the rose, the pomegranate, the lemon and orange groves are in perfection, and the whole country glowing in full bloom. Indeed, there is everything which can catch the poet's eye, but you know, *Sine Venere, friget Apollo*, and, until some Azorian nymph shall warm my heart into love, the beauties of nature will hardly warm my imagination into poesy.

I must confess, however, that friendship induced me to make an effort this way. I have been confined to my chamber for some time by an indisposition; and while in duress I commenced a poetical effusion to you, and had actually completed a page, when, recovering my liberty, there were so many strange objects to attract the attention, and I thought it so much less trouble to manufacture bad prose than bad poetry, that I dismounted from Pegasus, whom, by the by, I found a confounded hard trotter. Now, as you are professedly one of the *genus irritabile*, I think you cannot employ your leisure better than in serving me an Horatian dish *secundum artem*. Give my warmest affection to your father, mother, and sisters, and be assured, my dear Will, whether rhyme or reason, your epistles will ever confer the highest gratification on your friend,

WM. H. PRESCOTT.

TO HIS FATHER AND MOTHER.

St. Michael's, March 15, 1816.

I cannot regret, my beloved parents, that the opportunities of writing have not been more frequent; for, although it would be cruel to inform you of distresses, while actually existing, which it was not in your power to alleviate, yet it is so soothing to the mind to communicate its griefs, that I doubt if I could refrain from it.

The windows in Rosto de Cão are constructed on much the same principle as our barn-doors. Their uncharitable quantity of light and a slight cold increased the inflammation with which I landed to such a degree, that, as I could not soften the light by means of blinds, which are unknown here, I was obliged to exclude it altogether by closing the shutters. The same cause retarded my recovery; for, as the sun introduced himself *sans cérémonie* whenever I attempted to admit the light, I was obliged to remain in darkness until we removed to the city, where I was accommodated with a room which had a northern aspect, and, by means of different thicknesses of baize nailed to the windows, I was again restored to the cheering beams of heaven. This confinement lasted from the 1st of November to the 1st of February, and during six weeks of it I was in such total darkness it was impossible to distinguish objects in the room. Much of this time has been beguiled of its tediousness by the attentions of A——— and H———, particularly the latter, who is a charming creature, and whom I regard as a second sister.

I have had an abundance of good prescriptions. Grandfather has strongly urged old Madeira as a universal nostrum, and my good uncle the doctor no less strenuously recommended beef-steak. I took their advice, for it cost me nothing; but, as following it cost me rather too dear, I adhered with Chinese obstinacy to bread and milk, hasty pudding, and gruel. This diet and the application of blisters was the only method I adopted to preserve my eye from inflammation.

I have not often, my dear parents, experienced depression of spirits, and there have been but few days in which I could not solace my sorrows with a song. I preserved my health by walking on the piazza with a handkerchief tied over a pair of goggles, which were presented to me by a gentleman here, and by walking some hundreds of miles in my room, so that I emerged from my dungeon, not with the emaciated figure of a prisoner, but in the florid bloom of a *bon vivant*. Indeed, everything has been done which could promote my health and happiness; but darkness has few charms for those in health, and a long confinement must exhaust the patience of all but those who are immediately interested in us. A person situated as I have been can be really happy nowhere but at home, for where but at home can he experience the affectionate solicitude of parents. But the gloom is now dissipated, and my eyes have nearly recovered their former vigor. I am under no apprehension of a relapse, as I shall soon be wafted to a land where the windows are of Christian dimensions, and the medical advice such as may be relied upon.

The most unpleasant of my reflections suggested by this late inflammation are those arising from the probable necessity of abandoning a profession congenial with my taste, and recommended by such favorable opportunities, and adopting one for which I am ill qualified, and have but little inclination.   It is some consolation, however, that this latter alternative, should my eyes permit, will afford me more leisure for the pursuit of my favorite studies.   But on this subject I shall consult my physician, and will write you his opinion.   My mind has not been wholly stagnant during my residence here.   By means of the bright eyes of H—— I have read part of Scott, Shakespeare, Travels through England and Scotland, the Iliad, and the Odyssey.   A—— has read some of the Grecian and Roman histories, and I have cheated many a moment of its tedium by composition, which was soon banished from my mind for want of an amanuensis.

CHAPTER IV.

1816.

HIS relations to the family of his venerable grandfather at St. Michael's, as the preceding letters show, were of the most agreeable kind, and the effect produced by his character on all its members, old and young, was the same that it produced on everybody. They all loved him. His grandmother, with whom, from the difference of their languages, he could have had a less free intercourse than with the rest, wept bitterly when he left them; and his patriarchal grandfather, who had, during his long life, been called to give up several of his house to the claims of the world, pressed him often in his arms on the beach, and, as the tears rolled down his aged cheeks, cried out, in the bitterness of his heart, " God knows, it never cost me more to part from any of my own children."

On the 8th of April, 1816, he embarked for London. His acute rheumatism and the consequent inflammation in his eye recurred almost of course, from the exposures incident to a sea life with few even of the usual allowances of sea comforts. He was, therefore, heartily glad when, after a passage prolonged to four and twenty days, two and twenty of which he had been confined to his state-room, and kept on the most meagre fare, his suffering eye rested on the green fields of old England.

In London he placed himself in the hands of Dr. Farre ; of Mr. Cooper, afterwards Sir Astley Cooper ; and of Sir William Adams, the oculist. He could not, perhaps, have done better. But his case admitted of no remedy and few alleviations ; for it was ascertained, at once, that the eye originally injured was completely paralyzed, and that for the other little could be done except to add to its strength by strengthening the whole physical system. He followed, however, as he almost always did, even when his hopes were the faintest, all the prescriptions that were given him, and submitted conscientiously to the privations that were imposed. He saw few persons that could much interest him, because evening society was forbidden, and he went to public places and exhibitions rarely, and to the theatre never, although he was sorely tempted by the farewell London performances of Mrs. Siddons and Mr. John Kemble. A friend begged him to use an excellent library as if it were his own; "but," he wrote to his father and mother, "when I look into a Greek or Latin book, I experience much the same sensation one does who looks on the face of a dead friend, and the tears not infrequently steal into my eyes." He made a single excursion from London. It was to Richmond; visiting at the same time Slough, where he saw Herschel's telescopes, Eton, Windsor, and Hampton Court, — all with Mr. John Quincy Adams, then our Minister at the Court of St. James. It was an excursion which he mentions with great pleasure in one of his letters. He could, indeed, hardly have made it more agreeably or more profitably. But this was his only pleasure of the sort.

A fresh and eager spirit, however, like his, could not stand amidst the resources of a metropolis so magnificent as London without recognizing their power. Enjoyments, therefore, he certainly had, and, if they were rare, they were high. Nothing in the way of art struck him so much as the Elgin Marbles and the Cartoons of Raphael. Of the first, which he visited as often as he dared to do so, he says, "There are few living beings in whose society I have experienced so much real pleasure," and of the last, that "they pleased him a great deal more than the Stafford collection." It may, as it seems to me, be fairly accounted remarkable, that one whose taste in sculpture and painting could not have been cultivated at home should at once have felt the supremacy of those great works of ancient and modern art, then much less acknowledged than it is now, and even yet, perhaps, not so fully confessed as it will be.

He went frequently to the public libraries and to the principal booksellers' shops, full of precious editions of the classics which he had found it so difficult to obtain in his own country, and which he so much coveted now. But of everything connected with books his enjoyment was necessarily imperfect. At this period he rarely opened them. He purchased a few, however, trusting to the future, as he always did.

Early in August he went over to Paris, and remained there, or in its neighborhood, until October. But Paris could hardly be enjoyed by him so much as London, where his mother tongue made everything seem familiar in a way that nothing else can. He saw, indeed, a good deal of what is external; although, even in this, he was checked by care for his eye, and by at least one decided access of inflammation. Anything, however, beyond the most imperfect view of what he visited was out of the question.

The following winter, which he passed in Italy, was probably beneficial to his health, so far as his implacable enemy, the rheumatism, was concerned, and certainly it was full of enjoyment. He travelled with his old schoolfellow and friend, Mr. John Chipman Gray, who did much to make the journey pleasant to him. After leaving Paris, they first stopped a day at La Grange to pay their respects to General Lafayette, and then went by Lyons, the Mont Cenis, Turin, Genoa, Milan, Venice, Bologna, and Florence to Rome. In Rome they remained about six weeks; after which, giving a month to Naples, they returned through Rome to Florence, and, embarking at Leghorn for Marseilles, made a short visit to Nismes, not forgetting Avignon and Vaucluse, and then hastened by Fontainebleau to Paris, where they arrived on the 30th of March. It was the customary route, and the young travellers saw what all travellers see, neither more nor less, and enjoyed it as all do who have cultivation like theirs and good taste. In a letter written to me the next year, when I was myself in Italy, he speaks with great interest of his visit there, and seems to regret Naples more than any other portion of that charming country. But twenty and also forty years later, when I was again in Italy, his letters to me were full, not of Naples, but of Rome. "Rome is the place," he said, "that lingers longest, I suppose,

In everybody's recollection ; at least, it is the brightest of all I saw in Europe." This was natural. It was the result of the different vistas through which, at widely different periods of his life, he looked back upon what he had so much enjoyed.

One thing, however, in relation to his Italian journeyings, though not remarkable at the time, appears singular now, when it is seen in the light of his subsequent career. He passed over the battle-fields of Gonsalvo de Cordova, and all that made the Spanish arms in Italy so illustrious in the time of Ferdinand and Isabella, without a remark, and, I suppose, without a thought. But, as he often said afterwards, and, indeed, more than once wrote to me, he was then fresh from the classical studies he so much loved ; Horace and Livy, I know, were suspended in the net of his travelling-carriage ; and he thought more, I doubt not, of Cæsar and Cicero, Virgil and Tacitus, than of all the moderns put together.

Indeed, the moderns were, in one sense, beyond his reach. He was unable to give any of his time to the language or the literature of Italy, so wholly were his eyes unfitted for use. But he was content with what his condition permitted ; — to walk about among the ruins of earlier ages, and occasionally look up a passage in an ancient classic to explain or illustrate them. The *genius loci* was at his side wherever he went, and showed him things invisible to mortal sight. As he said in one of his letters to me, it was to him " all a sacred land," and the mighty men of old stood before him in the place of the living.

A few days after he reached Paris, April 7, I arrived there from Germany, where I had been passing nearly two years ; and, as we both had accidentally the same banker, our lodgings had been engaged for us at the same hotel. In this way he was one of the very first persons I saw when I alighted. His parlor, I found, was darkened, and his eye was still too sensitive for any healthy use of it ; but his spirits were light, and his enthusiasm about his Italian journey was quite contagious. We walked a little round the city together, and dined that day with our hospitable banker very gayly. But this was the last of his pleasures in Paris. When we reached our hotel, he complained of feeling unwell, and I was so much alarmed by the state of his pulse that I went personally for his physician, and brought him back with me, fearing, as it was already late at night, that there might otherwise be some untoward delay. The result showed that I had not been unreasonably anxious. The most active treatment was instantly adopted, and absolute quiet prescribed. I watched with him that night; and, as I had yet made no acquaintances in Paris, and felt no interest there, so strong as my interest in him, I shut myself up with him, and thought little of what was outside the walls of our hotel till he was better.

I was, in fact, much alarmed. Nor was he insensible to his position, which the severity of the remedies administered left no doubt was a critical one. But he maintained his composure throughout, begging me, however, not to tell him that his illness was dangerous unless I should think it indispensable to do so. In three or four days my apprehensions were relieved. In eight or ten more, during which I was much with him, he was able to go out, and in another week he was restored. But it was in that dark room that I first learned to know him as I have never known any other person beyond the limits of my immediate family; and it was there that was first formed a mutual regard over which, to the day of his death, — a period of above forty years, — no cloud ever passed.

In the middle of May, after making a pleasant visit of a week to Mr. Daniel Parker [1] at Draveil, he left Paris, and went, by the way of Brighton, to London, where he remained about six weeks, visiting anew, so far as his infirmities would permit, what was most interesting to him, and listening more than he had done before to debates in the House of Lords and the House of Commons. But the country gave him more pleasure than the city. His eyes suffered less there, and, besides, he was always sensible to what is beautiful in nature. Two excursions that he made gratified him very much. One

---

[1] Mr. Parker was an American gentleman, who lived very pleasantly on a fine estate at Draveil, near Paris. Mr. Prescott was more than once at his hospitable château, and enjoyed his visits there much. It was there he first became acquainted with Mr. Charles King, subsequently distinguished in political life and as the President of Columbia College, who, after the death of the historian, pronounced a just and beautiful eulogium on him before the New-York Historical Society, Feb. 1st, 1859.

was to Oxford, Blenheim, and the Wye; in which the Gothic architecture of New-College Chapel and the graceful ruins of Tintern Abbey, with the valley in which they stand, most attracted his admiration, the last "surpassing," as he said, "anything of the sort he had ever seen." He came back by Salisbury, and then almost immediately went to Cambridge, where he was more interested by the manuscripts of Milton and Newton than by anything else, unless, perhaps, it were King's College Chapel. But, after all, this visit to England was very unsatisfactory. He spoke to me in one of his letters of being "invigorated by the rational atmosphere of London," in comparison with his life on the Continent. But still the state of his eyes, and even of his general health, deprived him of many enjoyments which his visit would otherwise have afforded him. He was, therefore, well pleased to turn his face towards the comforts of home.

Of all this, pleasant intimations may be found in the following letter to his friend Gardiner : —

LONDON, 29th May, 1817.

I never felt in my life more inclined to scold any one, my dear Gardiner, than I do to scold you at present, and I should not let you off so easily but that my return will prevent the benefits of a reformation. You have ere this received a folio of hieroglyphics which I transmitted to you from Rome.[a] To read them, I am aware, is impossible; for, as I was folding them up, I had occasion to refer to something, and found myself utterly unable to decipher my own writing. I preferred, however, to send them, for, although unintelligible, they would at least be a substantial evidence to my friend that I had not forgotten him. As you probably have been made acquainted with my route by my family, I shall not trouble you with the details.

Notwithstanding the many and various objects which Italy possesses, they are accompanied with so many *désagrémens*, — poor inns, worse roads, and, above all, the mean spirit and dishonesty of its inhabitants, — that we could not regret the termination of our tour. I was disappointed in France, that is to say, the country. That part of it which I have seen, excepting Marseilles, Nismes, Avignon, and Lyons, possesses few beauties of nature, and little that is curious or worthy of remark. Paris is everything in France. It is certainly unique. With a great parade of science and literary institutions, it unites a constant succession of frivolities and public amusements. I was pleased as long as the novelty lasted, and satiated in less than two months. The most cheerful mind must become dull amidst unintermitted gayety and dissipation, unless it is constructed upon a French anatomy.

[a] Written with his noctograph.

I left —— in a retired part of the city, diligently occupied with the transition of the Roman language into the Italian, and with the ancient French Provençal dialect. There are some men who can unravel problems in the midst of a ball-room. In the fall —— goes down to Italy.

I have now been a fortnight in London. Its sea-coal atmosphere is extremely favorable to my health. I am convinced, however, that travelling is pernicious, and, instead of making the long tour of Scotland, shall content myself with excursions to the principal counties and manufacturing towns in England. In a couple of months I hope to embark, and shall soon have the pleasure of recapitulating with you, my friend, my perils and experiences, and treading in retrospection the classic ground of Italy. I sincerely hope you may one day visit a country which contains so much that is interesting to any man of liberal education. . . . . .

I anticipate with great pleasure the restoration to my friends; to those domestic and social enjoyments which are little known in the great capitals of Europe. Pray give my warmest regards to your father, mother, and sisters, and *n'oubliez jamais*

Your sincerely affectionate

WM. H. PRESCOTT.

CHAPTER V.

1817 – 1824.

HE embarked from England for home at midsummer, and arrived before the heats of our hot season were over. His affectionate mother had arranged everything for his reception that could insure the rest he needed, and the alleviations which, for an invalid such as he was, can never be found except in the bosom of his family. Fresh paper and paint were put on his own room, and everything external was made bright and cheerful to welcome his return. But it was all a mistake. His eye, to the great disappointment of his friends, had not been strengthened during his absence, and could ill bear the colors that had been provided to cheer him. The white paint was, therefore, forthwith changed to gray, and the walls and carpet became green. But neither was this thought enough. A charming country-house was procured, since Nature furnishes truer carpets and hangings than the upholsterer; but the house was damp from its cool position, and from the many trees that surrounded it.[1] His old enemy, the rheumatism, therefore, set in with renewed force; and in three days, just as his father was driving out to dine, for the first time, in their rural home, he met them all hurrying back to the house in town, where they remained nearly two years, finding it better for the invalid than

---

[1] This account is taken from the memoranda of his sister, Mrs. Dexter, whose graceful words I have sometimes used both here and elsewhere in the next few pages.

any other.   It was a large, comfortable old mansion in Bedford Street, and stood where the Second Congregational Church now stands.

The winter of 1817 – 18 he passed wholly at home.   As he wrote to me, his "eyes made him a very domestic, retired man." He avoided strong light as much as he could ; and, extravagantly as he loved society, indulged himself in it not at all, because he found, or rather because he thought he found, its excitements injurious to him.   But his old schoolfellow and friend Gardiner, who was then a student-at-law in the elder Mr. Prescott's office, read some of his favorite classics with him a part of each day ; and his sister, three years younger than he was, shut herself up with him the rest of it, in the most devoted and affectionate manner, reading to him sometimes six or even eight hours consecutively.   On these occasions he used to place himself in the corner of the room, with his face to the angle made by the walls, and his back to the light.   Adjusted thus, they read history and poetry, often very far into the night, and, although the reader, as she tells me, sometimes dozed, he never did.   It was a great enjoyment to them both, — to her, one of the greatest of her life ; but it was found too much for her strength, and the father and mother interfered to restrain and regulate what was unreasonable in the indulgence.

It was during this period that he made his first literary adventure.   The North-American Review had then been in existence two or three years, and was already an extremely respectable journal, with which some of his friends were connected. It offered a tempting opportunity for the exercise of his powers, and he prepared an article for it.   The project was a deep secret ; and when the article was finished, it was given to his much trusted sister to copy.   He felt, she thinks, some misgivings, but on the whole looked with favor on his first-born.   It was sent anonymously to the club of gentlemen who then managed the Review, and nothing was heard in reply for a week or more.   The two who were in the secret began, therefore, to consider their venture safe, and the dignity of authorship, his sister says, seemed to be creeping over him, when one day he brought back the article to her, saying : "There ! it is good for nothing.   They refuse it.   I was a fool to send it."   The sister was offended. But he was not. He only cautioned her not to tell of his failure.

He was now nearly twenty-two years old, and it was time to consider what should be his course in life. So far as the profession of the law was concerned, this question had been substantially settled by circumstances over which he had no control. His earliest misgivings on the subject seemed to have occurred during his long and painful confinement at St. Michael's, and may be found in a letter, before inserted, which was written March 15th, 1816.

A little later, after consulting eminent members of the medical profession in London, he wrote more decisively and more despondingly : " As to the future, it is too evident I shall never be able to pursue a profession. God knows how poorly I am qualified, and how little inclined, to be a merchant. Indeed, I am sadly puzzled to think how I shall succeed even in this without eyes, and am afraid I shall never be able to draw upon my mind to any large amount," — a singular prophecy, when we consider that his subsequent life for nearly forty years was a persistent contradiction of it.

After his return home this important question became, of course, still more pressing, and was debated in the family with constantly increasing anxiety. At the same time he began to doubt whether the purely domestic life he was leading was the best for him. The experiment of a year's seclusion, he was satisfied, and so were his medical advisers, had resulted in no improvement to his sight, and promised nothing for the future if it should be continued. He began, therefore, to go abroad, gradually and cautiously at first, but afterwards freely. No harm followed, and from this time, except during periods when there was some especial inflammation of the eye, he always mingled freely in a wide range of society, giving and receiving great pleasure.

The consequence followed that might have been anticipated from a nature at once so susceptible and so attractive. He soon found one to whom he was glad to intrust the happiness of his life. Nor was he disappointed in his hopes ; for, if there was ever a devoted wife, or a tender and grateful husband, they were to be found in the home which this union made happy.

3   D

As he said in a letter long afterwards, "Contrary to the assertion of La Bruyère, — who somewhere says, that the most fortunate husband finds reason to regret his condition at least once in twenty-four hours, — I may truly say that I have found no such day in the quarter of a century that Providence has spared us to each other." And so it continued to the last. I am sure that none who knew them will think me mistaken. The lady was Susan, daughter of Thomas C. Amory, Esq., a successful and cultivated merchant, who died in 1812, and of Hannah Linzee, his wife, who survived him, enjoying the great happiness of her child, until 1845.

In the summer of 1819 I returned from Europe, after an absence of more than four years. The first friends who welcomed me in my home, on the day of my arrival, were the Prescott family; and the first house I visited was theirs, in which from that day I was always received as if I were of their kin and blood. William was then in the freshest glow of a young happiness which it was delightful to witness, and of which he thought for some months much more than he did of anything else. I saw him constantly; but it was apparent that, although he read a good deal, or rather listened to a good deal of reading, he studied very little, or not at all. Real work was out of the question. He was much too happy for it.

On the evening of the 4th of May, 1820, which was his twenty-fourth birthday, he was married at the house of Mrs. Amory, in Franklin Place. It was a wedding with a supper, in the old-fashioned style, somewhat solemn and stately at first; many elderly people being of the party, and especially an aged grandmother of the bride, whose presence enforced something of formality. But later in the evening our gayety was free in proportion to the restraints that had previously been laid upon it.[*]

The young couple went immediately to the house of the Prescott family in Bedford Street, — the same house, by a

---

[*] Prescott always liked puns, and made a good many of them, — generally very bad. But one may be recorded. It was *apropos* of his marriage to Miss *Amory*, for which, when he was joked by some of his young bachelor friends as a deserter from their ranks, he shook his finger at them, and repeated the adage of Virgil: —

"Omnia vincit Amor, et nos cedamus *Amori*."

pleasant coincidence, in which Miss Linzee, the mother of the bride, had been married to Mr. Amory five and twenty years before; and there they lived as long as that ample and comfortable old mansion stood.[*]

Another coincidence connected with this marriage should be added, although it was certainly one that augured little of the happiness that followed. The grandfathers of Mr. Prescott and Miss Amory had been engaged on opposite sides during the war for American Independence, and even on opposite sides in the same fight; Colonel Prescott having commanded on Bunker Hill, while Captain Linzee, of the sloop-of-war Falcon, cannonaded him and his redoubt from the waters of Charles River, where the Falcon was moored during the whole of the battle. The swords that had been worn by the soldier and the sailor on that memorable day came down as heirlooms in their respective families, until at last they met in the library of the man of letters, where, quietly crossed above his books, they often excited the notice alike of strangers and of friends. After his death they were transferred, as he had desired, to the Historical Society of Massachusetts, on whose walls they have become the memorials at once of a hard-fought field and of " victories no less renowned than those of war." A more appropriate resting-place for them could not have been found. And there, we trust, they may rest in peace so long as the two nations shall exist, — trophies, indeed, of the past, but warnings for the future.[4]

At the time of his marriage my friend was one of the finest-looking men I have ever seen; or, if this should be deemed in some respects a strong expression, I shall be fully justified, by those who remember him at that period, in saying that he was one of the most attractive. He was tall, well formed, manly in his bearing but gentle, with light-brown hair that was hardly changed or diminished by years, with a clear complexion and a ruddy flush on his cheek that kept for him to the last an appearance of comparative youth, but, above all, with a smile that was the most absolutely contagious I ever looked upon.

---

[*] It was pulled down in 1845, and we all sorrowed for it, and for the venerable trees by which it was surrounded.

[4] See Appendix B.

As he grew older, he stooped a little.   His father's figure was
bent at even an earlier age, but it was from an organic infirmity of the chest, unknown to the constitution of the son, who
stooped chiefly from a downward inclination which he instinctively gave to his head so as to protect his eye from the light.
But his manly character and air were always, to a remarkable
degree, the same.   Even in the last months of his life, when
he was in some other respects not a little changed, he appeared
at least ten years younger than he really was.   And as for the
gracious, sunny smile that seemed to grow sweeter as he grew
older, it was not entirely obliterated even by the touch of
death.   Indeed, take him for all in all, I think no man ever
walked our streets, as he did day by day, that attracted such
regard and good-will from so many; for, however few he might
know, there were very many that knew him, and watched him
with unspoken welcomes as he passed along.

A little before his marriage he had, with a few friends
nearly of his own age and of similar tastes, instituted a club
for purposes both social and literary.   Their earliest informal
gathering was in June, 1818.   On the first evening they numbered nine, and on the second, twelve.   Soon, the number was
still further enlarged; but only twenty-four were at any time
brought within its circle; and of these, after an interval of
above forty years, eleven still survive (1862).[5]

[5] The names of the members of this genial, scholarlike little club were,

*Alexander Bliss,	William Powell Mason,
*John Brazer,	John Gorham Palfrey,
*George Augustus Frederic Dawson,	Theophilus Parsons,
*Franklin Dexter,	Octavius Pickering,
*Samuel Atkins Eliot,	*William Hickling Prescott,
*William Havard Eliot,	Jared Sparks,
Charles Folsom,	*William Jones Spooner,
William Howard Gardiner,	*Jonathan Mayhew Wainwright,
John Chipman Gray,	John Ware,
*Francis William Pitt Greenwood,	Henry Warren,
*Enoch Hale,	*Martin Whiting,
Charles Greely Loring,	*Francis William Winthrop.

Those marked with an asterisk are dead; but it may be worth notice that,
although several of the most promising members of the club died so young
that the time for their distinction never came, more than half of the whole
number have been known as authors, no one of whom has failed to do
credit to the association in which his youth, in part at least, was trained.

Prescott, from his happy, social nature, as well as from his love of letters, was eminently fitted to be one of the members of such a club, and rarely failed to be present at its meetings, which he always enjoyed. In their earliest days, after the fashion of such youthful societies, they read papers of their own composition, and amused themselves by criticising one another, and sometimes their neighbors. As a natural consequence of such intercourse, it was not long before they began to think that a part, at least, of what they had written was too good to be confined to their own meetings; and chiefly, I believe, under Prescott's leading, they determined to institute a periodical, or rather a work which should appear at uncertain intervals, and be as little subject to rules and restrictions of any sort as their own gay meetings were. At any rate, if he were not the first to suggest the project, he was the most earnest in promoting it after it was started, and was naturally enough, both from his leisure and his tastes, made editor.

It was called "The Club-Room," and the first number was published February 5th, 1820. But its life, though it seems to have been a merry one, was short; for the fourth and last number appeared on the 19th of July of the same year. Nor was there any especial reason to lament its fate as untimely. It was not better than the average of such publications, perhaps not so good. Prescott, I think, brought but three contributions to it. The first is the leading article in the second number, and gives, not without humor, an account of the way in which the first number had been received when it was ushered into a busy, bustling world, too careless of such claims to its notice. The others were tales; one of which, entitled "The Vale of Alleriot," was more sentimental than he would have liked later; and one, "Calais," was a story which Allston, our great artist, used to tell with striking effect. Neither of them had anything characteristic of what afterwards distinguished their author, and neither could be expected to add much to the popular success of such a publication. The best of the contributions to it were, I think, three by Mr. Franklin Dexter, his brother-in-law; two entitled "Recollections," and the other, "The Ruins of Rome"; * the very last being, in fact, a humorous anticipation of the mean

* See a notice of him in the account of the Prescott Family, Appendix (A).

and miserable appearance Boston would make, if its chief edifices should crumble away, and become what those of the mistress of the ancient world are now. "And here ended this precious publication," as its editor, apparently with a slight feeling of vexation, recorded its failure. Not that he could be much mortified at its fate; for, if it was nothing else, it was an undertaking creditable to the young men who engaged in it so as to accustom themselves to write for the public, and it had, besides, not only enlivened their evenings, but raised the tone of their intercourse with each other.[7]

When the last number of "The Club-Room" appeared, its editor had been married two months. The world was before him. Not only was his decision made to give up the law as a profession, but he had become aware that he must find some other serious occupation to take its place; for he was one of those who early discover that labor is the condition of happiness, and even of content, in this world. His selection of a pursuit, however, was not suddenly made. It could not be. Many circumstances in relation to it were to be weighed, and he

[7] I cannot refuse my readers or myself the pleasure of inserting here a faithful account of Prescott's relations to this club, given to me by one of its original founders and constant supporters, in some sketches already referred to; I mean his friend Mr. William H. Gardiner.

"The club formed in 1818, for literary and social objects combined, at first a supper and afterwards a dinner club, was, to the end of our friend's days, — a period of more than forty years, — a source of high enjoyment to him. It came to be a peculiar association, because composed of men of nearly the same age, who grew up together in those habits of easy, familiar intercourse which can hardly exist except where the foundations are laid in very young days. He was, from the first, a leading spirit there, latterly quite the life and soul of the little company, and an object of particular affection as well as pride. He was always distinguished there by some particular *sobriquet*. At first we used to call him 'the gentleman,' from the circumstance of his being the only member who had neither profession nor ostensible pursuit. For many years he was called 'the editor,' from his having assumed to edit, in its day, the little magazine that has been mentioned, called 'The Club-Room.' Finally, he won the more distinguished title of 'the historian,' and was often so addressed in the familiar talk of the club. It comprised several of Mr. Prescott's most intimate personal friends. The most perfect freedom prevailed there. All sorts of subjects took their turn of discussion. So that, were it possible to recall particulars of his conversations at these meetings, extending through two thirds of his whole life, the reader would gain a very perfect idea of him as a social man. But the ἔπεα πτερόεντα are too fleeting for reproduction; and even their spirit and effect can hardly be gathered from mere general descriptions."

had many misgivings, and hesitated long. But his tastes and employments had always tended in one direction, and therefore, although the decision might be delayed, the result was all but inevitable. He chose a life of literary occupation ; and it was well that he chose it so deliberately, for he had time, before he entered on its more serious labors, to make an estimate of the difficulties that he must encounter in the long path stretched out before him.

In this way he became fully aware, that, owing to the infirmity under which he had now suffered during more than six of the most important years of his life, he had much to do before he could hope even to begin a career that should end with such success as is worth striving for. In many respects, the very foundations were to be laid, and his first thought was that they should be laid deep and sure. He had never neglected his classical studies, and now he gave himself afresh to them during a fixed portion of each day. But his more considerable deficiencies were in all modern literature. Of the English he had probably read as much as most persons of his age and condition, or rather it had been read to him ; but this had been chiefly for his amusement in hours of pain and darkness, not as a matter of study, and much less upon a regular system. French he had spoken a little, though not well, while he was in France and Italy ; but he knew almost nothing of French literature. And of Italian and Spanish, though he had learnt something as a school-boy, it had been in a thoughtless and careless way, and, after the injury to his sight, both of them had been neglected. The whole, therefore, was not to be relied upon ; and most young men at the age of four or five and twenty would have been disheartened at the prospect of attempting to recover so much lost ground, and to make up for so many opportunities that had gone by never to return. When to this is added the peculiar discouragement that seemed almost to shut out knowledge by its main entrance, it would have been no matter of reproach to his courage or his manhood, if he had turned away from the undertaking as one beyond his strength.

But it is evident that he only addressed himself to his task with the more earnestness and resolution. He began, I think wisely, with the English, being willing to go back to the very elements, and on the 30th of October, 1821, made a memorandum that he would undertake "a course of studies" involving—

"1. Principles of grammar, correct writing, &c.;

"2. Compendious history of North America;

"3. Fine prose-writers of English from Roger Ascham to the present day, principally with reference to their mode of writing,—not including historians, except as far as requisite for an acquaintance with style;

"4. Latin classics one hour a day."

The American history he did not immediately touch; but on the rest he entered at once, and carried out his plan vigorously. He studied, as if he had been a school-boy, Blair's Rhetoric, Lindley Murray's Grammar, and the prefatory matter to Johnson's Dictionary, for the grammatical portion of his task; and then he took up the series of good English writers, beginning with Ascham, Sir Philip Sidney, Bacon, Browne, Raleigh, and Milton, and coming down to our own times,—not often reading the whole of any one author, but enough of each to obtain, what he more especially sought, an idea of his style and general characteristics. Occasionally he noted down his opinion of them,—not always such an opinion as he would have justified or entertained later in life, but always such as showed a spirit of observation and a purpose of improvement. Thus, under the date of November, 1821, he says:—

"Finished Roger Ascham's 'Schoolmaster.' Style vigorous and polished, and even euphonious, considering the period; his language often ungrammatical, inelegant, and with the Latin idiom. He was one of the first who were bold and wise enough to write English prose. He dislikes rhyme, and thinks iambics the proper quantity for English verse. Hence blank verse. He was a critical scholar, but too fastidious.

"Milton, 'Reasons of Church Government.' Style vigorous, figurative to conceit; a rich and sublime imagination; often coarse, harsh; constant use of Latin idiom; inversion. He is very bold, confident in his own talent, with close, unrelenting argument; upon the whole, giving the reader a higher idea of his sturdy principle than of his affections."

In this way he continued nearly a year occupying himself with the good English prose-writers, and, among the rest, with the great preachers, Taylor, Tillotson, and Barrow, but not stopping until he had come down to Jeffrey and Gifford, whom he marked as the leading critics of our period. But during all this time, he gave his daily hour to the principal Latin classics, especially Tacitus, Livy, and Cicero ; taking care, as he says, to " observe their characteristic physiognomies, — not style and manner as much as sentiments, &c."

Having finished this course, he turned next to the French, going, as he intimates, " deeper and wider," because his purpose was not, as in the Latin, to strengthen his knowledge, but to form an acquaintance with the whole of French literature, properly so called. He went back, therefore, as far as Froissart, and did not stop until he had come down to Chateaubriand. It was a good deal of it read by himself in the forenoons, thus saving much time ; for in 1822 – 1823, except when occasional inflammation occurred, his eye was in a condition to do him more service than it had done him for many years, and he husbanded its resources so patiently, and with so much care, that he rarely lost anything by imprudence.

But French literature did not satisfy him as English had done. He found it less rich, vigorous, and original. He, indeed, enjoyed Montaigne, and admired Pascal, whom he preferred to Bossuet or to Fénélon, partly, I think, for the same reasons that led him to prefer Corneille to Racine. But Lafontaine and Molière stood quite by themselves in his estimation, although in some respects, and especially in the delineation of a particular humor or folly, he placed Ben Jonson before the great French dramatist. The forms of French poetry, and the rigorous system of rhymes enforced in its tragedies, were more than commonly distasteful to him.

While, however, he was thus occupied with French literature as a matter of serious study during parts of 1822 and 1823, he listened to a good deal of history read to him in a miscellaneous way for his amusement, and went through a somewhat complete course of the old English drama from Heywood to Dryden, accompanying it with the corresponding portions of August Wilhelm Schlegel's Lectures, which he greatly relished. During the same period, too, we read together, at my house, three or four afternoons in each week, the Northern Antiquities, published by Weber, Jamieson, and Scott, in 1815 ; a good many of the old national romances in Ritson and Ellis, Sir

3 *

Tristrem, Percy's Reliques, and portions of other similar collections, — all relating either to the very earliest English literature or to its connection with the Scandinavian and the Teutonic. It was his first adventure in this direction, and he enjoyed it not a little, — the more, perhaps, because he was then going on with the French, in which he took less interest.

In the autumn of 1823, following out the same general purpose to which he had now devoted two years, he began the Italian. At first he only read such books as would soonest make him familiar with the language, and so much of Sismondi's " Littérature du Midi' as would give him an outline of the whole field. Afterwards he took Ginguené and sometimes Tiraboschi for his guide, and went over an extraordinary amount of poetry, rather than prose, from Dante, and even from the " Poeti del Primo Secolo," to Metastasio, Alfieri, and Monti. It seems quite surprising how much he got through with, and it would be almost incredible, if his notes on it were not full and decisive. He wrote, in fact, more upon Italian literature than he had written upon either the English or the French, and it made apparently a much deeper impression upon him than the last. At different times he even thought of devoting a large part of his life to its study; and, excepting what he has done in relation to Spanish history, nothing of all he has published is so matured and satisfactory as two articles in the " North-American Review": one on Italian Narrative Poetry, published in October, 1824, and another on Italian Poetry and Romance, published in July, 1831, both to be noticed hereafter.

With what spirit and in what tone he carried on at this time the studies which produced an effect so permanent on his literary tastes and character will be better shown by the following familiar notes than by anything more formal : —

TO MR. TICKNOR.

Tuesday Morning, 8 o'clock, Dec. 15, 1828.

DEAR GEORGE,

I am afraid you will think my study too much like the lion's den ; the footsteps never turn outwards. I want to borrow more books ; viz. one volume of ancient Italian poetry ; I should like one containing specimens of Cino da Pistoia, as I suspect he was the best versifier in Petrarch's time ; also Ginguené ; also, some translation of Dante.

I spoke very rashly of Petrarch the other day. I had only read the first volume, which, though containing some of his best is on the whole, much less moving and powerful than Part II. It is a good way to read him chronologically; that is, to take up each sonnet and *canzone* in the order, and understanding the peculiar circumstances, in which it was written. Ginguené has pointed out this course.

On the whole, I have never read a foreign poet that possessed more of the spirit of the best English poetry. In two respects this is very striking in Petrarch; — the tender passion with which he associates every place in the country, the beautiful scenery about Avignon, with the recollections of Laura; and, secondly, the moral influence which his love for her seems to have had upon his character, and which shows itself in the religious sentiment that pervades more or less all his verses.

How any one could ever doubt her existence who has read Petrarch's poetry, is a matter of astonishment to me. Setting aside external evidence, which seems to me conclusive enough, his poetry could not have been addressed to an imaginary object; and one fact, the particular delight which he takes in the belief that she retains in heaven, and that he shall see her there, with the same countenance, complexion, bodily appearance, &c., that she had on earth, is so natural in a real lover, and would be so unlikely to press itself upon a fictitious one, that I think that it is worth noticing, as affording strong internal evidence of her substantial existence. I believe, however, that it is admitted generally now, from facts respecting his family brought to light by the Abbé de Sade, a descendant of her house.

The richness and perfection of the Italian in the hands of Petrarch is truly wonderful. After getting over the difficulty of some of his mystical nonsense, and reading a *canzone* two or three times, he impresses one very much; and the varied measures of the *canzone* put the facility and melody of verse-making to the strongest test. Gravina says, there are not two words in Petrarch's verses obsolete. Voltaire, I remember, says the same thing of the "Provincial Letters," written three hundred years later. Where is the work we can put our finger on in our own tongue before the eighteenth century and then say the same? Yet from long before Elizabeth's time there were no invasions or immigrations to new-mould the language.

I hope you are all well under this awful dispensation oʃ snow. I have shovelled a stout path this morning, and can report it more than a foot deep. A fine evening for the party at ——, and I dine at ——; so I get a morning and a half. Give my condolence to Anna, whom I hope to meet this evening, if the baby is well and we should not be buried alive in the course of the day.

Yours affectionately,

Wm. H. Prescott.

Being also shut up in the house by the snow-storm referred to, I answered him the same day with a long note entering into the question of the real existence of Laura, and the following rejoinder came the next day close upon the heel of my reply.

TO MR. TICKNOR.

Bedford Street, Dec. 17, 1828.

DEAR GEORGE,

I think better of snow-storms than I ever did before; since, though they keep a man's body in the house, they bring his mind out. I suppose, if it had been fair weather yesterday, I should not have had your little dissertation upon Madonna Laura, which interested as well as amused me. As to the question of the real existence of Madonna, I can have but little to say. . . . . . One thing seems to me clear, that the *onus probandi* is with those who would deny the substantiality of Laura; because she is addressed as a living person by Petrarch, and because no contemporary unequivocally states her to have been an ideal one. I say unequivocally, because the remark you refer to of one of the Colonna family seems to have been rather an intimation or a gratuitous supposition, which might well come from one who lived at a distance from the scene of attachment, *amour*, or whatever you call this Platonic passion of Petrarch's. The *Idealists*, however, to borrow a metaphysical term, would shift this burden of proof upon their adversaries. On this ground I agree with you, that internal evidence derived from poetry, whose essence, as you truly say, is fiction, is liable to great misinterpretation. Yet I think that, although a novel or a long poem may be written, addressed to, and descriptive of some imaginary goddess, &c. (I take it, there is not much doubt of Beatrice, or of the original of Fiammetta), yet that a long series of separate poems should have been written with great passion, under different circumstances, through a long course of years, from the warm period of boyhood to the cool retrospective season of gray hairs, would, I think, be, in the highest degree, improbable. But when with this you connect one or two external facts, e. g. the very memorandum, to which you refer, written in his private manuscript of Virgil, intended only for himself, as he expressly says in it, with such solemn, unequivocal language as this: "In order to preserve the melancholy recollections of this loss, I find a certain satisfaction mingled with my sorrow in noting this in a volume which often falls under my eye, and which thus tells me there is nothing further to delight me in this life, that my strongest tie is broken," &c., &c. Again, in a treatise "De Contemptu Mundi," a sort of confession in which he seems to have had a sober communion with his own heart, as I infer from Ginguené, he speaks of his passion for Laura in a very unambiguous manner. These notes or memoranda, intended only for his own eye, would, I think, in any court of justice be admitted as positive evidence of the truth of what they assert. I should be willing to rest the point at issue on these two facts.

Opening his poetry, one thing struck me in support of his sincerity, in seeing a sonnet, which begins with the name of the friend we refer to.

"Rotta e l' alta Colonna e 'l verde Lauro."

Vile puns, but he would hardly have mingled the sincere elegy of a friend with that of a fictitious creation of his own brain. This, I admit, is not safe to build upon, and I do not build upon it. I agree that it may be highly probable that investigators, Italian, French, and English, have feigned more than they found, — have gone into details, where only a few general facts could be hoped for; but the general basis, the real existence of some woman named Laura, who influenced the heart, the conduct, the intellectual character, of Petrarch, is, I think, not to be resisted. And I believe your decision does not materially differ from this.

I return the "Poeti del Primo Secolo." Though prosaic, they are superior to what I imagined, and give me a much higher notion of the general state of the Italian tongue at that early period than I had imagined it was entitled to. It is not more obsolete than the French in the time of Marot, or the English in the time of Spenser. Petrarch, however, you easily see, infused into it a warmth and richness — a splendor of poetical idiom — which has been taken up and incorporated with the language of succeeding poets. But he is the most musical, most melancholy, of all. Sismondi quotes Malaspina, a Florentine historian, as writing in 1280, with all the purity and elegance of modern Tuscan. But I think you must say, *Sat prata biberunt.* I have poured forth enough, I think, considering how little I know of the controversy.

I have got a long morning again, as I dine late. So, if you will let me have "Cary," [a] I think it may assist me in some very knotty passages, though I am afraid it is too fine [print] to read much.

Give my love to Anna, who, I hope, is none the worse for last night's frolicking.

Yours affectionately,

W. H. PRESCOTT.

He soon finished Dante, and of the effect produced on him by that marvellous genius, at once so colossal and so gentle, the following note will give some idea. It should be added, that the impression thus made was never lost. He never ceased to talk of Dante in the same tone of admiration in which he thus broke forth on the first study of him, — a noteworthy circumstance, because, owing to the imperfect vision that so crippled and curtailed his studies, he was never afterwards able to refresh his first impressions, except, as he did it from time to time, by reading a few favorite passages, or listening to them. [b]

TO MR. TICKNOR.

Jan. 21, 1824.

DEAR GEORGE,

I shall be obliged to you if you will let me have the "Arcadia" of Sannazaro, the "Pastor Fido," and the "Aminta," — together with the volumes of Ginguené, containing the criticism of these poems.

I have finished the Paradiso of Dante, and feel as if I had made a most

[a] Translation of Dante.

[b] We, however, both listened to the reading of Dante, by an accomplished Italian, a few months later; but this I consider little more than a part of the same study of the *altissimo poeta.*

important addition to the small store of my acquisitions. To have read the Inferno, is not to have read Dante ; his genius shows itself under so very different an aspect in each of his three poems. The Inferno will always be the most popular, because it is the most — indeed the only one that is at all — entertaining. Human nature is so delightfully constituted, that it can never derive half the pleasure from any relation of happiness that it does from one of misery and extreme suffering. Then there is a great deal of narrative, of action in the Inferno, and very little in the two other parts. Notwithstanding all this, I think the impression produced on the mind of the reader by the two latter portions of the work much the most pleasing. You impute a finer, a more exquisite (I do not mean a more powerful), intellectual character to the poet, and, to my notion, a character more deeply touched with a true poetical feeling.

The Inferno consists of a series of pictures of the most ingenious, the most acute, and sometimes the most disgusting bodily sufferings. I could wish that Dante had made more use of the *mind* as a source and a means of anguish. Once he has done it with beautiful effect, in the description of a *Barattiere*, I believe,[10] who compares his miserable state in hell with his pleasant residence on the banks of the Arno, and draws additional anguish from the comparison. In general, the sufferings he inflicts are of a purely physical nature. His devils and bad spirits, with one or two exceptions, which I remember you pointed out, are much inferior in moral grandeur to Milton's. How inferior that stupendous overgrown Satan of his to the sublime spirit of Milton, not yet stript of all its original brightness. I must say that I turn with more delight to the faultless tale of Francesca da Polenta, than to that of Ugolino, or any other in the poem. Perhaps it is in part from its being in such a dark setting, that it seems so exquisite, by contrast. The long talks in the Purgatorio and the dismal disputations in the Paradiso certainly lie very heavy on these parts of the work ; but then this very inaction brings out some of the most conspicuous beauties in Dante's composition.

In the Purgatorio, we have, in the first ten cantos, the most delicious descriptions of natural scenery, and we feel like one who has escaped from a dungeon into a rich and beautiful country. In the latter portions of it he often indulges in a noble tone of moral reflection. I look upon the Purgatorio, full of sober meditation and sweet description, as more à l'Anglaise than any other part of the Commedia. In the Paradiso his shocking argumentations are now and then enlivened by the pepper and salt of his political indignation, but at first they both discouraged and disgusted me, and I thought I should make quick work of the business. But upon reading further, — thinking more of it, — I could not help admiring the genius which he has shown in bearing up under so oppressive a subject. It is so much easier to describe gradations of pain than of pleasure, — but more especially when this pleasure must be of a purely intellectual nature. It is like a painter sitting down to paint the soul. The Scrip-

---

[10] My friend says, with some hesitation, " a Barattiere, *I believe.*" It was in fact a " Falsificatore," — *a counterfeiter*, — and not a *barrator* or *peculator*. The barrators are found in the twenty-first canto of the Inferno ; but the beautiful passage here alluded to is in the thirtieth.

tures have not done it successfully. They paint the physical tortures of hell, fire, brimstone, &c., but in heaven the only joys, i. e. animal joys, are singing and dancing, which to few people convey a notion of high delight, and to many are positively disagreeable.

Let any one consider how difficult, nay impossible, it is to give an entertaining picture of purely intellectual delight. The two highest kinds of pure *spiritual* gratification which, I take it, a man can feel, — at least, I esteem it so, — are that arising from the consciousness of a reciprocated passion (I speak as a lover), and, second, one of a much more philosophic cast, that arising from the successful exertion of his own understanding (as in composition, for instance). Now Dante's pleasures in the Paradiso are derived from these sources. Not that he pretends to write books there, but then he disputes like a doctor upon his own studies, — subjects most interesting to him, but unfortunately to nobody else. It is comical to see how much he plumes himself upon his successful polemical discussions with St. John, Peter, &c., and how he makes those good saints praise and flatter him.

As to his passion for Beatrice, I think there is all the internal evidence of its being a genuine passion, though her early death and probably his much musing upon her, exaggerated her good qualities into a sort of mystical personification of his own, very unlike the original. His drinking in all his celestial intelligence from her eyes, though rather a mystical sentimentalism, is the most glorious tribute that ever was paid to woman. It is lucky, on the whole, that she died when she was young, as, had she lived to marry him, he would very likely have picked a quarrel with her, and his Divine Comedy have lost a great source of its inspiration.

In all this, however, there was a great want of action, and Dante was forced, as in the Purgatorio, to give vent to his magnificent imagination in other ways. He has therefore made use of all the meagre hints suggested metaphorically by the Scriptures, and we have the three ingredients, light, music, and dancing, in every possible and impossible degree and diversity. The Inferno is a sort of tragedy, full of action and of characters, all well preserved. The Paradiso is a great melodrama, where little is said, but the chief skill is bestowed upon the machinery, — the getting up, — and certainly, there never was such a getting up, anywhere. Every canto blazes with a new and increased effulgence. The very reading of it by another pained my poor eyes. And yet, you never become tired with these gorgeous illustrations, — it is the descriptions that fatigue.

Another beauty, in which he indulges more freely in the last than in the other parts, is his unrivalled similes. I should think you might glean from the Paradiso at least one hundred all new and appropriate, fitting, as he says, "like a ring to a finger," and most beautiful. Where are there any comparisons so beautiful?

I must say I was disappointed with the last canto; but then, as the Irishman said, I expected to be. For what mortal mind could give a portrait of the Deity. The most conspicuous quality in Dante, to my notion, is simplicity. In this I think him superior to any work I ever read, unless it be some parts of the Scriptures. Homer's allusions, as far as I recollect, are not taken from as simple and familiar, yet not vulgar, objects, as are Dante's, — from the most common intimate relations of domestic life, for instance, to which Dante often with great sweetness of nature alludes.

I think it was a fortunate thing for the world, that the first poem in modern times was founded on a subject growing out of the Christian religion, or more properly on that religion itself, and that it was written by a man deeply penetrated with the spirit of its sternest creed. The religion indeed would have had its influence sooner or later upon literature. But then a work like Dante's, showing so early the whole extent of its powers, must have had an incalculable influence over the intellectual world, — an influence upon literature almost as remarkable as that exerted by the revelation of Christianity upon the moral world.

As to Cary, I think Dante would have given him a place in his ninth heaven, if he could have foreseen his Translation. It is most astonishing, giving not only the literal corresponding phrase, but the spirit of the original, the true Dantesque manner. It should be cited as an evidence of the compactness, the pliability, the sweetness of the English tongue. It particularly shows the wealth of the *old vocabulary*, — it is from this that he has selected his rich stock of expressions. It is a triumph of our mother tongue that it has given every idea of the most condensed original in the Italian tongue in a smaller compass in this translation, — his cantos, as you have no doubt noticed, are five or six lines shorter generally than Dante's. One defect he has. He does not, indeed he could not, render the naïve terms of his original. This is often noticeable, but it is the defect of our language, or rather of our use of it. One fault he has, one that runs through his whole translation, and makes it tedious ; viz. a too close assimilation to, or rather adoption of, the Italian idiom. This leads him often to take liberties not allowable in English, — to be ungrammatical, and so elliptical as to be quite unintelligible.

Now I have done, and if you ask me what I have been doing all this for, or, if I chose to write it, why I did not put it in my Commonplace, I answer, — 1st. That when I began this epistle, I had no idea of being so *lengthy* (as we say) ; 2d. That, in all pursuits, it is a great delight to find a friend to communicate one's meditations and conclusions to, and that you are the only friend I know in this bustling, money-getting world, who takes an interest in my peculiar pursuits, as well as in myself. So, for this cause, I pour into your unhappy ear what would else have been decently locked up in my *escritoire*.

I return you Petrarca, Tasso, Ginguené, Vols. I. – IV., and shall be obliged to you, in addition to the books first specified, for any translation, &c., if you have any of those books ; also for an edition — if you have such — of the Canterbury Tales, Vol. I., that contains a glossary at the bottom of each page below the text ; Tyrwhitt's being a dictionary.

Give my love to Anna, and believe me, dear George, now and ever,
Yours affectionately,
W. H. PRESCOTT.

Pursuing the Italian in this earnest way for about a year, he found that his main purposes in relation to it were accomplished, and he would gladly, at once, have begun the German, of which he knew nothing at all, but which, for a considerable period, he had deemed more important to the general scholarship at which he then aimed than any other modern language, and certainly more important than any one of which he did not already feel himself sufficiently master. "I am now," he recorded, two years earlier, in the spring of 1822, "twenty-six years of age nearly. By the time I am thirty, God willing, I propose, with what stock I have already on hand, to be a very well read English scholar ; to be acquainted with the classical and useful authors, prose and poetry, in Latin, French, and Italian, and especially in history ; I do not mean a critical or profound acquaintance. The two following years I may hope to learn German, and to have read the classical German writers ; and the translations, if my eye continues weak, of the Greek. And this is enough," he adds quietly, "for general discipline."

But the German, as he well knew, was much less easy of acquisition than any of the modern languages to which he had thus far devoted himself, and its literature much more unmanageable, if not more abundant. He was, however, unwilling to abandon it, as it afforded so many important facilities for the pursuits to which he intended to give his life. But the infirmity of his sight decided this, as it had already decided, and was destined later to decide, so many other questions in which he was deeply interested. After much deliberation, therefore, he gave up the German, as a thing either beyond his reach, or demanding more time for its acquisition than he could reasonably give to it. It seemed, in fact, all but an impossibility to learn it thoroughly ; the only way in which he cared to learn anything.

At the outset he was much discouraged by the conclusion to which he had thus come. The acquisition of the German was, in fact, the first obstacle to his settled literary course which his patience and courage had not been able to surmount, and for a time he became, from this circumstance, less exact and methodical in his studies than he had previously been. He recorded late in the autumn of 1824 : "I have read with no method and very little diligence or spirit for three months." This he found an unsatisfactory state of things. He talked

E

with me much about it, and seemed, during nearly a year, more unsettled as to his future course, so far as I can now recollect, than he had ever seemed to me earlier; certainly, more than he ever seemed to me afterwards.   Indeed, he was quite unhappy about it.

CHAPTER VI.

1824 – 1828.

AN accident — as is sometimes the case in the life of even the most earnest and consistent men — had now an influence on him not at all anticipated by either of us at the time, and one which, if it ultimately proved a guiding impulse, became such rather from the force of his own character than through any movement imparted to him from without.

I had, at this period, been almost exclusively occupied for two or three years with Spanish literature, and had completed a course of lectures on Spanish literary history, which I had delivered to the highest class in Harvard College, and which became, many years afterwards, the basis of a work on that subject. Thinking simply to amuse and occupy my friend at a time when he seemed much to need it, I proposed to read him these lectures in the autumn of 1824. For this purpose he came to my house in the early part of a succession of evenings, until the whole was completed ; and in November he determined, as a substitute for the German, to undertake the Spanish, which had not previously constituted any part of his plan of study.[1]

He made his arrangements for it at once, and we prepared together a list of books that he should read. It was a great

---

[1] He speaks of this in February, 1841, writing to Don Pascual de Gayangos, one of our mutual Spanish friends ; when, referring back to the year 1824, he says, "I heard Mr. Ticknor's lectures then with great pleasure."

and unexpected pleasure to me to find him launched on a course of study in which I had long been interested, and I certainly encouraged him in it as much as I could without being too selfish.

Soon after this, however, I left home with my family, and was absent during the greater part of the winter. My house was, of course, shut up, except that servants were left in charge of it; but it had been understood between us, that, as he had no Spanish books of his own, he should carry on his Spanish studies from the resources he would find in my library. On the 1st of December he began a regular drill in the language, with a teacher, and on the same day, by way of announcing it, wrote to me: —

"Your mansion looks gloomy enough, I promise you, and as I pass it sometimes in the evening, with no cheerful light within to relieve it, it frowns doubly dismal on me. As to the interior, I have not set my foot within its precincts since your departure, which, you will think, does not augur well for the Spanish. I propose, however, intruding upon the silence of the illustrious dead the latter part of this week, in order to carry off the immortal remains of Don Antonio de Solis, whom you, dear George, recommended me to begin with."

This was the opening of the Spanish campaign, which ended only with his life; and it is worth noting that he was already more than twenty-eight years old. A few days afterwards he writes: "I snatch a fraction of the morning from the interesting treatise of Monsieur Jossé on the Spanish language,[2] and from the 'Conquista de Mexico,' which, notwithstanding the time I have been upon it, I am far from having conquered."[3] But he soon became earnest in his work. On the 24th of January, 1825, he wrote to me again: —

"I have been much bent upon Spanish the last month, and have uncourteously resisted all invitations . . . . . to break in upon my course of reading. I begin to feel my way perceptibly in it now. Did you never, in learning a language, after groping about in the dark for a long while,

[2] Jossé, Elémens de la Grammaire de la Langue Espagnole.
[3] In the early part of his Spanish studies, as he here intimates, he was not much interested. At Christmas, 1824, he wrote to his friend Mr. Bancroft: "I am battling with the Spaniards this winter, but I have not the heart for it that I had for the Italians. I doubt whether there are many valuable things that the key of knowledge will unlock in that language"; — an amusing prediction, when we consider what followed.

suddenly seem to turn an angle, where the light breaks upon you all at once? The knack seems to have come to me within the last fortnight, in the same manner as the art of swimming comes to those who have been splashing about for months in the water in vain. . . . . . Will you have the goodness to inform me in your next, where I can find some simple treatise on Spanish versification, — also in which part of your library is the 'Amadis de Gaula.'[4] For I presume, as Cervantes spared it from the bonfire, you have it among your treasures. I have been accompanying my course with Sismondi and Bouterwek, and I have been led more than once to reflect upon the injustice you are doing to yourself in secluding your own manuscript Lectures from the world. Neither of these writers has gone into the subject as thoroughly as you have," &c., &c.[5]

On coming back after my absence, he began to write me notes in Spanish, borrowing or returning books, and sometimes giving his opinion about those he sent home. His style was not, indeed, of the purest Castilian, but it was marked with a clearness and idiomatic vigor which not a little surprised me. Three of these notes, which he wrote in March and April, 1825, still survive to give proof of his great industry and success; and one of them is curious for opinions about Solis, more severe than he afterwards entertained when he came to study that historian's work on the Conquest of Mexico as a part of the materials for his own.[6]

But, during the summer of 1825, his reading was very miscellaneous, and, excepting "Doblado's Letters on Spain," by Blanco White, no part of it, I think, was connected with his strictly Spanish studies. In the autumn, however, becoming much dissatisfied with this unsettled and irregular sort of life, he began to look round for a subject to which he could give continuous thought and labor. On the 16th of October he

---

[4] He remembered, no doubt, the boyish pleasure he had found in reading Southey's *rifacimento* of it. See *ante*, p. 10.

[5] This, with much more like it in the present letter and in other letters, which I do not cite, was founded in a mistake, made by his kindness for me. The Lectures were far from being what he supposed them to be. They needed to be entirely recast, before they could be presented to the public with any decent claims to thoroughness. In fact, "The History of Spanish Literature" did not appear until a long time afterwards, and then it bore very few traces of its academic origin.

[6] On another occasion, making some remarks about Ercilla's "Araucana," he says, in the same spirit, "Both Solis and Ercilla disgust the temperate reader by the little value they set upon the sufferings of the heathen." In this view of the matter I heartily concur with him.

recorded : " I have been so hesitating and reflecting upon what
I shall do, that I have, in fact, done nothing." And October
30th : " I have passed the last fortnight in examination of a
suitable subject for historical composition.' It is well to determine with caution and accurate inspection."

At first his thoughts were turned towards American history,
on which he had bestowed a good deal of rather idle time during the preceding months, and to which he now gave more.[7]
But Spanish literature began, unexpectedly to him, to have
stronger attractions. He read, or rather listened to, the whole
of Mariana's beautiful history, giving careful attention to some
parts of it, and passing lightly over the rest. And in connection with this, as his mind became more directed to such subjects, he listened with great interest to Mably's " Étude de
l'Histoire," — a work which had much influence in giving its
final direction to his life, and which he always valued both for
its acuteness and for its power of setting the reader to think
for himself. The result was that, at Christmas, after no little
reflection and anxiety, he made the following memorandum : —

" I have been hesitating between two topics for historical investigation, — Spanish history from the invasion of the Arabs to the consolidation
of the monarchy under Charles V., or a history of the revolution of
ancient Rome, which converted the republic into a monarchy. A third
subject which invites me is a biographical sketch of eminent geniuses,
with criticisms on their productions and on the character of their times.
I shall probably select the first, as less difficult of execution than the
second, and as more novel and entertaining than the last. But I must

7. As early as 1820, I find that he had been greatly impressed by reading
Gibbon's Autobiography with Lord Sheffield's additions, — a book which he
always regarded with peculiar interest, and which doubtless had its influence
in originally determining him to venture on historical composition. In one
of his letters written in 1845, he says, he finds memoranda of a tendency to
historical studies as early as 1819.

[8] Two or three years earlier than this date — probably in 1822 — I find
the following among his private memoranda : — " History has always been
a favorite study with me; and I have long looked forward to it, as a subject
on which I was one day to exercise my pen. It is not rash, in the dearth of
well-written American history, to entertain the hope of throwing light upon
this matter. This is my hope. But it requires time, and a long time, before
the mind can be prepared for this department of writing." He took time, as
we shall see, for it was seven years, at least, after this passage was written,
before he began the composition of his Ferdinand and Isabella. " I think,"
he says, " thirty-five years of age full soon enough to put pen to paper." As
it turned out, he began in earnest a little before he had reached thirty-four.

discipline my idle fancy, or my meditations will be little better than dreams. I have devoted more than four hours *per diem* to thinking or dreaming on these subjects."

But this delay was no matter of serious regret to him. He always deliberated long before he undertook anything of consequence, and, in regard to his examination of this very matter, he had already recorded : " I care not how long a time I take for it, provided I am diligent in all that time."

He was a little distracted, however, at this period, by the thought of writing something like a history or general examination of Italian literature. As we have noticed, he had in 1823 been much occupied with the principal Italian authors, and had found the study more interesting than any he had previously pursued in modern literature. A little later — that is, in the autumn of 1824 and the spring of 1825 — an accomplished Italian exile was in Boston, and, partly to give him occupation, and partly for the pleasure and improvement to be obtained from it, I invited the unfortunate scholar to come three or four times a week, and read aloud to me from the principal poets of his country. Prescott joined me in it regularly, and sometimes we had one or two friends with us. In this way we went over large portions of the " Divina Commedia," and the whole of the " Gerusalemme Liberata," parts of Ariosto's " Orlando Furioso," and several plays of Alfieri. The sittings were very agreeable, sometimes protracted to two or three hours, and we not only had earnest and amusing, if not always very profitable, discussions about what we heard, but sometimes we followed them up afterwards with careful inquiries. The pleasure of the meetings, however, was their great attraction. The Italian scholar read well, and we enjoyed it very much. In consequence of this, Prescott now turned again to his Italian studies, and made the following record : —

" I have decided to abandon the Roman subject. A work on the revolutions of Italian literature has invited my consideration this week, — a work which, without giving a chronological and minute analysis of authors, should exhibit in masses the most important periods, revolutions, and characters in the history of Italian letters. The subject would admit of contraction or expansion *ad libitum ;* and I should be spared — what I detest — hunting up latent, barren antiquities."

The last remark is noteworthy, because it is one of the many instances in which, after severe consideration, he schooled himself to do well and thoroughly what he much disliked to do, and what was in itself difficult.

But on the same occasion he wrote further : —

"The subject would require a mass of [general] knowledge and a critical knowledge of the Italian in particular. It would not be new, after the production of Sismondi and the abundant notices in modern Reviews. Literary history is not so amusing as civil. Cannot I contrive to embrace the *gift* of the Spanish subject, without involving myself in the unwieldy, barbarous records of a thousand years? What new and interesting topics may be admitted — not forced — into the reigns of Ferdinand and Isabella? Can I not indulge in a retrospective picture of the Constitutions of Castile and Aragon, — of the Moorish dynasties, and the causes of their decay and dissolution? Then I have the Inquisition, with its bloody persecutions; the Conquest of Granada, a brilliant passage; the exploits of the Great Captain in Italy, — a proper character for romance as well as history; the discovery of a new world, my own country; the new policy of the monarchs towards the overgrown aristocracy, &c., &c. A Biography will make me responsible for a limited space only; will require much less reading (a great consideration with me); will offer the deeper interest which always attaches to minute developments of character, and a continuous, closely connected narrative. The subject brings me to the point whence [modern] English history has started, is untried ground, and in my opinion a rich one. The age of Ferdinand is most important, as containing the germs of the modern system of European politics; and the three sovereigns, Henry VII., Louis XI., and Ferdinand, were important engines in overturning the old system. It is in every respect an interesting and momentous period of history; the materials authentic, ample. I will chew upon this matter, and decide this week."

In May, 1847, above twenty years afterwards, he noted in pencil on this passage, "This was the first germ of my conception of Ferdinand and Isabella."

But he did not, as he hoped he should, decide in a week, although, having advanced well towards a decision, he soon began to act as if it were already made. On the 15th of January, 1826, when the week had expired, he recorded : —

"Still doubting, looked through Hita's 'Guerras de Granada,' Vol. I. The Italian subject has some advantages over the Spanish. It will save me at least one year's introductory labor. It is in the regular course of my studies, and I am comparatively at home in literary history, particularly the Italian. This subject has not only exercised my studies, but my meditations, so that I may fairly estimate my starting ground at one year. Then I have tried this topic in public journals, and know the measure of my own strength in relation to it. I am quite doubtful of my capacity for doing justice to the other subject. I have never exercised my mind upon similar matters, and I have stored it with no materials for comparison. How can I pronounce upon the defects or virtues of the Spanish constitutions, when I am hardly acquainted with those of other nations? How can I estimate the consequences, moral, political, &c., of laws and institutions, when I have, in all my life, scarcely ever looked the subject in the face, or even read the most elementary treatise upon it? But will not a year's labor, judiciously directed, put me on another footing?"

After some further discussion in the nature of a soliloquy, he adds: —

"I believe the Spanish subject will be more new than the Italian; more interesting to the majority of readers; more useful to me by opening another and more practical department of study; and not more laborious in relation to authorities to be consulted, and not more difficult to be discussed with the lights already afforded me by judicious treatises on the most intricate parts of the subject, and with the allowance of the introductory year for my novitiate in a new walk of letters. The advantages of the Spanish topic, on the whole, overbalance the inconvenience of the requisite preliminary year. For these reasons, I subscribe to the History of the Reign of Ferdinand and Isabella, January 19th, 1826."

And then follows in pencil, — "A fortunate choice, May, 1847."

He therefore began in earnest, and, on the 22d of January, prepared a list of books such as he should require, and wrote a long letter to Mr. Alexander H. Everett, then our Minister at Madrid, an accomplished scholar himself, and one who was always interested in whatever regarded the cause of letters. They had already been in correspondence on the subject, and Mr. Everett had naturally advised his younger friend to come to Spain, and make for himself the collections he needed, at the same time offering to serve him in any way he could.

"I entirely agree with you," Prescott replied, "that it would be highly advantageous for me to visit Spain, and to dive into the arcana of those libraries which, you say, contain such ample stores of history, and I assure you, that, as I am situated, no consideration of domestic ease would detain me a moment from an expedition, which, after all, would not consume more than four or five months. But the state of my eyes, or rather eye, — for I have the use of only one half of this valuable apparatus, — precludes the possibility of it. During the last year this one has been sadly plagued with what the physicians are pleased to call a rheumatic inflammation, for which I am now under treatment. . . . . . I have always found travelling, with its necessary exposures, to be of infinite disservice to my eyes, and in this state of them particularly I dare not risk it.

"You will ask, with these disadvantages, how I can expect to succeed

4

in my enterprise. I answer, that I hope always to have a partial use of my eyes, and, for the rest, an intelligent reader, who is well acquainted with French, Spanish, and Latin, will enable me to effect with my ears what other people do with their eyes. The only material inconvenience will be a necessarily more tedious and prolonged labor. Johnson says, in his Life of Milton, that no man can compile a history who is blind. But although I should lose the use of my vision altogether (an evil not in the least degree probable), by the blessing of God, if my ears are spared me, I will disprove the assertion, and my chronicle, whatever other demerits it may have, shall not be wanting in accuracy and research.[*] If my health continues thus, I shall necessarily be debarred from many of the convivial, not to say social pleasures of life, and consequently must look to literary pursuits as the principal and permanent source of future enjoyment. As with these views I have deliberately taken up this project, and my progress, since I have begun to break ground, entirely satisfies me of the feasibility of the undertaking, you will not wonder that I should be extremely solicitous to bring within my control an ample quantity of original materials, such as will enable me to achieve my design, and such as will encourage me to pursue it with steady diligence, without fear of competition from any quarter."

But his courage and patience were put to a new and severe trial, before he could even place his foot upon the threshold of the great undertaking whose difficulties he estimated so justly. A dozen years later, in May, 1838, when the Ferdinand and Isabella was already published, he made a memorandum in pencil on the letter just cited : " This very letter occasioned the injury to the nerve from which I have never since recovered." Precisely what this injury may have been, I do not know. He calls it at first " a stiffness of the right eye," as if it were a recurrence there of the rheumatism which was always more or less in some part of his person ; but a few months afterwards he speaks of it as " a new disorder." It was, I apprehend, only the result of an effort too great for the enfeebled organ, and, whenever any considerable similar exertion during the

---

[*] " To compile a history from various authors, when they can only be consulted by others' eyes, is not easy, nor possible, without more skilful and attentive help than can be commonly obtained ; and it was probably the difficulty of consulting and comparing, that stopped Milton's narrative at the Conquest, — a period at which affairs were not very intricate, nor authors very numerous." — Johnson's Works, (London, 1816,) Vol. IX. p. 115. " This remark of the great critic," says Prescott, in a note to the Preface of Ferdinand and Isabella, (1837,) where it is cited, — " This remark, which first engaged my attention in the midst of my embarrassments, although discouraging at first, in the end stimulated my desire to overcome them." *Nitor in adversum* might have been his motto,

rest of his life was required from it, he used to describe the sensation he experienced as "a strain of the nerve." It was, no doubt, something of the sort on this occasion, and he felt for a time much discouraged by it.

The letter which it had cost him so much to write, because he thought it necessary to do it with uncommon care, was left in his portfolio to wait the result of this fresh and unexpected attack on the poor resources of his sight. It was a painful interval. Severe remedies were used. The cuppings then made on his temples left marks that he carried to his grave. But in his darkened room, where I constantly saw him, and sometimes read to him, his spirits never failed. He bated "no jot of heart or hope."

At last, after above four weary months, which he passed almost always in a dark room, and during which he made no record, I find an entry among his memoranda dated "June 4, 1826. A melancholy gap," he says, "occasioned by this new disorder in the eye. It has, however, so much abated this summer, that I have sent my orders to Madrid. I trust I may yet be permitted to go on with my original plan. What I can't read may be read to me. I will secure what I can of the foreign tongues, and leave the English to my secretary. When I can't get six, get four hours per day. I must not waste time in going too deeply or widely into my subject; or, rather, I must confine myself to what exclusively and directly concerns it. I must abjure manuscript and fine print. I must make memoranda accurate and brief of every book I read for this object. Travelling at this lame gait, I may yet hope in five or six years to reach the goal." In this, however, he was mistaken. It proved to be twice as much.

As soon as the order for books was despatched, he made his plan of work. It was as ample and bold as if nothing had occurred to check his hopes.

"My general course of study," he says, "must be as follows. 1. General Laws, &c. of Nations. 2. History and Constitution of England. 3. History and Government of other European Nations, — France, Italy to 1550, Germany, Portugal. Under the last two divisions, I am particularly to attend to the period intervening between 1400 and 1550. 4. General History of Spain, — its Geography, its Civil, Ecclesiastical, Statistical Concerns; particularly from 1400 to 1550. 5. Ferdinand's Reign *en gros.*

6. Whatever concerns such portions of my subject as I am immediately to treat of. The general division of it I will arrange when I have gone through the first five departments.

"This order of study I shall pursue, as far as my eyes will allow. When they are too feeble to be used, I must have English writers read to me, and then I will select such works as have the nearest relation to the department of study which I may be investigating."

Immediately after this general statement of his plan follows a list of several hundred volumes to be read or consulted, which would have been enough, one would think, to alarm the stoutest heart, and severely tax the best eyes. This, indeed, he sometimes felt to be the case. Circumstances seemed occasionally to be stronger than his strong will. He tried, for instance, soon after making the last record, to read a little, and, went at the most moderate rate, through half a volume of Montesquieu's " Ésprit des Lois," which was to be one of the first stepping-stones to his great fabric. But the trouble in his sight was so seriously aggravated by even this experiment, very cautiously made, that he recorded it as " a warning to desist from all further use of his eye for the present, if not for ever." In fact, for three months and more he did not venture to open a book.

At the end of that time he began to doubt whether, during the period in which it now seemed all but certain that he could have no use of his eye, and must often be shut up in a darkened room, he had not better, without giving up his main purpose, undertake some other work more manageable than one that involved the use of books in several foreign languages. On the 1st of October, therefore, he records, evidently with great regret : —

"As it may probably be some years before I shall be able to use my own eyes in study, or even find a suitable person to read foreign languages to me, I have determined to postpone my Spanish subject, and to occupy myself with an Historical Survey of English Literature. The subject has never been discussed as a whole, and therefore would be somewhat new, and, if well conducted, popular. But the great argument with me is, that, while it is a subject with which my previous studies have made me tolerably acquainted and have furnished me with abundance of analogies in foreign literatures, it is one which I may investigate nearly as well with my ears as with my eyes, and it will not be difficult to find good readers in the English, though extremely difficult in any foreign language. *Faustum sit.*"

A month, however, was sufficient to satisfy him that this was a mistake, and that the time which, with his ultimate purpose of writing a large work on Spanish history, he could afford to give to this intercalary project, could do little with a subject so broad as English literature. After looking through Warton's fragment and Turner's Anglo-Saxons, he therefore writes, November 5th, 1826 : —

"I have again, and I trust finally, determined to prosecute my former subject, the Reign of Ferdinand and Isabella. In taking a more accurate survey of my projected English Literary History, I am convinced it will take at least five years to do anything at all satisfactory to myself, and I cannot be content to be so long detained from a favorite subject, and one for which I shall have such rare and valuable materials in my own possession. But what chiefly influences me is the prospect of obtaining some one, in the space of a year, who, by a competent knowledge of foreign languages, will enable me to pursue my original design with nearly as great facility as I should possess for the investigation of English literature. And I am now fully resolved, that nothing but a disappointment in my expected supplies from Spain shall prevent me from prosecuting my original scheme ; where, at any rate, success is more certain, if not more easy."

The difficulty that resulted from the want of a competent reader was certainly a great one, and he felt it severely. He talked with me much about it, but for a time there seemed no remedy. He went, therefore, courageously through several volumes of Spanish with a person who understood not a word of what he was reading. It was awkward, tedious work, — more disagreeable to the reader, probably, than it was to the listener. But neither of them shrunk from the task, which sometimes, notwithstanding its gravity and importance, seemed ridiculous to both.[10]

At last he was satisfied that his undertaking to write history was certainly practicable, and that he could substantially make his ears do the work of his eyes. It was an important conclu-

---

[10] In a letter to me written in the summer of 1827, when I happened to be on a journey to Niagara, he says: "My excellent reader and present scribe reads to me Spanish with a true Castilian accent two hours a day, without understanding a word of it. What do you think of this for the temperature of the dog-days? and which should you rather be, the reader or the *readee*?" In a letter ten years later — Dec. 20, 1837 — to his friend Mr. Bancroft, he says, that among those readings by a person who did not know the language were seven quarto volumes in Spanish.

sion, and its date is, therefore, one of the turning points of his life. He came to it about the time he prepared the letter to Mr. Everett, and in consequence provided himself for a few months with a young reader of more accomplishments, who subsequently became known in the world of letters, and was among those who paid a tribute of graceful verse to the historian's memory.[11]

This, however, was only a temporary expedient, and he was desirous to have something which should be permanent. It cost not a little time and labor to fit anybody for duties so peculiar, and he had no time and labor to spare, especially if the embarrassment should recur as often as it had heretofore. Thinking, from my connection with Harvard College, where I was then at the head of the department of Modern Literature, that I might be acquainted with some young man who, on completing his academic career, would be willing to become his secretary for a considerable period, he addressed himself to me. I advised with the instructors in the four modern languages, who knew the especial qualifications of their pupils better than I did, and a fortunate result was soon reached. Mr. James L. English, who was then a member of the College, accepted a proposition to study his profession in the office of Mr. Prescott, senior, and of his son-in-law, Mr. Dexter, who was then associated with the elder Mr. Prescott as a counsellor, and at the same time to read and write for the son five or six hours every day. This arrangement did not, however, take effect until after Mr. English was graduated, in 1827 ; and it continued, much to the satisfaction of both parties, for four years. It was the happy beginning of a new order of things for the studies of the historian, and one which, with different secretaries or readers, he was able to keep up to the last.[12]

During the interval of almost a year, which immediately pre-

---

[11] Mr. George Lunt.

[12] Mr. Prescott's different readers and secretaries were, as nearly as I can remember and make out, — George R. M. Withington, for a short period, which I cannot exactly determine ; George Lunt, 1825 – 26 ; Hamilton Parker, 1826 – 27 ; James Lloyd English, 1827 – 31 ; Henry Cheever Simonds, 1831 – 85 ; E. Dwight Williams, 1835 – 40 ; George F. Ware, 1840 – 42 ; Edmund B. Otis, 1842 – 46 ; George F. Ware again, 1846 – 47 ; Robert Carter, 1847 – 48 ; John Foster Kirk, 1848 – 59.

ceded the commencement of Mr. English's services, nothing
is more striking than the amount and thoroughness of Mr.
Prescott's studies. It in fact was a broad basis that he now
began to lay, in defiance of all the difficulties that beset him,
for a superstructure which yet, as he clearly foresaw, could be
erected only after a very long interval, if, indeed, he should
ever be permitted to erect it. It was, too, a basis laid in the
most deliberate manner, slowly and surely; for, as he could not
now read at all himself, every page, as it was listened to, had to
be carefully considered, and its contents carefully appropriated.
Among the books thus read to him were Montesquieu's "Spirit
of Laws," Enfield's "History of Philosophy," Smith's "Wealth
of Nations," Hallam's "Middle Ages," Blackstone's "Commentaries," Vol. I., Millar's "English Government," the four concluding volumes of Gibbon, parts of Turner's "History of England," parts of Mosheim's "Ecclesiastical History" and of John
Müller's "Universal History," Mills's "History of Chivalry,"
the Memoirs of Commines, Robertson's "Charles the Fifth,"
and his "America," and Watson's "Philip the Second." Besides all this, he listened to translations of Plato's "Phædo," of
Epictetus, of the Meditations of Marcus Aurelius, and of Cicero's "Tusculan Questions" and "Letters"; and, finally, he
went in the same way through portions of Sismondi's "Répub-
liques Italiennes" in the original, as an experiment, and became persuaded, from the facility with which he understood it
when read at the rate of twenty-four pages an hour, that he
should meet with no absolutely insurmountable obstacle in the
prosecution of any of his historical plans. Everything, therefore, went according to his wish, and seemed propitious; but
his eyes remained in a very bad state. He was often in a dark
room, and never able to use them for any of the practical purposes of study.[18]

[18] He makes hardly a note about his opinion on the authors embraced in
his manifold studies this year, from want of sight to do it. But what he records about Robertson and Watson, brief as it is, is worth notice, because
these writers both come upon his chosen track. "Robertson's extensive subject," he says, "is necessarily deficient in connection; but a lively interest is
kept up by a perpetual succession of new discoveries and brilliant adventures,
seasoned with sagacious reflections, and enriched with a clear and vigorous
diction." In some remarks concerning Charles V., thirty years later, he does
Dr. Robertson the homage of calling him "the illustrious Scottish historian,"

Still, as always, his spirits rose with the occasion, and his courage proved equal to his spirits. He had a large part of the Spanish grammar read over to him, that he might feel quite sure-footed in the language, and then, confirming anew his determination to write the History of Ferdinand and Isabella, he pushed vigorously forward with his investigations in that direction.

He read, or rather listened to, Koch's "Révolutions de l'Europe"; Voltaire's "Essai sur les Mœurs"; Gibbon, so far as the Visigoths in Spain are concerned; and Conde's "Spanish Arabs." As he approached his main subject more nearly, he went through the reigns of several of the preceding and following Spanish sovereigns in Ferreras's General History of Spain, as well as in Rabbe, Morales, and Bigland; adding the whole of Gaillard's "Rivalité de la France et de l'Espagne," and of the Abbé Mignot's meagre "Histoire de Ferdinand et Isabelle." The geography of the country he had earlier studied on minute maps, when his eyes had for a short time permitted such use of them, and he now endeavored to make himself familiar with the Spanish people and their national character, by listening to such travellers as Bourgoing and Townsend. Finally, he finished this part of his preparation by going afresh over the concluding portions of Mariana's eloquent History; thus obtaining from so many different sources, not only a sufficient and more than sufficient mere basis for his own work, but from Mariana the best general outline for it that existing materials could furnish. It is not easy to see how he could have been more thorough and careful, even if he had enjoyed the full use of his sight, nor how, with such an infirmity, he could deliberately have undertaken and carried out a course of merely preparatory studies so ample and minute.

But he perceived the peculiar embarrassments, as well as the great resources, of his subject, and endeavored to provide against them by long consideration and reflection beforehand. In his Memoranda he says: —

but enters into no discussion of his peculiar merits. Of Watson, on the contrary, in his private notes of 1827, he says that he is " a meagre unphilosophical chronicler of the richest period of Spanish history "; an opinion substantially confirmed in the Preface to his own Philip II., in 1855, where a compliment is paid to Robertson at Watson's expense.

"I must not be too fastidious, nor too anxious to amass every authority that can bear upon the subject. The materials that will naturally offer themselves to me are abundant enough, in all conscience. Whatever I write will have the merit at least of novelty to an English reader. In such parts of the subject, therefore, as have been well treated by French writers, I had better take them pretty closely for my guides, without troubling myself to hunt more deeply, except only for corroborative authorities, which can be easily done. It is fortunate that this subject is little known to English readers, while many parts of it have been ably discussed by accessible foreign writers, — such as Marina and Sempere for the Constitution ; Llorente for the Inquisition ; the sixth volume of the Historical Transactions of the Spanish Academy for the influence and many details of Isabella's reign, &c. ; Fléchier for the life of Ximenes ; Varillas for the foreign policy of Ferdinand ; Sismondi for the Italian wars and for the general state of Italian and European politics in that age, while the reflections of this historian *passim* may furnish me with many good hints in an investigation of the Spanish history and politics."

This was the view he took of his subject, as he fully confronted it for the first time, and considered how, with such use of his eyes as he then had, he could best address himself to the necessary examination of his authorities. But he now, and for some time subsequent, contemplated a shorter work than the one he finally wrote, and a work of much less learned pretensions. As, however, he advanced, he found that the most minute investigations, such as he had above considered beyond his reach, would be both necessary and agreeable. He began, therefore, very soon, to examine all the original sources with painstaking perseverance, and to compare them, not only with each other, but with the interpretations that had subsequently been put upon them. He struck much more widely and boldly than he had intended or thought important. In short, he learned — and he learned it soon — that it is necessary for a conscientious author to read everything upon the subject he means to discuss ; the poor and bad books, as well as those upon which his reliance will ultimately be placed. He cannot otherwise feel strong or safe.

Mr. Prescott had just reached this point in his studies, when, in the autumn of 1827, Mr. English became his reader and secretary. The first collection of books and manuscripts from Madrid had been received a little earlier. But they had not yet been used. They had come at a most unlucky moment, when his eye was in a more than commonly suffering state, and

4 *

they presented anything but a cheerful prospect to him, as they lay unpacked and spread out on the floor of his study. As he said long afterwards, "In my disabled condition, with my Transatlantic treasures lying around me, I was like one pining from hunger in the midst of abundance." [14]

But he went to work in earnest with his new secretary. The room in which they sat was an upper one in the back part of the fine old house in Bedford Street, retired and quiet, and every way well fitted for its purpose. Mr. English, in an interesting letter to me, thus truly describes it.

"Two sides of the room," he says, "were lined with books from floor to ceiling. On the easterly side was a green screen, which darkened that part of the room towards which he turned his face as he sat at his writing-table. On the westerly side was one window covered by several curtains of light-blue muslin, so arranged that any one of them could be wholly or partially raised, and thus temper the light exactly to the ability of his eye to bear it, as the sky might happen to be bright or cloudy, or his eye more or less sensitive. In the centre of the room stood his writing-table, at which he sat in a rocking-chair with his back towards the curtained window, and sometimes with a green shade over his eyes. When we had a fire, he used only coke in the grate, as giving out no flame, and he frequently placed a screen between himself and the grate to keep off the glare of the embers. At the northwesterly corner of the room was the only window not partly or wholly darkened. It was set high up in the wall, and under it was my chair. I was thus brought a short distance from his left side, and rather behind him, — as a sailor would say, on his quarter. In this position I read aloud to him regularly every day, from ten o'clock in the forenoon to two in the afternoon, and from about six in the evening to eight."

They began by reading portions of Llorente's "Histoire de l'Inquisition"; but their first serious attack was on the chronicles of Andrés Bernaldez, not then printed, but obtained by him in manuscript from Madrid, — a gossiping, amusing book, whose accounts extend from 1488 to 1513, and are particularly important for the Moorish wars and the life of Columbus. But the young secretary found it very hard reading.

"A huge parchment-covered manuscript," he calls Bernaldez, "my old enemy; from whose pages I read and reread so many hours that I shall never forget him. Mr. Prescott considered the book a great acquisition, and would sit for hours hearing me read it in the Spanish, — at first with great difficulty and until I got familiar with the chirography. How he could understand me at first, as I blundered along, I could not conceive.

[14] Conquest of Peru, (1857), Vol. I. p. xvi.

If he was annoyed, — as he well might be, — he never betrayed his feelings to me.

"He seemed fully conscious of the difficulty of the task before him, but resolutely determined to accomplish it, if human patience and perseverance could do so. As I read any passages which he wished to impress on his memory, he would say, 'Mark that,' — that is, draw parallel lines in the margin with a pencil against it. He used also to take a note or memorandum of anything he wished particularly to remember, with a reference to it. His writing apparatus always lay open before him on the table, and he usually sat with his ivory style in hand, ready to make his notes of reference.[16] These notes I afterwards copied out in a very large round hand for his future use, and, when he began actually to write the history, would read them over and verify the reference by the original authority, if he required it. I think, however, he did not very often find it necessary to refer to the book, as he seemed to have cultivated his memory to a very high degree, and had, besides, a habit of reflecting upon and arranging in his mind, or 'digesting,' as he phrased it, the morning's reading while sitting alone afterwards in his study. A graphic phrase it was, too, considering that he took in through his ears I don't know how many pages at a four hours' session of steady reading. The wonder was, how he could find time to 'digest' such a load between the sessions. But thus he fixed the substance of what had been read to him in his mind, and impressed the results of the forenoon's work on his memory.

"When I first began to read to Mr. Prescott, his eye was in a very sensitive state, and he did not attempt to use it at all. After some months, however, it got stronger, and he would sit at the curtained window, with a volume open upon a frame on a stand, and read himself, marking passages as he went along. While so reading, he would frequently raise or lower, wholly or partially, one or more of the blue curtains. Each of them had its separate cord, which he knew as well as a sailor knows his ropes. Every little white cloud that passed across the sky required a change in the arrangement of these curtains, so sensitive was his eye to a variation of light imperceptible to me. But it was only a portion of the time that he could do this. His eye would give way or he would feel symptoms of returning trouble, and then, for weeks together, he would be compelled to take his old seat in the rocking-chair, and return to the slow process of listening and marking passages, and having his notes and memoranda read over to him as at first."

How sound and practical his general views were can be seen from his plan of work at this moment, when he had determined what he would do, but did not think himself nearly ready even to begin the actual composition of the History itself. In October, 1828, when they had been at work for a year in this preparatory reading, but during which his private

---

[16] His peculiar writing apparatus, already alluded to, will be presently described. It was the noctograph, which he had obtained in England.

memoranda, owing to the state of his eye, had been very meagre, he says : —

"By the intermixture of reading for a given chapter and then writing for it, I shall be able, with the relief which this alternate occupation will give my eyes, to accomplish a good deal with them, I trust. After I have finished Bernaldez's manuscript and the few remaining pages of Ferreras, and looked through the 'Modern Universal History' from the accession of the house of Trastamara to the end of the reigns of the Catholic kings, and looked into Marina's 'Theory of the Cortes,' which will scarcely require more than a fortnight, I shall be prepared to *begin to read* for my first chapter."

He added to this a syllabus of what, from the point of view at which he then stood, he thought might be the arrangement of his materials for the first two chapters of his work ; noting the length of time he might need to prepare himself to begin to write, and afterwards the time necessary to complete them. That he was willing to be patient is clear from the fact that he allowed two hundred and fifty-six days, or eight months and a half to this preparatory reading, although he had already been two years, more or less, on the work ; and that he was not to be discouraged by slowness of actual progress is equally clear, for, although it was above fourteen months before he finished this part of his task, yet at the end of that time his courage and hopes were as high as ever.

CHAPTER VII.

1829 — 1837.

THE long delay referred to in the last chapter was in part owing to a severe sorrow which fell on him in the winter of 1828 – 9, and stopped him in mid-career. On the 1st of February, the eldest of his two children died. It was a daughter, born on the 23d of September, 1824, and therefore four years and four or five months old, — a charming, gentle child of much promise, who had been named after her grandmother, Catherine Hickling. He had doted on her. His mother said most truly, writing to Mrs. Ticknor in 1825: "It is a very nice little girl, and William is one of the happiest fathers you ever saw. All the time he can spare from Italian and Spanish studies is devoted to this little pet." Mr. English remembers well how she used to be permitted to come into the study, and interrupt whatever work was going on there, much to his own satisfaction as well as to the father's, for her engaging ways had won the secretary's love too. The shock of her death was very great, and was, besides, somewhat sudden. I have seldom seen sorrow more deep; and, what was remarkable, the grandfather and grandmother were so much overcome by it as to need the consolation they would otherwise have gladly given. It was, indeed, a much distressed house.[1]

---

[1] In a letter dated June 30, 1844, to Don Pascual de Gayangos, who had just suffered from the loss of a young child, Mr. Prescott says, "A similar calamity befell me some years since. It was my favorite child, taken away at the age of four, when all the loveliness and vivacity of the character is opening upon us. I never can suffer again as I then did. It was my first heavy sorrow; and I suppose we cannot feel twice so bitterly."

But the father wrought out consolation for himself in his own way. A fortnight after the death of his child he records :—

"February 15th, 1829. — The death of my dearest daughter on the first day of this month having made it impossible for me at present to resume the task of composition, I have been naturally led to more serious reflection than usual, and have occupied myself with reviewing the grounds of the decision which I made in 1819 in favor of the evidences of the Christian revelation. I have endeavored and shall endeavor to prosecute this examination with perfect impartiality, and to guard against the present state of my feelings influencing my mind any further than by leading it to give to the subject a more serious attention. And, so far, such influence must be salutary and reasonable, and far more desirable than any counter influence which might be exerted by any engrossing occupation with the cares and dissipation of the world. So far, I believe, I have conducted the matter with sober impartiality."

What he did on this subject, as on all others, he did thoroughly and carefully. His secretary read to him the principal books which it was then considered important to go through when making a fair examination of the supernatural claims of Christianity. Among them, on the one side, were Hume's "Essays," and especially the one on Miracles; Gibbon's fifteenth chapter, and parts of the sixteenth ; Middleton's "Free Inquiry," which whatever were its author's real opinions, leans towards unbelief; and Soame Jenyns's somewhat easy discussion of the Evidences, which is yet not wanting in hidden skill and acuteness. On the other hand, he took Watson's "Apology"; Brown's "Lectures," so far as they are an amplification of his admirably condensed "Essay on Cause and Effect"; several of Waterland's treatises; Butler's "Analogy" and Paley's "Evidences," with the portions of Lardner needful to explain and illustrate them. The last three works he valued more than all the others. But I think he relied mainly upon a careful reading of the Four Gospels, and an especial inquiry into each one of the Saviour's miracles, as related by each of the Evangelists. This investigation he made with his father's assistance ; and, when it was over, he said that he considered such an examination, made with an old and learned lawyer, was a sufficient pledge for the severity of his scrutiny. He might have added, that it was the safer, because the person who helped him in making it was not only a man of uncommon fairness of mind, perspicacity, and wisdom, but one who was very cautious, and, on all matters of evidence, had a tendency to scepticism rather than credulity.

The conclusions at which he arrived were, that the narratives of the Gospels were authentic; that, after so careful an examination of them, he ought not to permit his mind to be disturbed on the same question again, unless he should be able to make an equally faithful revision of the whole subject; and that, even if Christianity were not a divine revelation, no system of morals was so likely to fit him for happiness here and hereafter. But he did not find in the Gospels, or in any part of the New Testament, the doctrines commonly accounted orthodox, and he deliberately recorded his rejection of them. On one minor point, too, he was very explicit. He declared his purpose to avoid all habits of levity on religious topics. And to this purpose, I believe, he adhered rigorously through life. At least, I am satisfied that I never heard him use light expressions or allusions of any kind when speaking of Christianity, or when referring to the Scriptures. His mind, in fact, was reverential in its very nature, and so was his father's.[2]

After a few weeks devoted to these inquiries, he resumed his accustomed studies. At the moment when they had been broken off, he was not employed regularly on his History. He had already stepped aside to write an article for the "North-American Review." During eight years he had been in the habit occasionally of contributing what he sometimes called "his peppercorn" to that well-established and respectable periodical; regarding his contributions as an exercise in writing which could not fail to be useful to him. His first experiments

---

[2] It was noticed by one of the members of his Club, — Dr. John Ware, whose judgment and acuteness render his observation important, — that Mr. Prescott was much interested whenever the subject of religion, or anything that claimed to be connected with the spiritual world, came up in the familiar discussions of their meetings. "He was always desirous," says Dr. Ware, "to hear something about magnetism, when that was in vogue, and still more about spiritual manifestations, when they came in fashion." This falls in with my own recollections and impressions. He went once certainly, and I think more than once, to witness the exhibitions of a medium. But no effect was produced on his mind. He was always slow of belief. His historical judgments prove this, and what he saw of "the manifestations," as they were called, rested on nothing like the evidence he was accustomed to require. Besides, they offended the sentiment of reverence, which, as I have said, was strong in his whole nature.

of this sort, saving always the youthful failure already recorded, were, I suppose, two short articles, in 1821, on Sprague's beautifully prize "Ode to Shakespeare," and on Byron's Letter upon Pope. These had been followed, with the regularity that marked almost everything he did, by a single article on some literary subject every succeeding year. It was an excellent discipline for him as a beginner, and although, from the slowness with which he necessarily worked, it took much time, he never, I think, seriously regretted the sacrifice it implied.

But now, being engrossed with his inquiries into early Spanish history, he preferred to take a subject immediately connected with them. He wrote, therefore, an article on Conde's "History of the Arabs in Spain," comprising a general view of the Arabian character and civilization. It was prepared with great care. He gave much time to previous reading and study on the subject, — I do not know exactly how much, but certainly three months, probably four, — and it was not till nearly seven months after he first began to collect materials for the article that it was completed ;[3] from which, however, should be deducted the sorrowful period of several weeks that preceded and followed his little daughter's death. But, after all, he did not send it to the periodical publication for which it had been written. He found, perhaps, that it was too important for his own ulterior purposes; certainly, that it was not fitted for the more popular tone of such a work as the "North American." Substituting for it, therefore, a pleasant article on Irving's "Conquest of Granada," which had cost him much less labor, but which was quite as interesting, he laid the one on Conde quietly aside, and finally, with some modifications, used it as the eighth chapter in the First Part of his "Ferdinand and Isabella," where it stands now, an admirable foreground to the brilliant picture of the siege and fall of Granada.[4]

[3] The manuscript notes for this article, now before me, are extraordinarily elaborate and minute. They fill two hundred and forty-four large foolscap pages, and have an index to them.

[4] Mr. Bancroft, in a review of "Ferdinand and Isabella," selects this chapter as a happy illustration of the faithful industry with which the work is written. "Let any American scholar," he says, "turn, for instance, to the chapter on the literature of the Saracens, and ask himself, how long a period would be required to prepare for writing it." — Democratic Review, (1838,) Vol. II. p. 162.

It was June, 1829, before he returned to his regular readings preparatory to the actual composition of Ferdinand and Isabella. In his more leisure hours, generally in the evening, he went over several works, half biography, half history, — such as Miss Aikin's "Queen Elizabeth," Voltaire's "Charles XII.," and Roscoe's "Lorenzo de' Medici" and his "Leo X.,"— to see if he could glean from them any ideas for the general management of his subject; while, for easy, finished narrative, he listened to large portions of Barante's "Ducs de Bourgogne," and studied with some care Thierry, — the marvellous, blind Thierry, —for whom he always felt a strong sympathy in consequence of their common misfortune, and to whose manner of treating history with a free citation of the old ballads and chronicles he was much inclined. From all this, perhaps, he gained little, except warnings what to avoid. At the same time, however, that he was doing it, he gave his forenoons to the direct, severe study of his subject. He advanced slowly, to be sure; for his eyes were in a very bad state, and he was obliged to depend entirely on his reader when going through even such important works as those of Marina and Sempere on the Cortes, and Palencia's Chronicle of the time of Henry IV. Still he got on, and, in the course of the summer, prepared an elaborate synopsis of the chief events to be discussed in his contemplated history; all chronologically arranged from 1454, when John II., Isabella's father, died, to 1516, the date of Ferdinand's death, which, of course, would close the work.

From this synopsis, and especially from the estimate it involved of the proportions of its different divisions, he, indeed, sometimes varied, as his ample materials were unrolled before him. But the whole plan, as he then digested it, shows that he had mastered the outline of his subject, and comprehended justly the relations and combinations of its various parts. He thought, however, that he could bring it all into two moderate volumes in octavo. In this he was mistaken. The work, from his thorough and faithful treatment of it, grew under his hands, and the world is not sorry that at last it was extended to three.

On the 6th of October, 1829, — three years and a half from

the time when he had selected his subject, and begun to work
upon it, — he finally broke ground with its actual composition.
He had then been three months reading and taking notes exclusively for the first chapter.   It was a month before that
chapter was finished, and afterwards it was all rewritten.
Two months more brought him to the end of the third chapter ; and, although the space filled by the three so greatly
overran the estimate in his synopsis as to alarm him, he still
felt that he had made good progress, and took courage.   He
was, in fact, going on at a rate which would make his History
fill five volumes, and yet it was long before he gave up the
struggle to keep it down to two.   Similar trouble he encountered all the way through his work.   He was constantly over-
running his own calculations, and unreasonably dissatisfied
with himself for his mistakes and bad reckoning.

Two things are noteworthy at this stage of his progress,
because one of them influenced the whole of his subsequent
life as an historian, and the other did much towards giving a
direction and tone to his discussion of the characters and reign
of Ferdinand and Isabella.

The first is his increased regard for Mably as a counsellor
and guide.   In January, 1830, after looking afresh through
some of Mably's works, there occurs the following notice of
him, chiefly with reference to his treatise " Sur l'Étude de
l' Histoire," which, as we have already noticed, had engaged
his careful attention five years earlier : [5] " He takes wide views,
and his politics are characterized by directness and good faith.
I have marked occasionally passages in the portions I have
looked over which will be worth recurring to.   I like particularly his notion of the necessity of giving an interest as well as
utility to history, by letting events tend to some obvious point
or moral ; in short, by paying such attention to the development of events tending to this leading result, as one would in
the construction of a romance or a drama."   A few days afterwards he records the way in which he proposes to apply this
principle to the " History of Ferdinand and Isabella."   With

[5] He calls Mably " a perspicuous, severe, shrewd, and sensible writer, full
of thought, and of such thoughts as set the reader upon thinking for
himself."

what success he subsequently carried it out in his "Conquest of Mexico" need not be told. In each instance he was aware of the direction his work was taking, and cites Mably as the authority for it. The same purpose is plain in the "Conquest of Peru," although the conditions of the case did not permit it to be equally applicable.[5]

The other circumstance to which I referred, as worthy of notice at this time, is Mr. Prescott's increased and increasing sense of the importance of what Don Diego Clemencin had done in his "Elogio de la Reina Doña Isabel," for the life of that great sovereign. This remarkable work, which, in an imperfect outline, its author had read to the Spanish Academy of History in 1807, he afterwards enlarged and enriched, until, when it was published in 1821, it filled the whole of the sixth ample volume of the Memoirs of that learned body. Mr. Prescott, above a year earlier, had consulted it, and placed it among the books to be carefully studied, but now he used it constantly. Later, he said it was "a most rich repository of unpublished facts, to be diligently studied by me at every pausing point in my history." And in a note at the end of his sixth chapter he pronounces it to be a work of inestimable service to the historian. These tributes to the modest, faithful learning of the Secretary of the Spanish Academy of History, who was afterwards its Director, are alike creditable to him who offered them, and to Don Diego de Clemencin, who was then no longer among the living, and to whom they could not, therefore, be offered in flattery.

[5] In 1841, when he was occupied with the "Conquest of Mexico," he says, "Have read for the tenth time, ' Mably sur l'Etude de l'Histoire,' full of admirable reflections and hints. Pity that his love of the ancients made him high gravel-blind to the merits of the moderns." This treatise, which Mr. Prescott studied with such care and perseverance, was written by Mably as a part of the course of instruction arranged by Condillac, Mably's kinsman, for the use of the heir to the dukedom of Parma, and it was printed in 1775. Mably was, no doubt, often extravagant and unsound in his opinions, and is now little regarded. How the author of "Ferdinand and Isabella" hit upon a work so generally overlooked, I do not know, except that nothing seemed to escape him that could be made to serve his purpose. On another occasion, when speaking of it, he implies that its precepts may not be applicable to political histories generally, which often require a treatment more philosophical. But that he consulted it much when writing the "Ferdinand and Isabella," and the "Conquest of Mexico," is not doubtful.

But while the historian of Ferdinand and Isabella valued Mably and Clemencin as trustworthy guides, he read everything, and judged and decided for himself concerning everything, as he went on. His progress, indeed, was on these and on all accounts slow. His eye at this period was not in a condition to enable him to use it except with the greatest caution. He sometimes felt obliged to consider the contingency of losing the use of it altogether, and had the courage to determine, even in that event, to go on with his history. How patient he must have been, we may judge from the fact, that, in sixteen months, he was not able to accomplish more than three hundred pages. But neither then, nor at any time afterwards, was he disheartened by the difficulties he encountered. On the contrary, although progress — perceptible progress — was very important to his happiness, he was content to have it very slow. Sometimes, however, he went on more easily, and then he was much encouraged. In the summer of 1832, when he had been very industrious for two months, he wrote to me, "I have disposed of three chapters of my work, which is pretty good hammering for a Cyclops." Such intervals of freer labor gave him a great impulse. He enjoyed his own industry and success, and his original good spirits did the rest.

As he advanced, his subject cleared up before him, and he arranged it at last in two nearly equal divisions; the first illustrating more particularly the domestic policy of the sovereigns, and bringing Isabella into the foreground; and the second making their foreign policy and the influence and management of Ferdinand more prominent. In each he felt more and more the importance of giving interest to his work by preserving for it a character of unity, and keeping in view some pervading moral purpose. One thing, however, disappointed him. He perceived certainly that it must be extended to three volumes. This he regretted. But he resolved that in no event would he exceed this estimate, and he was happily able to keep his resolution, although it cost him much self-denial to do it. He was constantly exceeding his allowance of space, and as constantly condensing and abridging his work afterwards, so as to come within it. To this part of his labor he gave full two years. It was a long time; but, as he advanced with a step assured by experience, his progress became at least more even and easy, if not faster.

The early part of the summer of 1835, which he passed at Pepperell, was peculiarly agreeable and happy. He felt that his work was at last completely within his control, and was approaching its termination. He even began to be impatient, which he had never been before.

In a pleasant letter to his friend Mr. Bancroft, dated Pepperell, June 17, 1835, he says:—

"I find the country, as usual, favorable to the historic Muse. I am so near the term of my labors, that, if I were to remain here six months longer, I should be ready to launch my cock-boat, or rather *gondola*,—for it is a heavy three-volume affair,—into the world. A winter's campaigning in the metropolis, however, will throw me back, I suppose, six months further. I have little more to do than bury and write the epitaphs of the Great Captain, Ximenes, and Ferdinand. Columbus and Isabella are already sent to their account. So my present occupation seems to be that of a sexton, and I begin to weary of it." [1]

A month later he went, as usual, to the sea-shore for the hot season. But, before he left the spot always so dear to him, he recorded the following characteristic reflections and resolutions:—

"July 12th, 1835.— In three days, the 15th, we leave Pepperell, having been here nearly ten weeks. We found the country in its barren spring, and leave it in the prime dress of summer. I have enjoyed the time, and may look back on it with some satisfaction, for I have not misspent it, as the record will show.

"On the whole, there is no happiness so great as that of a permanent and lively interest in some intellectual labor. I, at least, could never be tolerably contented without it. When, therefore, I get so absorbed by pleasures — particularly exciting pleasures — as to feel apathy, in any degree, in my literary pursuits, just in that degree I am less happy. No other enjoyment can compensate, or approach to, the steady satisfaction and constantly increasing interest of active literary labor, — the subject of meditation when I am out of my study, of diligent stimulating activity within, — to say nothing of the comfortable consciousness of directing my

---

[1] The mother of the future historian and statesman was an early friend of the elder Mrs. Prescott, and the attachment of the parents was betimes transferred to the children. From the period of Mr. Bancroft's return home, after several years spent in Europe, where his academic course was completed, this attachment was cemented by constant intercourse and intimacy with the Prescott family, and was never broken until it was broken by death. Some allusions to this friendship have already been made. More will be found hereafter.

powers in some channel worthy of them, and of contributing something to the stock of useful knowledge in the world. As this must be my principal material for happiness, I should cultivate those habits and amusements most congenial with it, and these will be the quiet domestic duties — which will also be my greatest pleasures — and temperate social enjoyments, not too frequent and without excess; for the excess of to-day will be a draft on health and spirits to-morrow. Above all, observe if my interest be weakened in any degree in my pursuits. If so, be sure I am pursuing a wrong course somewhere, — wrong even in an Epicurean sense for my happiness, — and reform it at once.

" With these occupations and temperate amusement, seek to do some good to society by an interest in obviously useful and benevolent objects. Preserve a calm, philosophical, elevated way of thinking on all subjects connected with the action of life. Think more seriously of the consequences of conduct. Cherish devotional feelings of reliance on the Deity. Discard a habit of sneering or scepticism. Do not attempt impossibilities, or, in other words, to arrive at certainty [as if] on questions of historic evidence; but be content that there is evidence enough to influence a wise man in the course of his conduct, — enough to produce an assent, if not a mathematical demonstration to his mind, — and that the great laws for our moral government are laid down with undeniable, unimpeachable truth."

A week after the date of these last reflections, he was quietly established at Nahant, having remained, as usual, two or three days in Boston to look after affairs that could not be attended to in the country. But he always disliked these periodical changes and removals. They broke up his habits, and made a return to his regular occupations more or less difficult and unsatisfactory. On this occasion, coming from the tranquillizing influences of Pepperell, where he had been more than commonly industrious and happy, he makes an amusing record of a fit of low spirits and impatience, which is worth notice, because it is the only one to be found in all his memoranda : —

"July 19th. — Moved to Nahant yesterday. A most *consumed* fit of vapors. The place looks dreary enough after the green fields of Pepperell. Don't like the air as well either, — too chilly, — find I bear and like hot weather better than I used to. Begin to study, — that is the best way of restoring equanimity. Be careful of my eyes at first, till accommodated to the glare. Hope I shall find this good working-ground, — have generally found it so. This ink is too pale to write further. Everything goes wrong here."

But he had a good season for work at Nahant, after all. He wrote there, not only the troublesome account of the Conquest of Navarre, but the brilliant chapters on the deaths of Gonsalvo de Córdova and Ferdinand, leaving only the administration and fall of Cardinal Ximenes for a dignified close to the whole narrative part of the history, and thus giving a sort of tragical *dénouement* to it, such as he desired. This he completed in Boston, about the middle of November.

A chapter to review the whole of his subject, and point it with its appropriate moral, was, however, still wanted. It was a difficult task, and he knew it; for, among other things, it involved a general and careful examination of the entire legislation of a period in which great changes had taken place, and permanent reforms had been introduced. He allowed five months for it. It took above seven, but it is an admirable part of his work, and worth all the time and labor it cost him.

At last, on the 25th of June, 1836, he finished the concluding note of the concluding chapter to the History of Ferdinand and Isabella. Reckoning from the time when he wrote the first page, or from a period a little earlier, when he prepared a review of Conde on the Spanish Arabs, which he subsequently made a chapter in his work, the whole had been on his hands a little more than seven years and a half; and, deducting nine months for illness and literary occupations not connected with his History, he made out that he had written, during that time, at the rate of two hundred and thirty-four printed pages a year. But he had read and labored on the subject much in the two or three years that preceded the beginning of its absolute composition, and another year of corrections in the proof-sheets followed before it was fairly delivered to the world at Christmas, 1837. He was, therefore, exact, even after making all the deductions that can belong to the case, when, in his general estimate, he said that he had given to the work ten of the best years of his life.

CHAPTER VIII.

1837 – 1838.

DOUBTS ABOUT PUBLISHING THE "HISTORY OF FERDINAND AND ISABELLA." — FOUR COPIES PRINTED AS IT WAS WRITTEN. — OPINIONS OF FRIENDS. — THE AUTHOR'S OWN OPINION OF HIS WORK. — PUBLISHES IT. — HIS LETTERS ABOUT IT. — ITS SUCCESS. — ITS PUBLICATION IN LONDON. — REVIEWS OF IT IN THE UNITED STATES AND IN EUROPE.

STRANGE as it may seem, it is nevertheless true, that after these ten years of labor on the Ferdinand and Isabella, and with the full happiness he felt on completing that work, Mr. Prescott yet hesitated at last whether he should publish it or not. As early as 1833, and from that time forward, while the composition was going on, he had caused four copies of it to be printed in large type on one side only of the leaf. For this he had two reasons. If he should determine to publish the work in London, he could send a fair, plain copy to be printed from ; — and, at any rate, from such a copy he might himself, whenever his eye could endure the task, revise the whole personally, making on the blank pages such corrections and alterations as he might find desirable. This task was already accomplished. He had gone over the whole, a little at a time, with care. Some portions he had rewritten. The first chapter he wrote out three times, and printed it twice, before it was finally put in stereotype, and adjusted to its place as it now stands.

Still he hesitated. He consulted with his father, as he always did when he doubted in relation to matters of consequence. His father not only advised the publication, but told him that "the man who writes a book which he is afraid to publish is a coward." This stirred the blood of his grandfather in his veins, and decided him.[1]

He had, however, the concurrent testimony of judicious and

[1] Griswold's Prose Writers of America, 1847, p. 372.

faithful friends. Mr. Sparks, the historian, in a note dated February 24th, 1837, says : " I have read several chapters, and am reading more. The book will be successful, — bought, read, and praised." And Mr. Pickering, the modest, learned, philosophical philologist, to whom he submitted it a little later, sent him more decisive encouragement under date of May 1st.

My dear Sir,
Being uninterrupted last evening, I had an opportunity to finish the few pages that remained of your work, and I now return the volumes with many thanks. I cannot, however, take leave of them without again expressing the high satisfaction I feel that our country should have produced such a work, — a work which, unless I am much mistaken, will live as long as any one produced by your contemporaries either here or in England.
I am, my dear sir, with the warmest regard,
Very truly yours,
John Pickering.

His friend Mr. Gardiner had already gone over the whole of the three volumes with his accustomed faithfulness, and with a critical judgment which few possess. He had suggested an important alteration in the arrangement of some of the early chapters, which was gladly adopted, and had offered minor corrections and verbal criticism of all sorts, with the freedom which their old friendship demanded, but a considerable part of which were, with the same freedom, rejected ; the author maintaining, as he always did, a perfect independence of judgment in all such matters.

How he himself looked upon his ten years' labor may be seen by the following extracts from his memoranda, before he passed the final, fatal bourn of the press. After giving some account of his slow progress and its causes, he says, under date of June 26th, 1836, when he had recorded the absolute completion of the History : —

" Pursuing the work in this quiet, leisurely way, without over-exertion or fatigue, or any sense of obligation to complete it in a given time, I have found it a continual source of pleasure. It has furnished food for my meditations, has given a direction and object to my scattered reading, and supplied me with regular occupation for hours that would otherwise have filled me with *ennui*. I have found infinite variety in the study, moreover, which might at first sight seem monotonous. No historical labors, rightly conducted, can be monotonous, since they afford all the variety of pursuing a chain of facts to unforeseen consequences, of comparing doubtful and

5   G

contradictory testimony, of picturesque delineations of incident, and of analysis and dramatic exhibition of character. The plain narrative may be sometimes relieved by general views or critical discussions, and the story and the actors, as they grow under the hands, acquire constantly additional interest. It may seem dreary work to plod through barbarous old manuscript chronicles of monks and pedants, but this takes up but a small portion of the time, and even here, read aloud to, as I have been, required such close attention as always made the time pass glibly. In short, although I have sometimes been obliged to whip myself up to the work, I have never fairly got into it without deriving pleasure from it, and I have most generally gone to it with pleasure, and left it with regret.

"What do I expect from it, now it is done? And may it not be all in vain and labor lost, after all? My expectations are not such, if I know myself, as to expose me to any serious disappointment. I do not flatter myself with the idea that I have achieved anything very profound, or, on the other hand, that will be very popular. I know myself too well to suppose the former for a moment. I know the public too well, and the subject I have chosen, to expect the latter. But I have made a book illustrating an unexplored and important period, from authentic materials, obtained with much difficulty, and probably in the possession of no one library, public or private, in Europe. As a plain, veracious record of facts, the work, therefore, till some one else shall be found to make a better one, will fill up a gap in literature which, I should hope, would give it a permanent value, — a value founded on its utility, though bringing no great fame or gain to its author.

"Come to the worst, and suppose the thing a dead failure, and the book born only to be damned. Still it will not be all in vain, since it has encouraged me in forming systematic habits of intellectual occupation, and proved to me that my greatest happiness is to be the result of such. It is no little matter to be possessed of this conviction from experience."

And again, in the following October, when he had entirely prepared his work for the press, he writes : —

"Thus ends the labor of ten years, for I have been occupied more or less with it, in general or particular readings, since the summer of 1826, when, indeed, from the disabled state of my eyes, I studied with little spirit and very little expectation of reaching this result. But what result? Three solid octavos of facts, important in themselves, new in an English dress, and which, therefore, however poor may be the execution of the work, must have some value in an historic view. With the confidence in its having such a value, however humble it may be, I must rest contented. And I now part with the companion of so many years with the cheering conviction, that, however great or little good it may render the public, it has done much to me, by the hours it has helped to lighten, and the habits of application it has helped to form."

He caused the whole to be stereotyped without delay. This mode he preferred, because it was one which left him a more complete control of his own work than he could obtain in any other way, and because, if it rendered corrections and alterations more difficult, it yet insured greater typographical accuracy at the outset. Mr. Charles Folsom, a member of the pleasant club that had been formed many years before, superintended its publication with an absolute fidelity, good taste, and kindness that left nothing to desire ; although, as the author, when referring to his friend's criticisms and suggestions, says, they made his own final revision anything but a sinecure. It was, I suppose, as carefully carried through the press as any work ever was in this country. The pains that had been taken with its preparation from the first were continued to the last.

That it was worth the many years of patient, conscientious labor bestowed upon it, the world was not slow to acknowledge. It was published in Boston by the American Stationers' Company, — a corporate body that had a short time before been organized under favorable auspices, but which troubles in the financial condition of the country and other causes did not permit long to continue its operations. The contract with them was a very modest one. It was dated April 10th, 1837, and stipulated on their part, for the use of the stereotype plates and of the engravings, already prepared at the author's charge. From these, twelve hundred and fifty copies might be struck off at the expense of the Company, who were to have five years to dispose of them. The bargain, however, was not, in one point of view, unfavorable. It insured the zealous and interested co-operation of a large and somewhat influential body in the sale and distribution of the work, — a matter of much more importance at that time than it would be now, when bookselling as a business and profession in the United States is so much more advanced. Otherwise, as a contract, it was certainly not brilliant in its promise. But the author thought well of it ; and, since profit had not been his object, he was entirely satisfied.

I was then in Italy, having been away from home with my family nearly two years, during which I had constantly received letters from him concerning the progress of his work. On this occasion he wrote to me, April 11th, 1837, the very day after the date of his contract, as follows : —

" If your eyes are ever greeted with the aspect of the old North [American Review] in your pilgrimage, you may see announced the 'History of Ferdinand and Isabella, 3 vols. 8vo,' as in press, which means, will be out in October. The American Stationers' Company — a company got up with a considerable capital for the publication of expensive works — have contracted for an edition of twelve hundred and fifty copies. I find the stereotype plates, which cost not a great deal more than the ordinary mode of composition, and they the paper and all other materials, and pay me a thousand dollars. The offer was a liberal one, and entirely answers my purpose of introducing the work into the channels of circulation, which I could not have effected by so small an inducement as a commission to a publisher. The Company, as proprietors of the edition, have every motive to disseminate it, and they have their agencies diffused through every part of the United States. What has given me most satisfaction is the very handsome terms in which the book has been recommended by Messrs. Pickering and Sparks, two of the committee for determining on the publication by the Company, and the former of whom before perusal, expressed himself, as I know, unfavorably to the work as a *marketable* concern, from the nature of the subject. My ambition will be fully satisfied, if the judgments of the few whose good opinion I covet are but half so favorable as those publicly expressed by these gentlemen. . . . . .

" I must confess I feel some disquietude at the prospect of coming in full bodily presence, as it were, before the public. I have always shrunk from such an exhibition, and, during the ten years I have been occupied with the work, few of my friends have heard me say as many words about it. When I saw my name — harmonious 'Hickling' and all — blazoned in the North American, it gave me, as S—— would say, 'quite a turn,' — anything but agreeable. But I am in for it. Of one thing I feel confident, — that the book has been compiled from materials, and with a fidelity, which must make it fill a *hiatus deflendus* in Spanish history. For the same reasons, I cannot think that I have much to fear from criticism ; not to add, that the rarity of my materials is such, that I doubt if any but a Spaniard possesses the previous knowledge of the whole ground for a fair and competent judgment of my historical accuracy. But enough and too much of this egotism ; though I know you and Anna love me too well to call it egotism, and will feel it to be only the unreserved communication made around one's own fireside.":

A great surprise to all the parties concerned followed the publication. Five hundred copies only were struck off at first ; that number being thought quite sufficient for an experiment so doubtful as this was believed to be. No urgency was used to have the whole even of this inconsiderable edition ready for early distribution and sale. But during several days the demand was so great, that copies could not be prepared by the bookbinder as fast as they were called for. Three fifths of the whole number were disposed of in Boston before any could be spared to go elsewhere, and all disappeared in five weeks.

In a few months, more copies were sold than by the contract it had been assumed could be disposed of in five years ; and from the beginning of May, 1838, — that is, in the course of four months from its first publication, — the History itself stood before the public in the position it has maintained ever since. A success so brilliant had never before been reached in so short a time by any work of equal size and gravity on this side of the Atlantic. Indeed, nothing of the sort had approached it.

"But," as his friend Mr. Gardiner has truly said, "this wonderfully rapid sale of a work so grave, beginning in his own town, was due in the first instance largely to its author's great personal popularity in society, and may be taken as a signal proof of it. For Mr. Prescott had acquired earlier no marked reputation as an author. As a mere man of letters, his substantial merits were known only by a few intimate friends ; perhaps not fully appreciated by them. To the public he was little known in any way. But he was a prodigious favorite with whatever was most cultivated in the society of Boston. Few men ever had so many warmly attached personal friends. Still fewer — without more or less previous distinction or fame — had ever been sought as companions by young and old of both sexes as he had been. When, therefore, it came to be known that the same person who had so attracted them by an extraordinary combination of charming personal qualities was about to publish a book, — and it was known only a very short time before the book itself appeared, — the fact excited the greatest surprise, curiosity, and interest.

"The day of its appearance was looked forward to and talked of. It came, and there was a perfect rush to get copies. A convivial friend, for instance, who was far from being a man of letters, — indeed, a person who rarely read a book, — got up early in the morning, and went to wait for the opening of the publisher's shop, so as to secure the first copy. It came out at Christmas, and was at once adopted as the fashionable Christmas and New Year's present of the season. Those who knew the author read it from interest in him. No one read it without surprise and delight. Mr. Daniel Webster, the statesman, who knew Prescott well in society, was as much surprised as the rest, and spoke of him as a comet which had suddenly blazed out upon the world in full splendor.

"Such is the history of this remarkable sale at its outbreak. Love of the author gave the first impetus. That given, the extraordinary merits of the work did all the rest."

Meantime negotiations had been going on for its publication in London. My friend had written to me repeatedly about them, and so unreasonably moderate were his hopes, that, at one time, he had thought either not to publish it at all in the United States, or to give away the work here, and make his chief venture in England. As early as the 29th of December, 1835, he had written to me in Dresden, where I then was : —

"Before closing my letter, I shall detain you a little about my own affairs. I have nearly closed my *magnum opus*, — that is, I shall close it, and have a copy of it printed, I trust, early next autumn. I print, you know, only four copies, designing, whether I publish it here or not, to have it printed in England. . . . .

"Although the subject has nothing in it to touch the times and present topics of interest and excitement particularly, yet, as filling up a blank of importance in modern history, I cannot but think, if decently executed, that it will not be difficult to find some publisher in London who would be interested in it. You know that lucre is not my object. I wish, if possible, to give the work a fair chance under fair auspices. As to the merits of the work, it will be easy to form a judgment, since the book-seller will have the advantage of a fair printed copy. Now I wish your advice, how I had best proceed? If you should be in London next winter, my course would be clear. I would send the book to you, and doubt not you would put it in a train for getting it into the world, if any respectable *accoucheur* could be found to take charge of it. If you should not be there, as is most probable, can you advise me what to do next? . . . . .

"I think it possible I may print the book here simultaneously. —— offered the other day to take the concern off my hands, if I would give him the first impression of a certain number of copies. As I have no illusory hopes of a second, I don't know that I can do better. But I am persuaded the work, if worth anything, is suited to a European market, — at least, enough to indemnify the publisher. Else ten years nearly of my life have been thrown away indeed. I hope you will not lose your patience with this long-winded prosing, and will excuse this egotism, from the importance of the subject to myself. As to the trouble I occasion you, I know you too well to think you will require an apology."

To this I replied from Dresden, February 8th, 1836 : —

"You speak more fully about your *opus magnum*, and therefore I answer more fully than I did before. It must be a proud thought to you that you are so near the end of it; and yet I think you will leave it with the same feeling of regret with which Gibbon left his Decline and Fall. What, then, will you do to fill up the first void? Is it out of the question that you should fetch out your copy yourself, and get the peace of conscience that would follow making the arrangements for its publication in person? I hope not. For we could easily manage to meet you in England two years hence, and I assure you, my own experience leads me to think it no very grave matter to travel with wife and children. But let us suppose you do not. What then? I remain by the suggestion in my last letter, that Colonel Aspinwall is the man to take charge of it, provided neither you nor I should be in London, although, if both of us were on the spot, he would be the man with whom I think we should earliest advise in all publishing arrangements. His place as our Consul-General in London is something in talking to publishers. His character, prompt, business-like, firm, and honorable, is still more. And then, if I mistake not, he has a good deal of practice with these people ; for he certainly makes Irving's bargains, and, I believe, has managed for —— and others. This *practice*, too, is a matter of moment."

Very fortunately for the author of Ferdinand and Isabella, Colonel Aspinwall was soon afterwards in Boston, which is his proper home, and in whose neighborhood he was born. He at once undertook in the pleasantest manner the pleasant commission which was offered him, and a mutual regard was the consequence of the connection then formed, which was never afterwards broken or impaired ; so much was there in common between the characters of the two high-minded and cultivated men.

In the autumn of 1836, one of the four printed copies, carefully corrected, was therefore, sent to Colonel Aspinwall, accompanied by a letter dated October 28th, in which the author says : ——

" With regard to the arrangements for publication, which you have been kind enough to allow me to trust to you, I can only say that I shall abide entirely by your judgment. I certainly should not disdain any profits which might flow from it, though I believe you will do me the justice to think that I have been influenced by higher motives in the composition of the work. If I have succeeded, I have supplied an important *desideratum* in history, but one which, I fear, has too little in it of a temporary or local interest to win its way into public favor very speedily. But if the bookseller can wait, I am sure I can."

The first attempts with the trade in London were not encouraging. Murray, the elder, to whom the book was at once offered, declined promptly to become its publisher ; probably without an examination of its merits, and certainly without a thorough one. Longman took more time, but came to the same conclusion. The author, as might have been expected, was chagrined, and, with the openness of his nature, said so, in his letters both to Colonel Aspinwall and to me.

" Murray's decision," he wrote to the former, " was too prompt to be final with me : but Longman has examined the matter so deliberately, that I am convinced there is little reason to suppose the book can be regarded as a profitable concern for a London publisher. It will undoubtedly prejudice the work to go a-begging for a patron, and my ill-success will thus acquire a disagreeable notoriety not only there, but here, where nothing is known of my foreign negotiations. I think it best, therefore, to take Uncle Toby's advice on the occasion, and say nothing about it to any one. For the copy in your possession, you had best put it out of sight. It will soon be replaced by one of the Boston edition in a more comely garb. If you should have proposed the work before receiving this to any other person, I shall not care to hear of its refusal from you, as it will disgust me with the book before it is fairly born."

Similar feelings he expressed even more strongly two days later. But this state of things was not destined to last long. Before the letter which was intended to discourage any further proposition in London had reached Colonel Aspinwall, Mr. Richard Bentley had accepted an offer of the book. A few days after learning this, the author wrote to me in a very different state of mind from that in which he had written his last letters.

BOSTON, May 16, 1837.

MY DEAREST FRIEND,

I told you in my last that no arrangement for the publication had been made in England. I was mistaken, however, as I soon afterwards received a letter from Colonel Aspinwall, informing me of one with Bentley, by which he becomes proprietor of one half of the copyright, and engages to publish forthwith an edition at his own cost and risk, and divide with me the profits. He says, " It will be an object for him to get out the work in elegant style, with engravings, vignettes, &c." This is certainly much better, considering the obscurity of the author and the absence of all temporary allusion or interest in the subject, than I had a right to expect. My object is now attained. I shall bring out the book in the form I desired, and under the most respectable auspices on both sides of the water, and in a way which must interest the publisher so deeply as to secure his exertions to circulate the work. My bark will be fairly launched, and if it should be doomed to encounter a spiteful puff or two of criticism, I trust it may weather it.

But he encountered no such adverse blasts. Immediately after the appearance of the book at Christmas, 1837, but with the imprint of 1838, a very long and able article on it by his friend Mr. Gardiner, who, as we have seen, had just assisted in preparing it for the press, was published in the " North-American Review." [2] A little later, another friend, the Rev. Mr. Greenwood, — whose name it is not possible to mention without remembering what sorrow followed the early loss of one whose genius was at once so brilliant and so tender, — wrote a review for the " Christian Examiner," no less favorable than that of Mr. Gardiner. [3] Others followed. An excellent notice by Mr. John Pickering appeared in the " New York Review," — true, careful, and discriminating. [4] And the series of the more elaborate American discussions was closed in the " Democratic Review " of the next month by Mr. Bancroft, — himself an historian already of no mean note, and destined to

[2] January, 1838.   [3] March, 1838.   [4] April, 1838.

yet more distinction on both sides of the Atlantic. Of course, there were many other notices in periodical publications of less grave pretensions, and still more in the newspapers; for the work excited an interest which had not been at all foreseen. It was read by great numbers who seldom looked into anything so solid and serious. It was talked of by all who ever talked of books. Whatever was written or said about it was in one tone and temper; so that, as far as the United States were concerned, it may be regarded as successful from the moment of its appearance.

Nor did the notices which at the same time came from England show anything but good-will towards the unknown and unheralded claimant for the higher class of literary honors. They were written, of course, by persons who had never before heard of him, but their spirit was almost as kindly as if they had been dictated by personal friendship. The "Athenæum" led off with a short laudatory article, which I believe, was from the pen of Dr. Dunham, who wrote the summary History of Spain and Portugal in Lardner's Cabinet Cyclopædia.[a] An article, however, in the "Edinburgh Review," a little later, was much more satisfactory.[b] It was the first examination that the work obtained in England from one whose previous special knowledge of the reign of Ferdinand and Isabella enabled him to do it thoroughly. Its author was Don Pascual de Gayangos, a learned and accomplished Spanish gentleman, then resident in London, who wrote the Castilian and the English with equal purity and elegance, and of whose kindly connection with Mr. Prescott it will be necessary for me to speak often hereafter. He made in his article on the "Ferdinand and Isabella" a faithful and real review of the work, going over its several divisions with care, and giving a distinct opinion on each. It was more truly an examination of the work, and less a dissertation on the subject, than is common in such articles, and on this account it will always have its value.

To this succeeded in June an article in the "Quarterly Review," by an English gentleman familiar with everything Spanish; I mean Mr. Richard Ford, who wrote the "Handbook of Spain," — a brilliant work, not without marks of prejudice,

[a] 1838, pp. 42 – 44. [b] January, 1839.

5 *

CHAPTER IX.

1838.

PASSING over the multitude of notices that appeared concerning the "History of Ferdinand and Isabella," it will be pleasant to see how the author himself felt in the first flush of his unexpected honors. I was then in Paris, and ten days after the book was published in Boston he wrote to me as follows : —

"BOSTON, Jan. 6, 1838.

"MY DEAR FRIEND,

"It is long since I have seen your handwriting; though only a few weeks since I received a most kind and welcome epistle from Anna. Your friends here say your are not going to hold out your four years, and I could not help thinking that the complexion of Anna's sentiments looked rather *homeish*.[1] I wish it may prove so. You will, at least, be spared, by your return, sundry long communications from me, with a plentiful dash of egotism in them.

"There is some excuse for this, however, just now, which is a sort of epoch in my life, — my literary life at least. Their Catholic Highnesses have just been ushered into the world in three royal octavos. The bantling appeared on a Christmas morning, and certainly has not fallen stillborn, but is alive and kicking merrily. How long its life may last is another question. Within the first ten days half the first edition of five hundred copies (for the publishers were afraid to risk a larger one for our market) has been disposed of, and they are now making preparations for a second edition, having bought of me twelve hundred and fifty copies. The sale, indeed, seems quite ridiculous, and I fancy many a poor soul thinks so by this time. Not a single copy has been sent South, — the publishers not choosing to strip the market while they can find such demand here.

"In the mean time the book has got summer-puffs in plenty, and a gale to the tune of ninety pages from the old 'North American.' S—— facetiously remarked, that 'the article should be called the fourth volume of the

---

[1] I went abroad, with my family, for Mrs. Ticknor's health, in 1835, intending to stay abroad four years, if, as her physicians feared, so much time might be necessary for her restoration. She was well in three, and we gladly came home a few months after the date of this letter.

History.' It was written by Gardiner, after several months' industrious application, — though eventually concocted in the very short space of ten days,[2] which has given occasion to some oversights. It is an able, learned, and most partial review; and I doubt if more knowledge of the particular subject can easily be supplied by the craft on the other side of the water, — at least without the aid of a library as germane to the matter as mine, which, I think, will not readily be met with. I feel half inclined to send you a beautiful critique from the pen of your friend Hillard, as much to my taste as anything that has appeared. But *pudor vetat.*

"In the mean time the small journals have opened quite a cry in my favor, and while one of yesterday claims me as a Bostonian, a Salem paper asserts that distinguished honor for the witch-town. So you see I am experiencing the fate of the Great Obscure, even in my own lifetime. And a clergyman told me yesterday, he intended to make my case — the obstacles I have encountered and overcome — the subject of a sermon. I told him it would help to sell the book, at all events.

"'Poor fellow!' — I hear you exclaim by this time, — 'his wits are actually turned by this flurry in his native village, — the Yankee Athens!' Not a whit, I assure you. Am I not writing to two dear friends, to whom I can talk as freely and foolishly as to one of my own household, and who, I am sure, will not misunderstand me? The effect of all this — which a boy at Dr. Gardiner's school, I remember, called *fungum popularitatem* — has been rather to depress me, and S—— was saying yesterday, that she had never known me so out of spirits as since the book has come out. The truth is, I appreciate, more than my critics can do, the difficulty of doing justice to my subject, and the immeasurable distance between me and the models with which they have been pleased to compare me. . . . . .

"From two things I have derived unfeigned satisfaction; one, the delight of my good father, who seems disposed to swallow — without the requisite allowance of salt — all the good-natured things which are said of the book, and the other, the hearty and active kindness of the few whom I have thought and now find to be my friends. I feel little doubt that the work, owing to their exertions, when it gets to the Southern cities where I am not known, will find a fair reception, — though, of course, I cannot expect anything like the welcome it has met here.[3] I feel relieved, however, as well as the publishers, from all apprehensions that the book will burn their fingers, whatever it may do to the author's. . . . . .

"I have sent a copy for you to Rich [London], who will forward it according to your directions. I suppose there will be no difficulty in sending it over to Paris, if you remain there. Only advise him thereof. . . . . . A favorable notice in a Parisian journal of respectability would be worth a good deal. But, after all, my market and my reputation rest principally with England, and if your influence can secure me, not a friendly, but a

---

[2] He had, as has been noticed, gone over the whole work before it was published, and had done it with a continual consultation of the authorities on which its facts and statements were founded. He was, therefore, completely master of the subject, and wrote with an authority that few reviewers can claim.

[3] See *ante*, p. 100.

fair notice there, in any of the three or four leading journals, it would be the best thing you ever did for me, — and that is no small thing to say. But I am asking what you will do without asking, if any foreigner could hope to have such influence. I know that the *fiat* of criticism now-a-days depends quite as much on the temper and character of the reviewer as the reviewed, and, in a work filled with facts dug out of barbarous and obsolete idioms, it will be easy to pick flaws and serve them up as a sample of the whole. But I will spare you further twaddle about their Catholic Highnesses."

A little later, April 30, 1838, in his private Memoranda, after giving a detailed account of the circumstances attending its publication, the contracts for printing, and the printing itself, — all which he thus laid up for future use, — he goes on : —

" Well, now for the result in America and England thus far. My work appeared here on the 25th of December, 1837. Its birth had been prepared for by the favorable opinions, *en avance*, of the few friends who in its progress through the press had seen it. It was corrected previously as to style, &c., by my friend Gardiner, who bestowed some weeks, and I may say months, on its careful revision, and who suggested many important alterations in the form. Simonds [4] had previously suggested throwing the introductory ' Section 2 ' on Aragon into its present place, it first having occupied the place after Chapter III. The work was indefatigably corrected, and the references most elaborately and systematically revised by Folsom. . . . . .

" From the time of its appearance to the present date, it has been the subject of notices, more or less elaborate, in the principal reviews and periodicals of the country, and in the mass of criticism I have not met with one unkind, or sarcastic, or censorious sentence ; and my critics have been of all sorts, from stiff conservatives to levelling loco-focos. Much of all this success is to be attributed to the influence and exertions of personal friends, — much to the beautiful dress and mechanical execution of the book, — and much to the novelty, in our country, of a work of research in various foreign languages. The topics, too, though not connected with the times, have novelty and importance in them. Whatever is the cause, the book has found a degree of favor not dreamed of by me certainly, nor by its warmest friends. It will, I have reason to hope, secure me an honest fame, and — what never entered into my imagination in writing it — put, in the long run, some money in my pocket.

" In Europe things wear also a very auspicious aspect so far. The weekly periodicals — the lesser lights of criticism — contain the most ample commendations on the book ; several of the articles being written with spirit and beauty. How extensively the *trade* winds may have helped me along, I cannot say. But so far the course has been smooth

[4] Mr. Henry C. Simonds, who was Mr. Prescott's reader and secretary for four years, — an accomplished young scholar, for whom he felt a very sincere regard. Mr. Simonds died two years after this date, in 1840.

and rapid. Bentley speaks to my friends in extravagant terms of the book, and states that nearly half the edition, which was of seven hundred and fifty copies, had been sold by the end of March.[5] In France, thanks to my friend Ticknor, it has been put into the hands of the principal savans in the Castilian. Copies have also been sent to some eminent scholars in Germany. Thus far, therefore, we run before the wind."

I will not refuse myself the pleasure of inserting what I had already written to him from Paris, February 20th, when, the London copy he had sent me having failed to come to hand, I had read the first volume of " Ferdinand and Isabella " in an American copy which had reached a friend in that city : —

" I have got hold of the first volume, and may, perchance, have the luck to see the others. It has satisfied all my expectations ; and when I tell you that I wrote to Colonel Aspinwall from Berlin, nearly two years ago, placing you quite at the side of Irving, you will understand how I feel about it. I spoke conscientiously when I wrote to Aspinwall, and I do the same now. You have written a book that will not be forgotten. The Dedication to your father was entirely anticipated by me, — its tone and its spirit, — everything except its beautiful words. He is happy to have received a tribute so true and so due, — so worthy of him and so rarely to be had of any."

But in the midst of the happiness which his success naturally produced, trouble came upon him. The family had gone, as usual, to Pepperell early in the summer of 1838, when a severe illness of his mother brought them suddenly back to town, and kept them there above two months, at the end of which she was happily restored, or nearly so.

" Moved from Pepperell," he says in his private Memoranda, " prematurely, June 26th, on account of the distressing illness of my mother, which still, July 16th, detains us in this pestilent place, amidst heats which would do credit to the tropics. The same cause has prevented me from giving nearly as many hours to my studies as I should otherwise have done, being in rather an industrious mood. My mother's health, apparently improving, may permit me to do this."

But the next notice, July 27th, is more comfortable : —

" Been a month now in Boston, which I find more tolerable than at first. The heat has much abated, and, indeed, a summer residence here has many alleviations. But I should never prefer it to a summer at Nahant. Have received an English copy of ' Ferdinand and Isabella.' Better paper,

[5] Mr. Bentley had requested me to tell Mr. Prescott that he was proud of having published such a book, and that he thought it would prove the best he had ever brought out.

blacker ink, more showy pages, but, on the whole, not so good type, and, as the printer did not receive the corrections in season for the last three chapters, there are many verbal inaccuracies.   The plates are good, — the portrait of Columbus exquisite, and about as much like him, I suppose, as any other.   On the whole, Bentley has done fairly by the work.   My friend Ticknor brings me home a very favorable report of the opinions expressed of the work by French and English scholars.   If this report is not colored by his own friendship, the book will take some rank on the other side of the water."

As he intimates, I was just then returned from Europe after an absence of three years.   He met me at the cars on my arrival from New York, where I had landed ; but his countenance was sad and troubled with the dangerous illness of his mother, then at its height.   I saw him, however, daily, and talked with him in the freest and fullest manner about his literary position and prospects ; giving him, without exaggeration, an account of the opinions held in England and France concerning his work, which he could not choose but find very gratifying.

I had, in fact, received the book itself before I left Paris, and had given copies of it to M. Guizot, M. Mignet, Count Adolphe de Circourt, and M. Charles Fauriel.   The last three, as well as some other friends, had expressed to me their high estimation of it, in terms very little measured, which were, in their substance, repeated to me later by M. Guizot, when he had had leisure to read it.   Four persons better qualified to judge the merits of such a work could not, I suppose, have then been found in France ; and the opinion of Count Circourt, set forth in the learned and admirable review already alluded to, would, I think, subsequently have been accepted by any one of them as substantially his own.

In England, where I passed the spring and early summer, I found the same judgment was pronounced and pronouncing. At Holland House, then the highest tribunal in London on the subject of Spanish history and literature, Lord Holland and Mr. John Allen, who were both just finishing its perusal, did not conceal from me the high value they placed upon it ; Mr. Allen telling me that he regarded the introductory sections on the constitutional history of Aragon and Castile — which, it will be remembered, were three times written over, and twice printed, before they were finally given to the press for publication — as possessing a very high merit as statesmanlike discussions, and as better than anything else extant on the same subject.* Southey, whom I afterwards saw at Keswick, and from whose judgment on anything relating to Spanish history few would venture to appeal, volunteered to me an opinion no less decisive.[7]

The more important Reviews had not yet spoken; but, remembering the wish expressed by my friend in a letter to me already cited, — though, as he intimated, not needing such an expression, — I made, through the ready kindness of Lord Holland, arrangements with Mr. McVey Napier, the editor of the "Edinburgh Review," for the article in that journal by Don Pascual de Gayangos, of which an account has already been given. Mr. Lockhart, the Aristarch of the "Quarterly Review," had not read the book when I spoke to him about it, but he told me he had heard from good authority that "it was one that would last"; and the result of his own examination of it was Mr. Ford's review, Mr. Ford himself having been, I suppose, the authority referred to. Mr. Hallam, to whom I sent a copy in the author's name, acknowledged its receipt in a manner the most gratifying, and so did Mr. Milman; both of these distinguished and admirable men becoming afterwards personally attached to Mr. Prescott, and corresponding with him, from time to time, until his death. These, and some others like them, were the suffrages that I bore to my friend on my return home early in July, and to which, in the passages I have cited from his Memoranda, he alludes. They were all of one temper and in one tone. I had heard of no others, and had, therefore, no others to give him. At home

---

* I ought, perhaps, to add here, that, by common consent of the scholars of the time, the opinion of no man in England, on such a point, would have been placed before Mr. Allen's.

[7] Mr. Prescott was especially gratified with this opinion of Mr. Southey, because he had much feared that the rejection of his book by the Longmans was the result of advice from Southey, whose publishers they were, and who was often consulted by them respecting the publication of such works. But the Longmans declined it, as Southey himself told me, only because they did not, at the time, wish to increase their list of new publications. The same cause, I subsequently understood, had governed the decision of Murray, who did not even give the book to anybody for getting a judgment on its merits.

II

its success, I found, was already fully assured.   As Dr. Channing had told him, "Your book has been received here with acclamation." [*]

[*] A year after its publication, the author records very naturally, among his private Memoranda: " Dec. 25, 1838.   The anniversary of the appearance of their Catholic Highnesses Ferdinand and Isabella, God bless them!   What would I have given last year to know they would have run off so glibly?" I think about twenty-eight hundred copies had been sold in the United States when this record was made, — only a foretaste of the subsequent success. On the 1st of January, 1860, the aggregate sales in the United States and England amounted to seventeen thousand seven hundred and thirty-one.

CHAPTER X.

1837 – 1838.

WHEN the "Ferdinand and Isabella" was published, in the winter of 1837 – 8, its author was nearly forty-two years old. His character, some of whose traits had been prominent from childhood, while others had been slowly developed, was fully formed. His habits were settled for life. He had a perfectly well-defined individuality, as everybody knew who knew anything about his occupations and ways.

Much of what went to constitute this individuality was the result of his infirmity of sight, and of the unceasing struggle he had made to overcome the difficulties it entailed upon him. For, as we shall see hereafter, the thought of this infirmity, and of the embarrassments it brought with it, was ever before him. It colored, and in many respects it controlled, his whole life.

The violent inflammation that resulted from the fierce attack of rheumatism in the early months of 1815 first startled him, I think, with the apprehension that he might possibly be deprived of sight altogether, and that thus his future years would be left in "total eclipse, without all hope of day." But from this dreary apprehension, his recovery, slow, and partial as it was, and the buoyant spirits that entered so largely into his constitution, at last relieved him. He even, from time to time, as the disease fluctuated to and fro, had hopes of an entire restoration of his sight.

But before long, he began to judge things more exactly as they were, and saw plainly that anything like a full recovery of his sight was improbable, if not impossible. He turned his thoughts, therefore, to the resources that would still remain to him. The prospect was by no means a pleasant one, but he looked at it steadily and calmly. All thought of the profession which had long been so tempting to him he gave up. He saw that he could never fulfil its duties. But intellectual occupation he could not give up. It was a gratification and resource which his nature demanded, and would not be refused. The difficulty was to find out how it could be obtained. During the three months of his confinement in total darkness at St. Michael's, he first began to discipline his thoughts to such orderly composition in his memory as he might have written down on paper, if his sight had permitted it. "I have cheated," he says, in a letter to his family written at the end of that discouraging period, — "I have cheated many a moment of tedium by compositions which were soon banished from my mind for want of an amanuensis."

Among these compositions was a Latin ode to his friend Gardiner, which was prepared wholly without books, but which, though now lost, like the rest of his Latin verses, he repeated years afterwards to his Club, who did not fail to think it good. It is evident, however, that, for a considerable time, he resorted to such mental occupations and exercises rather as an amusement than as anything more serious. Nor did he at first go far with them even as a light and transient relief from idleness ; for, though he never gave them up altogether, and though they at last became a very important element in his success as an author, he soon found an agreeable substitute for them, at least so far as his immediate, every-day wants were concerned.

The substitute to which I refer, but which itself implied much previous reflection and thought upon what he should commit to paper, was an apparatus to enable the blind to write. He heard of it in London during his first residence there in the summer of 1816. A lady, at whose house he visited frequently, and who became interested in his misfortune, "told him," as he says in a letter to his mother, "of a newly invented machine by which blind people are enabled to write. I have," he adds, "before been indebted to Mrs. Delafield for an ingenious candle-screen. If this machine can be procured, you will be sure to feel the effects of it."

He obtained it at once; but he did not use it until nearly a month afterwards, when, on the 24th of August, at Paris, he wrote home his first letter with it, saying, " It is a very happy invention for me." And such it certainly proved to be, for he never ceased to use it from that day; nor does it now seem possible that, without the facilities it afforded him, he ever would have ventured to undertake any of the works which have made his name what it is.[1]

The machine — if machine it can properly be called — is an apparatus invented by one of the well-known Wedgewood family, and is very simple both in its structure and use. It looks, as it lies folded up on the table, like a clumsy portfolio, bound in morocco, and measures about ten inches by nine when unopened. Sixteen stout parallel brass wires fastened on the right-hand side into a frame of the same size with the cover, much like the frame of a school-boy's slate, and crossing it from side to side, mark the number of lines that can be written on a page, and guide the hand in its blind motions. This framework of wires is folded down upon a sheet of paper thoroughly impregnated with a black substance, especially on its under surface, beneath which lies the sheet of common paper that is to receive the writing. There are thus, when it is in use, three layers on the right-hand side of the opened apparatus; viz. the wires, the blackened sheet of paper, and the white sheet, — all lying successively in contact with each other, the two that are underneath being held firmly in their places by the framework of wires which is uppermost. The whole apparatus is called a *noctograph.*

When it has been adjusted, as above described, the person using it writes with an ivory style, or with a style made of some harder substance, like agate, on the upper surface of the blackened paper, which, wherever the style presses on it, trans-

[1] This very apparatus, the first he ever had, it still extant. Indeed, he never possessed but one other, and that was its exact duplicate. The oldest is nearly used up. But, although he never had more than two for himself, he caused others to be made for persons suffering under infirmities like his own, — not unfrequently sending them to those who were known to him only as needing such help.

fers the coloring matter of its under surface to the white paper beneath it, — the writing thus produced looking much like that done with a common black-lead pencil.

The chief difficulty in the use of such an apparatus is obvious. The person employing it never looks upon his work ; never sees one of the marks he is making. He trusts wholly to the wires for the direction of his hand. He makes his letters and words only from mechanical habit. He must, therefore, write straight forward, without any opportunity for correction, however gross may be the mistakes he has made, or however sure he may be that he has made them ; for, if he were to go back in order to correct an error, he would only make his page still more confused, and probably render it quite illegible. When, therefore, he has made a mistake, great or small, all he can do is to go forward, and rewrite further on the word or phrase he first intended to write, rarely attempting to strike out what was wrong, or to insert, in its proper place, anything that may have been omitted. It is plain, therefore, that the person who resorts to this apparatus as a substitute for sight ought previously to prepare and settle in his memory what he wishes to write, so as to make as few mistakes as possible. With the best care, his manuscript will not be very legible. Without it, he may be sure it can hardly be deciphered at all.

That Mr. Prescott, under his disheartening infirmities, — I refer not only to his imperfect sight, but to the rheumatism from which he was seldom wholly free, — should, at the age of five-and-twenty or thirty, with no help but this simple apparatus, have aspired to the character of an historian dealing with events that happened in times and countries far distant from his own, and that are recorded chiefly in foreign languages and by authors whose conflicting testimony was often to be reconciled by laborious comparison, is a remarkable fact in literary history. It is a problem the solution of which was, I believe, never before undertaken ; certainly never before accomplished. Nor do I conceive that he himself could have accomplished it, unless to his uncommon intellectual gifts had been added great animal spirits, a strong, persistent will, and a moral courage which was to be daunted by no obstacle that he might deem it possible to remove by almost any amount of effort.[2]

That he was not insensible to the difficulties of his undertaking, we have partly seen, as we have witnessed how his hopes fluctuated while he was struggling through the arrangements for beginning to write his "Ferdinand and Isabella," and, in fact, during the whole period of its composition. But he showed the same character, the same fertility of resource, every day of his life, and provided, both by forecast and self-sacrifice, against the embarrassments of his condition as they successively presented themselves.

The first thing to be done, and the thing always to be repeated day by day, was to strengthen, as much as possible, what remained of his sight, and at any rate, to do nothing that should tend to exhaust its impaired powers. In 1821, when he was still not without some hope of its recovery, he made this memorandum. "I will make it my principal purpose to restore my eye to its primitive vigor, and will do nothing habitually that can seriously injure it." To this end he regulated his life with an exactness that I have never known equalled. Especially in whatever related to the daily distribution of his time, whether in regard to his intellectual labors, to his social enjoyments, or to the care of his physical powers, including his diet, he was severely exact, — managing himself, indeed, in this last respect, under the general directions of his wise medical adviser, Dr. Jackson, but carrying out these directions with an ingenuity and fidelity all his own.

He was an early riser, although it was a great effort for him to be such. From boyhood it seemed to be contrary to his nature to get up betimes in the morning. He was, therefore, always awaked, and after silently, and sometimes slowly and with reluctance, counting twenty, so as fairly to arouse himself,

[2] The case of Thierry — the nearest known to me — was different. His great work, "Histoire de la Conquête de l'Angleterre par les Normands," was written before he became blind. What he published afterward was dictated, — wonderful, indeed, all of it, but especially all that relates to what he did for the commission of the government concerning the Tiers État, to be found in that grand collection of "Documents inédits sur l'Histoire de France," begun under the auspices and influence of M. Guizot, when he was minister of Louis-Philippe.

he resolutely sprang out of bed; or, if he failed, he paid a forfeit, as a memento of his weakness, to the servant who had knocked at his chamber-door.[3] His failures, however, were rare. When he was called, he was told the state of the weather and of the thermometer. This was important, as he was compelled by his rheumatism — almost always present, and, when not so, always apprehended — to regulate his dress with care ; and, finding it difficult to do so in any other way, he caused each of its heavier external portions to be marked by his tailor with the number of ounces it weighed, and then put them on according to the temperature, sure that their weight would indicate the measure of warmth and protection they would afford.[4]

As soon as he was dressed, he took his early exercise in the open air. This, for many years, was done on horseback, and, as he loved a spirited horse and was often thinking more of his intellectual pursuits than of anything else while he was riding, he sometimes caught a fall. But he was a good rider, and was sorry to give up this form of exercise and resort to walking or driving, as he did, by order of his physician, in the last dozen years of his life. No weather, except a severe storm, prevented him at any period from thus, as he called it, " winding himself up." Even in the coldest of our very cold winter mornings, it was his habit, so long as he could ride, to see the sun rise on a particular spot three or four miles from town. In a letter to Mrs. Ticknór, who was then in Germany, dated March, 1836, — at the end of a winter memorable for its extreme severity, — he says, " You will give me credit for some spunk when I tell you that I have not been frightened by the cold a single morning from a ride on horseback to Jamaica Plain and back again before breakfast. My mark has been

---

[3] When he was a bachelor, the servant, after waiting a certain number of minutes at the door without receiving an answer, went in and took away the bed-clothes. This was, at that period, the office of faithful Nathan Webster, who was remembered kindly in Mr. Prescott's will, and who was for nearly thirty years in the family, a true and valued friend of all its members.

[4] As in the case of the use of wine, hereafter to be noticed, he made, from year to year, the most minute memoranda about the use of clothes, finding it necessary to be exact on account of the rheumatism which, besides almost constantly infesting his limbs, always affected his sight when it became severe.

to see the sun rise by Mr. Greene's school, if you remember where that is." When the rides here referred to were taken, the thermometer was often below zero of Fahrenheit.

On his return home, after adjusting his dress anew, with reference to the temperature within doors, he sat down, almost always in a very gay humor, to a moderate and even spare breakfast, — a meal he much liked, because, as he said, he could then have his family with him in a quiet way, and so begin the day happily. From the breakfast-table he went at once to his study. There, while busied with what remained of his toilet, or with the needful arrangements for his regular occupations, Mrs. Prescott read to him, generally from the morning papers, but sometimes from the current literature of the day. At a fixed hour — seldom later than ten — his reader, or secretary, came. In this, as in everything, he required punctuality; but he noted tardiness only by looking significantly at his watch; for it is the testimony of all his surviving secretaries, that he never spoke a severe word to either of them in the many years of their familiar intercourse.

When they had met in the study, there was no thought but of active work for about three hours.[*] His infirmities, however, were always present to warn him how cautiously it must be done, and he was extremely ingenious in the means he devised for doing it without increasing them. The shades and shutters for regulating the exact amount of light which should be admitted; his own position relatively to its direct rays, and to those that were reflected from surrounding objects; the adaptation of his dress and of the temperature of the room to his rheumatic affections; and the different contrivances for taking notes from the books that were read to him, and for impressing on his memory, with the least possible use of his sight, such portions of each as were needful for his imme-

---

[*] I speak here of the time during which he was busy with his Historics. In the intervals between them, as, for instance, between the " Ferdinand and Isabella " and the " Mexico," between the " Mexico " and " Peru," &c., his habits were very different. At these periods he indulged, sometimes for many months, in a great deal of light, miscellaneous reading, which he used to call " literary loafing." This he thought not only agreeable, but refreshing and useful; though sometimes he complained bitterly of himself for carrying his indulgences of this sort too far.

6

diate purpose, — were all of them the result of painstaking experiments, skilfully and patiently made.   But their ingenuity and adaptation were less remarkable than the conscientious consistency with which they were employed from day to day for forty years.

In relation to all such arrangements, two circumstances should be noted.

The first is, that the resources of his eye were always very small and uncertain, except for a few years, beginning in 1840, when, from his long-continued prudence or from some inscrutable cause, there seemed to be either an increase of strength in the organ, or else such a diminution of its sensibility as enabled him to use it more, though its strength might really be diminished.

Thus, for instance, he was able to use his eye very little in the preparation of the " Ferdinand and Isabella," not looking into a book sometimes for weeks and even months together, and yet occasionally he could read several hours in a day if he carefully divided the whole into short portions, so as to avoid fatigue.   While engaged in the composition of the " Conquest of Mexico," on the contrary, he was able to read with considerable regularity, and so he was while working on the " Conquest of Peru," though, on the whole, with less.[*]

But he had, during nearly all this time, another difficulty to encounter.   There had come on prematurely that gradual alteration of the eye which is the consequence of advancing years, and for which the common remedy is spectacles.   Even when he was using what remained to him of sight on the

---

[*] How uncertain was the state of his eye, even when it was strongest, may be seen from memoranda made at different times within less than two years of each other.   The first is in January, 1829, when he was full of grateful feelings for an unexpected increase of his powers of sight.   " By the blessing of Heaven," he says, " I have been enabled to have the free use of my eye in the daytime during the last weeks, without the exception of a single day, although deprived, for nearly a fortnight, of my accustomed exercise. I hope I have not abused this great privilege."   But this condition of things did not last long.   Great fluctuations followed.   In August and September he was much discouraged by severe inflammations; and in October, 1830, when he had been slowly writing the " Ferdinand and Isabella " for about a year, his sight for a time became so much impaired that he was brought — I use his own words — " seriously to consider what steps he should take in relation to that work, if his sight should fail him altogether."

"Conquest of Mexico" with a freedom which not a little animated him in his pursuits, he perceived this discouraging change. In July, 1841, he says: "My eye, for some days, feels dim. 'I guess and fear,' as Burns says." And in June, 1842, when our families were spending together at Lebanon Springs a few days which he has recorded as otherwise very happy, he spoke to me more than once in a tone of absolute grief, that he should never again enjoy the magnificent spectacle of the starry heavens. To this sad deprivation he, in fact, alludes himself in his Memoranda of that period, where, in relation to his eyes, he says: "I find a misty veil increasing over them, quite annoying when reading. The other evening B—— said, 'How beautiful the heavens are with so many stars!' I could hardly see two. It made me sad."

Spectacles, however, although they brought their appropriate relief, brought also an inevitable inconvenience. They fatigued his eye. He could use it, therefore, less and less, or if he used it at all, beyond a nicely adjusted amount, the excess was followed by a sort of irritability, weakness, and pain in the organ which he had not felt for many years. This went on increasing with sad regularity. But he knew that it was inevitable, and submitted to it patiently. In the latter part of his life he was able to use his eye very little indeed for the purpose of reading, — in the last year, hardly at all. Even in several of the years preceding, he used it only thirty-five minutes in each day, divided exactly by the watch into portions of five minutes each, with at least half an hour between, and always stopping the moment pain was felt, even if it were felt at the first instant of opening the book. I doubt whether a more persistent, conscientious care was ever taken of an impaired physical power. Indeed, I do not see how it could have been made more thorough. But all care was unavailing, and he at last knew that it was so. The decay could not be arrested. He spoke of it rarely, but when he perceived that in the evening twilight he could no longer walk about the streets that were familiar to him with his accustomed assurance, he felt it deeply. Still he persevered, and was as watchful of what remained of his sight as if his hopes of its restoration had continued unchecked. Indeed, I think he always trusted that he was saving something by his anxious care; he always believed that great prudence on one day would enable him to do a little more work on the next than he should be able to do without so much caution.

The other circumstance that should be noticed in relation to the arrangements for his pursuits is, the continually increased amount of light he was obliged to use, and which he could use without apparent injury.

In Bedford Street, where he first began his experiments, he could, from the extreme sensitiveness of his eye, bear very little light. But, even before he left that quiet old mansion, he cut out a new window in his working-room, arranging it so that the light should fall more strongly and more exclusively upon the book he might be using. This did very well for a time. But when he removed to Beacon Street, the room he built expressly for his own use contained six contiguous windows; two of which, though large, were glazed each with a single sheet of the finest plate-glass, nicely protected by several curtains of delicate fabric and of a light-blue color, one or more of which could be drawn up over each window to temper the light while the whole light that was admitted through any one opening could be excluded by solid wooden shutters. At first, though much light was commonly used, these appliances for diminishing it were all more or less required. But, gradually, one after another of them was given up, and, at last, I observed that none was found important. He needed and used all the light he could get.

The change was a sad one, and he did not like to allude to it. But during the last year of his life, after the first slight access of paralysis, which much disturbed the organ for a time, and rendered its action very irregular, he spoke plainly to me. He said he must soon cease to use his eye for any purpose of study, but fondly trusted that he should always be able to recognize the features of his friends, and should never become a burden to those he loved by needing to be led about. His hopes were, indeed, fulfilled, but not without the sorrow of all. The day before his sudden death he walked the streets as freely as he had done for years.

Still, whatever may have been the condition of his eye at

any period, — from the fierce attack of 1815 to the very end of his life, — it was always a paramount subject of anxiety with him. He never ceased to think of it, and to regulate the hours, and almost the minutes, of his daily life by it. Even in its best estate he felt that it must be spared; in its worst, he was anxious to save something by care and abstinence. He said, " he reckoned time by eyesight, as distances on railroads are reckoned by hours."

One thing in this connection may be noted as remarkable. He knew that, if he would give up literary labor altogether, his eye would be better at once, and would last longer. His physicians all told him so, and their opinion was rendered certain by his own experience; for whenever he ceased to work for some time, as during a visit to New York in 1842 and a visit to Europe in 1850, — in short, whenever he took a journey or indulged himself in holidays of such a sort as prevented him from looking into books at all or thinking much about them, — his general health immediately became more vigorous than might have been expected from a relief so transient, and his sight was always improved; sometimes materially improved. But he would not pay the price. He preferred to submit, if it should be inevitable, to the penalty of ultimate blindness, rather than give up his literary pursuits.

He never liked to work more than three hours consecutively. At one o'clock, therefore, he took a walk of about two miles, and attended to any little business abroad that was incumbent on him, coming home generally refreshed and exhilarated, and ready to lounge a little and gossip. Dinner followed, for the greater part of his life about three o'clock, although, during a few years, he dined in winter at five or six, which he preferred, and which he gave up only because his health demanded the change. In the summer he always dined early, so as to have the late afternoon for driving and exercise during our hot season.

He enjoyed the pleasures of the table, and even its luxuries, more than most men. But he restricted himself carefully in the use of them, adjusting everything with reference to its effect on the power of using his eye immediately afterwards, and especially on his power of using it the next day. Occasional indulgence when dining out or with friends at home he found useful, or at least not injurious, and was encouraged in it by his medical counsel. But he dined abroad, as he did everything of the sort, at regulated intervals, and not only determined beforehand in what he should deviate from his settled habits, but often made a record of the result for his future government.

The most embarrassing question, however, as to diet, regarded the use of wine, which, if at first it sometimes seemed to be followed by bad consequences, was yet, on the whole, found useful, and was prescribed to him. To make everything certain, and settle the precise point to which he should go, he instituted a series of experiments, and between March, 1818, and November, 1820, — a period of two years and nine months, — he recorded the exact quantity of wine that he took every day, except the few days when he entirely abstained. It was Sherry or Madeira. In the great majority of cases — four fifths, I should think — it ranged from one to two glasses, but went up sometimes to four or five, and even to six. He settled at last, upon two or two and a half as the quantity best suited to his case, and persevered in this as his daily habit, until the last year of his life, during which a peculiar regimen was imposed upon him from the peculiar circumstances of his health. In all this I wish to be understood that he was rigorous with himself, — much more so than persons thought who saw him only when he was dining with friends, and when, but equally upon system and principle, he was much more free.

He generally smoked a single weak cigar after dinner, and listened at the same time to light reading from Mrs. Prescott. A walk of two miles — more or less — followed; but always enough, after the habit of riding was given up, to make the full amount of six miles' walking for the day's exercise, and then, between five and eight, he took a cup of tea, and had his reader with him for work two hours more.

The labors of the day were now definitively ended. He came down from his study to his library, and either sat there or walked about while Mrs. Prescott read to him from some amusing book, generally a novel, and, above all other novels, those of Scott and Miss Edgeworth. In all this he took great solace. He enjoyed the room as well as the reading, and, as he moved about, would often stop before the books, — especially his favorite books, — and be sure that they were all in their proper places, drawn up exactly to the front of their respective shelves, like soldiers on a dress-parade, — sometimes speaking of them, and almost to them, as if they were personal friends.

At half past ten, having first taken nearly another glass of wine, he went to bed, fell asleep quickly, and slept soundly and well. Suppers he early gave up, although they were a form of social intercourse much liked in his father's house, and common thirty or forty years ago in the circle to which he belonged. Besides all other reasons against them, he found that the lights commonly on the table shot their horizontal rays so as to injure his suffering organ. Larger evening parties, which were not so liable to this objection, he liked rather for their social influences than for the pleasure they gave him; but he was seen in them to the last, though rarely and only for a short time in each. Earlier in life, when he enjoyed them more and stayed later, he would, in the coldest winter nights, after going home, run up and down on a plank walk, so arranged in the garden of the Bedford-Street house that he could do it with his eyes shut, for twenty minutes or more, in order that his system might be refreshed, and his sight invigorated, for the next morning's work.[7] Later, unhappily, this was not needful. His eye had lost the sensibility that gave its value to such a habit.

In his exercise, at all its assigned hours, he was faithful and exact. If a violent storm prevented him from going out, or if the bright snow on sunny days in winter rendered it dangerous for him to expose his eye to its brilliant reflection, he would dress himself as for the street and walk vigorously about the colder parts of the house, or he would saw and chop fire-wood, under cover, being, in the latter case, read to all the while.

The result he sought, and generally obtained, by these efforts was not, however, always to be had without suffering. The

---

[7] Some persons may think this to have been a fancy of my friend, or an over-nice estimate of the value of the open air. But others have found the same benefit who needed it less. Sir Charles Bell says, in his journal, that he used to sit in the open air a great deal, and read or draw, because *on the following day*, he found himself so much better able to work. Some of the best passages in his great treatises were, he says, written under these circumstances.

first mile or two of his walk often cost him pain — sometimes sharp pain — in consequence of the rheumatism, which seldom deserted his limbs; but he never on this account gave it up; for regular exercise in the open air was, as he well knew, indispensable to the preservation of whatever remained of his decaying sight. He persevered, therefore, through the last two suffering years of his life, when it was peculiarly irksome and difficult for him to move; and even in the days immediately preceding his first attack of paralysis, when he was very feeble, he was out at his usual hours. His will, in truth, was always stronger than the bodily ills that beset him, and prevailed over them to the last.[*]

[*] On one occasion, when he was employed upon a work that interested him because it related to a friend, he was attacked with pains that made a sitting posture impossible. But he would not yield. He took his noctograph to a sofa, and knelt before it so as to be able to continue his work. This resource, however, failed, and then he laid himself down flat upon the floor. This extraordinary operation went on during portions of nine successive days.

CHAPTER XI.

1837 – 1838.

MR. PRESCOTT'S SOCIAL CHARACTER. — REMARKS ON IT BY MR. GARDINER AND MR. PARSONS.

A TRUE and sufficient understanding of Mr. Prescott's modes of life cannot be obtained without a more detailed account than has been thus far given of his social relations, and of the exactness with which he controlled and governed them.

"Never was there," says his friend Mr. Gardiner, in an interesting paper addressed to me, on this side of our friend's character, — "Never was there a man, who, by natural constitution, had a keener zest of social enjoyment in all its varieties. His friend Mr. Parsons says of him, that one of the 'most remarkable traits of this remarkable man was his singular capacity of enjoyment. He could be happy in more ways, and more happy in every one of them, than any other person I have ever known.' This may be a strong manner of stating the characteristic referred to ; but so far as respects one of his chief sources of happiness, — social enjoyment, — the idea would seem to be exemplified by the very different kinds of society from which he appeared to derive almost equal pleasure.

"So, in regard to his capacity of imparting pleasure to others, Mr. Parsons makes an equally strong statement ; but it is one I fully concur in. 'If I were asked,' he says, 'to name the man, whom I have known, whose coming was most sure to be hailed as a pleasant event by all whom he approached, I should not only place Prescott at the head of the list, but I could not place any other man near him.' I also must bear testimony, that I never have known any other man whose company was so universally attractive, — equally so to men and to women, to young and to old, and to all classes that he mingled with.

"With these capacities for both giving and receiving the highest degree of pleasure in social entertainment, there is no cause for wonder that this should have been with him a favorite pursuit. The wonder is, rather, that he should have always — at least after the first effervescence of youth — have kept it in such perfect subordination to those more important pursuits which were the business, and at the same time, on the whole, the highest enjoyment, of his life. I use the term pursuit, applying it to the one object no less than the other ; for this it is which constitutes the peculiarity. Both were pursued at the same time, ardently and systematically. Neither was sacrificed to the other for any great length of time. He felt that a due

G *   1 proportion of each — literary labor and social amusement — was essential to his happiness, and he studied the philosophy of life, both theoretically and practically, with reference to his own natural temper and constitution, to ascertain in what proportions they could best be combined to answer his whole purpose.

"These proportions varied certainly at different times. There was a natural tendency of the graver pursuits to predominate more and more as he advanced in age, but never to the entire exclusion of a perfectly youthful enjoyment of whatever society he sought. There were, too, periods of close retirement, — chiefly during his *villegiaturas* as he used to call his country life, — when he devoted himself, for a time almost exclusively, to his studies and compositions, with little addition to the agreeable social circle and quiet domestic life of his own and his father's family. But there were also corresponding periods of great relaxation, — what he used to call his 'loafing times,' — not always of short duration either, — especially in the interval between one long labor finished and the beginning of another. At these periods he gave himself up to a long holiday, dividing his time almost wholly between the lightest literature and a great deal of social amusement. There was usually something of this, though for a shorter term, when he first returned to the city, after a summer or autumn campaign at Pepperell. And seldom, when away from Pepperell, was he so hard at work as not to enjoy an ample allowance of social pleasure. Nay, at the period of his life when he used to pass a long summer, as well as autumn, at Pepperell, — that is, before either he or his father had a house on the sea-shore, — it was his custom to find an excuse for an occasional visit of a day or two to the city, when he always arranged for, and counted upon, at least one gay meeting of old friends at the dinner-table. After he became a summer inhabitant of Nahant, living in the unavoidable publicity of a fashionable watering-place, the difficulty was to guard against the intrusion of too much company, rather than to get the quantum he required. This was among the causes which led him, in later years, to forsake Nahant for his more quiet sea-shore residence at Lynn. But, wherever his residence was, frequent recreations of society — domestic, fashionable, literary, and convivial — were as much a part of his plan of life as the steady continuance of historical studies and labors of authorship.

"Yet, both before and after the publication of his 'Ferdinand and Isabella,' — the first notice, be it remembered, even to his personal friends, of his extraordinary merits as a man of letters, — he was scrupulously observant of hours. Though indulging so freely, and with such a zest, in this round of various society, he would never allow himself to be drawn by it into very late sittings. This was partly, no doubt, from domestic considerations regarding the general habit of his father's household, continued afterwards in his own, but mainly because he began the day early, and chose to keep his study hours of the morrow unimpaired. Except, therefore, on some extraordinary and foreseen occasions of his earlier days, carefully arranged for beforehand, he used to make a point of quitting the company, of whatever kind, and whatever might be its attractions, at his hour. This was, for a long time, ten o'clock. It did not mean ten o'clock or thereabouts, as most men would have made it; but at ten precisely he would insist on going, in spite of all entreaty, as if to an engagement of the last importance.

"I remember particularly one instance to illustrate this. It occurred at some time while he was yet a member of his father's family, but, I think, after his marriage, and certainly before he had published himself to the world as an author, — that is, while he was scarcely known to many persons as one engaged in any serious occupation. The case left an impression, because on this occasion Mr. Prescott, though not in his own house, was not a guest, but the entertainer, at a restaurateur's, of an invited company of young men, chiefly of the *bon-vivant* order. He took that mode sometimes of giving a return dinner to avoid intruding too much on the hospitality of his father's roof, as well as to put at ease the sort of company which promised exuberant mirth. His dinner hour was set early; purposely, no doubt, that all might be well over in good season. But it proved to be a prolonged festivity. Under the brilliant auspices of their host, who was never in higher spirits, the company became very gay, and not at all disposed to abridge their gayety, even after a reasonable number of hours. As the hour of ten drew near, I noticed that Prescott was beginning to get a little fidgety, and to drop some hints, which no one seemed willing to take, — for no one present, unless it were myself, was aware that time was of any more importance to our host than it was to many of his guests. Presently, to the general surprise, the host himself got up abruptly, and addressed the company nearly as follows : ' Really, my friends, I am very sorry to be obliged to tear myself from you at so very unreasonable an hour ; but you seem to have got your sitting-breeches on for the night. I left mine at home, and must go. But I am sure you will be very soon in no condition to miss me, — especially as I leave behind that excellent representative,' — pointing to a basket of several yet uncorked bottles, which stood in a corner. ' Then you know,' he added, ' you are just as much at home in this house as I am. You can call for what you like. Don't be alarmed, — I mean on *my* account. I abandon to you, without reserve, all my best wine, my credit with the house, and my reputation to boot. Make free with them all, I beg of you, — and, if you don't go home till morning, I wish you a merry night of it.' With this he was off, and the Old South clock, hard by, was heard to strike ten at the instant."

Mr. Gardiner, in the preceding remarks, refers more than once to the opinions of Professor Theophilus Parsons on Mr. Prescott's social character. They are contained in a paper which this early and intimate friend of the historian was good enough to give me ; but there are other portions of the same paper so true, and so happily expressed, that I should be unjust to my readers, if I were not to give them more than the glimpses afforded in Mr. Gardiner's remarks.

Speaking of Mr. Prescott's "marvellous popularity," Mr. Parsons goes on : —

"I do not speak of this as his *success* in society, for that would imply that he sought for popularity and aimed at it, and this would be wholly untrue. It was not perhaps undesired, and it certainly was neither un-

known nor unwelcome to him.   But it came, not because he made any
effort to procure it, but simply because it was *inevitable*, by which I mean
that it was the necessary effect of the combination of certain qualities in
his character.   Foremost among these, undoubtedly, was his universal,
constant, and extreme kindness of heart, and its fitting exponent in as
sweet a temper as ever man had.   But even these would not have sufficed,
but for his capacity for sympathy, a quality which is not always the companion of a real benevolence. . . . . . If Prescott never demanded or desired
that others should stand around and bow to him, it was not because he
could have no reason for claiming this.   For all whom he came near felt,
what he never seemed to feel, that there was, if not some renunciation of
right, at least a charming forgetfulness of self, in the way in which he
asserted no superiority over any, but gave himself up to the companion of
the moment, with the evident desire to make him as happy as he could.
And his own prompt and active sympathy awoke the sympathy of others.
His gayety became theirs.   He came, always bringing the gift of cheerfulness, and always offering it with such genuine cordiality, that it was sure
to be accepted, and returned with increase.   No wonder that he was just
as welcome everywhere as sunshine.   If I were asked to name the man
whom I have known, whose coming was most sure to be hailed as a pleasant event by all whom he approached, I should not only place Prescott at
the head of the list, but I could not place any other man near him.   And
with all this universal sympathy there was never any sacrifice or loss of
himself.   He did not go willingly to others because his mind had no home
of its own.   When we see one seeking society often, and enjoying it with
peculiar relish, we can hardly forbear thinking that he thus comes abroad
to find necessary recreation, and that, even if he be content at home, his
joys are elsewhere.   Nothing could be less true of Prescott.   It would
have been equally difficult for one who knew him only in his home activi-
ties and his home happiness, or only in the full glow of his social pleasures, to believe that he knew but half of the man, and that the other half
was quite as full of its own life, and its own thorough enjoyment, as the
half he saw."

CHAPTER XII.

1837.

MR. PRESCOTT'S INDUSTRY AND GENERAL CHARACTER BASED ON PRINCIPLE AND ON SELF-SACRIFICE. — TEMPTATIONS. — EXPEDIENTS TO OVERCOME THEM. — EXPERIMENTS. — NOTES OF WHAT IS READ TO HIM. — COMPOSES WITHOUT WRITING. — SEVERE DISCIPLINE OF HIS MORAL AND RELIGIOUS CHARACTER. — DISLIKES TO HAVE HIS HABITS INTERFERRED WITH. — NEVER SHOWS CONSTRAINT. — FREEDOM OF MANNER IN HIS FAMILY AND IN SOCIETY. — HIS INFLUENCE ON OTHERS. — HIS CHARITY TO THE POOR. — INSTANCE OF IT.

MR. PRESCOTT early discovered what many, whose social position makes no severe demand on them for exertion, fail to discover until it is too late, — I mean, that industry of some sort and an earnest use of whatever faculties God has given us, are essential to even a moderate amount of happiness in this world. He did not, however, come to this conclusion through his relations with society. On the contrary, these relations during the most exposed period of his youth were tempting him in exactly the opposite direction, and thus rendering his position dangerous to his character. He was handsome, gay, uncommonly entertaining, and a great favorite wherever he went. The accident to his sight obviously excluded him from the professions open to persons of his own age and condition, and his father's fortune, if not great, was at least such as to relieve the son, with whose misfortune his whole family felt the tenderest sympathy, from the necessity of devoting himself to any occupation as a means of subsistence. A life of dainty, elegant idleness was, therefore, as freely open to him as it was to any young man of his time; and his infirmities would no doubt have excused him before his friends and the world, if he had given himself up to it. His personal relations, in fact, no less than his keen relish of social enjoyments and his attractive qualities as a mere man of society, all seemed to solicit him to a life of self-indulgence.

But he perceived betimes that such a life would be only one long mistake, — that it might satisfy the years of youth, when the spirits are fresh, and the pursuit of pleasure has been checked neither by sorrow nor by disappointment, but that it must leave the graver period of manhood without its appropriate interests, and old age without its appropriate respect. "It is of little moment," he therefore recorded, for his own warning and government, as early as 1822, — "it is of little moment whether I succeed in this or that thing, but it is of great moment that I am habitually industrious." This conclusion was reached by him three years before he began his search for a subject to which he could devote serious and consecutive labor. But it was eight years after the occurrence of the accident that had shut him out from the field of adventure in which most of those who had been his companions and friends were already advancing and prosperous.[1]

And these eight years had been full of silent, earnest teachings. The darkness in which he had so often been immured for weeks and months together had given him leisure for thoughts which might otherwise never have come to him, or which would have come with much less power. Notwithstanding his exuberant spirits, he had suffered hours of *ennui*, which, in a free and active life, and amidst the pleasures of society, would have been spared to him. The result, therefore, to which he was brought by the workings of his own mind, was, that, to be happy, he must lead a life of continuous, useful industry, — such as he would at last enjoy if it were faithfully persisted in, and if it tended to the benefit of others.

We have seen how ingenious he was in inventing for himself the mechanical contrivances indispensable to the labor and study on which, with his imperfect sight, he so much depended. But there was another obstacle in his way of a different sort, and one still more difficult and disagreeable to encounter. He did not love work. He could do it, and had done it often, but

[1] The same thought is often repeated in his Memoranda, but nowhere in stronger terms than in a paper written twenty-seven years later. and showing that he adhered to his conviction on the subject through life. "I am convinced," he says, "that whether *clairvoyant* or stone-blind, intellectual occupation — steady, regular literary occupation — is the only true vocation for me, — indispensable to my happiness."

only under some strong stimulus. He had, for instance, commonly learned his lessons well in boyhood, because he respected Dr. Gardiner, and was sure to be punished, if he had neglected them. At college, he considered a certain moderate amount of scholarship necessary to the character of a gentleman, and came up to his own not very high standard with a good degree of alacrity. And he had always desired to satisfy and gratify his father, whose authority he felt to be gentle as well as just, and whose wishes were almost always obeyed, even in his earlier and more thoughtless years. But the present purpose of his life demanded a different foundation from all this, — one much deeper and much more solid. He was now to be a scholar, and to work not only faithfully, but gladly, — almost disinterestedly; for without such work, as he well knew, no permanent and worthy result could be obtained, — no ultimate intellectual success achieved. " Be occupied *always*," he therefore recorded firmly at the outset of his new life.

But his nature — buoyant, frolicsome, and simple-hearted — and his temperament — strong, active, and wilful — long contended against his wise determination. While he was engaged with his French and Italian studies, he did not, indeed, find industry difficult; for such studies were both pleasant and light. But when they were over, and he was persuaded that German was inaccessible to him, his exertions relaxed. " I have read with no method, and very little diligence or spirit, for three months," he said in 1824. " To the end of my life, I trust, I shall be more avaricious of time, and never put up with a smaller average than seven hours of intellectual occupation *per diem*. Less than that cannot discharge my duties to mankind, satisfy my own feelings, or give me a rank in the community of letters." But a few months afterwards he finds it needful to adopt new resolutions of reform. He complains bitterly that he " really works less than an hour a day," and determines that it shall at any rate be five hours, — a determination, however, which he makes only to be mortified again and again, that he can, with much effort, hardly come up to three or four. And so it went on for two years of alternating struggles and failures. Even after he had entered on the composition of the " Ferdinand and Isabella," it was not much better. The habit of industry indispensable to success was hard to be acquired. Resolutions, such as he had been long in the habit of making, but which, from their nature, should rather have been called good purposes, would not do it. He broke them continually. Some other expedient, therefore, — one more absolute and of more stringent authority, — must be resorted to, or he must fail.[2]

A good deal annoyed with himself, he turned to what had earlier been a favorite mode of compelling himself to keep his own good resolutions, — I mean a system of pecuniary mulcts and penalties. In college, he began this practice, which he continued through his whole life, by punishing himself with a moderate fine, to be paid, after certain neglects or offences, to some charity. But this had not quite enough of the essential character of punishment in it, since he was liberally supplied with money, and loved to give it away almost as well as his mother did. He therefore adopted another mode, that proved a little more effectual. He made bets, of some consequence, with such of his college friends as would take them, to the effect that he would avoid or would do certain things, in relation to which he was sure he should be mortified to have them know he had failed. But it was a whimsical peculiarity of these bets, to be on such subjects, or in such forms, that commonly nobody but himself could know whether he had lost or won. The decision was left to his own honor. It should be added, therefore, that, as such bets were made wholly for his own improvement, he was never at this period known to exact a forfeit when his adversary had lost. He considered his success as his true winning, and had no wish that anybody should be punished for it. He desired only to punish himself, and therefore, when he had lost was sure to proclaim himself the loser and pay the bet. When he had won, he said nothing.

It was to this last form of stimulus or punishment, therefore, that he resorted, when he found his industry in relation

---

[2] There is a characteristic allusion to this frailty in his notice of a good resolution which he made at the end of one of his memorandum-books, and to which he refers in the first words of the next: " I ended the last book with a good resolution. I shall never be too old to *make* them. See if I shall ever be old enough to *keep* them."

to the composition of the " Ferdinand and Isabella" not only flagging, but so seriously falling off that he began to be alarmed for the final result.   In September, 1828, he gave a bond to Mr. English, then acting as his reader and secretary, to pay him a thousand dollars, if, within one year from that date, he had not written two hundred and fifty pages of his history, " the object being," as he said, " to prevent further vacillation until he had written so much as would secure his interest in going through with it."   He did not incur the penalty, and thirteen years afterwards he recorded his conviction that the arrangement had been wise.   " I judged right," he said, " that when I had made so large an investment of time and labor, I should not flag again."

But Mr. English's account of the affair is more minute, and is not a little curious as an expression of Mr. Prescott's character.

" The bond or agreement made," he writes to me, " bound each of us to take from the other the amount Mr. Prescott should himself decide to be won on certain wagers written by himself and sealed up.   I never saw them, and do not, to this day, know the subject of the bets.   I took his word that they were made to gratify some fancy of his own, and that they were so proportioned that the odds were much in my favor, — for instance, that he risked in the proportion of one hundred to my twenty. This contract, I suppose, continued to his death ; at any rate, he never notified me that it had ceased.   He often added new wagers, or increased the amount of the old ones, as we have written our signatures with fresh dates over and over again on the bottom and margins of the sheets at numerous times since 1831,[*] down to within a few years of his death.   He would bring the paper to my office so folded that I could not read what was written in it, and, with a smile, ask me to sign again.   I always did so at his request, without knowing what I signed, having the most implicit confidence that it was only a harmless affair, and leaving it wholly to him to decide whether I lost or won.   I remember his paying me two winnings, — one, several years ago, of twenty or thirty dollars, — the other, somewhere about ten years ago, of one hundred.   He afterwards called on me to pay a loss of twenty or thirty, I forget which.   He would come into my office with a smile, lay down his money, and say, ' You remember that bond ? you have won that, and go out with a laugh.   On the other occasion, ' You have lost this time, and must pay me twenty or thirty dollars,' whichever it was.   I handed him the money without remark.   He laughed and said, that, on the whole, I was in pocket so far, but he could not tell how it would be next time, and went out without anything more said on either side."

[*] In 1831, Mr. English ceased to act as Mr. Prescott's secretary.

This document is lost, but another, not unlike it, and, what is remarkable, made with another friend, while the first bond was yet in full force, is preserved, and is very minute and stringent. Both prove that work was often painfully unwelcome to him, even when he had been long accustomed to it, and that not unfrequently, in order to rouse himself to a proper exertion of his faculties, he was willing to call in the aid of some foreign, direct stimulus. And this he did from a deliberate persuasion that it was a duty he owed to himself, to employ the talents that had been given to him "as ever in the great Taskmaster's eye." His literary memoranda afford abundant proof of this. Indeed, they are throughout a sort of monument of it, for they were made in a great degree to record his shortcomings, and to stimulate his uncertain industry. They contain many scores of phrases, like these, scattered over more than twenty years of the most active and important part of his life.

"I have worked lazily enough, latterly, or, rather, have been too lazy to work at all. — Ended the old year [1834] very badly. The last four weeks absolute annihilation. — Another three months, since the last entry, and three months of *dolce far niente*. Not so *dolce* either. Fortunately for the good economy and progress of the species, activity — activity, mental or physical — is indispensable to happiness."

On another occasion, after enumerating the work he had done during the preceding six months, he says : —

"There is the sum total of what I have done in this *dizzy-pated* winter, which has left me in worse health and spirits, and with less to show in any other way, than any past winter for ten years, — nay, twenty, — *proh pudor!*"

And again, in 1845 : —

"I find it as hard to get under way as a crazy hulk that has been hauled up for repairs. But I will mend, and, that I may do so, will make hebdomadal entries of my laziness. I think I can't stand the repetition of such records long."

But the very next week, in reference to the "Conquest of Peru," which he was then writing, he says : —

"*Horresco referens!* I have actually done nothing since last entry. . . . . . If I can once get in harness and at work, I shall do well enough. But my joints are stiff, I think, as I grow old. So, to give myself a start, I have made a wager with Mr. Otis,* that I will reel off at least one page

* Mr. Edmund B. Otis, who was then acting as his secretary.

per diem, barring certain contingencies. If I can't do this, it must be a gone case, and Pizarro may look to have his misdeeds shown up by a better pen."

No doubt, in these passages of his private Memoranda, and in many more, both earlier and later, of the same sort, there is high coloring. But it was intentional. The main object of the whole record for nearly forty years was to stimulate his industry, and to prevent himself from relapsing into the idleness, or into the light and pleasant occupations, that constantly tempted him from his proper studies. As he intimates in the last extract, when he was well entered on a subject and the impetus was obtained, he generally enjoyed his work, and felt the happiness and peace of conscience which he knew he could get in no other way. But the difficulty was, to obtain the impetus. After finishing one work, he did not like to begin another, and, even when he had completed a single chapter, he was often unwilling to take up the next. When he moved from the town to the country, or from the country to the town, he did not naturally or easily fall into his usual train of occupations. In short, whenever there was a pause, he wanted to turn aside into some other path, rather than to continue in the difficult one right before him ; but he very rarely went far astray, before he had the courage to punish himself and come back.

But, besides being intended for a rebuke to the idle and light-hearted tendencies of his nature, his Memoranda were designed to record the various experiments he made to overcome the peculiar difficulties in his way, and thus assist him to encounter others more successfully. Some of these bear the same marks of ingenuity and adaptation which characterized his mechanical contrivances for sparing his sight, and were near akin to them.

The notes that were taken from the books read to him, or which he was able to read himself, were made with very great care. They varied in their character at different periods, going more into detail at first than they did later. But they were always ample, abundant. I have now before me above a thousand pages of them, which yet cover only a small portion of the ground of " Ferdinand and Isabella." From these, and similar masses of manuscript, were selected, when they were wanted, such materials and hints as would suit the purpose of any given chapter or division of the work that might be in hand, and these again were transcribed by themselves, in a very plain hand, for use. If his eye served him tolerably well, he read such of these selected notes as were most important, with great care, repeatedly, until he felt himself to be absolute master of their contents. If they were not so important, they were read to him, rarely less than six times, — generally more, — "some," he says, "a dozen times," — so that he might not only comprehend their general scope, but be able to judge of any varieties involved in their separate statements, whether of opinion or of fact.

When he had thus collected all needful materials, he began the task of composition in his memory, — very difficult, from the detail into which it was necessarily carried, and from the exactness that was to be observed in each step as he advanced. Of its value and importance he was early aware, and, as he gradually surmounted the peculiar embarrassments it presented, he relied on it more and more exclusively, until at last he attained an extraordinary power in its use and application.

In 1824, he said, that, before composing anything, he found it necessary "to ripen the subject by much reflection in his mind." This, it will be remembered, was when he had not even begun his preliminary Spanish studies, and had, in fact, hazarded nothing more serious than an article for the "North-American Review." But, as soon as he had entered on the composition of the "Ferdinand and Isabella," he felt fully its great importance and wide consequences. Within a fortnight, he recorded: "Never take up my pen, until I have travelled over the subject so often, that I can write almost from memory." It was really desirable to write, not almost, but altogether, from memory. He labored, therefore, long for it, and succeeded, by great and continuous efforts, in obtaining the much-coveted power. "Think concentratedly," he says, "when I think at all." And again, "Think closely, gradually concentrating the circle of thought." [5]   At last, in 1841, when he was

---

[5] Again, November 10, 1839, he records: "Think continuously and closely before taking up my pen; make the corrections chiefly in my own mind; not

employed on the "Mexico," he records, after many previous memoranda on the subject: "My way has lately been to go over a large mass, — over and over, till ready to throw it on paper." And the next year, 1842, he says: " Concentrate more resolutely my thoughts the first day of meditation, — going over and over, — thinking once before going to bed, or in bed, or before rising, — prefer the latter. And after one day of chewing the cud should be [i. e. ought to be] ready to write. It was three days for this chapter." — [" Conquest of Mexico," Book V., Chapter II.] Sometimes it was longer, but, in general, a single whole day, or two or three evenings, with the hours of his exercise in riding or walking, were found to be sufficient for such careful meditation.[a]

The result was remarkable — almost incredible — as to the masses he could thus hold in a sort of abeyance in his mind, and as to the length of time he could keep them there, and consider and reconsider them without confusion or weariness. Thus, he says that he carried in his memory the first and second chapters of the fifth book of the " Conquest of Peru," and ran over the whole ground several times before beginning to write, although these two chapters fill fifty-six pages of printed text ; and he records the same thing of chapters fifth, sixth, and seventh, in the second book of " Philip the Second," which

---

attempt to overlook my noctographs; very trying to the eye. If I would enjoy composition, write well, and make progress, I must give my whole soul to it, so as not to know the presence of another in the room; going over the work again and again (not too fastidious, nor formal); thinking when walking and dressing, &c.; and not too scrupulous, hesitating, in my final corrections. It is a shame and a sin to waste time on mere form. Have been very contented and happy here [Pepperell]; fine weather, and pleasing occupation."

[a] In preparing Chapter III., of the Introduction to the " Conquest of Peru," — about thirty printed pages, — he records that, after having done all the necessary reading, he studied five days on the memoranda he had made, reflected on them one day more, and then gave four days to writing the text, and five to writing the notes.   Gibbon, too, used to compose in his mind; but it was in a very different way, and with very different results. He prepared only a paragraph at a time, and that he did, as he says, in order " to try it by the ear." (Misc. Works, 1814, Vol. I. p. 230.) I think the effect of this loud recital of his work to himself is plain in the well-known cadence of his sentences.   Mr. Prescott never, so far I as know, repeated his chapters aloud.   His mental repetition was generally done when he was riding, or walking, or driving.

make together seventy-two pages, and on which he was employed sixty-two days.[7]

He frequently kept about sixty pages in his memory for several days, and went over the whole mass five or six times, moulding and remoulding the sentences at each successive return. But this power did not remain in full vigor to the last. When he was writing the third volume of "Philip the Second," he found that he could not carry more than about forty pages in his mind at once, and spoke to me of it as a sad failure of memory, which no doubt, it was in one point of view, although in another, it can be regarded only as an expression of the surprising power at one time reached by a faculty which in its decline was still so marvellous. But, whatever might be the amount that he had thus prepared in his mind, he went over it five or six times, as a general rule, — sometimes more, — and once, at least, he did it, for a single chapter, sixteen times, — an instance of patient, untiring labor for which it will not be easy to find a parallel.[8]

Writing down by the help of his apparatus what had been so carefully prepared in his memory was a rapid and not disagreeable operation, especially in the composition of his "Conquest of Mexico," and of his later works, when the habit of doing it had become fixed and comparatively easy. As the sheets were thrown off, the secretary deciphered and copied

---

[7] His words are: "The batch — all run over in my mind several times, from beginning to end, before writing a word — has been got out, reading, thinking, and writing, in sixty-two days."

[8] Dionysius of Halicarnassus (De Compositione Verborum, Ed. Schaefer, 1808, p. 406) says, that Plato continued to correct and polish the style of his Dialogues when he was eighty years old. 'Ο δὲ Πλάτων τοὺς ἑαυτοῦ διαλόγους κτενίζων καὶ βοστρυχίζων καὶ πάντα τρόπον ἀναπλέκων οὐ διέλιπεν ὀγδοήκοντα γεγονὼς ἔτη. See, also, the well-considered remarks on a careful revision of style by good writers of all ages, in the twenty-first of Mr. George P. Marsh's Lectures on the English Language (New York, 1860), — a book full of rich, original thought and painstaking, conscientious investigation. "Literary Biography," he says, "furnishes the most abundant proofs, that, in all ages, the works which stand as types of language and composition have been of slow and laborious production, and have undergone the most careful and repeated revision and emendation." This, I have no doubt, is what Dionysius meant, when he said that Plato did not cease to comb and curl and braid the locks of his Dialogues, even when he was eighty years old, — an odd figure of speech, but a very significant one.

them in a large round hand, — and then they were laid aside, generally for some months, or even longer, that the subject might cool in the author's mind, and the imperfections of its treatment become, in consequence, more readily apparent to him. At the end of this period, or whenever the time for a final revision had come, he chose the hours or the minutes in each day — for they were often only minutes — when his eye would permit him to read the manuscript himself, and then he went over it with extreme care. This he held to be an important process, and never, I think, trusted it wholly to the ear. Certainly he never did so, if he could possibly avoid it. He believed that what was to be read by the eye of another should be, at least once, severely revised by the eye of its author.

As the proof-sheets came from the press, his friend Mr. Folsom corrected them, suggesting, at the same time, any emendations or improvements in the style that might occur to him, with the freedom of an old friendship, as well as with the skill and taste of a well-practised criticism; and then the author having himself passed judgment upon the suggestions thus offered to him, and having taken such as he approved, — rarely more than one third, or even one fifth, — the whole was delivered to the unchanging stereotype.[*]

This process, from the first breaking ground with inquiries into the subject to the final yielding of the completed work to the press, was, no doubt, very elaborate and painstaking; but it seems to me that it was singularly adapted to the peculiar difficulties and embarrassments of Mr. Prescott's case, and I do not suppose that in any other way he could have accomplished so much, or have done it so well. But, whether this were so

---

[*] Mr. Folsom — who had known him from the period of his college life — made before the American Academy, soon after his friend's death, some very graceful and appropriate remarks on his modes of composition, with which his "Cambridge Aldus," as Prescott was wont to call Mr. Folsom, was especially familiar. On the same occasion, other more general, but not less interesting, remarks on his life and character were made by the Rev. Dr. George E. Ellis of Charlestown, the Hon. Charles G. Loring of Boston, and Professor Theophilus Parsons of Harvard College, — the last two, like Mr. Folsom, members of the Club to which Mr. Prescott so many years belonged. — See the "Proceedings of the American Academy of Arts and Sciences," Vol. IV. pp. 149 – 163.

or not, the great labor it implied, added to the unceasing care he was compelled to practise for forty years, in order to protect his health, and preserve and prolong the failing powers of the single eye that remained to him, so as to enable him to pursue the minute historical investigations which seemed to be forbidden by the conditions of his life, is a very extraordinary spectacle. It is, no less, one full of instruction to those who think that a life without serious occupation can be justified either by the obstacles or the temptations it may be called to encounter.

But there is another side of his character, which should not be left out of view, and yet one which I cannot approach except with misgiving; I mean that which involves the moral and religious elements of his nature. Of these, so far as a belief in Christianity is concerned, and a conscientious and repeated examination of its authority as a revelation, I have already spoken. His life, too, devoted to hard labor, — often physically painful, — with the prevalent idea not only of cultivating his own faculties, and promoting his own improvement, but of fulfilling his duties towards his fellow-men, was necessarily one of constant careful discipline, but behind all this, and deeper than all this, lay, as its foundation, his watchfulness over his moral and religious character, its weaknesses and its temptations.

With these he dealt, to a remarkable degree, in the same way, and on the same system, which he applied to his physical health and his intellectual culture. He made a record of everything that was amiss, and examined and considered and studied that record constantly and conscientiously. It was written on separate slips of paper, — done always with his own hand, — seen only by his own eye. These slips he preserved in a large envelope, and kept them in the most reserved and private manner. From time to time, when his sight permitted, — and generally on Sunday, after returning from the morning service, — he took them out and looked them over, one by one. If any habitual fault were, as he thought, eradicated, he destroyed the record of it; if a new one had appeared, he entered it on its separate slip, and placed it with the rest for future warning and reproof. This habit, known only to the innermost circle of those who lived around his heart, was persevered in to the last. After his death the envelope was found, marked, as it was known that it would be, "To be burnt." And it *was* burnt. No record, therefore, remains on earth of this remarkable self-discipline. But it remains in the memory of his beautiful and pure life, and in the books that shall be opened at the great day, when the thoughts of all hearts shall be made manifest.

Probably to those who knew my friend only as men commonly know one another in society, and even to the many who knew him familiarly, these accounts of his private habits and careful self-discipline may be unexpected, and may seem strange. But they are true. The foundations of his character were laid as deep as I have described them, — the vigilance over his own conduct was as strict. But he always desired to have as little of this seen as possible. He detested all pretence and cant. He made no presumptuous claims to the virtues which everybody, who knew him at all, knew he possessed. He did not, for instance, like to say that he acted in any individual case from " a sense of duty." He avoided that particular phrase, as he more than once told me he did, and as I know his father had done before him, because it is so often used to hide mean or unworthy motives. I am pretty sure that I never heard him use it ; and on one occasion, when a person for whom he had much regard was urging him to do something which, after all, could only end in social pleasures for both of them, and added as an ultimate argument, " But can't you make *a duty* of it ? " — he repeated the words to me afterwards with the heartiest disgust. But, during his riper years, nobody, I think, ever saw anything in him which contradicted the idea that he was governed by high motives. It was only that he was instinctively unwilling to parade them, — that he was remarkably free from anything like pretension.

He carried this very far. To take a strong example, few persons suspected him of literary industry till all the world knew what he had done. Not half a dozen, I think, out of his own family, were aware, during the whole period in which he was employed on his " Ferdinand and Isabella," that he was occupied with *any* considerable literary undertaking, and hardly

7   J

anybody knew what it was. Most of his friends thought that he led rather an idle, unprofitable life, but attributed it to his infirmity, and pardoned or overlooked it as a misfortune, rather than as anything discreditable. On one occasion a near connection, whom he was in the habit of meeting in the most familiar and pleasant manner at least once a week, affectionately urged him to undertake some serious occupation as a thing essential to his happiness, and even to his respectable position in society. And yet, at that moment, he had been eight years laboring on his first great work ; and, though thus pressed and tempted, he did not confess how he was employed.[10]

He was sensitive from his very nature as well as from the infirmities that beset him ; and this sensitiveness of temperament made it more than commonly disagreeable to him to have his exact habits interfered with or intruded upon. But he did not willingly permit his annoyance to be seen, and few ever suspected that he felt it. When he was riding or taking his long walks, he was, as we have seen, in the habit of going over and over again in his memory whatever he might last have composed, and thus correcting and finishing his work in a way peculiarly agreeable to himself. Of course, under such circumstances, any interruption to the current of his thoughts was unwelcome. And yet who of the hundreds that stopped him in his daily walks, or joined him on horseback, eager for his kindly greeting or animated conversation, was ever received with any other than a pleasant welcome ? During one winter, I know that the same friend overtook him so often in his morning ride, that he gave up his favorite road to avoid a kindness which he was not willing to seem to decline. His

[10] As early as 1821, he showed signs of this sensitiveness, which so remarkably characterized all his literary labors. After indicating two or three persons, one of whom he might consult when he should be writing a review for the " North American," he adds: " Nor shall any one else, if I can help it, know that I am writing." This occasional reticence — so complete, so absolute, as it was in the case of the " Ferdinand and Isabella " — is a remarkable trait in the character of one who was commonly open-hearted almost to weakness. I do not believe that three persons out of his own home knew that he was writing that work until it was nearly completed. Indeed, I am not aware that anybody knew it for several years except myself, his family, and those who helped him abroad in collecting materials.

father and he understood one another completely on this point. They often mounted at the same time, but always turned their horses in different directions.

Nor was there in his intercourse at home or abroad — with strangers or with his familiar friends — any noticeable trace of the strict government to which he subjected his time and his character. In his study everything went on by rule. His table and his papers were always in the nicest order. His chair stood always in the same spot, and — what was important — in the same relations to the light. The furniture of the room was always arranged in the same manner. The hours, and often even the minutes, were counted and appropriated. But when he came out from his work and joined his family, the change was complete, — the relaxation absolute. Especially in the latter part of his life, and in the cheerful parlor of the old homestead at Pepperell, surrounded by his children and their young friends, his gay spirits were counted upon by all as an unfailing resource. The evening games could not be begun, the entertaining book could not be opened, until he had come from his work, and taken his accustomed place in the circle which his presence always made bright.

In society it was the same. He was never otherwise than easy and unconstrained. It would have been difficult to find him in a company of persons where any one was more attractive than he was. But he never seemed to be aware of it, or to make an effort to distinguish himself. The brilliant things he sometimes said were almost always in the nature of repartees, and depended so much for their effect on what had gone before that those who saw him oftenest and knew him best remember little of his conversation, except that it was always agreeable, — often full of drollery, — occasionally sparkling. But it was one of its peculiarities, that it became sometimes amusing from its carelessness, — running into blunders and inconsequences, not unlike Irish bulls, which nobody seemed to enjoy so heartily as he did, or to expose with such happy gayety. Eminently natural he always was, — everybody saw it who met him, — and in this quality resided, no doubt, much of the charm of his personal intercourse.

But it was certainly remarkable that one who lived so many

hours of each day by such rigorous rules, and who subjected himself constantly to a discipline, physical, intellectual, and moral, so exact, should yet have been thus easy, unconstrained, and even careless in all societies, at home and abroad, — with his children hardly more than with persons whom he saw for the first time. Such apparent contradictions — such a union of qualities and characteristics which nature commonly holds carefully asunder — were not always intelligible to those who occasionally caught glimpses of them, without being constantly near enough to see how they were produced, or how they acted upon each other. It was a combination which could, I conceive, have been originally found or formed in no nature that had not that essential goodness and sweetness for which the best training is but a poor substitute; and they could have been brought into such intimate union by no solvent less active than his charming spirits, which seemed to shed brightness over his whole character. His sunny smile was absolutely contagious, — his cordial, easy manners were irresistible. All who approached him felt and acknowledged their influence, and few thought of what might lie beneath them.

One trait of his character, however, which, from its nature, was less obvious than the traits expressed by his general manners, should be especially noticed, — I mean his charity to the poor. His liberality in contributing to whatever would improve and benefit the community was necessarily known of many. Not so his private generosity. This he had, as it were, inherited. His mother's greatest happiness, beyond the circle of her family, was found in a free-handed beneficence. In the latter part of her life, when her resources were much beyond the claims that could be made on them by children already independent, she avoided all personal expense, and gave more than half her income to the poor. Her son fully shared her spirit. While she lived, he co-operated with her, and, after her death, her pensioners were not permitted, so far as money could do it, to feel their loss.

But, from his earliest manhood, he was always free and liberal. In many years he gave away more than he intended to do, and more than he afterwards thought he ought to have done. But this did not prevent him from repeating the mis-

take or the miscalculation. Indeed, though he was considerate
and careful, as well as liberal, in his contributions to public institutions, he was very impulsive in his private charities. An
instance happily recorded by Mr. Robert Carter, who was his
secretary for about a year, in 1847 – 1848, will better explain
this part of his character than a page of generalities.

"One bitter cold day," he says, "I came to the study as usual at half
past ten. Mr. Prescott went to work immediately on two long and important letters, one to Señor de Gayangos at Madrid, the other to Count Circourt at Paris, which he was very anxious to have finished in season to go
by that week's mail to Europe. There was barely sufficient time to get
them ready before the mail closed. They were about half done when
twelve o'clock, his hour for exercise, arrived. He was so anxious to get
them off that he did what I had never known him to do before; he relin-
quished his walk, and kept at his writing-case, telling me to go out and
stretch my legs, but to be sure and return at one o'clock, when he would
have the letters ready to be copied. I offered to remain and copy as he
wrote, but he said there would be time enough if I came back at one
o'clock. He never would allow me to work for him beyond the hours
stipulated in our agreement, and was very careful not to encroach upon
my time, even for a minute, though he often made me take holidays. I
strolled about the city for half an hour, and on my way back passing
through Broad Street, where the Irish congregate, met one Michael Sulli
van, whom I know. He seemed to be in trouble, and I inquired what
ailed him. He said he had been sick and out of work, and had no money,
and his family were starving with cold. I went with him to the den
where he lived, and found his wife and three or four small children in a
wretched loft over a warehouse, where they were lying on the floor huddled
in a pile of straw and shavings, with some rags and pieces of old carpet
over them. The only furniture in the room was a chair, a broken table,
and a small stove, in which were the expiring embers of a scanty handful
of coal, which they had begged from neighbors equally poor. The mer-
cury was below zero out of doors, and the dilapidated apartment was not
much warmer than the street. I had no time to spare, and the detention,
slight as it was, prevented me from getting back to Mr. Prescott's till a
quarter past one. His manuscript lay on my desk, and he was walking
about the room in a state of impatience, I knew, though he showed none,
except by looking at his watch. As I warmed my chilled hands over the
fire, I told him, by way of apology, what had detained me. Without
speaking, he stepped to a drawer where scraps of writing paper were kept,
took out a piece, and, laying it on my desk, told me to write an order on
Mr. —— (a coal dealer with whom he kept an account always open for
such purposes) for a ton of coal, to be delivered without delay to Michael
Sullivan, Broad Street. He then went to his bell-rope, and gave it a vehe-
ment pull. A servant entered as I finished the order. 'Take this,' he
said, 'as quick as you can to Mr. ——, and see that the coal is delivered
at once. What is the number of the house in Broad Street?'

"I had neglected to notice the number, though I could find the place readily myself. I therefore suggested to Mr. Prescott, that, as there were probably twenty Michael Sullivans in Broad Street, the coal might not reach the right man, unless I saw to it in person, which I would do when I went to dinner at half past two o'clock.

"'Thank you! thank you!' he said; 'but go at once, there will be time enough lost in getting the coal.'

"I reminded him of the letters. 'Go! go! never mind the letters. Gayangos and Circourt will not freeze if they never got them, and Mrs. O'Sullivan may, if you don't hurry. Stay! can the man be trusted with money? or will he spend it all for drink?' He pulled out his pocket-book. I told him he could be trusted. He handed me five dollars. 'See that they are made comfortable, at least while this cold spell lasts. Take time enough to see to them; I shall not want you till six. Don't let them know I sent the money, or all Broad Street will be here begging within twenty-four hours.'

"I relieved Mr. O'Sullivan, as Mr. Prescott persisted in calling him, and, when I returned at six, I entered in the account-book, ' Charity five dollars.' 'Always tell me when you know of such cases,' he said, ' and I shall be only too happy to do something for them. I cannot go about myself to find them out, but I shall be always ready to contribute.'

"He did not let the matter rest there, but kept playfully inquiring after my friends Mr. and Mrs. O'Sullivan, until I satisfied him by ascertaining that he had found employment, and could provide for his family. After that he never alluded to them again." [11]

[11] From the New York "Tribune," as copied into the " Prescott Memorial," New York, 1859. Sullivan was, no doubt, a Catholic, as were most of the poor Irish, who then herded in Broad Street. But Prescott cared not a whit what was the religion of the poor he helped. It was enough that they were suffering.

CHAPTER XIII.

1837.

THE summer of 1836, when the composition of " Ferdinand and Isabella " was completed, and the following eighteen months, during which it was carried through the press and its success made sure, constituted a very happy period in Mr. Prescott's life. The inexperienced author speculated, indeed, more than he needed to have done on the risks of his venture, and felt concerning the final result a good deal of nervous curiosity, which, if it did not amount to anxiety, was something very near to it. But he soon began to consider what he should do when the holidays in which he was indulging himself should come to an end. For some time he was very uncertain. It was his way in such cases to doubt long.

At one period, he determined, if the " Ferdinand and Isabella " should be coldly received, to take up some lighter subject, for which, with all his distrust of himself, he could not doubt his competency. Several subjects came readily to his thoughts, but none tempted him so much as Molière, on whose character and works he had, in 1828, written a pleasant article for the " North American Review," — the " Old North," as he used to call it. As soon, therefore, as he had corrected the last sheets of the " Catholic Sovereigns," he wrote to me about his new project, knowing that I was in Paris, where I might help him in collecting materials for it. This was in September, 1837.[1]

---

[1] He had, somewhat earlier, a considerable fancy for literary history, of which he often spoke to me. When he was half through the composition of

It was not difficult to do all he desired. I advised with M. Jules Taschereau,[2] who, besides his other claims on the republic of letters, had then recently published the second edition of his "Life of Molière," — altogether the best book on its subject, though with an air of greater learning than might have been anticipated from the brilliant character of the genius to whom it is devoted. Having made sure of the assistance of M. Taschereau, I at once undertook the commission, and wrote to my friend how I proposed to execute it. He replied in the postscript to a letter already extending to four sheets, which he thus characterizes : —

"My letter resembles one of those old *higglety-pigglety* houses that have been so much tinkered and built upon that one hardly knows the front from the rear. I have got to-day your letter of November 24th, — a kind letter, showing that you are, as you always have been ever since you came into the world, thinking how you can best serve your friends. I am truly obliged by your interest in the little Molière purchases, and, if anything occurs to you of value that I have omitted, pray order it. . . . . . My design is to write a notice of his life and works, which, without pretence (for it would be but pretence) to critical skill in the French language or drama, would make an agreeable book for the parlor table. . . . . . As the thing, in my prosy way, would take two or three years, I don't care to speak of it to any one else.

"But my heart is set on a Spanish subject, could I compass the materials, viz. the Conquest of Mexico, and the anterior civilization of the Mexicans, — a beautiful prose epic, for which rich virgin materials teem in Simancas and Madrid, and probably in Mexico. I would give a couple of thousand dollars that they lay in a certain attic in Bedford Street. But how can I compass it in these troubled times, — too troubled, it would seem, for old Navarrete to follow down the stream of story, which he has carried to the very time of Cortés."[3]

his "Ferdinand and Isabella," and hastening to finish it, he recorded: "But, after all, literary history is more consonant with my taste, my turn of mind, and all my previous studies. The sooner I complete my present work, the sooner I shall be enabled to enter upon it. So *festina*."

[2] Now (1862) the head of the Imperial Library at Paris.

[3] He refers to the remarkable work — mainly documentary — entitled "Coleccion de Viages y Descubrimientos que hicieron por Mar los Españoles desde fines del Siglo XV. coordinada é ilustrada por Don Martin Fernandez de Navarrete." Madrid, 1825 – 37. 5 Tomos, 4to. It begins, of course, with Columbus; but it comes down only to Loaisa and Saavedra, without touching the expedition of Cortés for the Conquest of Mexico; or even approaching that of the Pizarros for the Conquest of Peru. The manuscript materials for both of these, however, as we shall see hereafter, were placed by Navarrete, who had collected them for publication, with true Spanish generosity, at the disposition of Mr. Prescott.

The result of the matter was, that I sent him a collection of about fifty volumes, which, for anybody who wished to write a pleasant life of Molière, left little to be desired, and nothing for one whose purpose was general literary criticism, rather than curious biographical or bibliographical research. But before he had received the purchase I had thus made for him, the success of his " Ferdinand and Isabella" had happily turned his attention again to the Spanish subject, which lay nearest his heart. On the sixth of April, he wrote to me concerning both the "Mexico" and the "Molière," telling me, at the same time, of a pleasant acquaintance he had made, which promised much to favor his Spanish project, and which, in the end, did a great deal more, giving him a kind, true, and important friend.

" I have been much gratified," he says, " by the manner in which the book has been received by more than one intelligent Spaniard here, in particular by the Spanish Minister, Don Angel Calderou de la Barca, who has sent me a present of books, and expresses his intention of translating my History into Castilian. In consequence of this, as well as to obtain his assistance for the other crotchets I have in my head, I paid a visit to New York last week, — a momentous affair, for it would be easier for you to go to Constantinople. Well, I saw his *Spanishship*, and was very much pleased with him, — a frank, manly *caballero*, who has resigned his office from a refusal to subscribe the late democratic constitution. He is quite an accomplished man, and in correspondence with the principal Spanish scholars at home, so that he will be of obvious use to me in any project I may have hereafter. He told me he had sent a copy of the work to the Royal Academy of History, and should present one to the Queen, if he had not retired from office. There's a feather in my cap !

" In New York I saw your old friends the L———a, and passed an evening with them. It is ten years to a month since I was there with you. . . . .

" The New-Yorkers have done the handsome thing by me, — that is, the book. But sink the shop ! I have dosed you and Anna with quite enough of it. The truth is, I always talk to you and Anna as I should to my own flesh and blood ; and if you do not so take it, I shall make a pretty ridiculous figure in your eyes. But I will venture it.

" I believe I have not written to you since the arrival of the French books [about Molière] all safe and sound. Never was there so much *multum* in so little *parvo*, — and then the '*damage*' a mere *bagatelle*. How much am I obliged to you, not only for thinking, but for thinking in the right place and manner, for me, and for acting as well as thinking. I begin to believe I have Fortunatus's wishing-cap while you are in Europe. For that reason, perhaps, I should show more conscience in putting the said wishing-cap on my head. Well, the wish I have nearest at heart, God knows, is to see you and Anna and the *petites* safe on this side of the water again. And that will come to pass, too, before long. You will

7 *

find us a few years older. Father Time has thinned out the loose hairs from some craniums, and shaken his vile dredging-box over others. For myself, I have turned forty, since you went away, — an ugly corner, that takes a man into the shadow of life, as it were. But better be in the shadow with the friends you love, than keep in the everlasting sunshine of youth, — if that were possible, — and see them go down into the valley without you. One does not feel his progress, when all around is going on at the same rate. I shall not, however, give up entirely my claims to be reckoned young, since a newspaper this very week styles me 'our young and modest townsman.' I suppose you will admit one epithet to be as true as the other."

As we have seen, the period that followed the publication of " Ferdinand and Isabella " was not fruitful in literary results. Except a pleasant article on Lockhart's " Life of Scott," which he prepared for the " North American Review," he wrote nothing during that winter, — not even his accustomed private memoranda. No doubt, he was, in one sense, idle, and he more than once spoke of these months afterwards with regret and pain ; but the vacation, though a pretty long one, seems not to have been entirely amiss in its occupations or its consequences. He read, or rather listened to much reading ; light and miscellaneous in general, but not always so. Sometimes, indeed, during his protracted holidays, it was of the gravest sort ; for, while his work was going through the press, he occupied himself again with careful inquiries into the authority and doctrines of the Christian religion. He read Marsh on the origin of the first three Gospels in his Prolegomena to the translation of " Michaelis "; the first volume — being all then published — of Norton's " Genuineness of the Gospels," to whose learning and power he bore testimony in a note to the " Ferdinand and Isabella "; Newcome's " Harmony "; Paley's " Evidences "; Middleton's " Free Inquiry "; and Gibbon's famous chapters, — works the last three of which he had considered and studied before. A little later he read Norton's " Statement of Reasons," and Furness on the Four Gospels ; but he did not go so thoroughly as he had in his previous inquiries into the orthodox doctrines, as they are called ; for, as he said, he was more and more satisfied that they were unfounded. After expressing himself decidedly on these points, and coming to the general conclusion that " the study of polemics or biblical critics will tend neither to settle principles nor clear up doubts, but rather to confuse the former and multiply the latter," he concludes with these striking words : —

" To do well and act justly, to fear and to love God, and to love our neighbor as ourselves, — in these is the essence of religion. To do this is the safest, our only safe course. For what we can believe, we are not responsible, supposing we examine candidly and patiently. For what we do, we shall indeed be accountable. The doctrines of the Saviour unfold the whole code of morals by which our conduct should be regulated. Who, then, whatever difficulties he may meet with in particular incidents and opinions recorded in the Gospels, can hesitate to receive the great religious and moral truths inculcated by the Saviour as the *words of inspiration?* I cannot, certainly. On these, then, I will rest, and for all else

' Wait the great teacher Death, and God adore.' "

When he had come to the conclusion that the " Ferdinand and Isabella " was a successful book, and likely to last, — a result at which he arrived very slowly, — he abandoned the idea of writing the Life of Molière, and turned, with a decided purpose, to the History of the Conquest of Mexico, which had been, for some time, interesting and tempting him in a way not to be resisted. One cause of his long hesitation was the doubt he felt whether he could obtain the materials that he deemed necessary for the work. He had written for them to Madrid, in April, 1838; but before a reply could reach him, weary of a vacation which, reckoning from the time when he finished the composition of " Ferdinand and Isabella," was now protracted to nearly two years, and quite sure that on all accounts he ought to be at work again, he began cautiously to enter on his new subject with such books as he could command.[4]

In June he records that he had read with much care Humboldt's " Researches concerning the Institutions of the Ancient inhabitants of America," and his " New Spain." It was his earliest acquaintance with the works of this great man, except that, when writing an account of the first voyage of Columbus for his " Ferdinand and Isabella," he had resorted to that mine of knowledge and philosophy, the " Examen Critique de l'Histoire

[4] He felt the need of a grave subject, and of success in it, as, I think, he always did after he had once begun his historical career. " Mere ephemeral success," he records in 1838, " still less paltry profit, will not content me, I am confident."

et de la Géographie du Nouveau Continent." [5] The two works
he now studied are, however, in some respects, of more significance, and he thus notes his opinion of them : —

" Humboldt is a true philosopher, divested of local or national prejudices, fortified with uncommon learning, which supplies him with abundant illustrations and analogies.   Like most truly learned men, he is
cautious and modest in his deductions, and, though he assembles very
many remarkable coincidences between the Old World and the New in
their institutions, notions, habits, &c., yet he does not infer that the New
World was peopled from the Old, — much less from what particular
nation, as more rash speculators have done."

The notes to his " Conquest of Mexico " abound in similar
expressions of admiration for the great traveller ; a man who,
as an observer of nature, was once said by Biot (a competent
judge, if anybody was) to have been equalled by none since the
days of Aristotle.

But though my friend was much interested in these works,
and, during the year 1838, read or ran over many others of less
moment relating to the geography and physical condition of
that part of America to which they relate, he did not yet begin
to labor in earnest on his " Conquest of Mexico."   In September, his disinclination to work was very strong.

" I have been indolent," he says, " the last fortnight. It is not easy to
go forward without the steady impulse of a definite object.   In the uncertainty as to the issue of my application in Spain, I am without such
impulse.   I ought always to find sufficient in the general advantages re-
sulting from study to my mental resources, — advantages to be felt on
whatever subject my mind is engaged.   But I am resolved to mend, and
to employ all the hours my reader is with me, and something more, when
my eye will serve.   Of one thing I am persuaded.   No motives but those
of an honest fame and of usefulness will have much weight in stimulating
my labors.   I never shall be satisfied to do my work in a slovenly way,
nor superficially.   It would be impossible for me to do the job-work of a
literary hack.   Fortunately, I am not obliged to write for bread, and I
never will write for money."

One anxiety, which had troubled him for a time, was removed in the following winter by the prompt courtesy of Mr.
Washington Irving.   It was not such an anxiety as would have
occurred to everybody under the same circumstances, nor one
that would have been always so readily and pleasantly removed as it was in the present case, by the following correspondence : —

[5] Ferdinand and Isabella, Part I. Chap. XVI., notes.

MR. PRESCOTT TO MR. IRVING.

BOSTON, Dec. 31, 1838.

MY DEAR SIR,

If you will allow one to address you so familiarly who has not the pleasure of your personal acquaintance, though he feels as if he had known you for a long time. Our friend Mr. Cogswell,* who is here on a short visit, has mentioned to me a conversation which he had with you respecting the design I had formed of giving an account of the Conquest of Mexico and Peru. I hope you will excuse me if I tell you how the matter stands with me.

Soon after I had despatched their Catholic Highnesses, Ferdinand and Isabella, I found the want of my old companions in the long hours of an idle man's life, and, as I looked round for something else, the History of Cortés and Pizarro struck me as the best subject, from its growing out of the period I had become familiar with, as well as from its relation to our own country. I found, too, that I had peculiar facilities for getting such books and manuscripts as I needed from Madrid, through the kindness of Señor Calderon, whom you know.

The only doubts I had on the subject were respecting your designs in the same way, since you had already written the adventures of the early discoverers. I thought of writing to you, to learn from you your intentions, but I was afraid it might seem impertinent in a stranger to pry into your affairs. I made inquiries, however, of several of your friends, and could not learn that you had any purpose of occupying yourself with the subject; and, as you had never made any public intimation of the sort, I believe, and several years had elapsed since your last publication of the kind, during which your attention had been directed in another channel, I concluded that you had abandoned the intention, if you had ever formed it.

I made up my mind, therefore, to go on with it, and, as I proposed to give a pretty thorough preliminary view of the state of civilization in Mexico and Peru previous to the Conquest, I determined to spare no pains or expense in collecting materials. I have remitted three hundred pounds to Madrid for the purchase and copying of books and manuscripts, and have also sent for Lord Kingsborough's and such other works relating to Mexico as I can get from London.† I have also obtained letters to individuals in Mexico for the purpose of collecting what may be of importance to me there. Some of the works from London have arrived, and the drafts from

---

* The reference here is to Mr. J. G. Cogswell, the well-known head of the Astor Library, New York, to whose disinterestedness, enthusiasm, and knowledge that important institution owes hardly less of its character and success than it does to the elder Mr. Astor, whose munificence founded it, or to the younger Mr. Astor, who, in the same spirit, has sustained it and increased its resources. Mr. Cogswell, from his youth, was intimate in the Prescott family, and always much cherished by every member of it; so that, being on equally intimate and affectionate terms with Mr. Irving, he was the best possible person to arrange such a delicate affair between the parties.

† This he had done about nine months earlier.

Madrid show that my orders are executing there.   Such works as can be got here in a pretty good collection in the College library I have already examined, and wait only for my books from Spain.

This is the state of affairs now that I have learned from Mr. C. that you had originally proposed to treat the same subject, and that you requested him to say to me, that you should relinquish it in my favor.   I cannot sufficiently express to you my sense of your courtesy, which I can very well appreciate, as I know the mortification it would have caused me, if, contrary to my expectations, I had found you on the ground ; for I am but a dull sailor from the embarrassments I labor under, and should have found but sorry gleanings in the field which you had thoroughly burnt over, as they say in the West.   I fear the public will not feel so much pleased as myself by this liberal conduct on your part, and I am not sure that I should have a right in their eyes to avail myself of it.[s]   But I trust you will think differently when I accept your proffered courtesy in the same cordial spirit in which it was given.

It will be conferring a still further favor on me, if you will allow me occasionally, when I may find the want of it, to ask your advice in the progress of the work.   There are few persons among us who have paid much attention to these studies, and no one, here or elsewhere, is so familiar as yourself with the track of Spanish adventure in the New World and so well qualified certainly to give advice to a comparatively raw hand. Do not fear that this will expose you to a troublesome correspondence.   I have never been addicted to much letter-writing, though, from the specimen before you, I am afraid you will think those I do write are somewhat of the longest.

Believe me dear Sir, with great respect,

Your obliged and obedient servant,

WM. H. PRESCOTT.

P. S.   Will you permit me to say, that if you have any materials in your own library having a bearing on this subject, that cannot be got here, and that you have no occasion for yourself, it will be a great favor if you will dispose of them to me.

MR. IRVING TO MR. PRESCOTT.

NEW YORK, Jan. 18, 1839.

MY DEAR SIR,

Your letter met with some delay in reaching me, and since the receipt of it I have been hovering between town and country, so as to have had no quiet leisure for an earlier reply.

I had always intended to write an account of the " Conquest of Mexico," as a suite to my " Columbus," but left Spain without making the

---

[s] A similar idea is very gracefully expressed in the Preface to the Conquest of Mexico, where, after relating the circumstance of Mr. Irving's relinquishment of the subject, Mr. Prescott adds: " While I do but justice to Mr. Irving by this statement, I feel the prejudice it does to myself in the unavailing regret I am exciting in the bosom of the reader."

requisite researches.   The unsettled life I subsequently led for some years, and the interruptions to my literary plans by other occupations, made me defer the undertaking from year to year.   Indeed, the more I considered the subject, the more I became aware of the necessity of devoting to it great labor, patient research, and watchful discrimination, to get at the truth, and to dispel the magnificent *mirage* with which it is enveloped.   For, unless this were done, a work, however well executed in point of literary merit, would be liable to be subverted and superseded by subsequent works, grounded on those documentary evidences that might be dug out of the chaotic archives of Spain.   These considerations loomed into great obstacles in my mind, and, amidst the hurry of other matters, delayed me in putting my hand to the enterprise.

About three years since I made an attempt at it, and set one of my nephews to act as pioneer and get together materials under my direction, but his own concerns called him elsewhere, and the matter was again postponed.   Last autumn, after a fit of deep depression, feeling the want of something to rouse and exercise my mind, I again recurred to this subject. Fearing that, if I waited to collect materials, I should never take hold of them, and knowing my own temperament and habits of mind, I determined to dash into it at once; sketch out a narrative of the whole enterprise, using Solis, Herrera, and Bernal Diaz as my guide-books; and, having thus acquainted myself with the whole ground, and kindled myself into a heat by the exercise of drafting the story, to endeavor to strengthen, correct, direct, and authenticate my work by materials from every source within my reach.

I accordingly set to work, and had made it my daily occupation for about three months, and sketched out the groundwork for the first volume, when I learned from Mr. Cogswell that you had undertaken the same enterprise.   I at once felt how much more justice the subject would receive at your hands.   Ever since I had been meddling with the theme, its grandeur and magnificence had been growing upon me, and I had felt more and more doubtful whether I should be able to treat it *conscientiously*, — that is to say, with the extensive research and thorough investigation which it merited.   The history of Mexico prior to the discovery and conquest, and the actual state of its civilization at the time of the Spanish invasion, are questions in the highest degree curious and interesting, yet difficult to be ascertained clearly from the false lights thrown upon them. Even the writings of Padre Sahagun perplex one as to the degree of faith to be placed in them.   These themes are connected with the grand enigma that rests upon the primitive population and civilization of the American continent, and of which the singular monuments and remains scattered throughout the wilderness serve but as tantalizing indications.

The manner in which you have executed your noble " History of Ferdinand and Isabella" gave me at once an assurance that you were the man to undertake the subject.   Your letter shows that I was not wrong in the conviction, and that you have already set to work on the requisite preparations.   In at once yielding up the thing to you, I feel that I am but doing my duty in leaving one of the most magnificent themes in American history to be treated by one who will build up from it an enduring monument in the literature of our country.   I only hope that I may live to see your work executed, and to read in it an authentic account of that conquest, and a satisfactory discussion of the various questions which since my boyhood have been full of romantic charm to me, but which, while they excited my imagination, have ever perplexed my judgment.

I am sorry that I have no works to offer you that you have not in the Boston libraries. I have mentioned the authors I was making use of. They are to be found in the Boston Athenæum, though I doubt not you have them in your own possession. While in Madrid, I had a few chapters of Padre Sahagun copied out for me, relating merely to some points of the Spanish invasion. His work you will find in Lord Kingsborough's collection. It professes to give a complete account of Mexico prior to the conquest, its public institutions, trades, callings, customs, &c., &c. Should I find among my books any that may be likely to be of service, I will send them to you. In the mean time do not hesitate to command my services in any way you may think proper.

I am scrawling this letter in great haste, as you will doubtless perceive, but beg you will take it as a proof of the sincere and very high respect and esteem with which I am

Your friend and servant,

WASHINGTON IRVING.*

MR. PRESCOTT TO MR. IRVING.

BOSTON, Jan. 25, 1839.

MY DEAR SIR,

You will be alarmed at again seeing an epistle from me so soon, but I cannot refrain from replying to your very kind communication. I have read your letter with much interest, and — I may truly say, as to that part of it which animadverts on the importance of the theme, as illustrating the Mexican Antiquities — with some dismay. I fear you will be sadly disappointed, if you expect to see a solution by me of those vexed questions which have bewildered the brains of so many professed antiquarians. My fingers are too clumsy to unravel such a snarl. All I propose to do in this part of the subject is, to present the reader such a view of the institutions and civilization of the conquered people as will interest him in their fortunes. To do this, it will not be necessary, I hope, to involve myself in those misty speculations which require better sight than mine to penetrate, but only to state facts as far as they can be gathered from authentic story.

* How Mr. Prescott felt on receiving this letter, may be seen from the following note enclosing it to me, the day it came to hand : —

JANUARY, 21st.

MIO CARISSIMO,

I told you that I wrote to Irving, thanking him for his courtesy the other day. Here is his response, which I thought you would like to see. He puts me into a fright, by the terrible responsibilities he throws on the subject, or rather on the man who meddles with it.

Ever thine,

W. H. PRESCOTT.

For this part of the subject, therefore, I have not attempted to collect manuscripts, of which I suppose there is a great number in the libraries of Mexico, — at least, there was in Clavigero's time, — but I shall content myself with the examination of such works as have been before the public, including, indeed, the compilation of Lord Kingsborough, and the great French work, "Antiquités Mexicaines," since published, the chief value of both of which, I suspect, except the chronicle of Sahagun in the former, consists in their pictorial illustrations. My chief object is the Conquest, and the materials I am endeavoring to collect are with the view to the exhibition of this in the most authentic light.

It will give you satisfaction to learn that my efforts in Spain promise to be attended with perfect success. I received letters last week from Madrid, informing me that the Academy of History, at the instance of Señor Navarrete, had granted my application to have copies taken of any and all manuscripts in their possession having relation to the Conquest of Mexico and Peru, and had appointed one of their body to carry this into effect. This person is a German, named Lembke, the author of a work on the early history of Spain, which one of the English journals, I remember, rapped me over the knuckles for not having seen.[10] This learned Theban happens to be in Madrid for the nonce, pursuing some investigations of his own, and he has taken charge of mine, like a true German, inspecting everything and selecting just what has reference to my subject. In this way he has been employed with four copyists since July, and has amassed a quantity of unpublished documents illustrative of the Mexican Conquest, which, he writes me, will place the expedition in a new and authentic light. He has already sent off two boxes to Cadiz, and is now employed in hunting up the materials relating to Peru, in which, he says, the Library appears to be equally rich. I wish he may not be too sanguine, and that the manuscripts may not fall into the hands of Carlist or Christino, who would probably work them up into musket-waddings in much less time than they were copying.

The specifications of manuscripts, furnished me by Dr. Lembke, make me feel nearly independent of Mexico, with which the communications are now even more obstructed than with Spain. I have endeavored to open them, however, through Mr. Poinsett and the Messrs. Barings, and cannot but hope I shall succeed through one or the other channel.

I had no idea of your having looked into the subject so closely yourself, still less that you had so far broken ground on it. I regret now that I had not communicated with you earlier in a direct way, as it might have

[10] Geschichte von Spanien, von Friederich Wilhelm Lembke, Erster Band. Hamburg, 1831, 8vo. It goes no farther than about the year A. D. 800, and therefore could not have been of the least importance to one writing the History of Ferdinand and Isabella, who lived seven hundred years later. Dr. Lembke, indeed, rendered good service to Mr. Prescott in collecting the materials for the "Conquests" of Mexico and Peru; but he wrote no more of his own History of Spain, which was, however, continued by Heinrich Schäfer, down to about 1100, — a period still far from that of the Catholic Sovereigns, — besides which Schäfer's work did not appear until 1844, six years after the appearance of the "Ferdinand and Isabella." So much for the clairvoyance of the English journalist.

x

saved both, or rather one of us, some previous preparation ; for during the summer and autumn I have been occupied with the investigation of the early Mexican history, having explored all the sources within my reach here, and being stopped by the want of [more of] them.

Now that I have gone on so far with my preparations, I can only acknowledge your great courtesy towards me with my hearty thanks, for I know well that whatever advantage I might have acquired on the score of materials would have been far — very far — outweighed by the superiority in all other respects of what might fall from your pen. And your relinquishing the ground seems to impose on me an additional responsibility, to try to make your place good, from which a stouter heart than mine might well shrink. I trust, however, that in you I shall find a generous critic, and allow me to add, with sincerity, that the kind words you have said of the only child of my brain have gratified me, and touched me more deeply than anything that has yet reached me from my countrymen.

Believe me, my dear sir,

With sincere respect,

Your friend and servant,

WM. H. PRESCOTT.

Since writing this chapter, and, in fact, since this work itself was finished and sent to press, the third volume of the charming "Life and Letters of Washington Irving, by his Nephew, Pierre M. Irving," has been published. It contains the following additional interesting facts upon the subject of the Conquest of Mexico : —

"Mr. Irving," says his biographer, "was now busy upon the History of the Conquest of Mexico, and it was upon this theme that he was exercising that 'vein of literary occupation' alluded to at the close of the foregoing letter [to Mrs. Van Wart, his sister]. He had not only commenced the work, but had made a rough draught to form the groundwork of the first volume, when he went to New York to procure or consult some books on the subject. He was engaged in the 'City Library,' as it is commonly designated, though its official style is 'The New York Society Library,' then temporarily in Chambers Street, when he was accosted by Mr. Joseph G. Cogswell, the eminent scholar, afterwards so long and honorably connected with the Astor Library. It was from this gentleman that Mr. Irving first learned that Mr. Prescott, who had a few months before gained a proud name on both sides of the Atlantic, by his 'History of Ferdinand and Isabella,' now had the work in contemplation upon which he had actively commenced. Cogswell first sounded him, on the part of Mr. Prescott, to know what subject he was occupied upon, as he did not wish to come again across the same ground with him. Mr. Irving asked, 'Is Mr. Prescott engaged upon an American subject?' 'He is,' was the reply. 'What is it? Is it the Conquest of Mexico?' 'It is,' answered Cogswell. 'Well then,' said Mr. Irving, 'I am engaged upon that subject ; but tell Mr. Prescott I abandon it to him, and I am happy to have this opportunity of testifying my high esteem for his talents and my sense of the very courteous manner in which he has spoken of myself and my writings, in his " Ferdinand and Isabella," though they interfered with a part of the subject of his history.' "

About five years later, Mr. Irving, then our Minister in Spain, received from Mr. Prescott a copy of his " History of the Conquest of Mexico," in the Preface to which he makes his public acknowledgment to Mr. Irving for giving up the subject.

How Mr. Irving received it will appear from the following account by his biographer. " ' I need not say,' writes Mr. Irving to me, in noticing its receipt, ' how much I am delighted with the work. It well sustains the high reputation acquired by the " History of Ferdinand and Isabella." ' Then, adverting to the terms of Mr. Prescott's handsome acknowledgment in the Preface, to which I had called his attention, he adds: ' I doubt whether Mr. Prescott was aware of the extent of the sacrifice I made. This was a favorite subject, which had delighted my imagination ever since I was a boy. I had brought home books from Spain to aid me in it, and looked upon it as the pendant to my Columbus. When I gave it up to him, I, in a manner, gave him up my bread; for I depended upon the profit of it to recruit my waning finances. I had no other subject at hand to supply its place. I was dismounted from my *cheval de bataille*, and have never been completely mounted since. Had I accomplished that work, my whole pecuniary situation would have been altered. . . . . . When I made the sacrifice, it was not with a view to compliments or thanks, but from a warm and sudden impulse. I am not sorry for having made it. Mr. Prescott has justified the opinion I expressed at the time, that he would treat the subject with more close and ample research than I should probably do, and would produce a work more thoroughly worthy of the theme. He has produced a work that does honor to himself and his country, and I wish him the full enjoyment of his laurels.' " — Life of Irving, 1863, Vol. III. pp. 138 sqq., and 148 sqq.

. There are few so beautiful passages as this in literary history, deformed as it often is with the jealousies and quarrels of authorship. One, however, not unlike it will be found subsequently in this volume, when we come to the relations between the author of the " History of Philip the Second," and the author of " The Rise of the Dutch Republic."

CHAPTER XIV.

1839 – 1842.

UNTIL some time after the appearance of "Ferdinand and Isabella," Mr. Prescott wrote very few letters to anybody, and most of those he did write are lost. He corresponded, of course, with his family, in 1816 and 1817, when he was in Europe, and he wrote subsequently to one or two personal and household friends, whenever he or they happened to be away from Boston. These letters, so far as they have been preserved, I have used in the preceding narrative. But his life, though he was much in society in Boston, was — both from preference and from his peculiar infirmities — in one sense very retired. He travelled hardly at all, thinking that the exposures involved by journeys injured his eye, and therefore the occasions on which he wrote letters to his family were very rare. At the same time, his urgent and steady occupations made it difficult for him to write to others, so that he had no regular correspondence from 1818 to 1839 with any single person. In one of the few letters that he wrote before he became known as an author, he says that in the preceding three months he had written to but two persons, — to both on business ; and in another letter, equally on business, but written a little later, he says, that the friend to whom it was addressed would "hardly know what to make of it" that he should write to him at all.

With his private Memoranda, begun in 1820, and continued to the last, so as to fill above twelve hundred pages, the case is somewhat different, although the result is nearly the same. Ample enough they certainly are from the first, and, for their private purposes, they are both apt and sufficient. But nearly or quite the whole of the earlier two-thirds of this minute record is filled with an account of his daily studies, of his good resolutions, often broken, and of his plans for the future, often disappointed. Such records were from their nature only for himself, and only of transient interest even to him.

But after the success of the "Ferdinand and Isabella," his relations to the world were changed, and so, in some degree, were his hopes and purposes in life. While, therefore, until that time, his correspondence and Memoranda furnish few materials for his life, they constitute afterwards not only the best, but the largest, part of whatever may be needful to exhibit him as he really was. I begin, therefore, at once with the letters and Memoranda of 1839, for, although some of them look much ahead, and talk about his "History of Philip the Second," while he was yet busy with the "Conquest of Mexico," and before he had even taken in hand that of Peru, still they show what, at the time, were his occupations and thoughts, and give proof of the providence and forecast which always constituted important traits in his character, and contributed much to his success in whatever he undertook.

The first of his letters belonging to this period is one containing his views on a subject which has by no means yet lost the whole of its interest as a public question, — that of international copyright.

TO WASHINGTON IRVING.

BOSTON, Dec. 24, 1839.

MY DEAR SIR,

I received some weeks since a letter from Dr. Lieber, of Columbia College, South Carolina, in which he informed me, that measures were to be taken in Congress, this session, for making such an alteration in our copyright law as should secure the benefits of it to foreigners, and thus enable us to profit in turn by theirs. He was very desirous that I should write, if I could not see you personally, and request your co-operation in the matter. I felt very reluctant to do so, knowing that you must be much better acquainted than I was with the state of the affair, and, of course, could judge much better what was proper to be done. My indefatigable correspondent, however, has again written to me, pressing the necessity of communicating with you, and stating in confidence, as he says, that Mr.

Clay is to bring in a bill this session, and that Mr. Preston[1] is to make the speech, &c. Mr. Preston told him that it would be very desirable to have a brief memorial, signed by the persons most interested in the success of the law, and that you were the proper person to prepare it. If anything be done, there can be no doubt that you are the one who, from your literary position in the country, should take the lead in it. Whether anything effectual can be done seems to me very doubtful.

Such a law is certainly demanded by every principle of justice. But I suspect it is rather late in the day to talk of justice to statesmen. At all events, one of those newspapers which they are now turning out every week here, and which contains an octavo volume of the new publications, at sixpence apiece, will, I am afraid, be too cogent an argument in favor of the present state of things, to be refuted by the best memorial ever drafted. Still we can but try, and, while the effort is making by the best men in Congress, it may be our duty to try.

Of all this, however, you can best judge. I can only say, that, if you will prepare a paper, I shall be very glad, when it has been signed in your city, to do all in my power to get such signatures to it here as will give it most weight. I trust I shall not appear to you officious in this matter, for I can well understand, from my own feelings, how distasteful this sort of work must be to you.

It will give you pleasure, I flatter myself, to know that I have completely succeeded in my negotiations in Spain. Señor Navarrete, with whom you were acquainted in Madrid, has very liberally supplied me with copies of his entire collection of manuscripts relating to Mexico and Peru, which it is improbable from his advanced age that he will ever publish himself. Through his aid I have also obtained from the Academy copies of the collections made by Muñoz and by its former President, Vargas y Ponce, — making all together some five thousand pages, all in fair condition, — the flower of my Spanish veterans.

From Mexico, through my good friend Calderon, who is now gone there, you know, as minister, I look for further ammunition, — though I am pretty independent of that now. I have found some difficulty in collecting the materials for the preliminary view I propose of the Aztec civilization. The works are expensive, and Lord Kingsborough's is locked up in chancery. I have succeeded, however, in ferreting out a copy, which, to say truth, though essential, has somewhat disappointed me. The whole of that part of the story is in twilight, and I fear I shall at least make only moonshine of it. I must hope that it will be good moonshine. It will go hard with me, however, but that I can fish something new out of my ocean of manuscripts.

As I have only half an eye of my own, and that more for show than use, my progress is necessarily no more than a snail's gallop. I should be very glad to show you my literary wares, but I fear you are too little of a locomotive in your habits to afford me that great pleasure. Though I cannot see you bodily, however, I am sitting under the light of your countenance, — for you are ranged above me (your immortal part) in a

---

[1] William C. Preston, then in the Senate of the United States from South Carolina.

goodly row of octavos, — not in the homespun garb, but in the nice costume of Albemarle and Burlington Streets.

My copy of the Sketch-Book, by the by, is the one owned by Sir James Mackintosh, and with his pencillings in the margin. It was but last evening that my little girl read us one of the stories, which had just enough of the mysterious to curdle the blood in the veins of her younger brother, who stopped up both his ears, saying he " would not hear such things just as he was going to bed," and as our assertions that no harm would come of it were all in vain, we were obliged to send the urchin off to his quarters with, I fear, no very grateful feelings towards the author.

At about the same time that he wrote thus to Mr. Irving, he received three letters from eminent historians, which gave him much pleasure. The first is

FROM M. J. C. L. DE SISMONDI.

Sir,

I have just received your letter from Boston, of the 1st of July, with the beautiful present which accompanies it. It has touched me, it has flattered me, but at the same time it has made me experience a very lively regret. I had found on my arrival at Paris, the last year, the English edition of your beautiful work. The address alone had informed me that it was a present of the author, and I have never known how it arrived to me. On my return here I wrote you on the 22d of July, to express to you my entire gratitude, the interest with which I had seen you cast so vivid a light over so interesting a period of the history of our Europe, my astonishment at your having attained such rich sources of learning, which are for the most part interdicted to us ; my admiration, in fine, for that force of character, and, without doubt, serenity of spirit, which had assisted you in pursuing your noble enterprise under the weight of the greatest calamity which can attend a man in his organs, and especially a man of letters, — the loss of sight. I do not remember what circumstance made me think that you lived at New York, and it is thither that I directed my letter to you, but I took care to add to your name, " Author of the History of Ferdinand and Isabella," and I represented to myself that your fellow-countrymen ought to be sufficiently proud of your book for the directors of the post of one of your largest cities to know your residence, and send you my letter. It is more than a year since that, and in the interval you have been able to learn how firmly established is the success of your work, and my suffrage has lost the little worth it might have had. I am mortified nevertheless to have been obliged to appear insensible to your kindness. . . . . .

I cannot believe that, after ten years so usefully, so happily employed, you lay aside the pen. You are now initiated into the History of Spain, and it will be much more easy to continue it than to begin it. After Robertson, after Watson, the shadows thicken upon the Peninsula ; will you not dissipate them ? Will you not teach us what we have so much need of knowing? Will not you exhibit this decay over more rapid, from the midst of which you will extract such important lessons? Consider that the more you have given to the public, the more it would have a right to demand of you. Permit me to join my voice to that of the public in this demand, as I have done in applauding what you have already done.

Believe me, with sentiments of the highest consideration,

Sir,

Your obedient servant,

J. C. L. de Sismondi.

Chênes, près Genève, Sept. 1, 1839.

The next letter referred to, which is one from the author of the "Histoire de la Conquête de l'Angleterre par les Normands," himself quite blind, is very interesting on all accounts,

FROM M. P. AUGUSTIN THIERRY.

Monsieur,

Pardonnez moi d'avoir tardé si longtemps à vous remercier du présent que vous avez eu la bonté de me faire. Deux causes ont contribué à ce retard : d'abord j'ai voulu lire en entier votre bel ouvrage, et les aveugles lisent lentement ; ensuite j'ai voulu vous envoyer, comme un bien faible retour, deux volumes qui étaient sous presse ; je prends la liberté de vous les offrir. Je ne saurais, Monsieur, vous exprimer tout le plaisir que m'a fait la lecture de votre " Histoire du Règne de Ferdinand et d'Isabelle." C'est un de ces livres également remarquables pour le fond et pour la forme, où se montrent à la fois des études approfondies, une haute raison et un grand talent d'écrivain. On sent que vos recherches ont pénétré au fond du sujet, que vous avez tout étudié aux sources, les origines nationales et provinciales, les traditions, les mœurs, les dialectes, la législation, les coutumes ; vos jugements sur la politique intérieure et extérieure de la monarchie Espagnole au 15ème siècle sont d'une grande fermeté et d'une complète impartialité ; enfin il y a dans le récit des événements cette clarté parfaite, cette gravité sans effort et sobrement colorée, qui est selon moi le vrai style de l'histoire.

Vous avez travaillé ce sujet avec prédilection, parceque là se trouvent les prolégomènes de l'histoire du nouveau monde où votre pays tient la première place ; continuez, Monsieur, à lui élever le monument dont vous voulez de poser la base. J'apprends avec peine que votre vue se perd de nouveau, mais je suis sans inquiétude pour vos travaux à venir ; vous serez comme moi, vous répéterez le devise du stoicien *Sustine, abstine*, et vous exercerez les yeux de l'âme à défaut des yeux du corps. Croyez, Monsieur, à ma vive sympathie pour une destinée qui sous ce rapport ressemble à la mienne et agréez avec mes remerciments bien sincères l'expression de ma haute estime et de mon dévouement.

P. Aug. Thierry.

Paris, le 17 Mars, 1840.

The last of the three letters from writers of historical reputation is one

FROM PATRICK FRASER TYTLER.

84 Devonshire Place [London], Monday, Feb. 24, 1840.

MY DEAR SIR,

I trust you will pardon my so addressing you, but it is impossible for me to use any colder terms, in acknowledging your letter and the accompanying present of your " History of Ferdinand and Isabella." To the high merit of the work, and to the place it has now confessedly taken in European literature, I was no stranger; but to receive it as a mark of your approbation and regard, and to be addressed from the New World as a brother laborer, greatly enhances the gift. I am indeed much encouraged when I find that anything I have done, or rather attempted to do, has given you pleasure, because I can sincerely say that I feel the value of your praise. You are indeed a lenient critic, and far overrate my labors, but it will, I believe, be generally found that they who know best, and have most successfully overcome, the difficulties of historical research are the readiest to think kindly of the efforts of a fellow-laborer.

I trust that you are again engaged on some high historical subject, and sincerely hope that your employing an amanuensis is not indicative of any return of that severe calamity which you so cheerfully and magnanimously overcame in your " Ferdinand and Isabella." At present I am intently occupied with the last volume of my " History of Scotland," which embraces the painful and much-controverted period of Mary. I have been fortunate in recovering many letters and original papers, hitherto unknown, and hope to be able to throw some new light on the obscurer parts of her history; but it is full of difficulty, and I sometimes despair. Such as it is, I shall beg your kind acceptance of it and my other volumes as soon as it is published.

Believe me, dear Sir,

With every feeling of respect and regard,

Most truly yours,

PATRICK FRASER TYTLER.

Other letters followed, of which one, characteristic of its author, may be here inserted.

FROM SAMUEL ROGERS, ESQ.

MY DEAR SIR,

How ungrateful must you have thought me in neglecting so long to thank you for your invaluable present; but, strange as it may be, I really imagined that I had done so in a letter to our excellent friend Mr. Ticknor; and, if I have not expressed what I felt, I have not felt the less; for I cannot tell you the delight with which I have read every page of your

8

History, — a history so happy in the subject, and, what is now a thing almost unknown, so well studied in the execution, — which, wherever it comes, interests old and young, and is nowhere more esteemed than in the cities of Spain. Thinking of it as I must, it can be no small consolation to me to learn that in what I have done, or rather attempted to do, I have given the author any pleasure, early or late. At my age, much as I may wish for it, I have little chance of seeing you, though the distance lessens every day. But I am determined to live, if I can, till you have finished what I understand you are now writing ; a noble task, and every way well worthy of you.

Pray allow me to subscribe myself
Your much obliged and sincere friend,
SAMUEL ROGERS.

London, March 30, 1840.

The next letter belongs to the important series of those to the Spanish scholar who contributed so much to Mr. Prescott's success in preparing his " History of Philip the Second," [2] by collecting the larger portion of the materials for it.

TO DON PASCUAL DE GAYANGOS.

BOSTON, June 20, 1840.

MY DEAR SIR,
Our friend Ticknor has informed me, that you desired him to say to me, that there are some documents in the British Museum relating to Mexico, which may be of value to me. I am extremely obliged and flattered by the friendly interest you take in my literary labors, and I shall be glad to avail myself of the treasures in the Museum. By a letter, dated April 4th, which you must have received ere this, I mentioned to you, that I had received a large mass of manuscripts from Madrid.[3] As my friend Mr. Sparks, with whose high literary reputation you are probably acquainted, is going to London, where he will pass some months, I send by him a list of the documents which I possess relating to Mexico and Peru, that I may not receive duplicates of any from the British Museum. If there are others of real value there relating to the *Conquests* of these two kingdoms, I should be very glad to have copies of them, and Mr. Sparks, whose labors will require him to be much in the British Museum, will do whatever you may advise in regard to having the copies made, and will forward them to me. I shall be very glad if you can get some one to select and copy from the correspondence of Gonsalvo and the Catholic Kings, and Mr. Sparks will reimburse you for the charges incurred on this account. But I fear, to judge from the specimen you have sent me, it will not be easy to find one capable of reading such hieroglyphical characters as these worthy persons made use of.

I am glad to learn from Ticknor that you are on the eve of publishing

[2] See *ante*, p. 105.
[3] This letter does not seem to have been preserved.

your Spanish History. You have not mentioned the nature of the work, but I suppose from the direction of your studies, as far as I understand them, it is the Spanish Arabic History. If so it is a splendid theme, which exhibits the mingled influences of European and Asiatic civilization, wonderfully picturesque and striking to the imagination. It is a subject which, to be properly treated, requires one who has wandered over the scenes of faded grandeur, and stored his mind with the rich treasures of the original Arabic. Very few scholars are at all competent to the subject, and no one will rejoice more than myself in seeing it fall into your hands. But perhaps I have misapprehended your work, as in your letter to Mr. Ticknor you merely call it a "History of Spain," and I shall be obliged by your telling me, when you do me the favor to write, what is the precise nature and object of it. Since writing to you, I have received letters from my friend Calderon,[4] the Spanish Minister at Mexico, communicating sundry documents, which he has procured for me there, as the public offices have all been thrown open to him. This is very good luck. But the collections I had previously from Spain were drawn, in part, from the same source.

*   *   *   *   *

MEMORANDA.

August 14, 1840. — General Miller, a very gallant and intelligent Englishman, who has filled the highest posts in the revolutionary wars of South America, has been at Nahant the last fortnight, and leaves to-morrow. He brought letters to me, and I have derived great benefit as well as pleasure from his society. He has given me much information respecting military matters, and has looked into the accounts of the battles in my work, and pointed out a few inaccuracies.[5]

August 15, 1840. — Monsieur Thierry, the author of the "Conquest of England by the Normans," made the following remark in a letter the other day to Ticknor, which I cannot refuse myself the pleasure of transcribing, as it comes from one who is at the head of his art.

"Si je pouvais renouer nos conversations d'il y a deux ans, je ne vous parlerais de la question du Canada, morte aujourd'hui, mais de l'avenir littéraire des États Unis, qui semblent vouloir prendre en ce point, comme en tout le reste, leur revanche sur la vieille Angleterre. J'ai dit à votre ami M. Prescott, tout le plaisir que m'a fait son livre. C'est un ouvrage étudié à fond sur les sources, et parfaitement composé. Il y a là autant de talent de style, et plus de liberté d'ésprit, que chez les meilleurs historiens Anglais."

[4] See ante, p. 153.
[5] General Miller died in South America in 1861, sixty-six years old. An account of the early part of his career was written by his brother, John Miller, of which the second edition was published at London, in 2 vols., 8vo, 1829. It is an interesting book, involving a history of much that was important in the affairs of South America, and was translated into Spanish by General Torrijos, well known and much honored in the war of the Peninsula, 1809-1814.

TO DON PASCUAL DE GAYANGOS.

BOSTON, Feb. 1, 1841.

MY DEAR FRIEND,

At last I have received the welcome present of your volume on the "Spanish Arabs," and the manuscripts of the "Great Captain." I cannot sufficiently express to you my admiration of your work, published, too, as it should be, in so splendid a form. It far exceeds the expectations I had entertained, which, however, were great, knowing your own familiarity with the ground.* During the few days it has been in my possession, I have greedily run over it, as well as my eyes, aided by those of another, would allow, and, though I have travelled over the ground before, as far as Spanish writers have cleared the way, I now see how much was left obscure and misunderstood, and perverted by the best of them. The work you have selected for translation is most happily chosen, not only from its own merits, but from its embodying so many copious extracts from other sources, that it is in itself a sort of abridgment or encyclopædia of the choicest passages relating to the multifarious topics of which it treats. These certainly are of great interest and importance. But your own notes throw a light over the whole, which can only come from a life of previous study in this department.

I wish it had been my good fortune to have had such a guide in my poor attempts among the remains of Arabian Spain. And how much am I gratified to find my own labors, such as they are, noticed by you with the beautiful encomium, which, when I read your learned and accurate pages, I feel I am poorly entitled to. Your book must certainly supersede all that has gone before it on this topic, the learned but unsatisfactory — I did not know how unsatisfactory — labors of Condé, Masdeú, Casíri, Cardonne, &c. You have furnished a clear picture of that Asiatic portion of the Peninsular history without which the European cannot be rightly interpreted or understood. I, of course, have had time only to glance rapidly through these pages, and very imperfectly. I shall return to them with more deliberation, when I come to a good resting-place in my own narrative. I am just bringing my account of the state of the Aztec civilization to a close; the most perplexing and thorny part of my own subject, which has cost me two years' labor. But I have wished to do it as thoroughly as I could, and I work much slower than you do, and, I suspect, much less industriously.

From about this time he occasionally wrote letters to my eldest daughter, and sent them to her just as they came from his noctograph, without being copied. Some of them are inserted, to show how pleasantly he accommodated himself to the tastes and humors of a young person.

* " History of the Mohammedan Dynasties in Spain, from the Arabic of Al-Makkari, translated by Pascual de Gayangos," 4to, Vol. I., London, 1840; Vol. II., 1843; published by the " Oriental Translation Fund."

TO MISS TICKNOR.

Oct. 1, 1840.

MY DEAR ANIKA,[7]
You said you should like to try to make out my writing with my noctograph; so I will give you a specimen of it, and believe, if you can decipher it, you will be qualified to read Egyptian papyri or the monuments of Palmyra. When in Europe, some twenty years since, I met with this apparatus, and have used it ever since, by which my eyes have been spared, and those of others severely taxed. I hope you will never be reduced to so poor a substitute for pen and ink. But if you are, I hope you will find as obliging an amanuensis as you have been to me sometimes.

But to change the subject, and take up one which we were speculating upon this morning at the breakfast table, — Lord Byron. I think one is very apt to talk extravagantly of his poetry; for it is the poetry of passion, and carries away the sober judgment. It defies criticism from its very nature, being lawless, independent of all rules, sometimes of grammar, and even of common sense. When he means to be strong, he is often affected, violent, morbid; if striking, is very obscure, from dealing more in impressions than ideas. And partly from affectation, I suppose, partly from want of principle, and partly from the *ennui* and disgust occasioned by long self-indulgence and by naturally violent passions, he is led into extravagances which outrage the reader, offend the taste, and lead many persons of excellent principles and critical discernment to condemn him, both on the ground of moral and literary pretensions. This is true, the more the pity. But then there is, with all this smoke and fustian, a deep sensibility to the sublime and beautiful in nature, a wonderful melody, or rather harmony, of language, consisting, not in an unbroken flow of versification, like Pope or Campbell, but in a variety, — the variety of nature, — in which startling ruggedness is relieved by soft and cultivated graces. As he has no narrative hardly in "Childe Harold," he would be very tiresome, if it were not for this very variety of manner, so that what is a fault in itself produces a beautiful effect taken as a whole. He has great attractions, and, pouring out his soul unreservedly, turns up the depths of feeling which even those who acknowledge the truth of it would shrink from expressing themselves. — "There is a mess for you," as D—— says. When you have made this out, burn it, as a lady would say. *Addio!*

* * * * * *

TO MISS TICKNOR.

PEPPERELL, Oct. 25, 1840.

MY DEAR ANIKA,
You are so clever at hieroglyphics that I shall send you a little more of them to unravel at your leisure, and in time you may be qualified to make out a mummy wrapper or an obelisk inscription as well as Champollion or Dr. Young.

[7] A name he gave to her in order to distinguish her from her mother, whom he commonly called by her first name, which was also Anna.

We were glad to learn you had reached the Yankee Athens in safety. You set out in a true wind from "The Horn," [*] — a cornucopia certainly you had of it. You left us all very sad and melancholic. The traveller on these occasions finds new scenes to divert him. But they who are left behind see only the deserted halls, the vacant place at the board, which was lighted by the bright countenance of a friend. Absence seems to be a negative thing, but there is nothing so positive, nothing which touches us more sensibly than the absence of the faces we love from the seats in which we have been used to see them. The traveller has always the best of the bargain on these occasions, therefore.

Well, we shall soon be in the gay metropolis with you. We have had many warnings to depart. The leaves have taken *their* leave, one after another. The summer weather is quite spent, and almost the autumnal. The bright colors have faded, the naked trees stare around wildly, and, as the cold wind whistles through them, the shrivelled leaves that still hold out rattle like the bones of a felon hung in chains. The autumn seems to be dying, and wants only the cold winding-sheet of winter to close the scene. In fact, she is getting some shreds of this winding-sheet before the time, for, while I am writing, the snow-flakes are dancing before the window. There's a mess of romance for you, all done up in hiero-glyphics. When you read Mrs. Radcliffe, or Miss Porter, or Miss —— any other mumbler of scenery and sentiment, you'll find it all there. Your papa talks of Mr. T——'s sending me his book. Ask him if he has not mixed up Mr. T—— with Mr. D. T——, very different men, I wot. I am glad he has seen General Miller. He is worth a wilderness of ——, as Shakespeare says.

Tell your papa and mamma, their maxims of education have not fallen on deaf ears, nor a stony heart. But I believe this will be quite enough for once. I must begin with small doses. But it is such a comfort to find any who can read me without my eternal amanuensis at my elbows, who, to-day being Sunday, he is not now. Adieu, dear Anika. Do not forget Amory and E.'s love to Lizzy, and mine to your honored parents,

I hope your respected father gets on yet without his wig, ear-trumpet, and glasses! By the by, my mother lost her spectacles yesterday. All the town has been ransacked for them in vain. They were a gold pair. —— Do you think your father carried them off?

Once more *addio!*

Your affectionate uncle,[*]

WM. H. PRESCOTT.

[*] The name very often given on the southern coast of Massachusetts to "Cape Horn," which so many of the people of that part of the country double in search of whales. I spent two or three summers there with my family; and Mr. Prescott, when he visited us, used to be much amused with the familiar manner in which that very remote part of the world was spoken of, as if it were some small cape in the neighborhood. The letter in the text was written immediately after we had returned to Boston from a visit to Pepperell.

[*] There was no blood relationship between us, but the children on both sides were always accustomed to speak of us as "uncles" and "aunts," while all round their elders accepted the designation as a pleasant mark of affection.

TO DON PASCUAL DE GAYANGOS.

BOSTON, Feb. 28, 1841.

. . . . . I have run into a most interminable length of prosing, and could not do worse if I were writing to an absolute *far niente*, instead of one with whom minutes are gold-dust. You would smile if you were to see how I am writing with a writing-case made for the blind, in which I do not see a word of what I write; furnishing a scrawl as illegible as Gonsalvo's [10] for my secretary to transcribe. Adieu! my dear friend. Pray accept my sincere congratulations on the happy addition to your family circle. I can sympathize with you, counting two boys and a girl, the youngest of whom is ten years old. I should like to present them to you, but still better to take you by the hand myself. And, now that steam has annihilated time and space, that may come to pass.

I have received a letter from the Marquis Gino Capponi of Florence this morning, informing me that nearly half my work is translated into the language of Dante and Petrarch, and that the remainder would be completed before long under his supervision. You may know his reputation as a scholar, which is high in Italy.[11]

MEMORANDA.

March 21, 1841. — Am fairly now engaged, though not with thorough industry, in beating the bushes for the narrative [of the Conquest of Mexico]. — Last week have been considering the best *modus operandi*, and been looking over some celebrated narratives of individual enterprises, as Voltaire's "Charles XII." and Livy's Expedition of Hannibal, lib. 22, 23, — the last a masterly story, in which the interest, though suspended by necessary digression, — more necessary in a general history, — is never broken. The historian, the greatest of painters, shows his talent in pictures of natural scenery, the horrors of the Alps and Apennines, as well as in the delineation of passions. Voltaire's volume, so popular, is very inferior in literary merit. It bears much resemblance to the gossiping

[10] Nothing can well be more difficult to decipher than the handwriting of the Great Captain. I have one of his autograph letters, but am nearly ignorant of its contents.

[11] A distinguished scholar, statesman, and man; the head of a family mentioned by Dante, and great before Dante's time, as well as in many generations since. The present Marquis (1862) is now entirely blind, and was nearly so when he first interested himself in the translation of "Ferdinand and Isabella"; but he has never ceased to maintain a high place in the affairs of his country, as well as in the respect of his countrymen. He was at one time head of the government of Tuscany, and, notwithstanding his blindness, was President of the Council of Advice in State Affairs, during the anxious period of the transition of power to the Kingdom of Italy. Their common infirmity caused a great sympathy between the Marquis Capponi and Mr. Prescott.

memoir-writing of the nation, with little regard to historic dignity ; not much method, or apparently previous digestion of his subject. It has, however, the great requisite, in a work meant to be popular, that of interest. This is maintained by the studious exhibition of Charles's remarkable character, with all its petty infirmities and crazy peculiarities. The easy, careless arrangement of the narrative gives it a grace very taking. The style, like Livy's (*magis par quam similis*), easy and natural, gives additional charm. After all, Chambers's " History of the Rebellion of 1745 " is about as well-written, lively, and agreeable a narrative of an interesting event, and is managed altogether as skilfully, as any that I remember.

Have been looking over Irving's " Columbus " also ; a beautiful composition, but fatiguing, as a whole, to the reader. Why ? The fault is partly in the subject, partly in the manner of treating it. The discovery of a new world — the result of calculation and an energy that rose above difficulties that would have daunted a common mind — is a magnificent theme in itself, full of sublimity and interest. But it terminates with the discovery ; and unfortunately this is made before half of the first volume is disposed of. All after that event is made up of little details, the sailing from one petty island to another, all inhabited by savages, and having the same general character. Nothing can be more monotonous, and, of course, more likely to involve the writer in barren repetition. The chief interest that attaches to the rest of the story is derived from the navigator's own personal misfortunes, and these are not exciting enough to create a deep or strong sensation. Irving should have abridged this part of his story, and, instead of four volumes, have brought it into two. Posterity may do this for him. But it is better for an author to do his own work himself.

The Conquest of Mexico, though very inferior in the leading idea which forms its basis to the story of Columbus, is, on the whole, a far better subject, since the event is sufficiently grand, and, as the catastrophe is deferred, the interest is kept up through the whole. Indeed, the perilous adventures and crosses with which the enterprise is attended, the desperate chances and reverses and unexpected vicissitudes, all serve to keep the interest alive. On my plan, I go on with Cortés to his death. But I must take care not to make this tail-piece too long. A hundred pages will be quite enough.

TO MISS TICKNOR.

FITFUL HEAD [Nahant], July 25, 1841.

MY DEAR ANIKA,

What a nice quiet time you have had of it for reading or sleeping, or anything else that is rational. Has the spirit of improvement beset you in your solitude, and carried you through as much metaphysics and Spanish as it has your respected parents ? or have you been meandering among romances and poeticals ? You have read Irving's " Memoirs of Miss Davidson," I believe. Did you ever meet with any novel half so touching ? It is the most painful book I ever listened to. I hear it from the children, and we all cry over it together. What a little flower of Paradise ! Do you remember Malherbe's beautiful lines, — which I happen just now not to, —

> "Et comme une rose elle a vecu
> L'éspace d'un matin," —

and Young's, no less beautiful, —

> "She sparkled, was exhaled, and went to heaven"?

Her whole life was one dying day, — one long heart-break. How fitting that her beautiful character should be embalmed in the delicate composition of Irving! Read over her farewell to Ruremont, if you forget it. It is really a sad subject.

Well, we descend on "The Hole" on Tuesday next.[12] William Prescott 1st, 2d, and 3d will make the party. Three persons and one name, — just the opposite of my friends the Spaniards, who each have a dozen names at least. On Monday, the 2d of August, we embark on the great Providence Railroad; reach New Bedford, we hope, that evening; pass the night in that great commercial emporium of the spermaceti; and the next morning by *noon* shall embrace the dear "Toads in the Hole." And as we can't get away, and you won't turn us out the while, we shall besiege you till Friday; and, if you are tired of us, you can send us to see Mr. Swain,[13] or to the ancient city of Nantucket; not a literary emporium, though I believe it smells of the lamp pretty strong. I feel quite in the trim of a little vagabondizing, having fairly worked myself down. . . . . . Indeed, my father and I half arranged a little journey before visiting you, but I showed the white feather, as usual. I mean to date health and spirits and renovated industry from the visit to "Wood's Hole."

Don't you think our traveller, Palenque Stephens, would smile at our great preparations in the travelling line? I was in town yesterday, and saw a picture which came from Mexico, a full-length of Cortés, in armor the upper part of his body; his nether extremities in a sort of stockinet, like the old cavaliers of the sixteenth century, — a very striking and picturesque costume superior to my Spanish painting in execution. But it is too large, and carries an acre of canvas, seven feet by four and a half. I called a council of war as to the expediency of cutting his feet off, but Mr. Folsom came in at the moment, and said I never should forgive myself; so I have concluded to frame him, legs and all. But my wife thinks I shall have to serve him like the Vicar of Wakefield's great family picture, he is so out of all compass.

Well, here I am, dear Anika, at the end of my letter. Let us know if our arrangements can be altered for the better, — i. e. if you are to be without company. Love to your father and mother. All of us send much love to you and them.

Believe me, most truly,

Your affectionate uncle,

WM. H. PRESCOTT.

[12] We were then passing the summer at "Wood's Hole," on the southern shore of Massachusetts.

[13] On the adjacent island of Naushon, where Mr. Swain lived.

8 *

L.

MEMORANDA.

March 22, 1842. — My good friends the Ticknors received this last week a letter from Miss Edgeworth, containing a full critique on "Ferdinand and Isabella," which she had just been reading. She condemns my parallel of the English and Castilian queens, and also my closing chapter; the former as not satisfactory and full enough, and rather feeble; the latter as superfluous. I will quote two remarks of another kind : "It is of great consequence both to the public and private class of readers, and he will surely have readers of all classes, from the cottage and the manufactory to the archbishopric and the throne in England, and from Papal jurisdiction to the Russian Czar and the Patriarch of the Greek Church. The work will last," &c. If Jupiter grants me half the prediction, I shall be pretty well off for readers. The other sentence is towards the end of the critique : "Otherwise an individual ought not to expect that a single voice should be heard amidst the acclaim of universal praise with which his work has been greeted in Europe." — This from Miss Edgeworth.

I never worked for the dirty lucre. Am I not right in treasuring up such golden opinions from such a source ?

TO DON PASCUAL DE GAYANGOS.

BOSTON, March 27, 1842.

. . . . . I received from Mr. Everett by this steamer copies of a correspondence of the Tuscan ambassadors at Philip's court, giving some very interesting details of the proceedings, and all in favor of the monarch.[14] I wrote you to see Mr. Everett,[15] who will, I am sure, take pleasure in communicating with you. I have written to him by this packet, that I have asked you to call on him, as he was out when you went before. He is much occupied with perplexing affairs, but I have never found him too much so for his friends. Should you find any impediment to the examination in the State Office, he will use his influence in your favor, I am certain. And I think you had better get a letter from him to Mignet or Guizot. Lord Morpeth, who was here this winter, offered me his services to obtain anything I desired. But that will be too late for you, as he will not return till summer. But if there remains anything to be done then, let me know, and I can get at it through him.

TO DON PASCUAL DE GAYANGOS.

BOSTON, May 30, 1842.

MY DEAR FRIEND,

I have not written by the last packets, having nothing particular to say. I have received yours of the 2d of April, and am glad you have seen Mr.

[14] On the death of Don Carlos. He had now, as we have seen, been some time collecting materials for his History of Philip the Second.

[15] Then Minister of the United States in London. See post, for Mr. Prescott's correspondence with him.

Everett, and are pleased with him. I am sure he will give you any facility in his power for getting access to the French depositories. I should suppose a line from him to Mignet would be serviceable.

You have found the British Museum a much richer field than you had first anticipated, and the length of your stay in London, fortunately for me, will enable you to reap the harvest. You mention one or two chronicles or memoirs which you have met with there. I have always found a good, gossiping chronicle or memoir the best and most fruitful material for the historian. Official documents, though valuable on other accounts, contain no private relations; nothing, in short, but what was meant for the public eye. Even letters of business are very apt to be cold and general. But a private correspondence like Peter Martyr's, or a chronicle like Pulgar's, or Bernal Diaz's, or Bernaldez's, is a jewel of inestimable price. There is nothing so serviceable to the painter of men and manners of a distant age. Pray get hold of such in manuscript or in print.

I hope you will get for me whatever printed books fall in your way, useful for a history of that reign. And I shall be much obliged by your making out a list of all such as may be desirable for me hereafter to get, as you promise to do. I can then pick them up at my leisure. I find some referred to in Ferreras, and others in Nic. Antonio. I am truly glad you are going to Madrid soon, or in the course of a couple of years. I shall be most happy to leave the collection then all in your hands, and, while Irving is there, I am sure you can count on his services, if they can be worth anything to you to get access to any archives which may be under the control of the government. He has assured me of his cordial desire to promote my views and Ticknor's in our researches. You will bear in mind, in the copying, to get it done in as legible a hand as possible. I don't care for the beauty of it, so it is legible. I suppose in Paris, and I know in Madrid, the expense will be greatly lightened.

I am very much obliged by your great kindness in sending me your own collection of manuscripts. They have all reached me safely, as I desired Mr. Rich to inform you. They are a most curious and valuable collection to the historian of the period. But Charles V. has been handled by Robertson, and I have not the courage nor the vanity to tread where he has gone before. I do not think the history of his period will make as good a pendant to " Ferdinand and Isabella " as Philip the Second will. Philip's reign is the first step towards the decline, as Isabella's was the last step in the rise, of the Spanish monarchy. I hope to treat this great theme in all its relations, literary, social, and political. It will be a ten years' work. *Da, Jupiter, annos.*

FROM RICHARD FORD, ESQ.

Heavitree, near Exeter, June 5, 1842.

My dear Sir,

Permit me to offer you my very best thanks for the copy of your last edition of " Ferdinand and Isabella," which you have been so kind as to direct Mr. Bentley to send to me. I have lived so long in Spain, and particularly in the Alhambra, that the work possesses for me a more than ordinary interest, great as is that which it has inspired in readers of all countries. Indeed, it is a History of which America, and, if you will allow me to say so, England, has every reason to be most proud, and of which it may be justly said, as was said of Gibbon's, that, although the first to grapple with a vast subject, it has left no room for any future attempt.

I hope that, having now fleshed your pen, you will soon resume it, — *non in reluctantes dracones.* Our mutual friend Pascual de Gayangos has often suggested, as an almost virgin subject, the life of Philip the Second. The poor performance of Watson is beneath notice. What a new and noble field for you, what an object for a tour to Europe to inspect the rich archives of England, Paris, and Simancas, where, as I can tell you from personal inspection, the state papers, interlined by Philip himself, are most various and numerous. . . . . .

FROM P. F. TYTLER, ESQ.

LONDON, 34 Devonshire Place, June 6, 1842.

MY DEAR SIR,

I entreat your kind acceptance of a copy of the second edition of the "History of Scotland." A single additional volume — the ninth — will complete the work, bringing it down to the union of the crowns in 1603, and I then purpose, if God grant me health, to write an introductory dissertation on the more ancient history of Scotland in another volume. In the mean time, although still an unfinished work, I hope you will place it in your library as a testimony, slight indeed, but most sincere, of the pleasure and instruction your excellent History has given me, and, I may add, my family. I feel, too, that in the love of history, for its own sake, there is a common and congenial tie, which, although so far separated, binds us together, and that one who has, like you, so successfully overcome the difficulties of history, will make the readiest allowance for the errors of a brother.

I met some time ago at Lady Holland's a Spanish gentleman,[16] who informed me of your having wished him to examine for you the manuscripts in the State Paper Office about the time of Philip and Mary. When writing, or rather making collections for, my "Letters during the Reigns of Edward the Sixth and Mary," I made a good many transcripts connected with the history of Philip and Mary, which, if they could be of the least service to you, are much at your disposal.

Believe me, dear Sir,

With sincere regard and respect,
Very truly yours,
PATRICK FRASER TYTLER.

[16] Don Pascual de Gayangos.

CHAPTER XV.

1839 — 1844.

FROM the letter to Mr. Irving at the beginning of the last
chapter, we have seen that Mr. Prescott's earlier apprehension about the failure of his application at Madrid for manuscripts concerning the " Conquest of Mexico " was not well
founded. He had excellent friends to assist him, and they had
succeeded. The chief of them were Don Angel Calderon, Mr.
A. H. Everett, then our Minister in Spain, and Mr. Middleton,
his Secretary of Legation, who had been Mr. Prescott's classmate and college chum, — all of whom were earnest and help-
ful, — to say nothing of Dr. Lembke, who was in his service
for a considerable time, collecting manuscripts, and was both
intelligent and efficient. Mr. Prescott, therefore, no longer
feared that he should fail to obtain all he could reasonably
expect. But his industry, which he thought had needed only
this stimulus, did not come with the promise of abundant materials for its exercise. During three months he did very
little, and records his regrets more than once in terms not to
be mistaken.

In May, 1839, however, he was better satisfied with himself
than he had been for at least two years. " I have begun," he
says, " to lay my bones to the work in good earnest. The last

week I have read a variety of authors, — i. e. looked into them, affording illustration, in some way or other, of the Mexican subject. Yesterday I completed my forty-third birth and my nineteenth wedding day. If they do not prove happy days for me, it is my own fault." And again, a week later: "An industrious week for me. My eyes have done me fair service; and when I do not try them by exposure to light, the hot air of crowded rooms, and the other *et cæteras* of town life, I think I can very generally reckon on them for some hours a day. The last winter they have not averaged me more than one hour; my fault in a great measure, I suspect."

Except from occasional exposures to lights in the evening, I think he suffered little at this time, and, as he now put himself into rigorous training for work, and avoided everything that could interfere with it, I suppose it was the period when, for three or four years, he enjoyed more of the blessings of sight than he did during the rest of his life subsequent to the original injury. Certainly he used with diligence whatever he possessed of it, and sometimes seemed to revel presumptuously in the privileges its very partial restoration afforded him.

After two or three months of careful preliminary reading on the subject of Mexico generally, he formed a plan for the whole work much as he subsequently executed it, although, as in the case of the "Ferdinand and Isabella," he for a long time hoped it would not exceed two volumes. The composition he began October 14th, 1839. But he had gone only a few pages, when he became dissatisfied with what he had done, and rewrote them, saying, "One would like to make one's introductory bow in the best style"; and adds, "The scenery-painting with which it opens wants the pencil of Irving."

This, however, was only the beginning of his troubles. The first part of the work he had undertaken was difficult, and cost him more labor than all the rest. It involved necessarily the early traditions and history of Mexico, and whatever related to its peculiar civilization before the Conquest and during the period when that extraordinary event was going on. It is true, he soon discovered that much of what passes for curious learning in the manifold discussions of this obscure subject is only "mist and moonshine speculations," and that Humboldt is "the first, almost the last, writer on these topics, who, by making his theories conform to facts, instead of bending his facts to theories, truly merits the name of a philosopher." Notwithstanding, however, the small value he found himself able to place on most of the writers who had examined the Mexican traditions and culture, he read all who might be considered authorities upon the subject, and even many whose works were only in a remote degree connected with it. Thus, he not only went carefully over all that Humboldt had written, and all he could find in the old printed authorities, like Herrera, Torquemada, and Sahagun, together with the vast documentary collections of Lord Kingsborough, and the "Antiquités Mexicaines"; but he listened to the manuscript accounts of Ixtlilxochitl, of Camargo, Toribio, and Zuazo. He compared whatever he found in these with the oldest records of civilization in other countries, — with Herodotus, Champollion, and Wilkinson for Egypt; with Marco Polo and Sir John Mandeville for the East; and with Gallatin, Du Ponceau, McCulloh, Heckewelder, and Delafield for our own continent. Nothing, in short, seemed to escape him, and it was curious to see in his notes how aptly, and with what grace, he draws contributions from Elphinstone, Milman, and Lyell, — from Homer, Sophocles, Southey, and Schiller, — and, finally, what happy separate facts he collects from all the travellers who have at any time visited Mexico, beginning with old Bernal Diaz, and coming down to the very period when he himself wrote, — I mean to that of Bullock, Ward, and Stephens.

Such studies for the deep foundations of the epic superstructure he contemplated were, of course, the work of time, and demanded not a little patience, — more, in fact, of both than he had foreseen. He had reckoned for his Introduction one hundred pages. It turned out two hundred and fifty. He thought that he could accomplish it in six months. It took nearly a year and a half, not counting the year he gave to preparatory reading on Mexico generally. Three months, indeed, before he put pen to paper, his notes already filled four hundred pages; and subsequently, when he showed them to me, as the composition was in progress, their mass was still greater. I do not know an instance of more conscientious labor; the more worthy of note, because it dealt with subjects less agreeable to his tastes and habits than any others to which he ever devoted himself.[1]

For the rest of his History he prepared himself, not only by reading some of the great masters of historical narrative, but by noting down in what particulars their example could be useful to him. This he found a very pleasant and encouraging sort of work, and it enabled him to go on with spirit. Not that he failed to find, from time to time, interruptions more or less serious, which checked his progress. One of these interruptions occurred almost immediately after he had completed his severe labor on the Introduction. It was the project for a visit to England, which tempted him very much, and occupied and disturbed his thoughts more than it needed to have done. Speaking of his work on his History, he says: "Now, why should I not go ahead? Because I am thinking of going to England, to pass four months in the expedition, and my mind is distracted with the *pros* and *cons*." And, ten days later, he says: "Have decided, at length, — after as much doubt and deliberation as most people would take for a voyage round the world, — and decided *not* to go to England." He thought he had given up the project for life. Happily this was not the case.

Another interruption was caused by a threatened abridgment of his "Ferdinand and Isabella," the untoward effect of which

[1] After going carefully through with the hieroglyphical writing of the Aztecs, he says: "Finished notes on the hieroglyphical part of the chapter, — a hard, barren topic. And now on the astronomy, — out of the frying-pan into the fire. I find it, however, not so hard to comprehend as I had anticipated. Fortunately, the Aztec proficiency does not require a knowledge of the 'Principia.' Still it was enough to task all my mathematics, and patience to boot; it may be, the reader's, too."

On this part of his labors, Mr. Gardiner well remarks: "In earlier life he used to fancy that his mind was constitutionally incapable of comprehending mathematical truths, or at least of following out mathematical demonstrations beyond the common rules of arithmetic. It was a mistake. They were only hard for him, and uncongenial; and, at the period referred to, he avoided real intellectual labor as much as he could. But now, though with no previous training, he did overcome all such difficulties, whenever they lay in the way of his historical investigations, whether on the coins and currency of the time of Ferdinand and Isabella, or on the astronomy of the Aztecs. It is a striking proof of the power his will had acquired over his intellectual tastes and propensities."

he determined to forestall by making an abridgment of it himself. This annoyed him not a little. After giving an account of a pleasant journey, which our two families took together, and which greatly refreshed him, he goes on : —

> " The week since my return, lazy and listless and dreamy. O! *pot.* And I must now — thermometer at 90° in the shade — abandon my Mexican friends and the pleasant regions of the plateau for — *horresco referens* — an abridgment of my 'History of Ferdinand and Isabella.' . . . . . Nothing but the dire necessity of protecting myself from piracy induces me to do this unnatural work, — sweating down my full-grown offspring to the size of a pygmy, — dwarfing my own conception from, I trust, a manly stature, to the compass of a nursery capacity. I never was in love with my own compositions. I shall hammer over them now, till they give me the *vomito.*" [2]

Disgusted with his work, — which, after all, he never published, as the idea of the piratical abridgment was early given up by the bookselling house that threatened it, — he finished it as soon as he could. But whether it was the disagreeableness of the task or the earnestness of his labors, it was too much for him. He grew feeble and listless, and came, as already noticed in one of his letters, with his father, to visit us for a few days on the southern coast of Massachusetts at Wood's Hole, where the milder sea-breezes might, he thought, prove beneficial.

On the 9th of August he records : —

> " I have done nothing except the abridgment, since May 26, when I went on a journey to Springfield. My health must be my apology the last three weeks, and a visit, from which I returned two days since, to my friends at Wood's Hole, — an agreeable visit, as I anticipated. Nahant has not served me as well as usual this summer. I have been sorely plagued with dyspeptic debility and pains. But I am resolved not to heed them more, and to buckle on my harness for my Mexican campaign *in earnest* again, though with more reserve and moderation."

This was a little adventurous, but it was successful. He worked well during the rest of August at Nahant, and when, in the autumn, we visited him as usual at Pepperell, where he went early in September, we found him quite restored, and enjoying his studies heartily. The last days there were days of

---

[2] It should be remembered that, when he wrote this passage, he had just been describing this terrible scourge itself. (Conquest of Mexico, Vol. I. pp. 394, etc.) The same disgust is expressed in one of his letters at the time, in which he says that he went through the whole work in twenty-four days.

great activity, and he returned to Boston, as he almost always did, with no little reluctance. Writing at the end of October, he says :—

"Leave Pepperell on Wednesday next, November 3.   Yesterday and the afternoon previous, beginning at four P. M., I wrote on my Chapter IV. (Book III.) between eighteen and nineteen pages print, — or twelve pages *per diem*.   I shall soon gallop to the 'Finis' at this pace.   But Boston !   The word includes a thousand obstacles.   Can I not overcome them ?"

One of these obstacles, however, which he encountered as soon as he reached town, was a very pleasant one, and the source of much happiness to him afterwards.   He found there Lord Morpeth, now the Earl of Carlisle, who had just arrived on a visit to the United States, and who spent several weeks in Boston.   They soon became acquainted, and an attachment sprang up between them almost at once, which was interrupted only by death.

How warm it was on the part of Lord Morpeth will be plainly seen by the following letter, written not long after he left Boston.

LA HABANA, March 30, 1842.

MY DEAR PRESCOTT,
   You are about the first person in my life who has made me feel in a hurry to write to him ; and I have really forborne hitherto, from thinking it might cross your mind that you had got rather more of a bargain than you wished when we made our corresponding compact.   I am sure, you have a very faint idea of the pleasure I derive from the thoughts of the acquaintance which has been so short, and the friendship which is to be so lasting between us ; and whenever, as has, however, been very seldom the case, matters have not gone quite so pleasantly on my journey, and the question, " Was it worth while after all ? " would just present itself, " Yes, I have made acquaintance with Prescott," has been the readiest and most efficacious answer.   I stop, though, lest you should imagine I have caught the Spanish infection of compliments.   It is at least appropriate to write to you from Spanish ground.
   I have now been in this island about a fortnight, having spent most of the first week in Havana, and returned to it this afternoon from an expedition into the interior.   I was entrapped into a dreadfully long passage from Charleston in an American sailing packet, having been almost guaranteed a maximum of six days, whereas it took us thirteen.   Painfully we threaded the coast of Georgia and Florida,

"And wild Altama murmured to our woe."

However, we did arrive at last, and nothing can be conceived more picturesque than the entrance into this harbor under the beetling rock of the fortress, or so peculiar, un-English, un-American, un-Bostonian, as the appearance of everything — houses, streets, persons, vehicles — that meets your eye. I take it to be very Spanish, modified by the black population and the tropical growths. I have been on a ten days' expedition into the interior, and have visited sundry sugar and coffee estates. At one of these, the Count Fernandina's, I had great satisfaction in meeting the Calderons. I immediately felt that you were a link between us, and that I had a right to be intimate with them, which I found it was very well worth while to be on their own account also. There is great simplicity of character, as well as abundant sense and good feeling, about him, and I think her most remarkably agreeable and accomplished. I leave you to judge what a resource and aid they must have been to me in a country-house, where everybody else was talking Spanish. We did all think it a pity that you had not gone to visit them in Mexico; there is so much truth in the Horatian rule about "oculis subjecta fidelibus," but, my dear and good friend, perhaps you think that is not the epithet exactly to be applied to you. They rave, especially Madame C., of what they saw during their equestrian exploration in Mexico, the climate and the products of every latitude, the virgin forests, of everything but the state of society, which seems almost hopelessly disorganized and stranded. With respect to Cuban scenery, I think I can best condense my impression as follows : —

" Ye tropic forests of unfading green,
   Where the palm tapers and the orange glows,
Where the light bamboo weaves her feathery screen,
   And her far shade the matchless *ceiba* throws!

" Ye cloudless ethers of unchanging blue,
   Save when the rosy streaks of eve give way
To the clear sapphire of your midnight hue,
   The burnished azure of your perfect day!

" Yet tell me not, my native skies are bleak,
   That, flushed with liquid wealth, no cane-fields wave;
For Virtue pines, and Manhood dares not speak,
   And Nature's glories brighten round the slave."

Shall you be in a hurry to ask me to write again when you see what it brings upon you? I only wish you would pay me in kind by sending me any bit of a more favorite passage, a more special inspiration, a Pisgah morsel, out of your History, as it runs along. By the way, upon the subject of my last line, and as you know that I do not for the first time assume the function of saying things disagreeable and impertinent, I do not think that you seemed to possess quite *the sufficient* repugnance to the system of slavery. Come here to be duly impressed. Will you very kindly remember me to all the members of your family, from the *ex* to the growing Judge. If you ever have a mind to write to me, Sumner will be always able to ascertain my direction from Mr. Lewis. Give that good friend of ours my blessing; I wish it were as valuable as a wig. If I could give you a still stronger assurance of my wish to be always pleasantly remembered by you, it is that, excessively as I should like to hear from you at all times, I yet had rather you did not write when not entirely inclined to do so.   I set off for New Orleans next week.   You see, that I have had the good fortune to lose my election, which makes me more able to encourage the hope that we may yet meet again on the soil of your republic.   That would be very pleasant.

Believe me ever,

Your affectionate friend,

MORPETH.

There is no allusion to this new friendship among the literary memoranda, except the following, made immediately after Lord Morpeth was gone : —

"December 28th, 1841.   Finished text, twenty-three pages of print, and the notes to Chapter VIII.   Οἴ μοι, Οἴ μοι.   Not a page a day.   So much for dinners, suppers, Lord Morpeth, and nonsense.   I wish I may never have a worse apology, however, than his Lordship, — a beautiful specimen of British aristocracy in mind and manners.   But what has it all to do with the ' Conquest of Mexico ' ?   If I don't mend, my Spaniards will starve among the mountains.   I WILL ! "

And this time he kept his resolution.   During the rest of the winter of 1841 — 1842, he worked hard and successfully, but made few memoranda.   Under the 7th of May, however, I find the following : —

"Another long hiatus.   Since last entry paid two visits to New York, — a marvellous event in my history !   First, a visit, about three weeks since, I paid to meet Washington Irving before his departure for Spain.   Spent half a day with him at Wainwright's,[*] — indeed, till twelve at night. Found him delightful and — what, they say, is rare — wide awake.   He promises to aid me in all my applications.   Stayed but two days.   Second visit, April 25, and stayed till May 3 ; went to see an oculist, Dr. ——, at request of friends, — my own faith not equal to the minimum requisite, — the grain of mustard-seed.   I consumed about a week or more in inquiring about him and his cases.   Returned re infectâ.   Passed a very agreeable week, having experienced the warmest welcome from the good people of New York, and seen what is most worthy of attention in their society.   The life I have led there, leaving my eyes uninjured, shows that, when I do not draw on them by constant literary labors, I can bear a great exposure to light and company.   During my absence I have been to bed no night till twelve or later, and have dined every day with a dinner party in a blaze of light.   Now for the old Aztecs again. . . . . . Shall I not work well after my holiday ? "

[*] The Rev. Jonathan M. Wainwright, afterwards Bishop of the Diocese of New York.   He had been from an earlier period a friend of Mr. Prescott, a member of his Club in Boston, and for some time, as Rector of Trinity Church, his clergyman.   Bishop Wainwright died in 1854.

But he did not. He found it as hard as ever to buckle on his harness afresh, and complained as much as ever of his indolence and listlessness. He however wrote a few pages, and then broke off, and we went — I mean both our families went — to Lebanon Springs, of which he made the following record : —

"Next day after to-morrow, June 2, I am going a journey with our friends the Ticknors to Lebanon Springs, and then

· ' To fresh fields and pastures new.' "

"June 11. — Returned from my excursion on the 9th. Now to resume my historical labors, and, I trust, with little interruption. The week has passed pleasantly, amidst the rich scenery of Lebanon, Stockbridge, and Lenox, which last we have visited, making the Springs our *point d'appui*. There are few enjoyments greater than that of wandering amidst beautiful landscapes with dear friends of taste and sympathies congenial to your own."

From this time until the " Conquest of Mexico " was finished he was very active and industrious, suffering hardly any interruption, and working with an interest which was not less the result of his devotion to his task than of the nature of his subject. Sometimes he advanced very rapidly, or at the rate of more than nine printed pages a day ; almost always doing more and enjoying it more when he was in the country than anywhere else.

On the 2d of August, 1843, the whole of the work was completed ; three years and about ten months from the time when he began the actual composition, and above five years from the time when he began to investigate the subject loosely and listlessly. His labor in the last months had been too severe, and he felt it. But he felt his success too. " On the whole," he writes the day he finished it, " the last two years have been the most industrious of my life, I think, — especially the last year, — and, as I have won the capital, entitle me to three months of literary loafing." [4]

[4] The following are his own dates respecting the composition of the " Conquest of Mexico."
" May, 1838. — Began scattered reading on the subject, doubtful if I get my documents from Spain. Very listless and *for-niente*-ish for a year. Over-visiting and not in spirits.
" April, 1839. — Began to read in earnest, having received MSS. from Madrid.
" Oct. 14, 1839. — Wrote first page of Introduction at Pepperell.

A few months earlier he had sold the right of publishing "The Conquest of Mexico" from stereotype plates furnished by himself to the Messrs. Harper and Brothers of New York.

"They are to have five thousand copies," he says, "paying therefor seven thousand five hundred dollars in cash (deducting three months' interest) at the date of publication. The right is limited to one year, during which they may publish as many more copies as they please on the same terms. . . . . . I hope they may not be disappointed, for their sakes as well as mine. But this is a different contract from that which ushered 'Ferdinand and Isabella' into the world."

His arrangements with his publishers made it necessary for him to deliver them the stereotype plates of the completed work by the 15th of October, and thus caused a pressure upon him to which he resolved that he would never again expose himself. But he needed not to feel anxious or hurried. His work was all stereotyped on the 10th of September.

He went immediately to Pepperell, that he might begin the pleasant "literary loafing" he had proposed as his reward. "I promise myself," he says, "a merry autumn with lounging at my ease among friends and idle books; a delicious contrast after the hard summer's work I have done." A part of this we spent with him, and found it as gay as he had anticipated. But, as he approached its end, a sad disappointment awaited him. On the 28th of October, his father suffered a slight shock of paralysis and the next day he wrote to me as follows.

PEPPERELL, Sunday Evening.

MY DEAR GEORGE,

I suppose you may have heard through William of our affliction in the illness of my father. As you may get incorrect impressions of his condition, I will briefly state it.

His left cheek was slightly, though very visibly, affected by the paralysis, — his articulation was so confused that he was scarcely intelligible, — and his mind was sadly bewildered. He was attacked in this way yesterday about half past nine A. M. In a few hours his face was restored to its

"March 1, 1841. — Finished Introduction and Part I. of Appendix.

"August 2, 1843. — Finished the work. So the Introduction, about half a vol., occupied about as long as the remaining 2½ vols. of dashing narrative.

"August, 1841 - August, 1842. — Composed 562 pages of print, text and notes of the narrative.

"August, 1842 - August, 1843. — Composed 425 pp. print, text and notes; revised Ticknor's corrections and his wife's of all the work. Corrected, &c. proofs of nearly all the work. The last Book required severe reading of MSS."

usual appearance. His articulation was gradually improved, and to-day is nearly perfect; and his mind has much brightened, so that you would not detect any failing unless your attention were called to it. I have no doubt the present attack will pass away in time without leaving permanent consequences. But for the future, I should tremble to lift the veil. There is an oppressive gloom over the landscape, such as it never wore to my eyes before. God bless you and yours.

Most affectionately,

WM. H. PRESCOTT.

GEORGE TICKNOR, Esq.

Later, he records his feelings in the same tone.

"A cloud is thrown over our happy way of life by the illness of my dear father, who three days since was attacked by a stroke of paralysis, which affected his speech materially, and for the first time threw a darkness over that fine intellect. The effects of the shock have, thank Heaven, much passed away; and we may hope that it is not intended that so much wisdom and goodness shall be taken away from us yet. Still it has filled me with a sadness such as but one other event of my life ever caused; for he has been always a part of myself; to whom I have confided every matter of any moment; on whose superior judgment I have relied in all affairs of the least consequence; and on whose breast I have been sure to find ready sympathy in every joy and sorrow. I have never read any book of merit without discussing it with him, and his noble example has been a light to my steps in all the chances and perplexities of life. When that light is withdrawn, life will wear a new and a dark aspect to me."

As he fondly anticipated, his father's health was soon in a great measure restored, and he enjoyed life much as he had done for some years previous to this attack. Meantime the inevitable press went on, and the "Conquest of Mexico" was published on the 6th of December, 1843.

"It is," he says, "six years next Christmas, since 'Ferdinand and Isabella' made their bow to the public. This second apparition of mine is by no means so stirring to my feelings. I don't know but the critic's stings, if pretty well poisoned, may not raise a little irritation. But I am sure I am quite proof against the anodyne of praise. Not that I expect much either. But criticism has got to be an old story. It is impossible for one who has done that sort of work himself to feel any respect for it. How can a critic look his brother in the face without laughing? As it is not in the power of the critics to write a poor author up into permanent estimation, so none but an author who has once been kindly received can write himself down. Yet I shall be sorry if the work does not receive the approbation of my friends here and abroad — *and of the few*." [5]

[5] It seems singular now that he should have had any anxiety about the success of the "Conquest of Mexico." But he had. Above a year earlier, he recorded his doubts: "The Ticknors, who have read my manuscript

But there was no need of this misgiving, or of any misgiving whatever. The work was greeted from one end of the United States to the other with a chorus of applause, such as was never vouchsafed to any other, of equal gravity and importance, that had been printed or reprinted among us. Within a month after it appeared, more than a hundred and thirty newspapers from different parts of the country had been sent to the author, all in one tone. Within the same period, many of the booksellers' shops were exhausted of their supplies several times, so as to be unable to meet the current demand. And finally, for a fortnight after the fourth thousand was sold, the whole market of the country was left bare. The five thousand copies, provided for by the contract, which he thought could hardly be sold within a year, disappeared, in fact, in about four months. The sale of the work was, therefore, as remarkable as the applause with which it had been received on its appearance. The author ceased to be anxious, and the publishers were jubilant.[*]

An English edition was at the same time published by Mr. Bentley in London; the copyright, after considerable negotiation, having been sold to him on the author's behalf by his kind and excellent friend, Colonel Aspinwall, for six hundred and fifty pounds. A second edition was called for in the May following, and Baudry published one at Paris in the original soon afterwards. It had at once a great run in England and on the Continent.

Of course, the reviews of all kinds and sizes were prompt in their notices. At home the authors of such criticisms ran no risk. They were to deal with a writer whose character was fully settled, in his own country at least. There was, therefore, no difference of opinion among them, no qualification, no reserve; certainly none that I remember, and none of any moment. A beautiful article, written with great judgment and

relating to the Conquest, assure me that the work will succeed. Would they were my enemies that say so! But they are friends to the backbone." He had the same misgivings, I know, until the work had been published two or three weeks.

[*] This was the genuine fruit of a well-earned fame, as the earliest sales in Boston of the "Ferdinand and Isabella" were the honorable fruit of great social and personal regard. See *ante*, p. 101.

kindness, by Mr. George S. Hillard, appeared in the "North American Review" for January, 1844, and was followed by two of no less power and finish in the "Christian Examiner" by Mr. George T. Curtis, and in the "Methodist Quarterly" by Mr. Joseph G. Cogswell. These all came from the hands of personal friends. But friendship was not needed to help the success of a book which, while it was settled on an assured foundation of facts carefully ascertained, yet read, in the narrative portions, like a romance, and was written in a style often not less glowing than that of Scott, and sometimes reminding us of what is finest in "Ivanhoe," or "The Talisman."

The same verdict, therefore, soon arrived from England, where the book was necessarily judged without reference to its author. The articles in the "Athenæum" were, I think, the earliest; one of no small ability, which appeared rather late, by Charles Philips, Esq., in the "Edinburgh," was, on the whole, the most laudatory. But they were all in the same spirit. A long and elaborate criticism, however, in the "Quarterly," written by the Rev. Mr. Milman, now (1862) the Dean of St. Paul's, was the most carefully considered and thorough of any. It gratified Mr. Prescott very much by its strong, manly sense and graceful scholarship, but still more by the estimate which a person of such known elevation of character placed upon the moral tendencies of the whole work. It became at once the foundation of an acquaintance which ripened afterwards into a sincere personal friendship.

But Mr. Prescott did not suffer these things to have more than their due weight with him, or to occupy much of his time or thought. After giving a slight notice of them, he says: "It is somewhat enervating, and has rather an unwholesome effect, to *podder* long over these personalities. The best course is action, — things, not self, — at all events not self-congratulation. So now I propose to dismiss all further thoughts of my literary success."

TO CHARLES LYELL, ESQ.[7]

NAHANT, July 11, 1842.

MY DEAR MR. LYELL,

I understand from Mrs. Ticknor that you are to be in town this week, previous to sailing. I trust we shall have the pleasure of shaking hands with you and Mrs. Lyell again before you shake the dust of our republican soil off your feet. Perhaps your geological explorations may lead you among our cliffs again. If so, will you and Mrs. L. oblige us by dining and making our house your head-quarters for the day? I regret, my father and mother are absent in the country this week. But I need not say, that it will give my wife and myself sincere pleasure to see you both, though we had rather it should be in the way of "how d' ye do," than "good-by." Pray remember me most kindly to Mrs. Lyell, and believe me

Very faithfully yours,

WM. H. PRESCOTT.

TO DON PASCUAL DE GAYANGOS.

BOSTON, Jan. 30, 1843.

MY DEAR FRIEND,

From yours of December 25th, I find you are still in London. I hope you received mine of November 14th, informing you of Mr. Tytler's kind offer to place his extracts from the State Paper Office at my disposal, and that you also received my note of December 1st. When you have examined the papers in Brussels and Paris you will be able to form an estimate of what the copying them will cost. I think that the first twenty letters in Raumer's "History of the Sixteenth and Seventeenth Centuries" show that there are very important materials in the Bibliothèque Royale in Paris; and I should think it would be well to get copies of the very documents of which he gives some slight abstracts. They seem, several of them, to relate to the private life of Philip and his family, and interesting details of the court in his reign, and the latter part of that of Charles the Fifth.

The Venetian *Relazioni* are, I suppose, some of them quite important, considering the minuteness with which the ministers of that republic entered into the affairs of the courts where they resided. Mr. Everett speaks of Mansard's account of these *Relations* as affording all the information one could desire to guide one. If Mr. E. is right, the Archives du Royaume, in the Hôtel Soubise, must also contain much of interest relating to our subject. But to say truth, valuable as are official documents, such as

---

[7] This letter is inserted here, as the first in a very interesting correspondence, of which large portions will hereafter be given, and which was terminated only by Mr. Prescott's death. Mr. Lyell — now Sir Charles Lyell — was in July, 1842, just finishing his first visit to the United States, of which he afterwards published an account in 1845, — one of the most acute and just views of the character and condition of the people of the United States that has ever been printed.

treaties, instructions to ministers, &c., I set still greater store by those
letters, diaries, domestic correspondence, which lay open the characters
and habits of the great actors in the drama.   The others furnish the cold
outlines, but these give us the warm coloring of history, — all that gives it
its charm and interest.   Such letters as Peter Martyr's, such notices as the
Quincuagenas of Oviedo, and such gossiping chronicles as Bernal Diaz's,
are worth an ocean of state papers for the historian of life and manners,
who would paint the civilization of a period.   Do you not think so ?

TO DON PASCUAL DE GAYANGOS.

"Boston, Jan. 30, 1843.
. . . . . You will also probably see Señor Benavides, my translator.*
I am greatly obliged by the account which you have given me of him and
the other translators, who, I suppose, will now abandon the ground.   You
say Señor B. will controvert some of my opinions.   So much the better,
if he does it in a courteous spirit, as I have no doubt he will ; for if he
did not approve of the work on the whole, he would, I should suppose,
hardly take the trouble to translate it.   If he presents views differing on
some points from mine, the reader will have more lights for getting at
truth, which ought to be the end of history.   Very likely I have pleased
my imagination with a *beau ideal* ; for you know I am born a republican,
but not a fierce one, and in my own country, indeed, am ranked among
what in England would correspond with the conservatives.
I hope his work will be got up in creditable style, as regards typographical execution, as well as in more important matters.   I should like to
make a good impression on my adopted countrymen, and a good dress
would help that.   From what you say of Señor Benavides I augur favor-
ably for the work.   I hope he will see the last London edition, full of
errors as it is in the Castilian.   You will be good enough to send me
some copies when it is published.

FROM MR. GALLATIN.

New York, June 22, 1843.
Dear Sir,
I feel much obliged to you for the copy of Veytia's "Historia Antigua
de Mexico," sent me by Mr. Catherwood.   Unfortunately I have so far
forgotten Spanish, as everything else which I learnt late in life, that to read
it has become a labor ; and Veytia is not very amusing or inviting.   Still
his work deserves attention.   The authorities he quotes are precisely those
of Clavigero, and the two books were written independent of each other.
I have only run through Veytia, and I intend (if I can) to read it more
carefully.   But the result in my mind, so far as I have compared, is that,
beyond the one hundred years which preceded the Spanish conquest, the
Mexican history is but little better than tradition ; at least beyond the
limits of the valley of Mexico.   Our best historical authorities are, as it

* Of the "Ferdinand and Isabella."

seems to me, those which the Spaniards found and saw on their arrival, and the still existing monuments. But I should not indulge in such crude conjectures, and wait with impatience for your work, the publication of which please to hasten that I may have a chance to read it. Please to accept the assurance of my high regard and distinguished consideration, and to believe me,

> Dear Sir,
>> Your obedient and faithful servant,
>>> ALBERT GALLATIN.

TO DON PASCUAL DE GAYANGOS.

BOSTON, Nov. 30, 1843.

MY DEAR FRIEND,

I am glad to find by your letter of October 10, that you are so comfortably established in Madrid, and most happy that you are placed in the Arabic chair for which you are so well qualified.[9] It is much preferable to an African mission on every account, and I hope, whatever party comes uppermost in your land of *trastornos*, you will not be disturbed in it.[10] I am not very much surprised at the impediments you met with in the public libraries from their confused state, and from the apathy of those who have the care of them. How can the regard for letters flourish amidst such cruel civil dissensions ? But *meliora speremus*. In the mean time I do not doubt that your habitual perseverance and the influence of your position will give you access to what is of most importance. You say nothing of the Escorial, in speaking of the great collections. Is not that a repository of much valuable historic matter ? And is it not in tolerable order ? I believe it used to be.

It will be very hard if the Spaniards refuse me admittance into their archives, when I am turning my information, as far as in my power, to exhibit their national prowess and achievements. I see I am already criticised by an English periodical for vindicating in too unqualified a manner the deeds of the old Conquerors. If you were in England, I should be sure of one champion, at least, to raise a voice in my favor ! But I hope it will not be needed.

You are most fortunate in having access to such private collections as those of Alva, Santa Cruz, Infantado, &c. The correspondence of the admiral of the Armada, and that also of Requesens, must have interest. It was the archives of the Santa Cruz family of which Señor Navarrete spoke as containing materials relating to Philip the Second. Pray thank that kind-hearted and venerable scholar for his many courtesies to me. You will of course add to our collection whatever he and his brother Academicians publish in reference to this reign.

---

[9] In the University of Madrid.

[10] Don Pascual had some thought of going, in an official capacity, to Tunis, &c., so as to collect Arabic manuscripts. In fact, he did go later; but not at this time, and not, I think, burdened with official cares.

FROM MR. ROGERS.

My dear Sir,

At Paris, where I was idling away one of the autumn months, I received your welcome letter; and I need not say with what pleasure I discovered your volumes on my table when I returned to London. Let me congratulate you on an achievement at once so bloodless and so honorable to your country and yourself.

"It seems to me," says Mr. Hume to Mr. Gibbon, "that your countrymen, for almost a whole generation, have given themselves up to barbarous and absurd faction, and have totally neglected all polite letters. I no longer expected any valuable production ever to come from them."

May it not in some measure be said even now of England and France, and I fear also of America, — the many who would except themselves there being for the most part a multitude of fast writers and fast readers, who descend from one abyss to another?

That you may long continue in health and strength, to set a better example, is the ardent but disinterested wish of one who cannot live to avail himself of it.

Sincerely yours,

S. ROGERS.

London, Nov. 30, 1843.

FROM MR. HALLAM.

WILTON CRESCENT, London, Dec. 29, 1843.

My dear Sir,

I received, not long after your letter reached my hands, a copy of your "History of the Conquest of Mexico," which you had so kindly led me to expect; and should have sooner acknowledged it, if my absence from London soon afterwards had not retarded my perusal of it, and if I had not been forced to wait some weeks for an opportunity of sending my answer through our friend Mr. Everett.

I sincerely congratulate you on this second success in our historic field. If the subject is not, to us at least of the Old World, quite equal in interest to the "History of Ferdinand and Isabella," you have perhaps been able to throw still more fresh light on the great events which you relate, from sources hardly accessible, and at least very little familiar to us. It has left Robertson's narrative, the only popular history we had, very far behind. But I confess that the history of your hero has attracted me less than those chapters relating to Mexican Antiquities, which at once excite our astonishment and curiosity. Mr. Stephens's work had already turned our minds to speculate on the remarkable phenomenon of a civilized nation decaying without, as far as we can judge, any subjugation, (or, of one by a more barbarous people, this, though not unprecedented, is still remarkable,) and without leaving any record of its existence. Some facts, if such they are, mentioned by you, are rather startling, especially those of religious analogy to Jewish and Christian doctrines; but they do not all seem to rest on certain evidence. If true, we must perhaps explain them by help of the Norwegian settlement.

Your style appears to me almost perfect, and better, I think, than in your former history. You are wholly free from what we call Americanisms. Sometimes I should think a phrase too colloquial, especially in the notes.

I beg you to give my best regards to Mr. and Mrs. Ticknor, when you next see them, and I remain, my dear sir,

Very faithfully yours,
HENRY HALLAM.

FROM MR. EVERETT.

LONDON, Jan. 2, 1844.

MY DEAR SIR,

..... We have been reading the "Conquest of Mexico" about our fireside, and finish the second volume this evening. I enjoy it more than its predecessor. The interest is of a more epic kind; and reading it aloud is more favorable to attention and effect. I think its success complete. I hear different opinions as to its merit compared with "Ferdinand and Isabella." Old Mr. Thomas Grenville (the son of George, of Stamp Act fame, and the collector, I think, of the best private library of its size I know) gives the preference to "Ferdinand and Isabella." Mr. Hallam inclines, I think, to prefer "The Conquest." He said he thought the style was rather easier in the latter; but Mr. Grenville made precisely the same criticism as to "Ferdinand and Isabella," which he told me he thought the ablest modern history in the English language. This extraordinary and venerable person was eighty-eight years old on the 31st of December. On that day he walked from his house near Hyde Park Corner to Stafford House, and called on me on his way home; not seeming more fatigued than I should have been with the same circuit. I once asked him if he recollected his uncle, Lord Chatham, and he answered that he recollected playing ninepins with him at the age of fourteen.

I enclose you a letter from Mr. Hallam. The article on your book in the "Quarterly," as I learn from Dr. Holland, was written by Mr. Milman. Mr. Grenville spoke with great severity of the article on "Ferdinand and Isabella" which appeared in the same journal.

MEMORANDA.

January 7, 1844. — The first entry in the New Year. It begins auspiciously for this second child of my brain, as 1838 did for its elder brother. More than a hundred and thirty papers from different parts of the country,[11] and a large number of kind notes from friends, attest the rapid circulation of the work, and the very favorable regard it receives from the public. The principal bookstores here have been exhausted of their

[11] These were sent to him in a flood, chiefly by mail and by his publishers.

copies two or three times, though there has always been a supply at the inferior depots. The Harpers have not been able to send the books nearly as fast as ordered. I suppose the delay is explained by the time occupied in binding them.

From the prevalent (with scarcely an exception) tone of criticism, I think three things may be established in regard to this History, of which I had previously great doubts. 1. The Introduction and chapter in Appendix I. are well regarded by the public, and I did not spend my time injudiciously on them. 2. The last book, on the biography of Cortés, is considered a necessary and interesting appendage. 3. The style of the whole work is considered richer, freer, more animated and graceful than that of "Ferdinand and Isabella." This last is a very important fact, for I wrote with much less fastidiousness and elaboration. Yet I rarely wrote without revolving the chapter many times in my mind before writing. But I did not podder over particular phrases.

. . . . . Had I accepted half of my good friend Folsom's criticisms, what would have become of the style? Yet they had and will always have their value for accurate analysis of language and thought, and for accuracy of general facts. My Postscripts, written with least labor, have been much commended as to style.

FROM LORD MORPETH.

CASTLE HOWARD, Jan. 23, 1844.

MY DEAR PRESCOTT,

You will have thought me over-long in answering your most gracious and precious gift of your "Mexico," but I sent you a message that you were not to have a word from me about it till I had quite finished it, and, as I read it out loud to my mother and sister, this has not taken place so soon as you might have expected. And now my poor verdict will come after you are saturated with the public applause, and will care mighty little for individual suffrage. Still I will hope that, however careless you may be of the approbation, you will not be wholly indifferent to the pleasure with which our occupation has been attended. Nothing could be more satisfactory than to roll along through your easy, animated, and pictured periods, and your candid and discriminating, but unassuming, disquisitions, and to have my own interest and approval shared by those to whom I read ; and then further to find the wide circle without corroborate our verdict,

> "And nations hail thee with a love like mine."

. . . .

We are getting through the mildest winter almost ever remembered. Before you receive this, I probably shall be a member of the House of Commons, a re-entry upon public turmoil of which I do not at all relish the prospect. Are you beginning Pizarro? How you must have pleased Rogers by your mention of him. Pray give my kindest regards to your family.

Believe me, ever affectionately yours,

MORPETH.

TO THE REV. H. H. MILMAN.

Boston, Jan. 30, 1844.

My dear Sir,

If you will allow one to address you so familiarly who has not the honor to be personally known to you ; and yet the frequency with which I have heard your name mentioned by some of our common friends, and my long familiarity with your writings, make me feel as if you were not a stranger to me. I have learnt from my friend Mr. Everett that you are the author of a paper in the last London "Quarterly" on the "Conquest of Mexico." It is unnecessary to say with what satisfaction I have read your elegant and encomiastic criticism, written throughout in that courteous and gentlemanlike tone, particularly grateful as coming from a Transatlantic critic, who has no national partialities to warp his judgment. Speaking the same language, nourished by the same literature, and with the same blood in our veins, I assure you the American scholar, next to his own country, looks for sympathy and countenance to his fatherland more than to any other country in the world. And when he receives the expression of it from those whom he has been accustomed to reverence, he has obtained one of his highest rewards.

May I ask you to remember me kindly to Mr. and Mrs. Lyell and to Mr. Hallam, and believe me, my dear sir,

With great respect,

Your obliged and obedient servant,

WM. H. PRESCOTT.

TO JOHN C. HAMILTON, ESQ., NEW YORK.

Boston, Feb. 10, 1844.

My dear Mr. Hamilton,

I have read the notice of my work in the last "Democratic Review," and as you interested yourself to get it written, you may perhaps be pleased to know my opinion about it. I like it very much. It is written throughout in a very courteous and gentlemanlike spirit. As far as I am personally concerned, I should be very unreasonable were I not gratified by the liberal commendation of my literary labors.

The great question of the proper standard of historic judgment is one in which of course I must be at issue with the writer, — or rather one in which he chooses to be at issue with me. In managing the argument, he shows much acuteness and plausibility. Yet if we accept his views of it, some of the fairest names in the dark period of the Middle Ages, and of antiquity, will wear a very ugly aspect. The immorality of the act and of the actor seem to me two very different things ; and while we judge the one by the immutable principles of right and wrong, we must try the other by the fluctuating standard of the age. The real question is, whether a man was sincere, and acted according to the lights of his age. We cannot fairly demand of a man to be in advance of his generation, and where a generation goes wrong, we may be sure that it is an error of the head, not of the heart. For a whole community, including its best and wisest, will not deliberately sanction the habitual perpetration of crime. This would be an anomaly in the history of man. The article in the last London "Quarterly," from the pen of Milman, a clergyman of the Church of England, you know, expressly approves of my moral estimate of Cortés. This is from a great organ of Orthodoxy. One might think the "Democratic" and the "Quarterly" had changed sides. Rather funny, *n'est ce pas?*

As to the question of fact, — what Cortés did, or did not do, — the "Reviewer" has leaned exclusively on one authority, that of the chronicler Diaz, an honest man, but passionate, credulous, querulous, and writing the reminiscences of fifty years back. Truth cannot be drawn from one source, but from complicated and often contradictory sources.

I think you will hardly agree that the Conqueror deserved censure for not throwing off his allegiance to the Emperor, and setting up for himself. However little we can comprehend the full feeling of loyalty, I think we can understand the baseness of treason. But I will not trouble you with an argument on this topic. I must say, however, that I respect the "Democratic," and am sure the "North American" contains few articles written with more ability than this, much as I differ from some of the positions taken in it.

I have run, I find, into an unconscionable length of line, which I hope you will excuse. Pray remember me kindly to your wife and daughter, and believe me,

Very sincerely, your friend,

WM. H. PRESCOTT.

FROM PATRICK FRASER TYTLER, ESQ.

84 Devonshire Place, April, 1844.

MY DEAR SIR,

Your precious present of the "History of Mexico," and the kind letter which accompanied it, found me entangled with my ninth and last volume of the "History of Scotland," and the winding up my imperfect labors. This must be my apology for a delay which has weighed heavily on my conscience, but I could not bear the idea of dipping into, or giving a hasty perusal to anything proceeding from your pen, and Cortés was deferred till Elizabeth and King Jamie were at rest. And now, my dear sir, let me thank you most sincerely for the delight and the instruction which I have received. "Ferdinand and Isabella" had prepared me to expect much; but in the "Conquest of Mexico" you have outstript yourself, and produced a work which can instruct the wisest, and charm and interest the youngest reader; which combines a pathetic and stirring narrative with some of the gravest lessons that can be derived from history. How you should have achieved such a work, under the continued privation to which you allude so simply and beautifully in your Preface, is to me, I own, little less than miraculous; for, composed under every advantage of individual consultation and research, "Mexico" would be a noble monument of labor and genius. Long, very long may you live to conquer such difficulties as would overwhelm any inferior mind.

9 *

Believe me, my dear Mr. Prescott, with sincere regard and respect, most truly yours,

PATRICK FRASER TYTLER.

P. S.   I have sent along with this the ninth and last volume of my "History of Scotland," with some manuscripts, letters, and extracts, relating to the times of Philip and Mary, which I copied from the originals in the State Paper Office.   These are entirely at your service, if they can be of the least assistance in the researches into this period which I understood you at one time contemplated.

FROM THE REV. H. H. MILMAN.

Cloisters, Westminster Abbey, April 12, 1844.

MY DEAR SIR,
I reproach myself for having delayed so long to acknowledge the note in which you expressed your gratification at the notice of your Mexican work in the "Quarterly Review."   I assure you that nothing could give me greater pleasure than finding an opportunity of thus publicly, though anonymously, declaring my high opinion of your writings.   Our many common friends have taught me to feel as much respect for your private character as your writings have commanded as an author.   I was much amused, after I had commenced the article, with receiving a letter from our friend Lord Morpeth, expressing an anxious hope that justice would be done to the work in the "Quarterly Review."   Without betraying my secret, I was able to set his mind at rest.

Can we not persuade you to extend your personal acquaintance with our men of letters, and others whose society you would appreciate, by a visit to England?   Perhaps you might not find much to assist you in your researches (if report speaks true, that you are engaged on the Conquest of Peru), which you cannot command in America, yet even in that respect our libraries might be of service.   But of this I am sure, that no one would be received with greater cordiality or more universal esteem.

If this be impossible or impracticable, allow me to assure you that I shall be delighted if this opening of our correspondence should lead to further acquaintance, even by letter.   I shall always feel the greatest interest in the labors of one who does so much honor to our common literature. In letters we must be brethren, and God grant that we may be in political relations, and in reciprocal feelings of respect and regard.

Believe me, my dear sir, ever faithfully yours,

H. H. MILMAN.

CHAPTER XVI.

1844.

IT has, I believe, been generally thought that Mr. Prescott's style reached its happiest development in his "Conquest of Mexico." No doubt, a more exact finish prevails in many parts of the "Ferdinand and Isabella," and a high authority has said that there are portions of "Philip the Second" written with a vigor as great as its author has anywhere shown.[1] But the freshness and freedom of his descriptions in the "Mexico," especially the descriptions of scenery, battles, and marches, are, I think, not found to the same degree in either of his other histories, and have rendered the style of that work singularly attractive. Certainly, it is a style well fitted to its romantic subject, although it may be one which it would have been adventurous or unwise to apply, in the same degree, to subjects from their nature more grave and philosophical.

But whatever Mr. Prescott's style may at any period have been, or in whichever of his works its development may have been most successful, it was unquestionably the result of much consideration and labor, and of very peculiar modes of composition. With what self-distrust he went back, when he was already above twenty-five years old, and toiled through Murray's English Grammar, and Blair's Rhetoric, as if he were a schoolboy, and how he followed up these humble studies with a regular investigation of what was characteristic in all the great English prose-writers, from Roger Ascham down to our own times, we have already seen. It was a deep and solid

---

[1] Letter from Dean Milman.

foundation, laid with a distinct purpose, that cannot be mistaken, and one which, in years subsequent, well repaid the weary hours it cost him. I remember how conscientious and disagreeable these labors were, for he sometimes grew impatient and complained of them. But he persevered, as he always did in what he deliberately undertook.

He determined, however, at the same time, that, whatever his style might be, it should be his own.

" Every one," he said at the outset of his severer studies, " pours out his thoughts best in a style suited to his own peculiar habits of thinking.

" The best method for a man of sense to pursue is to examine his own composition, after a sufficiently long period shall have elapsed for him to have forgotten it. He will then be in a situation to pronounce upon his own works as upon another's.[2] He may consult one or two good friends in private. Their opinions will be valuable, inasmuch as they will in all probability be more honest and sincere than a printed criticism, and, moreover, they will not exert the same depressing influence on the spirits that a reverence for public criticism is apt to beget. I am inclined to believe that it would be for a man's interest as an author never to consult a printed criticism on his own publications." [3]

These were wise and wary conclusions to have been reached so early in his literary life, and they were substantially adhered to through the whole of it. He did not, however, refrain from reading the criticisms that appeared on his larger works, because they were unfavorable. None, it is true, were really such. But whether he read them or not, he judged and corrected whatever he wrote with the assistance of at least one friend, exactly in the way he has here indicated; maintaining, however, at all times, an entire independence of opinion as to his own style.

Imitation he heartily dreaded. Five years before he began his " Ferdinand and Isabella," he said : " Model myself upon no manner. A good imitation is disgusting, — what must a

[2] " In order to correct my own history advantageously," he said, nine years later, when he was just beginning to write his " Ferdinand and Isabella," " I must never revise what I have written until after an interval of as many years as possible."

[3] I think the tone of these remarks about " printed criticisms " is owing to certain notices of the " Club-Room " that appeared about that time, and which I know somewhat annoyed him. He would hardly have made them later, when he wrote an article on Sir Walter Scott, where he speaks very slightingly of reviewers and their criticisms.

bad one be?" "Rely on myself for criticism of my own compositions." "Neither consult nor imitate any model for style, but follow my own natural current of expression."

This sort of independence, however, made him only more rigorous with himself. When he had been four months employed on his "Ferdinand and Isabella," he made this memorandum:—

Two or three faults of style occur to me in looking over some former compositions.[4] Too many adjectives; too many couplets of substantives, as well as adjectives, and perhaps of verbs; too set; sentences too much in the same mould; too formal periphrasis instead of familiar; sentences balanced by *ands*, *buts*, and semicolons; too many precise, emphatic pronouns, as *these*, *those*, *which*, &c., instead of the particles *the*, *a*, &c.

He even went into an elaborate inquiry as to the punctuation he should adopt, and as to the proper use of capital initials, recording the whole with care for his own government. But, after all his pains, he failed for a long time to satisfy himself. Every word he wrote of the early chapters of the "Ferdinand and Isabella" was rewritten, when he came to prepare that work for the press. So was the beginning of the "Mexico," and I think also that of the "Peru." One reason of this, especially in the first instance, was, that he thought he had been too elaborate. He early said, "On the whole, I think, with less fastidiousness I should write better." And, long before he published his "Ferdinand and Isabella," he deliberately recorded:—

With regard to the style of this work I will only remark that most of the defects, such as they are, may be comprehended in the words *trop soigné*. At least, they may be traced to this source. The only rule is, to write with freedom and nature, even with homeliness of expression occasionally, and with alternation of long and short sentences; for such variety is essential to harmony. But, after all, it is not the construction of the sentence, but the tone of the coloring, which produces the effect. If the sentiment is warm, lively, forcible, the reader will be carried along without much heed to the arrangement of the periods, which differs exceedingly in different standard writers. Put life into the narrative, if you would have it take. Elaborate and artificial fastidiousness in the form of expression is highly detrimental to this. A book may be made up of perfect sentences and yet the general impression be very imperfect. In fine, be engrossed with the thought, and not with the fashion of expressing it.

4 Probably articles in the "Club-Room" and the "North American Review."

As he advanced with his work, he grew less and less anxious for anything like a formal exactness in his style, or rather, perhaps I should say, he became more and more persuaded of the importance of freedom.

"I am now convinced from experience," he says, after four years' trial, "that fastidious care and precision as to style, when composing, are fatal to excellence as well as to rapidity of writing, excluding many not merely legitimate expressions, but positive graces and beauties of language, as well as nature and ease."

No doubt he profited all his life by the pains he early took with his style, and certainly he never regretted it, minute and troublesome as it had been.   Nor did he ever cease to scrutinize with patience what he had freely composed, and to correct it, even in the proof-sheets, with severity.   But undoubtedly, too, his first draft in his noctograph was made every year with increasing boldness and ease.   In this respect he was like a person who in his childhood has been trained to good manners, and in his riper years proves the gentleness of his breeding without remembering or in any way showing the rules by which he had been drilled to it.

But at last the day of reckoning came.   "The History of Ferdinand and Isabella," on which he had labored so long and so conscientiously, was published, and all the Reviews, or almost all of them, made a point of discussing its style.   None complained, except the "London Quarterly," in which a somewhat dashing, but on the whole brilliant and favorable article appeared, written by Mr. Richard Ford, the distinguished Spanish scholar, with whom afterwards Mr. Prescott became personally acquainted, and enjoyed a pleasant correspondence. This article Mr. Prescott read carefully more than once.   It somewhat disturbed his equanimity, and led him to an examination of his style as compared with that of English writers whose purity and excellence are acknowledged.   He gave several days to the task, the unpleasantness of which did not prevent him from making it thorough, and then he recorded his deliberate and singularly candid opinion as follows : —

The only strictures [in this article] which weigh a feather with me are those on my style, in forming which I have taken much pains, and of the success of which I am not the best judge. This I may say, however, that of the numerous notices of the work, both in this country and in Europe, while almost all have commended more or less — and some excessively — the diction, none, that I am aware, have censured it. Many of these critics are scholars, entirely competent to form a judgment on its merits ; more so, to judge from their own styles, than the critic in question. I have received and seen many letters from similar sources to the same effect. Indeed, the work could not have obtained its rapid and wide popularity, had the execution been *bad* in this all-important respect.

I say not this to lay a flattering unction to my soul, but to put myself on my guard against rashly attempting a change in a very important matter on insufficient grounds, and thus, perhaps, risking for the future one of the most essential elements of past success. Nevertheless, I have devoted several days to a careful scrutiny of my defects, and to a comparison of my style with that of standard English writers of the present time.

Master Ford complains of my text as being too formal, and my notes as having too much levity. This shows some versatility in me, at all events. As regards the former, it seems to me, the first and sometimes the second volume affords examples of the use of words not so simple as might be ; not objectionable in themselves, but unless something is gained in the way of strength or of coloring it is best to use the most simple, *unnoticeable* words to express ordinary things ; ex. gr. " to send " is better than " to transmit " ; " crown descended " better than " devolved " ; " guns fired " than " guns discharged " ; " to name," or " call," than " to nominate " ; " to read " than " peruse " ; " the term," or " name," than " appellation," and so forth. It is better also not to encumber the sentence with long, lumbering nouns ; as, " the relinquishment of," instead of " relinquishing " ; " the embellishment and fortification of," instead of " embellishing and fortifying " ; and so forth. I can discern no other warrant for Master Ford's criticism than the occasional use of these and similar words on such commonplace matters as would make the simpler forms of expression preferable. In my third volume, I do not find the language open to much censure.

As to the notes, it is doubtless bad taste to shock the current of feeling, where there is much solemnity or pathos in the text, by unseasonable jests. But I do not find such in such places. In regard to them I do not find anything to alter in any particular in future.

My conclusion from the whole is, — after a very honest and careful examination of the matter, — that the reader may take my style for better or worse as it now is formed, and that it is not worth while for me to attempt any alteration in it until I meet a safer critic to point out its defects than Master Ford.

One more conclusion is, that I will not hereafter vex myself with anxious thoughts about my style when composing. It is formed. And if there be any ground for the imputation that it is too formal, it will only be made worse in this respect by extra-solicitude. It is not the defect to which I am predisposed. The best security against it is to write with less elaboration ; a pleasant recipe, which conforms to my previous views. This determination will save me trouble and time. Hereafter what I print shall undergo no ordeal for the style's sake, except only the grammar, and *that* I may safely trust to my Harvard Aldus.[5]

To the latter part of this decision he did not adhere. He asked counsel to the end of life about his works before they were printed, and corrected them with no less care than he had done earlier. But he never interfered with the general characteristics of his style, nor permitted any friend or critic to do it.

"A man's style," he said, as a final settlement of his opinion on the whole matter, — "a man's style, to be worth anything, should be the natural expression of his mental character, and where it is not, the style is either painfully affected, or it falls into that conventional tone which, like a domino at a masquerade, or the tone of good-breeding in society, may be assumed by anybody that takes pains to acquire it; fitting one person as well as another, and belonging to anybody, — nobody. The best consequence of such a style is, that it offends no one. It delights no one, for it is commonplace. It is true that genius will show itself under this coating, as an original will peep out under a domino. But this is not the best dress for it. The best, undoubtedly, for every writer, is the form of expression best suited to his peculiar turn of thinking, even at some hazard of violating the conventional tone of the most chaste and careful writers. It is this alone which can give full force to his thoughts. Franklin's style would have borne more ornament, — Washington Irving could have done with less, — Johnson and Gibbon might have had much less formality, and Hume and Goldsmith have occasionally pointed their sentences with more effect. But, if they had abandoned the natural suggestions of their genius, and aimed at the contrary, would they not in mending a hole, as Scott says, have very likely made two?

"There are certain faults which no writer must commit: false metaphors; solecisms of grammar; unmeaning and tautological expressions; for these contravene the fundamental laws of all writing, the object of which must be to express one's ideas clearly and correctly. But, within these limits, the widest latitude should be allowed to taste and to the power of unfolding the thoughts of the writer in all their vividness and originality. Originality — the originality of nature — compensates for a thousand minor blemishes.

"Of one thing a writer may be sure, if he adopt a manner foreign to his mind he will never please. Johnson says, 'Whoever would write in a good style, &c., &c., must devote his days and nights to the study of Addison.'[6] Had he done so, or had Addison formed his style on Johnson's,

---

[5] Mr. Folsom.

[6] Johnson is a little more cautious in his phraseology, but the substance of his meaning, so far as it was needed for the purpose in hand, is given in the text with sufficient precision. His exact words are: "Whoever wishes to attain an English style, *familiar, but not coarse, and elegant, but not ostentatious*, must give his days and his nights to the volumes of Addison." It is the last sentence in Addison's Life, and was, no doubt, intended, by its position, for a sort of epigrammatic effect.

what a ridiculous figure each would have cut ! One man's style will no more fit another, than one man's coat, or hat, or shoes will fit another. They will be sure to be too big, or too small, or too something, that will make the wearer of them ill at ease, and probably ridiculous.

" It is very easy for a cool, caustic critic, like Brougham, to take to pieces the fine gossamer of Dr. Channing's style,[1] which has charmed thousands of readers in this country and in Europe, and the Doctor would be a fool to give up his glorious mystifications — if they are such — for the home-spun, matter-of-fact materials out of which a plainer and less imaginative mind would make its tissue. It would be impossible for Brougham — in his way of writing, tolerably set and sometimes pedantic, with an occasional air of familiarity that matches the rest of the sentences badly enough — to ascend into the regions of the true sublime, as Dr. Channing does, or to call up such a strong sense of the beautiful. It may be the best style for criticism, however, — the best for the practical, ordinary uses of life. But I should not advise the Doctor to take it up, and still less the Ex-Chancellor to venture into the Doctor's balloon, or — as his admirers might think — his chariot of fire.

" How many varieties of beauty and excellence there are in this world ! As many in the mental as the material creation, and it is a pedantic spirit which, under the despotic name of taste, would reduce them all to one dull uniform level. A writer who has succeeded in gaining the public favor should be cautious how he makes any innovation in his habitual style. The form of expression is so nicely associated with the idea expressed, that it is impossible to say how much of his success is owing to the one or the other. It is very certain, however, that no work in any of the departments of the belles-lettres can dispense with excellence of style of some kind or other. If this be wanting, a work, however sound or original in the conception, can hardly be popular, for it cannot give pleasure or create interest, — things essential in every kind of composition which has not science *exclusively* for its end.

" Let the writer, therefore, who has once succeeded in gaining the public suffrages, — the suffrages of the higher public, the well-educated, — let him beware how he tampers with the style in which he has before approached them. Let him be still more slow to do this in obedience to the suggestions of a few ; for style is the very thing which, all-important as it is, every well-educated man is competent to judge of. In fact, he had better not make any serious innovation in it, unless, like Sharon Turner or Jeremy Bentham, it is the object of such universal censure as shows he has succeeded in spite of it, and not in consequence of it. Innovation is not reform in writing any more than in politics. The best rule is to dispense with all rules except those of grammar, and to consult the natural bent of one's genius."

Saving the last sweeping sentence, — which I suspect was

[1] This refers to a somewhat bitter review of Dr. Channing, in the " Edinburgh " for October, 1829, by Lord Brougham, — a man who could no more comprehend Dr. Channing, as an eminent person who knew him well once said, than Dickens could comprehend Laplace.

N

prompted by the half-play upon the word "rules," and to whose doctrine the author of the "Conquest of Mexico" and of "Philip the Second" by no means conformed in his own practice, — I do not know where, within the same compass, so much good sense on the subject of style is uttered with so much spirit and point.

But, whatever we may think of the opinions contained in these striking extracts, one fact is plain from them; I mean that, while their author was willing and even glad to profit by Mr. Ford's criticisms in the "Quarterly Review," he was thoroughly independent in the use he made of them, and thoroughly determined that, at all hazards, his style should be his own, and should not be materially modified by anybody's unfavorable opinion of it, unless he were satisfied the opinion was just. In this he was right. The success of the "Ferdinand and Isabella" had no doubt given him increased confidence in his manner of writing, and the habit of composing entirely in his memory had given him both greater freedom and greater facility.[*]   But, even before this, his style had become substantially what it always was after he was tolerably advanced in the "Ferdinand and Isabella." It had, in fact, from its first proper formation, been settled on foundations too deep to be shaken.

Instead, therefore, of writing more anxiously, in consequence of Mr. Ford's criticisms, he wrote more freely. While he was employed on his next work, "The Conquest of Mexico," he made such memoranda as the following: "I will write *calamo currente*, and not weigh out my words like gold-dust, which they are far from being." "Be not fastidious, especially about phraseology. Do not work for too much euphony. It is lost in the mass." "Do not elaborate and *podder* over the style." "Think more of general effect; don't quiddle."

When the "Mexico" was published, he found no reason to regret the indulgence he had thus granted to himself in its

[*] " Tried to write with imperfect *pre-thinking*, i. e. thinking, as Irving said to me, with a pen. It won't do for bad eyes. It requires too much correcting. The correcting in the mind and writing from memory suit my peculiarities bodily, and, I suspect, mental, better than the other process." He was approaching the end of the " Conquest of Mexico" when he wrote this.

composition. He learned, at once, from the Reviews and in many other ways, that his manner was regarded as richer, freer, more animated and graceful than it had been in his " Ferdinand and Isabella." " This," he says, " is a very important fact; for I wrote with much less fastidiousness and elaboration. Yet I rarely wrote without revolving the chapter half a dozen times in my mind. But I did not *podder* over particular phrases. Had I accepted half of my good friend Folsom's corrections, what would have become of my style? Yet they had, and always will have, their value for accurate analysis of language and thought." *

From this time to the end of his life, — a period of fifteen years, — he makes hardly any memoranda on his style, and none of any consequence. Nor was there reason why he should. His manner of writing was, from the time he published " The Conquest of Mexico," not only formed but sanctioned ; and sanctioned, not only by the public at large, but by those whose opinion is decisive. Mr. Milman's review of that work, and the conclusion of one in the " Christian Examiner" by Mr. George T. Curtis, — in both of which the remarks on his style are very beautiful, and, as I know, gave Mr. Prescott much pleasure, — left no doubt in his mind touching this point. Hallam, too, noticed by Sir James Mackintosh as singularly parsimonious in commendation, wrote to Mr. Prescott, December 29th, 1843 : " Your style appears to me to be nearly perfect." With these judgments before him, and others hardly less valued and safe, he had no motive for reconsidering his style, if he had desired, for any reason, to do so. But he was too wise to desire it.

It may, perhaps, seem singular to those who knew him little, that such a style should have been formed by such a process ; that the severe, minute rules and principles in which it was originally laid should have been, as it were, cavalierly thrown aside, and a manner, sometimes gay and sparkling, sometimes rich and eloquent, but always natural and easy, should have

---

* Mr. Folsom had the excellent habit of noting whatever occurred to him as doubtful, no less than what he regarded as a blemish, thinking that such minute suggestions were due to the author. I speak as one who has profited by his skill and kindness.

been the result. This, however, was characteristic of his whole moral constitution and conduct, and was in harmony with the principles and habits that in other respects governed his life. Thus every day in his study he was rigorous with himself, and watchful of those he employed; but in his family and with his friends nobody was more free, gay, and unexacting. Those who met him only at the dinner-table, or in general society, would be surprised to learn that his wine even there was carefully measured, and that, if he seemed to indulge as much as others did, and to enjoy his indulgence more, it was all upon a system settled beforehand, just as much as was his spare everyday diet at home. How vigilant he was in whatever regarded his character; how strictly he called himself to account in those solitary half-hours on Sunday when he looked over the secret record of his failings and faults, we have seen; but who ever saw restraint in his manner when he was with others; who ever saw him when he seemed to be watchful of himself, or to be thinking of the principles that governed his life? And just so it was with his style. He wrote rapidly and easily. But the rules and principles on which his manner rested, even down to its smallest details, had been so early and so deeply settled, that they had become like instincts, and were neither recurred to nor needed when he was in the final act of composition.[10]

But there was one charm in Mr. Prescott's style which, I think, was much felt, without being much understood by the great mass of his readers. He put not a little of his personal character into it; a great deal more, I think, than is common with writers of acknowledged eminence. The consequence was, that the multitudes who knew him in no way except as an author were yet insensibly drawn to him by the qualities that made him so dear to his friends as a man, and felt, in some degree, the attachment that is commonly the result only

---

[10] There are some remarks by Mr. Prescott on purity of style, in his Memoir of Mr. John Pickering (Massachusetts Historical Society's Collections, 8vo, Third Series, Vol. X. pp. 210, 211), which are valuable. But they relate chiefly to the danger of Americanisms, as they are called, Mr. Prescott maintaining that "one and the same language cannot have two standards of purity." See also what Mr. Marsh says in his excellent Lectures on the English Language (1860), pp. 446 sqq.

of personal intercourse. They seemed to know him more than they know other authors whom they have never seen ; and, as most of us have favorite writers without being able always to explain why they are such, he became peculiarly so to many, who yet never stopped to inquire what was the cause of an interest so agreeable to them.

To this result — the insensible communication to his works of so much that belonged to himself personally and to his inmost nature — two circumstances, immediately connected with the infirmity of his sight, I doubt not, contributed.

The first of these circumstances was the long and severe thought which he felt himself compelled to give in the course of his investigation of any subject, before he began to write on it. For, after he had collected the materials for any chapter, or other less definite portion of his subject, — that is, after everything about it in the way of authority or opinion had been read to him, and he had caused it all to be embodied in short notes, to which he listened again and again, as the only way to make himself master of their contents, — then he sat down, as we have seen, in silence, and gave to the whole the benefit of the most vigorous action of his own mind. Being generally unable to look at all at the notes which had been thus prepared for him, he turned every fact or circumstance in the case on which he was employed over and over again in his memory, and examined on every side whatever related to it. While doing this, he put the greatest stress he was able to put on his faculties, and urged his mind to the most concentrated and unbroken action, so as to make sure that he had mastered all the details. And this process was sometimes long-continued. I knew one instance in which, after preparatory investigations which occupied only two days, he gave yet three days more to the mere shaping and moulding of his materials. The result was sure. The general outline was right, if it was in his power to make it so. But no other process, I suppose, could have so completely digested and harmonized his materials, or made them so completely a part of himself; no other process could have tinged his works so largely and so deeply with what was most characteristic of his own mind and temperament ; nothing could have made so certain to the reader his love of truth, of justice, of liberty, of toleration. And for these and other kindred qualities, thus insensibly but thoroughly infused into the very materials and fabric of his tissues, though almost never seen on their surface, the reader, after a little experience, came to trust the author, and take a personal interest in him, without considering or knowing exactly why he did it. The chord of sympathy between them was invisible, indeed, but it was already there, and it was strong enough to hold them together.

But thus far in the process of his work not a phrase or sentence had been adjusted or thought out. The composition, as that word is commonly understood, was still to be done. And here again his infirmity was a controlling influence, and is to be counted among the secrets of a manner which has been found at once so simple and so charming. He was compelled to prepare everything, down to the smallest details, in his memory, and to correct and fashion it all while it was still held there in silent suspense; after which he wrote it down, by means of his noctograph, in the freest and boldest manner, without any opportunity really to change the phraseology as he went along, and with little power to alter or modify it afterwards. This, I doubt not, was among the principal causes of the strength as well as of the grace, ease, and attractiveness of his style. It gave a life, a freshness, a freedom, both to his thoughts and to his mode of expressing them. It made his composition more akin than it could otherwise have been to the peculiar fervor and happiness of extemporaneous discussion. It not only enabled but it led him to address his reader, as it were, with his natural voice, so that those who never heard a word from his lips seemed yet, in this way, to find something like its effects in the flow and cadence of his sentences.

By such processes and habits, Mr. Prescott's style, which he began to form with a distinct purpose in 1822, became, before he had finished the "Ferdinand and Isabella," fifteen years afterwards, in its essential characteristics, what it is in all his published historical works. At first, this mode of composition — so different from the common one of composing while the pen is in the author's hand, excited and influenced as most writers are by its mechanical movements, and by the associations they awaken — was difficult and disagreeable. But I never knew him to give up any good thing for either of these reasons. On the contrary, he always went on the more earnestly. And the extent to which, in this particular case, he succeeded, was remarkable. For, as we have seen, he was able to carry what was equal to sixty pages of printed matter in his memory for many days, correcting and finishing its style as he walked or rode or drove for his daily exercise.

In 1839, therefore, after going carefully over the whole ground, he said, as we have noticed, "My conclusion is, that the reader may take my style for better or for worse, as it now is." And to this conclusion he wisely adhered. His manner became, perhaps, a little freer and easier, from continued practice, and from the confidence that success necessarily brings with it; but, in its essential elements and characteristics, it was never changed.

CHAPTER XVII.

1844 — 1845.

"AND now," he says on the 3d of February, 1844, — "now I propose to break ground on 'Peru.' I shall work the mine, however, at my leisure. Why should I hurry?" Nor did he. On the contrary, he procrastinated, as usual, from an unwillingness to begin hard work. He sat to Mr. Joseph Ames for his portrait in oils, an excellent piece of coloring, now in the possession of Mr. James Lawrence, and to Mr. Richard S. Greenough for a bust, now in the possession of Mrs. Prescott, beautiful as a work of art, and very valuable as a happy likeness at the period when it was taken. But the sittings to these artists consumed a good deal of time, and broke up many days in February and March. He was, however, too willing to be idle.

In the middle of April he made a visit to New York, partly out of listlessness, and partly in order to settle some trifling affairs with his publishers. It was designed to fill only a few days; but, by the solicitations of friends and the eagerness to become acquainted with him on the part of those who had not earlier enjoyed that pleasure, it proved to be a visit of a fortnight, and a very gay and happy one.

"Three weeks since," he says under date of May 5th, 1844, "I went to New York, thinking I might pass a couple of days. It turned out twelve, and then I found it no easy matter to break away from friends who, during my stay there, feasted and fêted me to the top of my constitution. Not a day in which I rose before nine, dined before five or six, went to bed before twelve. Two years ago I did not know half a dozen New-Yorkers; I have now made the acquaintance of two hundred at least, and the friendship, I trust, of many. The cordiality with which I was greeted is one of the most gratifying tributes I have received from my country men, coming as it did from all classes and professions. It pleased me that the head of the Roman Catholic clergy, Archbishop Hughes, a highly respectable person, should openly thank and commend me for 'the liberality I had shown in my treatment of the Catholics.'[1] I have stood the tug of social war pretty well. Yet, on the whole, it was too long a time for such excitement. Five days should be the limit. The faculties become weary, and the time does not move so fleetly as in the regular occupations at home. How could I stand then a season in London? I shall not try. Nor shall I ever exceed two, or at most three days, in a great American city."

During all this time — I mean during the autumn, winter, and spring of 1843 and 1844 — he thought very little of his "Conquest of Peru." He even, for a large part of the period, made few entries among his literary memoranda; and when he began the record again, after an absolute silence of almost three months, he says, in relation to this unwonted neglect, that it was indeed a very long interval, and that such long intervals were proof either of great occupation or great idleness. "The latter," he adds, "will account for this."

He had, however, not been so wholly idle as such self-reproach might seem to imply. He had listened to the Inca Garcilasso's important Commentaries on the earliest history and traditions of Peru; to some of the more familiar and common writers who cover the same ground; and to a manuscript of Sarmiento, President of the Royal Council of the Indies, who had travelled in that part of South America immediately after its conquest, and who is one of the most ample and trustworthy authorities for its early condition. It was not, indeed, much to have accomplished in so long a time, nor was any of it difficult or disagreeable; but his interruptions had been many and inevitable. During his father's illness he had watched

---

[1] In connection with this well-deserved commendation from a man so eminent, may be aptly mentioned a remark which the late President John Quincy Adams made to Mr. Edmund B. Otis, who, during four years, rendered excellent and kind service to Mr. Prescott, as his secretary. "Mr. Adams said, that Mr. Prescott possessed the two great qualifications of an historian, who should be apparently without country and without religion. This," Mr. Otis adds, "he explained by saying that the history should not show the political or religious bias of the historian. It would be difficult, Mr. Adams thought, to tell whether Mr. Prescott were a Protestant or a Catholic, a monarchist or a republican." See Appendix (O).

10

him with a care that interfered not a little with his own regular occupations, and during his convalescence had accompanied him in many a long walk, from which he derived no little pleasure and consolation. But his father, whose faculties had not been impaired by his illness, was now restored to as much physical health as he was ever likely to enjoy, and, from his nature, rather preferred to be independent in his out-of-door exercise than to be assisted or accompanied. The son, therefore, after nine months of "literary loafing," as he called it, instead of three, which he had proposed to himself, turned resolutely to his new work.

He did not need to make a collection of materials for it. That had been done when he gathered his ample stores for the " Conquest of Mexico." His first studies were on Cieza de Leon, the careful geographer of Peru, contemporary almost with its conquest; on Diego Fernandez de Palencia, a somewhat tedious chronicler of the country at the same period; on Fernando Montesinos, who lived a century later, and is much less trustworthy; and on the crude collections of Lord Kingsborough, made in our own time, but marked with the credulity and rashness of the time of the Pizarros. This reading, and more of the same sort during the summer of 1844, all related to the mythical rather than to the historical period of Peruvian Antiquities; and before the month of August was ended the mere notes and references for this part of his subject filled above three hundred compact pages. It was not, indeed, so important as the corresponding period of the Mexican annals, but it was interesting, and had its peculiar attractions. He made his plan for it, accordingly, and, having accumulated notes to the amount of eighty large sheets, allowed five or six months for the work, and a hundred pages. But here, as in the case of the " Mexico," he was mistaken, although his error was less considerable. It took eight months and made a hundred and eighty pages; more troublesome and disagreeable from the nature of the subject than any other part of the work, and in some respects more so than the Introduction to the " Conquest of Mexico."

But before he could put pen to paper, the course of his studies was again interrupted, first by the death of his brother

Edward,[2] which occurred at sea on a voyage to Europe, and afterwards by a journey to Niagara on account of his daughter's health, which for some months had given cause for anxiety. At last, however, after reading Alfieri's life to quicken his courage, he began his work in earnest. " I find it very difficult," he said, " to screw up my wits to the historic pitch ; so much for the vagabond life I have been leading ; and breaking ground on a new subject is always a dreary business."

He wrote the first sentences on the 12th of August, 1844, a little more than a year from the time when he had completed his " Conquest of Mexico." He was at Nahant, where — what with the rheumatism which often troubled him much in that damp climate, and the interruptions of company, which at such a watering-place could not always be avoided, he found his progress both slow and uneasy. But he made vigorous efforts with himself, and succeeded, before he left the sea-shore, so far as to make the following record : —

Industry good, and with increased interest. Spirits — an amiable word for temper — improved. Best recipe, occupation with things, not self.

At Pepperell, where, as was his custom, he passed the early autumn, he pursued his labors in a manner still more satisfactory to himself.

" Industry," he says, referring to the good effects of a tranquil country-life, — " industry, as usual, excellent ; interest awakened ; progress sensible ; the steam is up."

And again a few days later : —

I have got my working-tackle on board, and should be delighted not to quit these highland solitudes till they are buried under snow-drifts. Now, how glorious they are to eye and car and every other sense, — the glories of an American autumn. Surely a man is better, and forms a better estimate of life and its worthlessness here in the country than anywhere else.

The town, as he anticipated, was less favorable to work. When he had been there some time, he noted : " Nearly three weeks in town, and not looked at ' Peru.' The old sin of the town. Shall I never reform ? " Still, after the pressure of

[2] For a notice of his brother Edward, see Appendix (A), on the Prescott family.

affairs which had accumulated during his absence was removed, and a little gay lounging among his friends was over, he was going on well again, when he was stopped by a great sorrow. His father died suddenly on Sunday morning, the 8th of December, and an hour afterwards I received from him the following note : —

> MY DEAR FRIEND,
>
> I write to tell you, what you may learn from other sources, and what will give you much pain. My father was taken with a fainting turn this morning, about eight o'clock, which has terminated fatally. Nathan, who takes this, will give you the account.
>
> We are all very tranquil, as my writing to you now shows. Do not come till after church, as nothing can be done now.
>
> Your affectionate
>
> WM. H. PRESCOTT.

I went to him, of course, as soon as the morning services were over, and found him tranquil, indeed, but more tenderly and more easily moved than I had ever seen him before, and more than I ever saw him afterwards. His mind was sorrowfully filled with the thought of the great tie that had been so suddenly broken, and of the consequences that must follow. He could talk only of his father or of his desolate mother ; and, although I saw him again before the day was ended, and each succeeding day afterwards for some time, it was still the same. He was unable to think continuously on any other subject. There was, however, nothing violent or extravagant in his sorrow. He saw things as they really were. He did not seem so much oppressed with the idea of his immediate loss, as with the idea that it was one he should never cease to feel. And in this he judged himself rightly. He was always afterwards more or less sensible of the void that had been left by the death of his father, and recurred to it frequently in conversation with me, down even to one of the last times I saw him.

The evening after the funeral there seemed to be more of bitterness in his grief than there had been before. The day had been raw and cheerless, with much wind and dust in the streets as the procession passed along. His eye had been seriously troubled by it, and was still painful. I noticed how close he had followed the body as we turned in, all on foot, to enter the crypt under St. Paul's Church, and that his head at that moment was almost brought in contact with the sad drapery of the hearse. "Yes," he said, "my eye suffered very much from the wind and dust that came out of the passage, and *he* protected me to the last, as he always had."

It was long before he could settle himself to his work again. The world had assumed a new look to him, and its ways seemed harder to tread. Burdens were hereafter to rest on his shoulders which had earlier been borne by another. Counsels were to fail on which he had always relied. Much business was to be done requiring both time and thought. More than two months, therefore, elapsed before he returned to his literary labors, and when he did he found it impossible to recover, in a manner at all satisfactory to himself, the thoughts with which he had intended to go on, and which, before his father's death, lay all settled and spread out in his memory. He found, as he said, that they had been effaced as completely as if they had been wiped out by a sponge. He began, therefore, a new chapter, without absolutely finishing the one on which he had till then been employed.

He was soon cheered on his course by the following letter from Alexander von Humboldt, which he justly deemed "as high a recompense as he could receive in this way": —

MONSIEUR,

Dans la crainte, que peut être la première expression de ma juste admiration, addressée, au moment où je recevais votre important ouvrage sur le Méxique, ne vous soit pas parvenue, je donne ce peu de lignes à Mons. Lieber, qui nous est cher, et qui part pour votre beau pays. Après avoir déployé le grand et noble talent d'historien de l'Europe dans la Vie de Ferdinand et d'Isabelle, — après avoir retracé des événements que les calamités recentes de l'Espagne rendent doublement instructives aux peuples "qui oublient et apprennent peu," — Mons. Prescott a daigné jetter une vive lumière sur un pays qui a eu l'independance avant les éléments de la liberté civile ; mais auquel je tiens par tous les liens de la reconnaissance et des souvenirs, croyant avoir le faible mérite d'avoir fait connaître le premier, par des observations astronomiques et des mesures de hauteur, la merveilleuse configuration du Méxique, et le reflèt de cette configuration sur les progrès et les entrâves de la civilization. Ma satisfaction a été bien grande en étudiant ligne par ligne votre excellent ouvrage, Monsieur. On est un juge sévère, souvent enclin à l'injustice, lorsqu'on a eu la vivante impression des lieux et que l'étude de l'histoire antique dont je me suis occupée avec prédilection a été suivie sur le sol même, où une partie des grands événements s'est passée. La sévérité est désarmée, Monsieur, à la lecture de votre "Conquête du Méxique." Vous peignez avec succès parce que vous avez vu des yeux de l'esprit, du sens intérieur. C'est un bonheur pour moi, citoyen du Méxique, d'avoir vécu assez longtemps pour vous lire ; pour vous parler de ma reconnaissance des expressions de bienveillance dont vous avez honoré mon nom. L'Amérique Espagnole, bien malheureuse aujourd'hui, déchirée par d'ignobles guerres intestines — trop grande heureusement, pour que l'importation d'un joug étranger soit possible — trouvera avec toute société humaine son équilibre intérieur. Je ne désespère pas. Je dirai avec Christophe Colomb, dans le rêve à la rivière de Belom : Que le Seigneur tient dans son pouvoir une longue hérédité d'années ; *muchas heredades tiene el Señor y grandisimas.*[a] Si je n'étais tout occupé de mon Cosmos — d'une Physique du Monde — que j'ai l'imprudence d'imprimer, j'aurais voulu traduire votre ouvrage dans la langue de mon pays.

Je suis heureux de savoir que votre santé s'est solidement améliorée, et que nous pouvons espérer vos travaux sur le Pérou et son antique et mystérieuse civilization.

Agréez, Monsieur, je vous prie, l'expression renouvelée du respectueux attachement avec lequel j'ai l'honneur d'être,

Monsieur,

Votre très humble et très obéissant serviteur,
ALEXANDRE DE HUMBOLDT.

À Sans Souci, ce 26 Octobre, 1844.

On devrait se rappeler un jour, que lorsque j'ai publié mon Atlas du Méxique et l'Essai Politique il n'existait aucune autre carte du pays, que celle qu'Alzate a offert à l'Académie des Sciences à Paris.

Such a letter was, as he intimated, an honor second to few that he could receive. Other honors, however, were not wanting. Four months later — in February, 1845 — he was elected into the French Institute, as a Corresponding Member of the Academy of Moral and Political Science, and into the Royal Society of Berlin, as a Corresponding Member of the Class of Philosophy and History. He had no intimation of either until

---

[a] The words which Humboldt has here cited from memory, and which he has a little spiritualized, are found in a letter which Columbus wrote from Jamaica, July 7, 1503, to Ferdinand and Isabella, giving an eloquent and solemn account of a vision which he believed himself to have had on the coast of Veragua, — one of the magnificent illusions which occasionally filled his mind, and persuaded him that he was inspired and commissioned of Heaven to discover the passage to the Indies, and perhaps the terrestrial Paradise. The exact words referred to by Humboldt are, *muchas heredades tiene El, grandisimas.* They refer to God, and, with the context, intimate that Columbus himself was to receive some of these reserved "heredades," — *possessions, or inheritances.*

he received the diploma announcing it; and it was not until some weeks afterwards, April 23d, 1845, that he made the following entry among his literary memoranda:—

In my laziness I forgot to record the greatest academic honor I have received,—the greatest I shall ever receive,—my election as Corresponding Member of the French Institute, as one of the Academy of Moral and Political Science.   I was chosen to fill the vacancy occasioned by the death of the illustrious Navarrete.   This circumstance, together with the fact, that I did not canvass for the election, as is very usual with the candidates, makes the compliment the more grateful to me.

By the last steamer I received a diploma from the Royal Society of Berlin also, as Corresponding Member of the Class of Philosophy and History.   This body, over which Humboldt presides, and which has been made famous by the learned labors of Niebuhr, Von Raumer, Ranke, &c., &c., ranks next to the Institute among the great Academies of the Continent.   Such testimonies, from a distant land, are the real rewards of a scholar.   What pleasure would they have given to my dear father!   I feel as if they came too late!

Similar remarks, as to the regret he felt that his father could no longer share such honors with him, he had made earlier to more than one of his friends, with no little emotion.[4]   They were honors of which he was always naturally and justly proud,—for they had been vouchsafed neither to Bowditch nor to Irving,—but sorrow for a time dimmed their brightness to him.   As Montaigne said on the death of Boëtie, "We had everything in common, and, now that he is gone, I feel as if I had no right to his part."

Of the election at Berlin, which, according to the diploma, was made in February, 1845, I have no details; but at Paris, I believe, the forms were those regularly observed.   On the 18th of January, 1845, M. Mignet, on behalf of the Section of History, reported to the Academy of Moral and Political Science the names of those who were proposed as candidates

---

[4] This seems, indeed, to have been his first feeling on receiving the intelligence.   Dr. George Hayward, the distinguished surgeon, met him on the steps of the post-office as he came with the official notice of his election to the Institute in his hand, and told me a few days afterwards, that, while Mr. Prescott showed without hesitation how agreeable to him was the intelligence he had received, he added immediately a strong expression of his regret that the unsolicited and unexpected honor had not come to him before the death of his father.   Mr. Parsons, Mr. Prescott's early friend, has sent me a statement somewhat similar.   Both agree entirely with my own recollections and those of his family, as to his feelings at the same period.

to fill the place of Navarrete, who had died the preceding year; viz. in the first rank, Mr. Prescott; in the second rank, *ex æquo*, Mr. Turner and Mr. Bancroft; in the third, Mr. Dahlmann. M. Mignet at this meeting explained the grounds for his report, and the President inquired whether the Academy would confine itself to the list of candidates thus offered. M. Bérenger,[5] without proposing to add the name of M. Cesare Cantù, called the attention of the Section to his claims. M. Mignet and M. Cousin then spoke, and the subject was passed over. At the next meeting, — that of January 25th, — when the subject came up in course, no discussion took place; and on the 1st of February, when the election was made, Mr. Prescott was chosen by eighteen ballots out of twenty, one being for Mr. Bancroft and one blank.

In a letter of business to his friend, Colonel Aspinwall, at London, dated March 30th, Mr. Prescott says, with his accustomed frankness : —

You will be pleased to learn that by the last steamer I received a diploma of Corresponding Member of the Institute of France, to fill the vacancy occasioned by the death of the Spanish historian Navarrete. This academic honor is often canvassed pretty zealously for; but, as I got it without the asking on my part, it is the more welcome. I don't know how they came to think of an out-of-the-way Yankee for it.[6]

MEMORANDA.

June 30, 1844. — Nahant, where lighted the 28th. Returned from my tour to Trenton and Niagara Falls on the 25th, being fifteen days. A most romantic excursion of eleven hundred miles through the whole length of the great Empire State, which the traveller sees in all its glory of vegetation and wonderful fertility, — its noble streams, lofty woods, and matchless cataracts, — the valley of the Mohawk, the broad Hudson, with its navy of little vessels, the Erie Canal, winding like a silver snake through its cultivated fields, — its cities and villages rising up like fairy creations in the wide expanse of its clearings, and all the evidences of a busy, thriving population amidst the wreck of gigantic forests, that show the contest with savage nature had not been of very long date. It is indeed the "Empire State," and Niagara is a fitting termination to such a noble tour. But I grow twaddling. A pleasant tour of a couple of weeks — not more — with pleasant companions (mine were so), is not a

[5] Not the poet, who spelt his name differently, but a distinguished jurist and statesman.

[6] See Appendix (D), for other literary honors.

bad break into the still life of the student. It gives zest to the quiet course of literary labor. Yet it is not easy, after such a vagabond life, to come up to the scratch. The hide gets somewhat insensible to the spur of lofty ambition, — that last infirmity which the poet speaks of. Yet may I never be insensible to it.

July 21, 1844. — Industry and literary ardor improve. Been reading, or rather listening to, Alfieri's Life, — a strange being, with three ruling passions, literary glory, love, and horses! the last not the least powerful. His literary zeal — by fits only, it is true — is quite stimulating, and, like Gibbon's Memoirs, rouses the dormant spark in me. It is well occasionally to *reinvigorate* by the perusal of works so stirring to the flagging student. I ought not to flag with such an audience as I am now sure to have. Life out of Boston, whether at Nahant or Pepperell, very favorable to regular studious habits and scholar-like ardor. My *ideal* would be best accomplished by a full six months' residence in the quiet country. But would my general vigor, and especially that of the stomach, allow it ? I fear not. This is a good place for effective work, even in the dogdays. But my eyes are better in the country, and rheumatism becomes a formidable enemy on these bleak and misty shores.

The face of nature, whether here or in the country, is most tranquillizing, and leads to contemplative occupation. I feel as if my studies, family, and the sight of a few friends, — *non brevi intervallo*, — not convivial friends, would answer all my desires, and best keep alive the best source of happiness in me; literary ambition, not the mere ambition of fame, — I have obtained that, — but of advancing the interests of humanity by the diffusion of useful truth. I have been more truly gratified by several messages I have received since the publication of the "Conquest," thanking me for the solace I had afforded in a sick-chamber, than by commendations from higher sources. Yet I read with satisfaction a passage in our Minister Wheaton's letter from Berlin this week, in which he says: "M. de Humboldt never ceases praising your book, and he is not a little difficult in his judgment of those who venture on his American ground." Humboldt is the most competent critic my work has to encounter.

This week I have been reviewing my notes for the Introduction, already reaching to seventy sheets, and not done yet. I have been arranging under what heads I must distribute this *farrago* of facts and fiction. The work of distribution, by the appropriate figure for each sentence, will be no joke.

Been to town twice last week, — most uncommon for me, — once to see my friend Calderon, returned as Minister from Spain, and once to see my poor friend Sumner, who has had a sentence of death passed on him by the physicians. His sister sat by his side, struck with the same disease. It was an affecting sight to see brother and sister, thus hand in hand, preparing to walk through the dark valley.[7] I shall lose a good friend in Sumner, and one who, though I have known him but a few years, has done me many kind offices.

[7] It is not necessary to say that Mr. Sumner recovered from this attack. The prognostications relating to his sister were unhappily fulfilled.

O

August 18, 1844. — Began Chapter I. of Book I., the Introduction of the " Conquest of Peru," on Monday, August 12th ; wrote 8 noctograph — 10 pp. print, — slow work and not particularly to my mind either. I have found it best to alter my plan, and throw military policy into another chapter, and continue this chapter by treating of the civil administration, else it comes cart before the horse.

My spirits this season at Nahant have been variable, and my temper ditto ; I am convinced that I am to expect contentment only, or rather chiefly, from *steady and engrossing literary occupation.* When one work is finished, don't pause too long before another is begun, and so on till eyes, ears, and sense give way ; then resignation ! I doubt even the policy of annual journeys ; am clear against episodical excursions for a few days in addition to the one journey of two weeks at most. I suspect my summer migrations for residence will be enough for health, and better for spirits. Locomotion *riles* up all the wits, till they are as muddy as a dirt-puddle, and they don't settle again in a hurry. Is it not enough to occupy myself with my historical pursuits, varying the scene by change of residence suited to the season, and by occasionally entertaining and going into society, — occasionally, not often ? What a cursed place this is for rheumatism and company, yet good for general vigor. No dog-days here, and all might be working-days if I had pluck for it.

TO DON PASCUAL DE GAYANGOS.

PEPPERELL, Oct. 18, 1844.

MY DEAR FRIEND,

I am glad to receive your very kind letter of August 28th, and to learn that you have at length accomplished the *residencia* at Simancas. Fifty-two days was a long while, and, if you had had the command of all your time, would have enabled you to have sifted, at the rapid rate at which you go on, half the library. But what absurd rules ! I think you made the most of that precious hour allowed for the *papeles reservados.* Your use of ciphers stood you in good stead. It was a rare piece of fortune to have stumbled on such a budget, which nobody else has. But how can a government wish to exclude the light from those who are occupied with illustrating its history, necessarily compelling the historian to take partial and limited views, and that, too, of events three hundred years old ! There will be a great *trastorno* when the archives are poured into the Escorial.*

TO COUNT ADOLPHE DE CIRCOURT.

BOSTON, Jan. 30, 1845.

MY DEAR SIR,

I am truly obliged by your kind letter, and the beautiful pieces of

* It was proposed to remove the collections of Simancas to the Escorial and there unite all the documents of the kingdom relating to the national history, as had been so admirably done in Seville for the history of Spanish America.

criticism from your pen which accompanied it.   I have read them with the greatest pleasure.   The account of the Venetian language is full of novel historical details, as well as of architectural criticisms, that carry me back to those witching scenes where in earlier life I passed some very happy days.   The sketch of the German pastor Hebel is conceived in the tranquil and beautiful spirit which so well accords with his own life and character.   And the translations of the Tartar poems have all the freshness of original composition, with a singular coloring of thought altogether different from the European.   Why do you not gather these little gems of criticism together, which you thus scatter at random, into one collection, where they may be preserved as the emanation of one and the same mind ?   I was talking this over with Ticknor the other day, and we both agreed that few volumes of any one author would present such a rich variety of criticism and disquisition on interesting and very diversified topics.   And yet you write with the ease and fulness of one who had made each of these topics his particular study.   I assure you I am saying to you what I have said to our common friend, and he, with a superior judgment to mine, fully confirmed.

I must also thank you for M. Chevalier's article in the "Journal des Débats," which contains a spirited analysis of my historical subject.   It is very kind in him to bestow so much time on it, and I have now written to thank him ; and shall request his acceptance of a copy of the American edition of the work, which I shall send this week by the New York packet, with another copy to the French translator.   I esteem myself fortunate in the prospect of seeing my thoughts clothed in the beautiful tongue of Racine and Rousseau.   Did I mention to you that the work is in process of translation in Berlin and in Rome ?   In Mexico, a Spanish translator has undertaken to make such alterations (according to his prospectus) as shall accommodate my religious ideas and my opinions of modern Mexico more satisfactorily to the popular taste !

Should you find leisure to write the notice which you contemplate in the "Bibliothèque Universelle," you will, of course, have the kindness to forward me a copy ; though I trust you will not allow this subject to make such demands on your time as my former history did, or else the publication of a new work by me will be no day of jubilee to you.

A little while before I had the pleasure of receiving your letter, I met with a domestic calamity of which I shall allow myself to speak to one who has shown such a friendly interest in my literary reputation.   This is the death of my father, who has been my constant companion, counsellor, and friend from childhood to the present time ; for we have always lived under the same roof together.   As he had the most cultivated tastes himself, and took the deepest interest in my literary career, his sympathy had become almost a necessary part of my existence ; and now that he is gone life wears a new aspect, and I feel that much of the incentive and the recompense of my labors is withdrawn from me.   But I have no right to complain ; he was spared to me, in the full possession of his powers of head and heart, to a good old age.   I take the liberty to enclose you a little obituary notice of him from the pen of our friend Ticknor, as I know you will read what he has written with pleasure, and it gratifies my own feelings to think that one for whom I feel as high a regard as your

self, in a distant land, should hold my father's name in honor. I hope
you will not think this is a weakness.

I pray you, my dear Sir, to accept the assurance of the sincere respect
with which I remain

Your obliged friend,

WM. H. PRESCOTT.

MEMORANDA.

February 6, 1845.— A long interval since my last entry, and one preg-
nant with important and most melancholy results to me, for in it I have
lost my father, my counsellor, companion, and friend from boyhood to the
hour of his death. This event took place on Sunday morning, about
eight o'clock, December 8th, 1844. I had the sad comfort of being with
him in his last moments, and of witnessing his tranquil and beautiful
death. It was in keeping with the whole tenor of his mild and philosophical life. He had complained of a slight obstruction or uneasiness in his
left side for ten days before, and the bad weather confined him in the
house, and prevented his getting his customary exercise. The physicians
thought it a rheumatic affection. But he did not feel confidence in this.
His strength became impaired by confinement, and half an hour before his
death, while in the library in which he spent so many happy and profitable hours of his life, he was taken with a faintness. His old domestic,
Nathan Webster, was there with him, and immediately ran for assistance.
My father recovered, but soon after relapsed. He was laid on the floor,
and we were all apprehensive of a recurrence of the melancholy attack
with which he had been visited at Pepperell, the year preceding. But his
mind was not affected otherwise than with the languor approaching to in-
sensibility which belongs to faintness. On the speedy arrival of the
physician he was carried up stairs to his own apartment, in the arms of the
family, and in fifteen minutes his spirit took its departure to a happier
world. On an examination, it was found that the arteries leading from
the heart had not conducted off the blood, and the pressure of this had
caused the uneasy sensation. The machinery was worn out. The clock —
to borrow the simile of the poet — had run down, and stopped of its own
accord.

He lived to a good old age, being eighty-two August 19th, 1844, and
we have certainly great reason for gratitude that he was spared to us so
long, and that he did not, even then, outlive his noble faculties. To have
survived the decay of his mind would have been a blow which even he,
with all his resignation, could not well have borne. But the temporary
cloud of the preceding year had passed away, and he died in the full possession of the powers which he has now returned, strengthened and increased
by unceasing industry and careful cultivation, into the hands of his merci-
ful Father. Yet, though there is much, very much to be thankful for, it
is only time that can reconcile me to the rupture of a tie that has so long
bound us closely together. It is a great satisfaction that his eminent virtues have been so justly appreciated by the community in which he lived.
Rarely has a death excited such wide and sincere sorrow. For his high
intellectual character commanded respect ; but his moral qualities, his

purity of principle, his high sense of honor, his sympathy with others, especially those who stood most in need of it, insured veneration and love. Yet those only who have dwelt under his roof, and enjoyed the sweet pleasures of the most intimate domestic intercourse, can estimate the real extent of his excellence. The nearer the intimacy, the deeper and more constant was the impression produced by his virtues. His character stood the test of daily, hourly inspection.

It would be most ungrateful in me not to acknowledge the goodness of that Providence which has spared such a friend to be the guide of my steps in youth, and my counsellor in riper years. And now that he is gone, it must be my duty and my pleasure to profit by this long intercourse, and to guide myself through the rest of my pilgrimage by the memory of his precepts and the light of his example. He still lives, and it must be my care so to live on earth as to be united with him again and forever.

I have not felt in heart to resume my historical labors since his death, and my time has been much engrossed by necessary attention to family affairs. But I must no longer delay to return to my studies, although my interest in them is much diminished, now that I have lost my best recompense of success in his approbation. Yet to defer this longer would be weakness. It will at least be a satisfaction to me to pursue the literary career in which he took so much interest, and the success of which, it is most consoling for me to believe, shed a ray of pleasure on the evening of his days.

CHAPTER XVIII.

1844 – 1845.

PUBLICATION OF A VOLUME OF MISCELLANIES. — ITALIAN LITERATURE. — CONTROVERSY WITH DA PONTE. — CHARLES BROCKDEN BROWN. — BLIND ASYLUM. — MOLIÈRE. — CERVANTES. — SCOTT. — IRVING. — BANCROFT. — MADAME CALDERON. — HISTORY OF SPANISH LITERATURE. — OPINIONS OF REVIEW-WRITING.

JUST at this time — the winter of 1844 – 5 — Mr. Prescott made an arrangement with Bentley in London for publishing a volume of Miscellanies, entitled in the English edition, "Critical and Historical Essays"; chiefly articles from the "North American Review," for which, though his contributions had already become rare, and subsequently ceased altogether, he wrote with some regularity for many years.

The subjects he had discussed were almost wholly literary, and, having little relation to anything local, political, or personal, were likely, on many accounts, to be read with interest in England. He therefore selected a few of his contributions as a specimen, and sent them to his friend Colonel Aspinwall, in London, with a good-humored letter, dated November 15th, 1844, in which he says : —

As the things are already in print, and stale enough here, I can't expect the London publishers will give much for them. Possibly they may not be willing to give a farthing. I would not advise them to. But you will probably think best to ask something, as I shall still have to select and dress them up a little. But, though I will not insist on a compensation if I can't get it, I had rather not have them published than to have them appear in a form which will not match with my other volumes in size. I would add, that at all events I should be allowed a dozen copies for myself. If Bentley, who should have the preference, or Murray, do not think them worth the taking, I would not go further with the trumpery. Only, pray see that they are returned safely to your hands to be destroyed.

Now, I hope this will not put you to much trouble. It is not worth it, and I do not intend it. Better accede to any proposition, — as far as profits are concerned, they must be so trifling, — than be bothered with negotiations. And, after all, it may be thought this *rechauffé* of old bones is not profitable enough to make it worth while for a publisher to undertake it at all. If so, I shall readily acquiesce. There will be no labor lost.

Bentley, however, thought better of the speculation than the author did, and accepted, with a just *honorarium*, the whole of what, a few months later, was sent to him. It made a handsome octavo volume, and appeared in the summer of 1845; but there was prefixed to it an engraved portrait, which, though great pains were taken to have it a good one, was a total failure.[1] The articles were fourteen in number, marking very well the course of the author's studies, tastes, and associations during the preceding twenty years. Some of them had cost him no little labor; all were written with a conscientious fidelity not common in such contributions to the periodical press. They were therefore successful from the first, and have continued to be so. An edition by the Harpers at New York appeared contemporaneously with Bentley's; a second London edition was called for in 1850; and these have been followed by others both in England and the United States, making in all, before the end of 1860, a sale of more than thirteen thousand copies. The misgivings of the author, therefore, about his "*rechauffé* of old bones" were soon discovered to be groundless.

The first article in the volume, reckoning by the date of its composition, is on "Italian Narrative Poetry," and was originally published in the "North American Review" for October, 1824. At that time, or a little earlier, Mr. Prescott had, it will be remembered, occupied himself much with the literature of Italy, and, among other things, had taken great pleasure in listening to an accomplished Italian, who had read parts of Dante, Tasso, Ariosto, and Alfieri, in a succession of mornings, to two or three friends who met regularly for the purpose. He was, therefore, in all respects, well qualified to discuss any department of Italian literature to which he might direct a more especial attention. The choice he made on this occasion was fortunate; for narrative poetry is a department in which Italian genius has had eminent success, and his treatment

---

[1] When he sent me a copy of the English edition, he said, in the note accompanying it: "You will recognize everything in it except the portrait."

of the subject was no less happy than the choice; especially, I think, in whatever regarded· his judgments on Politian, Berni, and Bojardo.

But excellent and pleasant as was the article in question, it was not satisfactory to a very respectable Italian, then living in the United States, who seems to have been more keenly sensitive to the literary honor of his country than he needed to have been. This gentleman, Signor Lorenzo Da Ponte, had been the immediate successor of Metastasio as Imperial Poet — *Poeta Cesareo* — at Vienna, and had early gained much reputation by writing to " Don Giovanni " the *libretto* which Mozart's music has carried all over the world. But the life of the Imperial Poet had subsequently been somewhat unhappy; and, after a series of adventures and misfortunes, which he has pleasantly recorded in an autobiography published in 1823, at New York, he had become a teacher of his native language in that metropolis, where he was deservedly much regarded and respected.

Signor Da Ponte was an earnest, — it may fairly be said, — an extravagant admirer of the literature of his native country, and could ill endure even the very cautious and inconsiderable qualifications which Mr. Prescott had deemed it needful to make respecting some of its claims in a review otherwise overflowing with admiration for Italy and Italian culture. In this Signor Da Ponte was no doubt unreasonable, but he had not the smallest suspicion that he was so; and in the fervor of his enthusiasm he soon published an answer to the review. It was, quaintly enough, appended to an Italian translation, which he was then editing, of the first part of Dodsley's " Economy of Human Life," and fills nearly fifty pages.[2]

---

[2] The title-page is, " Economia della Vita Humana, tradotta dal Inglese da L. Giudelli, resa alla sua vera lezione da L. Da Ponte, con una traduzione del medesimo in verso rimato della Settima Parte, che ha per titolo La Religione, *con varie lettere dei suoi allievi.* E con alcune osservazioni sull' articolo quarto, pubblicato nel *North American Review* il mese d'Ottobre 1824, *ed altre Prose e Poesie.* Nuova Yorka, 1825 " (16mo, pp. 141). This grotesquely compounded little volume is now become so rare, that, except for the kindness of Mr. Henry T. Tuckerman, who found it only after long search, I should probably now have been unable to obtain the use of a copy of it. I, however, recollect receiving one from the author when it first appeared, and the circumstances attending and following its publication.

As a matter almost of course, an answer followed, which appeared in the "North American Review" for July, 1825, and is reprinted in the "Miscellanies." It treats Signor Da Ponte with much respect, and even kindness; but, so far as it is controversial in its character, its tone is firm and its success complete. No reply, I believe, was attempted, nor is it easy to see how one could have been made. The whole affair, in fact, is now chiefly interesting from the circumstance that it is the only literary controversy, and indeed I may say the only controversy of any kind, in which Mr. Prescott was ever engaged, and which, though all such discussion was foreign from his disposition and temperament, and although he was then young, he managed with no little skill and decision.

In the same volume is another review of Italian Literature, published six years later, 1831, on the "Poetry and Romance of the Italians." The curious, who look into it with care, may perhaps notice some repetition of the opinions expressed in the two preceding articles. This is owing to the circumstance that it was not prepared for the journal in which it originally appeared, and in which the others were first published. It was written, as I well remember, in the winter of 1827 – 8, for a leading English periodical, and was gladly accepted by its scholar-like editor, who in a note requested the author to indicate to him the subjects on which he might be willing to furnish other articles, in case he should indulge himself further in the same style of writing. But, as the author did not give permission to send his article to the press until he should know the sort of editorial judgment passed on it, it happened that, by a series of accidents, it was so long before he heard of its acceptance, that, getting wearied with waiting, he sent for the paper back from London, and gave it to the "North American Review." Mr. Prescott adverts to these coincidences of opinion in a note to the article itself, as reprinted in the "Miscellanies," but does not explain the reason for them.

The other articles in the same volume are generally of not less interest and value than the three already noticed. Some of them are of more. There is, for instance, a pleasant "Life of Charles Brockden Brown," our American novelist, in which,

perhaps, his merits are overstated.   At least, the author afterwards thought so himself; but the task was voluntarily undertaken as a contribution to the collection of biographies by his
friend Mr. Sparks, in 1834, and he felt that it would be somewhat ungracious to say, under such circumstances, all he might
otherwise have deemed becoming.   No doubt, too, he thought
that Brown, who died in 1810, and was the best of the pioneers
in romantic fiction on this side of the Atlantic, had a claim to
tenderness of treatment, both from the difficult circumstances
in which he had been placed, and from the infirmities which
had carried him to an early grave.   It should, however, be
understood, while making these qualifications, that the Life
itself is written with freedom and spirit, and shows how well
its author was fitted for such critical discussions.

Another article, which interested him more, is on the condition of those who suffer from the calamity which constituted
the great trial of his own life, and on the alleviations which
public benevolence could afford to their misfortunes.   I refer,
of course, to the blind.

In 1829, by the exertions mainly of the late excellent Dr.
John D. Fisher, an "Asylum for the Blind," now known as
"The Perkins Institution," was established in Boston, — the
earliest of such beneficent institutions that have proved successful in the United States, and now one of the most advanced in
the world.   It at once attracted Mr. Prescott's attention, and
from its first organization, in 1830, he was one of its trustees,
and among its most efficient friends and supporters.[a]

He began his active services by a paper published in the
"North American Review" in July, 1830, explaining the
nature of such asylums, and urging the claims of the one in
which he was interested.   His earnestness was not without

---

[a] A substantial foundation for this excellent charity was laid somewhat
later by Colonel Thomas H. Perkins, so well known for his munificence to
many of our public institutions.   He gave to it an estate in Pearl Street,
valued at thirty thousand dollars, on condition that an equal sum should be
raised by subscription from the community.   This was done; and the institution bears in consequence his honored name.   In the arrangements for this
purpose Mr. Prescott took much interest, and bore an important part, not
only as a trustee of the "Asylum," but as a personal friend of Colonel
Perkins.

fruits ; and the institution which he helped with all his heart to found is the same in which, under the singularly successful leading of Dr. Samuel G. Howe, a system has been devised for printing books so as to enable the blind to read with an ease before deemed unattainable, and is the same institution in which, under the same leading, the marvel has been accomplished of giving much intellectual culture to Laura Bridgman, who, wholly without either sight or hearing, has hardly more than the sense of touch as an inlet to knowledge. Mr. Prescott's sympathy for such an institution, so founded, so managed, was necessarily strong, and he continued to serve it with fidelity and zeal as a trustee for ten years, when, its success being assured, and other duties claiming his time and thoughts more urgently, he resigned his place.

Some parts of the article originally published in the " North American Review," in order to give to the Boston Asylum for the Blind its proper position before the public, are so obviously the result of his personal experience, that they should be remembered as expressions of his personal character. Thus, in the midst of striking reflections and illustrations connected with his general subject, he says : —

The blind, from the cheerful ways of men cut off, are necessarily excluded from the busy theatre of human action. Their infirmity, however, which consigns them to darkness, and often to solitude, would seem favorable to contemplative habits, and the pursuits of abstract science and pure speculation. Undisturbed by external objects, the mind necessarily turns within, and concentrates its ideas on any point of investigation with greater intensity and perseverance. It is no uncommon thing, therefore, to find persons sitting apart in the silent hours of evening for the purpose of composition, or other purely intellectual exercise. Malebranche, when he wished to think intensely, used to close his shutters in the daytime, excluding every ray of light ; and hence Democritus is said to have put out his eyes in order that he might philosophize the better ; a story, the veracity [*] of which Cicero, who relates it, is prudent enough not to vouch for.

Blindness must also be exceedingly favorable to the discipline of the memory. Whoever has had the misfortune, from any derangement of that organ, to be compelled to derive his knowledge of books less from the eye than the ear, will feel the truth of this. The difficulty of recalling what has once escaped, of reverting to or dwelling on the passages

* Addison so uses the word, and I suppose his authority is sufficient. But *veracity* is strictly applicable only to a person, and not to a statement of facts.

read aloud by another, compels the hearer to give undivided attention to the subject, and to impress it more forcibly on his own mind by subsequent and methodical reflection. Instances of the cultivation of this faculty to an extraordinary extent have been witnessed among the blind.[5]

And, near the end of the article, he says, in a noble tone, evidently conscious of its application to himself: —

There is no higher evidence of the worth of the human mind, than its capacity of drawing consolation from its own resources under so heavy a privation, so that it not only can exhibit resignation and cheerfulness, but energy to burst the fetters with which it is encumbered.[6]

These words, it should be remembered, were written at the moment when their author was just stretching forth his hand, not without much anxiety, to begin the composition of his "Ferdinand and Isabella," of which the world knew nothing and suspected nothing for nearly ten years. But the words, which had little meaning to others at that time, are instinct with the spirit which in silence and darkness animated him to his bold undertaking, and not only carried him through it, but gave to the rest of his life its direction and character.[7]

The other articles in this volume, published in 1845, less need to be considered. One is a short discussion on Scottish popular poetry, written as early as the winter of 1825 – 6, and published in the following summer, when he was already busy with the study of Spanish, and therefore naturally compared the ballads of the two countries.[8] Another is on Molière, dating from 1828, and was the cause of directing his thoughts, ten years later, while he was uncertain about his success as an historian, to inquiries into the life of that great poet.[9] A third is on Cervantes, and was written as an amusement in 1837, immediately after the "Ferdinand and Isabella" was com-

---

[5] Critical and Historical Essays, London, 1850, pp. 40, 41.

[6] Ibid., p. 59. There are also some striking remarks, in the same tone, and almost equally applicable to himself, in his notice of Sir Walter Scott's power to resist pain and disease, with the discouragements that necessarily accompany them. Ibid., pp. 144, 145.

[7] I think he took pleasure, for the same reason, in recording (Article on Molière) that "a gentleman dined at the same table with Corneille for six months, without suspecting the author of the Cid."

[8] Critical and Historical Essays, pp. 55 sqq.

[9] Ibid., pp. 247 sqq.

pleted, and before it was published.   And a fourth and fifth,
on Lockhart's Life of Scott and on Chateaubriand, followed
soon afterwards, before he had been able to settle himself down
to regular work on his " Conquest of Mexico."

A few others he wrote, in part at least, from regard for
the authors of the books to which they relate.   Such were a
notice of Irving's "Conquest of Granada";[10] a review of the
third volume of Bancroft's "History of the United States";
one of Madame Calderon's very agreeable "Travels in Mexico,"
which he had already ushered into the world with a Preface;
and one on my own " History of Spanish Literature."   This
last, which was published in January, 1850, and which, therefore, is not included in the earliest edition of the "Miscellanies," was the only review he had written for seven years.
His record in relation to it is striking : —

October 25th, 1849. — Leave Pepperell to-morrow ; a very pleasant
autumn and a busy one.   Have read for and written an article in the
" North American Review " on my friend Ticknor's great work ; my last
effort in the critical line, amounting to forty-nine sheets noctograph !   The
writing began the 12th, and ended the 21st of the month ; not bad as to
industry.   No matter how often I have reviewed the ground, I must still
review it again whenever I am to write, — when I sit down to the task.[11]
Now, Muse of History, never more will I desert thy altar !   Yet I shall
have but little incense to offer.

This promise to himself was faithfully kept.   He never
wrote another article for a review.

In this, I do not doubt, he was right.   He began, when
he was quite young, immediately after the failure of the
" Club-Room," and wrote reviews upon literary subjects of
consequence, as an exercise well fitted to the general course
of studies he had undertaken, and as tending directly to the
results he hoped at last to reach.   It was, he thought, a
healthy and pleasant excitement to literary activity, and an

[10] It may be worth notice here, that, in the opening of this review, written in 1829, Mr. Prescott discusses the qualifications demanded of an historian, and the merits of some of the principal writers in this department of
literature.

[11] This is among the many proofs of his conscientious care in writing.   He
had read my manuscript, and had made ample notes on it ; but still, lest he
should make mistakes, he preferred to go over the printed book, now that he
was to review it.

obvious means of forming and testing his style. For twelve years, therefore, beginning in 1821, he contributed annually an article to the "North American Review." At one time he thought of writing occasionally, from the same motives, for the more eminent English periodicals; but from this he was diverted partly by accident, but chiefly by labors more important and pressing. Indeed, from 1833, when he was in the midst of his "Ferdinand and Isabella," to 1837, when its composition was completed, he found no time for such lighter occupations; and, during the last six and twenty years of his life, his contributions were only eight, nearly all of which were undertaken from motives different from those that had prompted his earlier efforts. As far as he himself was concerned, review-writing had done its work, and he was better employed.[12]

But, besides his own engrossing occupations, he had another reason for abandoning the habit of criticising the works of others. He had come to the conclusion that this form of literary labor is all but worthless. In his review of the Life of Scott, he had noticed how little of principle is mingled with it, and in his memoranda five years later, when his own

[12] Even before the publication of the "Ferdinand and Isabella" he had begun to see the little value of American Reviews. This is plain from the following extract from a letter discovered since this memoir was finished, and dated October 4, 1837. It was addressed from Pepperell by Mr. Prescott to his friend, Mr. Gardiner, in Boston.

"The last number of the 'North American' has found its way into our woods. I have only glanced at it, but it looks uncommonly weak and waterish. The review of Miss Martineau, which is meant to be double-spiced, is no exception. I don't know how it is; but our critics, though not pedantic, have not the business-like air, or the air of the man of the world, which gives manliness and significance to criticism. Their satire, when they attempt it, — which cannot be often laid to their door, — has neither the fine edge of the 'Edinburgh,' nor the sledge-hammer stroke of the 'Quarterly.' They twaddle out their humor as if they were afraid of its biting too hard, or else they deliver axioms with a sort of smart, dapper conceit, like a little parson laying down the law to his little people. I suppose the paltry price the 'North' pays (all it can bear, too, I believe) will not command the variety of contributions, and from the highest sources, as with the English journals. Then, in England, there is a far greater number of men highly cultivated, — whether in public life or men of leisure, — whose intimacy with affairs and with society, as well as books, affords supplies of a high order for periodical criticism. For a' that, however, the old 'North' is the best periodical we have ever had, or, considering its resources, are likely to have, for the present."

experiences of it had become abundant, he says : " Criticism
has got to be an old story. It is impossible for one who has
done that sort of work himself to have any respect for it. How
can one critic look another in the face without laughing ? " He
therefore gave it up, believing neither in its fairness, nor in its
beneficial effect on authors or readers. Sir James Mackintosh,
after long experience of the same sort, came to the conclusion
that review-writing was a waste of time, and advised Mr.
Tytler, the historian, who had occasionally sent an article to
the " Edinburgh," to abandon the practice ; [19] and in the same
spirit, De Tocqueville, writing at the end of his life, said, somewhat triumphantly : " Je n'ai jamais fait de ma vie un article
de revue." I doubt not they were all right, and that society,
as it advances, will more and more justify their judgment.

[18] Mr. Prescott's articles in the " North American Review " are as follows,
those marked with an asterisk (*) constituting, together with the Life of
Charles Brockden Brown, the volume published in London with the title of
"Critical and Historical Essays," and in the United States with that of
" Biographical and Critical Miscellanies " : —

1821. Byron's Letters on Pope.
1822. Essay-Writing.
1823. French and English Tragedy.
1824. Italian Narrative Poetry.*
1825. Da Ponto's Observations.*
1826. Scottish Song.*
1827. Novel-Writing.
1828. Molière.*
1829. Irving's Granada.*
1830. Asylum for the Blind.*
1831. Poetry and Romance of the Italians.*
1832. English Literature of the Nineteenth Century.
1837. Cervantes.*
1838. Lockhart's Life of Scott.*
1839. Kenyon's Poems.
1839. Chateaubriand.
1841. Bancroft's United States.*
1842. Mariotti's Italy.
1843. Madame Calderon's Mexico.*
1850. Ticknor's Spanish Literature.*

At one period, rather early, he wrote a considerable number of short articles for some of our newspapers; and even in the latter part of his life
occasionally adopted this mode of communicating his opinions to the public.
But he did not wish to have them remembered. " This sort of ephemeral
trash," he said, when recording his judgment of it, " had better be forgotten
by me as soon as possible."

CHAPTER XIX.

1845 – 1848.

ON the 4th of May, 1845, Mr. Prescott made, with his own hand, what is very rare in his memoranda, a notice of his personal feelings and domestic relations. It is simple, touching, true; and I recollect that he read it to me a few days afterwards with the earnest tenderness which had dictated it.

"My forty-ninth birthday," he says, "and my twenty-fifth wedding-day; a quarter of a century the one, and nearly half a century the other. An English notice of me last month speaks of me as being on the sunny side of thirty-five. My life *has* been pretty much on the sunny side, for which I am indebted to a singularly fortunate position in life; to inestimable parents, who both, until a few months since, were preserved to me in health of mind and body; a wife, who has shared my few troubles real and imaginary, and my many blessings, with the sympathy of another self; a cheerful temper, in spite of some drawbacks on the score of health; and easy circumstances, which have enabled me to consult my own inclinations in the direction and the amount of my studies. Family, friends, fortune, — these have furnished me materials for enjoyment greater and more constant than is granted to most men. Lastly, I must not omit my books; the love of letters, which I have always cultivated and which has proved my solace — invariable solace — under afflictions mental and bodily, — and of both I have had my share, — and which have given me the means of living for others than myself, — of living, I may hope, when my own generation shall have passed away. If what I have done shall be permitted to go down to after times, and my soul shall be permitted to mingle with those of the wise and good of future generations, I have not lived in vain. I have many intimations that I am now getting on the shady side of the hill, and as I go down, the shadows will grow longer and darker. May the dear companion who has accompanied me thus far be permitted to go with me to the close, ' till we sleep together at the foot ' as tranquilly as we have lived."

Immediately after this entry occurs one entirely different,

and yet not less characteristic. It relates to the early chapters of his " Conquest of Peru," which, it will be remembered, he had begun some months before, and in which he had been so sadly interrupted by the death of his father.

May 11th, 1845. — Finished writing — not corrected yet, from secretary's illness — Chapters I. and II. of narrative, text. On my noctograph these two chapters make just twenty-nine sheets, which will scarcely come to less than thirty-eight pages print. But we shall see, when the copy, by which I can alone safely estimate, is made. I began composition Wednesday ; finished Saturday noon ; about three days, or more than twelve pages print *per diem*. I never did so much, I think, before in the same time, though I have done more in a single day. At this rate, I should work up the " Peru " — the two volumes — in just about two months. Lord, deliver me ! What a fruitful author I might become, were I so feloniously intent ! *Felo de se*, it would be more than all others.

I have great doubts about the quality of this same homespun that has run off so rapidly. I never found it *so hard to come to the starting-point. The first chapter was a perfectly painful task*, as painful as I ever performed at school.[1] I should not have scraped over it in a month, but I bound myself by a forfeit against time. Not a bad way (*Mem.*) to force things out, that might otherwise rot. from stagnation. A good way enough for narrative, which requires only a little top-dressing. But for the philosophy and all that of history, one must delve deeper, and I query the policy of haste. It is among possibilities that I may have to rewrite said first chapter, which is of the generalizing cast. The second, being direct narrative, was pleasant work to me, and as good, I suppose, as the raw material will allow. It is not cloth of gold by a long shot ! A hero that can't read ! I must look at some popular stories of highwaymen.

May 18th, 1845. — The two chapters required a good deal of correction ; yet, on the whole, read pretty well. I now find that it only needed a little courage at the outset to break the ice which had formed over my ideas, and the current, set loose runs on naturally enough. I feel a return of my old literary interest ; am satisfied that this is the secret of contentment, of happiness, for me ; happiness enough for any one in the passing [day] and the reflection. I have written this week the few notes to be hitched on here and there. They will be few and far between in this work. The Spanish quotations corroborative of the text must be more frequent.

The summer of 1845 he passed entirely at Pepperell ; the first he had so spent for many years. It was, on the whole, a most agreeable and salutary one. The earliest weeks of the season were, indeed, saddened by recollections of his father,

---

[1] This is the first chapter and is on the civilization of the Incas.

peculiarly associated with everything about him on that spot
where from his infancy their intercourse had been more free
and unbroken than it could be amidst the business and cares
of the town. The mingled feelings of pleasure and sadness
which scenes and memories like these awakened are, I think,
very naturally and gracefully expressed in a letter, addressed
to Mrs. Ticknor, at Geneseo, New York, where we were passing the summer for her health, in frequent intercourse with
the cultivated family of the Wadsworths, to which our friend
alludes among the pleasures of our condition.

PEPPERELL, June 19, 1845.

MY DEAR ANNA,

I took a letter out of the post-office last evening which gladdened my
eyes, as I recognized the hand of a dear friend; and now take the first
return of daylight to answer it, and, as you see, with my own hand,
though this will delay it; for I cannot trust my broken-down nags to a
long heat.

I am rejoiced to hear that you are situated so much to your mind.
Fine scenery, with the rural quiet broken only by agreeable intercourse
with two or three polished families; pleasant drives; books; the last
novel that is good for anything, and, of course, not very new; old books,
old friends, and most of these *at corresponding distances;* — what could
one desire more for the summer, except, indeed, not to be baked alive
with the heat, and a stomach not beset by the foul fiend Dyspepsia,
abhorred by gods and men, who has laid me on my back more than one
day here? But we should not croak or be ungrateful. And yet, when
the horn is filled with plenty, it is apt to make the heart hard.

We lead a very rational way of life. A morning ride among these
green lanes, never so green as in the merry month of June, when the
whole natural world seems to be just turned out of the Creator's hand;
a walk at noon, under the broad shades that the hands of my father prepared for me; a drive at evening, with Will or the Judge [2] officiating in
the saddle as squire of dames to Miss B—— or to Miss C——, who
happens to be on a visit here at present; the good old stand-by, Sir
Walter, to bring up the evening. Nor must I omit the grateful fumes of
the segar to help digestion under the spreading branches of the old oilnut-
trees. So wags the day. "How happily the hours of Thalaba went

---

[2] It was customary, in the affectionate intercourse of Mr. Prescott's family,
to call the eldest son sometimes Will and sometimes "the Colonel," because
his great-grandfather, of Bunker Hill memory, had been a Colonel; but the
youngest son, who was much of a pet, was almost always called "the Judge,"
from the office once held by his grandfather. The historian himself long
wore the sobriquet of "the Colonel," which Dr. Gardiner gave him in his
school-boy days, and it was now handed down to another generation by
himself.

by!" I try between-whiles to pick some grains of gold out of the Andes. I hope the manufacture will not turn out mere copper-wash.

June 20.

Another day has flitted by, and with it my wife has flitted also; gone to town for a cook. O the joys, the pains of housekeeping! The "neat-handed Phyllis" who prepares our savory messes is in love, and fancies herself homesick. So here I am monarch of all I survey, — a melancholy monarchy! The country never looked so charming to my eyes; the fields were never spread with a richer green; the trees never seemed so flourishing; the streams never rolled fuller or brighter; and the mountain background fills up the landscape more magnificently than ever. But it is all in mourning for me How can it be otherwise? Is it not full of the most tender and saddening recollections? Everything here whispers to me of *him;* the trees that he planted; the hawthorn hedges; the fields of grain as he planned them last year; every occupation, — the rides, the rambles, the social after-dinner talks, the evening novel, — all speak to me of the friend, the father, with whom I have enjoyed them from childhood. I have good bairns, as good as fall to the lot of most men; a wife, whom a quarter of a century of love has made my *better* half; but the sweet fountain of intellectual wisdom of which I have drunk from boyhood is sealed to me forever. One bright spot in life has become dark, — dark for this world, and for the future how doubtful!

I endeavor to keep everything about me as it used to be in the good old time. But the spirit which informed it all, and gave it its sweetest grace, is fled. I have lead about the heart-strings, such as I never had there before. Yet I never loved the spot half so well.

I am glad to hear that George is drinking of the old Castilian fount again, so much at his leisure. I dare say, he will get some good draughts at it in the quiet of Genesco. I should like to break in on him and you some day. *Quien sabe?* as they say in the land of the *hidalgo.* If I am obliged to take a journey, I shall set my horses that way. But I shall abide here, if I can, till late in October.

Pray tell your old gentleman, that I have had letters from the Harper's expressing their surprise at an advertisement they had seen of a volume of "Miscellanies, Biographical and Critical," in the London papers, and that this had led to an exchange of notes, which will terminate doubtless in the republication of the said work here, in the same style with its historical predecessors.

My mother has not been with us yet. She is conducting the great business of transmigration, and we get letters from her every other day. The days of the auld manse are almost numbered.[*]

The children send love to you and Anika. Elizabeth says she shall write to you soon. Pray remember me to your *caro sposo,* and believe me always

Most truly and affectionately yours,
WM. H. PRESCOTT.

[*] They were then removing from Bedford Street to Beacon Street, and the old house in Bedford Street was about to be pulled down.

But, notwithstanding the discouragements suggested in the preceding letter, his work went on well in the country. His habits were as regular as the most perfect control of his own time could enable him to make them, and the amount of exercise he took was more than usual; for the heats of the interior, so much greater than anything of the sort to which he had been accustomed on the sea-coast, had made the assaults of his old enemy, the dyspepsia, more active than ever, and had compelled him to be more than ever in the open air. He rose, as he always did, early, and, unless prevented by rain, got an hour and a half in the saddle before breakfast. At noon he walked half an hour in the shade of his own trees, and towards evening drove an hour and a half, commonly stopping so as to lounge for a mile or two on foot in some favorite woodland. In this way he went through the summer without any very severe attack, and did more work than usual.[4] One result of it, however, was, that he became more than ever enamored of his country life, and hoped that he should be able to enjoy it for at least six months in every year. But he never did. Indeed, he was never at Pepperell afterwards as long, in any summer, as he was during this one.

On reaching town, he established himself at once in a house he had bought in Beacon Street, overlooking the fine open ground of the Mall and the old Common. The purchase had been made in the preceding spring, when, during the adjustment of his father's affairs, he determined on a change of residence, as both useful and pleasant. He did not, however, leave the old house in Bedford Street without a natural regret. When he was making his first arrangements for it, he said, "It will remove me from my old haunts and the scenes of many a happy and some few sad hours. May my destinies be as fortunate in my new residence!"

The process of settlement in his new house, from which he expected no little discomfort, was yet more disagreeable than he had anticipated. He called it, "a month of Pandemonium;

[4] He records, for instance, that he wrote in June two chapters, one of twenty-five, and the other of twenty-six printed pages, in four days, adding: "I never did up so much yarn in the same time. At this rate, Peru would not hold out six months. Can I finish it in a year? Alas for the reader!"

an unfurnished house coming to order; parlors without furniture; a library without books; books without time to open them. Old faces, new faces, but not the sweet face of Nature."

Early in December, however, the removal was complete; the library-room, which he had built, was filled with his books; a room over it was secured for quiet study, and his regular work was begun. The first entry in his memoranda after this revolution was one on the completion of a year from his father's death. "How rapidly," he says, "has it flitted. How soon will the little [remaining] space be over for me and mine! His death has given me a new position in life, — a new way of life altogether, — and a different view of it from what I had before. I have many, many blessings left; family, friends, fortune. May I be sensible of them, and may I so live that I may be permitted to join *him* again in the long hereafter."

He was now in earnest about the "Conquest of Peru," and determined to finish it by the end of December, 1846. But he found it very difficult to begin his work afresh. He therefore, in his private memoranda, appealed to his own conscience in every way he could, by exhortation and rebuke, so as to stimulate his flagging industry. He even resorted to his old expedient of a money wager. At last, after above a month, he succeeded. A little later, he was industrious to his heart's content, and obtained an impulse which carried him well onward.

His collection of materials for the "History of the Conquest of Peru" he found to be more complete even than that for the corresponding period in Mexico. The characters, too, that were to stand in the foreground of his scene, turned out more interesting and important than he had anticipated, and so did the prominent points of the action and story. No doubt the subject itself, considered as a whole, was less grave and grand than that of the "Conquest of Mexico," but it was ample and interesting enough for the two volumes he had devoted to it; and, from the beginning of the year 1846, he went on his course with cheerfulness and spirit.

Once, indeed, he was interrupted. In March he "strained," as he was wont to describe such an access of trouble, the nerve of the eye severely. "Heaven knows how," he says, "probably by manuscript-digging; and the last fortnight, ever since March 10th, I have not read or written, in all, five minutes on my History, nor ten minutes on anything else. My notes have since been written by ear-work; snail-like progress. I must not use my eye for reading nor writing a word again, till restored. When will that be? *Eheu! pazienza!*"

It was a long time before he recovered any tolerable use of his sight; — never such as he had enjoyed during a large part of the time when he was preparing the "Conquest of Mexico." On the 4th of May, 1846, he records: —

My fiftieth birth-day; a half-century! This is getting on with a vengeance. It is one of those frightful halting-places in a man's life, that may make him reflect a little. But half a century is too long a road to be looked over in half an hour; so I will defer it — till when? But what have I done the last year? Not misspent much of it. The first eleven months, from April 26th, 1845, to March 26th, 1846, I wrote five hundred and twenty pages, text and notes, of my "Conquest of Peru." The quantity is sufficient, and, in the summer especially, my industry was at fever-heat. But I fear I have pushed the matter indiscreetly.

My last entry records a strain of the nerve, and my eye continued in so disabled a state that, to give it a respite and recruit my strength, I made a journey to Washington. I spent nearly a week there, and another at New York on my return, which, with a third on the road, took up three weeks. I was provided with a very agreeable fellow-traveller in my excellent friend, Charles Sumner. The excursion has done me sensible benefit, both bodily and mental. I saw much that interested me in Washington; made many acquaintances that I recollect with pleasure; and in New York I experienced the same hearty hospitality that I have always found there. . . . . . I put myself under Dr. Elliott's hands, and his local applications to the eye were of considerable advantage to me. The application of these remedies, which I continue to use, has done much to restore the morbid circulation, and I have hope that, with a temperate use of the eye, I may still find it in order for going on with my literary labors. But I have symptoms of its decay not to be mistaken or disregarded. I shall not aspire to more than three hours' use of it in any day, and for the rest I must *facit per alium.*[5] This will retard my progress; but I have time enough, being only half a century old; and why should I press?

5 *Qui facit per alium, facit per se.* A pun made originally by Mr. T. Bigelow, a distinguished lawyer of this neighborhood, who was at one time Speaker of the House of Representatives, and otherwise much connected with the government of the Commonwealth. The pleasantry in question may be found happily recorded at p. 110 of a little volume of "Miscellanies," published in 1821, by Mr. William Tudor, a most agreeable and accomplished person, who died as our *Chargé d'Affaires* in Brazil. Mr. Bigelow, still re-

But in these hopes he soon found himself disappointed. He with difficulty strengthened his sight so far that he was able to use his eye half an hour a day, and even this modicum soon fell back to ten minutes. He was naturally much disheartened by it. "It takes the strength out of me," he said.

But it did not take out the courage. He was abstinent from work, and careful; he used the remedies appointed; and economized his resources of all kind as well as he could. The hot weeks of the season, beginning June 25th, except a pleasant excursion to Albany, in order to be present at the marriage of Miss Van Rensselaer and his friend, Mr. N. Thayer, were passed at Nahant, and he found, as he believed, benefit to his eye, and his dyspepsia, from the sea-air, although it was rude in itself and full of rheumatism. He was even able, by perhaps a rather too free use of the active remedies given him, to read sometimes two hours a day, though rarely more than one and a half; but he was obliged to divide this indulgence into several minute portions, and separate them by considerable intervals of repose.

The rest of the season, which he passed at Pepperell, was equally favorable to effort and industry. His last chapter — the beautiful one on the latter part of Gasca's healing administration of the affairs of Peru, and the character of that wise and beneficent statesman — was finished in a morning's gallop through the woods, which were then, at the end of October, shedding their many-colored honors on his head. The last notes were completed a little later, November 7th, making just about two years and three months for the two volumes. But he seems to have pushed his work somewhat indiscreetly at last; for, when he closed it, the resources of his sight were again considerably diminished.

The composition of the "Conquest of Peru" was, therefore, finished within the time he had set for it a year previously, and, the work being put to press without delay, the printing was completed in the latter part of March, 1847; about two

membered by a few of us, as he was in Mr. Tudor's time, for "his stores of humor and anecdote," was the father of Mrs. Abbott Lawrence, and the grandfather of Mr. James Lawrence, who, as elsewhere noted, married the only daughter of Mr. Prescott the historian.

years and nine months from the day when he first put pen to paper. It made just a thousand pages, exclusive of the Appendix, and was stereotyped under the careful correction and supervision of his friend, Mr. Folsom, of Cambridge.

While it was passing through the press, or just as the stereotyping was fairly begun, he made a contract with the Messrs. Harper to pay for seven thousand five hundred copies on the day of publication at the rate of one dollar per copy, to be sold within two years, and to continue to publish at the same rate afterwards, or to surrender the contract to the author at his pleasure ; terms, I suppose, more liberal than had ever been offered for a work of grave history on this side of the Atlantic. In London it was published by Mr. Bentley, who purchased the copyright for eight hundred pounds, under the kind auspices of Colonel Aspinwall ; again a large sum, as it was already doubtful whether an exclusive privilege could be legally maintained in Great Britain by a foreigner.

An author rarely or never comes to the front of the stage and makes his bow to the public without some anxiety. The present case was not an exception to the general rule. Notwithstanding the solid and settled reputation of " Ferdinand and Isabella," and the brilliant success of the " Conquest of Mexico," their author was certainly not free from misgivings when his new argosy was launched. He felt that his subject had neither the breadth and importance of the subjects of those earlier works, nor the poetical interest that constituted so attractive an element in the last of them. About negligence in the matter of his style, too, he had some fears ; for he had written the " Conquest of Peru " with a rapidity that might have been accounted remarkable in one who had the free use of his eyes, turning off sometimes sixteen printed pages in a day, and not infrequently ten or a dozen. About the statement of facts he had no anxiety. He had been careful and conscientious, as he always was ; and, except for mistakes trifling, accidental, and inevitable, honest criticism, he knew, could not approach him.

But whatever might have been his feelings when the " Conquest of Peru " first came from the press, there was soon nothing of doubt mingled with them. The reviews, great and small, at home and in Europe, spoke out at once loudly and plainly; but the public spoke yet louder and plainer. In five months five thousand copies of the American edition had been sold. At about the same time, an edition of half that number had been exhausted in England. It had been republished in the original in Paris, and translations were going on into French, German, Spanish, and Dutch. A more complete success in relation to an historical work of so much consequence could, I suppose, hardly have been asked by any author, however much he might previously have been favored by the public.*

MEMORANDA.

May 18th, 1845. — I received the "Edinburgh Review" this week. It contains an article on the "Conquest of Mexico," written with great spirit and elegance, and by far the most cordial as well as encomiastic I have ever received from a British journal; much beyond, I suspect, what the public will think I merit. It says, — Nothing in the conduct of the work they would wish otherwise, — that I unite the qualifications of the best historical writers of the day, Scott, Napier, Tytler, — is emphatic in the commendation of the style, &c., &c. I begin to have a high opinion of Reviews! The only fault they find with me is, that I deal too hardly with Cortés. Shade of Montezuma! They say I have been blind several years! The next thing, I shall hear of a subscription set on foot for the blind Yankee author. But I have written to the editor, Napier, to set it right, if he thinks it worth while. Received also twenty columns of "newspaperial" criticisms on the "Conquest," in a succession of papers from Quebec. I am certainly the cause of some wit, and much folly, in others.

In relation to the mistake in the "Edinburgh Review" about his blindness, he expressed his feelings very naturally and very characteristically, when writing immediately afterwards, to his friend, Colonel Aspinwall, London. He was too proud to submit willingly to commiseration, and too honest to accept praise for difficulties greater than he had really overcome.

"I am very much obliged to you," he wrote May 15th, 1845, "for your kind suggestion about the error in the 'Edinburgh Review' on my blindness. I have taken the hint and written myself to the editor, Mr. Napier, by this steamer. I have set him right about the matter, and he can correct it, if he thinks it worth while. I can't say I like to be called

* To January 1, 1860, there had been sold of the American and English editions of the "Conquest of Peru," 16,965 copies.

11 *

blind. I have, it is true, but one eye; but that has done me some service, and, with fair usage, will, I trust, do me some more. I have been so troubled with inflammations, that I have not been able use it for months, and twice for several years together."

The following letter from the editor of the " Edinburgh Review " to Mr. Everett, then American Minister in London, and the subsequent memorandum of Mr. Prescott himself, show the end of this slight matter.

FROM MACVEY NAPIER, ESQ.

EDINBURGH, June 10, 1845.

DEAR SIR,

A short absence in the country has till now prevented me from acknowledging the receipt of the flattering letter of the 2d with which you have been pleased to honor me, covering a very acceptable enclosure from Mr. Prescott.

Thank God, there is an extensive as well as rich neutral territory of science and literature, where the two nations may, and ever ought to meet, without any of those illiberal feelings and degrading animosities which too often impart a malignant aspect to the intercourse and claims of civil life; and it has really given me high satisfaction to find, that both you and Mr. Prescott himself are satisfied that his very great merits have been kindly proclaimed in the article which I have lately had the pleasure of inserting in the " Edinburgh Review."

I hope I may request that, when you shall have any call otherwise to write to Mr. Prescott, you will convey to him the expression of my satisfaction at finding that he is pleased with the meed of honest approbation that is there awarded to him.

I am truly glad to learn from that gentleman himself, that the statement as to his *total* blindness, which I inserted in a note to the article, on what I thought good authority, proves to be inaccurate; and from his wish — natural to a lofty spirit — that he should not be thought to have originated or countenanced any statement as to the additional merits of historical research which so vast a bereavement would infer, I shall take an opportunity to correct my mistake; a communication which will, besides, prove most welcome to the learned world.

With respect to the authorship of the article, there needs to be no hesitation to proclaim it. With the exception of a very few editorial insertions and alterations, which do not by any means enhance its merits, it was wholly written by Mr. Charles Phillipps, — a young barrister and son of Mr. Phillipps, one of the Under-Secretaries of State for the Home-Department. He is the author of some other very valuable contributions. You are quite at liberty to mention this to Mr. Prescott.

I have the honor to remain, with very great esteem, dear sir,
Your obliged and faithful servant,
MACVEY NAPIER.

To HIS EXCELLENCY E. EVERETT, LONDON.

MEMORANDUM.

August 10th, 1845. — The editor of last "Edinburgh Review" has politely inserted a note correcting the statement, in a preceding number, of my blindness, on pretty good authority, — viz. myself. So I trust it will find credit.

TO DON PASCUAL DE GAYANGOS.

PEPPERELL, Sept. 28, 1845.

. . . . . The Gasca manuscript, which I believe is in the box, will be in perfect season, as I am yet a good distance from that period.' I have been very industrious this summer, having written half a volume in these quiet shades of Pepperell. This concludes my first volume, of which the Introduction, about one hundred and fifty pages, took me a long while. The rest will be easy sailing enough, though I wish my hero was more of a gentleman and less of a bandit. I shall not make more than a brace of volumes, I am resolved. Ford has sent me his "Handbook of Spain." What an *olla podrida* it is ! — criticism, travels, history, topography, &c., &c., all in one. It is a perfect treasure in its way, and will save me the trouble of a voyage to Spain, if I should be inclined to make it before writing "Philip." He speaks of you like a gentleman, as he ought to do ; and I have come better out of his hands than I did once on a time.

Have you got the copy of my "Miscellanies" I ordered for you ? You will see my portrait in it, which shows more imagination than anything else in the book, I believe. The great staring eyes, however, will show that I am not blind, — that's some comfort.

TO DON PASCUAL DE GAYANGOS.

BOSTON, Nov. 18, 1845.

. . . . . And now, my dear friend, I want to say a word about the manuscripts, which I found awaiting me on my return to town. I have as yet, with the aid of my secretary's eyes, looked through only about half of them. They are very precious documents. The letters from San Geronimo de Yuste have much interest, and show that Charles the Fifth was not, as Robertson supposed, a retired monk, who resigned the world, and all the knowledge of it, when he resigned his crown. I see mentioned in a statement of the manuscripts discovered by Gonzales, printed in our newspapers and written by Mr. Wheaton, our Minister at Berlin, that one of these documents was a diary kept by the Major Domo Quixada and Vasquez de Molina, the Emperor's private secretary, to be transmitted to Doña Juana, the Princess of Portugal ; which journal contains a minute account of his health, actions, and conversation, &c., and that the diary furnished one great source of Gonzales's information. It is now, I sup-

' An important MS. relating to the administration of Gasca in Peru.

pose, too late to get it, as most probably the situation of the manuscript is not known to the clerks of the archives. Mignot told a friend of mine that he should probably publish some of the most important documents he had got from Gonzales before long. I have no trouble on that score, as I feel already strong enough with your kind assistance. The documents relating to the Armada have extraordinary interest. The despatches of Philip are eminently characteristic of the man, and show that nothing, great or little, was done without his supervision. We are just now exploring the letters of the Santa Cruz collection. But this I have done only at intervals, when I could snatch leisure. In a week or two I hope to be settled.

TO DON PASCUAL DE GAYANGOS.

BOSTON, Aug. 31, 1846.

. . . . . The translation* appears faithful, as far as I have compared it. As to its literary execution in other respects, a foreigner cannot decide. But I wish you would give my thanks to the translator for the pleasure it has given me. His notes on the whole are courteous, though they show that Señor Sabau has contemplated the ground often, from a different point of view from myself. But this is natural. For am I not the child of democracy? Yet no bigoted one, I assure you. I am no friend to bigotry in politics or religion, and I believe that forms are not so important as the manner in which they are administered. The mechanical execution of the book is excellent. It gives me real pleasure to see myself put into so respectable a dress in Madrid. I prize a translation into the noble Castilian more than any other tongue. For if my volumes are worthy of translation into it, it is the best proof that I have not wasted my time, and that I have contributed something in reference to the institutions and history of the country which the Spaniards themselves would not willingly let die.

TO THE CAVALIERE EUGENIO ALBÈRI, FLORENCE.

BOSTON, Oct. 18, 1846.

MY DEAR SIR,
I have great pleasure in acknowledging the receipt of the six volumes of *Relazioni*, which you have been so obliging as to send me through Mr. Lester.

It is a work of inestimable value, and furnishes the most authentic basis for history. Your method of editing it appears to me admirable. The brief but comprehensive historical and chronological notices at the beginning, and your luminous annotations throughout, put the reader in possession of all the information he can desire in regard to the subjects treated in the *Relazioni*. At the close of the third volume, on the Ottomans, you place an Index of the contents of the volume, which is a great convenience.

* Of "Ferdinand and Isabella," by Sabau.

I suppose, from what you say in the Preface, there will be a full Index of the whole when completed.

I have a number of Venetian *Relazioni* in manuscript, copied from the libraries of Berlin and Gotha. They relate to the court of Philip the Second, on which you must now, I suppose, be occupied, and I shall look forward to the conclusion of your learned labors with the greatest interest. Many of your manuscripts, I see, are derived from the Marquis Gino Capponi's collection. It must be very rich indeed. — I am much grieved to learn that his eyes have now failed him altogether. My own privations in this way, though I have the partial use of my eyes, make me feel how heavy a blow it is to a scholar like him. It is gratifying to reflect that he bears up under it with so much courage, and that the misfortune does not quench his generous enthusiasm for letters. Pray give my sincere respects and regards to him, for, though I never saw him, I had the pleasure formerly of communicating with him, and I know his character so well that I feel as if I knew him personally.

FROM MISS MARIA EDGEWORTH.

EDGEWORTH'S TOWN, Aug. 28, 1847.

DEAR SIR,

Your Preface to your "History of the Conquest of Peru" is most interesting; especially that part which concerns the author individually. That delicate integrity which made him apprehend that he had received praise or sympathy from the world on false pretences, converts what might have been pity into admiration, without diminishing the feeling for his suffering and his privations, against which he has so nobly, so perseveringly, so successfully struggled. Our admiration and highest esteem now are commanded by his moral courage and truth.

What pleasure and pride — honest, proper pride — you must feel, my dear Mr. Prescott, in the sense of difficulty conquered; of difficulties innumerable vanquished by the perseverance and fortitude of genius! It is a fine example to human nature, and will form genius to great works in the rising generation and in ages yet unborn.

What a new and ennobling moral view of posthumous fame! A view which short-sighted, narrow-minded mediocrity cannot reach, and probably would call romantic, but which the noble-minded realize to themselves, and ask not either the sympathy or the comprehension of the commonplace ones. You need not apologize for speaking of yourself to the world. No one in the world, whose opinion is worth looking to, will ever think or call this "egotism," any more than they did in the case of Sir Walter Scott. Whenever he spoke of himself it was with the same noble and engaging simplicity, the same endearing confidence in the sympathy of the good and true-minded, and the same real freedom from all vanity which we see in your addresses to the public.

As to your judgments of the advantages peculiar to each of your Histories, — the "Conquest of Mexico" and the "Conquest of Peru," — of course you, who have considered and compared them in all lights, must be accurate in your estimate of the facility or difficulty each subject prosented; and you have well pointed out in your Preface to "Peru" the difficulty of making out a unity of subject, — where, in fact, the *first* unity ends, as we may dramatically consider it, at the third act, when the conquest of the Incas is effected, — but not the conquest of Peru for Spain, which is the thing to be done. You have admirably kept the mind's eye upon this, the real end, and have thus carried on, and prolonged, and raised, as you carried forward, the interest sustained to the last moment happily by the noble character of Gasca, with which terminates the history of the mission to Peru.

You sustain with the dignity of a just historian your mottoes from Claudian and from Lope de Vega. And in doing this *con amore* you carry with you the sympathy of your reader. The cruelties of the Spaniards to the inoffensive, amiable, hospitable, trusting Peruvians and their Incas are so revolting, that, unless you had given vent to indignation, the reader's natural, irrepressible feelings would have turned against the narrator, in whom even impartiality would have been suspected of want of moral sense.

I wish that you could have gone further into that comparison or inquiry which you have touched upon and so ably pointed out for further inquiry, — How far the want of political freedom is compatible or incompatible with happiness or virtue? You well observe, that under the Incas this experiment was tried, or was trying, upon the Peruvians, and that the contrary experiment is now trying in America. Much may be *said*, but much more is to be seen, on both sides of this question. There is a good essay by a friend of mine, perhaps of yours, the late Abbé Morellet, upon the subject of *personal* and *political* freedom. I wonder what your negroes would say touching the comforts of slavery. They seem to feel freedom a curse, when suddenly given, and, when unprepared for the consequences of independence, lie down with the cap of liberty pulled over their ears and go to sleep or to death in some of our freed, lazy colonies and the empire of Hayti. But, I suppose, time and motives will settle all this, and waken souls in black bodies as well as in white. Meanwhile, I cannot but wish you had discussed a little more this question, even if you had come upon the yet more difficult question of races, and their unconquerable, or their conquerable or exhaustible differences. Who could do this so well?

I admire your adherence to your principle of giving evidence in your notes and appendices for your own accuracy, and allowing your own opinions to be rejudged by your readers in furnishing them with the means of judging which they could not otherwise procure, and which you, having obtained with so much labor and so much favor from high and closed sources, bring before us *gratis* with such unostentatious candor and humility.

I admire and favor, too, your practice of mixing biography with history; genuine sayings and letters by which the individuals give their own character and their own portraits. And I thank you for the quantity of information you give in the notices of the principal authorities to whom you refer. These biographical notices add weight and value to the authorities, in the most agreeable manner; — though I own that I was often mortified by my own ignorance of the names you mention of great men, your familiars. — You have made me long to have known your admirable friend, Don Fernandez de Navarrete, of whom you make such honorable and touching mention in your Preface.

I must content, myself, however, — and comfortably well I do content myself, — with knowing your dear friend Mr. Ticknor, whom I do esteem and admire with all my heart, as you do.

You mention Mr. O. Rich as a bibliographer to whom you have been obliged. It occurred to me that this might be the Mr. O. Rich residing in London, to whom Mr. Ticknor had told me I might apply to convey packets or books to him, and, upon venturing to ask the question, Mr. Rich answered me in the most obliging manner, confirming, though with great humility, his identity, and offering to convey any packets I might wish to send to Boston.

I yesterday sent to him a parcel to go in his next box of books to Mr. Ticknor. In it I have put, addressed to the care of Mr. Ticknor, a very trifling offering for you, my dear sir, which, trifling as it is, I hope and trust your good nature will not disdain, — half a dozen worked *marks* to put in books ; and I intended those to be used in your books of reference when you are working, as I hope you are, or will be, at your *magnum opus*, — the History of Spain. One of those marks, that which is marked in green silk, "Maria E—— for Prescott's works" !!! is my own handiwork every stitch ; in my eighty-first year, — eighty-two almost, — I shall be eighty-two the 1st of January. I am proud of being able, even in this trifling matter, to join my young friends in this family in working *souvenirs* for the great historian.

Believe me, my dear Mr. Prescott, your much obliged and highly gratified friend, and admiring reader and *marker*,

MARIA EDGEWORTH.

TO DON PASCUAL DE GAYANGOS.

BOSTON, Jan. 27, 1848.

. . . . . I have been overhauling my Philip the Second treasures, and making out a catalogue of them. It is as beautiful a collection, printed and manuscript, I will venture to say, as history-monger ever had on his shelves. How much am I indebted to you ! There are too many of your own books in it, however, by half, and you must not fail to advise me when you want any or all of them, which I can easily understand may be the case at any time.

FROM M. AUGUSTIN THIERRY.

MONSIEUR,

Pardonnez moi le long retard que j'ai mis à vous remercier du précieux envoi que vous avez eu la bonté de me faire ; la lenteur de mes lectures d'aveugle, surtout en langue étrangère, le peu de loisir que me laisse le triste état de ma santé et des travaux impérieux auxquels j'ai peine à suffire, voilà quelles ont été les causes de ma négligence apparente à remplir un devoir de gratitude et de haute estime pour vous. Je voulais avoir complètement lu vos deux nouveaux et très remarquables volumes. Je trouve que, pour le fond, pour les recherches, la netteté et la justesse des vues, ils sont égaux à vos précédentes publications, et que peut-être ils les surpassent pour la forme. Le style est sobre et ferme, l'exposition nette et la partie dramatique de l'histoire vivement traitée. Poursuivez, Monsieur, des travaux dont le succès égale le mérite, et qui ont rendu votre nom illustre de ce côté-ci de l'Atlantique ; donnez leur toute l'étendue que vos projets comportaient, et ne vous laissez pas décourager par la menace d'un mal qui, — j'en ai fait l'expérience, — est, dans la carrière d'historien, une gêne, un embarras, mais nullement un obstacle.

Vous me demandez si la nécessité, mère de toute industrie, ne m'a pas suggéré quelques méthodes particulières, qui atténuent pour moi les difficultés du travail d'aveugle. Je suis forcé d'avouer que je n'ai rien d'intéressant à vous dire. Ma façon de travailler est la même qu'au tems où j'avais l'usage de mes yeux, si ce n'est que je dicte et me fais lire ; je me fais lire tous les matériaux que j'emploie, car je ne m'en rapporte qu'à moi-même pour l'exactitude des recherches et le choix des notes. Il résulte de là une certaine perte de temps. Le travail est long, mais voilà tout ; je marche lentement mais je marche. Il n'y a qu'un moment difficile, c'est le passage subit de l'écriture manuelle à la dictée ; quand une fois ce point est gagné, on ne trouve plus de véritables épines. Peut-être, Monsieur, avez-vous déjà l'habitude de dicter à un secrétaire ; si cela est, mettez vous à la faire exclusivement, et ne vous inquiétez pas du reste. En quelques semaines vous deviendrez ce que je suis moi-même, aussi calme, aussi présent d'esprit pour tous les détails du style que si je travaillais avec mes yeux, la plume à la main. Ce n'est pas au point où vous êtes parvenu qu'on s'arrête ; vous avez éprouvé vos forces ; elles ne vous manqueront pas ; et le succès est certain pour tout ce que vous tenteres déformais. Je suivrai de loin vos travaux avec la sympathie d'un ami de votre gloire ; croyez le, Monsieur, et agréez avec mes remerciments les plus vifs, l'assurance de mes sentiments d'affection et d'admiration.

P. AUGUSTIN THIERRY.

22 Février, 1848.

FROM MR. HALLAM.

WILTON CRESCENT, LONDON, July 18, 1848.

MY DEAR SIR,

I hope that you will receive with this letter, or at least very soon afterwards, a volume which I have intrusted to the care of our friend, Mr. Bancroft.* It contains only the gleanings of the harvest, and I can hardly find a sufficiently modest name for it. After thirty years I found more to add, and, I must say, more to correct, in my work on the "Middle Ages," than could well be brought into the foot-notes of a new edition. I have consequently produced, under the title "Supplemental Notes,"

* Then Minister of the United States in London.

almost a new volume, but referring throughout to the original work, so that it cannot be of any utility to those who do not compare the two. This is, perhaps, rather a clumsy kind of composition, and I am far from expecting much reputation by it: but I really hope that it may be useful to the readers of the former volumes. A great deal required expansion and illustration, besides what I must in penitence confess to be the oversights and errors of the work itself. I have great pleasure, however, in sending copies to my friends, both here and what few I possess in the United States; and among them I am proud to rank your name, separated as we are by the Atlantic barrier, which at my age it would be too adventurous to pass. Rumors have from time to time reached me, that, notwithstanding the severe visitation of Providence under which you labor, you have contemplated yourself so arduous a voyage. May you have health and spirits to accomplish it, while I yet remain on earth! But I have yesterday entered my seventy-second year.

I will not speak of the condition of Europe. You have been conversant with the history of great and rapid revolutions; but nothing in the past annals of mankind can be set by the side of the last months. We rejoice in trembling, that God has hitherto spared this nation; but the principles of disintegration, which France and Germany are so terribly suffering under, cannot but be at work among us.

I trust that you are proceeding as rapidly as circumstances will permit with your fourth great History, that of Philip the Second. It always appears marvellous to me, how you achieve so much under so many impediments.

Believe me, my dear sir,

Most faithfully yours,
HENRY HALLAM.

TO MRS. LYELL.

NAHANT, FITFUL HEAD, Aug. 5, 1848.

. . . . . We are passing our summer in our rocky eyrie at Nahant, taking in the cool breezes that blow over the waters, whose spray is dashing up incessantly under my window. I am idly-busy with looking over my Philip the Second collection, like one who looks into the dark gulf, into which he is afraid to plunge. Had I half an eye in my head, I should not "stand shivering on the brink" so long. The Ticknors are at a very pleasant place on the coast, some twenty miles off, at Manchester. I hear from them constantly, but see them rarely.

FROM THE EARL OF CARLISLE.

LONDON, Nov. 18, 1848.

MY DEAR PRESCOTT,

I sadly fear that, if a strict investigation of my last date took place, it would be found that I had lagged behind the yearly bargain; and I fear I am the delinquent. I will honestly own why I put off writing for some

Q

time; I wished to have read your "Peru" before I did so, and to tell you what I thought of it. I will carry my honesty further, and intrepidly avow, that I still labor under the same disqualification, though in fact this is both my shame and my merit, for I am very sure it would have been a far more agreeable and delightful occupation to me than the many tedious, harassing shreds of business which engross and rule all my hours. I can as honestly tell you, that I have heard very high and most concurrent praise of it, and there are many who prefer it to "Mexico." I wonder what you are engaged upon now; is it the ancient project of "Philip the Second"?

Europe is in the meanwhile acting history faster than you can write it. The web becomes more inextricable every day, and the tissues do not wear lighter hues. I think our two Saxon families present very gratifying contrasts, on the whole, to all this fearful pother.

You will probably be aware, that my thoughts and feelings must have of late been mainly concentrated upon a domestic bereavement,[10] and, at the end of my letter, you will read a new name. After my long silence, I was really anxious to take a very early opportunity of assuring you that it inherits and hopes to perpetuate all the esteem and affection for you that were acquired under the old one. My dear friend, absence and distance only rivet on my spirit the delight of claiming communion with such a one as yours; for I am sure it is still as bright, gentle, and high-toned, as when I first gave myself to its spell.

I must not write to his brother-historian without mentioning that Macaulay tells me the two first volumes of his History will be out in less than a fortnight. Tell Sumner how unchangedly I feel towards him, though, I fear, I have been equally guilty to him.

Does Mrs. Ticknor still remember me?

   Ever, my dear Prescott,

         Affectionately yours,

           CARLISLE.

[10] The death of his father, sixth Earl of Carlisle.

CHAPTER XX.

1848.

SOMEWHAT earlier than the period at which we are now arrived, — in fact, before the "Conquest of Peru" was published, — an interesting circumstance occurred connected immediately with the "History of Philip the Second," which Mr. Prescott was at this time just about to undertake in earnest, and for which he had been making arrangements and preparations many years. I refer to the fact, now well known, that Mr. J. Lothrop Motley, who has since gained so much honor for himself and for his country as an historian, was — in ignorance of Mr. Prescott's purposes — already occupied with a kindred subject.[1] The moment, therefore, that he was aware of this condition of things and the consequent possibility that there might be an untoward interference in their plans, he took the same frank and honorable course with Mr. Prescott, that Mr. Prescott had taken in relation to Mr. Irving, when he found that they had both been contemplating a "History of the Conquest of Mexico." The result was the same. Mr. Prescott, instead of treating the matter as an interference, earnestly encouraged Mr. Motley to go on, and placed at his disposition such of the books in his library as could be useful to him. How amply and promptly he did it, Mr. Motley's own account will best show. It is in a letter, dated at Rome, 26th February, 1859, — the day he heard of Mr. Prescott's

---

[1] "The Rise of the Dutch Republic," not published until 1856.

death, — and was addressed to his intimate friend, Mr. William Amory, of Boston, Mr. Prescott's much loved brother-in-law.

It seems to me but as yesterday, though it must be now twelve years ago, that I was talking with our ever-lamented friend Stackpole[2] about my intention of writing a history upon a subject to which I have since that time been devoting myself. I had then made already some general studies in reference to it, without being in the least aware that Prescott had the intention of writing the "History of Philip the Second." Stackpole had heard the fact, and that large preparations had already been made for the work, although "Peru" had not yet been published. I felt naturally much disappointed. I was conscious of the immense disadvantage to myself of making my appearance, probably at the same time, before the public, with a work, not at all similar in plan to Philip the Second, but which must, of necessity, traverse a portion of the same ground.

My first thought was inevitably, as it were, only of myself. It seemed to me that I had nothing to do, but to abandon at once a cherished dream, and probably to renounce authorship. For I had not first made up my mind to write a history, and then cast about to take up a subject. My subject had taken me up, drawn me on, and absorbed me into itself. It was necessary for me, it seemed, to write the book I had been thinking much of, even if it were destined to fall dead from the press, and I had no inclination or interest to write any other. When I had made up my mind accordingly, it then occurred to me that Prescott might not be pleased that I should come forward upon his ground. It is true, that no announcement of his intentions had been made, and that he had not, I believe, even commenced his preliminary studies for Philip. At the same time, I thought it would be disloyal on my part not to go to him at once, confer with him on the subject, and, if I should find a shadow of dissatisfaction on his mind at my proposition, to abandon my plan altogether.

I had only the slightest acquaintance with him at that time. I was comparatively a young man, and certainly not entitled, on any ground, to more than the common courtesy which Prescott never could refuse to any one. But he received me with such a frank and ready and liberal sympathy, and such an open-hearted, guileless expansiveness, that I felt a personal affection for him from that hour. I remember the interview as if it had taken place yesterday. It was in his father's house, in his own library, looking on the garden. House and garden, honored father and illustrious son, — alas! all numbered with the things that were! He assured me that he had not the slightest objection whatever to my plan, that he wished me every success, and that, if there were any books in his library bearing on my subject that I liked to use, they were entirely at my service. After I had expressed my gratitude for his kindness and cordiality, by which I had been, in a very few moments, set completely at ease, — so far as my fears of his disapprobation went, — I also, very naturally stated my opinion, that the danger was entirely mine, and that it

[2] Mr. J. L. Stackpole, a gentleman of much cultivation, and a kinsman of Mr. Motley by marriage, was suddenly killed by a railroad accident in 1847.

was rather wilful of me thus to risk such a collision at my first venture, the probable consequence of which was utter shipwreck.   I recollect how kindly and warmly he combated this opinion, assuring me that no two books, as he said, ever injured each other, and encouraging me in the warmest and most earnest manner to proceed on the course I had marked out for myself.

Had the result of that interview been different, — had he distinctly stated, or even vaguely hinted, that it would be as well if I should select some other topic, or had he only sprinkled me with the cold water of conventional and commonplace encouragement, — I should have gone from him with a chill upon my mind, and, no doubt, have laid down the pen at once ; for, as I have already said, it was not that I cared about writing *a* history, but that I felt an inevitable impulse to write *one particular history*.

You know how kindly he always spoke of and to me ; and the generous manner in which, without the slightest hint from me, and entirely unexpected by me, he attracted the eyes of his hosts of readers to my forthcoming work, by so handsomely alluding to it in the Preface to his own, must be almost as fresh in your memory as it is in mine.

And although it seems easy enough for a man of world-wide reputation thus to extend the right hand of fellowship to an unknown and struggling aspirant, yet I fear that the history of literature will show that such instances of disinterested kindness are as rare as they are noble.*

To this frank and interesting statement I can add, that Mr. Prescott told it all to me at the time, and then asked me whether I would not advise him to offer Mr. Motley the use of his *manuscript* collections for "Philip the Second," as he had already offered that of his *printed books*.   I told him, that I thought Mr. Motley would hardly be willing to accept such an offer ; and, besides, that, if there were anything peculiarly his own, and which he should feel bound to reserve, as giving especial authority and value to his History, it must be the materials he had, at so much pains and cost, collected from the great archives and libraries all over Europe.   The idea, I confess, struck me as somewhat extravagant, and no doubt he would have felt pain in giving away personal advantages so obvious, so great, and so hardly earned ; but, from the good-

* The whole of this striking letter is to be found in the Proceedings of the Massachusetts Historical Society for 1858, 1859, pp. 266 – 271.   It is a true and touching tribute to Mr. Prescott's personal character and intellectual eminence, the more to be valued, since, in 1860, Mr. Motley was elected to the place left vacant in the French Institute by Mr. Prescott's death, — an honor not only fit in itself, but peculiarly appropriate, since it preserves the succession of Spanish historians in the same chair unbroken, from the time of Navarrete's election, half a century earlier.

ness of his nature, I have no doubt that he was capable of the sacrifice.

In due time, as we have seen, the " Conquest of Peru " was published ; and Mr. Prescott naturally turned to the next great work he was to undertake, and which had been ten years, at least, among his well-digested plans for the future.

His position for such an undertaking was, in many respects, fortunate. The state of his eyes indeed was bad, and his general health seemed a little shaken. But he was only fifty-two years old ; his spirits and courage were as high as they had been in his youth ; his practice as a writer and his experience of the peculiar difficulties he had to encounter were as great as they well could be ; and, above all, success had set a seal on his previous brilliant efforts which seemed to make the future sure.

Still he paused. The last sheets of the " Conquest of Peru " were corrected for the press, and the work was therefore entirely off his hands, in March, 1847 ; as, in fact, it had been substantially since the preceding October. But in March, 1848, he could not be said to have begun in earnest his studies for the reign of Philip the Second. This long hesitation was owing in part to the reluctance that always held him back from entering promptly on any new field of labor, and partly to the condition of his sight.

The last, in fact, had now become a subject of such serious consideration and anxiety, as he had not felt for many years. The power of using his eye — his only eye, it should always be remembered — had been gradually reduced again, until it did not exceed one hour a day, and that divided into two portions, at considerable intervals from each other. On examination, the retina was found to be affected anew, and incipient *amaurosis,* or decay of the nerve, was announced. Hopes were held out by an oculist who visited Boston at this period, and whom Mr. Prescott consulted for the first time, that relief more or less considerable might still be found in the resources of the healing art, and that he might yet be enabled to prosecute his labors as well as he had done. But he could not accept these hopes, much as he desired to do so. He knew that for thirty-four years one eye had been compelled to do the work of

two, and that the labor thus thrown upon the single organ —
however carefully he had managed and spared it — had been
more than it could bear. He felt that its powers were decaying; in some degree, no doubt, from advancing years, but more
from overwork, which yet could not have been avoided without abandoning the main hopes of his literary life. He therefore resorted for counsel to physicians of eminence, who were
his friends, but who were not professed oculists, and laid his
case before them. It was not new to them. They had known
it already in most of its aspects, but they now gave to it again
their most careful consideration. The result of their judgment coincided with his own previously formed opinion; and,
under their advice, he deliberately made up his mind, as he
has recorded it, " to relinquish *all* use of the eye for the future
in his studies, and to be content if he could preserve it for the
more vulgar purposes of life."

It was a hard decision. I am not certain that he made it
without a lingering hope, such as we are all apt to indulge,
even in our darkest moments, concerning whatever regards
health and life; — a hope, I mean, that there might still be a
revival of power in the decayed organ, and that it might still
serve him, in some, degree, as it had done, if not to the same
extent. But if he had such a hope, he was careful not to foster it or rely on it. His record on this point is striking and
decisive.

Thus was I in a similar situation with that in which I found myself
on beginning the "History of Ferdinand and Isabella"; — with this
important difference. Then I had hopes to cheer me on; the hope of
future improvement, as the trouble then arose from an excessive sensibility of the nerve. But this hope has now left me, and forever. And
whatever plans I am to make of future study must be formed on the same
calculations as those of a blind man. As this desponding conviction
pressed on me, it is no wonder that I should have paused and greatly
hesitated before involving myself in the labyrinth of researches relating to
one of the most busy, comprehensive, and prolific periods of European
history. The mere sight of this collection from the principal libraries
and archives of Europe, which might have daunted the resolution of a
younger man, in the possession of his faculties, filled me with apprehension bordering on despair; and I must be pardoned if I had not the
heart to plunge at once into the arena, and, blindfold as I was, engage
again in the conflict.

And then I felt how slow must be my progress. Any one who has had occasion to consult numerous authorities, — and those, too, in foreign languages, — for every sentence, will understand *how* slow and perplexing. And though, once entered on this career, I could have gone on in spite of obstacles, as, at times, I had already done, yet I hesitated before thus voluntarily encountering them.

The first six months after the publication of my "Peru" were passed in that kind of literary loafing in which it is not unreasonable to indulge after the completion of a long work. As I tired of this, I began to coquet with my Philip the Second, by reading, or rather listening to, the English histories which had any bearing on the story, and which could show me the nature and compass of it. Thus, I have heard Robertson's "Charles the Fifth," Watson's "Philip the Second," Ranke's "Popes," and other works of Ranke and Von Raumer done into English, and Dunham's volume relating to the period in his "Spain and Portugal." I have, also, with the aid of my Secretary, turned over the title-pages and got some idea of the contents of my books and manuscripts; — a truly precious collection of rarities, throwing light on the darkest corners of this long, eventful, and, in some respects, intricate history.

The result of the examination suggests to me other ideas. There is so much incident in this fruitful reign, — so many complete and interesting episodes, as it were, to the main story, — that it now occurs to me I may find it expedient to select *one* of them for my subject, instead of attempting the *whole*. Thus, for example, we have the chivalrous and fatal expedition of Don Sebastian and the conquest of Portugal; the romantic siege of Malta; the glorious war of the revolution in the United Provinces. This last is by far the greatest theme, and has some qualities — as those of unity, moral interest, completeness, and momentous and beneficent results — which may recommend it to the historian, who has the materials for both at his command, in preference to the Reign of Philip the Second.

One obvious advantage to me in my crippled state is, that it would not require more than half the amount of reading that the other subject would. But this is a decision not lightly to be made, and I have not yet pondered it as I must. Something, I already feel, I must do. This life of *far niente* is becoming oppressive, and "I begin to be aweary of the sun." I am no longer young, certainly; but at fifty-two a man must be even more crippled than I am to be entitled to an honorable discharge from service.

With such mingled feelings, — disheartened by the condition of his eye, and yet wearied out with the comparative idleness his infirmity had forced upon him, — it is not remarkable that he should have hesitated still longer about a great undertaking, the ample materials for which lay spread out before him. Just at this time, too, other things attracted his attention, or demanded it, and he gladly occupied himself with them, feeling that they were at least an apology for not turning at once to his severer work.

One of these was a Memoir of Mr. John Pickering, a wise, laborious, accurate scholar, worthy every way to be the son of that faithful statesman, who not only filled the highest places in the government under Washington, but was Washington's personal, trusted friend. This Memoir the Massachusetts Historical Society had appointed Mr. Prescott to prepare for its Collections, and his memorandum shows with what feelings of affection and respect he undertook the work assigned to him.

"It will not be long," he says, "but, long or short, it will be a labor of love; for there is no man whom I honored more than this eminent scholar, estimable alike for the qualities of his heart and for the gifts of his mind. He was a true and kind friend to me; and, from the first moment of my entering on my historic career down to the close of his life, he watched over my literary attempts with the deepest interest. It will be a sad pleasure for me to pay an honest tribute to the good man's worth."

The Memoir is not long nor eulogistic; but as a biography it is faithful and sincere, and renders to Mr. Pickering's intellectual and moral character the honors it so richly deserved. The style throughout is simple and graceful, without the slightest approach to exaggeration; such, in short, as was becoming the modest man to whose memory the Memoir itself was devoted.[4]

Another of the subjects that occupied a good deal of his time during the spring of 1848 was a careful revision which he gave to my manuscript "History of Spanish Literature," then nearly ready for the press. It was an act of kindness for which I shall always feel grateful, and the record of which I preserve with care, as a proof how faithful he was and how frank. It took him some weeks, — too many, if he had not then been more than usually idle, or, at least, if he had not deemed himself to be so.

But he was not really idle. In comparison with those days of severe activity which he sometimes gave to his "Mexico," when his eyes permitted him to do for two or three hours a day what he could never do afterwards, his work might not

[4] It is in the "Collections of the Massachusetts Historical Society," Third Series, Vol. X.

12

now be accounted hard ; but still, during the summer of 1848, it was real work, continuous and effective.

The great subject of the reign of Philip the Second had, as I have already intimated, been many years in his mind. As early as the spring of 1838, when he had only just sent to Madrid for the materials on which to found his histories of the Conquest of Mexico and Peru, and while he was still uncertain of success about obtaining them, he said : " Should I succeed in my present collections, who knows what facilities I may find for making one relative to Philip the Second's reign, — a fruitful theme if discussed under all its relations, civil and literary as well as military, the last of which seems alone to have occupied the attention of Watson."

In fact, from this time, although he may occasionally have had doubts or misgivings in relation to his resources for writing it, the subject itself of the reign of Philip the Second was never long out of his mind. Somewhat more than a year later he says : " By advices from Madrid this week, I learn that the archives of Simancas are in so disorderly a state, that it is next to impossible to gather materials for the reign of Philip the Second. I shall try, however " ; — adding that, unless he can obtain the amplest collections, both printed and manuscript, he shall not undertake the work at all.

The letters to which he refers were very discouraging. One was from Dr. Lembke, who had so well served him in collecting manuscripts and books for his Conquests of Mexico and Peru, but who seemed now to think it would be very difficult to get access to the archives of Simancas, and who was assured by Navarrete, that, even if he were on the spot, he would find everything in confusion, and nobody competent to direct or assist his researches. The other letter, which was from the Secretary of the American Legation, — his old college friend, Middleton, — was still more discouraging.

" I enclose you," he writes, " Lembke's letter, and confirm what he says as to the difficulty of getting at the Simancas papers, or even obtaining any definite notion of their subjects. A young gentleman who had free access to them during six months, under the auspices of a learned professor, assured me that, with the exception of those relating to the Bourbon dynasty (i. e. since 1700), the papers are all thrown together without order or index. Whatever step, therefore, you may be inclined to take in the matter, would be a *speculation*, and the question is, whether it would be worth your while."[4]

But, as Mr. Prescott well knew, Simancas must necessarily be the great depository for original, unpublished documents relating to the reign of Philip the Second, the collection of which was begun there by that monarch ; and he therefore determined to persevere in his efforts, and by some means obtain access to them. Indeed, as we have all along seen, he was not of a temper readily to give up anything important which he had once deliberately undertaken.

Just at this moment, however, he was deprived of the services of Dr. Lembke. That gentleman had become obnoxious to the Spanish government, and was ordered out of the country with hardly the formality of a warning. But his first refuge was Paris, and there he was again able to be useful to Mr. Prescott. M. Mignet and M. Ternaux-Compans opened to him freely their own rich manuscript collections, and indicated to him yet other collections, from which also he caused copies to be made of documents touching the affairs of Philip. But Dr. Lembke, I think, remained in Paris only a few months, and never was able to return to Madrid, as he intended and hoped when he left it. His services to Mr. Prescott, therefore, which had been, up to this time, both important and kind, could no longer be counted upon.

Happily, however, Mr. Prescott was now able to turn to Don Pascual de Gayangos, the Spanish scholar, who, as we have noticed, had written eighteen months earlier a pleasant article in the "Edinburgh Review" on "Ferdinand and Isabella," and who was now in London publishing for "The Oriental Fund Society" his translation of Al Makkari on the Mohammedan rule in Spain. Some correspondence of a friendly nature had already passed between them,[5] and Mr. Prescott

---

[4] These letters were written in 1839. In 1841, Mr. Middleton ceased to be connected with the Spanish Legation. When Mr. Prescott received the last results of his friend's care for his wants, he said: "I have received another supply, — the last of the manuscripts from Middleton, in Madrid. I lose there a good friend, who has been efficient and true in his labors for me."

[5] I have not been able to procure the earliest letters in the correspondence between Mr. Prescott and Don Pascual de Gayangos, and suppose they are lost. The earliest one that has come to my hands is from Don Pascual, and

now asked Don Pascual's counsel and aid in collecting the materials he needed for his work on the reign of Philip the Second. He could not have addressed himself more fortunately. Don Pascual entered into the literary projects of Mr. Prescott, as we have already seen, in his previous correspondence, with great disinterestedness and zeal. He at once caused above eighteen hundred pages of manuscript to be copied in the British Museum and the State-Paper Office, London, and went with an assistant, to the remarkable collection of Sir Thomas Phillips, in Worcestershire, where he again obtained much that proved valuable. Subsequently he visited Brussels, and, with letters from Mr. Van de Weyer, the accomplished Minister of Belgium in London, was permitted to take copies of whatever could be found in the archives there. Still later, he went to Paris, and, assisted by M. Mignet, discovered other rich materials, which were immediately transcribed and sent to their destination. The mass of manuscripts was, therefore, in 1842, already considerable.

But Spain was, after all, the country where the chief materials for such a subject were to be found ; and nobody knew this better than Mr. Prescott. While, therefore, he neglected no resource outside of the Pyrenees ; and while, by the kindness of Mr. Edward Everett, our statesman at once and our scholar, who happened then to be in Florence ; by that of Dr. Ferdinand Wolf of Vienna, learned in everything Spanish ; and by that of Humboldt and Ranke, at Berlin, each *primus inter pares* on such matters, he had obtained a great deal that was most welcome from the public offices and libraries of Tuscany, Austria, Prussia, and Gotha, — still he kept his eye fastened on Spain, as the main resource for his great undertaking.

is dated Dec. 1, 1839. From this I infer that Mr. Prescott had written to him on the 30th of March preceding, to thank him for his review of the "Ferdinand and Isabella," and on the 6th of July concerning his literary projects generally ; but that illness and absence from London had prevented Don Pascual from answering earlier. On the 28th of December, 1841, Mr. Prescott records in his memoranda : "I have had the satisfaction to learn from that accomplished scholar, Gayangos, that he will undertake the collection of manuscripts for me relating to Philip the Second's history, so far as it can be effected in Paris and London." A part of Mr. Prescott's correspondence with Don Pascual about the materials for a history of Philip the Second has already been given, as its dates required, while Mr. Prescott was employed on his "Conquest of Peru."

And here again he was fortunate. Don Pascual de Gayangos, having finished his important work for the "Oriental Fund," naturally returned to Madrid, with whose University he became connected as Professor of Arabic Literature. This was in 1842, and from that time he never ceased to send Mr. Prescott, not only rare books in large numbers, but manuscripts, both original and copied, of the greatest value.[7] Already, in 1849, these collections seemed to be complete; but for several years more they were continued and increased. The muniment rooms of the great families in Spain — the Alvas, the Santa Cruz, and others — were thrown open; the Public Archives, the National Library, in short, whatever could be used as a resource, were all visited and examined. In 1844, Don Pascual spent nearly two months at Simancas, under the most favorable auspices, and brought away and subsequently secured, from this great treasure-house and tomb of the Spanish government and its diplomacy, spoils which one less familiar with the history of the times would hardly have been able to discover amidst the confusion that had so long reigned there undisturbed.

The collection thus made with great labor in the course of nearly twenty years is, no doubt, one of the richest and most complete ever made on any subject of historical research. Setting aside the books in Mr. Prescott's library that relate only incidentally to the affairs of Spain in the sixteenth century, the number of which is very considerable, there are above three hundred and seventy volumes that regard especially the times of Philip the Second; and, when the manuscript copies that had been made for him all over Europe were brought together and bound, they made fifteen thick folios, not counting those which came to him already bound up, or which still remain unbound, to the amount of eight or ten volumes more.[8] It needed many

---

[7] In a letter to Don Pascual, dated March 27, 1842, he says: "I wish you could spend only three months in Spain, and I should ask no better luck." And again, July 14: "It will be very fortunate for me, if you can visit both Paris and Spain. It will leave me nothing to desire." Before the year was over, this wish was most unexpectedly fulfilled.

[8] The greater part of his rich collection of manuscripts for the "Mexico," "Peru," and "Philip the Second," stood together, well bound in morocco, and made quite a striking appearance in his library. He sometimes called this part of it "his Serraglio."

skilful, kind, and faithful hands in many countries to form such a collection ; but without the assistance of a scholar to superintend and direct the whole, like Don Pascual de Gayangos, full of knowledge on the particular subject, proud of his country, whose honor he knew he was serving, and disinterested as a Spanish *hidalgo* of the olden temper and loyalty, Mr. Prescott could never have laid the foundations he did for his " History of Philip the Second," or executed his purpose so far and so well.

Some of these treasures arrived in the course of the last two or three years of his life ; but most of them were already on his shelves in the summer of 1848, when he had not yet given himself up to severe labor on his " History of Philip the Second," and when, indeed, as we have seen, he was complaining of his idleness. But he was somewhat unjust to himself on this point now, as he had occasionally been before. He had not, in fact, been idle during the summer. When the autumn set in and he returned to town, he had read, or rather listened to, San Miguel's " Historia de Felipe Segundo," published between 1844 and 1847 in four goodly octavos ; the " Histoire de l'Espagne," by Weiss ; the portion of Tapia's " Civilizacion Española," which covers the sixteenth century ; and the corresponding parts of Sismondi's " Histoire des Français," and of Lingard's " History of England." But, above all, he had read and studied Ranke's " Spanish Empire " ; a book which whoever writes on the history of Spain must, if he is wise, consider carefully in all its positions and conclusions. In his memoranda Mr. Prescott truly describes Ranke as " acute and penetrating ; gathering his information from sources little known, especially the reports of the Venetian Ambassadors." [*] " His book," the personal memoranda go on, " contains inestimable material for a more minute and extended history. It is a sort of skeleton, the bone-work of the monarchy. It must be studied for the internal administration, the financial system, the domestic politics, &c. ; — just the topics neglected by Watson and the like common, uncommonplace writers. The historian of Philip the Second will be largely indebted to Ranke, to his original acuteness and to his erudition."

[*] Since published at Florence, under the able editorship of the Cavaliere Eugenio Albèri.

This portion of Ranke's work, therefore, became now to Mr. Prescott what Clemencin's dissertation on Queen Isabella had been in the composition of his History of the Catholic Sovereigns. Indeed, foreseeing from the outset how important it would be, and finding it ill printed in the English translation, he caused four copies of the part touching Philip the Second to be struck off on a large type, so that, whenever his eye would permit the indulgence, he might recur to it as to his manual and guide. It makes in this form barely one hundred and sixty-eight pages in octavo; and being printed on thick paper and only on one side of each leaf, so as to render every letter perfectly distinct, it was as well fitted to its peculiar purpose as it could be. Probably he never looked on it for ten minutes together at any one time; but we have already noticed how thoughtful and ingenious he was in whatever related to the means of encountering the many obstacles laid in his way by his great infirmity, and how little he cared for money or ease when anything of this sort was to be accomplished. This reprint of Ranke was, in truth, one of his contrivances for an end that never was long absent from his thoughts.

CHAPTER XXI.

1848 – 1850.

WHILE Mr. Prescott was going on with his "Philip the Second" as well as he could, considering the slow process for work to which he was now reduced, — "dull sailing," as he called it, — he was surprised by a tempting invitation to write a history of the Second Conquest of Mexico, — the one, I mean, achieved by General Winfield Scott in 1847. The subject was obviously a brilliant one, making, in some respects, a counterpart to the history of the first conquest under Cortés; and, as to the bookselling results that would have accrued from such a work glowing with the fervent life Mr. Prescott's style would have imparted to it, and devoted to the favorite national hero of the time, there can be no doubt they would have exceeded anything he had ever before dreamed of as the profits of authorship. But his course in another direction was plainly marked out, and had long been so. Contemporary events, transient and unsettled interests, personal feelings and ambitions, had never entered into his estimates and arrangements for a literary life. He felt that he should hardly know how to deal with them. He therefore declined the honor, — and an honor it certainly was, — without hesitation. "The theme," he said, "would be taking; but I had rather not meddle with heroes who have not been under ground two centuries at least." [1]

---

[1] He often expressed this feeling. In a letter to me in 1856, he says: "I belong to the sixteenth century, and am quite out of place when I sleep elsewhere," — a remark which reminds one of old Bernal Diaz, who, it has been said, wore his armor so long and so constantly in the conquest of Mexico, that afterwards he could not sleep in comfort without it.

His weeks at Pepperell in the subsequent autumn of 1849 were agreeable, as they always were, but not as fruitful of literary results as they had been in many preceding years. "The delicious stillness of the fields," he writes soon after his emigration there from Nahant, "is most grateful after the incessant, restless turmoil of the ocean, whose melancholy beat makes no music like the wind among the boughs of the forest. The sweet face of Nature is the only face that never grows old, — almost the only one that we never tire of."

But in truth the trouble lay deeper. He could do little work. His eyes were in a very bad state, and sometimes occasioned him much suffering. He therefore was able to "Philippize," as he called it, very little; and when he returned to town at the end of October, he recorded that he had had "a pleasant *villeggiatura*," but added: "The country is now dark with its sad autumnal splendors. Is it not my true home? Monadnock and his brotherhood of hills seemed to look gloomily on me as I bade them farewell. What may betide me of weal or woe before I see them again?"

But this was not a permanent state of feeling with him. During that autumn and winter, he went slowly, but with much regularity, over the whole ground, which, as he foresaw, must be occupied by a history of Philip the Second and his times, endeavoring to get a bird's-eye view of it in its general relations and proportions without descending to details. When he had done this, he felt that the time for a final decision as to the nature and form which his labors should take was come, and he made it promptly and decisively.

"I have, indeed," he says, looking back over the eighteen months' deliberation on this subject, and considering at the same time the bad condition of his eyes and of his general health, — "I have, indeed, hardly felt courage to encounter the difficulties of a new work, *de longue haleine*, in my crippled state. But if I am crippled, I am not wholly disabled yet; and I have made up my mind to take the subject — the whole subject — of Philip the Second. I can, by a little forecast, manage so that it will cost me no more labor or research than a fraction of the subject, which I should treat, of course, more *in extenso*. I must select the most important and interesting features of the reign, and bring these, and these only, into as clear a light as possible. All the wearisome research into constitutional, financial, ecclesiastical details, I must discard, or at least go into them sparingly; — only so as to present a background to the great transactions of the reign.

12 *

"The brilliant passages are numerous, and must be treated, of course, with reference to one another, as well as to their individual merit, so as to preserve their respective proportions, and harmonize into one whole. A dominant and central interest for the mighty and richly varied panorama must be ever kept in view. The character of Philip will be the dominant principle controlling every other; and his policy will be the central object of interest, to which almost every event in the reign must be in a great degree referred. That policy, doubtless, will be found to be the establishment of the Roman Catholic religion and of absolute power. These were the ends ever kept in view by him, and they must be so, therefore, by his historian, as furnishing the true clew to his complicated story.

"There will be no lack of great events of the highest interest and the most opposite character; the war with the Turks, and the glowing battle of Lepanto; the bloody revolt of the Moriscos; the conquest of Portugal, and, preceding it, the Quixotic expedition of Don Sebastian; the tragic domestic story of Don Carlos, and the mysterious adventures of Antonio Perez; the English invasion, and the gallant days of the Armada; and above all, and running through all, the glorious war of the Netherlands, — the war of freedom then begun and not yet ended.

"As for portraits, great events call forth great men, and there is good store of them, — Don John of Austria, frank and chivalrous; the great Duke of Alva, a name of terror; William of Orange, the Washington of Holland; Farnese, the greatest captain of his times; Don Sebastian, the theme for romance rather than history; contemporary foreign princes, Henry the Fourth, Elizabeth, &c., and at home Charles the Fifth in his latter days, of which so little has hitherto been known; and Philip the Second, the master-spirit, who, in the dark recesses of the Escorial, himself unseen even by his own subjects, watches over the lines of communication which run out in every direction to the farthest quarters of the globe. . . . .

"I propose to go on with sober industry, — the *festina lente* sort, — working some four hours a day, and if the whole should run to four volumes, which is enough, I may get out two at a time, allowing four years for each brace. *Da, Jupiter annos!* But I must mend my habits, or I shall not get out a volume in as many centuries. . . . .

"I am not sure that it will not be better for me to call the work *Memoirs*, instead of *History*, &c. This will allow a more rambling style of writing, and make less demand on elaborate research, and so my eyes and my taste both be accommodated."

To these general remarks he added, as he was wont in such cases, a synopsis or summary of the whole work he was about to undertake, — one intended to suggest the different subjects and points upon which he should chiefly concentrate his attention, but not intended to govern his treatment of the details. It was a sort of outline map, and was made in February, 1849.

But his doubts and anxieties at that time, and for a long while afterwards, were very considerable, both as to the form

of his work, whether memoirs or history, and as to the amount
of labor which his advancing years and infirmities might warrant him in hoping to bestow upon it. While his mind continued thus unsettled, he talked with me much on the embarrassments he felt, and I endeavored to strengthen him in a purpose
of taking up the whole subject under the gravest forms of
regular history, and treating it with absolute thoroughness as
such ; anxious neither as to how slow his progress might be,
nor how laborious it might prove.

One ground of my judgment at that time [*] — but unhappily
one which failed at last — was, that I counted upon a long life
for him, like that of his father and of his mother. But I felt,
too, whether he lived many years, as I fondly hoped, or few,
that the most active and earnest occupation of his faculties was
necessary to his own happiness, and that he would become dis-
contented with himself, if he should not fulfil his own idea of
what his subject implied in its widest and most serious requisitions. I did not, in short, believe that he would be satisfied to
write *Memoirs* of Philip the Second after having written the
History of Ferdinand and Isabella. Nor did I believe that
scholars or the public would be better satisfied than he would
be himself.

He expresses his state of mind on this subject in his memoranda : —

June 28th, 1849. — At Nahant, where we arrived on the 23d, after a
week of tropical heats in town, that gave me the dyspepsia. These summer months were once my working months. But now, alas! all times
and places are alike to me. I have even ceased to make good resolutions,
— the last infirmity of feeble minds. Since last summer, what have I
done? My real apology for doing nothing is still my health, which
hedges me round, whichever way I attempt to go. Without eyes I cannot read. Yet I constantly try to do something, and as constantly strain
the nerve. An organic trouble causes me pain, if I sit and write half an
hour, so that I am baffled and disheartened, and I find it *impossible* (shall
I say the coward's word?) to get up a lively interest, — the interest I felt
in happier days in my historical labors.

Yet I am determined to make one serious trial before relinquishing the

[*] This was in 1849. He did not determine to write a history rather than
memoirs, until he came to the troubles in the Netherlands, in October, 1851.
And the change of purpose is to be noted after page 360 of the first volume
of the American edition.

glorious field, on which I have won some laurels, and on which I had promised myself a long career. I will make up my mind to dispense with my eyes nearly all the time. I will dictate, if I cannot write. I will secure three hours every day for my work, and, with patience, I may yet do something.[a]

I will not seek to give that minute and elaborate view of the political and economical resources of the country which I attempted in "Ferdinand and Isabella," and for which I have such rich materials for this reign. But I must content myself with a more desultory or a picturesque view of things, developing character as much as possible, illustrating it by the anecdote, and presenting the general features of the time and the court. The work in this way, though not profound, may be amusing, and display that philosophy which consists in the development of human passion and character.

Great events, told with simplicity, will interest the reader, and the basis on which the narrative throughout will rest will be of the most authentic kind, enabling me to present facts hitherto unknown, and, of course, views and deductions not familiar to the student of history. The book will lose much of its value compared with what it might have had under happier auspices; but enough may remain to compensate both the reader and myself for the time bestowed on it. But, then, I must proceed on the right principle; content with accomplishing what the embarrassments of my situation will permit me to accomplish, without aiming at what, by its difficulties, would disgust me in its progress, and by its failure in the end bring only mortification and chagrin. I will try.

The conditions were hard, and the first efforts he made to break ground were anything but cheerful or encouraging; for his eyes were in a very bad state, and he was otherwise not a little disordered. After an experiment of nearly a month, he says : —

Looked over various works for an introductory chapter. Worked about three hours *per diem*, of which with my own eyes (grown very dim, — alas ! perceptible in this strong light) about thirty minutes a day. I can manage with this to make progress on a less searching plan of study. Am now prepared *to think*. But after this long repose, the business of fixing thought is incredibly difficult. It must be done.

And it *was* done. On the 29th of July, 1849, at Nahant, he records : "Last Thursday (July 26th), at 6 P. M., began the composition of Chapter First of 'Philip the Second,' whether memoirs or history time will show. Heavy work this starting. I have been out of harness too long."

[a] He did not, in fact, succeed in getting so much work as this out of himself in the summer and autumn of 1849.

At Pepperell, where he went with his accustomed eagerness on the 6th of September, his eyes were rather worse than they had been at Nahant, and he was more troubled with dyspepsia and his other chronic ailments. But he worked, against wind and tide, as earnestly, if not as hopefully, as if both had been in his favor.

On his return to town, about the end of October, he talked with me afresh concerning his plans in relation to " Philip the Second," of which he had been able to complete only two chapters. On the whole, he was confirmed in his decision that he would take the entire reign of that monarch for his subject, and not any episode of it, however brilliant, like the war with the Turks, or the siege of Malta, or however important, like the grand tragedy of the contest with the Netherlands. But he did not feel strong enough to make more of it than memoirs, as distinguished from history. On the first point, I concurred with him entirely; on the last, I regretted his decision, but submitted to it, if not as to something inevitable, at least as to a result concerning which his health and years afforded grounds, of which he was to judge rather than anybody else.

His decision, however, which seemed then to be final, had one good effect immediately. He worked more freely, and for a time made a degree of progress that satisfied himself. But about Christmas his strength began to fail. He lost flesh visibly, and his friends, though they certainly did not look on the state of his health with anxiety, yet felt that more than ordinary care had become necessary. He himself did not share their feelings ; but he had other doubts and misgivings more disheartening than theirs. In February, 1850, he said : " Increasing interest in the work is hardly to be expected, considering it has to depend so much on the ear. As I shall have to depend more and more on this one of my senses, as I grow older, it is to be hoped that Providence will spare me my hearing. It would be a fearful thing to doubt it."

Happily he was never called to encounter this terrible trial. Not infrequently, indeed, a suspicion occurred to him, especially about this period, that the acuteness of his hearing was impaired, as, in truth, I think it was, but in so small a degree, that he was rarely admonished of it, even by his own fears, and certainly never so much as to interfere with the course which his studies necessarily took. But whenever the thought came to him of what might possibly be the result in this respect, darkness seemed to settle on his thoughts; and, although his elastic spirits soon obtained the mastery, it was not until after a struggle such as they had not heretofore been summoned to make. A few of my conversations with him on this subject were among the most painful that I remember ever to have had. But the most painful of them were later, in the last two years of his life.

In the early spring of 1850, finding that he was less able to work than he had previously been, and that he could not command his thoughts for the concentrated efforts he had always found important to success, he made a journey southward, to anticipate the milder season. He was accompanied by his daughter, by Mrs. Charles Amory, by Mrs. Howland Shaw, and by his brother-in-law, Mr. William Amory, — a party as agreeable as affection and friendship could have collected for him. I chanced to be in Washington when he arrived there, and was witness to the pleasure with which he was everywhere received. All sorts of hospitalities were offered to him by General Taylor, then President of the United States; by the Calderons, his old and faithful friends; by the British Minister, Sir Henry Bulwer; by our own great New-England statesman, Mr. Webster, who had always entertained the sincerest veneration for the elder Mr. Prescott, and always welcomed the son as worthy of his ancestry; in short, he was received by whatever was eminent in the diplomatic society of Washington, or among those collected there to administer our own affairs, with a distinction not to be mistaken or misinterpreted. His friends sought eagerly to enjoy as much of his society as he could give them, and strangers gladly seized the opportunity to know personally one with whom in so many other ways they were already familiar. But he was little in a condition to accept the kindness which under different circumstances would have been so pleasant to him. He was not well. He was not happy. He felt that he needed the comforts and the solace to which he was accustomed at home. He remained in Washington, therefore, only a short time, and then returned to Boston.

The comforts of home, however, were not all that he needed. He needed a change of life for a time, — something that should, as it were, renew, or at least refresh and strengthen the resources of a constitution which had so long been touched with infirmities, not of the gravest sort, indeed, but yet constantly so pressing on the springs of life, and so exhausting their elasticity, that neither his physical nor his mental system was any longer capable of the severe efforts which he had always claimed from them, and almost always with success.

After some time, therefore, the project of visiting England, which he had partly entertained at different times for many years, but had constantly rejected, recurred with new force. His friends, who had heretofore urged it on the ground of the personal enjoyment he could not fail to derive from such a visit, now urged it on the stronger ground of health, and of the sort of renovation which so great a change of climate and of his modes of life and thought often give to the whole moral and physical constitution at the age which he had now reached. He acknowledged the force of what they pressed upon him, but still he hesitated. His domestic life was so wisely regulated; everything about him was so carefully adjusted and adapted, by the watchfulness of affection, to his peculiar infirmities, and the wants they entailed on him; in short, his condition in his own home, and with his daily occupations, was so entirely such as demanded only gratitude to God, that he naturally felt unwilling to interrupt its long-settled, even, and happy course. But the strong hours conquered, as they always must in what regards health and life. The reasons for a European excursion grew every week more distinct and decisive, and at last he yielded.

He embarked from New York the 22d day of May, 1850. On board the steam-packet in which he took passage he found, as he did everywhere, the kindness that was drawn out by the magnetism of his own affectionate nature, and by his obvious infirmities, added to the strong interest he had excited as an author. He was at once provided with readers for all the hours when he was well enough to listen, and among them were some members of the Middleton family of South Carolina, who were connections of his old classmate, and who became at once not only interesting and agreeable companions, but personal friends.   Notwithstanding, therefore, the usual tribute of sea-sickness, which he paid like others, and complained of as bitterly, his passage was far from being disagreeable.

Just so it was when, at midnight, on Monday, the 3d of June, the vessel on which he was embarked arrived in the Mersey, at Liverpool.   The first voice he heard through the darkness, from a boat which came alongside five minutes after the steamer's anchor had been dropped, was that of an English friend whose face he had not seen for three and thirty years, but whose regard had survived unimpaired from the days when they had been together almost as boys in Italy.   At the house of that friend, Mr. Alexander Smith, he found at once an affectionate reception, and remained there hospitably entertained until two days later, when he hurried up to London.

"On Wednesday, June 5th," he says in his second letter to Mrs. Prescott, "I came by railway to 'London town,' through the English garden, lawns of emerald green, winding streams, light arched bridges, long lines stretching out of sight between hedges of hawthorn, — all flowering, — rustic cottages, lordly mansions, and sweeping woods; flocks of sheep, and now and then peasants shearing off the fat fleeces; cattle of the Durham breed, but all more or less white, often wholly so, — white as snow; the whole landscape a miracle of beauty, all of the cultivated sort, too tame on the whole; and before I reached the great leviathan, I would have given something to see a ragged fence, or an old stump, or a bit of rock, or even a stone as big as one's fist, to show that man's hand had not been combing Nature's head so vigorously.   I felt I was not in my own dear, wild America."

London hospitality had met him at Liverpool.   Lady Lyell, to whom, like everybody else who was permitted to become really acquainted with her during her visits to the United States, he was already much attached, had sent him charming words of welcome, which he received as he stepped on shore in the night.[4]   Mr. Lawrence, too, his friend and kinsman, then

---

[4] I add the answer to Lady Lyell's kind note, welcoming him to England.

TO LADY LYELL.

Liverpool, June 4, 1850.

My dear Lady Lyell,

I have just received your kind note, in the midst of trunks, *luggage* (you

American Minister at the Court of St. James, had begged him in the same way to be in season for a large diplomatic dinner which he was to give on the evening that Mr. Prescott would naturally reach London. Others had, in other ways, sent salutations both courteous and cordial. It was all very flattering and kindly, and, accompanied as he was by his faithful and intelligent secretary, Mr. Kirk, he did not, from the moment of his landing, feel for an instant that he was either alone or upon a stranger soil.

On reaching London, he drove at once to Mivart's Hotel, where lodgings had been engaged for him ; but he had hardly alighted when Sir Charles Lyell entered and gave him his first London greeting, which he loved always afterwards to remember for its affectionate warmth. The dinner at Mr. Lawrence's he had declined, being too fresh from a long journey to enjoy it ; but he took tea a little later with Lady Lyell, and went with her to the evening party at the Minister's, which followed the more serious dinner, and was, in fact, a part of it. His introduction to much of what was most distinguished in English society, including Lord Palmerston and several others of the Ministers, could hardly have been more agreeable or more graceful.

It was on this occasion that he first saw the Milmans, with whom he had long felt acquainted, and to whom he soon became personally much attached. It was then, too, that he first saw the venerable mother of his friend Lord Carlisle, and many other persons of distinction, his meeting with whom he often afterwards recalled with peculiar pleasure. But that with Lord Carlisle went to his heart, and well it might, for it was warmer than he intimates it to have been, even in a letter to

see my Yankee breeding), and all the other custom-house trumpery from which it is so difficult a matter, after a voyage, to disentangle one's self. I am passing a day here with an old friend, and to-morrow shall take the eleven o'clock train for London. Many thanks for your agreeable invitation, which I shall have the pleasure of answering in person to-morrow evening. I have declined an invitation to dine with our Minister, as I shall not be in condition to dine, so soon after my journey, with an array of Ministers and Ministers' ladies. But I shall be in first-rate condition for seeing friends whom I value so much as you and your husband.

Pray remember me warmly to him, and believe me, my dear Lady Lyell, &c.

Mrs. Prescott, in which he says, that it made him "feel as awkward as a young girl." A person who was present said that Lord Carlisle almost embraced him. But he remained at this first London party only a little while. He was too tired after his journey.

From this moment his table was covered with cards and invitations. His preference and pleasure were undoubtedly for the more cultivated and intellectual society which received him on all sides with earnest cordiality; but he was also the fashion. He was invited everywhere. He was the lion of the season.[5]

His own letters to his family, and his more intimate friends, will show this in the simplest and pleasantest manner.

TO MRS. PRESCOTT.

LONDON, Tuesday, June 11, 1850.

DEAREST SUSAN,

I returned last evening from a visit to the Horners, Lady Lyell's parents and sisters, a very accomplished and happy family-circle. They occupy a small house, with a pretty lawn stretching between it and the Thames, that forms a silver edging to the close-shaven green. The family gather under the old trees, on the little shady carpet, which is sweet with the perfumes of flowering shrubs, and you see sails gliding by and stately swans of which there are several hundreds on the river. Any injury to those birds is visited with a heavy penalty. The next day, Sunday, after dinner, — which we took at four, — we strolled through Hampton Court and its royal park. The entrance to the park is not more than half a mile from Mr. H.'s house. We spent a couple of hours in rambling over it, — a most superb green lawn stretching in all directions, covered with avenues of stately trees planted in the time of William and Mary, mostly the English elm. Troops of deer were standing and lying idly round, and every now and then we started a hare. Whole companies of rooks — a bird seen everywhere here — sailed over the tops of the trees, — such

---

[5] The Nepaulese Princes were in London that year, and were much stared at for their striking costumes and magnificent diamonds. Alluding to this circumstance, Mr. Lockhart, the first time he met Mr. Prescott, said, playfully, but not without a touch of the cynical spirit always in him, that "he was happy to make the acquaintance of Mr. Prescott, who, as he had heard, was the great lion of London, — he and the Nepaulese Princes." "You forget the hippopotamus!" retorted Mr. Prescott. It was not, perhaps, the most auspicious and agreeable beginning of an acquaintance, but it did not prevent them from being a good deal together afterwards, and liking each other much. A parting dinner with Ford and Stirling at Lockhart's was always remembered by Mr. Prescott as peculiarly gay and gratifying.

trees! In front of the old palace were broad red gravel walks through the green turf, with artificial basins of water. In short, the real scene looked like the picture in our camera at Pepperell. Here was the favorite residence of William and Mary, and of their predecessor, the merry Charles the Second, whose beauties, by the hands of Sir Peter Lely, still decorate the walls. I fancied, as I strolled through the grounds, I could see the gallant prince and his suite sauntering among the lordly avenues, playing with his spaniels and tossing crumbs to the swans in the waters. We walked home at twilight, hearing the nightingale at his evening song, and the distant cuckoo, sounding so like the little toy the children play with!

The next day we had our picnic at Box-Hill, — a sweet, romantic spot in Surrey, on a high hill, looking over half the country, and fragrant with the odors of the box, which rises here into trees. There was a collection of seven and twenty persons in all, friends of the family. So we spread our cloth in a shady spot, and produced our stores of good things, and with the aid of a little of the spiritual with the material, we had a merry time of it. T—— A—— will tell you all about it, as he returns by the next steamer; so he intends, at least, at the present moment. The P——s return by it also. To think that I should have missed them! William was at just such a picnic last year, and I heard many kind things of him. He made some good friends here, and left everywhere, I believe, a good impression. I have written to our Minister at Madrid to look him up, for I have not yet heard from him. Unlucky enough! but I think he must soon turn up.[*]

* * * * *

Friday noon.

I have so many things to tell you of since my last date, and so little time to do it in, dear Susan, that I don't know which to take, — the Ascot races, dinner at Sir Robert Peel's, — or I will begin (probably end) with the visit to Lady S——s, which I was about to make when I left off. I went at eleven, and found myself in the midst of a brilliant saloon, filled with people, amongst whom I could not recognize one familiar face. You may go to ten parties in London, be introduced to a score of persons in each, and in going to the eleventh party not see a face that you have ever seen before; so large is the society of the Great Metropolis! I was soon put at my ease, however, by the cordial reception of Lord and Lady C——, who presented me to a number of persons.

In the crowd I saw an old gentleman, very nicely made up, stooping a good deal, very much decorated with orders, and making his way easily along, as all, young and old, seemed to treat him with deference. It was the Duke, — the old Iron Duke, — and I thought myself lucky in this opportunity of seeing him. Lord C—— asked me if I would like to know him, and immediately presented me to him. He paid me some pretty compliments, on which I grew vain at once, and I did my best to

* The reference is to Mr. Prescott's eldest son, who had been some time in Europe, but with whom Mr. Prescott had found it difficult to come into communication at this time. The son did not yet know that his father had thought of leaving America, and he was, in fact, now in Africa.

repay him in coin that had no counterfeit in it. He is a striking figure, reminding me a good deal of Colonel Perkins in his general air,[7] though his countenance is fresher. His aquiline nose is strongly cut, as in earlier days, when I saw him at the head of his troops in Paris, and his large forehead has but few wrinkles. He does not show the wear and tear of time and thought, and his benevolent expression has all the *iron* worked out of it. He likes the attention he receives in this social way, spending half an hour in working his way quietly through the rooms, and, having received the general homage, disappears. He wore round his neck the ribbons and ornaments of the Golden Fleece, and on his coat the diamond-star of the Order of the Garter. He is in truth the lion of England, not to say of Europe, and I could not take my eyes off him while he remained.

We had a stately dinner at Sir Robert's, — four and twenty guests. He received us in a long picture-gallery. The windows of the gallery at one end look out on the Thames, its beautiful stone bridges with lofty arches, Westminster Abbey with its towers, and the living panorama on the water. The opposite windows look on the Green Gardens behind the palace of Whitehall, — gardens laid out by Cardinal Wolsey, and near the spot where Charles the First lived and lost his life on the scaffold. The gallery is full of masterpieces, especially Dutch and Flemish, — among them the famous *Chapeau de Paille*, which cost Sir Robert over five thousand pounds, or twenty-two thousand dollars. In his dining-room are also superb pictures, — the famous one by Wilkie, of John Knox preaching, which did not come up to the idea I had formed from the excellent engraving of it; and Waagen, the German critic, who was there, told me, as I said this to him, that I was perfectly correct in the judgment. So I find I am a connoisseur! There was a portrait of Dr. Johnson, by Reynolds, — *the* portrait owned by Mrs. Thrale, and engraved for the Dictionary. What a *bijou* !

We sat at dinner, looking out on the moving Thames. We dined at eight, but the twilight lingers here till half past nine o'clock at this season. Sir Robert was exceedingly courteous to his guests; told some good stories, at which some laughed immoderately; showed us his pictures, his collection of autographs, &c. He has the celebrated letter, written by Nelson, in which he says, " If I die, *frigate* will be found written on my heart." [8]

---

[7] The resemblance to the Duke of Wellington of the late Colonel Thomas H. Perkins, already referred to as a munificent merchant of Boston, was often noticed and very obvious.

[8] An anecdote of this dinner, connected with an account of another, is happily given by Mr. Stirling, in a little memoir of Mr. Prescott, which was originally published in " Fraser's Magazine," for March, 1869, and was subsequently printed privately, with additions.

"Amongst the many occasions when it was the good fortune of the author of this sketch to meet Mr. Prescott, there is one which has especially stamped itself on his memory. It was on a delightful summer day, at a dinner given at the ' Trafalgar,' at Greenwich, by Mr. Murray, of Albemarle Street. Of that small and well-chosen circle, the brightest lights are, alas! already

Is not this a fine life ?   I am most sincerely tired of it.   Not that I do not enjoy the social meetings, and there are abundant objects of interest. But I am weary of the dissipation, and would not exchange my regular domestic and literary occupations in the good old Puritan town for this round of heedless, headless gayety, — not if I had the fortune of the Marquis of Westminster, the richest peer in England.   It is hard work to make a *life* of pleasure.   Wherever you go, you see wealth, splendor, and fashion, — horses, carriages, houses, all brilliant and gorgeous ; — but nothing like repose, and not always good taste.   All seem to be eagerly pursuing the goddess Pleasure, — hard to be caught, and vanishing in the grasp.   If I could bring it with a wish, August 15th would be here in

quenched.   The festive humor of Ford will no more enliven the scene he loved so well; nor will the wit of Lockhart and the wisdom of Hallam ever more brighten or adorn banquets like that at which they met their fellow-laborer from the New World.   Everything was in perfection, — the weather, the preliminary stroll beneath the great chestnut-trees in Greenwich Park, the cool upper room with its balcony overhanging the river, the dinner, from the profatory water-souchy to the ultimate devilled white-bait, the assortment, spirits, and conversation of the guests.   On our return to town in the cool of the summer night, it was the good fortune of the present writer to sit beside Mr. Prescott, on the box of the omnibus which Mr. Murray had chartered for his party.   It was there that the historian related to him the fortunes of his first historical work, as told above.   He likewise described with great zest a more recent incident of his life.   Some days before that, he had dined with the late Sir Robert Peel.   With the punctuality which was very noticeable amidst all the bustle of Mr. Prescott's endless London engagements, he was in Whitehall gardens at the precise moment indicated on the card of invitation.   It followed, as a natural result, that he was for some minutes the sole occupant of the drawing-room.   In due time, Sir Robert walked in, very bland and a little formal, somewhat more portly than he appeared on the canvas of Lawrence, somewhat less rotund than he was wont to be figured in the columns of *Punch*.   Although not personally known to his host, Mr. Prescott took for granted that his name had been announced. It was to his great surprise, therefore, that he found himself addressed in French.   He replied in the same language, idly musing whether he had been mistaken for somebody else, or whether to speak French to all persons from beyond the sea was the etiquette of British statesmanship, or the private predilection of Peel.   After some introductory topics had been got over, he was still further mystified by finding the dialogue turned towards the drama, and being complimented on his great success in that unfamiliar walk of letters. The astonished historian was making the reply which his native modesty dictated, when a second guest, a friend of his own, entered, and addressed both of them in English.   Mr. Prescott had been mistaken for M. Scribe, — a blunder ludicrous enough to those who know the contrast that existed between the handsome person of the historian, and the undistinguished appearance of the most prolific of modern playwrights.   By a curious chance, M. Scribe did not arrive until a large party of political and literary celebrities were seated at dinner, and Mr. Prescott concluded his story by remarking on the graceful kindness with which Sir Robert hastened to meet him at the door, and smoothed the foreigner's way to a place amongst strangers."

less than no time,* — and then, Ho for Yankee-land! Mr. Rogers has just sent me a message to say, that he must at least shake hands with me. How kind is this! although his house is crowded with visitors, he sees no one but his physicians.

Remember me kindly to George and Anna, and to any other friends. Kiss mother and Lizzie, and believe me, dearest,

Your loving husband,

WM. H. PRESCOTT.

TO MISS PRESCOTT.

LONDON, June 14, 1850.

MY DEAR LIZZIE,

As your mother tells me that you are to write me this week, I will do the same good turn to you. What shall I tell you about? There are so many things that would interest you in this wonderful city. But first of all, I think on reflection, you judged wisely in not coming. You would have had some lonely hours, and have been often rather awkwardly situated. Girls of your age make no great figure here in society. One never, or very rarely, meets them at dinner-parties, — and they are not so numerous in the evening parties as with us, unless it be the balls. Six out of seven women whom you meet in society are over thirty, and many of them over forty and fifty, — not to say sixty. The older they are, the more they are dressed and diamonded. Young girls dress little, and wear very little ornament indeed. They have not much money to spend on such costly luxuries. At the Ascot races yesterday, I happened to be next to Lady ——, a very pleasing girl, the youngest sister of Lord ——. She seemed disposed to bet on the horses; so I told her I would venture anywhere from a shilling to a sovereign. She said she never bet higher than a shilling, but on this occasion would go as high as half a crown. So she did, — and lost it. It was quite an exciting race, between a horse of Lord Eglinton's, named "Flying Dutchman," and a little mare of Lord Stanley's,[10] named "Canezou." The former had won on several occasions, but the latter had lately begun to make a name in the world, and Lord Stanley's friends were eagerly backing her. It was the most beautiful show in the world.

But I will begin with the beginning. I went with the Lawrences. We went by railway to Windsor, then took a carriage to Ascot, some half-dozen miles distant. The crowds of carriages, horses, &c. on the road filled the air with a whirlwind of dust, and I should have been blinded but for a blue veil which was lent me to screen my hat and face. The Swedish Minister, who furnished these accommodations, set the example by tying himself up. On reaching Ascot, we were admitted to the *salon*, which stands against the winning-post, and which is occupied by the Queen, when there. It was filled with gay company, all in high spirits. Lord Stanley was looking forward to a triumph, though he talked coolly about it. He is one of the ablest, perhaps the ablest, debater

---

* The period at which he then proposed to embark for home.

10 Now (1862) the Earl of Derby.

in Parliament, and next Monday will make a grand assault on the Cabinet. This is the way he relieves himself from the cares of public life. I suspect he was quite as much interested in the result of the race yesterday as he will be in the result of the Parliamentary battle on Monday.

The prize, besides a considerable stake of money from subscription, was a most gorgeous silver vase, the annual present of the Emperor of Russia for the Ascot races. It represents Hercules taming the horses of Diomede, beautifully sculptured, making an ornament for a sideboard or a table, some five feet in height, and eighteen inches square. What a trophy for the castle of the Earl of Derby, or for the Eglinton halls in Scotland!

The horses were paraded up and down before the spectators, — betting ran very high, — men and women, nobles and commoners, who crowd the ground by thousands, all entering into it. Five horses started on a heat of two miles and a half. The little bay mare led off gallantly, — "Flying Dutchman" seemed to lose ground, — the knowing ones began to shake, — and the odds rose in "Canezou's" favor, — when, just as they were within half a mile of the goal, Lord Eglinton's jockey gave his horse the rein, and he went off in gallant style, — not running, but touching the ground in a succession of flying leaps that could hardly have brushed the wet from the grass, for it began to rain. There was a general sensation; bets changed; the cry was for the old favorite; and as the little troop shot by us, "Flying Dutchman" came in at the head, by the length of several rods, before all the field. Then there was a shouting and congratulations, while the mob followed the favorite horse as if they would devour him. He was brought directly under our windows, and Lady Eglinton felt, I have no doubt, as much love for him at the moment as for any of her children. It was a glorious triumph, and the vase was hers, — or her lord's, whom I did not see. Now I did not feel the least excited by all this, but excessively tired, and I would not go to another race, if I could do it by walking into the next street; that is, if I had to sit it out, as I did here, for three mortal hours. How hard the English fine people are driven for amusement!

Coming home, we drove through the royal park at Windsor, among trees hundreds of years old, under which troops of deer were lazily grazing, secure from all molestation. The Thames is covered with swans, which nobody would dare to injure. How beautiful all this is! I wish, dear Lizzie, you could have a peep at the English country, with its superb, wide-stretching lawns, its numerous flocks of sheep, everywhere dotting the fields, and even the parks in town, and the beautiful white cows, all as clean as if they had been scrubbed down. England, in the country, is without a rival. But in town, the houses are all dingy, and most of them as black as a chimney with the smoke. This hangs like a funeral pall over the city, penetrating the houses, and discoloring the curtains and furniture in a very short time. You would be amused with the gay scene which the streets in this part of the town present. Splendid equipages fill the great streets as far as the eye can reach, blazing with rich colors, and silver mountings, and gaudy liveries. Everything here tells of a proud and luxurious aristocracy. I shall see enough of them to-day, as I have engagements of one kind or another to four houses, before bed-time, which is now with me very regularly about twelve, — sometimes later, but I do not like to have it later.

Why have I no letter on my table from home? I trust I shall find one there this evening, or I shall, after all, have a heavy heart, which is far from gay in this gayety.

Your affectionate father,

WM. H. PRESCOTT.

The account of his presentation at Court is much in the same style with the last. It is addressed to Mrs. Prescott, and, after an introduction on slight subjects, goes on as follows: —

Thursday, 6 P. M.

Well, the presentation has come off, and I will give you some account of it before going to dine with Lord Fitzwilliam. This morning I breakfasted with Mr. Monckton Milnes, where I met Macaulay, — the third time this week. We had also Lord Lyttleton, — an excellent scholar, — Gladstone, and Lord St. Germans, — a sensible and agreeable person, — and two or three others. We had a lively talk; but I left early for the Court affair. I was at Lawrence's at one, in my costume: a chapeau with gold lace, blue coat, and white trousers, begilded with buttons and metal, — the coat buttons up, single-breasted, to the throat, — a sword, and patent-leather boots. I was a figure, indeed! But I had enough to keep me in countenance. I spent an hour yesterday with Lady M., getting instructions for demeaning myself. The greatest danger was, that I should be tripped up by my own sword. On reaching St. James's Palace we passed up-stairs through files of the guard, — beef-eaters, — and were shown into a large saloon, not larger than the great room of the White House, but richly hung with crimson silk, and some fine portraits of the family of George the Third. It was amusing, as we waited there an hour, to see the arrival of the different persons, diplomatic, military, and courtiers. All, men and women, blazing in all their stock of princely finery; and such a *power* of diamonds, pearls, emeralds, and laces, the trains of the ladies' dresses several yards in length! Some of the ladies wore coronets of diamonds that covered the greater part of the head, others necklaces of diamonds, and emeralds that were a size perfectly enormous. I counted on Lady ——'s head two strings of diamonds, rising gradually from the size of a fourpence to the size of an English shilling, and thick in proportion. Lady —— had emeralds mingled with her diamonds, of the finest lustre, as large as pigeon's eggs. The *parure* was not always in the best taste. The Duchess of ——'s dress was studded with diamonds along the border and down the middle of the robe, — each of the size of half a nutmeg. The young ladies, a great many of whom were presented, were dressed generally without ornament. I tell all this for Lizzie's especial benefit. The company were at length permitted one by one to pass into the presence-chamber, — a room of about the same size as the other, with a throne and gorgeous canopy at the farther end, before which stood the little Queen of the mighty Isle, and her consort, surrounded by her ladies in waiting. She was rather simply dressed, but he was in a Field-Marshal's uniform, and covered, I should think, with all the orders of Europe. He is a good-looking person, but by no means so good-looking as the portraits of him. The Queen is better looking than you might expect. I was presented by our Minister, according to the directions of the Chamberlain, as the historian of Ferdinand and Isabella, in due form, — and made my profound obeisance to her Majesty, who made a very dignified courtesy, as she made to some two hundred others, who were presented in like manner. Owing to there having been no drawing-room for a long time, there was an unusual number of presentations of young ladies; but very few gentlemen were presented. I made the same low bow to his Princeship, to whom I was also presented, and so bowed myself out of the royal circle, without my sword tripping up the heels of my nobility. As I was drawing off, Lord Carlisle, who was standing on the edge of the royal circle, called me, and kept me by his side, telling me the names of the different lords and ladies, who, after paying their obeisance to the Queen, passed out before us. He said, he had come to the drawing-room to see how I got through the affair, which he thought I did without any embarrassment. Indeed, to say truth, I have been more embarrassed a hundred times in my life than I was here, I don't know why; I suppose, because I am getting old. I passed another hour in talking and criticising, especially with Lady T——, whom E—— D—— knew, and with Lady M—— H—— and Lord M——, all of whom happened to gather in that part of the room. I had also some talk with Sir Robert Peel and his wife, who has the remains of beauty, and whose daughter, much admired, according to Lord C., has much beauty herself. I talked also for some time with the old Iron Duke, who had more gold than iron about him to-day, and looked very well, although his utterance is not perfectly distinct, and he is slightly deaf.

After the drawing-room, I went at five to Stafford House, the Duchess of Sutherland's, where I lunched, and spent a couple of hours in rambling through the rooms of the magnificent palace ornamented with hundreds of the most exquisite paintings and statues, and commanding a beautiful view of Hyde Park. Nothing can be more kind than the behavior of the whole of Lord C.'s relatives to me. Luckily for me, they are of the best families in England. They treat me, one and all, as if I were one of themselves. What can be so grateful to the wanderer in a foreign land, as to find himself at once among friends, who seem to be friends of an old standing? If I were to tell you of the cordial and affectionate greetings they give me, I should seem more vain than I seem now, I fear, — if possible. But you will feel that I am talking to you, and do not say half I should if I were really talking.

I am most desirous to embark by September 1st, but I must see four or five specimens of English country-life; and Parliament — confound it — will not rise before the middle of August, unless the Ministry are upset, which may be. I have invitations to Lord Lansdowne's, the Duke of Northumberland's, Lord Fitzwilliam's, the Duke of Argyll's, and all that kith and kin, — and several other places. Lord Carlisle wants me to go first to Castle Howard, then to old Nawarth Castle, on the borders, which he has entirely restored since the fire, and the family spend some weeks there. I am afraid all this will carry me into September. But if so,

13

I shall abridge some of the visits.   I shall try to embark by the first of September.

Your loving husband,

WM. H. PRESCOTT.

To his mother he begins a letter in London, June 20th, but continues it from the Bishop of Oxford's palace.

CUDDESDON PALACE, June 23.

You will be surprised at the date of my continuation, perhaps, dear mother.   I am about seven miles from Oxford, at the residence of the Bishop, called Cuddesdon Palace; a very old building, and the mansion occupied from ancient times by his predecessors.   The present Bishop is the son of the famous Wilberforce.   He is a very handsome man, polished in his manners, and an eloquent preacher.   He invited me to stay here two or three days.   We have besides a dozen persons in the house, — a brother bishop, Thirlwall, who wrote the "History of Greece," an amiable and unpretending scholar; the Lawrences; Lord and Lady Castlereagh, &c.   It is very convenient for me, as I am to-morrow to receive the degree of Doctor of Laws from Oxford University.   The Marquis of Northampton,[11] who is also here, is to receive a degree at the same time, and a special convocation has been called for the purpose.   After the ceremony we all lunch at the Vice-Chancellor's, and return in the evening to London.   I came down to Oxford yesterday in the train with the Lawrences. The Bishop was obliged unluckily to remain in London till this morning, to attend the christening of the last royal infant.   He had arranged, therefore, that we should dine with the Principal of one of the Colleges in Oxford, after which, at ten, we drove over to Cuddesdon.   Lord Northampton and I came over together, and I found him a lively, sensible person, full of interesting anecdote.   He has travelled a good deal, and is much connected with science and scientific men.   Before going to bed, the whole household — guests included — went to the chapel, a very pretty building erected by the present Bishop, and heard the evening service, — very solemn, and parts of it chanted by the domestics of the house.   There are two chaplains attached to the establishment.   My bedroom looks out on a lawn, dotted with old trees, over whose tops the rooks are sailing and cawing, while a highly gifted nightingale is filling the air with his melody.   I am writing, you must understand, at five o'clock in the afternoon, while the rest of the household have gone to the afternoon service in the parish church.   I went there this morning, and heard the Bishop preach.   He arrived here from London, late last night, after we had all retired to rest. The church is one I should much like you to see.   It is of the greatest antiquity, — parts of it going back to the times of the Plantagenets, — to the reigns, indeed, of Henry the Third and John.   Is not that a glorious antiquity?   We sat in the venerable pile, where prayer and praise had

---

[11] President of the Royal Society.   He died the next year.

ascended for nearly seven centuries. The crumbling walls have been restored by the present Bishop, a man of great architectural taste. The light streams in through the stained panes, on which the arms and names of a long roll of bishops, from the beginning of the fourteenth century, were colored. The service was performed with a ceremony quite Roman-Catholic. The chant was conducted by all the congregation, as it seemed to me, and a great deal of the service read by us was chanted. The sermon was adapted, or meant to be adapted, to a parish church; but I did not acquiesce in the views of the preacher, though the tones of his voice would have melted the most obdurate heart. They started an unfortunate urchin who had fallen asleep, and whom he paused in his sermon to admonish in a very pastoral but decided tone. There must be little danger of the good Bishop's flock going to sleep, I should think, with *this* sort of improvement of the discourse. In truth, he is so eloquent that there must be very little danger of it at any rate. I walked with some of the ladies for a long while under the old elms in the grounds, after church.

I wish you could see the pretty picture — the English picture — under my window; — the green lawn, as smooth as velvet and of as deep a verdure. There are circular beds of roses, and yellow and purple flowers, gayly set out in one part of it, clumps of stately elms, and cypresses throwing masses of shadow over the turf, and several of the party, returned from church, stretched out under the trees, while the great birds, the rooks, are wheeling in the air, and the woods are alive, as the evening sun is withdrawing his fiercer rays. For it has been "real" warm to-day.

Cuddesdon stands on a high terrace, and from the grounds, which are not extensive, you have a wide view of the rich vale of the Isis, as it winds through Oxfordshire. The pastures are covered with white or white-streaked cattle, that look as if they had been groomed like horses, so clean and shining are they, and flocks of sheep, that always speckle an English landscape. Then there is a beautiful chime of bells, that has twice sent its musical echoes to-day over hill and dale, filling the air and the heart with a sober Sabbath melody. Then just beyond the grounds, around the old church, lies the country churchyard, where rest the mortal part of many a brave soul that lived in the times of the Edwards and Henrys. What is there like these old links of Time, that bind us to the past, — as much our past as it is John Bull's?

To-morrow morning we go to Oxford, for the ceremony of *Doctorizing* which takes place in the theatre, before the Bigwigs. Our household all go over to do us honor, and eat the Vice-Chancellor's lunch, who wrote me a note inviting me to bring my friends. So fare you well, dear mother. Pray be careful of your health. Do stay, if you can, some time with Susan at Nahant. Give my love to her and Lizzie, with as many kisses as you please, and tell my dear wife she must take this for her letter this time, as I intend to write to Ticknor. God bless you all.

Your affectionate son,

WM. H. PRESCOTT.

He was at Cuddesdon, as we have seen, partly in order to be

near Oxford, when he was "called up" there, as the phrase is, to be made a Doctor of Civil Law. Of this he gives a more distinct account in the following letter than I find elsewhere.

TO MR. TICKNOR.

LONDON, June 26, 1850.

MY DEAR GEORGE,

I must thank you for your kind letter by the Asia, which made her trip in ten days and a bittock. I had written to my mother from Oxford that I should send you a line by this steamer; so you will consider me, if you please, as quick on the trigger as yourself.

Well, here I am in the hurry-scurry of London, up to my ears in dances, dinners, and breakfasts, some of the last at 10 A. M., some at 5 P. M., to say nothing of luncheons, the most beautiful of which that I have seen, was yesterday at Lansdowne House. I am booked up for dinners to the middle of July, and then I intend to stop, as I may take a week for a trip to Holland, — the land of my historic *avenir*. Meanwhile I have invitations of one kind or another, often three or four a day. So I shall not go to sleep till bedtime certainly; and I believe, though I have been here but three weeks, I have been industrious enough to be able to form a pretty good judgment of the stuff of which London society is made. On the whole, it is a very extraordinary kind of life, and, as far as health is concerned, agrees with me wonderfully. My eyes and many et-ceteras are improved, and even the digestive organs, which must form the great *pièce de resistance* in the battle, so far come up to the mark gloriously. Yet it is a life, which, were I an Englishman, I should not desire a great deal of; two months, at most, although I think, on the whole, the knowledge of a very curious state of society, and of so many interesting and remarkable characters, well compensates the bore of a voyage. Yet I am quite sure, having once had this experience, nothing would ever induce me to repeat it. As I have heard you say, it would not pay.

The world here are all in great agitation and suspense as to the fate of the Ministry. It hangs, you know, on the vote of the Commons on the Greek question. I will not trouble you with the details, with which you are too good a reader of English politics not to be familiar. I was in the House of Peers at the grand charge of Lord Stanley, and have heard some speeches in the Commons, but not the best. If government do not get a majority of over thirty, at least, it is understood they will go out, and then there will be such a scramble, for they reign by the weakness and division of their opponents. The voting on this motion will, I imagine, cause no less division in the government ranks. It is curious to see the interest shown by the women in political matters.

What will interest you more than the contest is the assault made so brutally by Brougham on your friend Bunsen. I was present, and never saw anything so coarse as his personality. He said the individual took up the room of two ladies. Bunsen is rather fat, as also Madame and his daughter, — all of whom at last marched out of the gallery, but not until eyes and glasses had been directed to the spot, to make out the unfortunate individual, while Lord Brougham was flying up and down, thumping the table with his fist, and foaming at the mouth, till all his brother-peers, including the old Duke, were in convulsions of laughter. I dined with Bunsen and Madame the same day, at Ford's. He has since received scores of condoling visits, as well as the most conciliatory communications from Lord Palmerston, &c., &c. It will, probably, end in providing a place for the Corps Diplomatique, who have hitherto been shuffled with "distinguished foreigners" into the vacant space around the throne.

* * *

I returned day before yesterday from a visit to the Bishop of Oxford, Wilberforce, you know; one of the best-bred men, and most pleasing in conversation, that I have met with. However canny he may be in his church politics, he is certainly amiable, for uniform good-breeding implies a sacrifice of self that is founded on benevolence. There was some agreeable company at the house, among them a lady, very well read, the daughter of a Bishop, who told me she had never heard the *name* of Dr. Channing! I gave her a great shock by telling her I was a Unitarian. The term is absolutely synonymous, in a large party here, with Infidel, Jew, Mohammedan; worse even, because regarded as a wolf in sheep's clothing.

On Monday morning our party at the Bishop's went to Oxford, where Lord Northampton and I were Doctorized in due form. We were both dressed in flaming red robes (it was the hottest day I have felt here) and then marched out in solemn procession with the Faculty, &c., in their black and red gowns, through the public street, looking, that is, we, like the victims of an *auto de fé;* though, I believe, on second thoughts, the *san benito* was yellow. The house was well filled by both men and women. The Archæological Society is holding its meetings there. We were marched up the aisle; Professor Phillimore made a long Latin exposition of our merits, in which each of the adjectives ended, as Southey said in reference to himself on a like occasion, in *issimus;* and amidst the cheers of the audience we were converted into Doctors. We lunched with the Vice-Chancellor, who told me I should have had a degree on Commemoration-day, the regular day; but he wrote about me to the Dean of St. Paul's, who was absent from town, and so an answer was not received until too late. He did not tell me that the principal object of the letter was to learn my faith, having some misgivings as to my heresy. M—— wrote him word that he thought my books would be found to be vouchers enough for me to obtain a degree. So a special convocation was called, and my companion in the ceremony was a better man than a military chief, like Lord Gough. I like Lord Northampton very much. He was at the Bishop's, and we drove together from Cuddesdon to Oxford.[12] He is a man of very active mind. He told me some good anecdotes; among others, an answer of the Duke to a gentleman who asked him if he had

---

[12] Mr. Prescott had already received more than one honorary degree at home; but, with his accustomed ingenuousness and simplicity, remembering how lavishly and carelessly such distinctions are conferred by most of our American colleges, he could not repress his satisfaction that he was "now a *real* Doctor."

not been surprised at the battle of Waterloo. The Duke coldly replied, "I never was surprised, as well as I can remember, till now, in my life." Did you ever hear of his fine answer to a lady who was glorifying his victories? "A victory, ma'am, is the saddest thing in the world, except a defeat." Now that Sidney Smith is gone, Rogers furnishes the nicest touches in the way of repartee. His conversation even in his dilapidated condition, on his back, is full of salt, not to say cayenne. I was praising somebody's good-nature very much. "Yes," he said, "so much good-nature, that there is no room for good-sense." Perhaps you have heard of a good thing of Rogers's, which Lord Lansdowne told me the other day he *heard* him say. It was at Lord Holland's table, when Rogers asked Sir Philip Francis (the talk had some allusion to Junius) if he, Sir Philip, would allow him to ask a certain question. "Do so at your peril," was the amicable reply. "If he is Junius," said Rogers in an undertone to his neighbor, "he must be Junius *Brutus.*"

Since writing the preceding, I have passed half an hour with Lockhart in his own quarters. He showed me some most interesting memorials of Scott; among the rest the diary, in which the trembling character, more and more trembling, and the tottering thoughts showed the touch of apoplexy. Very affecting, is it not?

Macaulay has gone to Scotland to look over topography; among the rest, the scene of the massacre of Glencoe. I have met him several times, and breakfasted with him the other morning. His memory for quotations and illustration is a miracle, — quite disconcerting. He comes to a talk, like one specially crammed. Yet you may start the topic. He told me he should be delivered of twins on his next publication, which would not be till '53. I was glad to hear him say this, though it will be a disappointment to brethren of the trade, who think a man may turn out historicals, like romances and calicoes, by the yard. Macaulay's first draught — very unlike Scott's — is absolutely illegible from erasures and corrections. He showed me a sheet just written. I found *cls* as an abridgment of castle, and all on that plan. This draft he copies always, with alteration, &c. This shows more care than I had supposed. He tells me he has his moods for writing. When not in the vein, he does not press it. Johnson, you remember, ridiculed this in Gray. H—— told me that Lord Jeffrey once told him that, having tripped up Macaulay in a quotation from "Paradise Lost," two days after Macaulay came to him and said, "You will not catch me again in the Paradise"; at which Jeffrey opened the volume and took him up in a great number of passages at random, in all of which he went on, correctly repeating the original. Was not this a miraculous *tour d'esprit?* Macaulay does not hesitate to say now, that he thinks he could restore the first six or seven books of the "Paradise" in case they were lost.

The world here is agitated by the debate still going on in the Commons, on which the fate of the Ministry depends. Lord Palmerston made a most able defence evening before last. The Speaker says he never heard one superior to it since he has presided there, nearly a dozen years. His wife heard the whole of it, and seems to feel the full glory which has come upon her husband. Yet, although it has made a good rally for the party, the issue is very doubtful. Day before yesterday I dined with your friend Kenyon. I found him kind and most cordial. It is the first time I have seen him; no fault of his, for he has called, and repeatedly asked me to dine; nor of mine, for I have called also. But meeting any particular body in London is a small chance, — too small to be counted on by any person. I have seen much of the Milmans and Lyells. Nothing can be kinder. Lord Carlisle and his whole kith and kin, ditto. These I had some right to count upon, but, in truth, the expressions of kindness from utter strangers have been what I had no right to anticipate. I avail myself so much of this friendly feeling that I flatter myself I shall see as much of London (the interior) in six weeks as most of its inhabitants would in as many months. Twice this week I kept my ground in the ball-room till ghost-time had passed, once till an hour after dawn. Am I not a *fast boy*?

Of all the notabilities no one has struck me more than the Iron Duke. His face is as fresh as a young man's. He stoops much and is a little deaf. It is interesting to see with what an affectionate and respectful feeling he is regarded by all, — not least by the Queen.

Do you know, by the way, that I have become a courtier, and affect the royal presence? I wish you could see my gallant costume, gold-laced coat, white inexpressibles, silk hose, gold-buckled patent slippers, sword, and chapeau, &c. This and my Cardinal's robe on Monday! Am I not playing the fool as well as my betters? No wonder that the poet who lived in London should find out that "The world 's a stage, and all the men," &c. But I must conclude this long talk, so pleasant with a dear friend, but not without thanking you for so kindly condensing my character into twelve hundred words; better than if you had had more words allowed to tell it in.[18] L———, in the haste of my departure, asked if he could not refer to some one, and I told him you; for I had rather be in your hands than in any other man's alive. If I had not been in yours, I should have been in his. I hope to get something better than the paralysis effigy which L——— got of me an hour before sailing, as I am engaged to sit for my portrait next week to an excellent artist, Richmond, in the same style as our Cheney, for Lord Carlisle; a thing I did not expect to do again.

With ever so much love to Anna, and Anika, and little Lizzie,

   I remain, dear George,

     Always affectionately yours,

        WM. H. PRESCOTT.

TO MRS. PRESCOTT.

         LONDON, Sunday, June 30, 1850.

DEAREST SUSAN,

I go this afternoon to the Dean of St. Paul's to lunch and hear his afternoon service in the great Cathedral. I shall call for our good friend Lady Lyell, and take her with me. What shall I tell you of the past

---

[18] A notice of Mr. Prescott, which I prepared for a publication at New York, entitled "Illustrious Americans," where I was limited to twelve hundred words, as it was only intended to explain a portrait of him.

week? I will run over my engagements for yesterday and a day or two coming, that you may know my whereabouts. I was invited to a rural party at a Mrs. Lawrence's, Ealing Park, where went the Duke of Cambridge. But I could not go, having engaged to visit Lambeth, the old palace of the Archbishop of Canterbury, with my friends the Milmans. And friends they are; I wish you knew Mrs. M., you would so like her. Her letter to me last summer was a fair index to her character.

I received your letter, enclosing that of Amory, to whom I shall write this week. But I write so much to you, that it really leaves me little time for others. But writing to you is my chief happiness, as it is talking with my best friends, you and mother. Well, where was I? At the Queen's. — (The servant has just brought me a note from Alison, inviting me most cordially to make his house in Glasgow my head-quarters, should I visit Scotland, where he goes in a day or two. That is kind from a brother of the craft.) — After some of the company had paid their respects, dancing began. The Queen danced a quadrille very gracefully with the Prince of Prussia. The crowd in the neighborhood of the Queen was intense, and the heat suffocating. I strolled through the whole suite of magnificent apartments, all filled with a blaze of beauty, simply attired in the young, and of age bejewelled from head to foot, — the men in their picturesque diplomatic costumes, or military or court-dresses blazing with diamond-crosses and ribbons, and noble orders. It was a gorgeous sight. At midnight we went to supper, the Queen leading in the procession, while the whole band played the grand national air. The supper-table ran through the whole length of the immense hall, the farther end of which was hung with gold or gilt shields of great size and lighted up with a thousand lights. The rest of the room was in comparative darkness. It was a grand stage effect, which I did not much admire. The servants stood next to the wall. They were as many as could stand at the tables, which at the end were united by a transverse table. They were all gold and finery, so that I felt very diffident of calling on them for anything. The Queen kept her state at the head of the room, and, as well as her guests, was on the inside of the tables. The supper was magnificent, especially in fruits and confectionery. You know I have a failing in the way of confectionery, and the English have varieties that would make the fortune of a Yankee. After supper, dancing again, till I saw one young lady in a waltz before the Queen, who never waltzes, go down with a thump that I thought might have broken a bone. Two other couples had the like fate that evening. The floors are of hard wood and polished. At two her Majesty retired. So could not I; for my carriage was more than an hour in getting to the door, and the daylight was broad in the streets before I laid my head on the pillow. There is the Court Ball! And from one you may learn all. We are now in great stir here for the accident which has befallen Sir Robert Peel; I called there to-day, and left my card, as do half London. It is curious to see the interest excited. A police-officer is stationed at the gates to prevent disorder, and bulletins are handed round to the crowd, containing the last report of the physicians. You will see the particulars in the newspapers. It is a serious, very probably a fatal accident.

July 3d. — Sir Robert Peel is dead! The news has given a shock to the whole town. He died in his dining-room, — the very room where I was with him a fortnight ago. It seems a frivolous thing, this dining and dancing in the midst of death. I am getting a-weary of the life, I assure you.

Fourth of July. — William came in upon me to-day at noon. He arrived in the Southampton steamer from Gibraltar. He has been in Africa and Southern Spain, and, as his letters remained in Paris by his orders, he heard nothing of my being in London till he received a note from our Minister in Madrid. He looks very well, just as he did when he sailed, except that he is as black as a Moor from the African sun. It was a merry meeting on both sides. He is very simple and unaffected in his manners, and is full of his adventures. He has brought with him your daguerrotype, the sight of which, dear, was as welcome to me as the sight of him. He has left some articles in Paris, and I think I shall let him run over there for a few days. On the 20th, I shall go with him for a week to Belgium; then take him with me to a few country-places, and early in September I shall embark. If Parliament did not continue sitting till the middle of August, I should not be so late. With love to mother and Lizzie, and to E. Dexter,

I remain your loving husband,
WM. H. PRESCOTT.

My eyes are much better, and health generally very good. William compliments me by saying I look younger than when he left.

I am now writing to Amory,[14] and shall send the letters to-day. It is a fine day, and I go at noon on my expedition to Greenwich with Ford, Lockhart, Hallam, Stirling, Rawlinson, Cummings, the African lion-hunter, &c. William is to be one of the party. I sat up with him late last night after my return from dinner, till one o'clock, hearing his Southern adventures, and indulging with him in the fume of cigars.

TO MRS. PRESCOTT.

Wednesday evening. — Just returned from the Countess Grey's. A small party of ten. I sat between two ladies, whose united ages amounted to one hundred and fifty, Lady —— and Lady ——. There was also a charming lady there to whom I lost my heart, dear wife, some three weeks since. Don't be jealous, she is over seventy, — Lady Morley, a most natural, lively, benevolent body. I know you would like her. I really think the elder bodies here are very charming. In fact, nobody is old. I have not seen any up to one I have left in Beacon Street. What a delightful letter from mother! Your letters of June 30th came in this afternoon. I have sent your nice little notes to Lady Lyell and Mrs. Smith. How good it was in them to write! Your note to me was a shabby one. You must

[14] His younger son, William Amory Prescott.
13 *

not write the less that others write.   I shall answer Anna Ticknor by a good letter this mail for her kindness in thinking of me.

TO MRS. TICKNOR.

LONDON, July 18, 1850.

Thank you, my dear Anna, for so kindly thinking of me in the practical way of a letter.   I knew your superscription before I broke the seal, and it was "good for sair e'en."   I did mean to answer you with a bigger letter, but on returning home this evening after a visit to the city, I found my friends here had cut out work enough for Mr. Kirk,[15] which could not be passed over.   To-morrow I go to the Continent, an historical tour, for a few days.

I have now seen life in London and its environs, wealth, wit, and beauty, and rank ; sometimes without either ; women talking politics, men talking nonsense ; literary breakfasts, fashionable dinners, convivial dinners, political dinners ; lords without pretension, citizens with a good deal, literary lions, fashionable lions, the Nepaulese, the hippopotamus, &c., &c. But I have not seen an old woman.   As to age, nobody, man or woman, is old here.   Even Miss Berry is but *getting* old.   I forgot, however, Miss Joanna Baillie, — decidedly old, much older than her sister.   What a little world it is !   Everything is drawn into the vortex, and there they swim round and round, so that you may revolve for weeks, and not meet a familiar face half a dozen times.   Yet there is monotony in some things, — that everlasting turbot and shrimp-sauce.   I shall never abide a turbot again.

The dinners are very agreeable, if you are planted between agreeable people.   But what a perilous affair the settling of the respective grades, as you move in solemn procession to the banquet !   It is a nation of *castes*, as defined as those in India.   But what cordial hearts are sometimes found under the crust of shyness and reserve !   There are some, however, so invincibly shy that they benumb the faculties of any one, — at least, any stranger who approaches them.

I have found the notabilities here pretty much as I had supposed. Macaulay is the most of a miracle.   His *tours* in the way of memory stagger belief.   He does not go about much now, except at breakfast.   I lost a pleasant dinner with him on Monday at Denison's.   His talk is like the labored, but still unintermitting, jerks of a pump.   But it is anything but wishy-washy.   It keeps the mind, however, on too great a tension for table-talk.   The Milmans are the most lovable people I have met with, always excepting our friends the Lyells and Lord Carlisle and his family. These are the people whom I have seen the most of, and enjoyed the most ; — invariable kindness, shown not merely in passing hospitality, but active measures for promoting one's happiness in every way that a stranger could desire.   I have seen Rogers several times, that is, all that is out of the bed-clothes.   His talk is still *sauce piquante*.   The best thing on record of his late sayings is his reply to Lady ———, who at a

[15] His secretary.

dinner-table, observing him speaking to a lady, said, "I hope, Mr. Rogers, you are not attacking me!" "Attacking you!" he said, "why, my dear Lady ———, I have been all my life defending you." Wit could go no further.

Since writing the above, I have returned from a dinner with Lockhart. We had only Ford, Stirling, and Major Rawlinson. Carlyle was invited, but was unwell. He came the other day to a place five minutes after I left it, and I sat next but two to him at a dinner-table some time since, and never knew I was in his company. Odd enough! It proves he did not talk loud that day. So I have never seen him; is it not droll? Yet there are many men I should have more cared to see. Lockhart showed us the diary of Sir Walter. He (Lockhart) had two copies of it printed for himself. One of them was destroyed in printing the Memoir, for which he made extracts.

But I must bid you good-night, dear Anna, as it is midnight. The iron tongue strikes it as I write these words. Good night, dear friend. Much love to George and to Anika. Thank your husband for his kind letter, which he will be kind enough to consider partly answered in this. Love to little Lizzie.

Believe me, now and ever,
    Yours affectionately,
        WM. H. PRESCOTT.

CHAPTER XXII.

1850.

THE expedition to the Continent was begun the next day after the last letter was written, and on the afternoon of the day following, July 20th, Mr. Prescott was in Paris. But he did not stop there. He was in brilliant Paris hardly two days, and one of them was a Sunday. He left it on the 22d, and on the 23d wrote from Antwerp to Mrs. Prescott a long letter, from which I select the portion that has a general interest.

TO MRS. PRESCOTT.

ANTWERP, July 23, 1850.

In Brussels I found myself in the heart of the Middle Ages. Old buildings of stone, curiously carved, immense gables and fantastic architraves, and cornices of the houses; churches with antique Gothic spires. The Place Royale, in which my hotel stood, was the spot on which Charles the Fifth abandoned the crown in presence of the most royal assembly that ever met in Brussels. What do I dream of at night? Not Charles the Fifth, but Boston. That is a fact; but my waking dreams were of the sixteenth century. I visited the Hôtel de Ville, a most glorious municipal monument of the Middle Ages, standing as it stood when, directly in front of it, those gallant nobles, Egmont and Horne, were beheaded on a public scaffold by order of Alva. I visited the house, a fine old Gothic edifice, still standing, from which the Flemish patriots walked out to the scaffold, and from the windows of which Alva witnessed the execution. What a square that is! If I don't make something out of my visit to Brussels and its glorious squares, I don't know what there is in eyesight. Yet I do know what there is in the *want* of it too well. My eyes, however, have been much better of late, and I read some every day. Then the noble cathedral of Brussels, dedicated to Saint Gudule; the superb organ filling its long aisles with the most heart-thrilling tones, as the voices of the priests, dressed in their rich robes of purple and gold, rose in a chant that died away in the immense vaulted distance of the cathedral. It was the service for the dead, and the coffin of some wealthy burgher, probably, to judge from its decorations, was in the choir. A number of persons were kneeling and saying their prayers in rapt attention, little heeding the Protestant strangers who were curiously gazing at the pictures and statues with which the edifice was filled. I was most struck with one poor woman who was kneeling at the shrine of the saint, whose marble corpse, covered by a decent white gauze veil, lay just before her, separated only by a light railing. The setting sun was streaming in through the rich colored panes of the magnificent windows, that rose from the floor to the ceiling of the cathedral, some hundred feet in height. The glass was of the time of Charles the Fifth, and I soon recognized his familiar face, the *whapper-jaw* of the Austrian line. As I heard the glorious anthem rise up to Heaven in this time-honored cathedral, which had witnessed generation after generation melt away, and which now displayed the effigies of those, in undying colors, who had once worshipped within its walls, I was swept back to a distant period, and felt I was a contemporary of the grand old times when Charles the Fifth held his Chapters of the Golden Fleece in this very building.

But in truth I do not go back quite so far. A silly woman, with whom I came into Paris, said when I told her it was thirty years since I was here, " Poh ! you are not more than thirty years old !" — and on my repeating it, still insisted on the same flattering ejaculation. The Bishop of London, the other day, with his amiable family, told me they had settled my age at forty, and that is just the age at which Richmond's portrait, so excellent, puts me ! So I am convinced there has been some error in the calculation. Ask mother how it is. They say here that gray hairs, particularly whiskers, may happen to anybody, even under thirty. On the whole, I am satisfied, I am the youngest of the family.

I had a note to M. de Praet, Leopold's Minister, who lives with him in his palace at Brussels. Mr. Van der Weyer expressed a desire that I should see Leopold, and gave me the letter for that purpose. It would have been an easy matter, as the king is very accessible, with very little form, and, as he is a clever person, is an interesting one in the line of crowned heads. But Fate has decided otherwise. On calling, I found his Belgian Majesty was not to come to-day (I am writing Tuesday, the 23d) from his country-place, and had sent for his Minister, half an hour before, to come to him. As I was to leave Brussels in a couple of hours, I left the note, with my regrets, and thus the foundation of what might have been a permanent friendship between us — I mean, of course, Leopold and me — was entirely destroyed ! At three, I left Brussels for Antwerp, another of the great historical cities of the Low Countries. Our road lay through fat meadows, wheat spreading out for miles, all yellow as gold, and as high as a man's head ; fields of the most tender green checkering the landscape ; rows of willow trees, elms, and lindens, all in straight lines ; hedges of hawthorn ; such a fruitful country as your eye never rested on. It beats England all hollow. The women in the fields, reaping and binding the sheaves ; the cattle all speckled white and black, suggesting lots of cream, delicious butter, and Dutch cheeses, — such as Mr. B—— sent me, you know ; cottages wretchedly poor, shaded by old

trees, and enchanting creepers and wild-flowers ; the whole as level as a
bowling-green.   Dear Susan, I never see anything beautiful in nature or
art, or hear heart-stirring music in the churches, the only place where music
does stir my heart, without thinking of you, and wishing you could be by
my side, if only for a moment.   But I shall be by yours before September
is closed.   I mean to take my passage, on my return to England, for
the 7th.

To-morrow I go by steam to Rotterdam, take a peep into Holland, and
see "the broad ocean lean against the land."   It will be but a peep. —
But fare thee well.   Good night, dear.   Love to mother and Lizzie, and a
hearty kiss, by way of good night, to both of them.   Remember me to
Elizabeth and the Ticknors, and believe me,

Your affectionate husband,

WM. H. PRESCOTT.

He made a little excursion in Holland, and, returning to
Antwerp five days afterwards, wrote to his daughter on the
28th another long letter, like the last to Mrs. Prescott, but one
from which, as in that case, I omit such details as are of a
domestic nature and do not belong to the public.

TO MISS PRESCOTT.

ANTWERP, Sunday, July 28, 1850.

DEAR LIZZIE,

From Antwerp I went to Rotterdam, Delft, the Hague, Haarlem, and
Amsterdam.   At Delft I saw the spot on which William of Orange, the
hero of the Netherlands, was standing when he was assassinated ; the
very spot is indicated by a tablet in the wall.   He was just coming down-
stairs when he was shot by the assassin.   The pistol has been preserved,
and is so long that it could hardly have been presented without touching
William's body in the narrow passage.   Was it not an interesting spot to
me ?   I wish you could have been with me on the visit to Holland.   Life
is so different there from what it is anywhere else.   Your mother would
revel in its neatness.   The great streets of Rotterdam and Amsterdam are
filled with women, all busily engaged in different labors, some of which
with us are performed by men.   They were all dressed in neat caps, and
with no bonnets or shawls, — so it seemed as if we were in some great
house, instead of being out of doors.   We went to the little town of
Broek, remarkable even here for its extravagant neatness.   The streets
looked as if they had been scoured down every day.   We went into
stables where the accommodations for cows were as nice as those usually
for the masters and mistresses.   They have a front-door to each of the
houses, which is never opened except for weddings and funerals.   One
thing would have delighted you in all the Dutch towns, the quantities
of little babies, the prettiest little rosy-faced things in the world, and
without a speck on their clothes.   How the Dutch mammas manage their

babies and their other handiwork, I don't comprehend. But every woman almost seems to have one of them in her arms. On the whole, I was much pleased with my bird's-eye view of the people, men and women, although the former do smoke intensely, not hesitating to light their pipes and cigars in the carriage or at the breakfast-table.

On the 29th of July he was again in his old quarters at Mivart's Hotel. His object, however, was not London or London society; but English country life, and what is best in it. He began, therefore, a series of visits, with which, according to his previous arrangements, he was to close his European excursion; stopping, however, one day for a most agreeable dinner at Lord Carlisle's, to which he had promised himself before he went over to Holland.

His first country visit was a charming one to Ham's Hall, in Warwickshire, where he went with a kinsman and friend of the statesman who is the master of that noble and luxurious establishment. The three days they spent there were most agreeable in all respects, involving, as they did, excursions with a brilliant party to Kenilworth, Warwick, and Stoneleigh Abbey. But he was obliged to hurry away in order to keep an engagement for a great annual festival observed at Alnwick Castle, in Northumberland, and of which he gives a full account in the following letter to his daughter, — familiar certainly in its whole tone, but the better and more agreeable because it is so.

TO MISS PRESCOTT.

ALNWICK CASTLE, August 8, 1850.

MY DEAR LIZZIE,

It was very good of you to write me such a charming letter, and so very interesting. I received it here in the ancient castle of the Percy's; and it was more pleasant to my sight than the handwriting — if I could meet with it — of Harry Hotspur himself. So I cannot do better than to answer it by some account of the magnificent place where I am now quartered. We reached it three days since in a heavy rain. It rains in England twice as much as with us; and in the North and in Scotland four times as much, I understand. But nobody minds rain; and the ladies jump into their saddles or put on their walking-shoes as soon in a drizzle or a light shower as in sunshine. I wonder they do not grow web-footed, as I have told them. I received a note from the Duke a day or two before I left London, advising me to be in time for dinner, and it was just after the first bell rang that our carriage drove up. Alnwick Castle stands at the end of the town, from which it is cut off by high walls and towers, — and it looks out on a bold hilly country, with the river Alne flowing below its walls. My chamber, where I am now writing, overlooks a wide stretch of border land, made famous by many a ballad; and away to the west rise the blue hills of Cheviot, with Chevy Chase between, and farther to the west is the field of Flodden. Is it not a stirring country? Then to look on it from the towers of Alnwick!

I went down to dinner, and found the Duke with a few friends, waiting for the ladies. He gave us a cordial welcome. He was no stranger to me, as I have met both him and the Duchess in London. He is a good-looking man, with light hair, blue eyes, rather tall, frank and cordial in his manners. He has been a captain in the navy. He immediately took me to a window, and showed me the battle-ground, where Malcolm, who succeeded Macbeth, was slain, when besieging Alnwick. A little stone cross still marks the spot. In fifteen minutes the company assembled in the drawing-room to the number of forty. The dining-room is very large, as you may imagine, to accommodate so many persons. There was a multitude of servants, and the liveries, blue, white, and gold, of the Duke were very rich. We had also our own servants to wait on us. The table was loaded with silver. Every plate was silver, and everything was blaz- oned with the Northumberland arms. The crest is a lion, and you see the lion carved on the stone-work displayed in sugared ornaments on the table, in the gilt panelling of the rooms, &c. As you enter the town of Alnwick, a stone column some sixty feet high is seen, surmounted by a colossal lion, and four monsters of the same family in stone lie at its base. The Northumberland lion has his tail always sticking out straight, which has proved too strong a temptation for the little boys of Alnwick, who have amused themselves with breaking off that ornamental appendage to a little lion sculptured on a bridge below the house. After dinner, which was a great London dinner over again, we retreated to the drawing-room, where a concert was prepared for us, the musicians having been brought from London, three hundred miles distant. The room was hung round with full-length portraits of the Duke's ancestors, some of them in their robes of state, very showy. I went to bed in a circular room in one of the towers, with a window, shaped something like a rose, set into a wall from five to six feet thick. In the morning I waked up, and heard the deep tones of the old clock announcing seven. My head was full of the stout Earl of Northumberland who

> " A vow to God did make,
> His pleasure in the Scottish woods," &c.

As I looked out of the window, I saw myself to be truly in an old baronial fortress, with its dark walls, and towers gloomily mustered around it. On the turrets, in all directions, were stone figures of men, as large as life, with pikes, battle-axes, &c., leaning over the battlements, appar- ently in the act of defending the castle, — a most singular effect, and to be found only in one or two fortresses. It reminded me of the description in Scott of the warders pacing to and fro on the battlements of " Nor- ham's castled steep," while the banner of Northumberland waved high in the morning breeze. It was a glorious prospect, which called up the old border minstrelsy to memory, and I felt myself carried back to the days when the Douglas came over the borders. The dwelling of the family is the keep of the castle, the interior fortress. It was entirely rebuilt on the old foundations by the Duke's grandfather. But in conforming to them he has been led into such a quantity of intricacies, odd-shaped rooms, perplexing passages, out-of-the-way staircases, &c., that it is the greatest puzzle to find one's own room, or anybody's else. Even the partition-walls are sometimes five feet thick. The whole range of towers, which are offices for domestics and for the Duke's men of business, together with the walls, are of the ancient Norman structure ; and the effect of the whole, as seen from different points of view, is truly majestic. The print which I send you may give you some idea of the castle, though not a very good one.

At a quarter past nine the whole household assembled for prayers in the chapel, to the number, it might be, of over a hundred. Services were performed by the Duke's chaplain, and at parts of them every one knelt. Prayers in this way are read every morning in the English houses that I have seen, and, where there is no chaplain, by the master. It is an excellent usage, and does much for the domestic morals of England. From prayers we go to the breakfast-table, — an informal meal. After the breakfast the company disperses to ride, to walk, to read, &c.

One day I amused myself with going over the different towers exploring the secrets of the old castle, with a party of ladies who could not be persuaded to descend into the dungeon, which is still covered by its iron grating in the floor above. The good old times ! One day I took a ride with Lord M—— in the park, to see the ruins of Hulm Abbey. The park is a noble piece of ground, surrounded by a ring fence, a high wall of ten miles in circumference. It is carpeted with beautiful verdure, filled with old trees, and watered by the river Alne, which you cross at fords when there are no bridges. As you drive along over the turf and among the green thickets, you start hares and pheasants, and occasionally a troop of deer. The Duke has some red deer, which at times it is not pleasant for the pedestrian to meet. Lord O—— told me that he was with a party once, when a stag of this kind planted himself in the path, and, on the carriage's advancing, rushed against the horses, and plunged his horns into the heart of one of them, who reared and fell dead. On reaching the Abbey we found the Duchess with a party of ladies had just arrived there, in two carriages drawn by four horses each, with postilions whose gay liveries looked pretty enough among the green trees. The Abbey is in a deep valley, a charming cultivated spot. The old monks always picked out some such place for their nest, where there was plenty of sweet water and food for their cattle, and venison to boot. We wandered over the ruins, over which Time had thrown his graceful mantle of ivy, as he always does over such ruins in England. From the topmost tower the eye ranged along a beautiful landscape, closed by the Cheviots. In coming home, which we all did at a gallop, we found lunch ready for us, at half-past two o'clock. This, too, is an informal meal, but it is a substantial one at Alnwick. After lunch we again took care of ourselves as we liked till dinner. In shooting-time the park affords a noble range

x

for the sportsman, and plenty of trout are caught in the streams. Those of less murderous intent frequent the library, a large room stored with some thousands of volumes, — some of them old enough, — and hung round with family portraits. In this pleasant room I have passed some agreeable hours, with persons who seemed to take the greatest pleasure in hunting up things for me most worthy of notice. English country-life brings out all the best qualities of the Englishman.

At seven o'clock again came the dinner, for which we dress as much as in town. One day we all dined — the men — at a public dinner of all the great tenant farmers in the county. The building was of boards and sail-cloth, and lighted with hundreds of gas-lights. There were about a thousand persons, and the Duke and his guests sat at a long table, raised above the others, and, as it ran crosswise also to these, it commanded the whole hall. It was an animated sight, especially as the galleries were filled with the ladies of the Castle and the County. I luckily had laid in a good lunch ; for as to eating in such a scramble, it is hopeless. There was a good deal of speaking, and, among others, Lawrence did credit to himself and his country. I bargained with the Duke that I should not be called upon. Without this I would not have gone. But I did not get off without some startling allusions, which made my hair stand on end, for fear I should be obliged to answer them. But they told me it was not intended. The Duke himself spoke half a dozen times, as president of the feast. He always spoke well, and the enthusiasm was immense ; — cheering, *hip hurrahs*, till my head ached. Our Minister's speech was most heartily received, showing a good-will towards Yankees which was very gratifying. It was an animating sight, the overflow of soul and sound. But I had rather have eaten my cheese-cakes alone in a corner, like Sancho Panza.

On returning to the castle we found an informal dinner prepared for us, and in another room a superb desert of cakes, ices, and confectionery. The tables, both at breakfast and lunch, are ornamented with large vases of flowers of the most brilliant colors, with clusters of white and purple grapes of mammoth size, pine-apples, peaches, &c. Talking of flowers, it is the habit now to surround the houses in the country with beds of flowers, arranged in the most artificial forms, diamonds, circles, &c. The flowers are disposed after some fanciful pattern, so as to produce the effect of brilliant carpeting, and this forms quite a study for the English dames. And such flowers ! If they had our autumnal woods, they would undoubtedly dispose the trees so as to produce the best effects of their gaudy colors.

Another day we went in to see the peasantry of the great tenants dine, some sixteen hundred in number, or rather we saw them for half an hour after dinner. The Duke and the Duchess took the head of the hall ; and I thought the people, dressed in their best, to whom the dinner was given, as they drank off healths to their noble hosts, would have gone mad with enthusiasm. I nearly did so from the noise. The Duke, on allusion to his wife, brought her forward ; and she bowed to the multitude. It was altogether a pretty sight. Persons in their condition in England are obliged to be early accustomed to take part in these *spectacles*, and none do it better than our excellent host and hostess. They are extremely beloved by their large tenantry, who are spread all over the County of Northumberland.

The Duke has shown the greatest desire to promote the education and comfort of his peasantry. "He wants us all to be comfortable," one of them said to me; and the consequence is he is universally beloved by them. Both he and his wife visit the poor cottages constantly; and she has a large school of her own, in which she assists in teaching the children. One of the prettiest sights was the assembly of these children in one of the Castle courts, making their processions in the order of their schools; that of the Duchess being distinguished by green jackets. The Duke and Duchess stood on the steps, and the little children, as they passed, all made their bows and courtesies, a band playing all the while. Afterwards came the feasting. It was a happy day for the little urchins, — a visit to the Castle; and I am told there was no such thing as getting any study out of them for days previous; — and I will answer for it there will be none for days to come. As they all joined in the beautiful anthem, "God save the Queen," the melody of the little voices rose up so clear and simple in the open court-yard, that everybody was touched. Though I had nothing to do with the anthem, some of my *opera tears*, dear Lizzie, came into my eyes, and did me great credit with some of the John and Jeannie Bulls by whom I was surrounded.

Edinburgh, August 11th. — Here I am in the Scottish capital, dear Lizzie, where we have met Mr. Kirk, on his Northern pilgrimage, and to save time I am dictating this letter to him. But I must leave Edinburgh till another time, and wind up now with Alnwick. When it was known I was going, I had a quantity of invitations all along my route, and memoranda given me to show how I could best get to the different places. I took them all kindly, as they were meant, but can go to none. One of them, Lord and Lady O——, would have given me an interesting place, for it is the only one which still preserves the famous breed of Chillingham cattle, snow-white and still as untamed as zebras. The estate is really that of Lord O——'s father, a blind old peer, whose wife told me in London that she had read my histories aloud to him. So he might have known me without his eyes. My friendly hosts remonstrated on my departure, as they had requested me to make them a long visit, and " I never say what I do not mean," said the Duke, in an honest way. And when I thanked him for his hospitable welcome, "It is no more," he said, "than you should meet in every house in England." That was hearty. They urged me next time to bring your mother. I rather think I shall! They invited me also to their place at Stanwick; a pretty spot, which they like better than Alnwick, living there in less state, which, as I learn from others, he keeps up no more than is absolutely necessary. He goes from Alnwick to Keilder, where he and the Duchess pass a couple of months with never more than two friends, the house being so small that the dinner-room is also the sitting-room. We can do better than this at the *Highlands*; Heaven bless the place dearer to me than Highlands or Lowlands in any other quarter of the globe!

Yesterday we went to Abbotsford, Melrose Abbey, and Dryburgh. Shade of Scott! I had a note from Lockhart, which instructed the housekeeper to let me and my friends take our fill of the hallowed precincts. As I looked through the iron grating of Dryburgh, and saw the stone sarcophagus of the great minstrel, it seemed as if I was looking with you, dear, through the iron bars that fence in the marble sarcophagus of our great and good Washington. But I must finish. To-morrow for the North, — Loch Katrine, Loch Lomond, Inverary Castle, where I shall halt for a few days. I have told William he ought to write to you, but he says the family have given up writing to him, so he leaves it all to me. How do you like that? I am glad you take so much comfort in ——; I know you would. Pray remember me to the dear girl, and to ——, and to ——, when you write her. I mean to write to her soon. But you see what long letters I send to Fitful Head. Kiss your mother for me. I know you are a comfort to her; you cannot be otherwise. With much love to your grandmother and Aunt Dexter, I remain,

Your affectionate father,

WM. H. PRESCOTT.

His more general but still very familiar views of English society may perhaps be better gathered from a letter written after he had crossed into Scotland, than from those written on the other side of the Tweed.

TO MR. TICKNOR.

EDINBURGH, Aug. 16, 1850.

DEAR GEORGE,

As I could not send you a letter from Alnwick Castle by my regular amanuensis, I have deferred sending it till I came here, and have taken the liberty to carry off one of the Alnwick note-papers, to give you a more vivid idea of my late whereabouts. I was much pleased with my short residence there, liking my noble host and his Duchess very much. They are in truth excellent people, taking an active interest in the welfare of their large tenantry. The Duke is doing much to improve the condition of his estates. His farmers and tenants appear, from the glance I had at them, — that was at feeding hours, — to be a thriving, contented people, and overflowing with loyalty to the noble house of Percy. But I have written particulars of my visit to Lizzie, in a letter, which, if you feel curious, I dare say she will show you, as I wish all my letters to be read by you and Anna, if you desire it. I passed also some days with Mr. A——, a great landed proprietor in Warwickshire; quite an amiable, cultivated person, who has taken an active interest in colonial affairs in Parliament. We had some agreeable people in the house, and I saw a good deal of the neighboring country, in the society of our friend T——, through whom I became acquainted with Mr. A——. Mr. A——'s wife is T——'s cousin. But for my adventures here, I shall refer you also to family letters. I am now at Edinburgh en route for the North, and propose to be at Inverary Castle at the end of three days, taking the way of Stirling, Loch Katrine, &c.

I have been now long enough in London society, I believe, to understand something of it, and something also of English country life, — far the noblest phase. Yet neither one nor the other, as they are conducted in the great houses, would be wholly to my taste. There is an *embarras de richesses*; one would want more repose. I am told the higher English themselves discover something of this taste, and that there is less of profuse hospitality than of yore. This is somewhat attributed to the railroads, which fetch and carry people with the utmost facility from the most distant quarters. It was a great affair formerly to make journeys of two or three hundred miles; arrangements were made long beforehand, and the guests stayed long after they got there. But now-a-days they slip in and off without ceremony, and the only place where the old state of things perfectly exists is in a county like Cornwall, too rough for railways, — at least for many. Your railroad is the great leveller after all. Some of the old grandees make a most whimsical lament about it. Mrs. ——'s father, who is a large proprietor, used to drive up to London with his family, to attend Parliament, with three coaches and four. But now-a-days he is tumbled in with the unwashed, in the first class, it is true, — no better than ours, however, — of the railway *carriages*; and then tumbled out again into a common cab with my Lady and all her little ones, like any of the common pottery.

There are a good many other signs of the times to be seen in the present condition of the aristocracy. The growing importance of manufactures and moneyed capitalists is a wound, not only to the landed proprietors, but to the peers, who, it is true, are usually the greatest landed proprietors in the country. The last man raised to the peerage was a banker, a man of sense, whom I have met several times. Another peer, Lord C——, — or some such name, I may not have got it right, — whose brother, a well-known baronet, — I forget his name (I have a glorious memory for forgetting, and they say that is an excellent kind of memory), — was raised to the House of Lords not many years since, — actually, I mean, the first nominative, Lord C——, applied to the Queen the other day to *dis-peer* him. After a grave consideration of the matter with the Privy Council, it was decided that it was not in the power of the Crown to do so, and the poor man was obliged to pocket his coronet, and make the best of it. Sir Robert Peel showed his estimate of titles by his curious injunction on his family; as indeed he had shown it through his whole life. A person who, I believe, is well acquainted with the matter, told me that the Queen urged the title of Earl on Sir Robert when he went out of office; but he steadily declined it, requesting only that her Majesty and the Prince would honor him by sitting for their portraits for him. Two indifferent full-lengths were accordingly painted for him by Winterhalter, the Flemish artist, and form one of the principal ornaments, as the guide-book would say, of Sir Robert's house. Peel, it is well known, was a good deal snubbed in his earlier life, when he first became a Cabinet Minister, by the aristocracy; so that he may have felt satisfaction in showing that he preferred to hold the rank of the Great Commoner of England to any that titles could give him. Yet it seems almost an affectation to prevent their descending to his posterity, though it is true it was only as far as they were meant as the reward of his own services.

He had too much pride, it seems, to digest this.   As to the inferior aristocracy of baronets, knights, &c., there is many an old commoner that would refuse it, with contempt.   You know our friend Hallam's decision in regard to a baronetcy, though he did not express himself like one of the old family of T——, who, when he was told that it was intended to make him a baronet, begged that it might be commuted to a knighthood, that the disgrace might not descend to his posterity.   I had the story from one of the aristocracy myself.   You won't understand from all this that I think titles have not their full value, real and imaginary, in England.   I only mention it as a sign of the times, — that they have not altogether the prestige which they once had, and the toe of the commoner galls somewhat the heel of the courtier.

You know Sir Robert left to Lord Mahon and Mr. Cardwell the care of his papers.   The materials will all be easily at hand if they biographize.   Peel told Mr. A——, whose estate lies near to Tamworth, that he preserved all his correspondence, except invitations to dinner; and on one occasion, wanting an important letter in a great hurry in the House of Commons, he was able to point out the file in which it was kept so exactly, that his friend Lord L—— went to Tamworth and got it for him in the course of a few hours.   His death seems to have broken the knot which held together rather an anomalous party.   Many speculations there are about them, as about a hive of bees ready to swarm, of which one cannot tell where it will settle.   The persons most important in the party are Sir James Graham and Gladstone, two of the best speakers, indeed, if not the very best, in the House of Commons.   They are pledged, however, to the Corn-Law movement, and into whatever scale the Peelites may throw themselves, there seems to be a general impression that there can be no decidedly retrograde movement in regard to the Corn-Laws, at least at present.   The experiment must be tried; and the diversity of opinion about it among the landholders themselves seems to show that it is far from having been tried yet.

Before I left town, almost all your friends had flown, — the Lyells, Hallam, the excellent Milmans, Lord Mahon, T. Phillips, — all but good Kenyon, whom, by the by, I saw but twice, and that was at his hospitable table, though we both made various efforts to the contrary, and poor Mr. Rogers, who, far from flying, will probably never walk again, — all are gone, and chiefly to the Continent.   Ford has gone to Turkey, Stirling to Russia; Lockhart remains to hatch new Quarterlies.   He is a fascinating sort of person, whom I should fear to have meddle with me, whether in the way of praise or blame.   I suspect he laughs in his sleeve at more than one of the articles which come out with his *imprimatur*, and at their authors too.   I had two or three merry meetings, in which he, Stirling, and Ford were met in decent conviviality.

But I must conclude the longest, and probably the last, epistle I shall ever send you from the Old World, and I hope you will never send me one from that same world yourself.   Pray remember me most lovingly to Anna and Anika, with kind remembrance, moreover, to Gray, and Hillard, and Everett, when you see them.   No American Minister has left a more enviable reputation here.   Lawrence, with very different qualities, is making himself also equally acceptable to the English.   *Addio, mio caro.*

With many thanks for your most interesting letter on our Yankee politics, — more interesting to me here even than at home, — I remain

Affectionately yours,

WM. H. PRESCOTT.

He hastened from Edinburgh, and pushed on to Inverary Castle, the Duke of Argyll's, picking up on the way Sir Roderick Murchison and Professor Sedgwick, who were bound to the same hospitable port. There he remained for a few days, but days of great enjoyment, and then turned his face southward, feeling, at the same time, that he had the happiness of turning it towards his home. But great pleasures and great festivities still awaited him on the hospitable soil of Old England. Of these, the most ample and agreeable accounts will be found in the following letters.

TO MRS. PRESCOTT.

CASTLE HOWARD, August 24th, 1850.

DEAR WIFE,

Here we are at Castle Howard, by far the most magnificent place I have yet seen. But I will begin where I left off. After bidding adieu to the Duke and his charming wife at Inverary Castle, we sailed down Loch Coyle and up the Clyde with Lady Ellesmere, and reached Glasgow at eight. I posted at once to Alison's, and was cordially received by him and Madame. He lives in an excellent house, surrounded by a handsome park. I found a company of ladies and gentlemen, and passed the hours pleasantly till midnight, when I returned to Glasgow. Alison has a noble library, and in the centre of it is a great billiard-table, which, when he wrote, he covered with his authorities. Droll enough ! He showed me a handsome tribute he had paid to me in the last edition of his History. He had a cheerful fire in my bedroom, expecting me to stay. But it was impossible. The next morning we left for Naworth Castle, where I was to meet Lord Carlisle.

This is a fine old place, of the feudal times, indeed. In the afternoon we arrived, and saw the towers with the banners of the Howards and Dacres flying from the battlements, telling us that its lord was there. He came out to greet us, dressed in his travelling garb, — for he had just arrived, — with his Scotch shawl twisted round his body. Was it not kind in him to come this distance — a hundred and fifty miles — solely to show me the place, and that when he was over head and ears in preparations for the Queen ? What a superb piece of antiquity, looking still as when Lord Surrey's minstrel

> " Forsook, for Naworth's iron towers,
>   Windsor's sweet groves and courtly bowers."

It was partially injured by fire ; but Lord Carlisle has nearly restored it,

and in the best taste, by copying the antique.   Fortunately the walls of
the building, with its charming old ivy and eglantines, are unscathed, and
a good deal of the interior.   It stands proudly over a deep ravine, bristled
with pines, with a running brook brawling below ; a wild scene, fit for a
great border fortress.   The hall is a hundred feet long and thirty high,
hung round with armorial quarterings of the family.   Before dinner we
visited the rich old ruins of Lanercost Abbey, which stand on Lord C.'s
grounds ; walking miles through the wildest mountain scenery to get at
it.   Every one we met showed a respect for the lord of the domain,
which seemed to be mingled with warmer feelings, as he spoke kindly to
each one, asking them about their families, &c.   Indeed, it is very gratifying to see the great deference shown to Lord Carlisle all along the
route, on my way to Castle Howard.   Every one seemed to know him,
and uncover themselves before him.   Lady E—— told me — what I have
often heard — that he was more generally beloved than any man in the
country.

We found on our return a game dinner smoking for us, for which we
were indebted to Mr. Charles Howard, a younger brother, and Baron
Parke,[1] his father-in-law, who had been slaughtering grouse and black-
cock on the moors.   Our table was laid on the dais, the upper part of the
long hall, with a great screen to keep off the cold, and a fire such as
belted Will Howard himself never saw, for it was of coal, of which
Lord C. has some mines in the neighborhood.   The chimney, which has
a grate to correspond, is full twelve feet in breadth ; a fine old baronial
chimney, at which they roasted whole oxen I suppose.   We all soon felt
as if we could have snapped our fingers at " Belted Will," if he had
come to claim his own again.   There are some fine old portraits in the
hall ; among them one of this hero and his wife, who brought the estate
into the Howard family.   She was a Dacre.   The embrasures of the
drawing-room windows of this old castle are about ten feet thick.   I have
got some drawings of the place which Lady —— gave me, and which
will give you a better idea of it.   Next morning we took up our march
for Castle Howard, — seventeen miles from York.   You can follow me on
the map.

We arrived about six ; found Lady Mary Howard in a pony phaeton
with a pair of pretty cream-colored steeds, waiting for us at the station,
three miles distant.   There was a rumble, so that all the party were accommodated.   The scenery was of a different character from that of Naworth.
Wide-spreading lawns, large and long avenues of beech and oak, beautiful
pieces of water, on which white swans were proudly sailing, an extensive
park, with any quantity of deer, several of them perfectly white, grazing
under the trees, all made up a brilliant picture of the softer scenery of
England.   We passed under several ornamented stone arches by a lofty
obelisk of yellow stone, and at length came in full view of the princely
palace of the Howards.

It is of clear yellow stone, richly ornamented with statues and every
kind of decoration.   It makes three sides of a square, and you will form
some idea of its extent, when I tell you that a suite of rooms continues

---

[1] Now Lord Wensleydale (1862).

round the house six hundred feet in length. I have seen doors open through the whole front of the building, three hundred feet, as long as Park Street, — a vista indeed. The great hall, rising to the top of the house, is gorgeous with decoration, and of immense size. The apartments and the interminable corridors are filled with master-pieces of art, painting and sculpture. In every room you are surrounded with the most beautiful objects of *virtù*, — tables of porphyry and Oriental alabaster, vases of the most elegant and capricious forms, &c. The rooms are generally not large, but very lofty and richly gilt and carved, and many of them hung with old Gobelins tapestry. Critics find much fault with the building itself, as overloaded with ornament. It was built by Van brugh, who built Blenheim, — both in the same ornamental style.

Nothing could be more cordial than the reception I met with. Lady Carlisle reminds me so of mother ; so full of kindness. If you could see the, not attention, but affection, which all the family show me, it would go to your heart. I spoke yesterday of writing to my late charming hostess, the Duchess of Argyll, and the kind old lady insisted on being my secretary instead of William. So I went into her dressing-room, and we concocted half a dozen pages, which she wrote off, at my dictation, as rapidly, and with as pretty a hand, as her granddaughter. We found only some of the family here ; Lady Dover, the widow of Lord Dover and sister of Lord Carlisle, and her two daughters. Last evening we had another arrival, the splendid Duchess of Sutherland among others, and William's friend, young Lord Dufferin. I drove over with Lady Mary in the pony phaeton to the station. Some went on horseback, and two showy barouches, with four horses each, one of bays, the other grays, with young postilions in burnished liveries. It was a brilliant show as we all came merrily over the park, and at full gallop through the villages in the neighborhood.

All now is bustle and preparation for the royal visit, which is to come off on Tuesday, the 27th, — to take up two days. The Queen and Prince, with four children, and five and twenty in their suite, chiefly domestics. Lord Carlisle's family, brothers and sisters, and sons and daughters, will muster over twenty. So that he has really not asked another, besides Will and myself, except those in attendance on the Queen. He has put off having my portrait engraved till after these festivities, and has actually had it brought down here, where he has hung it up beside the Prince's and the Queen's, for her Majesty to look at. This is a sample of all the rest, and I suppose you won't think me a ninny for telling you of it.

The dining-room will be such as the Queen cannot boast of in Buckingham Palace. It is to be the centre of the famous Picture Gallery one hundred and fifty feet long. This centre is an octagon of great height, and a table has been made, of hexagon shape, twenty feet across each way. It is to hold thirty-six, the number of guests and residents of the Castle. On one of the days a lunch for double the number will be spread, and people invited, when two long ends are to be added to the table, running up the gallery. You may imagine the show in this splendid apartment, one side of which is ornamented with statues, and with the costliest pictures of the Orleans Collection ; the other, with a noble

14

library in rich bindings; the windows opening on a velvet lawn and a silver sheet of water. But this will not be seen at the dinner hour of eight. The centre of the table will be occupied with candelabra, pyramids of lights and flowers, and we shall all be able to see the way in which her gracious Majesty deports herself. But I believe I must wind up my yarn, and spin some for somebody else.

I must tell you of one of my accomplishments. Last night we played billiards; — the game of pool, a number of gentlemen and ladies. Each person has three lives. All had lost their lives but Lord Dufferin and myself. He had three and I had only one. The pool of sixpences would go to the victor. There was a great sensation, as he, being a capital player, had deprived many of their lives; that is, pocketed their balls. I struck him into a pocket, which cost him one life, — a general shout, — the whole house was there. He missed his stroke and pocketed himself; thus he lost two lives and we were equal. The stir was great, — all shouting, as I played, "Hit him there, you can't fail! kill him!" &c., &c. We fought round and round the table and he took off his coat. So did not I, but buttoned up mine. As he missed a hazard and left his ball exposed, the silence was breathless. I struck him into the pocket amidst a shout that made the castle ring again. It was just twelve o'clock when I retired with my laurels and sixpences. Will, who is an excellent player, missed fire on this occasion, and I, who am a poor one, had all his luck.

I have taken my passage, and paid for it, on board the Niagara, the same vessel I came out in, for September 14th, a week later than I intended. But I found I should be too much hurried by the 7th. This will give me three weeks in old Pepperell. But it will take me old New York. I shall write to you once more. Love to mother and Lizzie. I shall write E. Dexter by this. Don't forget me also to the Ticknors and other old friends, and believe me, dearest wife,

Your ever-loving husband,

W. H. P.

August 26th. — Having nothing else to do, as there is just now a general lull in the breeze and I have some leisure, I will go on with my domestic chat. I left off, — let me see, — Sunday. In the evening we had little games, &c., of conversation, as at Pepperell. But the chief business was lighting up the splendid pictures so as to see the best effect; arranging the lights, &c. Beautiful pictures by any light. Before retiring we heard prayers in the noble hall; all the household, including a large troop of domestics. The effect in this gorgeous room, as large and as richly ornamented as an Italian church, was very fine. Yesterday, the weather fair, we drove over the park. First I went with Lady Mary, who whipped me along in her pony-carriage. After lunch I and Will went with Lady Caroline Lascelles and Captain Howard in a barouche and four, postilions and outriders all in gay liveries, spotless white leather pantaloons, and blue and silver coats and hats. We dashed along over the green sod, always in the park, startling the deer, and driving often into the heart of the woods, which are numerous in this fine park. We all prayed for as fine a day for the morrow for the royal advent. The house looks magnificently in the sunshine, as you drive up to it!

Alas! it is always so in this country, the morrow has come, and a drenching rain, mortifying to all loyal subjects, and a great pity. A great awning has been raised for the Queen over the steps of the principal entrance. It is now five o'clock. In an hour the royal *cortége* will be here. There has been such a fuss all day. Everybody has been running about arranging and deranging, — some carrying chairs, some flower-pots, some pictures, some vases, &c., &c. Such a scampering! I help on with a kind word, and encourage the others, and especially comfort my kind host with assurances of the weather changing! Gas has been conducted into the great dome over the hall, and "God save the Queen" blazes out in fiery characters that illuminate the whole building.

Such a quantity of fine things, beautiful flowers and fruits, have arrived to-day from the Duchess of Sutherland's place at Trentham, and from the Duke of Devonshire's at Chatsworth! The Duke is brother to Lady Carlisle. A large band will play during dinner at one end of the long gallery, and the Duke of Devonshire has sent his band for music in the evening. We had our partners and places at table assigned us this morning. There will be eight or ten more men than women, thirty-six in all. I go in with Lady Caroline Lascelles, and sit next to Sir George Grey, the Cabinet Minister, — who accompanies the Queen, — next the Duchess of Sutherland, and next Lord Carlisle and the Queen. So you see I shall be very near her Majesty, and, as the table is circular, I could not be better placed, — another instance of the kindness with which I have been treated.

A quantity of policemen have arrived on the ground before the house, as the royal train will be greeted by all the loyal people in the neighborhood, and a body of military are encamped near the house to keep order. There is such a turn-out of coaches and four, with gay liveries and all. Plague on the weather! But it only drizzles now. The landscape, however, looks dull, and wants the lights to give it effect.

August 28th, Wednesday. — I have a little time to write before luncheon, and must send off the letter then to London to be copied. Received yours this morning, complaining I had not written by the last. You have got the explanation of it since. To resume. The Queen, &c., arrived yesterday in a pelting rain, with an escort of cavalry, — a pretty sight to those under cover. Crowds of loyal subjects were in the park in front of the house to greet her. They must have come miles in the rain. She came into the hall in a plain travelling-dress, bowing very gracefully to all there, and then to her apartments, which occupy the front of the building. At eight we went to dinner, all in full dress, but mourning for the Duke of Cambridge; I, of course, for President Taylor! All wore brooches or tight pantaloons. It was a brilliant show, I assure you, — that immense table, with its fruits and flowers, and lights glancing over beautiful plate, and in that superb gallery. I was as near the Queen as at our own family table. She has a good appetite, and laughs merrily. She has fine eyes and teeth, but is short. She was dressed in black silk and lace, with the blue scarf of the Order of the Garter across her bosom. Her only ornaments were of jet. The Prince, who is certainly a handsome and very well-made man, wore the Garter with its brilliant buckle round his knee, a showy star on his breast, and the collar of a foreign order round his neck.   Dinner went off very well, except that we had no music ; a tribute to Louis-Philippe at the Queen's request, — too bad ![2] We drank the royal healths with prodigious enthusiasm.

After the ladies retired, the Prince and the other gentlemen remained half an hour, as usual.   In the evening we listened to some fine music, and the Queen examined the pictures.   Odd enough the etiquette.   Lady Carlisle, who did the honors like a high-bred lady as she is, and the Duchess of Sutherland, were the only ladies who talked with her Majesty. Lord Carlisle, her host, was the only gentleman who did so, unless she addressed a person herself.   No one can sit a moment when she chooses to stand.   She did me the honor to come and talk with me, — asking me about my coming here, my stay in the Castle, what I was doing now in the historic way, how Everett was, and where he was, — for ten minutes or so ; and Prince Albert afterwards a long while, talking about the houses and ruins in England, and the churches in Belgium, and the pictures in the room, and I don't know what.   I found myself now and then trenching on the rules by interrupting, &c. ; but I contrived to make it up by a respectful " Your Royal Highness," " Your Majesty," &c.   I told the Queen of the pleasure I had in finding myself in a land of friends instead of foreigners, — a sort of stereotype with me, — and of my particular good fortune in being under the roof with her.   She is certainly very much of a lady in her manner, with a sweet voice.

The house is filled with officials, domestics, &c.   Over two hundred slept here last night.   The grounds all round the house, as I write, are thronged with thousands of men and women, dressed in their best, from the adjacent parts of the country.   You cannot stir out without seeing a line of heads through the iron railing or before the court-yard.   I was walking in the garden this morning (did I tell you that it is a glorious day, luckily ?) with the Marchioness of Douro, who was dressed in full mourning as a lady in waiting, when the crowd set up such a shout ! as they took her for the Queen.   But I must close.   God bless you, dear !

WILLIAM H. PRESCOTT.

TO MRS. PRESCOTT.

LONDON, Sept. 5, 1850.

DEAREST WIFE,

I send you a few lines, my last from England, to bring up my history to as late a date as possible.   I told you of the royal festivities at Castle Howard, and you will get still more particulars from the account in the " Illustrated News," which I hope you have provided yourself with.   The Queen went off in royal state.   In the evening after came off the ball, at

[2] Louis-Philippe died at Clermont, Monday, August 26th, 1850, and, as the Queen was on her way the next day to Castle Howard, the train was stopped, when passing near Clermont, long enough for Prince Albert to make a visit of condolence to the ex-Queen.   With all this fresh in their recollection, it was, I suppose, regarded as a considerate and graceful tribute to the affliction of the French family to request that festive music might be omitted at the dinner.

which I danced three quadrilles and two country-dances, — the last two with the Duchess of Sutherland, — and it was four in the morning, when we wound up with the brave old dance of Sir Roger de Coverley. I spent a day longer at Castle Howard, driving about with Lady Mary Howard in her pony phaeton over the park to see her village pensioners. When I left early the next day, we had an affectionate leave-taking enough; I mean all of us together, and as I know it will please you to see how much heart the family have shown to me, I will enclose a note I received at Trentham from old Lady Carlisle, and another from her granddaughter, the Duchess of Argyll. We all parted at the railway station, and I shall never see them more!

From Castle Howard we proceeded to Trentham in Staffordshire, the Duchess of Sutherland's favorite seat, and a splendid place it is. We met her at Derby, she having set out the day before us. We both arrived too late for the train. So she put post-horses to her barouche, and she and Lady Constance, a blooming English girl looking quite like Lizzie, and Will and I, posted it for thirty-six miles, reaching Trentham at ten in the evening, — an open barouche and cool enough. But we took it merrily, as indeed we should not have got on at all that night, if we had not had the good luck to fall in with her Grace.

Trentham is a beautiful place; the grounds laid out in the Italian style for an immense extent; the gardens with plots of flowers so curiously arranged that it looks like a fine painting, with a little lake studded with islands at the end, and this enclosed by hills dark with forest-trees. Besides these noble gardens, through which the Trent flows in a smooth current, there is an extensive park, and the deer came under my windows in the morning as tame as pet lambs. The Duchess spent the former part of the afternoon in taking us round herself to all the different places, walking and sometimes boating it on the Trent; for they extend over a great space. The green-houses, &c. are superb, and filled with exquisite flowers and fruit: and the drawing-rooms, of which there is a suite of ten or twelve, very large, open on a magnificent conservatory, with marble floors, fountains, and a roof of glass, about five times as big as Mrs. R.'s, tell E. The rooms are filled with the choicest and most delicate works of art, painting, sculpture, bijouterie of all kinds. It is the temple of Taste, and its charming mistress created it all. As I was coming away, she asked me to walk with her into the garden, and led me to a spot where several men were at work having a great hole prepared. A large evergreen tree was held up by the gardener, and I was requested to help set it in the place and to throw some shovelfuls of earth on it. In fact, I was to leave an evergreen memorial, "which," said she, "my children shall see hereafter, and know by whom it was planted." She chose to accompany us to the station, and by the way took us to the great porcelain manufactory of Stoke, where she gave Will a statuette of the Prince of Wales, very pretty, and me an exquisite little vase, which you will be so happy as to take care of under a glass cover. Her own rooms contain some beautiful specimens of them. Is she not a Duchess? She is, every inch of her; and what is better, a most warm-hearted, affectionate person, like all the rest of the generous race of Howard. They always seem employed on something. The Duchess of Argyll, I remember, was never unemployed, — reading, or working, or drawing, which she does uncommonly well. The tenderness of the mother and daughter for each other is pleasing enough. We came to be present at the christening of the hope of the family, — Lord Stafford's first-born son. It took place in the church, which is attached to a wing of the mansion. The family occupied a gallery at the end of the chapel, and the ceremony was witnessed by all the village.

I had intended to go to Lord Ellesmere's, agreeably to a general invitation, but found that Lord and Lady Ellesmere were in Ireland, called there by the illness of a daughter. So we went to Chatsworth, the famous seat of the Duke of Devonshire. He is absent, but had written to the housekeeper to show us all the place, to have the fountains play, — one of which springs up two hundred feet or more, — and to prepare lunch for me. I found the servants prepared to receive us, and we passed several hours at his magnificent place, and fared as well as if its noble proprietor had been on the spot to welcome us. I shall, after a day here, go to Lady Theresa Lewis, at Lord Clarendon's place, then to Baron Parke's, Ampthill, for a day or two ; then to the Marquis of Lansdowne's,[3] and then huzza for home! Pray for the good steamer Niagara ; a good steamer, and a good captain, and I trust a good voyage.

Sept. 9th. — Just received yours and E.'s charming letters ; — alas ! by my blunder (the last ?) I was startled by mother's illness. Thank God all is right again. I could not afford to have anything happen to her while I am away.

Your affectionate husband,

WM. H. PRESCOTT.

And so ended, in unbroken enjoyment, the most brilliant visit ever made to England by an American citizen not clothed with the *prestige* of official station.[4] That Mr. Prescott deeply

[3] The visit to Lord Lansdowne's failed ; but before he reached London he made a most agreeable one at Baron Parke's, now Lord Wensleydale.

[4] A whimsical proof that Mr. Prescott was a lion in London during his visit there may be found in the following note of the venerable Miss Berry, — Horace Walpole's Miss Berry, — with whom Dean Milman had invited Mr. Prescott and himself to dine, but, owing to Mr. P.'s engagements, he had been obliged to offer their visit above a fortnight ahead of the time when he proposed it.

MISS BERRY TO THE REV. MR. MILMAN.

June 20, 1850.

Having insured my life at more than one of the most respectable insurance-companies, I venture to accept of your most agreeable proposal for next Saturday fortnight! and shall rejoice to see you and Mrs. Milman accompanied by one whose works I have long admired, and to whose pen I am indebted for some of the liveliest interests and the most agreeable hours that can exist for an octogenarian, like your obliged and attached friend,

M. BERRY.

felt the kindness he received — especially that of the Lyells, the Milmans, and " all the blood of all the Howards " — is plain from his letters, written in the confidence and simplicity of family affection. How much of this kindness is to be attributed to his personal character rather than to his reputation as an author, it is not easy to tell. But, whatever portion of it resulted from the intercourse and contact of society ; whatever was won by his sunny smile and cordial, unconstrained ways, — he seemed to recognize without accurately measuring it, and by the finer instincts of his nature to appreciate it as something more to be valued and desired, than any tribute of admiration which might have become due to him from his works before he was personally known.

After he returned home, when the crowded life he had led for three or four months, with its pleasures and excitements, was seen from a tranquil distance, he summed up the results of his visit in the following passage, carefully recorded among his Memoranda at the end of October, 1850.

On the whole, what I have seen raises my preconceived estimate of the English character. It is full of generous, true, and manly qualities ; and I doubt if there ever was so high a standard of morality in an aristocracy which has such means for self-indulgence at its command, and which occupies a position that secures it so much deference. In general, they do not seem to abuse their great advantages. The respect for religion — at least for the forms of it — is universal, and there are few, I imagine, of the great proprietors who are not more or less occupied with improving their estates, and with providing for the comfort of their tenantry, while many take a leading part in the great political movements of the time. There never was an aristocracy which combined so much practical knowledge and industry with the advantages of exalted rank.

The Englishman is seen to most advantage in his country home. For he is constitutionally both domestic and rural in his habits. His fireside and his farm, — these are the places in which one sees his simple and warm-hearted nature most freely unfolded. There is a shyness in an Englishman, — a natural reserve, — which makes him cold to strangers, and difficult of approach. But once corner him in his own house, a frank and full expansion will be given to his feelings, that we should look for in vain in the colder Yankee, and a depth not to be found in the light and superficial Frenchman, — speaking of nationalities, not individualities.

The Englishman is the most truly rural in his tastes and habits of any people in the world. I am speaking of the higher classes. The aristocracy of other countries affect the camp and the city. But the English love their old castles and country seats with a patriotic love. They are fond of country sports. Every man shoots or hunts. No man is too old to be in the saddle some part of the day, and men of seventy years and more follow the hounds and take a five-barred gate at a leap. The women are good whips, are fond of horses and dogs, and other animals. Duchesses have their cows, their poultry, their pigs, — all watched over and provided with accommodations of Dutch-like neatness. All this is characteristic of the people. It may be thought to detract something from the feminine graces which in other lands make a woman so amiably dependent as to be nearly imbecile. But it produces a healthy and blooming race of women to match the hardy Englishmen, — the finest development of the physical and moral nature which the world has witnessed. For we are not to look on the English gentleman as a mere Nimrod. With all his relish for field sports and country usages, he has his house filled with collections of art and with extensive libraries. The tables of the drawing-rooms are covered with the latest works sent down by the London publisher. Every guest is provided with an apparatus for writing, and often a little library of books for his own amusement. The English country-gentleman of the present day is anything but a Squire Western, though he does retain all his relish for field sports.

The character of an Englishman, under this its most refined aspect, has some disagreeable points which jar unpleasantly on the foreigner not accustomed to them. The consciousness of national superiority, combined with natural feelings of independence, gives him an air of arrogance, though it must be owned that this is never betrayed in his own house, — I may almost say, in his own country. But abroad, where he seems to institute a comparison between himself and the people he is thrown with, it becomes so obvious that he is the most unpopular, not to say odious, person in the world. Even the open hand with which he dispenses his bounty will not atone for the violence he offers to national vanity.

There are other defects which are visible even in his most favored circumstances. Such is his bigotry, surpassing everything, in a quiet passive form, that has been witnessed since the more active bigotry of the times of the Spanish Philips. Such, too, is the exclusive, limited range of his knowledge and conceptions of all political and social topics and relations. The Englishman, the cultivated Englishman, has no standard of excellence borrowed from mankind. His speculation never travels beyond his own little — *great-little* — island. That is the world to him. True, he travels, shoots lions among the Hottentots, chases the grizzly bear over the Rocky Mountains, kills elephants in India and salmon on the coast of Labrador, comes home, and very likely makes a book. But the scope of his ideas does not seem to be enlarged by all this. The body travels, not the mind. And, however he may abuse his own land, he returns home as hearty a John Bull, with all his prejudices and national tastes as rooted as before. The English — the men of fortune — all travel. Yet how little sympathy they show for other people or institutions, and how slight is the interest they take in them! They are islanders, cut off from the great world. But their island is, indeed, a world of its own. With all their faults, never has the sun shone — if one may use the expression in reference to England — on a more noble race, or one that has done more for the great interests of humanity.

CHAPTER XXIII.

1850 – 1852.

VOYAGE HOME. — LETTERS TO FRIENDS IN ENGLAND. — BEGINS TO WORK AGAIN. — PEPPERELL. — "PHILIP THE SECOND." — CORRESPONDENCE.

ON the 14th of September, Mr. Prescott embarked at Liverpool, to return home, on board the Niagara, — the same good ship on which he had embarked for Europe nearly four months earlier at New York, and in which he now reached that metropolis again, after a fortunate passage of thirteen days. At Liverpool he stopped, as he did on his arrival there, at the hospitable house of his old friend Smith ; and the last letter he wrote before he went on board the steamer, and the first he despatched back to England, after he was again fairly at home, were to Lady Lyell, with whom and Sir Charles he had probably spent more hours in London than with anybody else, and to both of whom he owed unnumbered acts of kindness.

TO LADY LYELL.

LIVERPOOL, September 13, 1850.

MY DEAR LADY LYELL,

I am now at Liverpool, or rather in the suburbs, at my friend's house. It is after midnight, but I cannot go to sleep without bidding you and your husband one more adieu. I reached here about five o'clock, and find there are seventy passengers ; several ladies, or persons that I hope are so, for they are not men. But I look for little comfort on the restless deep. I hope, however, for a fair offing. You will think of me sometimes during the next fortnight, and how often shall I think of you, and your constant kindness to me ! You see I am never tired of asking for it, as I sent you the troublesome commission of paying my debts before I left, and, I believe, did not send quite money enough. Heaven bless you !
With kind remembrances to Sir Charles, believe me, my dear friend,
Most affectionately yours,
WM. H. PRESCOTT.

Can you make out my hieroglyphics ? [1]

[1] This letter was written with his noctograph.

14 *

U

TO LADY LYELL.

BOSTON, September 30, 1850.

MY DEAR LADY LYELL,

I write you a line to tell you of my safe arrival on the other side of the great pond — I beg pardon — *lake*. We had a fair passage, considering the season, some thumping and tumbling about and constant head-winds, but no very heavy gales, such as fall due at the equinox. I was lucky enough to find a lady on board who was not sick, and who was willing to read aloud; so the *ennui* of the voyage was wonderfully lightened by "Vanity Fair" and Mr. Cumming's lion-stories. I had the good fortune to find all well on returning, and the atmosphere was lighted up with a sunny light, such as I never saw on the other side of the water, at least during my present journey. I do not believe it will be as good for my eyes as the comfortable neutral tints of England, — merry England, not from its climate, however, but from the warm hearts of its people. God bless them! I have no time to think over matters now, busy in the midst of trunks and portmanteaus, some emptying, some filling, for our speedy flight to Pepperell. But once in its welcome shades, I shall have much to think over, — of dear friends beyond the water. Yesterday, who should pop in upon me but Dr. Holland, fresh from Lake Superior. It seemed like an apparition from Brook Street, so soon and sudden. He and Everett and Ticknor will dine with me to-day, and we shall have a comfortable talk of things most agreeable to us all. Dr. H. sails in the "Canada" to-morrow. The grass does not grow under his feet. I sent Anna Ticknor yesterday the beautiful present, all in good order. She went down in the afternoon to her sea-nest, and her husband comes up to-day. Possibly she may come and dine with us too. She was right glad to see me, and had a thousand questions to ask; so I hope she will come and get answers to some of them to-day. To-morrow we flit, and a party of young people go along with us. So we shall not be melancholy. Adieu, my dear friend. Pray remember me most kindly to your husband and your family. My wife joins in loving remembrances to you, and desires to thank you for your kind note.

Believe me, my dear Lady Lyell, here and everywhere,
                    Affectionately yours,

                                        WM. H. PRESCOTT.

Give my love to the Milmans, when they return. I shall write them from Pepperell.

Very soon he wrote to Dean Milman.

PEPPERELL, Mass., October 10, 1850.

MY DEAR FRIEND,

I have at length reached my native land, and am again in my country quarters, wandering over my old familiar hills, and watching the brilliant changes of the leaf in the forests of October, the finest of the American months. This rural quiet is very favorable for calling up the past, and many a friendly face on the other side of the water comes up before me, and none more frequently than yours and that of your dear wife.

Since I parted from you, I have been tolerably industrious. I first passed a week in Belgium, to get some acquaintance with the topography of the country I am to describe. It is a wonderful country certainly, — rich in its present abundance as well as in its beautiful monuments of art and its historic recollections. On my return to England, I went at once into the country, and spent six weeks at different places, where I saw English life under a totally new aspect. The country is certainly the true place in which to see the Englishman. It is there that his peculiar character seems to have the best field for its expansion ; a life which calls out his energies physical as well as mental, the one almost as remarkable as the other.

The country life affords the opportunity for intimacy, which it is very difficult to have in London. There is a depth in the English character, and at the same time a constitutional reserve, sometimes amounting to shyness, which it requires some degree of intimacy to penetrate. As to the hospitality, it is quite equal to what we read of in semi-civilized countries, where the presence of a stranger is a boon instead of a burden. I could have continued to live in this agreeable way of life till the next meeting of Parliament, if I could have settled it with my conscience to do so. As to the houses, I think I saw some of the best places in England, in the North and in the South, with a very interesting dip into the Highlands, and I trust I have left some friends there that will not let the memory of me pass away like a summer cloud. In particular, I have learned to comprehend what is meant by "the blood of the Howards," — a family in all its extent, as far as I have seen it, as noble in nature as in birth. . . . . .

I had a pretty good passage on my return, considering that it was the season of equinoctial tempests. I was fortunate in finding that no trouble or sorrow had come into the domestic circle since my departure, and my friends were pleased to find that I had brought home substantial proofs of English hospitality in the addition of some ten pounds' weight to my mortal part. By the by, Lord Carlisle told the Queen that I said, "Instead of John Bull, the Englishman should be called John Mutton, for he ate beef only one day in the week, and mutton the other six"; at which her Majesty, who, strange to say, never eats mutton herself, was pleased to laugh most graciously.

The day after I reached Boston I was surprised by the apparition of my old neighbor, Dr. Holland, just returned from an excursion to Lake Superior. It was as if a piece of Brook Street had parted from its moorings, and crossed the water. We were in a transition state, just flitting to the country, but I managed to have him, Everett, and Ticknor dine with me. So we had a pleasant *partie carrée* to talk over our friends, on the other side of the salt lake. What would I not give to have you and Mrs. Milman on this side of it. Perhaps you may have leisure and curiosity some day, when the passage is reduced to a week, as it will be, to see the way of life of the American aborigines. If you do not, you will still be here in the heart of one who can never forget the kindness and love he has experienced from you in a distant land.

Pray remember me most affectionately to Mrs. Milman, to whom I shall soon write, and believe me, my dear friend,

Very sincerely yours,

W. H. PRESCOTT.

He found it somewhat difficult to settle down into regular habits of industry after his return home. But he did it. His first weeks were spent at Pepperell, where I recollect that I passed two or three merry days with him, when our common friend, Mr. Edward Twisleton, who had been very kind to him in England, made him a visit, and when the country was in all the gorgeous livery of a New England autumn.

The subsequent winter, 1850 – 51, was spent as usual, in Boston. But his eyes were in a bad state, and his interruptions so frequent, that he found it impossible to secure as many hours every day for work as he desired. He therefore was not satisfied with the results he obtained, and complained, as he often did, somewhat unreasonably, of the ill effects of a town life. Indeed, it was not until he made his *villeggiatura* at Pepperell, in the autumn of 1851, that he was content with himself and with what he was doing.

But from this time he worked in earnest. He made good resolutions and kept them with more exactness than he had commonly done ; so that, by the middle of April, 1852, he had completed the first volume of his " Philip the Second," and was plunging with spirit into the second. I remember very well how heartily he enjoyed this period of uncommon activity.

It was at this time, and I think partly from the effect of his visit to England, that he changed his purpose concerning the character he should give to his " History of Philip the Second." When he left home he was quite decided that the work should be *Memoirs*. Soon after his return he began to talk to me doubtfully about it. His health was better, his courage higher. But he was always slow in making up his mind. He therefore went on some months longer, still really undetermined, and writing rather memoirs than history. At last, when he was finishing the first volume, and came to confront the great subject of the Rebellion of the Netherlands, he perceived clearly that the gravest form of history ought to be adopted.

" For some time after I had finished the ' Peru,' " he says, " I hesitated whether I should grapple with the whole subject of Philip *in extenso*, and when I had made up my mind to serve up the whole barbecue, instead of particular parts of it, I had so little confidence in the strength of my own vision, that I thought of calling the work 'Memoirs' and treating the subject in a more desultory and superficial manner than belongs to regular history. I did not go to work in a business-like style until I broke ground on the troubles of the Netherlands. Perhaps my critics may find this out."

I think they did not. Indeed, there was less occasion for it than the author himself supposed. The earlier portions of the history, relating as they do to the abdication of Charles V. and the marriage of Philip with Mary of England, fell naturally into the tone of memoirs, and thus they make a more graceful vestibule to the grand and grave events that were to follow than could otherwise have been arranged for them, while, at the same time, as he advanced into the body of his work and was called on to account for the war with France, and describe the battles of St. Quentin and Gravelines, he, as it were, inevitably fell into the more serious tone of history, which had been so long familiar to him. The transition, therefore, was easy, and was besides so appropriate, that I think a change of purpose was hardly detected. One effect of it, however, was soon perceptible to himself. He liked his work better, and carried it on with the sort of interest which he always felt was important, not only to his happiness, but to his success.

From this time forward — that is, from the period of his return home — his correspondence becomes more abundant. This was natural, and indeed inevitable. He had made acquaintances and friendships in England, which led to such intercourse, and the letters that followed from it show the remainder of his life in a light clearer and more agreeable than it can be shown in any other way. Little remains, therefore, but to arrange them in their proper sequence.

TO MR. FORD.

PEPPERELL, Mass., U. S., October 12, 1850.

Here I am, my dear Ford, safe and sound in my old country quarters, with leisure to speak a word or two to a friend on the other side of the Atlantic. I had a voyage of thirteen days, and pretty good weather for the most part, considering it was the month when I had a right to expect to be tumbled about rudely by the equinoctial gales. We *had* some rough gales, and my own company were too much damaged to do much for me.

But angel woman, God bless her! always comes when she is wanted, — and sometimes when she is not, — and I found one in a pretty little Yankee lady, who had the twofold qualifications of being salt-water-proof, and of being a good reader. So, thanks to her, I travelled through "Vanity Fair" for the second time, and through Cumming's African exploits, quite new to me. And so killing his lions helped me to kill my time; the worst enemy of the two. It was with a light heart, however, that I descried the gray rocks of my native land again.

I am now about forty miles from town, on my old family acres, which do not go back to the time of the Norman conquest, though they do to that of the Aborigines, which is antiquity for a country where there are no entails and the son seldom sits under the shadow of the trees that his father planted. It is a plain New England farm, but I am attached to it, for it is connected with the earliest recollections of my childhood, and the mountains that hem it round look at me with old familiar faces. I have had too many friends to greet me here to have as much time as I could wish to myself, but as I wander through my old haunts, I think of the past summer, and many a friendly countenance on the other side of the water comes before me. Then I think of the pleasant hours I have had with you, my dear Ford, and of your many kindnesses, not to be forgotten; of our merry Whitebait feed with John Murray, at Royal Greenwich, which you are to immortalize one day, you know, in the "Quarterly,"

"So savage and tartarly."

And that calls to mind that prince of good fellows, Stirling, and the last agreeable little dinner we three had together at Lockhart's. Pray remember me most kindly to the great Aristarch and to Stirling. That was not my final parting with the latter worthy, for he did me the favor to smoke me into the little hours the morning before I left London for my country campaign. And I had the pleasure of a parting breakfast with you, too, in Brook Street, as you may recall, on my return. God bless you both! Some day or other I shall expect to see you twain on this side of the great salt lake, if it is only to hunt the grizzly bear, of which amiable sport John Bull will, no doubt, become very fond when Cumming has killed all the lions and camelopards of the Hottentot country.

In about a fortnight I shall leave my naked woods for the town, and then for the *Casas de España.* And when I am fairly in harness, I do not mean to think of anything else; not even of my cockney friends in the great-little isle. If there is any way in which I can possibly be of use to you in the New World, you will not fail to tell me of it with all frankness. Pray remember me most kindly to your daughters.

Y mando siempre su amigo quien le quiere de todo corazon

Y. S. M. B.

GUILLERMO H. PRESCOTT.

TO THE EARL OF CARLISLE.

BOSTON, November 12, 1850.

MY DEAR CARLISLE,

I have the pleasure of sending you Allston's Sketches, of which I spoke to you. They are the first draughts of some of his best pictures; among them the "Uriel," which the Duchess of Sutherland has at Trentham. Generally, however, they have remained mere sketches which the artist never worked up into regular pictures. They have been much esteemed by the critics here as fine studies, and the execution of this work was intrusted to two of our best engravers. One of them is excellent with crayons; * quite equal to Richmond in the portraits of women. . . . . .

I now and then get a reminder of the land of roast mutton by the sight of some one or other of your countrymen who emerges from the steamers that arrive here every fortnight. We are, indeed, one family. Did I ever repeat to you Allston's beautiful lines, one stanza of the three which he wrote on the subject? *Les voilà!*

> " While the manners, while the arts,
> That mould a nation's soul,
> Still cling around our hearts,
> Between let ocean roll,
> Our joint communion breaking with the sun,
> Yet still from either beach
> The voice of blood shall reach,
> More audible than speech:
> ' We are one.' "

Is it not good? . . . . .

Farewell, my dear friend. I think of you mixed up with Castle Howard and brave old Naworth, and many a pleasant recollection.

Once more, *mio caro, addio.*

Always thine,

WM. H. PRESCOTT.

FROM MR. LOCKHART.

MY DEAR MR. PRESCOTT,

Your basket of canvas-backs arrived here a day after your note, and the contents thereof proved to be in quite as good condition as they could have been if shot three days before in Leicestershire. I may say I had never before tasted the dainty, and that I think it entirely merits its reputation; but on this last head, I presume the *ipse dixit* of Master Ford is "a voice double as any duke's."

Very many thanks for your kind recollections. I had had very pleasing accounts of you and other friends from Holland on his return from his rapid expedition. He declares that, except the friends, he found everything so changed, that your country seemed to call for a visit once in five years, and gallant is he in his resolution to invade you again in 1855. I

* Cheney.

wish I could muster leisure or pluck, or both, for such an adventure. Let me hope meanwhile that long ere '55 we may again see you and Everett and Ticknor here, where surely you must all feel very tolerably at home.

Believe me always very sincerely yours,

J. G. LOCKHART.

December 27, 1850.

TO THE EARL OF CARLISLE.

BOSTON, January 14, 1851.

MY DEAR CARLISLE,

I have the pleasure of sending you by this steamer a work of which I happen to have two copies, containing the portraits of some dozen Yankee notabilities, which may perhaps interest you. The likenesses, taken from daguerrotypes, are sometimes frightfully, odiously like. But some of the heads, as those of Taylor, our present President, besides being true, are not unpleasing likenesses. The biographical sketches are written for the most part, as you will see, in the Ercles vein. My effigy was taken in New York, about an hour before I sailed for England, when I had rather a rueful and lackadaisical aspect. The biographical notice of me is better done than most of them, in point of literary execution, being written by our friend Ticknor.

Pray thank your brother Charles for his kindness in sending me out the reports of your Lectures. I, as well as the rest of your friends here, and many more that know you not, have read them with great pleasure, and, I trust, edification. The dissertation on your travels has been reprinted all over the country, and, as far as I know, with entire commendation. Indeed, it would be churlish enough to take exception at the very liberal and charitable tone of criticism which pervades it. If you are not blind to our defects, it gives much higher value to your approbation, and you are no niggard of that, certainly. Even your reflections on the black plague will not be taken amiss by the South, since they are of that abstract kind which can hardly be contested, while you do not pass judgment on the peculiar difficulties of our position, which considerably disturbs the general question. Your remarks on me went to my heart. They were just what I would wish you to have said, and, as I know they came from your heart, I will not thank you for them. On the whole, you have set an excellent example, which, I trust, will be followed by others of your order. But few will have it in their power to do good as widely as you have done, since there are very few whose remarks will be read as extensively, and with the same avidity, on both sides of the water.

TO THE EARL OF CARLISLE.

BOSTON, U. S., January 27, 1851.

MY DEAR CARLISLE,

I wrote you from the country that, when I returned to town, I should lose no time in endeavoring to look up a good painting of the Falls of Niagara. I have not neglected this; but, though I found it easy enough to get paintings of the grand cataract, I have not till lately been able to meet with what I wanted. I will tell you how this came about. When Bulwer, your Minister, was here, I asked him, as he has a good taste in the arts, to see if he could meet with any good picture of Niagara while he was in New York. Some time after, he wrote me that he had met with "a very beautiful picture of the Falls, by a Frenchman." It so happened, that I had seen this same picture much commended in the New York papers, and I found that the artist's name was Lebron, a person of whom I happened to know something, as a letter from the Viscount Santarem, in Paris, commended him to me as a "very distinguished artist," but the note arriving last summer, while I was absent, I had never seen Mr. Lebron. I requested my friend, Mr. ———, of New York, on whose judgment I place more reliance than on that of any other connoisseur whom I know, and who has himself a very pretty collection of pictures, to write me his opinion of the work. He fully confirmed Bulwer's report; and I accordingly bought the picture, which is now in my own house.

It is about five feet by three and a half, and exhibits, which is the most difficult thing, an entire view of the Falls, both on the Canada and American side. The great difficulty to overcome is the milky shallowness of the waters, where the foam diminishes so much the apparent height of the cataract. I think you will agree that the artist has managed this very well. In the distance a black thunder-storm is bursting over Goat Island and the American Falls. A steamboat, "The Maid of the Mist," which has been plying for some years on the river below, forms an object by which the eye can measure, in some degree, the stupendous proportions of the cataract. On the edge of the Horseshoe Fall is the fragment of a ferry-boat which, more than a year since, was washed down to the brink of the precipice, and has been there detained until within a week, when, I see by the papers, it has been carried over into the abyss. I mention these little incidents that you may understand them, being something different from what you saw when you were at Niagara; and perhaps you may recognize some change in the form of the Table-Rock itself, some tons of which, carrying away a carriage and horses standing on it at the time, slipped into the gulf a year or more since.

I shall send the painting out by the "Canada," February 12th, being the first steamer which leaves this port for Liverpool, and, as I have been rather unlucky in some of my consignments, I think it will be as safe to address the box at once to you, and it will await your order at Liverpool, where it will probably arrive the latter part of February.

I shall be much disappointed if it does not please you well enough to hang upon your walls as a faithful representation of the great cataract; and I trust you will gratify me by accepting it as a *souvenir* of your friend across the water. I assure you it pleases me much to think there is anything I can send you from this quarter of the world which will give you pleasure. . . . . .

Pray remember me most affectionately to your mother and sister, who, I suppose, are now in town with you.

And believe me, dearest Carlisle,

Ever faithfully yours,

W. H. PRESCOTT.

TO THE EARL OF CARLISLE.

BOSTON, May 29, 1851.

MY DEAR CARLISLE,

I am off in a couple of days for the great cataract. I like to refresh my recollections of it every few years by a visit in person; and I have a pleasant party to accompany me. I wish you were one of them. How I should like to stroll through the woods of Goat Island with you, my dear Carlisle, and talk over the pleasant past, made so pleasant the last year by you and yours. By the by, the Duke of Argyll sent me an address which he made some time since at Glasgow, in which he made the kindest mention of me. It was a very sensible discourse, and I think it would be well for the country if more of the aristocracy were to follow the example, which you and he have set, of addressing the people on other topics besides those of a political or agricultural nature, — the two great hobbies of John Bull.

So you perceive Sumner is elected after twenty ballotings. His position will be a difficult one. He represents a coalition of the Democratic and Free-Soil parties, who have little relation to one another. And in the Senate the particular doctrine which he avows finds no favor. I believe it will prove a bed filled more with thorns than with roses. I had a long talk with him yesterday, and I think he feels it himself. It is to his credit that he has not committed himself by any concessions to secure his election. The difficulty with Sumner as a statesman is, that he aims at the greatest abstract good instead of the greatest good practicable. By such a policy he misses even this lower mark; not a low one either for a philanthropist and a patriot.

You and your friends still continue to manage the ship notwithstanding the rough seas you have had to encounter. I should think it must be a perplexing office until your parties assume some more determinate character, so as to throw a decided support into the government scale.

Pray remember me most affectionately to your mother and to Lady Mary, and to the Duchess of Sutherland, whom I suppose you see often, and believe me, my dear Carlisle,

Always most affectionately your friend,

W. H. PRESCOTT.

TO MRS. MILMAN.

BOSTON, February 16, 1852.

How kind it was in you, my dear Mrs. Milman, to write me such a good letter, and I am afraid you will think little deserved by me. But if I have not written, it is not that I have not thought often of the happy days I have passed in your society and in that of my good friend the Dean, — God bless you both! You congratulated me on the engagement of my daughter.* It is a satisfactory circumstance for us every way; and

* His only daughter to Mr. James Lawrence, eldest son of Mr. Abbott Lawrence, who was then Minister of the United States in London.

the character of the *fiancé* is such, I believe, as to promise as much happiness to the union as one could expect.   Yet it is a hard thing to part with a daughter, — an only daughter, — the light of one's home and one's heart.   The boys go off, as a thing of course; for man is a migratory animal.   But a woman seems part of the household fixtures.   Yet a little reflection makes us feel that a good connection is far better than single blessedness, especially in our country, where matrimony is the destiny of so nearly all, that the few exceptions to it are in rather a lonely and anomalous position.

What a delightful tour you must have had in Italy!   It reminds me of wandering over the same sunny land, five and thirty years ago, — a prodigious reminiscence.   It is one of the charms of your situation that you have but to cross a narrow strait of some twenty miles to find yourself transported to a region as unlike your own as the moon, — and, to say truth, a good deal more unlike.   This last *coup d'etat* shows, as Scriblerus says,

> " None but themselves can be their parallel."

I am very glad to learn from your letter that the Dean is making good progress in the continuation of his noble work.   I have always thought it very creditable to the government that it has bestowed its church dignities on one so liberal and tolerant as your husband.   I do not think that the royal patronage always dares to honor those in the Church, whom the world most honors.

Have you seen Macaulay of late?   He told me that he should not probably make his bow to the public again before 1853.   It seems that his conjecture was not wrong, the false newspapers notwithstanding.   But one learns not to believe a thing, for the reason that it is affirmed in the newspapers.   Our former Minister, Bancroft, has a volume in the press, a continuation of his American history, which will serve as a counterpart to Lord Mahon's, exhibiting the other side of the tapestry.

I hope history is in possession of all the feuds that will ever take place between the two kindred nations.   In how amiable a way the correspondence about the Prometheus has been conducted by Lord Granville!   John Bull can afford to make apology when he is in the wrong.   The present state of things in Europe should rather tend to draw the only two great nations where constitutional liberty exists more closely together.

I am very glad that our friend Mr. Hallam is to have the satisfaction of seeing his daughter so well married.   He has had many hard blows, and this ray of sunshine will, I hope, light up his domestic hearth for the evening of life.   Pray present my congratulations most sincerely to him and Miss Hallam.

We are now beginning to be busy with preparations for my daughter's approaching nuptials, which will take place, probably, in about a month, if some Paris toggery, furniture, &c., as indispensable as a bridegroom or a priest, it seems, come in due time.   The affair makes a merry stir in our circle, in the way of festive parties, balls, and dinners.   But in truth there is a little weight lies at the bottom of my heart when I think that the seat at her own board is to be forever vacant. Yet it is but a migration to the next street. How can parents consent to a match that places an ocean betwixt them and their children?

But I must bring my prosy talk to a close. I feel, now that I have my pen in hand, that I am by your side, with your husband and your family, and our friends the Lyells; or perhaps rambling over the grounds of royal Windsor, or through dark passages in the Tower, or the pleasant haunts of Richmond Hill; at the genial table of the charming lady "who came out in Queen Anne's day," or many other places with which your memory and your husband's, your kindly countenances and delightful talk, are all associated. When I lay my head on my pillow, the forms of the dear friends gather round me, and sometimes I have the good luck to see them in midnight visions, — and I wake up and find it all a dream.

Pray remember me most kindly to the Dean and your sons, and to Lady Lyell, whom, I suppose, you often see, and believe me, my dear Mrs. Milman,

Always most affectionately yours,

WM. H. PRESCOTT.

TO THE EARL OF CARLISLE.

BOSTON, April 7, 1852.

DEAREST CARLISLE,

Lawrence wrote me a little while since that you remarked you could now say for once that I was in your debt. It may be so; but I wonder if I have not given you two to one, or some such odds. But no matter; in friendship, as in love, an exact tally is not to be demanded.

Since I had last the pleasure of hearing from you, there has been a great revolution in your affairs, and the *ins* have become *outs*. Is it not an awkward thing to be obliged to face about, and take just the opposite tacks; to be always on the attack instead of the defence! What a change! First to break with your Minister of Foreign Affairs, who was in so much glory, fighting the battle so stoutly when I was in London! And then to break up altogether, and surrender the field to the Protectionists! We are most of us protectionists, more or less, in my part of the country, with which doctrines I found very little sympathy when I was in England. I wonder if that policy can possibly get the upper hand again with you. The *revocare gradum* is always a difficult step, more difficult than any two forward. Can the present Cabinet possibly stand on one leg, and that the lame one of protection? We at the North have long been trying to get the scale of duties raised, but in vain. *Nil retrorsum*. What hot work you will have in the coming election! It would be almost worth a voyage to see. Yet I doubt if any candidate will spend a hundred thousand upon it, as was the case, I believe, in your own county not many years ago.

Sumner has not been anxious to make a display in Congress. In this he has judged well. The session has been a tame one, so far. He made a short speech on the Kossuth business, and a very good one; — since that, a more elaborate effort on the distribution of our wild lands, so as to favor the new, unsettled States. According to our way of thinking, he was not so successful here. I suppose he provides you with his parliamentary eloquence. We are expecting Kossuth here before long. I am glad he takes us last. I should be sorry that we should get into a scrape by any ill-advised enthusiasm. He has been preaching up doctrines of intervention (called by him non-intervention) by no means suited to our policy, which, as our position affords us the means of keeping aloof, should be to wash our hands of all the troubles of the Old World.

What troubles you are having now, in France especially. But revolution is the condition of a Frenchman's existence apparently. Can that country long endure the present state of things, — the days of Augustus Cæsar over again ?

Have you seen Bancroft's new volume ? I think this volume, which has his characteristic merits and defects, showy, sketchy, and full of bold speculations, will have interest for you. Lord Mahon is on the same field, surveying it from an opposite point of view. So we are likely to have the American Revolution well dissected by able writers on opposite sides at the same time. The result will probably be doubt upon everything.

In the newspaper of to-day is a letter, to be followed by two others, addressed to Bryant, the poet-editor of the New York "Evening Post," from Sparks, himself the editor of Washington's papers. I think you must have known Sparks here. He is now the President of Harvard University, the post occupied by Everett after his return. Sparks has been sharply handled for the corruption of the original text of Washington, as appeared by comparisons of some of the originals with his printed copy. Lord Mahon, among others, has some severe strictures on him in his last volume. Sparks's letters are in vindication of himself, on the ground that the alterations are merely verbal, to correct bad grammar and obvious blunders, which Washington would have corrected himself, had he prepared his correspondence for the press. He makes out a fair case for himself, and any one who knows the integrity of Sparks will give him credit for what he states. As he has some reflections upon Lord Mahon's rash criticism, as he terms it, I doubt not he will send him a copy, or I would do it, as I think he would like to see the explanation.

I suppose you breakfast sometimes with Macaulay, and that he dines sometimes with you. I wish I could be with you at both. I suppose he is busy on his new volume. When will the new brace be bagged ? I remember he prophesied to me not before 1853, and I was very glad to hear from him, that his great success did not make him hurry over that historic ground. A year or two extra is well spent on a work destined to live forever.

And now, my dear friend, I do not know that there is anything here that I can tell you of that will much interest you. I am poddering over my book; still Philippizing. But " it is a far cry to Loch Awe "; which place, far as it is, by the by, I saw on my last visit to Europe under such delightful auspices, with the Lord of the Campbells and his lovely lady, God preserve them ! I have been quite industrious, for me, this winter, in spite of hymeneal merry-making, and am now on my second volume. But it is a terrible subject, so large and diffuse, — the story of Europe.

I told Bentley to send Lady Mary a copy of my "Miscellanies" two months since, which contains an engraved portrait of me from a picture by Phillips, painted when in London for Mr. Stirling. The engraving is a good one; better, I suspect, than the likeness. . . . . .

You will think, by the length of my yarn, that I really think you are returned to private life again, and have nothing in the world to do. But a host of pleasant recollections gather round me while I converse with you across the waters, and I do not like to break the spell. But it is time. I must not close without thanking you for the kind congratulations which you sent me some weeks since on my daughter's approaching nuptials. It is all over now, and I am childless, and yet fortunate, if it must be so. Does not your sister the Duchess part with her last unmarried daughter very soon? The man is fortunate, indeed, who is to have such a bride. Pray say all that is kind for me to the Duchess, whose kindness to me is among the most cherished of my recollections in my pleasant visit to merry England.

Farewell, dear Carlisle. Believe me always

Affectionately yours,

Wm. H. Prescott.

TO LADY LYELL.

Boston, April 18, 1852.

My dear Lady Lyell,

Since I last wrote, we have had another wedding in my family, as you have no doubt heard. Indeed, you prove how well you are posted up about us, and the kind part you take in our happiness, by the little souvenir which you sent to Lizzy at the time of the marriage.* We like to have the sympathy of those who are dear to us in our joys and our sorrows. I am sure we shall always have yours in both, though I hope it will be long before we have to draw on it for the latter. Yet when did the sun shine long without a cloud, — lucky, if without a tempest. We have had one cloud in our domestic circle the last fortnight, in the state of my mother's health. She was confined to the house this spring by an injury, in itself not important, to her leg. But the inaction, to which she is so little accustomed, has been followed by loss of strength, and she does not rally as I wish she did. Should summer ever bless us, of which I have my doubts, I trust she will regain the ground she has lost. But I guess and fear! Eighty-five is a heavy load; hard to rise under. It is like the old man in the Arabian Nights, that poor Sinbad could not shake off from his shoulders. Elizabeth's marriage has given occasion to a good deal of merry-making, and our little society has been quite astir in spite of Lent. Indeed, the only Fast-day which the wicked Unitarians keep is that appointed by the Governor as the "day of fasting, humiliation, and prayer." It comes always in April. We keep it so appropriately, that I could not help remarking the other day, that it would be a pity to have it abolished, as we have so few fête days in our country.

* The marriage of his only daughter to Mr. Lawrence, already mentioned.

CHAPTER XXIV.

1852.

POLITICAL OPINIONS. — CORRESPONDENCE WITH MR. BANCROFT, MR. EVERETT, AND MR. SUMNER. — CONVERSATION ON POLITICAL SUBJECTS.

OF Mr. Prescott's political opinions there is little to be said. That he was sincerely and faithfully attached to his country — to his whole country — nobody ever doubted who heard him speak on the subject. His letters when he was in England, flattered as few men have been by English hospitality, are as explicit on this point as was the expression of his every-day feelings and thoughts at home. But, with all his patriotic loyalty, he took little interest in the passing quarrels of the political parties that, at different times, divided and agitated the country. They were a disturbing element in the quiet, earnest pursuit of his studies ; and such elements, whatever they might be, or whencesoever they might come, he always rejected with a peculiar sensitiveness ; anxious, under all circumstances, to maintain the even, happy state of mind to which his nature seemed to entitle him, and which he found important to continuous work. He was wont to say, that he dealt with political discussions only when they related to events and persons at least two centuries old.

Of friends who were eminent in political affairs he had not a few ; but his regard for them did not rest on political grounds. With Mr. Everett, whom he knew early during his college life, and who, as Secretary of State, represented the old Whig party, he had always the most kindly intercourse, and received from him, as we have seen, while that gentleman was residing in Italy in 1840 and 1841, and subsequently while he so ably represented the United States as our Minister in London, efficient assistance in collecting materials for the " History of Philip the Second." With Mr. Bancroft, who had an inherited claim on his regard, and whom he knew much from 1822, he stood in relations somewhat more intimate and familiar, and always maintained them, though he never sympathized with his friend in the decidedly democratical tendencies that have marked his brilliant career as a statesman. With Mr. Sumner his personal acquaintance began later, — not till the return of that gentleman from Europe in 1840; but from the first, it was cordial, and in the last two or three years of his life he took much interest in the questions that arose about Kansas, and voted for Mr. Fremont as President in preference to either of the other candidates. During his whole life, however, he belonged essentially, both in his political feelings and in his political opinions, as his father always did, to the conservative, school of Washington and Hamilton, as its doctrines are recorded and developed in the " Federalist."

With the three eminent men just referred to, whom all will recognize as marking with the lustre of their names the opposite corners of the equilateral triangle formed by the three great political parties that at different times during Mr. Prescott's life preponderated in the country, he had a correspondence, sometimes interrupted by the changing circumstances of their respective positions, but always kindly and interesting. The political questions of the day appeared in it, of course, occasionally. But whenever this occurred, it was rather by accident than otherwise. The friendship of the parties had been built on other foundations, and always rested on them safely.

The earliest letters to Mr. Bancroft that I have seen are two or three between 1824 and 1828; but they are unimportant for any purposes of biography. The next one is of 1831, and is addressed to Northampton, Massachusetts, where Mr. Bancroft then lived.

TO MR. BANCROFT.

Boston, April 30, 1831.

MY DEAR FRIEND,

We jog on in much the same way here, and, as we are none of us Jacksonists, care little for the upsetting of cabinets, or any other mad pranks, which doubtless keep you awake at Northampton, for I perceive you are doing as many a misguided man has done before you, quitting the sweets of letters for the thorny path of politics. I must say I had rather drill Greek and Latin into little boys all my life, than take up with this trade in our country. However, so does not think Mr. ——, nor Mr. ——, nor Mr. &c., &c., &c., who are much better qualified to carry off all the prizes in literature than I can be. Your article on the Bank of the United States produced quite a sensation, and a considerable contrariety of opinion.[1] Where will you break out next? I did not think to see you turn out a financier in your old age! I have just recovered from a fit of sickness, which has confined me to my bed for a fortnight. I think the weather will confine me to the house another fortnight. Do you mean to make a flying trip to our latitudes this vacation? We should be glad to see you. In the mean time I must beg you to commend me to your wife, and believe me,

Most affectionately your friend,

WM. H. PRESCOTT.

TO MR. BANCROFT.

PEPPERELL, October 4, 1887.

MY DEAR BANCROFT,

Since we returned here, I have run through your second volume with much pleasure.[2] I had some misgivings that the success of the first,[3] and still more that your political hobbyism, might have made you, if not careless, at least less elaborate. But I see no symptoms of it. On the contrary, you have devoted apparently ample investigation to all the great topics of interest. The part you have descanted on less copiously than I had anticipated — perhaps from what I had heard you say yourself — was the character and habits of the Aborigines; but I don't know that you have not given as ample space to them — considering, after all, they are but incidental to the main subject — as your canvas would allow.[4] You certainly have contrived to keep the reader wide awake, which, considering that the summary nature of the work necessarily excluded the interest derived from a regular and circumstantial narrative, is a great thing. As you have succeeded so well in this respect, in the comparatively barren parts of the subject, you cannot fail as you draw nearer our own times.

I see you are figuring on the Van Buren Committee for concocting a public address. Why do you coquet with such a troublesome termagant as politics, when the glorious Muse of History opens her arms to receive you? I can't say I comprehend the fascination of such a mistress; for which,—I suppose, you will commiserate me.

Well, I am just ready to fly from my perch, in the form of three pon-

[1] An article in the "North American Review," by Mr. Bancroft.
[2] Then just published.
[3] Published in 1834.
[4] The sketch of the Indians was reserved for Mr. Bancroft's third volume, and was, in fact, made with a great deal of care.

15

derous octavos. Don't you think there will be a great eagerness to pay seven dollars and a half for an auld warld's tale of the fifteenth century, in these rub-and-go times? [a] You are more fortunate than I, for all who have bought your first, will necessarily buy the second volume; as subscribers to a railroad are obliged to go on deeper and deeper with the creation of new stock, in order to make the old of any value, as I have found by precious experience. Nevertheless, I shall take the field in December, *Deo volente*, all being in readiness now for striking off, except the paper.

With the sincere hope that your family continue in health, and that you may be blessed yourself with good health and restored spirits, I am

Ever truly yours,

WM. H. PRESCOTT.

TO MR. BANCROFT.

Saturday P. M. (Indorsed May 5, 1838.)

DEAR BANCROFT,

I return the review with my hearty thanks.[b] I think it is one of the most delightful tributes ever paid by friendship to authorship. And I think it is written in your very happiest manner. I do not believe, in estimating it so, I am misled by the subject, or the writer, for I have not been very easy to please on the score of puffs, of which I have had full measure, you know, from my good-natured friends. But the style of the piece is gorgeous, without being over-loaded, and the tone of sentiment most original, without the least approach to extravagance or obscurity. Indeed, the originality of the thoughts and the topics touched on constitute its great charm, and make the article, even at this eleventh hour, when so much has been said on the subject, have all the freshness of novelty. In this I confess, considering how long it had been kept on the shelf, I am most agreeably disappointed. As to the length, it is, taken in connection with the sort of critique, just the thing. It will terrify none from venturing on it, and I am sure a man must be without relish for the beautiful, who can lay it down without finishing.

Faithfully yours,

WM. H. PRESCOTT.

P. S. There is one thing which I had like to have forgotten, but which I shall not forgive. You have the effrontery to speak of my having passed the prime of life, some dozen years ago. Why, my youthful friend, do you know what the prime of life is? Molière shall tell you: "Hé bien! qu'est ce que cela, soixante ans? C'est la fleur de l'âge cela." Prime of life, indeed! People will think the author is turned of seventy. He was a more discreet critic that called me "young and *modest*"!

---

[a] There were heavy financial troubles in the winter of 1837 – 8.

[b] The article in the "Democratic Review," by Mr. Bancroft, on the "Ferdinand and Isabella." It has been noticed *ante*, p. 104.

TO MR. BANCROFT.

Thursday morning, November 1, 1838.

DEAR BANCROFT,

I return you Carlyle with my thanks. I have read as much of him as I could stand. After a very candid desire to relish him, I must say I do not at all. I think he has proceeded on a wrong principle altogether. The French Revolution is a most lamentable comedy (as Nick Bottom says) of itself, and requires nothing but the simplest statement of facts to freeze one's blood. To attempt to color so highly what nature has already overcolored is, it appears to me, in very bad taste, and produces a grotesque and ludicrous effect, the very opposite of the sublime or beautiful. Then such ridiculous affectations of new-fangled words! Carlyle is even a bungler at his own business; for his creations, or rather combinations, in this way, are the most discordant and awkward possible. As he runs altogether for dramatic, or rather picturesque effect, he is not to be challenged, I suppose for want of original views. This forms no part of his plan. His views certainly, as far as I can estimate them, are trite enough. And, in short, the whole thing, in my humble opinion, both as to *forme* and to *fond*, is perfectly contemptible. Two or three of his articles in the Reviews are written in a much better manner, and with elevation of thought, if not with originality. But affectation,

" The trail of the serpent is over them all."

Mercy on us, you will say, what have I done to bring such a shower of twaddle about my ears? Indeed, it is a poor return for your kindness in lending me the work, and will discourage you in future, no doubt. But to say truth, I have an idle hour; my books are putting up.[7]

Thierry I will keep longer, with your leave. He says " he has made friends with darkness." There are we brothers.

Faithfully yours,

WM. H. PRESCOTT.

TO MR. SUMNER.[8]

BOSTON, April 18, 1839.

MY DEAR SIR,

Our friend Hillard[9] read to me, yesterday, some extracts from a recent letter of yours, in which you speak of your interviews with Mr. Ford,[10]

[7] For moving to town.

[8] Mr. Sumner was then in Europe, and Mr. Prescott was not yet personally acquainted with him.

[9] George S. Hillard, Esq., author of the charming book, " Six Months in Italy," first printed in 1853 in Boston, and subsequently in London, by Murray, since which it has become a sort of manual for travellers who visit Florence and Rome.

[10] Already noticed for his review in the " London Quarterly " of " Ferdinand and Isabella," and for his subsequent personal friendship with Mr. Prescott.

who is to wield the scalping-knife over my bantling in the "Quarterly."
I cannot refrain from thanking you for your very efficient kindness towards me in this instance, as well as for the very friendly manner in which
you have enabled me to become acquainted with the state of opinion on
the literary merits of my History in London. It is, indeed, a rare piece
of good fortune to be thus put in possession of the critical judgments of
the most cultivated society, who speak our native language. Such information cannot be gathered from Reviews and Magazines, which put on a
sort of show dress for the public, and which are very often, too, executed
by inferior hands. Through my friend Ticknor, first, and subsequently
through you, I have had all the light I could desire; and I can have no
doubt, that to the good-natured offices of both of you I am indebted for
those *prestiges* in my favor, which go a good way towards ultimate success.
I may truly say, that this success has not been half so grateful to my feelings as the kind sympathy and good-will which the publication has drawn
forth from my countrymen, both at home and abroad.

Touching the "Quarterly," . . . . . I had half a mind, when I learned
from your letters that it was to take up "Ferdinand and Isabella," to
send out the last American edition, for the use of the reviewer (who, to
judge from his papers in the "Quarterly," has a quick scent for blemishes,
and a very good knowledge of the Spanish ground), as it contains more
than a hundred corrections of inadvertencies and blunders, chiefly verbal,
in the first edition. It would be hard, indeed, to be damned for sins
repented of; but, on the whole, I could not make up my mind to do it,
as it looked something like a sop to Cerberus; and so I determined to
leave their Catholic Highnesses to their fate. Thanks to your friendly
interposition, I have no doubt, this will be better than they deserve; and,
should it be otherwise, I shall feel equally indebted to you. Any one who
has ever had a hand in concocting an article for a periodical knows *quantum valet*. But the οἱ πολλοί know nothing about it, and of all journals
the "Edinburgh" and the "Quarterly" have the most weight with the
American, as with the English public.

You are now, I understand, on your way to Italy, after a campaign
more brilliant, I suspect, than was ever achieved by any of your countrymen before. You have, indeed, read a page of social life such as few
anywhere have access to; for your hours have been passed with the great,
not merely with those born to greatness, but those who have earned it for
themselves,

                    "Colla penna e colla spada."

In your progress through Italy, it is probable you may meet with a
Florentine nobleman, the Marquis Capponi.[11] Mr. Ellis,[12] in a letter
from Rome, informed me, that he was disposed to translate "Ferdinand
and Isabella " into the Italian; and at his suggestion I had a copy forwarded to him from England, and have also sent a Yankee one, as more
free from inaccuracies. I only fear he may think it presumptuous. He

11 The Marquis Gino Capponi. See *ante*, p. 175, note.
12 Rev. Dr. George E. Ellis, of Charlestown, Mass.

had never seen the book, and I can easily divine fifty reasons why he would not choose to plague himself with the job of translating when he has seen it.   He is a man of great consideration, and probably fully occupied in other ways.   But after the intimation which was given me, I did not choose to be deficient on my part ; and I only hope he may understand, that I do not flatter myself with the belief that he will do anything more than take that sort of interest in the work which, as one of the leading *savans* in Italy, I should wish him to feel for it.   I am sincerely desirous to have the work known to Continental scholars who take an interest in historical inquiries.   I shall be obliged to you if you will say this much to him, should you fall in with him.

I shall be further obliged to you, should you return to London, if you will, before leaving it for the last time, ascertain from Bentley whether he is making arrangements for another edition, and in what style.   I should be sorry to have the work brought out in an inferior dress, for the sake of the *tocher*.   Above all, he must get a rich portrait, *coute que coute*, of my heroine.   I have written him to this effect, and he has promised it, but " it is a far cry to Loch Awe," and, when a man's publisher is three thousand miles off, he will go his own gait.   I believe, however, he is disposed to do very fairly by me.   Thus you see my gratitude for the past answers the Frenchman's definition of it, a lively sense of favors to come.   I shall trust, however, without hesitation, to the same friendly spirit which you have hitherto shown for my excuse in your eyes.

Adieu, my dear sir.   With sincere wishes that the remainder of your pilgrimage may prove as pleasant and profitable to you as the past must have been, I am (if you will allow me to subscribe myself)

Very truly your obliged friend and servant,

WM. H. PRESCOTT.

TO MR. EVERETT.[12]

BOSTON, May 21, 1840.

MY DEAR MR. EVERETT,

I enclose a note to Mr. Grahame,[14] who is now residing at Nantes for the benefit of his daughter's health, who, as Mr. Ellis informs me, is married to a son of Sir John Herschel.

Touching the kind offices I wish from you in Paris, it is simply to ascertain if the Archives (the Foreign Archives, I think they are called) under the care of Mignet contain documents relating to Spanish history during the reign of Philip the Second.   A Mr. Turnbull,[15] who, I see, is now publishing his observations on this country and the West Indies, assured me last year, that the French government under Bonaparte caused the papers, or many of them, relating to this period, to be transferred from Simancas to the office in Paris.   Mr. Turnbull has spent some time both in Madrid and Paris, and ought to know.   If they are there, I should like to know if I can obtain copies of such as I should have occasion for,

[12] Mr. Everett was then about embarking for Europe.
[14] J. Grahame, Esq., author of the History of the United States.
[15] D. Turnbull, Esq., who published a book on Cuba, &c., in 1840.

and I shall be obliged by your advising me how this can best be done. I shall not attempt to make a collection, which will require similar operations in the principal capitals of Europe, till I have learnt whether I can succeed in getting what is now in Spain, which must be, after all, the principal *dépôt*. My success in the Mexican collection affords a good augury, but I fear the disordered condition of the Spanish archives will make it very difficult. In the Mexican affair, the collections had been all made by their own scholars, and I obtained access to them through the Academy. For the "Philip the Second" I must deal with the government. There is no hurry, you know, so that I beg you will take your own time and convenience for ascertaining the state of the case.

I return you the Lecture on Peru, in which you have filled up the outlines of your first. Both have been read by me with much pleasure and profit ; though it must be some years before I shall work in those mines myself, as I must win the capital of Montezuma first.

I pray you to offer my wife's and my own best wishes to Mrs. Everett, and with the sincere hope that you may have nothing but sunny skies and hours during your pilgrimage, believe me, my dear Mr. Everett,

Most truly and faithfully yours,

Wm. II. Prescott.

FROM MR. EVERETT.

Paris, July 27, 1840.

My dear Sir,

I have lost no time in instituting inquiries as to the documents which may be accessible in Paris, on the subject of Philip the Second. My first recourse was to M. Mignet. He is the keeper of the Archives in the Department of Foreign Affairs. From him I learned that his department contains nothing older than the seventeenth century. I learned, however, from him, that Napoleon, as Mr. Turnbull informed you, caused not only a part, but the whole, of the archives of Simancas to be transferred to Paris. On the downfall of the Empire, everything was sent back to Spain, excepting the documents relating to the History of France, which, somehow or other, remained. These documents are deposited in the *Archives du Royaume, Hôtel Soubise*. Among them is the correspondence of the successive Ministers of Spain in France with their government at Madrid. These papers are often the originals ; they are not bound, nor indexed, but tied up in *liasses*, and M. Mignet represented the labor of examining them as very great. He showed me some of the bundles, which he had been permitted to borrow from the *Archives du Royaume*, but I did not perceive wherein the peculiar difficulty of examining them consisted. He has examined and made extracts from a great mass of these documents for the History of the Reformation which he is writing. He showed me a large number of manuscript volumes, containing these extracts, which he had caused to be made by four copyists. He had also similar collections from Brussels, Cassel, and Dresden, obtained through the agency of the French Ministers at those places. I have made an arrangement to go to the *Archives du Royaume* next week, and see these documents. I think M. Mignet told me there were nearly three hundred bundles, and, if I mistake not, all consisting of the correspondence of the Ministers of Spain in France.

My next inquiry was at the *Bibliothèque Royale.*[16] The manuscripts there are under the care of an excellent old friend of mine, Professor Hase, who, in the single visit I have as yet made to the library, did everything in his power to facilitate my inquiry. In this superb collection will, I think, be found materials of equal importance to those contained in the *Archives du Royaume.* A very considerable part of the correspondence of the French Ministers at Madrid and Brussels, for the period of your inquiry, is preserved, — perhaps all ; and there are several miscellaneous pieces of great interest if I may judge by the titles.

FROM MR. EVERETT.

PARIS, August 22, 1840.

MY DEAR SIR,

Since my former letter to you, I have made some further researches, on the subject of materials for the History of Philip the Second. I passed a morning at the *Archives du Royaume,* in the ancient *Hôtel Soubise,* inquiring into the subject of the archives of Simancas ; and in an interview with M. Mignet, he was good enough to place in my hands a report made to him, by some one employed by him, to examine minutely into the character and amount of these precious documents. They consist of two hundred and eighty-four bundles, as I informed you in my former letter, and some of these bundles contain above a couple of hundred pieces. They are tied up and numbered, according to some system of Spanish arrangement, the key of which (if there ever was any) is lost. They do not appear to follow any order, either chronological, alphabetical, or that of subjects; and an ill-written, but pretty minute catalogue of some of the first bundles in the series is the only guide to their contents. M. Mignet's amanuensis went through the whole mass, and looked at each separate paper ; and this, I think, is the only way in which a perfectly satisfactory knowledge of the contents of the collection can be obtained. I had time only to look at two bundles. I took them at a venture, being *Liasses* A 55 and A 56; selecting them, because I saw in the above-named catalogue that they contained papers which fell within the period of the reign of Philip the Second. I soon discovered that these documents were far from being confined to the correspondence of the Spanish Ministers in France. On the contrary, I believe, not a paper of that description was contained in the bundles I looked at. There were, however, a great number of original letters of Philip himself to his foreign Ministers. They appeared in some cases to be original draughts, sometimes corrected in his own handwriting. Sometimes they were evidently the official copies, originally made for the purpose of being preserved in the archives of the Spanish government. In one case, a despatch, apparently prepared for transmission, and signed by Philip, but for some reason not sent, was preserved

[16] Now the *Bibliothèque Impériale.*

with the official copy. In some cases there were letters in several different states, from a first draught, through one or two corrected forms, till the letter was reduced to a satisfactory condition. This was strikingly the case with the Latin letter to Elizabeth of England, of 23d August, 1581, warmly expostulating against the reception of Portuguese fugitives, and particularly Don Antonio, and threatening war if his wishes were not complied with. Further reflection, perhaps, convinced Philip, that this kind of logic was not the best adapted to persuade Queen Elizabeth, and a draught of another letter, *minus* the threat, is found in the bundle. Of some of the letters of Philip I could not form a satisfactory idea whether they were originals or copies, and if the latter, in what stage prepared. Those of this class had an indorsement, purporting that they were "in cipher," in whole or in part. Whether they were deciphered copies of originals in cipher, or whether the indorsement alluded to was a direction to have them put in cipher, I could not tell. It is, in fact, a point of no great importance, though of some curiosity in the literary history of the materials.

Besides letters of Philip, there are official documents and reports of almost every description; and I should think, from what I saw of the contents of the collection, that they consist of the official papers emanating from and entering the private cabinet of the king, and filed away, the first in an authentic copy, the last in the original, from day to day. The letters of Philip, though not in his handwriting, were evidently written under his dictation; and I confess, the cursory inspection I was able to give them somewhat changed my notion of his character. I supposed he left the mechanical details of government to his Ministers, but these papers exhibit ample proof that he himself read and answered the letters of his ambassadors. Whether, however, this was the regular official correspondence with the foreign Ministers, or a private correspondence kept up by the King, of which his Secretaries of State were uninformed, I do not know; but from indications, which I will not take up your time in detailing, I should think the former. Among the papers is a holograph letter of Francis the First to the wife of Charles the Fifth, after the treaty of Madrid, by which he recovered his liberty. They told me, at the Archives, that no obstacles existed to copying these documents, and that it would be easy to find persons competent to examine and transcribe them.

TO MR. EVERETT.

NAHANT, September 1, 1840.

MY DEAR SIR,

I have received your letter of the 27th of July, and it was certainly very kind of you to be willing to bury yourself in a musty heap of parchments so soon after your arrival in the most brilliant and captivating of European capitals. I should have asked it from no one, and should have been surprised at it in almost any other person. Your memoranda show that, as I had anticipated, a large store of original materials for Philip the

Second's reign is in the public libraries there; possibly enough to authorize me to undertake the history without other resources, though still I cannot but suppose that the Spanish archives must contain much of paramount importance not existing elsewhere. I have received from Middleton this very week a letter, informing me that he and Dr. Lembke, my agent in Madrid, have been promised the support of several members of government and influential persons in making the investigations there. By a paper, however, which he sends me from the *archivero* of Simancas, I fear, from the multitude and disorderly state of the papers, there will be great embarrassment in accomplishing my purpose. I wrote some months since to Dr. Lembke, — who is a German scholar, very respectable, and a member of the Spanish Academy, and who has selected my documents for the "Conquest of Mexico," — that, if I could get access to the Madrid libraries for the "Philip the Second" documents, I should wish to complete the collection by the manuscripts from Paris, and should like to have him take charge of it. It so happens, as I find by the letter received from Middleton, that Lembke is now in Paris, and is making researches relating to Philip the Second's reign. This is an odd circumstance. Lembke tells him (Middleton) he has found many, and has selected some to be copied, and that he thinks he shall "be able to obtain Miguet's permission to have such documents as are useful to me copied from his great collection."

.   .   .   .   .   .

TO MR. EVERETT.

Boston, February 1, 1841.

My dear Sir,

I must thank you for your obliging letter of November 27th, in which you gave me some account of your disasters by the floods, and, worse, from illness of your children. I trust the last is dissipated entirely under the sunny skies of Florence. How the very thought of that fair city calls up the past, and brushes away the mists of a quarter of a century! For nearly that time has elapsed since I wandered a boy on the banks of the Arno.

Here all is sleet and "slosh," and in-doors talk of changes, political not meteorological, when the *ins* are to turn *outs*. There is some perplexity about a Senator to Congress, much increased by your absence and J. Q. Adams's presence. Abbott Lawrence, who was a prominent candidate, has now withdrawn. It seems more fitting, indeed, that he should represent us in the House than the Senate. Both Choate [17] and Dexter [18] have been applied to, and declined. But it is now understood that Mr. C. will consent to go. The sacrifice is great for one who gives up the best practice, perhaps, in the Commonwealth.

If you remain abroad, I trust, for the credit of the country, it will be in some official station, which is so often given away to unworthy partisans. There is no part of our arrangements, probably, which lowers us

[17] The Hon. Rufus Choate.
[18] The Hon. Franklin Dexter, Mr. Prescott's brother-in-law.

15 *

so much in foreign estimation, as the incompetence, in one way or another, of our representatives abroad.

I have received the books from the Marquis Capponi of which he spoke to you, and also a very kind letter informing me of the arrangements for the translation of the Catholic Kings into the beautiful tongue of Petrarch and Dante. I see, from the Prospectus which he sends me, that I am much honored by the company of the translated. The whole scheme is a magnificent one, and, if it can be carried through, cannot fail to have a great influence on the Italians, by introducing them to modes of thinking very different from their own. I suppose, however, the censorship still holds its shears. It looks as if the change so long desired in the copyright laws was to be brought about, or the Associates could hardly expect indemnification for their great expenses. Signor Capponi is, I believe, a person of high accomplishments, and social as well as literary eminence. In my reply to him, I have expressed my satisfaction that he should have seen you, and taken the liberty to notice the position you have occupied in your own country; though it may seem ridiculous, or at least superfluous, from me, as it is probable he knows it from many other sources.

I am much obliged by your communication respecting the "Relazioni degli Ambasciatori Veneti." It is a most important work, and I have a copy, sent me by Mariotti. The subsequent volumes (only three are now published) will cover the reign of Philip the Second and supply most authentic materials for his history, and I must take care to provide myself with them.[19] When you visit Rome, if you have any leisure, I shall be obliged by your ascertaining if there are documents in the Vatican germane to this subject. Philip was so good a son of the Church, that I think there must be. Should you visit Naples, and meet with an old gentleman there, Count Camaldoli, pray present my sincere respects to him. He has done me many kind offices, and is now interesting himself in getting some documents from the archives of the Duke of Monte Leone, the representative of Cortés, who lives, or vegetates, in Sicily.

Lembke is now in Paris, and at work for me. Sparks is also there, as you know, I suppose. He has found out some rich deposits of manuscripts relating to Philip, in the British Museum. The difficulty will be, I fear, in the *embarras de richesses*. The politics of Spain in that reign were mixed up with those of every court in Europe. Isabel's were fortunately confined to Italy and the Peninsula.

I pray you to remember us all kindly to your wife, and to believe me, my dear Mr. Everett,

Most truly your obliged friend,

WM. H. PRESCOTT.

[19] The "Relazioni degli Ambasciatori Veneti," published by Professor Eugenio Albèri, of Florence, — a scholar whose learning fits him singularly for the task. The first volume was published in 1839, and I think the fifteenth and last has recently appeared. Meantime Signor Albèri has edited, with excellent skill, the works of Galileo, in sixteen volumes, 1842–1856. He assisted Mr. Prescott in other ways.

FROM MR. EVERETT.

FLORENCE, September 21, 1841.

MY DEAR SIR,

I duly received your favor of the 30th of April. I delayed answering it till I should have executed your commissions, which, upon the whole, I have done to my satisfaction. I immediately addressed a note to the Marquis Gino Capponi, embodying the substance of what you say on the subject of his offer to furnish you with copies of his "Venetian Relations." He was then absent on a journey to Munich, which I did not know at the time. He has since returned, but I have not seen him. Since the loss of his sight, he leads a very secluded life, and is, I think, rarely seen but at M. Vieusseux's Thursday-evening *Conversazione;* which, as I have been in the country all summer, I have not attended. I infer from not hearing from him, that he thinks the "Relazioni" will be published within five years, and that consequently it will not be worth while to have them transcribed. But I shall endeavor to see him before my departure. The Count Pietro Guicciardini readily placed in my hands the manuscripts mentioned by you in yours of the 30th of April, which I have had copied at a moderate rate of compensation. They form two hundred pages of the common-sized foolscap paper, with a broad margin, but otherwise economically written, the lines near each other, and the hand quite close, though very legible. I accidentally fell upon copies of two autograph letters of Philip the Second, — the one to the Pope, the other to the Queen of Portugal, — on the subject of the imprisonment of Don Carlos, while I was in search of something else in the Magliabecchian. They are not intrinsically very interesting. But, considering the author and the subject, as they are short, each two pages, I had them copied. I experienced considerable difficulty in getting the document in the "Archivio Mediceo" copied. For causes which I could not satisfactorily trace, the most wearisome delays were interposed at every step, and I despaired for some time of success. The Grand Duke, to whom I applied in person, referred the matter, with reason, to the Minister. The Minister was desirous of obliging me, but felt it necessary to take the opinion of the Official Superintendent of the department, who happens to be the Attorney-General, who is always busy with other matters. He referred it to the Chief Archivist, and he to the Chief Clerk. Fortunately the *Archivio* is quite near my usual places of resort ; and, by putting them in mind of the matter frequently, I got it, after six weeks, into a form in which the Minister, Prince Corsini, felt warranted in giving a peremptory order in my favor.

* * * * * *

FROM MR. EVERETT.

LONDON, April 20, 1842.

MY DEAR Sir,

I have to thank you for your letter of the 27th March, which I have just received, and I am afraid that of the 29th December, which you sent me by Mr. Gayangos, is also still to be acknowledged.   After playing bo-peep with that gentleman all winter, I requested him to give me the favor of his company at breakfast to-day.   I had Mr. Hallam and Lord Mahon, who has been in Spain, with other friends, to meet him, and found him an exceedingly pleasant, intelligent person.   I hope to see more of him during the summer, which he passes here.

Mr. Rich sent me the other day a copy of the third edition of your book, for which I am truly obliged to you.   I find your History wherever I go, and there is no American topic which is oftener alluded to in all the circles which I frequent, whether literary or fashionable.   It is a matter of general regret that you are understood to pass over the reign of Charles the Fifth in your plans for the future.   Mr. Denison expressed himself very strongly to that effect the other day, and, though everybody does justice to the motive as a feeling on your part, I must say that I have not conversed with a single person who thinks you ought to consider the ground as preoccupied by Robertson.   He was avowedly ignorant of all the German sources, had but partial access to the Spanish authorities, and wrote history in a manner which does not satisfy the requirements of the present day.

I am glad you are not disappointed in the manuscripts I procured you at Florence.   The account of the Tuscan Minister at Madrid is of course to be read with some allowance for the strong disposition he would have to see everything in the most favorable light, in consequence of his master's desire to conciliate the favor of Philip the Second.   The contents of the Archives of Simancas, which M. de Gayangos will get you at Paris, whatever they may do for the moral character of Philip, will throw new light on his prodigious capacity for business.   The conduct of the affairs of his mighty empire seems to have centred in his own person. . . . . .

Pray remember my wife and myself most kindly to your parents and Mrs. Prescott, and believe me ever most faithfully yours,

EDWARD EVERETT.

TO MR. SUMNER.

PEPPERELL, September 11, 1842.

Many thanks for your kind proposition, my dear Sumner.   My wife's *veto* is not the only one to be deprecated in the matter.[20]   You forgot the *Conquistador*, Cortés, a much more inexorable personage.   He will not grant me a furlough for a single day.   In truth, ague, company, and the terrible *transition* week[21] — a word of horror — have so eaten into my time of late, that I must buckle on harness now in good earnest.   I don't know anything that would please me better than the trip to New York with you, except, indeed, to shake hands once more with Morpeth. But that pleasure I must forego.   I shall trouble you, however, with a

[20] To visit New York with Mr. Sumner, in order to take leave of Lord Morpeth, then about to embark for England.

[21] Moving from Pepperell to Boston, always annoying to him.

note to him, and will send it to you by the 20th. If you should leave before that, let me know, as I will not fail to write to him. He must be quite aboriginal by this time.[22] Pray get all the particulars of his tour out of him.

Here I am in the midst of green fields and misty mountains, absolutely revelling in the luxury of rustic solitude and study. Long may it be before I shall be driven back to the *sumum strepitumque Romæ.*[23]

Remember me kindly to Lieber and Hillard, and believe me,

Ever faithfully yours,

WM. H. PRESCOTT.

TO MR. SUMNER.

PEPPERELL, October 4, 1842.

I am truly obliged to you, my dear Sumner, for giving me the *carte du pays* of the last week so faithfully. Why, what a week you had of it ! You celebrated our noble friend's departure[24] in as jolly a style as any Highlander or son of green Erin ever did that of his friend's to the world of spirits, — a perpetual wake, — wake, indeed, for you don't seem to have closed your eyes night or day. Dinners, breakfasts, suppers, "each hue," as Byron says, "still lovelier than the last." I am glad he went off under such good auspices, — New York hospitality, and you to share it with him. Well, peace to his *manes !* I never expect to see another peer or commoner from the *vater-land* whom I shall *cotton to,* as Madam B—— says, half so much.

I am pegging away at the Aztecs, and should win the mural crown in three months, were I to stay in these rural solitudes, where the only break is the plague of letter-writing. But Boston ; the word comprehends more impediments, more friends, more enemies, — alas ! how alike, — than one could tell on his fingers. *Addio !* love to Hillard, and, when you write, to Longfellow, whom I hope Lord M. will see, and believe me

Very affectionately yours,

WM. H. PRESCOTT.

TO MR. EVERETT.

BOSTON, November 29, 1843.

MY DEAR SIR,

It was very kind in you to write to me by the last steamer, when you were suffering under the heavy affliction with which Providence has seen fit to visit you.[25] I believe there can scarcely be an affliction greater than

---

[22] Lord Morpeth had visited some of our North American Indians.

[23] This quotation, comparing Boston with Rome in its days of glory, reminds one irresistibly of the words of Virgil's shepherd : —

> "Urbem quam dicunt Romam, Melibœe putavi,
> Stultus ego, huic nostræ similem."

[24] Lord Morpeth's embarkation for England.

[25] The death of his eldest daughter, — singularly fitted to gratify affection and to excite a just pride in her parents.

that caused by such a domestic loss as yours; so many dear ties broken, so many fond hopes crushed. There is something in the relation of a daughter with a mind so ripe and a soul so spotless as yours, which is peculiarly touching, and more so perhaps to a father's heart than to any other. There is something in a female character that awakens a more tender sympathy than we can feel for those of our own sex, — at least I have so felt it in this relation. I once was called to endure a similar misfortune. But the daughter whom I lost was taken away in the dawn of life, when only four years old. Do you remember those exquisite lines of Coleridge, —

> " Ere sin could blight, or sorrow fade,
> Death came with timely care,
> The opening bud to heaven conveyed,
> And bade it blossom there."

I think I can never know a sorrow greater than I then experienced.

And yet, if such was the blow to me, what must this be to you, where promise has ripened into so beautiful a reality. You have, indeed, all the consolation that can be afforded by the recollection of so delightful a character, and of a life that seems to have been spent in preparation for a glorious future. Now that she is gone, all who knew her — and there are many here — bear testimony to her remarkable endowments, and the surpassing loveliness of her disposition. If any argument were needed, the existence and extinction here of such a being would of itself be enough to establish the immortality of the soul. It would seem as reasonable to suppose, that the blossom, with its curious organization and its tendencies to a fuller development, should be designed to perish in this immature state, as that such a soul, with the germ of such celestial excellence within it, should not be destined for a further and more noble expansion. It is the conviction of this immortality which makes the present life dwindle to a point, and makes one feel that death, come when it will, separates us but a short space from the dear friend who has gone before us. Were it not for this conviction of immortality, life, short as it is, would be much too long. But I am poorly qualified to give consolation to you. Would that I could do it!

You will be gratified to know that my father, of whose illness I gave you some account in my last, has continued to improve, and, as he continues to get as much exercise as the weather of the season will permit, there is little doubt his health will be re-established.

Before this, you will have received a copy of the "Conquest of Mexico" from Rich, I trust. When you have leisure and inclination to look into it, I hope it may have some interest for you. You say I need not fear the critical brotherhood. I have no great respect for them in the main, but especially none for the lighter craft, who, I suspect, shape their course much by the *trade*-winds. But the American public defer still too much to the leading journals. I say, too, much, for any one who has done that sort of work understands its value. One can hardly imagine that one critic can look another soberly in the face. Yet their influence makes their award of some importance, — not on the ultimate fate of a work, for I believe that, as none but the author can write himself up *permanently,* so none other can write him down. But for present success the opinion of the leading journals is of moment.

My parents and wife join with me in the expression of the warmest sympathy for Mrs. Everett, with which believe me, my dear Mr. Everett,

Most faithfully yours,

WM. H. PRESCOTT.

TO MR. SUMNER.

FITFUL HEAD, August 21, 1844.

MY DEAR SUMNER,

I am delighted that you are turning a cold shoulder to Æsculapius, Galen, and *tutti quanti*. I detest the whole brotherhood. I have always observed that the longer a man remains in their hands, and the more of their cursed stuff he takes, the worse plight he is in. They are the bills I most grudge paying, except the bill of mortality, which is very often, indeed, sent in at the same time.

I have been looking through Beau Brummell. His life was the triumph of impudence. His complete success shows that a fond mother should petition for her darling this one best gift, *da, Jupiter, impudence ;* and that includes all the rest, wit, honor, wealth, beauty, &c., or rather is worth them all. An indifferent commentary on English high life !

Did I tell you of a pretty present made to me the other day by an entire stranger to me ? It was an almond stick cut in the woods of the Alhambra at Granada, and surmounted by a gold *castellano* of the date of Ferdinand and Isabella, set in gold on the head of the stick, which was polished into a cane. The coin bears the effigies of Ferdinand and Isabella, with the titles, &c., all somewhat rudely stamped. Is it not a pretty conceit, such a present ?

My mother has been quite unwell the last two days, from a feverish attack, now subsided ; but we were alarmed about her for a short time. But we shall still " keep a parent from the sky," I trust.

Pray take care of yourself, and believe me

Always faithfully yours,

WM. H. PRESCOTT.

TO MR. EVERETT.

BOSTON, May 15, 1845.

MY DEAR SIR,

I take the liberty to enclose a note, which you will oblige me by forwarding to Mr. Napier, the editor of the " Edinburgh Review." [26] If anything additional is necessary as to the address, will you have the goodness to set it right ?

In the last number of his journal is a paper that you may have read, on the " History of the Conquest of Mexico," in a foot-note of which the

[26] To correct a mistake in the preceding number of the " Edinburgh Review," about the degree of his blindness. See *ante,* p. 249.

reviewer says that I have been blind some years. Now I have one eye that does *some* service to *me*, if not to the *state*, and I do not half like to be considered as stone-blind. The next thing I shall hear of a subscription for the poor blind author! So I have written to the Scotch Aristarch just to say that, though I have at times been, and was, particularly during the composition of "Ferdinand and Isabella," deprived of all use of my eyes, yet they have so far mended, at least one of them, — for the other is in Launcelot Gobbo's state, or his father's, I believe, — that I can do a fair share of work with it by daylight, though, it is true, I am obliged to use a secretary to decipher my hieroglyphics made by writing with a case used by the blind. I am entitled to some allowance on this score for clerical errors, some of which, occasionally, have been detected just in time to save me from the horrors of a comic blunder. I have no right, however, nor desire, to claim the merit of such obstacles vanquished, as are implied by *total* blindness. He will set it right, if he thinks it worth the trouble. But very likely he will think John Bull would not care a fig if I had one eye or a score in my cranium, and so let it go.

I was much pleased with the article in the Edinburgh. It is written with spirit and elegance, and in a hearty tone of commendation, which I should be glad to merit, and which runs off much more freely, at any rate, than is usual in British journals. Could you do me the favor to inform me who was the author?

We are still permitted to be represented by you, though, as you perceive, more from a very natural diffidence on the part of any one to succeed you in that perilous post, than from any fault of Mr. Polk. I trust that the excitement produced by the vaunt of that eminent personage anent the Oregon matter has subsided in England. That it should have existed at all was not easily comprehended here, where we perfectly understood that our new chief could not distinguish betwixt a speech from the throne and one on the floor of Congress. He was only talking to Buncombe. There is a very general feeling here that you may be willing to subside, after your diplomatic, into a literary career, and take the vacant post in the neighborhood.[27] But I suppose you have heard more than enough on that matter.

I pray you to remember me kindly to Mrs. Everett, and believe me, my dear sir,

Yours with sincere regard,

WM. H. PRESCOTT.

TO MR. SUMNER.

PEPPERELL, August 15, 1845.

MY DEAR SUMNER,

Thank you for your Discourse, which I have read — notes and all — with great pleasure and great instruction.[28] You have amassed a heap of

[27] The Presidency of Harvard College.

[28] "The True Grandeur of Nations," an Oration delivered before the city authorities of Boston, July 4th, 1845, maintaining the extreme doctrines of the Peace Society.

valuable and often recondite illustration in support of a noble cause. And who can refuse sympathy with the spirit of philanthropy which has given rise to such a charming ideal ? — but a little too unqualified.

" There can be no war that is not dishonorable." I can't go along with this ! No ! by all those who fell at Marathon ; by those who fought at Morgarten and Bannockburn ; by those who fought and bled at Bunker's Hill ; in the war of the Low Countries against Philip the Second, — in all those wars which have had — which are yet to have — freedom for their object, — I can't acquiesce in your sweeping denunciation, my good friend.

I admire your moral courage in delivering your sentiments so plainly in the face of that thick array of " well-padded and well-buttoned coats of blue, besmeared with gold," which must have surrounded the rostrum of the orator on this day. I may one day see you on a crusade to persuade the great Autocrat to disband his million of fighting-men, and little Queen Vic to lay up her steamships in lavender !

You have scattered right and left the seeds of a sound and ennobling morality, which may spring up in a bountiful harvest, I trust, — in the Millennium, — but I doubt.

I shall be in town in a few days, when I shall hope to see you. Meantime remember me kindly to Hillard, and believe, dear Sumner,

Most affectionately yours,

WM. H. PRESCOTT.

TO MR. SUMNER.

HIGHLANDS, October 2, 1846.

MY DEAR SUMNER,

I thank you heartily for your Phi Beta Kappa Oration, which I received a few days since. I was then up to the elbows in a bloody " battle-piece." [29] I thought it better to postpone the reading of it till I could go to it with clean hands, as befits your pure philosophy.

I have read, or rather listened to it, notes and all, with the greatest interest ; and when I say that my expectations have not been disappointed after having heard it cracked up so, I think you will think it praise enough. The most happy conception has been carried out admirably, as if it were the most natural order of things, without the least constraint or violence. I don't know which of your sketches I like the best. I am inclined to think the Judge's. For there you are on your own heather, and it is the tribute of a favorite pupil to his well-beloved master, gushing warm from the heart. Yet they are all managed well, and the vivid touches of character and the richness of the illustration will repay the study, I should imagine, of any one familiar with the particular science

---

[29] An oration entitled " The Scholar, the Jurist, the Artist, the Philanthropist," delivered before the Phi Beta Kappa Society in Harvard College, 1846. It is mainly devoted to a delineation of the characters of John Pickering, Esq., Judge Story, Washington Allston, the artist, and the Rev. Dr. Channing. Mr. Prescott alludes here to one phrase in it, touching the artist: " No more battle-pieces."

W

you discuss. Then your sentiments certainly cannot be charged with inconsistency. Last year you condemned wars *in toto*, making no exception even for the wars of freedom.[20] This year you condemn the *representation* of war, whether by the pencil or pen. Marathon, Salamis, Bunker Hill, the retreat from Moscow, Waterloo, great and small, — speaking more forcibly than all the homilies of parson or philanthropist, — are *all* to be blotted from memory, equally with my own wild skirmishes of barbarians and banditti. Lord deliver us! Where will you bring up? If the stories are not to be painted or written, such records of them as have been heedlessly made should by the same rule be destroyed. And I don't see, if you follow out your progress to perfection, but what you will one day turn out as staunch an Omar, or Iconoclast, as any other of glorious memory.

I laugh; but I fear you will make the judicious grieve.

I puer, — *ut declamatio fias,* as some satirist may say.

But fare thee well, dear Sumner. Whether thou deportest thyself *sand mente* or *mente insanâ,* believe me

Always truly yours,

WM. H. PRESCOTT.

TO MR. BANCROFT.

BOSTON, March 5, 1852.

MY DEAR BANCROFT,

Uncle Isaac[21] sent me yesterday a copy of your new volume, and you may be sure it occupied me closely during a good part of the day. Of course I could only glance over its contents, reading with a relish some of the most striking pictures, — at least, those that would catch the eye most readily on a rapid survey. I recognize the characteristic touches of your hand everywhere, bold, brilliant, and picturesque, with a good deal of the poetic and much more of philosophy. You have a great power of condensing an amount of study and meditation into a compact little sentence, quite enviable. Your introduction, — your description of the working of the Reformation in its Calvinistic aspect especially; your remarks on the political tendencies of the Old World institutions and the New World; your quiet rural pictures of New England and Acadian scenes and scenery; stirring battle-pieces, Quebec in the foreground, and Braddock's fall, and Washington's rise, — told very simply and effectively; — I have read these with care and much interest. Of course one should not pronounce on a work without reading it through, and this I shall do more leisurely. But I have no doubt the volume will prove a very attractive one, and to the English as well as the Yankee reader, though to the Englishman it opens a tale not the most flattering in the national annals.

Why did you not mention your resources, so ample and authentic, in your Preface? Every author has a right to do this, and every reader has a right to ask it. Your references do not show the nature of them suf-

---

[20] See the last preceding letter, dated August 15, 1845.

[21] Isaac P. Davis, Esq., uncle to Mrs. Bancroft.

ficiently, as I think. But I suppose you have your reasons. I am glad you have another volume in preparation, and I can only say, God speed!

With kind remembrances to your wife, believe me, my dear Bancroft,

Faithfully yours,

WM. H. PRESCOTT.

TO MR. BANCROFT.

BOSTON, December 20, 1852.

Thank you, dear Bancroft, for the second volume of the work immortal. It gives me a mingled sensation of pleasure and pain to receive it; pleasure to see what you have done, pain at the contrast with what I have done the last year or two. But it will operate as a spur to my enterprise, I hope.

I have only glanced over the volume, and listened carefully to the first chapters. It is a volume not to be taken at a leap, or at a sitting, especially by an American. You have given a noble platform for the Revolution by making the reader acquainted with the interior of English and Continental politics beyond any other work on the subject. I admire the courage as well as the sagacity you have shown in your chapter on the English institutions, &c. You have made John Bull of the nineteenth century sit for his portrait of the eighteenth, and rightly enough, as the islander changes little but in date. I do not know how he will like the free commentaries you have made on his social and political characteristics. But if he is tolerably candid he may be content. But honest Bull, as you intimate, is rather insular in his notions, bounded by the narrow seas. There is more depth than breadth in his character.

Now that your side has won the game, I wonder if you will be tempted away from the historic chair to make another diplomatic episode.[22] I shall be sorry, on the whole, if you are; for life is fleeting, though art be long, and you are now warm in harness, running your great race of glory well. I wonder if Mrs. B. does not agree with me? Yet St. James's might offer a sore temptation to any one that could get it.

Thackeray dines — at least I have asked him — with me on Thursday. I wish you could make one of a *partie carrée* with him.

With much love to your dear lady, believe me, dear Bancroft,

Affectionately yours,

WM. H. PRESCOTT.

TO MR. BANCROFT.

BOSTON, January 5, 1856.

DEAR BANCROFT,

It was very kind in you to take the trouble to read my volumes through so carefully, and to give me the results of your examination.[23] I am not

[22] The success of the Democratic party in the elections of 1852.

[23] The first two volumes of the "History of Philip the Second."

a little pleased that these are so favorable to me. It is no flattery to say that your opinion, with the allowance of the grain — perhaps a bushel — of salt on the score of friendship, is of more value to me than almost any other person's in the community; you are so familiar with the ground of the historian, and know from experience so well what difficulties lie in his path. The verbal inaccuracies you have pointed out I shall give heed to, as well as the two blunders of date and spelling. With respect to the *French* discourse at the abdication,[34] that is right. Flemish was the language of the people, but French was more commonly used by the nobility. It was the language of the court, and historians expressly state that on this occasion Philip excused himself from addressing the States on the ground of his inability to speak French. Cateau-Cambresis is also right, being the modern French usage. It is so written by Sismondi, by the editor of the "Granvelle Papers," and in the latest geographical gazetteers.

The book has gone off very well so far. Indeed, double the quantity, I think, has been sold of any of my preceding works in the same time. I have been lucky, too, in getting well on before Macaulay has come thundering along the track with his hundred horse-power. I am glad to hear you say that his Catholic Majesty is found in so many houses in New York. I have had some friendly notices from that great Babylon. Nothing has pleased me more than a note which I received last week from Irving (to whom, by the by, I had omitted to send a copy), written in his genial, warm-hearted manner. My publishers, whose reader had got into rather a hot discussion with the "Tribune," I understand, had led me to expect a well-peppered notice from that journal. But on the contrary, an able article, from the pen, I believe, of Mr. Ripley, who conducts the literary criticisms in its columns, dealt with me in the handsomest manner possible. Some fault was found, — not so much as I deserve, — mixed up with a good deal of generous approbation; a sort of criticism more to my taste than wholesale panegyric.

    .   .   .   .   .

I cannot conclude this collection of letters to the three eminent American statesmen, with whom Mr. Prescott most freely corresponded, better than with the following remarks on his conversation by his friend Mr. Parsons. "Never, perhaps," says Mr. Parsons, "did he suggest political, or rather party questions. He was himself no partisan and no extremist on any subject. He had valued friends in every party, and could appreciate excellence of mind or character in those who differed from him. But in this country, where all are free to be as prejudiced and violent as they choose, — and most persons take great care that this right shall not be lost for want of use, — it is seldom that political topics can be discussed with warmth,

[34] Of Charles the Fifth.

but without passion, or without the personal acerbity, which offended not only his good taste, but his good feelings. Perhaps he never sought or originated political conversation; but he would not decline contributing his share to it; and the contribution he made was always of good sense, of moderation, and of forbearance."

CHAPTER XXV.

1852 – 1854.

DEATH OF MR. PRESCOTT'S MOTHER. — PROGRESS WITH "PHILIP THE SECOND." — CORRESPONDENCE.

BUT while Mr. Prescott, after his return from England, was making such spirited advances with his work on "Philip the Second," and taking avowed satisfaction in it, another of the calamities of life, for which foresight is no preparation, came upon him. On Monday, the 17th of May, 1852, in the forenoon, a gentleman whom I met in the street stopped to tell me that Mrs. Prescott, the mother of my friend, was very ill. I had seen her only two evenings before, when she was in her own chamber, slightly indisposed, indeed, but still in her accustomed spirits, and seeming to enjoy life as much as she ever had. I was surprised, therefore, by the intelligence, and could hardly believe it. But I hastened to the house, and found it to be true. She had been ill only a few hours, and already the end was obviously near. How deeply that affliction was felt by her son I shall not forget; nor shall I forget the conversation I had with him in the afternoon, when all was over. His suffering was great. He wept bitterly. But above every other feeling rose the sense of gratitude for what he had owed to his mother's love and energy.

The impression of her loss remained long on his heart. In the subsequent July, when he went, as usual, to Nahant, he writes : —

July 4th, 1852. — Nahant, where we came on the first, — cold, dreary and desolate. I miss the accustomed faces. All around me how changed, yet not the scene. There all is as it always has been. The sea makes its accustomed music on the rocks below. But it sounds like a dirge to me. Yet I will not waste my time in idle lament. It will not bring back the dead, — the dead who still live, and in a happier world than this.

He did not, in fact, recover a tolerable measure of spirits until he reached Pepperell in the autumn.

"Left Nahant," he says, "September 6th, and came to the Highlands September 9th, full of good intent. Delicious solitudes; safe even from friends — for a time! Now for the Spanish battle-cry, 'St. Jago, and at them!'"

But three months later he writes : —

December 4th. — St. Jago has not done much for me after all. The gods won't help those that won't help themselves. I have dawdled away my summer, and have only to show for it Chapter XII., thirty-five pages of text and four pages of notes. Fie on it! I am now well read up for Chapter XIII., and — I mean to have a conscience and reform. We left Pepperell October 26th.

In the winter of 1852 — 3 he made good progress again in his work ; at least such progress as encouraged him, if it was not very rapid. By the 15th of May he had written the thirteenth and fourteenth chapters of the Second Book, and the first chapter of Book Third, making about ninety pages in print. October 3d he had gone on a hundred and sixty pages farther ; and, although he did not account it "railroad speed," he knew that it was an improvement on what he had done some months before. He was, therefore, better satisfied with himself than he had been, and more confident of success.

TO LADY LYELL.

Boston, January 11, 1853.

You have no idea of the weather you left behind you here.[1] The thermometer is at 50° at noon to-day, and the trees on the Common seem quite puzzled as to what to do about it. We took our cold, raw weather when you were here, at the bottom of Long Wharf, in Copp's Hill burying-ground, and the bleak Dorchester drive, to say nothing of the afternoon, when the great jet would not play for your entertainment. You have not forgotten these pleasant rambles, now that you are so far away. Thackeray has left us. His campaign was a successful one, and he said, "It rained dollars." He dined with me thrice, and was in good flow of spirits till a late hour generally. He went much to the Ticknors also. I do not think he made much impression as a critic. But the Thackeray vein is rich in what is better than cold criticism.

[1] Sir Charles and Lady Lyell had now made a second visit to the United States.

TO LADY LYELL.

BOSTON, March 1, 1853.

At length I have the pleasure to send you the little nothings by Colonel Lawrence, viz. a miniature pencil-case, to be worn round the neck, for ornament more than use. *Item*, an ivory stylus, more for use than ornament (the worse for wear, having been pared away, as it required sharpening an inch or more), with which I wrote all the "Conquest of Mexico." I gave to dear Mrs. Milman the stylus that indited "Peru." Anna Ticknor has the "Ferdinand and Isabella" one. My wife says she will not accept the one with which I am doing the *Philippics*. As that is agate-pointed, I think it will be able to run off as long a yarn as I shall care to spin.

TO MRS. MILMAN.

PEPPERELL, September 16, 1853.

MY DEAR MRS. MILMAN,

By the steamer which sailed this week I have done myself the pleasure to send you a couple of volumes, called, "Six Months in Italy." It is a book lately given to the world by a friend of mine, Mr. Hillard, an eminent lawyer in Boston, but one who has found leisure enough to store his mind with rich and various knowledge, and whose naturally fine taste fits him for a work like the present. The subject has been worn out, it is true, by book-makers; but Hillard has treated it in an original way, and as his style is full of animation and beauty, I think the volumes will be read with pleasure by you and by my good friend your husband.

Since I last wrote to you the Lyells have made their Crystal Palace trip to the New World, and passed some days with me at the seaside; and, as Lady Lyell has perhaps told you, I afterwards accompanied her to New York. It was a great pleasure to see them again, when we thought we had bid them a long, if not a last adieu. But that is a word that ought not to be in our vocabulary. They are to pass next winter, I believe, in the Canaries. They put a girdle round the earth in as little time almost as Puck.

My travels are from town to seaside, and from seaside to country. And here I am now among the old trees of Pepperell, dearer to me than any other spot I call my own.

The Lyells have been with us here, too, and I believe Lady Lyell likes my Pepperell home the best. It is a plain old farm, recommended by a beautiful country, glistening with pretty streams of water, well covered with woods, and with a line of hills in the background that aspire to the dignity of mountains. But what endears it most to me is that it has been the habitation of my ancestors, and my own some part of every year from childhood. It is too simple a place, however, not to say rude, to take any but an intimate friend to.

Pray remember me most kindly to your husband, and believe me, my dear Mrs. Milman, now and always,

Affectionately yours,

WM. H. PRESCOTT.

TO LADY LYELL.

BOSTON, December 25, 1853.

A merry Christmas to you, dear Lady Lyell, and to Lyell too, and good orthodox mince-pies to celebrate it with. I wonder where you are keeping it. Not where you will find it kept in as genial a way as in Old England. How much your countrymen, by the by, are indebted to Washington Irving for showing the world what a beautiful thing Christmas is, or used to be, in your brave little island. I was reading his account of it this morning, stuffed as full of racy old English rhymes as Christmas pudding is of plums. Irving has a soul, which is more than one can say for most writers. It is odd that a book like this, so finely and delicately executed, should come from the New World, where one expects to meet with hardly anything more than the raw material.

I don't know anything that has been stirring here of late that would have interest for you, or for us either, for that matter. It has been a quiet winter, quiet in every sense, for the old graybeard has not ventured to shake his hoary locks at us yet, or at least he has shed none of them on the ground, which is as bare as November. This is quite uncommon and very agreeable. But winter is not likely to rot in the sky, and we shall soon see the feathers dancing about us.

TO LADY LYELL.

BOSTON, February 26, 1854.

I dined with the Ticknors on Friday last, a snug little party, very pleasant. Anna has been in good health this winter, and in very good spirits. Good kind friends they are, and if you want to find it, be a little ill, or out of sorts yourself, and you will soon prove it.

I have been tolerably industrious for me this winter, and I hope to be in condition to make a bow to the public by the end of the year. . . . . . You have heard that my publishers, the Harpers, were burnt out last December. They lost about a million; one third perhaps insured. It is said they have as much more left. I should have made by the fire, as they had about half an edition of each of my books on hand, which they had paid me for. But I could not make money out of their losses, and I told them to strike off as many more copies, without charging them. Ticknor did the same. If all their authors would do as much by them, they would be better off by at least a couple of hundred thousand dollars than their report now shows.

16

TO LADY LYELL.

BOSTON, May 15, 1854.

I am hard at work now on a very amiable chapter in the "History of Philip the Second," the affair of Don Carlos, for which I fortunately have a good body of materials from different quarters, especially Spain. A romantic subject, Carlos and Isabella, is it not? Those who have read Schiller, and Alfieri, and Lord John Russell, who wrote a long tragedy on the matter, may think so. But truth is a sturdy plant, that bears too few of the beautiful flowers that belong to fiction, and the historian, who digs up the dry bones of antiquity, has a less cheering occupation than the poet, who creates and colors according to his own fancy. Some people, however, think history not much better than poetry, as far as fact is concerned. Those are most apt to think so who are let behind the scenes.

TO DEAN MILMAN.

LYNN, July 24, 1854.

MY DEAR FRIEND,

I had the pleasure of receiving a few days since a copy of your "History of Latin Christianity," which you were so kind as to send me through Murray, and for which I am greatly obliged to you. As I glance over the rich bill of fare which the "Contents" hold out, I only regret that I have not the eyes to go into it at once in a more thorough manner than can be done with the ear. But a recent strain of the nerve just before I left town has so far disabled me, that for some weeks I have scarcely ventured to look at the contents of a book. I have, however, listened to some portions of it, sufficient to give me an idea of the manner in which the work has been executed. I have been particularly struck with your admirable account of Becket, and the formidable struggle which the proud priest, in the name of religion, carried on with the royalty of England. I had thought myself pretty well acquainted with the earlier portions of English history, but I have nowhere seen the motives and conduct of the parties in that remarkable struggle so clearly unveiled. As you come down to later times, the subject may have greater interest for the general reader; but yet it can hardly exceed in interest those portions of the present volumes which discuss those great events and institutions the influence of which is still felt in the present condition of society.

I am not sufficiently familiar with ecclesiastical history to make my opinion of any value, it is true. Yet there are some points in the execution of such a work which may be apprehended by readers not bred in any theological school; and I am sure I cannot be mistaken when I express the firm conviction that these volumes will prove every way worthy of the enviable reputation which you now enjoy, both as a scholar and a friend of humanity.

I have been bringing my long-protracted labors on the first two volumes of my "Philip the Second" to a close. I have made arrangements for their publication next spring in England and the United States, though I may be yet longer delayed by the crippled condition of my eyes.

* * * * *

TO LADY LYELL.

PEPPERELL, September 27, 1864.

DEAR LADY LYELL,

Here we are in old Pepperell, after a week in which we have been in all the hubbub of the transition state. We have come much later than usual, for Lynn, with its green fields and dark blue waters, and the white sails glistening upon them under a bright September sun, was extremely lovely. Indeed, I think, if we were not so much attached to the old farm, we should hardly have thought it worth while to come here for a month, as we now do, and as we always shall do, I suppose. In fact, the topsy-turvy life, and all the bustle of moving from seaside to town, and town to country, is something like travelling on a great scale, and forms a very good substitute for it, just as that mammoth water-lily, the Victoria Regia, which you and I saw at Sion House, and which had always depended on a running stream for its existence, did just as well by Paxton's clever invention of keeping up a turmoil in a tank. The lily thought she was all the while in some bustling river, and expanded as gloriously as if she had been. I rather think the tank sort of turmoil is the only one that we shall have ; at all events, that my better half will, who I think will never see the vision even of New York before she dies. We have had a dismal drought all over the country, which lasted for more than two months. Luckily, the September rains have restored the vegetation, and the country looks everywhere as green as in the latter days of spring. Then there is an inexpressible charm in the repose, a sort of stillness which you almost hear, *poetica*, in the soft murmurs and buzzing sounds that come up from the fields and mingle with the sounds made by the winds playing among the trees. It makes quite an agreeable variety to the somewhat oppressive and eternal roar of the ocean. The wind as it sweeps through the forest makes a music that one never wearies of. But I did get tired of the monotonous beat of the ocean. I longed for another tune of Nature's, and now I have got it. .

CHAPTER XXVI.

RHEUMATISM AT NAHANT. — BOSTON HOMES SUCCESSIVELY OCCUPIED BY MR. PRESCOTT IN TREMONT STREET, SUMMER STREET, BEDFORD STREET, AND BEACON STREET. — PATRIARCHAL MODE OF LIFE AT PEPPERELL. — LIFE AT NAHANT AND AT LYNN.

DURING the year 1852 – 53, Mr. Prescott was much troubled with rheumatism, more than he had been for a long time, and was led seriously to consider whether his residence at Nahant, and his summer life on the edge of the ocean, must not be given up. He did not like the thought, but could not avoid its intrusion. Home was always a word of peculiar import to him, and any interference with his old habits and associations in relation to it was unwelcome.

Most of these associations had been settled for many years, and belonged especially to Boston. From 1808, when he was only twelve years old, his proper home, as we have seen, was always there, under the same roof with his father for thirty-six years, and with his mother for forty-four.

The first house they occupied was on Tremont Street, at the head of Bumstead Place, and the next was in Summer Street, contiguous to Chauncy Place, both now pulled down to make room for the heavy brick and granite blocks demanded by commerce. Afterwards they lived, for a few years, at the corner of Otis Place, nearly opposite their last residence; but in 1817, Mr. Prescott the elder purchased the fine old mansion in Bedford Street, where they all lived eight and twenty years. In 1845, the year following the death of the venerable head of the household, the remainder of the family removed to No. 55 in Beacon Street, the last home of the historian and his mother's last home on this side the grave.

As long as his father lived, which was until Mr. Prescott himself was forty-eight years old, and until all his children had been born, there was a patriarchal simplicity in their way of life that was not to be mistaken. The very furniture of the goodly old house in Bedford Street belonged to an earlier period, or, at least, though rich and substantial, it gave token of times gone by. The hospitality, too, that was so freely exercised there, and which, to all who were privileged to enjoy it, was so attractive, had nothing of pretension about it, and very little of recent fashion. It was quiet, gentle, and warm-hearted. Sometimes, but rarely, large parties were given, and always on Thanksgiving-day, our chief domestic festival in New England, the whole of the family, in all its branches, was collected, and the evening spent, with a few very intimate friends, in merry games. Once, I remember, Sir Charles and Lady Lyell were added to the party, and shared heartily in its cordial gayety, — romping with the rest of us, as if they had been to the manner born.[1]

The establishment in Beacon Street, where the historian spent the last thirteen winters of his life, was more modern and elegant. He had fitted it carefully to his peculiar wants and infirmities, and then added the comforts and luxuries of the time. But the hearty hospitality which had always been enjoyed under the old trees in Bedford Street was not wanting to his new home. He had inherited it from his grandfather and his father, and it was, besides, a part of his own nature. There was always a welcome, and a welcome suited to each case, — to the stranger who called from curiosity to see one whose name was familiar in both hemispheres, and to the friend who entered uninvited and unannounced. No house among us was more sought, none more enjoyed.

But Mr. Prescott never spent the whole of any one year in Boston. In childhood, he was carried every summer, at least once, to visit his grandmother in the family homestead at Pepperell. His father held such visits to be both a pleasure and a duty. The youthful son enjoyed them as happy seasons of holiday relaxation and freedom. Both of them naturally increased there a sort of familiar affection and intimacy, which

---

[1] Since this was written, I have fallen on a letter of Lady Lyell to Mr. Prescott, dated January 7, 1857, in which she says: " Shall I ever forget the Thanksgiving in Bedford Street? Never, as long as I live. It is now more than fifteen years ago, but still I see the rooms, the dinner-table, the blind-man's-buff, and the adjournment to your study to see Lord Kingsborough's ' Mexico.' "

in the bustle of the town and amidst the engrossing cares of the father's professional life could not be so thoroughly rooted and cultivated.

While the venerable grandmother lived, nothing could be more simple than the ways and manners in that old house, which was only one of the better sort of New England farm-houses ; small for our times, but not so accounted when it was built. Its furniture was comfortable, but already old, and dating from a period when grace and taste in such things were little considered. Its fare was country fare, abundant, health-ful, and keenly enjoyed with appetites earned by wandering about the large, fine farm, and breathing the pure mountain air of the region. None were gathered there, however, at this period, except the members of the little family, which, though of three generations, numbered as yet only six persons. In-deed, there was hardly room for more, and, besides this, the aged head of the household could not well enjoy any society save that of the persons nearest to her, for she had long been infirm, and was now nearly blind. But it was good for them all to be there. The influences of the place were salutary and happy. .

After the death of the much-loved grandmother in 1821, at the age of eighty-eight, a good deal of this was naturally changed. The essential characteristics of the quiet homestead were indeed preserved, and are to this day the same. But the two elder children of Mr. Prescott were already married, and room was to be found for them and for their families. A study was built for the future historian, that he might devote himself undisturbed to his books, and other additions were made for hospitality's sake. Everything, however, was done in the most unpretending way, and in keeping with the simplicity of the place and its associations.

At this period it was that I first became acquainted with Pepperell, and began, with my family, still young, to visit there a few days or more every-summer, when it was in our power to do so ; a practice which we continued as long as the elder Mr. Prescott lived, and afterwards until both our households had become so large that it was not always easy to accommo-date them. But although, in one way or another, the old house at Pepperell was often full, and sometimes crowded, yet so happy were the guests, and so glad were the two or three families there to receive their many friends, that no inconvenience was felt on either side.

Mr. Prescott the elder was nowhere so completely himself as he was at Pepperell; I mean, that his original character came out nowhere else so naturally and fully. He was about sixty years old when I first saw him there, after having long known him familiarly in Boston. He was very dignified, mild, and prepossessing in his general appearance everywhere; a little bent, indeed, as he had long been, but with no other mark of infirmity, and not many indications of approaching age. But in Pepperell, where the cares of professional life were entirely thrown off, he seemed another man, younger and more vigorous. His step on the soil that gave him birth was more elastic than it was elsewhere, and his smile, always kind and gentle, had there a peculiar sweetness. He loved to walk about the fields his father had cultivated, and to lounge under the trees his father had planted. Most of his forenoons were spent in the open air, superintending the agricultural improvements he understood so well, and watching the fine cattle with which he had stocked his farm, much to the benefit of the country about him.

After dinner, he preferred to sit long at table, and few were so young or so gay that they did not enjoy the mild wisdom of his conversation, and the stirring recollections and traditions with which his memory was stored, and which went back to the period when the spot where we were then so happy was not safe from the Indian's tomahawk. Later in the afternoon we generally took long drives, sometimes long walks, and in the evening we read together some amusing book, commonly a novel, and oftener than any others, one of Sir Walter Scott's or Miss Edgeworth's. They were very happy days.

The walks and drives about Pepperell and its neighborhood are pleasant and cheerful, but hardly more. It is a broken country, well watered and well cultivated, and the woodlands, now somewhat diminished by the encroachments of civilization, were, at the time of which I speak, abundant and rich, especially on the hills. How much the historian enjoyed this free and open nature, we have already had occasion often to notice, and shall find that it continued to the last. Everything at Pepperell was familiar and dear to him from the days of his childhood.

There is a charming shady walk behind the house, looking towards the Monadnock mountain, and there many a chapter of his Histories was composed, or conned over and fitted for the noctograph. On the other side of the road is an old grove of oaks, which he used to call the "Fairy Grove," because under its spreading shades he had told his children stories about fairies, who danced there on moonlight nights and brushed away the gathering dews from the grass. In the "Fairy Grove" he walked before dinner, and, as he loved companionship at that time of the day, I have walked many a mile with him in the path his feet had worn deep in the sod. Farther on is a piece of his woodland, to which he had given the name of "Bloody Grove," because he had associated it with a wild tradition of the Indian times. There, but more rarely, we walked in the rich twilight of our summer evenings. It was too far off from the house to be much frequented.

The drives were no less agreeable, and, like the walks, had their old associations and fancy names, in which we all delighted. One was Jewett's Bridge, over the Nashua, between Pepperell and Groton, where, when his grandfather had gone to fight the battle of Bunker Hill, and had taken all the able-bodied men with him, the women, dressed in their husbands' clothes, mounted guard with muskets and pitchforks, and absolutely arrested a man who was in the interest of the enemy, and took from his boots dangerous papers, which they sent to the Committee of Safety.[2] Another of the favorite drives was through rich meadows and woodlands, which in the declining light of the long afternoons were full of gentle beauty, and this he called the "Valley-Forge Drive," in memory of one of the darkest and most honorable periods of Washington's military life, although the association was provoked only by the circumstance that in one of the hollows which we used to pass there was a large blacksmith's-forge. And yet another, the longest drive of all, was to a bright valley, where in a hillside

[2] See Butler's "History of Groton," (Boston, 8vo, 1848,) p. 486.

the farmer who lived hard by, mistaking pyrites for silver ore, had gradually wrought a long gallery in the solid rock, chiefly with his own hands, sure that he should find hidden treasure at last, but died without the sight. And this little, quiet valley was always called "Glen Withershins," in memory of Edie Ochiltree, who was a great favorite in the old homestead at Pepperell.[3]

But wherever the afternoon drives or walks led us, or whatever were the whimsical associations connected with them, they were always cheerful and happy hours that we thus passed together. The woods were often made merry with our shouts and laughter; for the parties after dinner were never small, and no cares or anxious thoughts oppressed any of us. We were young, or at least most of us were so, when these gay local associations were all settled, and, as we grew older, we enjoyed them the more for the happy memories that rested on them. Certainly we never wearied of them.

After the death of the elder Mr. Prescott, his son preserved, as far as was possible, the accustomed tone and modes of life in his old rural home. Three generations could still be gathered there, and the house was enlarged and altered, but not much, to accommodate their increasing numbers. It was the son's delight, as it had been his father's, not only to have his own friends, but the friends of his children, share his cordial hospitality; and, if their number was often large enough to fill all the rooms quite as full as they should be, it was never so large as to crowd out the truest enjoyment.[4]

[3] In the evenings of one of our visits, we read aloud the whole of "The Antiquary," and I well remember, not only how it was enjoyed throughout, but how particular parts of it were especially relished. Edie's patriotism, in the last chapter but one, where that delightful old beggar, with not a penny in the world, enumerates the many rich blessings he would fight for, if the French should invade Scotland, brought tears into the eyes of more than one of the party, including the elder Mr. Prescott.

[4] Sometimes, indeed not unfrequently, he fancied that he should like to live at Pepperell eight months in the year, or even longer. But the thought of the snow-drifts, and the restraints and seclusion which our rigorous winters imply under the circumstances of such a residence, soon drove these fancies from his mind. Their recurrence, however, shows how strong was his attachment to Pepperell. Of this, indeed, there can be no doubt; but perhaps the most striking illustration of it is to be found in the fact, that, in whatever testamentary arrangements he at different times made, there was always

But, besides his houses in Boston and Pepperell, Mr. Prescott lived for many years a few weeks of every summer on the sea-coast. This habit was adopted originally less for his own sake than for that of his father, who, on the approach of old age, found the air of the ocean important to him during the hot season. As they had always lived together in town, so now they built their house together at Nahant, about fourteen miles from Boston; a rocky peninsula which juts out so far into the ocean, that even our most parching southwest winds in July

special and tender regard shown to this old farm, which his grandfather had rescued from the primeval forest, and which he himself held, as his father had done, by the original Indian title. The fact to which I refer is, that in successive wills he entailed the Pepperell estate in the strictest manner, although he perfectly well knew, at the time he did it, that any heir of his to whom it might descend could, by the very simple provisions of our statutes, break the entail, and convert the estate into an ordinary inheritance, as unfettered by conditions as if he had bought it. This, however, made no difference to Mr. Prescott. "It was," as Mr. Gardiner, who drew the wills in question, truly says, — "It was a matter of pure sentiment; for the estate is of very moderate value as a piece of salable property, not at all worthy, in that view, of unusual pains to preserve it for the benefit of remote descendants. Nor had Mr. Prescott, in truth, the smallest desire to perpetuate wealth in connection with his name to a distant generation. Property in general he was content to leave, after the death of those who were personally dear to him, and for whom he made special provisions, to the common operation of the laws of the land, and the accidents of life. Wealth he regarded only for its uses, and valued no more than other men. But his little Pepperell farm, simple and unostentatious as it is, he was as fond and as proud of as any baron of England is of his old feudal castle, and for very similar reasons. Hence he had the strongest desire that those few acres of native soil, which had been long in the family, — the home especially of the old hero of Bunker Hill, the favorite resort of that hero's son, the learned lawyer and judge, and afterwards of his grandson, the historian, — should always be held undivided by some one of the same name, blood, and lineage. He well understood, indeed, that he had no power in law to prevent the heir in tail from defeating this purpose; but he hoped and trusted that nothing but a last necessity would induce an inheritor of his blood to part with such a patrimonial possession for the little money it would produce. At any rate, he intended, so far as was possible by his own act and will, to secure its perpetual family transmission; though he duly estimated the chances that this, in the course of human vicissitudes, might not hold out for many generations beyond those which he could himself see.

"He attached similar feelings even to the old and valueless furniture of his grandsires, some relics of which remained in the Pepperell house; and, since he could not entail them, like the land, he takes care to bequeath all the movables of the house and farm to the first tenant in tail, who should come into possession of the estate, with a request that he would use means to transmit them to his successors."

and August are much cooled by the waves before they reach it. The purchase of the land was made in 1828, the year Mr. Prescott the elder retired from the bar; and their cottage of two stories — built without the slightest architectural pretensions, but full of resources for comfort, and carefully fitted to its objects and position — was occupied by them the next summer. In a hot day it is the coolest spot of the whole peninsula, and therefore among the coolest on the whole line of our coast. There, with the exception of the summer at Pepperell, following his father's death, and that of 1850, which he passed in England, he spent eight or ten weeks of every season for five and twenty years.

As he said in one of his letters, —

The house stands on a bold cliff overlooking the ocean, — so near that in a storm the spray is thrown over the piazza, — and as it stands on the extreme point of the peninsula, it is many miles out at sea. There is more than one printed account of Nahant, which is a remarkable watering-place, from the bold formation of the coast and its exposure to the ocean. It is not a bad place — this sea-girt citadel — for reverie and writing, with the music of the winds and waters incessantly beating on the rocks and broad beaches below. This place is called "Fitful Head," and Norna's was not wilder.

He had, however, different minds about Nahant at different periods, and generally felt more or less misgiving as to its benefits each year just before he was to begin his summer residence there. Sometimes he thought that the strong reflection from the bright ocean, which often filled the air with a dazzling splendor, was hurtful to his impaired sight. Almost always he perceived that the cool dampness, which was so refreshing, increased his rheumatic tendencies. And sometimes he complained bitterly that his time was frittered away by idlers and loungers, who crowded the hotels and cottages of that fashionable watering-place, and who little thought how he suffered as they sat gossiping with him in his darkened parlor or on his shady piazza.[5] But wherever he might live, as he well

---

[5] His Memoranda contain much on this annoyance of company. In one place he says: "I have lost a clear month here by company, — company which brings the worst of all satieties; for the satiety from study brings the consciousness of improvement. But this dissipation impairs health, spirits, scholarship. Yet how can I escape it, tied like a bear to a stake here? I will devise some way another year, or Nahant shall be 'Nae haunt of mine,'

knew, his life would be beset with all its old infirmities, and
as for visitors, his kindly nature and social propensities would
never permit him to be rigorous with his friends, and still less
with the strangers who were attracted by his reputation, and
whose calls it might seem churlish to refuse. He therefore
made the best he could of his residence at Nahant, even after
he had begun to entertain a serious doubt about its effects.
This was natural. The sharp, tonic air of the ocean undoubtedly invigorated him for his work, and kept down, in part at
least, his troublesome dyspepsia,[*] while, at the same time,
taking his principal exercise on horseback in the long twilight
of our summer evenings, he avoided, to a great degree, the
injurious effects of the dazzling noonday splendors of the place.
But his rheumatism at last prevailed. It was clearly aggravated by the damp air which penetrated everywhere at Nahant,
and against which flannels and friction were a very imperfect
defence.

As, therefore, he approached the confines of old age, he
found that he must make some change in his modes of life,
and arrange, if possible, some new compromise with his conflicting infirmities. But he hesitated long. While his father
lived, who found great solace at Nahant, he never failed to
accompany him there any more than to Pepperell, and never
seemed to shrink from it or to regret it, so important to him
was the society of that wise and gentle old man, and so necessary to his daily happiness.

But after his father's death, and again after his mother's, the
place in his eyes changed its character. It became cold, dreary,
and desolate ; it wanted, as he said, the accustomed faces. The
last strong link that connected him with it was broken, and he

as old Stewart [the portrait-painter] used to say." And in a letter to me
about the same time, August, 1840, he says: " We are here in a sort of
whirligig, — company morning, noon, and night, — company to dine twice a
week, — and, in short, all the agreeable little interruptions incident to a
watering-place or a windmill."

[*] But not always. In August, 1841, he says: " Nahant has not served me
as well as usual this summer. I have been sorely plagued with the dyspep-
tic debility and pains. But I am determined not to heed them." Sometimes
he seemed out of all patience with Nahant. Once he recorded: " An acre
of grass and old trees is worth a wilderness of ocean." He wrote this, however, at Pepperell, which he always loved.

determined to live there no more,—"his visit oft, but never his abode."

Having come to this final decision, he purchased, in the spring of 1858, a house on the shore of Lynn Bay, looking pleasantly over the waters to his old home at Nahant, and only half a dozen miles distant from it. It was a luxurious establishment compared with the simple cottage for which he exchanged it, and was less exposed to the annoyance of idle strangers or inconsiderate friends. Its chief attractions, however, were its mild sea-breezes, cool and refreshing, but rarely or never sharp and damp, like those at Nahant, and its drives, which could easily be extended into the interior, and carried into rural lanes and woodlands. He enjoyed it very much,— not, indeed, as he did Pepperell, which was always a peculiar place to him,— but he enjoyed it more than he did any other of his residences in town or country, spending ten or twelve weeks there every summer during the last five years of his life, embellishing its grounds, and making its interior arrangements comfortable and agreeable to his children and grandchildren, whom he gathered around him there, as he loved to do everywhere. Still, much was added to his happiness when, two years later, his only daughter, who had been married in 1852 to Mr. James Lawrence, was settled in a charming villa hardly a stone's throw from his door. After this he seemed to need nothing more, for she lived still nearer to him in Boston, and visited him at Pepperell every year with her children.

One thing at his Lynn home was and still is (1862) very touching. There was hardly a tree on the place, except some young plantations, which were partly his own work, and which he did not live to see grow up. But shade was important to him there as it was everywhere; and none was to be found in his grounds except under the broad branches of an old cherry-tree, which had come down from the days of the Quaker shoemakers who were so long the monarchs of the lands there and in all the neighborhood. Round the narrow circle of shade which this tree afforded him, he walked with his accustomed fidelity a certain length of time every day, whenever the sun prevented him from going more freely abroad. There he soon wore a path in the greensward, and so deep did it at last become, that now — four years since any foot has pressed it — the marks still remain, as a sad memorial of his infirmity. I have not unfrequently watched him, as he paced his wearisome rounds there, carrying a light umbrella in his hand, which, when he reached the sunny side of his circle, he raised for an instant to protect his eye, and then shut it again that the suffering organ might have the full benefit, not only of the exercise, but of the fresh air ; so exact and minute was he as to whatever could in the slightest degree affect its condition.[7]

But in this respect all his houses were alike. His sight and the care needful to preserve it were everywhere in his thoughts, and controlled more or less whatever he did or undertook.

[7] Since writing these sentences, a sonnet has been pointed out to me in a cutting from one of the newspapers of the time, which refers to the circle round the old cherry-tree.

> "No more, alas ! the soft returning Spring
> Shall greet thee, walking near thy favorite tree,
> Marking with patient step the magic ring
> Where pageants grand and monarchs moved with thee,
> Thou new Columbus ! bringing from old Spain
> Her ancient wealth to this awaiting shore ;
> Returning, stamped with impress of thy brain,
> Far richer treasures than her galleons bore.
> Two worlds shall weep for thee, the Old, the New,
> Now that the marble and the canvas wait
> In vain to cheer the homes and hearts so true
> Thy immortality made desolate,
> While angels on imperishable scroll
> Record the wondrous beauty of thy soul."

It was written, as I have learned since I copied it into this note, by a very cultivated lady of New York, Mrs. John Sherwood.

CHAPTER XXVII.

1853 — 1858.

MR. PRESCOTT went to Lynn on the 21st of June,
1853. He found it, as he recorded a few days afterwards, "a sober, quiet country, with the open ocean spread
out before him. What," he added, "can be better for study
and meditation? I hope to show the fruits of it, and yet, in
this tonic air, defy the foul fiend dyspepsia. At any rate, I
shall be less plagued with rheumatism."

His first season in his new villa, however, was not very fruitful in literary results, and he was little satisfied. It was hard
to get settled, and interruptions from affairs were frequent.
But his life there was not without its appropriate enjoyments.
He had visits from his friends Sir Charles and Lady Lyell,
and from the Earl and Countess of Ellesmere, and he was
with them all in a gay visit to New York, where they went
for the Exhibition of that year, to which Lord Ellesmere and
Sir Charles Lyell had come as Commissioners on behalf of the
British government. But, though these were interruptions,
they were much more than compensated for by the pleasure
they gave, and, after all, he made progress enough to insure
to him that feeling of success which he always found important
for sustaining his industry. In fact, by October he was so far
advanced with the second volume of "Philip the Second," that
he began to make calculations as to the number of pages it
might fill, as to the disposition of the remaining materials, and
as to the time when the whole would be ready for the press.
But his arrangements contemplated some postponement of the

publication beyond the time he had originally proposed for it. When noting this circumstance, he added, with characteristic good-humor, " The public, I fancy, will not object to waiting."

His results, however, in this case differed more than usual from his calculations. The space filled by the troubles of Philip with the Barbary powers, by the siege of Malta, and by the tragedy of Don Carlos, was more than double what he had reckoned for them. The consequence was, that the Morisco rebellion and the battle of Lepanto, which had been destined for the second volume, were necessarily postponed to the third. But all these subjects interested and excited him. From this time, therefore, he worked vigorously and well, and on the 22d of August, 1854, he finished the last note to the last chapter of the second volume.

On this occasion he made the following memoranda : —

By next spring, when I trust these volumes will be published, nearly eight years will have elapsed since the publication of the " Conquest of Peru," which was also in two volumes, and which was published in less than four years after the appearance of the " Conquest of Mexico." The cause of this difference is to be charged even more on the state of my eyes than on the difficulty and extent of the subject. For a long time after the " Peru " was published I hardly ventured to look into a book, and though I have grown bolder as I have advanced, my waning vision has warned me to manage my eye with much greater reserve than formerly. Indeed, for some time after I had finished the " Peru," I hesitated whether I should grapple with the whole subject of " Philip " *in extenso ;* and, when I made up my mind to serve up the whole barbecue instead of particular parts, I had so little confidence in the strength of my vision, that I thought of calling the work " Memoirs," and treating the subject in a more desultory and superficial manner than belongs to a regular history. I did not go to work in a business-like style till I broke ground on the troubles of the Netherlands. Perhaps my critics may find this out.

My first chapter was written in July, 1849, at Nahant ; my last of the second volume concluded at this date at Lynn, which allows about five years for the actual composition of the work, from which six months must be deducted for a visit to England.

The amount of the two volumes I reckon at about eleven hundred and fifty pages, one hundred and fifty more than a wise economy would have prescribed ; but I hope the reader will be the gainer by it. Nothing remains now but to correct the earlier portions of the work, especially those relating to Charles the Fifth, in which all my new things have been forestalled since I began to write by Mignet, Stirling, &c., — a warning to procrastinating historians. This tinkering, with a few biographical notices, ought not to take more than two or three months, if my eyes stand by me. But, *Quien sabe ?* The two months I have been here I have hardly had two weeks' use of the eye; so much for a stupid strain of the muscles, rather than the nerve, just before I left town.

In November he began to stereotype the work, at the rate of ten pages a day. Each volume held out a little more than his estimate, but the whole was completed in May, 1855, his friend Mr. Folsom revising it all with great care as it went through the press. It was not, however, immediately published. To suit the exigencies of the time, which, from severe financial embarrassments, were unfavorable to literary enterprise, it did not appear, either in England or in the United States, until November.

An adverse decision of the House of Lords as to the power of a foreigner to claim copyright in England had, however, cut him off from his brilliant prospects there; and in the United States he had changed his publishers, not from any dissatisfaction with them, — for, as he said, they had dealt well with him from first to last, — but from circumstances wholly of a financial character.

Six months after the publication of the first two volumes of "Philip the Second," he made the following notice of the result: —

A settlement made with my publishers here last week enables me to speak of the success of the work. In England it has been published in four separate editions; one of them from the rival house of Routledge. It has been twice reprinted in Germany, and a Spanish translation of it is now in course of publication at Madrid. In this country eight thousand copies have been sold, while the sales of the preceding works have been so much improved by the impulse received from this, that nearly thirty thousand volumes of them have been disposed of by my Boston publishers, from whom I have received seventeen thousand dollars for the "Philip" and the other works the last six months. So much for the lucre!

From the tone of the foreign journals and those of my own country, it would seem that the work has found quite as much favor as any of its predecessors, and, as the sales have been much greater than of any other of them in the same space of time, I may be considered to have as favorable a breeze to carry me forward on my long voyage as I could desire. This is very important to me, as I felt a little nervous in regard to the reception of the work, after so long an interval since the preceding one had appeared.

It is needless to add anything to a simple statement like this. The success of the work was complete, and has continued so.

The reviews of it on its first appearance were less numerous than they had been in the case of its predecessors. It was a foregone conclusion that the book would be equal to its subject; and, besides, the sale both in England and in the United States was so large and so prompt, that the public decision was, in fact, made quite as soon as the critics could have been heard. There was, however, no difference of opinion anywhere on the matter; and, if there had been, the favorable judgment of M. Guizot, in the "Edinburgh Review" for January, 1857, would have outweighed many such as are commonly pronounced by persons little competent to decide questions they so gravely claim to adjudicate.[1]

But while the publication of the first two volumes of the "History of Philip the Second" was going on, Mr. Prescott was occupied with another work on a kindred subject, and one which seemed to grow out of the circumstances of the case by a sort of natural necessity. I refer to the latter part of the reign and life of Philip's illustrious father. It was plain that the accounts of Gachard, drawn from manuscript sources, which had been already so well used in English by Stirling, and in French by Mignet,[2] respecting the life of Charles the Fifth after his abdication, were so different from the accounts given by Robertson, that his eloquent work could no longer serve as a sufficient link between the times of Ferdinand and Isabella and those of their grandson; still less between those of their grandson and Philip the Second. It had therefore more than once been suggested to Mr. Prescott that he should himself fill up the interval with an entirely new work on the reign of Charles the Fifth.

But this was a task he was unwilling to undertake. On the one hand, he had no wish to bring himself at all into competi-

[1] On the first of January, 1860, nearly 18,000 copies of these two volumes of the "History of Philip the Second" had been sold; but the number in England could not be given with exactness; although a few days later it was known that the number must have been greater than had been assumed in making up the above estimate.

[2] The Cloister Life of the Emperor Charles V., by William Stirling (London, 1852, 8vo). Charles-Quint, son Abdication, son Séjour et sa Mort au Monastère de Yuste, par M. Mignet (Paris, 1854, 8vo). Gachard, L. P., Retraite et Mort de Charles-Quint, au Monastère de Yuste (Bruxelles, 2 vol. 8vo, 1854, sqq.).

tion with the Scotch historian, who had so honorably won his laurels; and, on the other, the reign of Philip the Second opened to him a long vista of years all filled with labor; besides which the times of Charles the Fifth constituted a wide subject, for which he had made no collections, and which he had examined only as a portion of Spanish history intimately connected with the portions immediately preceding and following it, to which he had already devoted himself. Still, he admitted that something ought to be done in order to bring the concluding period of Robertson's History into harmony with facts now known and settled, and with the representations which must constitute the opening chapters of his own account of the reign of Philip the Second.

In May, 1855, therefore, he began to prepare a new conclusion to Robertson's "Charles the Fifth," and in the January following had completed it. It embraces that portion of the Emperor's life which followed his abdication, and makes about a hundred and eighty pages. It was not published until the succeeding December, the intervening months having been required to prepare and print the volumes of Robertson, to which the account of the last year of the Emperor's life, the one at Yuste, was to be the conclusion.

I was then in Europe, and on the 8th of December, 1856, he wrote to me: —

My "Charles the Fifth," or rather Robertson's, with my Continuation, made his bow to the public to-day, like a strapping giant with a little urchin holding on to the tail of his coat. I can't say I expect much from it, as the best and biggest part is somewhat of the oldest. But people who like a complete series will need it to fill up the gap betwixt "Ferdinand" and "Philip."

It had, however, the same sort of success with all his other works. Six thousand nine hundred copies were published in London and Boston before the end of eighteen hundred and fifty-nine.

As soon as his continuation of Robertson was completed, he gave a few weeks to the preparation of a Memoir of his friend and kinsman, Mr. Abbott Lawrence, who had died in the preceding month of August. It is a graceful and becoming tribute to an eminent man, who deserved well not only of

Massachusetts, where he was born and always lived, but of the country which he had faithfully served in many high capacities at home and abroad, and which had wellnigh called him to what, in the course of events, became the highest.[a] The Memoir is short, originally prepared for the National Portrait Gallery, and subsequently printed in a beautiful quarto form for private distribution.

In the beginning of March, 1856, he turned again to his "History of Philip the Second," and went on with it, not rapidly, perhaps, but still, with the exception of the time when he was partly occupied in correcting for the press his addition to "Charles the Fifth," his progress was good. He had a pleasant summer at Lynn, during the heats of the season, and enjoyed his life so well in the autumn at Pepperell, that he again thought he might make his holidays there longer in succeeding years. But he never did.

"Our autumn *villeggiatura*," he says, under date of October 30th, 1856, "has been charming, as usual, — the weather remarkably fine, — many of the days too *Indian-summerish*, however.[a] The vegetation has been remarkably fresh to a late period, from the great rains, and then fading, or rather flushing into a blaze of glorious colors, which, as they passed away, and the fallen leaves strewed the ground with their splendors, have been succeeded by wider reaches of the landscape and the dark-blue mountains in the distance. The old trees seem like friends of earlier days, still spreading out their venerable arms around me, and reminding me of him by whose hands so many of them were planted. No spot that I own is so full of tender reminiscences to me.

The time has been propitious, as usual, to mental, and, I trust, moral progress. I have worked *con amore*, as I always do in these quiet shades, though not with the *furore* of those times when I turned off sometimes

[a] Mr. Lawrence came very near being nominated by the Whig party's convention as their candidate for Vice-President of the United States, instead of Mr. Fillmore, on the same ticket with General Taylor. In that case, he would, on the death of General Taylor, have become President of the United States, as did Mr. Fillmore. Mr. Lawrence lacked very few votes of this high success; and I shall never forget the quiet good-humor with which, a few minutes after he knew that he had failed of the nomination as Vice-President, he came into my house, being my next-door neighbor, and told me of it.

[a] This peculiar New England season is well described in a note to the eighth sermon of a small collection first printed privately in 1812, and afterwards published, by the late Rev. James Freeman, one of the wise and good men of his time.

"The southwest is the pleasantest wind which blows in New England. In the month of October, in particular, after the frosts which commonly take fifteen pages in a day. But my eyes — my literary legs — grow feebler and feebler, as I near my grand climacteric. I hope it will be long, however, before I shall have to say, *Solve senescentem*. I would rather die in harness. Another year, I trust, we may get some way into December before going into town. But I don't know. It takes two to make a bargain in my family.

The winter that followed, 1856 – 7, was an unhappy one, and not without painful auguries. I was then in Italy. My letters informed me that my friend was suffering from severe headaches. He wrote me, in reply to inquiries on the subject, that it was true he had suffered from a new sort of troubles ; but he wrote lightly and pleasantly, as if it were a matter of little consequence. The greatest severity of his pain was from December to March. During that period, he was often unable to work at all, and from time to time, and generally for some hours every day, his sufferings were very severe.

On my return home in September, 1857, I found his appearance considerably changed. He was much better, I was assured, than he had been during the winter ; and the ever-watchful Mrs. Prescott told me that he had been able for several months to pursue his literary labors nearly every day, though cautiously and sometimes not without anxiety on her part. He was, I thought, not a sound man, as he was when I had last seen him, fifteen or sixteen months before ; for, although he suffered less pain in his head than he had for some time, he was seldom free from annoyance there. He, however, regarded the affection, in its different forms, as rheumatic, and as connected with all the kindred maladies that from his youth had been lurking in

place at the end of September, it frequently produces two or three weeks of fair weather, in which the air is perfectly transparent, and the clouds, which float in a sky of the purest azure, are adorned with brilliant colors. If at this season a man of an affectionate heart and ardent imagination should visit the tombs of his friends, the southwestern breezes, as they breathe through the glowing trees, would seem to him almost articulate. Though he might not be so rapt in enthusiasm as to fancy that the spirits of his ancestors were whispering in his ear, yet he would at least imagine that he heard the still, small voice of God. This charming season is called the Indian Summer, a name which is derived from the natives, who believe that it is caused by a wind which comes immediately from the court of their great and benevolent God, Cantantowwit, or the Southwestern God, the God who is superior to all other beings ; who sends them every blessing which they enjoy, and to whom the souls of their fathers go after their decease."

his system.   I would gladly have agreed with him, but, when
I occasionally observed that the pain he suffered flushed his
face and neck with a dark mahogany color, I could not drive
away the apprehensions that haunted me.

Still he was almost always able to occupy himself, at least
a part of each day, with his literary labors ; and in the first
weeks of the new year he wrote the opening chapters of the
Sixth Book of his " Philip the Second," or, if the concluding
paragraphs of the last of them were not absolutely committed
to paper at that time, they were composed, as was his custom,
in his memory, and were ready to be written down at the first
moment of leisure.   This was the condition of things at the end
of January, 1858.

But, though he did not feel himself strong and well during
the latter part of 1857 and in the opening days of 1858, still
he enjoyed life almost as he had done in its happiest years.
He not only worked, and did it well, but he took the same
sort of pleasure in society that he always had.   Dining with
friends, which had been his favorite mode of social enjoyment,
as it had been his father's, was continued, and especially dining
with a few ; an indulgence which he could not permit to be
interfered with.   One of the last of these occasions — I suppose
the very last, before his illness in February, 1858, interrupted
them for several months — is so happily described by his life-
long friend, Mr. Gardiner, that I take much pleasure in giving
his account of it entire.   He is speaking of a sort of dinners
that Prescott used to call *croneyings*, which he particularly
enjoyed, and of which there are occasional, though very rare
and slight, notices in his Memoranda.

" With what mingled emotions," says Mr. Gardiner, " I recall the *last*
of these occasions !   I am enabled to fix its date very nearly.   It was at
my own house, either on the last day of January, or one of the earliest
days of February, 1858.   It was a party so small that it hardly deserves
the name.   Prescott and two of his most intimate friends, besides myself
and my family, were all who filled a small round table.   He had suffered
during the past year from frequent and severe headaches ; a source of
more uneasiness to his friends than to himself, for he never attributed these
headaches to what the event proved them to be.   He thought them either
neuralgic, or a new phase of his old enemy, rheumatism ; nothing that
required extraordinary care.   For a few days past he had been unusually
free from them, and this day he was particularly bright and clear.   From

the beginning he was in one of his most lively and amusing moods.   The
ladies were induced by it to linger longer at the table than usual.   When
they had left, the whole company was reduced to only a party of four, but
of very old friends, each of whom was stored with many reminiscences of
like occasions, running far back into younger days.   Prescott overflowed
with the full tide of mirth belonging to those days.   It was a gush of rare
enjoyment.   After nearly five years, the date at which I write, I cannot
recall a thing that was said.   Probably nothing was said in itself worth
recalling, nothing that would bear to stand alone on cold paper.   But all
that quick-wittedness, lively repartee, sparkling humor, exceeding *naïveté*,
and droll manner of saying droll things, for which he was so remarkable
when he let himself out with perfect freedom, were brought into full play.
And then he laughed, as he only could laugh, at next to nothing, when
he was in one of these moods, and made us inevitably laugh too, almost
as the Cambridge Professor did, according to his own story.   He stayed,
too, considerably beyond his usual time, the rarest of all things with him.
But he had come bent on having ' a good time,' — it was so long, he said,
since he had had one, — and laid out for it accordingly.

" On comparing notes a few days afterwards with the two friends who
were present, we all agreed that we had not seen ' the great historian ' for
years in such a state of perfect youthful abandonment.

" It was a sad note of solemn warning which led us to make that comparison.   But the picture of him as he was that night, in all his merriment, will never fade from the memory — till all fades."

TO LADY LYELL.

Boston, November 4, 1854.

We passed a very quiet month in old Pepperell.   Susan was so fatigued
with the rather bustling life we led at Lynn, that I proposed we should
live like anchorites, bating the bread and water, in the country.   So we
had only the children and little ones.   One friend, the ex-Minister to England, spent indeed a couple of days with us.   Groton, the next town, you
know, to Pepperell, was his birthplace.   His father was a lieutenant in
my grandfather's regiment on the memorable day of Bunker Hill, when
British tyranny was so well humbled, you recollect.   The two brave companions in arms were great friends, and, being neighbors, often sipped
their *toddy* together in the same room where their descendants took their
champagne and sherry, the latter some of the *good* — I do not say the *best*
— fruits of our glorious Revolution.   It was rather interesting to think of
it, was it not ?   But poor Lawrence went from us to Groton to pass a few
days, and while there had a bad attack of — I don't know what, nor the
doctors either — great pains in the chest, pressure on the head, and insen-
sibility.   Yet they do not think it apoplectic in its character, but arising
from a disturbance of the liver, to which he has been subject.   Any way
it is very alarming.   It is the third attack of the kind he has had in six
weeks, and it makes all his friends " guess and fear " for the future.   He
is now on a very careful regimen, and pays little attention to business or

anything that can excite him. His loss would be a great one to this community, and it certainly would be inestimable to his family. There are few whom I should be more sorry to part with, for besides good sense and large practical information he has such a genial nature, with such frank and joyous manners as are not often found among us cold-blooded Yankees. I would not have you think from all this that he is at the point of death. On the contrary, I have just met him in the street, and looking very well. But his constitution is shaken.

Soon after our return to town your friends, the Governor-General of all the Canadas and lady, turned up again, to my great satisfaction, as I wished to see them, and have the opportunity of paying them some attention. I dined with them at the Ticknors day before yesterday, and to-day they dine with us. We shall have a dozen more friends, the *famille* Sears, the elder and younger branches, the Ticknors supported by Hillard, and our brave Ex-Consul Aspinwall. Do you think it will be prim and prosy? I wish you and your husband were to help us out with it. I like the Heads very much, the little I have seen of them ; well-bred, unaffected, and intellectual people, with uncommon good-nature for travellers, i. e. John Bull travellers.

TO LADY LYELL.

BOSTON, December 24, 1854.

Have you seen Lord Carlisle's volume of Travels? He sent it to me the other day, and it strikes me as a very agreeable record, and full of the noble sentiments which belong to him.

So poor Lockhart has paid the great debt. Was it not a touching thing that he should have died on the spot endeared to him by so many tender and joyous recollections, and of the same disease which destroyed Sir Walter too? I liked Lockhart, tho little I saw of him ; and a vein of melancholy tinged with the sarcastic gave an interesting piquancy to his conversation. I don't know that it made his criticism more agreeable to those who were the subjects of it.

TO LADY LYELL.

BOSTON, December 31, 1854.

Thank you, dear Lady Lyell, for your kind note and the likeness⁵ which accompanied it. It is charming ; the noble, expansive forehead, the little mouth that does — not speak. Nothing can be more perfect. It will make a nice *pendant* to Ticknor's, executed in the same way. This crystallotype — if that is the name it goes by with you as it does with us — is a miraculous invention, and one by no means auspicious to the engraver, or indeed the painter. Apollo, in old times, was the patron of the fine arts, and of painting among the rest. But in our days he is made to become painter himself.

⁵ Of Sir Charles Lyell.

TO LADY LYELL.

Boston, March 15, 1855.

I envy you your Continental tour, especially your visit to Berlin. It is a capital I should like well to see, if it were only to meet Humboldt, one of the very few men in the world whom one would take the trouble to walk a mile to see; now that the Iron Duke is dead, I hardly know another I would go half that distance to have a look at. I have had some very kind letters from Humboldt, who has always taken a friendly interest in my historical career; and, as this has lain in his path, it has enabled me to appreciate the immense services he has done to science and letters by his curious researches and his beautiful manner of exhibiting the results of them to the reader.

FROM LORD CARLISLE.

Castle Howard, March 20, 1855.

Optime et Carissime,

Nothing ever pleased me more, except perhaps your own most kind and indulgent verdict, than the opinion you enclosed to me from the erudite and weighty authority of Felton.[6] For, besides all his intrinsic titles to respect and deference as scholar, author, and critic, he had himself drunk in the inspiration of the self-same scenes, and knows how feebly the pale coloring of words can portray all the glowing realities of those classic shores. I will attend to your behest about the book when I get back to London. You will excuse me for guiding myself by Homeric precedent, so I shall presume to expect a Diomedean exchange of armor, and, in return for my light texture, to receive your full mail-clad "Philip the Second."

You will have perceived that we have been shifting scenes on our political stage with much rapidity and not a little complexity of plot. I appear myself before you in a new character.[7] Suppose you come and see how I comport myself in it. I had once an opportunity of showing you a real sovereign, and I can now treat you to the representation of a mock one. I will not guarantee, however, that I may not have to descend from my throne before you can reach its august presence.

I take up my abode in Ireland about Easter. I have a comfortable residence there, and a most agreeable view; not so sparkling as that over the Ægean and Cyclades, but over bright fresh green and a good outline of hill. I am quite serious in urging you to come. You may send Sumner too.

---

[6] Professor Felton, afterwards the much-loved President of Harvard College, edited and illustrated with his pleasant learning "The Diary in Turkish and Greek Waters," of Lord Carlisle (1855).

[7] As Viceroy of Ireland.

Peace be with you and yours at least, if it cannot be with the whole world.

Most affectionately,

CARLISLE.

TO LADY LYELL.

BOSTON, April 25, 1855.

I don't think I do myself quite justice in saying I am a fixture, because I stick to the easy-chair; for, after all, the mind is the man, and my mind has carried me over many a league since I saw you last, and far back, too, into other centuries. If I should go to heaven when I quit this dirty ball, I shall find many acquaintances there, and some of them very respectable, of the olden time; many whose letters I have read since their death, never intended for vulgar eyes to feed upon. Don't you think I should have a kindly greeting from good Isabella? Even Bloody Mary, I think, will smile on me; for I love the old Spanish stock, the house of Trastamara. But there is one that I am sure will owe me a grudge, and that is the very man I have been making two big volumes upon. With all my good-nature I can't wash him even into the darkest French gray. He is black and all black. My friend Madame Calderon will never forgive me. Is it not charitable to give Philip a place in heaven?

So Lord Carlisle has got the Irish sceptre. He has written kindly to ask me to visit him this summer, and see his vice-regal state. I should like nothing better; but I have my four acres of *lawn*, and ever so many greener acres of salt water to overlook, to say nothing of generations of descendants, who will be crying out for me like pelicans in the wilderness, should I abscond. An edition, by the by, of Carlisle's book is in the press here, and will come out under Felton's care. He went over the same ground, at about the same time with Lord C.

TO LADY LYELL.

BOSTON, June 17, 1855.

We are very busy just now preparing for our seaside flitting. It is a great pleasure to us that Elizabeth is to be so near us.* Her new house is on a larger scale, and every way a more ambitious affair, than ours. I expect to revel in babies, for William and his wife and nursery take up their quarters the first month with us.* I suppose Anna Ticknor, with whom I dined yesterday, — no one but the family, — has told you of Mr. Lawrence's illness. It is the old trouble, chiefly of the liver. A fortnight since as I walked with him round the Common, I told him he was losing ground and should go to Europe. I went in and saw his wife, and it was

* Mrs. James Lawrence, his only daughter, removed this season to a summer villa in his neighborhood at Lynn.

* His oldest son, then expected from Europe with his family.

arranged before I left, that he should take passage for England the 20th of June. That night he became very ill, and has been ever since in bed. He is now slowly mending, and, if well enough, will embark probably early in July; I should not think, however, before the middle of it. He just sent me from his sick-bed a scrap of paper, simply stating that "eighty years ago, June 17th, his father and my grandfather fought side by side on Bunker Hill," — a stirring reminiscence for a sick-bed.

FROM THE EARL OF ELLESMERE.

OXFORD, September 27, 1855.

DEAR MR. PRESCOTT,

Your kind and sad letter has remained long unacknowledged. It reached me at a moment when I was leaving London for an excursion less of pleasure than of business, a visit to the Paris Exhibition; and from my arrival there to my return a few days since I have been deprived of any use of my right hand by my usual enemy. If my right hand had more cunning than it pretends to, it could not convey what either Lady Ellesmere or myself feels on the frustration of the pleasant hope we had lately entertained of meeting again with the kind and good friend, whom I yet hope to meet, though not in this weary world.[10]

It seems but a day, but an hour, since he left us,
With no sign to prepare us, no warning to pain,
As we clung to the hand of which death has bereft us,
Little thinking we never should clasp it again.

We ought to have thought so; — to earth, for a season,
Worth, friendship, and goodness are lent, but not given;
And faith but confirms the conjecture of reason,
That the dearest to earth are the fittest for heaven.

I venture to quote the above, not as good, for they are my own, but as apposite, be they whose they may. They were written on the loss of a very valued friend and relative, Lord William Bentinck. We need no knell over the Atlantic to tell us of the frailty of human ties. I have personally been spared as yet, and no name is coupled with the horrors of our late Crimean despatches which directly concerns mine or me; but some have been reaped in this bloody harvest whom I know enough to value, and many — a son among the number — are exposed to the further chances of this awful and apparently interminable struggle. Nothing is on record since the siege of Jerusalem, unless it be some of the passages of the retreat from Moscow, which equals the sickening horrors of the "Times" of to-day; and we in England, though our people did what they could, and died in the Redan, have not the blaze of success to console us, which makes France forget its losses. I believe our cause is good. I cannot truly say that in other respects, as a nation, we have deserved other than severe trial, for we entered on this war, in my opinion, with much levity, ignorance, and presumption. I think we were right in going to war, and that we could not long have avoided it; but it is one thing to

[10] Mr. Abbott Lawrence.

face a great calamity calmly and sternly, from a sense of right and duty, and another to court the encounter with cheers and jeers and vaunting. I writhe under the government of Journalism. We are governed at home, and represented abroad, by a press which makes us odious to the world.

I am here at Oxford doing rather hard and unpaid service on a commission for shaping out and regulating the introduction of the changes directed by Parliament in the University; — a good deal of dry and heavy detail, but not without interest and some prospect of ultimate advantage. I lie on my back, and dignities drop into my mouth. I am appointed Lord-Lieutenant of Lancashire, for the excellent reason that there happens to be nobody else who comes within the usual category of qualifications of rank, residence, and political tendencies. It makes me a General of seven regiments of militia, an *Admiral*, and Custos Rotulorum, and covers me with silver-lace and epaulets! It does not, thank Heaven, in Lancashire convey, as in other counties, the power of recommending persons to the magistracy. The fact is, there is usually nothing to do in the office, but at present the militia does involve some business. . . . . .

E. ELLESMERE.

FROM MR. HALLAM.

PICKHURST BROOMLEY, Kent, December 5, 1855.

MY DEAR MR. PRESCOTT,

I must return you my best thanks for your very kind present of your "History of Philip the Second," which I received in town from Bentley last week. I only repeat the universal opinion in praising the philosophical depth of reflection, the justness of the sentiments, and the admirable grace of the style. I have not been lately in the way of seeing many people, but I am convinced that there will hardly be a difference of opinion upon the subject. If I regret anything, it is that you have so large a portion of your labor left behind.

You are quite right in supposing that the local interest about public events is unfavorable to literature. Macaulay's volumes will probably appear within a fortnight. He prints, I believe, twenty-five thousand copies, and they are all bespoken.

With my best wishes, believe me, my dear Mr. Prescott,
Very truly yours,
HENRY HALLAM.

TO MRS. MILMAN.

BOSTON, December 24, 1855.

I had a note from Macaulay the other day, in which he spoke of having just finished his book. I suppose ere now it is launched upon the great deep. I am glad that he has given me time to get out of the way with my little argosy, before taking the wind out of my sails. His readers on this side of the water count by thousands and tens of thousands. There is no man who speaks to such an audience as Macaulay. It is certainly a great responsibility. I was sorry to learn from him that he was confined to his house. When I was in England, he seemed to have too robust a constitution to be easily shaken by disease.

I gather my little circle of children and grandchildren about me to-morrow, to keep our merry Christmas. There will be a touch of sadness in it, however; for more than one seat will be made vacant by the death of poor Mr. Lawrence. His death has made a sad gap in our family gatherings. He will long live in the hearts of all who know him.

Pray remember me, my dear Mrs. Milman, in the kindest manner, to my good friend your husband, and to your family, and believe me

Very truly and affectionately yours,

WM. H. PRESCOTT.

TO COUNT ADOLPHE DE CIRCOURT.

BOSTON, April 7, 1856.

MY DEAR COUNT CIRCOURT,

I have read with the greatest pleasure your letter containing your remarks upon "Philip the Second." The subject is a difficult one to treat, and I have naturally felt a good deal of solicitude in regard to the judgment of competent critics upon it. The opinions, as far as I have gathered them from the criticisms that have appeared in England and in this country, have certainly been very friendly to me; but I cannot but feel that very few of those that criticise the work are particularly qualified to judge of it, for the simple reason, that they are not acquainted with the subject, or with the historic sources from which the narrative is derived. I was particularly gratified, therefore, to get an opinion from you so favorable on the whole to the execution of the task. And yet I am aware that, from a friend such as you are, not merely the *granum salis*, but a whole bushel of salt, to take our English measure, must be allowed. I have also had the pleasure of receiving this week a letter from Gachard, and no critic can be more qualified certainly in what relates to the Netherlands, and I hope you will not think it vanity in me when I say to you that his approval of my labors was conveyed in a tone of apparent candor and good faith which gave me sincere pleasure.

What gave me no less pleasure than your general commendation was the list of errata which accompanied it; not that I was happy to find I had made so many blunders, but that I possessed a friend who had the candor and sagacity to point them out. I am filled with astonishment when I reflect on the variety, the minuteness, and the accuracy of your knowledge. With this subject, thrown up by chance before you, you seem to be as familiar as if it had been your *spécialité*. I shall not fail to profit by your intelligent criticism, as my future editions in England and my own country will testify. Allow me to say, however, that your closing critique on a reading of Balbi, which I give in the notes, is not, I think, conformable to the author's meaning. This I gather from the context as well as from a more explicit statement on the subject by Calderon, another authority quoted by me, from whom the reasons given by me in the text are more especially derived. When the notice which you have been so kind as to write of the work appears, you will have the kindness to send it to me; and this reminds me that I have not been so fortunate as to receive an article which you promised some time since to send me on the career of Charles le Téméraire, a subject which has much interest for me, and which I trust you will not forget.

Do you know that our friends the Ticknors propose to visit Europe in the spring, and to pass a year or more on the Continent? I know you will like to take by the hand again this dear old friend, who has a mind as bright, and a heart as warm, as in earlier days. I know no one whose society I can so ill spare. I met your friend Mrs. —— last evening, and she spoke to me about you and Madame de Circourt, whom she spoke of as being in a very poor state of health. I was aware that she had suffered much from the deplorable accident which lately befell her; but I trust, for your sake and for that of the society of which she is so distinguished an ornament, that her apprehensions have exaggerated the amount of her illness.

I congratulate you on the termination of this unhappy war, which seemed likely to bring nothing but misery to all the parties engaged in it, though Napoleon may have found his account in the lustre which it has thrown upon the French arms; a poor compensation, after all, to a reflecting mind, for the inevitable evils of war. In the mean time you are blessed with an imperial baby, which, I suppose, is equivalent to half a dozen victories, and which will be worth more to Napoleon, if it can serve to perpetuate his dynasty. But whoever has read the past of France for the last thirty years will feel no great confidence in omens for the future.

We have some petty subjects for quarrelling with John Bull on hand just now, which may easily be disposed of, if the governments of the two countries are in a tolerably amiable mood. If they are not, I trust there is good sense and good feeling enough in the two nations to prevent their coming to blows about trifles which are not of the slightest real importance to either party. Unhappily, it does sometimes happen that disputes, which are founded on feeling rather than reason, are the most difficult for reasonable men to settle.

With constant regard, believe me, my dear Count Circourt,

Very truly your friend,

WM. H. PRESCOTT.

TO SIR CHARLES LYELL.

BOSTON, November 11, 1856.

I wrote to her [Lady Lyell] in my last letter, I think, that I was about to send something again in the historical way into the world. The greater part, however, is not my work, but that of a much bigger man. Robertson, you know, closes his "History of Charles the Fifth" with his reign, bestowing only two or three pages, and those not the most accurate, on his life after his abdication. As his reign comes between that of Ferdinand and Isabella and the reign of that virtuous monarch Philip the Second (who may be considered as to other Catholics what a Puseyite is to other Protestants), my publishers thought it would be a proper thing — that is a *good* thing — if I were to furnish a continuation of Robertson, for which I have the materials, so as to bring him within the regular series of my historical works. This I have accordingly done to the tune of some hundred and fifty pages, with comparatively little trouble to myself, having already touched on this theme in " Philip the Second." It was intended for the Yankee public in particular ; but Routledge brings it out in London in four editions at once ; and a copy of the largest octavo I have ordered him to send to you. Do not trouble yourself to read it, or thank me for it, but put it on your shelves, as a memento of friendship, very sincere, for you.

FROM DEAN MILMAN.

DEANERY ST. PAUL'S, December 1, 1856.

MY DEAR FRIEND,

The date of your last letter looks reproachfully at me, but I am sure that you will ascribe my long silence to anything rather than want of the most sincere and cordial friendship. I received it during our summer wanderings in Germany, where we passed many weeks — holiday-weeks — in great enjoyment, and, I rejoice and am thankful to be able to say, in uninterrupted, perhaps improved, health. We paid a visit to our friend Bunsen at Heidelberg, whom we found (I know not whether you made his acquaintance in England) in the dignity and happiness of literary quiet and labor, after having so honorably lost his high diplomatic position. He has a beautifully situated house, looking over the bright Neckar, and up to the noble ruins of the Castle. From thence we took the course of the fine Bavarian cities, Aschaffenburg, Wurtzburg, Bamberg, Nuremberg. At Donauwik we launched on the rapid Danube, and followed its stream to Vienna and to Pesth. To us the Danube is a noble stream, especially after its junction with the Inn, amid the magnificent scenery about Passau ; though I know that you Americans give yourselves great airs, and would think but lightly of the power and volume of such a river. From Vienna to Prague and Dresden. At Dresden we had the great pleasure of falling in with the Ticknors, whom I had frequently seen during their short stay in London ; and also with their most charming relative, our friend Mrs. Twisleton and her lord. Then to Berlin, and after a peep into Holland we found our way home. We, indeed, have been hardly settled at home (having paid some visits in the autumn) till within two or three weeks.

Among the parcels which awaited me on my arrival was your graceful and just tribute to the memory of our excellent friend, poor Mr. Lawrence. I should have read it with great interest for his sake if from another hand, — with how much more, when it came from you, executed with your accustomed skill and your pleasant style, heightened by your regret and affection.

I have not yet seen your concluding chapters (announced in this week's Athenæum) to the new edition of Robertson's "Charles the Fifth." I doubt not that you have found much to say, and much that we shall be glad to read, after Stirling's agreeable book. . . . . . (By the way, at the Goldene Kreus Hotel at Regensburg [Ratisbon], which was once a fine palace, they show the room in which John of Austria was born.) But his life is comparatively of trivial moment in the darkening tragedy (for you must allow it to gather all its darkness) of Philip the Second's later years. Though I would on no account urge you to haste incompatible with the full investigation of all the accumulating materials of those fearful times, yet you must not allow any one else to step in before you, and usurp the property which you have so good a right to claim in that awful impersonation of all that is anti-Christian in him who went to his grave with the conviction, that he, above all other men, had discharged the duties of a Christian monarch.

I am now, as you may suppose, enjoying my repose with all my full and unexhausted interest in literary subjects, in history especially, and poetry, (I trust that it will last as long as my life,) but without engaging in any severe or continuous labor. *Solve senescentem*, is one of the wisest adages of wise antiquity, though the aged horse, if he finds a pleasant meadow, may allow himself a light and easy canter. I am taking most kindly to my early friends, the classic writers ; having read, in the course of my later life, so much bad Greek and Latin, I have a right to refresh myself, and very refreshing it is, with the fine clear writings of Greece and Rome. . . . . .

So far had I written when, behold ! your second letter made its appearance, announcing your promised present of "Charles the Fifth." I at first thought of throwing what I had written behind the fire, but soon determined rather to inflict upon you another sheet, with my best thanks, and assurances that I shall not leave my neighbor Mr. Routledge long at peace. . . . . .

And now to close, my dear friend, I must add Mrs. Milman's kind love. She begs me to say that you have read her a lesson of charity towards Philip the Second, which she almost doubts whether your eloquence can fully enforce upon her. . . . . .

H. H. MILMAN.

Do come and see us again, or make me twenty years younger, that I may cross to you.

TO LADY MARY LABOUCHERE.

BOSTON, February 7, 1857.

MY DEAR LADY MARY,

It was with very great pleasure that I received the kind note in your handwriting, which looked like a friend that I had not looked upon for a long time. And this was followed soon after by the portrait of your dear mother, forwarded to me by Colnaghi from London. It is an excellent likeness, and recalls the same sweet and benevolent expression which has lingered in my memory ever since I parted from her at Castle Howard.

I have wished that I could think that I should ever see her again in her princely residence. But there is little chance, I fear, of my meeting her again in this world. Pray, when you next see her, give my most respectful and affectionate remembrances to her. You have been fortunate in keeping one parent from the skies so long. My own mother survived till some few years since, and we were never parted till death came between us. This is a blessing not to be estimated. And she was so good that her removal, at the age of eighty-four, was an event less to be mourned on her account than on ours who survived her.

I was extremely sorry to hear of Lord Ellesmere's severe illness. Sir Henry Holland gave me some account of it in a letter some time since. From what you write and what I have heard elsewhere, I fear that his restoration to health is still far from being complete.

I wish there were any news here that would interest you. But I lead a very quiet, domestic sort of life, which, as far as I am concerned, affords little that is new. I am at present robbed of both my sons, who are passing this winter in Paris, and probably will pass the next in Italy. The eldest has his wife and children with him, and I carry on a sort of nursery correspondence with my little granddaughter, who has almost reached the respectable age of five. My own daughter, Mrs. Lawrence, and her two children, live within a stone's-throw of me, both in Boston and in the country, where we pass our summers. And this doubles the happiness of life.

It is a pleasant thing for us that our two nations should have such kindly feelings as they now seem to have for one another. The little affair of the "Resolute" seems to have called them all out. We are brethren who have too large an inheritance in common of the past to forget it all for some petty quarrel about a thing which can be of no real importance to either.

I am glad to learn that the members of your own family are in such good health. I suppose you see little of Morpeth, to whom I write occasionally, and think myself lucky when I get an answer, especially when it comes through so kind a secretary as you. I am not likely to forget your features, for the charming portrait which you last sent me stands in a frame on a ledge of my book-case in the library, which is our sitting-room.

Pray remember me most kindly to your sisters and your brother Charles, and believe me, dear Lady Mary, with sincere regards to Mr. Labouchere,

Most truly and affectionately yours,
WM. H. PRESCOTT.

TO LADY LYELL.

Boston, April 4, 1857.

I believe I told you of my headaches, which Jackson considers as belonging to my rheumatic habits, and bred in the bone. Very bad habits they are. I am happy to say the aches have nearly subsided, though I have lost two good months by them. Agassiz, who dined with me on

17 *

Wednesday, filled me with envy by saying he had worked fifteen hours the day before. What is the man made of? The great book on Turtles has been delayed, from his desire to make it more complete. He has brought into it discussions on a great variety of themes terrestrial and celestial. It reminded me, I told him, of the old cosmographical myth of the Indians, where the world was said to rest on an elephant and the elephant on the back of a tortoise. For myself, I think it would be a great improvement if he would furnish a chapter on turtle-doves, with their tender associations, instead of the real turtle, whose best associations, as far as I know, are those connected with an alderman or a lord-mayor's feast. But Agassiz thinks he has not half exhausted the subject. . . . . .

FROM MR. IRVING.

SUNNYSIDE, August 25, 1857.

MY DEAR MR. PRESCOTT,

You say "you don't know whether I care about remarks on my books from friends, though they be brothers of the craft." I cannot pretend to be above the ordinary sensitiveness of authorship, and am especially alive to the remarks of a master-workman like yourself. I have never been less confident of myself and more conscious of my short-comings, than on this my last undertaking, and have incessantly feared that the interest might flag beneath my pen. You may judge, therefore, how much I have been gratified by your assurance that the interest felt by yourself and Mrs. Prescott on reading the work "went on *crescendo* from the beginning, and did not reach its climax till the last pages."

I thank you, therefore, most heartily, for your kind and acceptable letter, which enables me to cheer myself with the persuasion that I have not ventured into the field once too often; and that my last production has escaped the fate of the Archbishop of Granada's.

You hint a wish that I would visit your Northern latitudes, and partake of the good-fellowship that exists there; and, indeed, it would give me the greatest pleasure to enjoy communionship with a few choice spirits like yourself, but I have a growing dread of the vortex of gay society into which I am apt to be drawn if I stir from home. In fact, the habits of literary occupation, which of late years I have indulged to excess, have almost unfitted me for idle, gentlemanly life. Relaxation and repose begin to be insupportable to me, and I feel an unhealthy hankering after my study, and a disposition to relapse into hard writing.

Take warning by my case, and beware of literary intemperance.

Ever, my dear Prescott,

Yours very truly,

WASHINGTON IRVING.

TO LADY LYELL.

November 30, 1857.

When the times are bad, I fortunately have a snug retreat on my little farm of the sixteenth century, and an hour or two's conversation with my good friend Philip generally puts me at peace with the world. I suppose you eschew all books while you are on the wing. If you ever meet with an English one, and can get hold of Thackeray's last, "The Virginians," publishing in numbers, I believe, in England as well as here, I wish you would look at it, if only to read the first paragraph, in which he pays a very nice tribute to my old swords of Bunker Hill renown, and to their unworthy proprietor. It was very prettily done of him. I am well booked up now in regard to my English friends, first from the Ticknors, whom I have examined and cross-examined until I am well enough acquainted with their experiences, and now Sumner has arrived and given me four or five hours' worth of his in an uninterrupted stream, and a very pleasant raconteur he is, especially when he talks of the friends of whom I have such a loving remembrance on your side of the water. He seems to have had quite a triumphant reception. When a Yankee makes his appearance in London circles, the first question asked, I fancy, if they think him worth asking any about, is whether he is a pro-slavery man, or an anti-slavery, and deal with him accordingly. It would seem droll if, when an Englishman lights on our soil, the first question we should ask should be whether he was in favor of making the Chinese swallow opium, or whether he was opposed to it; as if that were not only the moral, but the social, standard by which everything was to be tested, and we were to cut him or caress him accordingly. But Sumner was hailed as a martyr, and enjoys — quite contrary to usage — the crown of martyrdom during his own lifetime. His ovation has agreed with him, and he goes to Washington this week. . . . . .

CHAPTER XXVIII.

1858 — 1859.

ON the 4th of February, 1858, in the afternoon, I happened to call on my friend for a little visit or a walk, that being the portion of the day in which, from our respective occupations, we oftenest saw each other. As I entered, the air of the servant who opened the door surprised me, and I hardly understood the words he uttered with great emotion, to tell me that Mr. Prescott was suddenly and seriously ill. He had, in fact, been seized in the street a couple of hours before, and the affection was evidently of the brain, and apoplectic.

The attack occurred just on his return from his accustomed walk in the early afternoon. Indeed, he reached home with some difficulty, and went, not without much effort, at once, and as it were instinctively and almost unconsciously, to his working study. His mind wandered for a few moments, and his powers of speech and motion were partly suspended. The earliest articulate words he uttered were to his wife, as she was tenderly leaning over him : " My poor wife ! I am so sorry for you, that this has come upon you so soon ! "

The symptoms were not formidable, and those that seemed most threatening yielded to remedies in the course of the afternoon. His venerable physician, Dr. Jackson, expressed himself to me at nine o'clock in the evening with much hopefulness, and the next day nearly all anxiety concerning an immediate recurrence of the disease was gone. But a mark had been made on his physical constitution which was never to be obliterated.

For the first two days he was kept almost entirely in bed, and in a state of absolute rest and quietness, with his room somewhat darkened. On the third day I saw him. He talked with me as clearly as he ever had when in full health, and with intellectual faculties as unclouded. But his utterance was slightly affected. His movements were no longer assured. A few words and many proper names did not come promptly at his summons. He occasionally seemed to see figures — especially the figure of a gentleman in black — moving about the room, though he was quite aware that the whole was an optical delusion. If he looked into a book, one line was strangely mingled with another, and the whole became confused and illegible. All this he explained to me in the simplest and clearest manner, as if he were speaking, not of his own case, but of that of another person. He was, in fact, not under the smallest misapprehension as to the nature of his attack, nor as to what might be its consequences at a moment's notice. Neither did he at all exaggerate his danger, or seem alarmed or anxious at the prospect before him. He saw his condition as his physicians and his family saw it, and as the result proved that it must have been from the first.

In five or six days he walked out with assistance; but he was put upon a rigorous, vegetable diet, and his strength returned slowly and imperfectly. After a few weeks the irregularity in his vision was corrected; his tread became so much more firm that he ventured into the streets alone; and his enunciation, except to the quick ear of affection, was again distinct and natural. But his utterance never ceased to be marked with a slight effort; proper names were never again so easily recalled as they had been; and, although his appropriate gait was recovered, it was at best a little slower than it had been, and, in the last weeks of his life, when I walked with him a good deal, he sometimes moved very heavily, and more than once called my attention to this circumstance as to a considerable change in his condition. In his general appearance, however, at least to a casual observer, in the expression of his fine manly countenance, and in his whole outward bearing, he seemed such as he had always been. Those, therefore, who saw him only as he was met in his accustomed walks, thought him quite recovered. But his family and his more intimate friends were too vigilant to be thus deluded. They knew, from the first, that he was no longer the same.

Reading was the earliest pleasure he enjoyed, except that of the society of his household and of a chosen few out of it. But it was only the lightest books to which he could listen safely, — novels and tales, — and it was only those he liked best, such as Miss Edgeworth's Helen and Scott's Guy Mannering, that could satisfy him enough to enable him to keep his attention fastened on them. Even of such he soon wearied, and turned with more interest, though not with conviction, to parts of Buckle's first volume on the "History of Civilization," then recently published.[1]

A very different and a stronger interest, however, he felt in listening, as he did a little later, to the accounts of cases of eminent men of letters resembling his own; to Adam Ferguson's, in the Memoirs of Lord Cockburn, which was full of encouragement, and to Scott's, in Lockhart's "Life," which, on the other hand, could not fail to sadden him, and yet which he insisted on following, through all its painful details, to its disheartening, tragical catastrophe.

This phasis of his disease, however, passed gradually away, and then he began to crave afresh the occupations and modes of life to which he had always been accustomed; — simple, both, as they could be, and laborious, but which had become seriously important to him from long habit. His physician advised a very moderate and cautious use of wine; a glass a day at first, and afterwards a little more, so as to increase his strength, and enable him to return, in some degree at least, to the studies that were so necessary to his daily happiness; still restricting him, however, to a merely vegetable diet. The prescriptions were rigorously obeyed; and he was able soon to take exercise in walking equal to four miles a day, which, if it was materially less than he had found useful and easy when he was in

---

[1] When Professor Playfair was suffering from his last painful disease, his affectionate attendants tried to amuse him with the early novels of Scott, then just in the course of publication, and other books of the same sort, which, when well, he much enjoyed. But now they soon became wearisome to him. "Try a little of Newton's 'Principia,'" said the dying philosopher; and, for a time, his attention was commanded.

full health, was yet much more than he had of late been able to sustain. It was, therefore, a great point gained, and he thankfully acknowledged it to be such. But still he marked the difference in his general strength, and knew its meaning.

Encouraged, however, by his improvement, such as it was, and permitted at least, if not counselled to it, by his medical adviser, he now adventured once more within the domain of his old and favorite studies. He did not, indeed, undertake to prepare anything for the fourth volume of " Philip the Second"; nor did he even go on to fill out the third to the full proportions into which he had originally determined to cast it. But the conclusion of the last chapter that he ever finished, a few paragraphs only — which, as was his wont, he had, I believe, composed before his attack and had preserved to a good degree in his memory — was now reduced to writing, and the manuscript completed so far as it was destined ever to be.

In April, 1858, he went to press with it, and in the course of the summer the stereotyping was finished; the whole having undergone, as it advanced, a careful revision from his ever-faithful friend, Mr. Folsom. In this part of the work of publishing, he took much pleasure; more, I believe, than he had before in any similar case. The reason is simple. He did not like to think that he was, in consequence of his diminished strength, obliged to reduce the amount of his intellectual exertions; and, while his present occupation was light and easy, he could feel that it was indispensable, and that it came now in regular course, instead of being taken up because he was unequal to work that was heavier. He expressed this to me with much satisfaction at Lynn one day after dinner, when he was near the end of his task; for, although he felt the fearful uncertainty of his condition, he did not like to think that he was in any degree yielding to it. His courage, in this respect, was absolute. It never faltered.

At Pepperell, where he went on the 25th of September, he ventured a little further. In 1844 two translations of his "Conquest of Mexico" had appeared in Mexico itself, one of which was rendered more than commonly important by the comments of Don José F. Ramirez at the end of the second volume, and the other by the notes of Don Lucas Alaman, a statesman and man of letters of no mean rank, who had long occupied himself with the history of his country. Mr. Prescott now busied himself with these materials, as, I think, he had done before, and prepared a considerable number of additions and emendations for a future edition of the original work.

"I am now amusing myself," he says, under the date of September 30th, "with making some emendations and additional notes for a new edition, some day or other, of the ' Conquest of Mexico.' Two Mexican translations of the work, enriched with annotations, furnish a pretty good stock of new materials for the purpose." The amount that he accomplished is considerable, and it will, I hope, be used hereafter, as its author intended it should be.

But though such labor was light compared with that needful in the prosecution of his studies for the "History of Philip the Second," if he had ventured to take them up in earnest, still little that he did during that summer and autumn was wholly free from painful effort. I witnessed it more than once while he was at Lynn, where headaches, though treated as of little account, yet gave occasion for grave apprehensions, — not the less grave, because their expression, which could have done only harm, was carefully forborne by those about him.

His occupations at Pepperell, however, can hardly have injured him. At any rate, he felt that what he had done had been an amusement rather than anything else; and when he left that much-loved region, with its cheerful drives and walks, and with all the tender associations that rested on it, — that tapestried the rooms of the old house and lighted up the whole landscape, and its waters, woods, and hills, — he made the following simple record : —

Pepperell, October 28th. — Return to town to-morrow. The country is now in its splendid autumn robe, somewhat torn, however, and draggled by the rain. I have been occupied with corrections and additions to my "Mexico." On my return to Boston shall resume my labors on "Philip," and, if my health continues as good as it has been this summer, shall hope to make some progress. But I shall not press matters. Our *villeggiatura* has been brightened by the presence of all the children and grandchildren, God bless them! And now we scatter again, but not far apart.

These touching words are the last he ever wrote in the

private Memoranda, which he had now kept above forty years, and there are no words in the whole mass of above twelve hundred pages that are more expressive of what was peculiar to him. His domestic affections were always uppermost in his character, and never more so than they were in the last weeks and months of his life ; indeed, I think, never so much and so manifestly. How he loved his children, — all his children, — how he delighted in his grandchildren, how he held them all "in his heart of heart," those who most knew him, knew best.

On his return to Boston, he looked stronger than he did when he left it four months earlier. His spirits were more natural ; sometimes as bright as they had ever been. He was in better flesh, and his muscular power was increased, although not much. But I think he never passed a day without a sense of the shadow that he knew must always rest on his way of life, whether it should be long or short.

During the first weeks after his coming to town, he was occupied with affairs that had accumulated during his absence. As usual, they somewhat wearied and annoyed him ; perhaps more than they had on other similar occasions. But he dismissed them from his thoughts as soon as he could, and then he seemed to turn with a sort of irresistible craving to the intellectual pursuits which long habit and conscientious devotion to them had made so important to his happiness.

About New Year of 1859, he spoke to me more than once of a change in his modes of life. He thought, as he told me, that, if his diet were made more nourishing, his general strength would be improved, and he should thus become capable of more labor in all ways, and especially upon his " Philip the Second." On this, however, he did not venture. His obedience to his medical director was exact to the last. He restrained himself rigorously to a vegetable diet, and never took more wine than was prescribed to him, as if it had been a medicine.

But he could not fully resist the temptation of his old books and manuscripts ; nor was he altogether discouraged by his wise professional adviser from making an inconsiderable and wary experiment with them. Indeed, something of the sort seemed to have become important for his health as well as for his spir-

z

its, which were now pining for the aliment that was demanded alike by his physical and moral constitution. During two or three weeks, therefore, he was occupied with that portion of the History of Philip the Second with which his fourth volume would necessarily open. His researches, no doubt, were not as laborious as they had sometimes been, when he was busy with a difficult subject. They were, in fact, entirely prefatory, involving only the plan of an opening chapter, and the general mode in which that part of the war of the Netherlands might be discussed, to which the volume itself was to be largely devoted. Even in this, I believe, he was careful, and gave much less time to work than was his wont. But whenever he thought, he thought intently. He could not help it. It was a habit which he had cultivated with so much care, that he could not now shake it off. It is possible, therefore, that his occupations during these weeks were among the causes that hastened the final event. But if they were, their influence must have been small. Nothing gave token of what, from inscrutable causes, was not only inevitable, but was near.

About a fortnight before his death, he suffered from an ague, which gave him so much pain, that it entirely interrupted his accustomed occupations. During the five or six days of its continuance, I spent the leisure of each afternoon with him. His strength was a good deal diminished, and he was generally lying on his sofa when I saw him; but never was he brighter or more agreeable, never more cheerful or more interesting. And so it continued to the end. I saw him only twice or three times afterwards; but those who were constantly with him, and watched every word and movement with affectionate solicitude, observed no change.

That his intellectual faculties were not affected, and that his temperament had lost little of its charming gayety, the letters and memoranda of the year leave no doubt. They were not, I suppose, always written without effort, but the effort was successful, which, in general, it would not have been, and in his case was so in consequence mainly of the original elements that had been so gently mixed in his whole nature.

TO MR. BANCROFT.

Boston, February 19 (indorsed 1858).

Dear Bancroft,

It is well enough for a man to be ill sometimes, if it is only to show to him the affectionate sympathy of his friends, though in truth this was hardly necessary to prove yours. Two weeks since I had a slight touch of paralysis, which should have fallen on a man of more flesh than I can boast. It was so slight, however, that the doctor thinks there was no rupture of any vessel in the brain. The effects of it have passed off, excepting only some slight damage in that part of the cranium which holds proper names. I am somewhat reduced, as much perhaps in consequence of the diet I am put upon as the disease; for meat and generous wine are proscribed for the present.

So you are to make your bow to the public in May; and the world, I have no doubt, as it shows signs of revival, will gladly wake from its winter's trance to receive you.

That is a charming paragraph which you have sent me, containing a letter wholly new to me,[2] and I look forward to the hours when I shall devour the coming volume, the one of greatest interest to me, and not one least difficult to you.

I hope your wife is in good health. Pray remember me most affectionately to her, and believe me

Ever faithfully your friend,

Wm. H. Prescott.

TO MR. BANCROFT.

Boston, April 8, 1858.

I am truly obliged to you, my dear Bancroft, for sending me your account of Bunker Hill battle, in which I am so much interested.[3] I have read it with the greatest care and with equal pleasure. It was a difficult story to tell, considering how much it has been disfigured by feelings of personal rivalry and foolish pretension. In my judgment, you have steered clear of all these difficulties, and have told the story in a simple though eloquent style, that cannot fail to win the confidence of your reader, and satisfy him that you have written with no desire but to tell the truth, after a careful study of the whole ground.

For the last thirty years or more the friends and kinsmen of the prominent chiefs in the action have been hunting up old Revolutionary survivors, most of whom had survived their own faculties, and extorting from them such views as could carry no conviction to a candid mind. My

---

[2] A remarkable letter from Colonel Prescott, the historian's grandfather, to the Committee of Safety, in Boston, August, 1774. See Bancroft's History, Vol. VII. (1858.) p. 99. Mr. Bancroft possesses the autograph of this vigorous, patriotic document.

[3] At the end of Vol. VII. of Bancroft's History, 1858, sent in the proof-sheet to Mr. Prescott.

father took no interest in all this, and made no effort to contradict the accounts thus given from time to time to the public. He thought, as I did, that these random statements would make no permanent impression on the public mind. He waited to see — what I, more fortunate than he, have now lived to see — an impartial account given of the action by the classical pen of the historian, whose writings are destined not merely for the present age, but for posterity. While you have done entire justice to my grandfather, you have been scrupulous in giving due praise to Putnam and Warren, and to the latter in particular you have paid an eloquent tribute, well deserved, and in your happiest manner.

You are now entering on the most brilliant and fascinating part of your grand subject, and I hope no political coquetry will have the power to entice you away in another direction until you have brought it to a completion. Since my apoplectic thump I have done nothing in the literary way, giving my wits a good chance to settle and come into their natural state again. I am rather tired of this kind of loafing, and am now beginning to fall into the old track, — but with caution. As I am on a vegetable diet, though the doctor has allowed me to mend my cheer with a little wine, I may hope to be armed against any future attack.

With affectionate remembrances to your wife, believe me, my dear Bancroft,

Always faithfully your friend,

WM. H. PRESCOTT.

TO LADY LYELL.

BOSTON, April 6, 1858.

MY DEAR LADY LYELL,

Susan wrote you last week an account of my apoplectic troubles, in which you take so affectionate an interest. The attack was one wholly unexpected by me, for I had nothing about me except the headaches of last year, which looked in that direction. I am not a plethoric, red-visaged gentleman, with a short neck and a portly paunch "with good capon lined," seeming to invite the attack of such an enemy. Nor am I yet turned of seventy, much less of eighty, when he takes advantage of decayed strength to fall upon his superannuated victim. But the fiend is no respecter of persons or ages. Yet I must acknowledge he has dealt rather kindly with me. The blow caused some consternation in my little circle, by sending my wits a wool-gathering for a few days. But they have gradually come to order again, and the worst thing that now remains is the *anchoritish* fare of pulse and water on which they have put me. Probably owing to this meagre diet more than to the disease, I have been somewhat reduced in strength. But as the doctor has now reinforced my banquet with a couple of glasses of sherry, I look confidently to regaining my former vigor, and gradually resuming my historical labors, — amusements I should say, for the hardest thing to do is to do nothing. We are made happy now by the return of Amory, who is soon to be followed by William and his family, who will make one household with us this summer at Lynn. It is a pleasant reunion to look forward to after our long separation. . . . . .

MEMORANDA.

April 18th, 1858. — More than five months since the last entry. During the first three I wrote text and notes of Book VI., Chapters I. and II., in all eighty-five pages print. On the 4th of February I had a slight apoplectic shock, which affected both sight and power of motion, the last but for a few moments.

The attack — so unexpected, though I had been troubled with head-aches through the winter, in a less degree, however, than in the preceding year — caused great alarm to my friends at first. Much reason have I to be grateful that the effects have gradually disappeared, and left no traces now, except a slight obscurity in the vision, and a certain degree of weakness, which may perhaps be imputable to my change of diet. For I have been obliged to exchange my carnivorous propensities for those of a more innocent and primitive nature, picking up my fare as our good parents did before the fall. In this way it is thought I may defy the foul fiend for the future. But I must not make too heavy or long demands on the cranium, and if I can get three or four hours' work on my historic ground in a day, I must be content.

TO MR. PARSONS.[*]

Boston, April 20, 1858.

Dear Theoph.,

I return you the vegetarian treatise, with many thanks. It furnishes a most important contribution to kitchen literature. From the long time I have kept it, you might think I have been copying the receipts. I marked some for the purpose, but soon found them so numerous, that I concluded to send to London for the book itself. I shall receive a copy in a few days. I was very sorry to hear that you had wounded yourself with a pruning-knife, and I trust long before this you have got over the effects of it. This is an accident that cannot befall me. The more's the pity. I wish with all my heart I could get up a little horticultural gusto, if it were only for multiplying and varying the pleasures of life.

God bless you, dear Theoph. Believe me, always affectionately yours,

WM. H. PRESCOTT.

TO LADY LYELL.

Boston, May 31, 1858.

My dear Lady Lyell,

It was a loving remembrance in you, that of my birthday. It shows you have a good memory, at least for your friends. Threescore years and two is a venerable age, and should lead one to put his house in order, es-

---

[*] This note needs a little explanation, and I will give it in the words of the friend to whom it is addressed. He says: "I had been advised to eat mainly vegetable food; and, noticing among the advertisements of London books one of a vegetarian cookery-book, I ordered it; and, when Prescott told me that he was strictly limited to a vegetable diet, I sent it to him."

pecially after such a thump on the cranium as I have had. I hope I shall round off threescore years and ten, at least, before I get another. I was greatly cheered the other day by finding in a biographical account of Adam Ferguson, that, after a severe paralytic shock at fifty, he survived on a vegetable diet to ninety-three, and wrote books, too, which people still continue to read. Indeed, it was thought that his vegetable fare served rather to clarify his wits. It is a very watery diet at any rate, better suited, I should say, to moral philosophy than to carnivorous history. Ferguson, however, wrote both.

I suppose in giddy London you don't get time to read much, that is, in the London season. Have you met with Bancroft's last volume, published at the beginning of the present month? It is occupied with a topic very interesting to us Yankees, and, in the closing chapters, does honor, of which it has been too long defrauded, to my grandfather, Colonel Prescott's memory. The book is written with spirit, but it is a pity he has not supported his story by a single note or reference. The reader must take it all on the writer's word. And yet his original materials are ample.

I suppose you have read Buckle; indeed, Anna Ticknor told me that you liked him much. I am sure your husband must relish his acute and liberal-minded speculations, and especially the intrepidity with which he enters upon fields of discussion on which English writers are apt to tread so daintily, not to say timidly. He doubts in the true spirit of a philosopher. And yet he dogmatizes in a style the most opposed to philosophy. He would make a more agreeable impression if, with his doubts, he would now and then show a little doubt of himself. But whatever defects of manner he may have, I suppose few readers will deny that his big volume is the book of the age.

I dined with the Ticknors last week; a quiet little meeting of only two or three guests. Everett, who was there, was in good trim. His Washington address, with its concomitants, has done as much for him as for the Monument, by building him up. I have not seen him in so good condition for a long while. . . . . . .

TO MADAME CALDERON.

LYNN, September 7, 1858.

MY DEAR MADAME CALDERON,

It is very long since I have exchanged a kindly greeting with you across the waters, — not since your return to Spain. I have kept some knowledge of your whereabouts, however, but not as much as I could desire, which nobody can give but yourself, — where you have been, where you are now staying, what you are doing. Is my good friend Calderon still coquetting with politics? Or is he living at ease, letting the world go by, like an honest cavalier, as I do? I hope, at all events, that both you and he are in good health, and in the enjoyment of all the happiness that this world can give. You will tell me something about all this when you write, won't you? For myself, I have been very well of late, though, during the last winter, in February, I experienced, what was little expected, an apoplectic attack. It alarmed my friends a good deal, and frightened me out of my wits for a time. But the effects have gradually passed off, leaving me only a slight increase of the obscurity in my vision. As I don't intend the foul fiend shall return again, I live upon vegetables and farinaceous matter, like the anchorites of old. For your apoplexy is a dangerous fellow, who lives upon good cheer, fat and red-faced gentlemen, who feed upon something better than beets and carrots. I don't care about the fare, but I should be sorry not to give the last touches to Philip the Prudent, and to leave him in the world in a dismembered condition! I am amusing myself now with putting through the press the third volume. This will make three fifths of the whole work. Five volumes are as heavy a load as posterity will be willing to take upon its shoulders; and I am ambitious enough to consign my wares to posterity. The book will make its appearance in December, and will give you and Calderon some winter evenings' readings, if you are not too much absorbed in the affairs of the public to have time for private matters. I am just now occupied with making some notes and corrections for a new edition of the "Conquest of Mexico." I have particularly good materials for this in the two Mexican translations of it, one of them having Alaman's notes, and the other those of Ramirez. I know very little about these eminent scholars, though I have somewhere a notice which was sent me of Alaman, put away so carefully and so long ago that I doubt if I can lay my hands on it. Could you not give me some little account of these two worthies, — of the offices they hold, their social position, and general estimation? Ramirez somewhere remarks that he belongs to the old Mexican race. This explains the difference of his views on some points from Alaman's, who has a true love for the "Conquistadores." On the whole, it is a trial, which few historians have experienced, to be subjected to so severe a criticism, sentence by sentence, of two of the most eminent scholars of their country. Though they have picked many holes in my finery, I cannot deny that they have done it in the best spirit and in the most courtly style. . . . . .

TO THE EARL OF CARLISLE.

BOSTON, December 27, 1858.

MY DEAR CARLISLE,

My eye was caught by the sight of your name this morning, as I was running over the columns of my daily paper, and I read an extract from a late address of yours at Hull, not so complimentary as I could have wished to my own country. The tone of remark, differing a good deal from the usual style of your remarks on us, is, I fear, not undeserved. The more 's the pity. I send you the extracts, for, as I suppose you intended it for our edification as well as for your own countrymen, I thought you might be pleased to see that it was quoted here. At any rate, I imagine you will be gratified with the candid and liberal style in which it is received. The Boston "Daily Advertiser" is one of our most respectable journals, and I may add that the opinions expressed in it perfectly coincide with those of several well-informed persons who have spoken to me on the matter, and for whose judgment you would entertain respect.

I am not willing, any more than the editor is, to agree with you in your desponding views as to the destinies of our country, and I should mourn for my race if I thought that the grand experiment we are making of the capacity of men for self-government should prove a failure. We must not be too hastily judged. We are a young people, and have been tried by the severest of all trials, uninterrupted prosperity; a harder trial than adversity for a nation as well as for an individual. We have many men of high intelligence as well as sound principle in the country, and, should exigencies arise to call them into action, I cannot doubt that they would take the place of the vaporing politicians who have been allowed too much to direct the affairs of the republic.

I have just come out with a third volume of "Philip the Second," and I hope ere this you have received a copy which I directed my publisher, Routledge, to send you at once.

Should he not have done so, you will oblige me much by advertising me of it, as I wish you to have all my literary bantlings from my own hand. I have done myself the pleasure also to send a copy to the Duchess and Lady Mary. I trust that you and yours are all in good health.

This reminds me of a blank in your circle, one dear and revered name, which I never omitted when I wrote to you. She has gone to a better world than this. I must thank you for sending me, through Everett, the miniature photograph of her, surprisingly like, considering the size. Pray remember me kindly to the Duchess and to Lady Mary, when you see them. My son and daughter desire their kindest remembrances to you, with which, believe me, my dear friend, always

Affectionately yours,

WM. H. PRESCOTT.

TO LADY LYELL.

BOSTON, January 10, 1859.

MY DEAR LADY LYELL,

I must not let another packet go without thanking you for the friendly invitation given by you and your husband to Susan and myself to visit you this spring; and although it will not be in our power to accept it, you will believe that we are not the less grateful to the loving hearts which dictated it. You, who put a girdle round the earth in as little time almost as Puck, can have no idea of the way in which we have struck our roots in the soil, as immovable as the great tree on the Common. As to my wife, a voyage to the moon would not be more chimerical in her eyes than a trip (as they pleasantly call it) across the Atlantic. She will die, without ever having got so far as New York. I do hope, however, that we are not destined never to meet again, though I think it must be in your husband's pursuit after science. The book of nature is a big one, and there are some pages in it on American antiquities which he has not yet read, I suppose. At all events, I hope we shall meet again in this lower world, before we get to the land of spirits. We should like to see each other in the form to which we have been accustomed, not in the guise of a shadow, or of a flickering flame, as Dante put his loving souls into the Inferno. Such a meeting would be only of the voice, without even a friendly grasp of the hand, to make the heart beat. It would be like a talk between friends, after a long absence on the different sides of a partition to divide them. Yet if we don't meet before long, I don't know, but I should rather postpone the interview till we have crossed the Styx. But you, I am told, are reversing the order of nature. I wonder where you got your recipe for it. Yet the youth of the body is, after all, easier to preserve than the youth of the soul. I should like a recipe for that. Life is so stale when one has been looking at it for more than sixty winters! It would be a miracle if the blood were not a little chilled. . . . . .

FROM MR. IRVING.

SUNNYSIDE, January 12, 1859.

MY DEAR MR. PRESCOTT,

I cannot thank you enough for the third volume of your "Philip," which you have had the kindness to send me. It came most opportunely to occupy and interest me when rather depressed by indisposition. I have read with great interest your account of the Rebellion of the Moriscoes, which took me among the Alpuxarras mountains, which I once traversed with great delight. It is a sad story, the trampling down and expulsion of that gallant race from the land they won so bravely and cultivated and adorned with such industry, intelligence, and good taste. You have done ample justice to your subject.

The battle of Lepanto is the splendid picture of your work, and has never been so admirably handled.

I congratulate you on the achievement of the volume, which forms a fine variety from the other parts of your literary undertakings.

Giving you my best wishes that you may go on and prosper, I remain, my dear Mr. Prescott,

Yours ever truly and heartily,

WASHINGTON IRVING.

WM. H. PRESCOTT, ESQ.

FROM LORD MACAULAY.*

HOLLY LODGE, KENSINGTON, January 8, 1859.

MY DEAR SIR,

I have already delayed too long to thank you for your third volume It is excellent, and, I think, superior to anything that you have written, parts of the "History of the Conquest of Mexico" excepted. Most of those good judges whose voices I have been able to collect, at this dead time of the year, agree with me. This is the season when, in this country, friends interchange good wishes. I do not know whether that fashion has crossed the Atlantic. Probably not, for your Pilgrim Fathers held it to be a sin to keep Christmas and Twelfth Day. I hope, however, that you

* This letter Mr. Prescott never had the pleasure of reading. It arrived a few days after his death.

will allow me to express my hope that the year which is beginning may
be a happy one to you.

Ever yours truly,

MACAULAY.

WM. H. PRESCOTT, ESQ., &c., &c.

TO SIR CHARLES LYELL.

BOSTON, January 23, 1859.

MY DEAR SIR CHARLES,

I have had the pleasure of receiving your friendly letter of December
31st, and must thank you for another, in which you so kindly invited my
wife and me to visit you in England. Nothing, you may well believe,
could give her and myself greater pleasure than to pass some time under
your hospitable roof, which would afford me the inexpressible satisfaction
of taking some friends again by the hand, whose faces I would give much
to see. But I have long since abandoned the thought of crossing the great
water, and the friends on the other side of it are, I fear, henceforth to find
a place with me only in the pleasures of memory. And pleasant recollections they afford to fill many an hour which the world would call idle, for
there is neither fame nor money to be made out of them. But one who
has crossed sixty (how near are you to that ominous line?) will have
found out that there is something of more worth than fame or money in
this world. I was last evening with Agassiz, who was in capital spirits at
the prospect of opening to the public a project of a great museum, for
which Frank Gray, as I suppose you know, left an appropriation of fifty
thousand dollars. There will be a subscription set on foot, I understand,
for raising a similar sum to provide a suitable building for the collection,
— a great part of which has already been formed by Agassiz himself, —
and the Governor, at a meeting of the friends of the scheme held the
other evening at James Lawrence's, gave the most cordial assurances of
substantial aid from the State. Agassiz expressed the greatest confidence
to me of being able in a few years to establish an institution, which would
not shrink from comparison with similar establishments in Europe. He
has been suffering of late from inflammation of the eyes, a trouble to
which he is unaccustomed, but for which he may thank his own imprudence. I am glad to learn that you are pursuing, with your usual energy,
your studies on Ætna. The subject is one of the greatest interest. I
must congratulate you on the reception of the Copley medal. However
we may despise, or affect to despise, the vulgar *volitare per ora*, it is a satisfaction to find one's labors appreciated by the few who are competent to
pronounce on their value.

Good by, my dear Lyell. With kindest remembrances to your wife,
believe me always faithfully yours,

WM. H. PRESCOTT.

This is the latest letter from my friend that has come to
my knowledge. Notes he continued to write afterwards. I
received several such down to within two or three days of his

death, and others, I doubt not, were sent to other persons in kindness or on business at the same period. In this and in all respects, he went on as usual. He seemed to himself to grow better and better, and was even in a condition to enjoy some of the pleasures of society. We had occasionally dined at each other's houses from the preceding spring, as he has noticed in his letters to Lady Lyell, already inserted; and, less than a week before his death, I was to have met a small party of friends at his own table. But a family affliction prevented his hospitality, and I was afterwards glad, as I well might be, that the dinner did not take place. Not that he would have failed in abstinence; but he was less strong than he believed himself to be, and less than we all hoped he was, so that the fatal blow then impending might, by the excitement of merely social intercourse, have fallen sooner than it otherwise would, or, at least, we might afterwards have believed that it had.

CHAPTER XXIX.

1859.

FROM day to day, after New Year of 1859, he seemed more to miss his old occupations. On the 27th of January, he talked decidedly of beginning again to work in good earnest on the "History of Philip the Second," and speculated on the question whether, if he should find his physical strength unequal to the needful exertion, he might venture to reinforce it by a freer diet. On the following morning — the fatal day — he talked of it again, as if his mind were made up to the experiment, and as if he were looking forward to his task as to the opening again of an old and sure mine of content. His sister, Mrs. Dexter, was happily in town making him a visit, and was sitting that forenoon with Mrs. Prescott in a dressing-room, not far from the study where his regular work was always done. He himself, in the early part of the day, was unoccupied, walking about his room for a little exercise; the weather being so bad that none ventured out who could well avoid it. Mr. Kirk, his ever-faithful secretary, was looking over Sala's lively book about Russia, "A Journey due North," for his own amusement merely, but occasionally reading aloud to Mr. Prescott such portions as he thought peculiarly interesting or pleasant. On one passage, which referred to a former Minister of Russia at Washington, he paused, because neither of them could recollect the name of the person alluded to; and Mr. Prescott, who did not like to find his memory at fault, went to his wife and sister to see if either of them could recall it for him. After a moment's hesitation, Mrs. Prescott hit upon it ; a circumstance which amused him not a little, as she so rarely took an interest in anything connected with public affairs, that he had rather counted upon Mrs. Dexter for the information. He snapped his fingers at her, therefore, as he turned away, and, with the merry laugh so characteristic of his nature, passed out of the room, saying, as he went, "How came *you* to remember?" They were the last words she ever heard from his loved lips.

After reaching his study, he stepped into an adjoining apartment. While there, Mr. Kirk heard him groan, and, hurrying to him, found him struck with apoplexy and wholly unconscious. This was about half past eleven o'clock in the forenoon. He was instantly carried to his chamber. In the shortest possible space of time, several medical attendants were at his bedside, and among them — and the chief of them — was his old friend and his father's friend, Dr. Jackson. One of their number, Dr. Minot, brought me the sad intelligence, adding his own auguries, which were of the worst. I hastened to the house. What grief and dismay I found there, needs not to be told. All saw that the inevitable hour was come. Remedies availed nothing. He never spoke again, never recovered an instant of consciousness, and at half past two o'clock life passed away without suffering.

He would himself have preferred such a death, if choice had been permitted to him. He had often said so to me and to others ; and none will gainsay, that it was a great happiness thus to die, surrounded by all those nearest and dearest to him, except one much-loved son, who was at a distance, and to die, too, with unimpaired faculties, and with affections not only as fresh and true as they had ever been, but which, in his own home and in the innermost circle of his friends, had seemed to grow stronger and more tender to the last.

Four days afterwards he was buried ; two wishes, however, having first been fulfilled, as he had earnestly desired that they should be. They related wholly to himself, and were as simple and unpretending as he was.

From accidental circumstances, he had always entertained a peculiar dread of being buried alive ; and he had, therefore, often required that measures should be taken to prevent all possibility of the horrors that might follow such an occurrence. His injunctions were obeyed. Of his absolute death it was not, indeed, permitted to doubt. It had occurred under circumstances which had been distinctly foreseen, and by a blow only too obvious, sure, and terrible. But still, as had been promised to him, a principal vein was severed, so that, if life should again be awakened, it might ebb silently away without any possible return of consciousness.

His other request was no less natural and characteristic. He desired that his remains, before they should be deposited in the house appointed for all living, might rest, for a time, in the cherished room where were gathered the intellectual treasures amidst which he had found so much of the happiness of his life. And this wish, too, was fulfilled. Silently, noiselessly, he was carried there. Few witnessed the solemn scene, but on those who did, it made an impression not to be forgotten. There he lay, in that rich, fair room, — his manly form neither shrunk nor wasted by disease; the features that had expressed and inspired so much love still hardly touched by the effacing fingers of death, — there he lay, in unmoved, inaccessible peace; and the lettered dead of all ages and climes and countries collected there seemed to look down upon him in their earthly and passionless immortality, and claim that his name should hereafter be imperishably associated with theirs.

But this was only for a season. At the appointed hour — his family, and none else, following — he was borne to the church where he was wont to worship. No ceremonies had been arranged for the occasion. There had been no invitations. There was no show. But the church was full, was crowded. The Representatives of the Commonwealth, then in session, had adjourned so as to be present; the members of the Historical Society, whose honored wish to take official charge of the duties of the occasion had been declined, were there as mourners. The whole community was moved; the poor whom he had befriended; the men of letters with whom he had been associated or whom he had aided; the elevated by place or by fortune, whose distinctions and happiness he had increased by sharing them; — they were all there. It was a sorrowful gathering, such as was never before witnessed in this land for the obsequies of any man of letters wholly unconnected, as he had been, with public affairs and the parties or passions of the time; — one who was known to most of the crowd collected around his bier only by the silent teachings of his printed works. For, of the multitude assembled, few could have known him personally; many of them had never seen him. But all came to mourn. All felt that an honor had been taken from the community and the country. They came because they felt the loss they had sustained, and only for that. And after the simple and solemn religious rites befitting the occasion had been performed,[1] they still crowded round the funeral train and through the streets, following, with sadness and awe, the hearse that was bearing from their sight all that remained of one who had been watched not a week before as he trod the same streets in apparent happiness and health. It was a grand and touching tribute to intellectual eminence and personal worth.

He was buried with his father and mother, and with the little daughter he had so tenderly loved, in the family tomb under St. Paul's Church; and, as he was laid down beside them, the audible sobs of the friends who filled that gloomy crypt bore witness to their love for his generous and sweet nature, even more than to their admiration for his literary distinctions, or to their sense of the honor he had conferred on his country.

Other expressions of the general feeling followed. The Massachusetts Historical Society; the Historical Societies of New York, of Pennsylvania, of Maryland, and of Illinois; the American Academy of Arts and Sciences; the American Antiquarian Society; the New England Genealogical Society; the Essex Institute, meeting on the spot where he was born; and the Boston Athenæum and Harvard College, with which, from his youth, he had been much connected, — each bore its especial and appropriate part in the common mourning. The multitudinous periodicals and newspapers of the country were filled with it, and the same tone was soon afterwards heard from no small portion of what is most eminent for

---

[1] By Mr. Prescott's clergyman, the Rev. Rufus Ellis, pastor of the First Congregational Church in Boston.

intellectual cultivation in Europe. There was no division of opinion. There was no dissentient, no hesitating voice, on either side of the Atlantic. All sorrowfully felt that a great loss had been sustained; that a brilliant and beneficent light had been extinguished.

APPENDIX.

18*

APPENDIX A.

THE PRESCOTT FAMILY.

(See p. 1.)

THE Prescott family belong to the original Puritan stock and blood of New England. They came from Lancashire, and about 1640, twenty years only after the first settlement at Plymouth and ten years after that of Boston, were established in Middlesex County, Massachusetts, where not a few of the honored race still remain.

Like most of the earlier emigrants, who left their native homes from conscientious motives, they were men of strongly marked characters, but of small estates, and devoted to mechanical and agricultural pursuits, — circumstances which fitted them as nothing else could so well have done for the trials and labors incident to their settlement in this Western wilderness. But, even among men like these, the Prescotts were distinguished from the first. They enjoyed, to an uncommon degree, the respect of the community which they helped to found, and became at once more or less concerned in the management of the entire Colony of Massachusetts, when those who took part in its affairs bore heavy burdens and led anxious lives.

John, the first emigrant, was a large, able-bodied man, who, after living some time in Watertown, established himself in Lancaster, then on the frontiers of civilization. There he acquired a good estate and defended it bravely from the incursions of the Indians, to whom he made himself formidable by occasionally appearing before them in a helmet and cuirass, which he had brought with him from England, where he was said to have served under Cromwell. His death is placed in 1683.

Of him are recorded by Mr. William Prescott, father of the historian, the following traditionary anecdotes, — given him by Dr. Oliver Prescott, — which may serve, at least, to mark the condition of the times when he lived.

"He brought over," says Mr. Prescott, "a coat of mail-armor and habiliments, such as were used by field-officers of that time. An aged lady informed Mr. Oliver Prescott[1] that she had seen him dressed in this armor. Lancaster (where Mr. Prescott established himself) was a frontier town, much exposed to the incursions of the Indians. John was a sturdy, strong man, with a stern countenance, and, whenever he had a difficulty with the Indians, clothed himself with his coat of armor, — helmet, cuirass, and gorget, — which gave him a fierce and frightful appearance. It is

---

[1] Born in 1731, and died in 1804.

related, that when, on one occasion, they stole a valuable horse from him, he put on his armor and pursued them, and after some time overtook the party that had his horse. They were surprised to see him alone, and one of the chiefs approached him with his tomahawk uplifted. John told him to strike, which he did, and, finding the blow made no impression on his cap, he was astonished, and asked John to let him put it on, and then to strike on his head, as he had done on John's. The helmet was too small for the Indian's head, and the weight of the blow settled it down to his ears, scraping off the skin on both sides. They gave him his horse, and let him go, thinking him a supernatural being.

" At another time the Indians set fire to his barn. Old John put on his armor and rushed out upon them. They retreated before him, and he let his horses and cattle out of the burning stable. At another time they set fire to his saw-mill. The old man armed cap-à-pied, went out, drove them off, and extinguished the fire."

Jonas, a son of the first emigrant, was born in 1648, and died in 1723, seventy-five years old. He lived in Groton. He was a captain of the yeomanry militia, at a time when the neighborhood of the savages made such a post important to the safety of the country ; and he was a justice of the peace when that office, also, implied a degree of consideration and authority now unknown to it.

Benjamin, one of the sons of Jonas, was born January 4, 1695 – 6. He represented his native town many years in the General Court of the Colony, was a colonel in the militia of his own county, and of the adjoining county of Worcester, and in the year before his death, which occurred in 1738, was delegated to the important service of defending the territorial rights of Massachusetts against the claims of New Hampshire, before a royal commission appointed to adjudge the case.[a]

Benjamin had three sons, each of whom distinguished himself in the line of life he had chosen.

The eldest, James, remained on the family estate at home, and cultivated and managed it. He passed through all the degrees of military rank, from that of an ensign to that of colonel. He represented Groton, for a long period, in the General Court, and was afterwards in the Colonial Governor's Council. At the outbreak of the Revolution, taking the popular side, he became a member of the Provincial Congress and of the Board of War, and, after the peace of 1783, was successively sheriff of the county and Judge of the Court of Common Pleas. He died, more than seventy-nine years old, in 1800, at Groton, where the family had then been settled above a century.

Oliver, the youngest son of Benjamin, was born in 1731. He was graduated at Harvard College in 1750, and became subsequently an eminent physician in Groton and its neighborhood. But, like others of his family, he turned to public affairs, both military and civil. In 1777, and for several years afterwards, he was of the Governor's Council, and in 1778 he became one of the major-generals in the service of the Commonwealth. A

[a] This has sometimes been otherwise stated, but the record leaves no doubt upon the matter. See Journal of the House of Representatives, August 12th, and October 13th, 1737.

severe illness in 1781 somewhat impaired his activity, and the same year he was appointed Judge of Probate for his native county of Middlesex, an office which he held, to the great acceptance of all, till his death. He, however, never ceased to be interested in his original profession, and, besides other marks of distinction for his medical knowledge, he received in 1791 the degree of Doctor in Medicine, *honoris causâ*, from Harvard College. He died in 1804, leaving several sons, the oldest of whom, Oliver, delivered an address before the Massachusetts Medical Society in 1813, on the *Secale cornutum* or *ergot*, which was found so important in relation to the use of that remedy, that, besides being reprinted in this country and in London, it was translated into French and German, and inserted in the thirteenth volume of the *Dictionnaire des Sciences Médicales*. He died at Newburyport in 1827.

William, the second son of Benjamin, and grandfather of the historian, was of a more bold and enterprising nature than his brother James, and has left a name which will not be forgotten. He was born in Groton on the 20th of February, 1726; but, in a spirit of adventure common throughout New England at that period, and not yet unknown, he preferred to remove farther into the land and establish himself in the primeval forest. This he did, before he was of age. But it was not necessary for him to go far. He removed only a few miles, and afterwards, when he had served as a soldier, caused the land on a part of which he had settled to be made a township, naming it after Sir William Pepperell, who had just then so much distinguished himself by the capture of Louisbourg. Pepperell is in the upper part of the county of Middlesex, just on the line of the State, and next to the town of Hollis, which is in New Hampshire. There, not above a mile from the border, he always lived, — or at least he always had his only home there, — holding his estate, as his great-grandson continues to hold it still in 1862, under the original Indian title. The Indians, indeed, long continued to be his near neighbors; so near, that there were periods of anxiety, during which those who went to the field with the plough did not feel safe unless their rifles stood leaning against the neighboring trees.

This was a rude training, no doubt; and living, as he did, among the savages, an unmarried man, it seems early to have given him soldierlike habits and tastes. At any rate, when he was twenty-seven years old, he was a lieutenant in the militia, and at twenty-nine, in the true spirit of adventure, entered, with the same rank, the regular service in the Colonial troops sent to remove the French from Nova Scotia. This was in 1755. But the service was a short, and not an agreeable one. On his return home, therefore, he left the army, and married Abigail Hale, a descendant, like himself, of the original Puritan stock of the country. It was a fortunate connection for the young soldier, who now seemed to have settled down on his farm for a peaceful and happy life, retaining only so much of his military tastes as was implied by accepting the command of the yeomanry of his neighborhood.

But troublesome times soon followed, and a spirit like his was sure to be stirred by them. This he early permitted to be seen and known. In August, 1774, he counselled his assembled townsmen to stand by the men of Boston in their resistance to the unjust and unconstitutional claims of the royal authority, and embodied their thoughts and purposes in a fervent letter which is still extant. "Be not dismayed," he said, "nor disheartened in this day of great trials. We heartily sympathize with you, and are always ready to do all in our power for your support, comfort, and relief, knowing that Providence has placed you where you must stand the first shock. We consider, we are all embarked in one bottom, and must sink or swim together."[3] Soon afterwards, in 1775, being recognized as a good soldier, who in Nova Scotia had become familiar with the discipline of a camp, and being, besides, no less known for his political firmness, he was made colonel of a regiment of minute-men, who, as their name implies, were to be ready at a moment's warning for any revolutionary emergency. It was a duty he loved, and it was not long before his courage and firmness were put to the test.[4]

On the 19th of April, 1775, within an hour after the news reached him of the skirmishes at Lexington and Concord, he hurried to Groton, and, collecting as many of his men as he could muster, and leaving orders for the rest to follow, marched to Cambridge, hoping to overtake the British troops; then in full retreat towards Boston. This, however, was impossible. But a force, full of the active and devoted spirit of the time, was rapidly collected at Cambridge, under the command of General Artemas Ward. By his orders, Colonel Prescott was despatched on the evening of June the 16th, with about a thousand men, to Charlestown, where, in the course of the night, he threw up a redoubt on Bunker's Hill, — or to speak more accurately on Breed's Hill, — and fought there, the next day, the first real battle of the Revolution, manfully putting in peril that reputation, which, to a soldier, is dearer than life, and which, if the cause he then espoused had failed, would have left his own name and that of his descendants blackened with the charge of rebellion. But things did not

[3] Bancroft's "History of the United States," Vol. VII. (Boston 1858), p. 99. This is the document already alluded to, (ante, p. 403, note,) as sent by Mr. Bancroft to Mr. Prescott the historian.

[4] Two circumstances in relation to this commission are worth notice. The first is, that, with a disregard to exactness not uncommon in times of great peril, the month and day of the month when the commission was issued are not given. The other is, that the President of "the Congress of the Colony of the Massachusetts Bay" who signed it is General Joseph Warren, who fell a few days later on Bunker Hill; and the justice of the peace before whom, on the 26th of May, 1775, Colonel Prescott took the oath of allegiance, was Samuel Dexter, one of the leading men of the Colony, — the grandfather of Mr. Franklin Dexter, who, nearly half a century later, married a granddaughter of the same Colonel Prescott, — a man of severe integrity, and of an original, strong, uncompromising character, who, during the short period in which his health allowed him to occupy himself with political affairs, exercised no small influence in the troubled commonwealth. A notice of him, by his son, the eminent lawyer, who died in 1816, may be found in the "Monthly Anthology" for 1810. Mr. Dexter, the elder, was the founder of the Dexter Lectureship of Biblical Literature in Harvard College. At the time when he signed the commission of Colonel Prescott, he was a member of the Provincial Congress. Colonel Prescott, it should be noted, served as colonel before he took the oath, namely, as early as the month of April.

so turn out. He was, indeed, defeated, — mainly for want of ammunition, — and driven from the hill, which he was among the last to leave. A brave resistance, however, had been made, and the defeat had many of the results of a victory. When Washington heard of it, he exclaimed, "The liberties of the country are safe"; [5] and Franklin wrote, "England has lost her Colonies forever." [6]

Colonel Prescott continued in the army until the end of 1776, [7] when, on the retirement of the American troops from Long Island, the excellent manner in which he brought off his regiment was publicly commended by General Washington. But from this period until his death, except during the autumn of 1777, when, as a volunteer with a few of his former brother-officers, he assisted in the capture of Burgoyne at Saratoga, he resided on his farm in Pepperell. He did not, however, withdraw himself entirely from public affairs. He served as a Representative in the Legislature of Massachusetts, and when the formidable insurrection known as "Shays's Rebellion" broke out in his own county of Middlesex, he hastened to Concord and assisted in protecting the courts of justice, and in preserving law and order. He died on the 13th of October, 1795, and was buried with the military honors becoming his life and character. His widow, an admirable person, full of gentleness and dignity, survived him many years, and died in 1821, at the advanced age of eighty-eight.

They had but one child, William, who was born on his father's farm, August the 19th, 1762, and lived there, in great simplicity, until 1776. His early education was entirely due to his mother, for whom he always felt a deep reverence, and of whom, late in his own life, he said: "She was more remarkable, than any one I have ever known, for her power of governing children and young people, and that without any austerity in her manner. They all respected, loved, and obeyed her. Her kindness won their hearts. I feel that I am indebted to her wise and affectionate government and guidance of my childhood and youth, — her daily counsels and instructions, — for whatever character and success I may have had in life." Considering what Mr. Prescott had become when he wrote these words, a more beautiful tribute could hardly have been paid to womanly tenderness and wisdom.

But, at the age of fourteen, he was placed under the instruction of "Master Moody," of Dummer Academy, in Essex County, then known as the best teacher of Latin and Greek in New England, and — what was of no less consequence to his pupils — wholly devoted to his duties, which he loved passionately. Nearly three years of careful training under such an instructor almost changed the boy to a man, and four years more at Harvard College, where he was graduated in 1783, completed the transformation.

But as he approached manhood, he felt the responsibilities of life

[5] Irving's "Life of Washington" (1855). Vol. I. p. 488.

[6] The last words of Vol. VII. of Bancroft's "History of the United States" (1858).

[7] His commission in the army of "The United Colonies," signed by John Hancock, President, and Charles Thomson, Secretary, is dated January 1, 1776, and constitutes him Colonel of the "Seventh Regiment of Foot." .

already crowding upon him. The first of these, and probably the one that pressed heaviest upon his thoughts, was the idea that, for the seven preceding years, he had been a burden upon the small means of his father, when he might rather have been a relief. This state of things he determined at once should no longer continue, and, from that moment, he never received any pecuniary assistance from his family. On the contrary, after the death of his father, whose life, like that of most military men of his time, had been one of generous hospitality, rather than of thrift, he assumed the debts with which the estate had become encumbered, and, for above a quarter of a century, made the most ample and affectionate arrangements for the support of his much-loved mother, who thus died in peace and happiness on the spot where she had lived above sixty years.

His earliest resource, when he began the world for himself, was one then common among us, and still not very rare, for young men who have left college without the means necessary to continue their education further. He became a teacher. At first, it was for a few months only, in Brooklyn, Connecticut; but afterwards for two years in Beverly, Massachusetts. Here he lived very happily in a cultivated society, and here he studied his profession under Mr. Dane, a learned jurist and statesman, who afterwards founded the Law Professorship in Harvard College that bears his name. During this period Mr. Prescott received an invitation to become a member of General Washington's household, where, while pursuing his legal studies, he would have acted as the private tutor of a youthful member of the family, to whom its great head was much attached. But the young law-student declined the offer, in consequence of his previous engagements, and his college classmate, Lear, took the coveted place.

Mr. Prescott began the practice of his profession in Beverly; but, at the end of two years, in 1789, finding the field there not wide enough for his purposes, he removed to the adjacent town of Salem, the shire town of the county, and the seat of much prosperous activity. His success, from the first, was marked and honorable, and it continued such so long as he remained there. During a part of the time, he entered a little, but only a little, into political life, serving successively as a Representative of Salem and as a Senator for the county of Essex in the Legislature of the State. But, although he took no selfish interest in the success of any party, he maintained then, as he did till his death, the opinions of the Federalists, who received their name from an early and faithful support of the Federal Constitution, and who subsequently devoted themselves to sustaining the policy and measures of Washington during his civil administration of the affairs of the country. In truth, however, while Mr. Prescott lived in Salem, he gave himself up almost exclusively to his profession, in which his talents, his integrity, and his industry gained for him so high a rank, that, as early as 1806, he was offered a seat on the bench of the Supreme Court of the Commonwealth; an offer repeated with much urgency in 1813, but one which, on both occasions, he declined, partly from the state of his family, but chiefly from considerations connected with his health. His refusal occasioned no little regret; for it was a place to which he was admirably adapted by the judicial character of his mind, by his moral courage, and by a singular power he had of holding any subject under advisement until the last moment, and then deciding it as promptly and firmly as if he had never hesitated.

But from 1803, when he ruptured a blood-vessel in his lungs, and was compelled, in consequence, to give up all severe occupation for many months, he was never an active or vigorous man. To relieve himself, therefore, from a kind of business which was quite as onerous as it was profitable, and which made his life in Salem more burdensome than he could well bear, he determined, in 1808, to remove to Boston. He did so, however, with reluctance. He had many kind friends in Salem, to whom he and his family were sincerely attached. He had passed there nineteen years of great professional usefulness, enjoying the respect of a very intelligent and thriving community. He had been happy much beyond the common lot, and he was by no means without misgivings at the thought of a change so important and decisive.

His removal, however, proved fortunate beyond his hopes. His professional business in Boston, while it was less oppressive than his business in Salem had been, insured him immediately an increased and ample income. Into public affairs he entered little, and only so far as his duty plainly required ; for political life was never agreeable to him, and, besides this, it interfered with his professional labors and the domestic repose he always loved and needed. But from 1809 he served for a few years in the Council of the Commonwealth, under Governor Gore and Governor Strong, and enjoyed all the confidence of those eminent and faithful magistrates, as they enjoyed all his. In 1814 he was elected, by the Legislature of Massachusetts, to be one of the delegates to the Convention which, in that year, met at Hartford, in Connecticut, to consider the condition of the New England States, exposed and neglected as they were by the general government, during the war then carrying on against Great Britain. It was inconvenient and disagreeable to him to accept the office. But he had no doubt that he ought to do it. Nor did he ever afterwards regret it, or fail to do justice to the honorable and high-minded men who were associated with him in its duties.

He went to that remarkable Convention, fearing, unquestionably, from the great excitement which then prevailed throughout New England on the subject of the war, that rash measures, tending to affect the integrity of the Union, might be suggested. But he was present through the whole session, and found his apprehensions entirely groundless. "No such measure," he said, "was ever proposed in the Convention, nor was there," in his opinion deliberately recorded long afterwards, "a member of that body who would have consented to any act, which, in his judgment, would have tended directly or indirectly to destroy or impair the union of the States." If there was ever a man loyal to the constitution and laws under which he lived, it was Mr. Prescott ; nor did he deem any one of his associates at Hartford, in this respect, less faithful than himself.

In 1818 he was appointed Judge of the Court of Common Pleas for the City of Boston, and accepted the office, thinking to hold it so as to facilitate his retirement from the practice of his profession. But he found it more laborious and engrossing than he had anticipated, and resigned it at the end of a year.

In 1820 – 21 he served as a delegate from the city of Boston to the

Convention for revising the Constitution of the Commonwealth of Massachusetts, and, on its first organization, was made chairman of the committee charged with the most difficult and perplexing subject that was submitted to that body for discussion and decision, — the representation of the people in their own government. It was not an enviable post; but, by his wisdom and moderation, by an energy and a firmness that were still always conciliating, and by a power of persuasion that rested on truth, he at last led the Convention to a decision, although, at one critical moment, it had seemed impossible to decide anything. The members of that body, therefore, as distinguished for talent and for personal character as any that was ever assembled in Massachusetts, always felt — even those who had differed from him — that they and the Commonwealth were under lasting obligations to his wisdom and integrity.

He continued at the bar until 1828, making in all above forty years of service to the law. During more than half of that time his practice was as extensive, as honorable, and as successful as that of any member of the profession in the State, which, while he belonged to it, numbered in its ranks such men as Sullivan, Parsons, Dexter, Otis, and Webster, all of whom, except the last, ceased to be members of the bar before he did. During the whole of his professional life he enjoyed, in an eminent degree, the kindly regard and sincere respect of his brethren, and of the different members of the courts before which he was called to practice, no one of whom ever, for a moment, imagined that any spot had fallen on the absolute purity and integrity of his character. Of his distinction as a jurist there was as little doubt. Mr. Daniel Webster, when, with much sensibility, he announced Mr. Prescott's death to the Supreme Court, then in session at Boston, well said of him, that "at the moment of his retirement from the bar of Massachusetts he stood at its head for legal learning and attainments."

The last sixteen years of his life were spent in the quietness of his home, where his original nature, disencumbered of the cares that had oppressed him during a very busy life, seemed to come forth with the freshness of youth. He read a great deal, especially on subjects connected with religion, ethics, metaphysics, and history, — all of them sciences of which he never tired. Agriculture, too, the occupation of some of his earlier days, had great charms for him; and he showed no little skill in cultivating the estate on which he was born, and where, during much of his life, and especially the latter part of it, he spent a happy portion of each year. But whether in the city, or at Pepperell, or on the seashore at Nahant, where, during many seasons, he passed the hottest weeks of our hot summers, he loved to be surrounded by his family, — his children and his grandchildren; and with them and among his private friends, he found in his declining years what, in the intervals of leisure during his whole life, he had most enjoyed and valued.

It was in this happy retirement that there broke in upon him the light which so gilded the mild evening of his days, — the success of his son as an historian, shedding new distinction on a name already dear to his country, and carrying that name far beyond the limits of the language spoken by all who had borne it before him. Mr. Prescott in the innermost circle of his friends never disguised the happiness his son's reputation gave him, although certainly, from the instinctive modesty of his nature, nothing could be more graceful than the way in which he expressed it.

But there is an end to everything earthly. In the autumn of 1843, while at his old home in Pepperell,[*] he had a slight attack of paralysis. He recovered from it, however, easily, and, except to the ever-watchful eyes of affection, seemed fully restored to his wonted health. But he himself understood the warning, and lived, though cheerfully and with much enjoyment of life, yet as one who never forgot that his time must be short, and that his summons could hardly fail to be sudden. In the last days of November, 1844, he felt himself slightly incommoded, — not, as before, in the head, but in the region of the heart. As late, however, as the evening before his death, no change was noticed in his appearance when he retired to bed, nor is it probable that, after a night of his usual comfortable rest, he noticed any change in himself when he rose the next morning. At any rate he went, as was his custom, quietly and directly to his library. But he had hardly reached it, when he perceived that the messenger of death was at his side. He therefore desired the faithful attendant, who had for many years been attached to his person, not to leave him, and a few moments afterwards, surrounded by the family he so much loved, in the full possession of his faculties, and with a peaceful trust in his Maker and in the blessedness of a future life, he expired without a struggle. It was Sunday, December the 8th, 1844, and on the following Wednesday he was buried in the crypt of St. Paul's Church.

While he was a young lawyer in Salem, Mr. Prescott was married, December 18th, 1793, to Catherine Greene Hickling, daughter o Thomas Hickling, Esq., earlier a merchant of Boston, but then, and subsequently until his death at the age of ninety-one, Consul of the United States in the island of St. Michael. It was a connection full of blessing to him and to his house during the fifty-one years that it pleased God to permit it to be continued. Few women have done more to relieve their husbands from the cares of life, and to bear for them even a disproportionate share of its burdens. Still fewer have, at the same time, made their influence felt abroad through society, as she did. But she was full of energy and activity, of health, cheerfulness, and the love of doing good. Probably no woman, in the position she occupied among us, ever gave her thoughts, her conversation, and her life in so remarkable a degree to the welfare of others. When, therefore, she died, May 17th, 1852, nearly eighty-five years old, it is not too much to say that her death was mourned as a public loss.[*]

Mr. and Mrs. Prescott had seven children, all of whom were born to them in Salem, between 1795 and 1806, but four died without reaching the age of a single year.

Of the other three the oldest was the historian.

The next was Catherine Elizabeth, who still survives (1862). She was born November 12th, 1799, and was married September 28th, 1819, to Franklin Dexter, son of Samuel Dexter, the eminent lawyer and statesman. Mr. Franklin Dexter was born in 1793, and, after a careful academical and professional education, and a visit to the most interesting and

* See *ante*, p. 190.   * See *ante*, p. 358.

cultivated portions of Europe, established himself as a lawyer in Boston. He rose early to distinction at the bar, and by his courage, his quickness of perception, his acute and manly logic, and an intellectual grasp which the strongest could not escape, he vindicated for himself a place in the front rank of a company of eminent men, such as New England had never before seen collected. But his tastes and his preferences led him into paths widely different from theirs. His mind turned instinctively to what was refined and beautiful. He loved letters more than law, and art more than letters; so that, perhaps without deliberately intending it, he always sought much of his happiness in both, and found it. When, therefore, he had reached an age at which, with a constitution of only moderate vigor, repose became desirable, and had obtained a fortune equal to the wants of one who never over-estimated the worth of what the world most desires, he gave himself more and more to the happiness of domestic life and to the pursuit of art, towards which, from an early period, he had — and perhaps rightly — thought his genius more inclined than to any other. But life was not long protracted. He died in 1857, leaving behind him in the minds of his contemporaries a persuasion, that, if his severe taste in what related even to his favorite pursuits, and the fastidious acuteness with which he looked quite through the ways of men, and detected the low motives which often lead to power, had not checked him in mid-career, he might have risen to an eminence where he would have left behind him not a few of the rivals to whom, during the active years of his life, he had willingly yielded the honors of success.

The only brother of the historian who lived beyond infancy was Edward Goldsborough, who was born at Salem, January 2d, 1804. At a suitable age, after the removal of his father to Boston, he was sent to the same school in which his elder brother had laid the foundation for his distinction. But his tendencies were not then towards intellectual culture, and, at his own earnest desire, he was placed in a counting-house, that he might devote himself to mercantile pursuits. A taste for letters was, however, somewhat to his own surprise, awakened in him a little later; and, with sudden but earnest efforts to recover the time that had been lost, he succeeded in obtaining a degree at Harvard College in 1825. Subsequently, he studied law with his father, under the most favorable circumstances; and after 1828, when he began the practice of his profession, he not only took his fair share of the business of the time, but, as so many of his family before him had done, he served the Commonwealth both in its Legislature and in its military organization, rising to the rank of colonel in the militia. This seemed for a time to satisfy a nature too eager for excitement and distinction. But after seven years of great activity, a change came over him. He was grown weary of a busy, bustling life, full of temptations which he had not always effectually resisted. His religious convictions, which from his youth had been strong, if not constant, now became paramount. He was pained that he had not better obeyed them, and, after many struggles, he resolutely determined to give himself up to them entirely. And he did it. He began at once a course of regular studies for the ministry, and in 1837 was settled as an Episcopalian clergyman in a retired parish of New Jersey, where he devoted himself earnestly to the duties he had assumed. But his labors were severe, and his health failed under them; slowly, indeed, but regularly. Still, no anxiety was felt for the result; and when he determined to visit the Azores, where several of his mother's family, as we have seen, had long resided, he embarked with every promise that the mild climate of those Fortunate Isles would restore the impaired forces of his physical constitution, and permit him soon to resume the duties he loved. But on the second day out, a sudden attack — perhaps apoplectic and certainly one of which there had been no warning symptom — broke down his strength at once; and early the next morning, April 11th, 1844, he died without a movement of his person, like one falling asleep, his watch held gently in his hand, as if he had just been noting the hour.

After his settlement as a clergyman in New Jersey, he was married to an excellent and devoted wife, who survived him only a few years, but they had no children.

William Hickling Prescott, the historian, as it has already been recorded, has three surviving children, viz. : —

1. William Gardiner Prescott, born January 27, 1826, and named after his father's friend, William Howard Gardiner, Esq. He was married November 6, 1851, to Augusta, daughter of Joseph Augustus Peabody, Esq., of Salem, and they have four children, —
   Edith, born April 20, 1853,
   William Hickling, born February 22, 1855,
   Linzee, born November 27, 1859, .
   Louisa, born February 19, 1863.

2. Elizabeth Prescott, born July 27, 1828, and married, March 16, 1852, to James Lawrence, Esq., son of the late Hon. Abbott Lawrence, Minister of the United States at the Court of St. James from 1849 to 1853. They have three children, —
   James, born March 23, 1853,
   Gertrude, born February 19, 1855,
   Prescott, born January 17, 1861.

3. William Amory Prescott, born January 25, 1830, and named after his mother's brother and his father's friend, William Amory, Esq. He is unmarried (1862).

APPENDIX B.

THE CROSSED SWORDS.

(See p. 51.)

COLONEL WILLIAM PRESCOTT, the grandfather of the historian, died, as has been mentioned, in 1795. Captain John Linzee, grandfather of the historian's wife, was born at Portsmouth, England, in 1743, but, establishing himself in the United States after the war of the Revolution was over, died at Milton, near Boston, in 1798. In process of time, the swords of these two opposing commanders came by transmission and inheritance to the historian, and were by him arranged, first over one of the bookcases in his quiet study in Bedford Street, and afterwards on the cornice of his library in Beacon Street. In either place the sight was a striking one, and generally attracted the attention of strangers. Mr. Thackeray, whose vigilant eye did not fail to notice it when he visited Mr. Prescott in 1852, thus alludes to it very happily in the opening of his "Virginians," published six years later : —

"On the library-wall of one of the most famous writers of America there hang two crossed swords, which his relatives wore in the great war of Independence. The one sword was gallantly drawn in the service of the king, the other was the weapon of a brave and honored republican soldier. The possessor of the harmless trophy has earned for himself a name alike honored in his ancestors' country and in his own, where genius like his has always a peaceful welcome."

By the thirteenth article of Mr. Prescott's will he provided for the disposition of these swords as follows : —

"The sword which belonged to my grandfather, Colonel William Prescott, worn by him in the battle of Bunker Hill, I give to the Massachusetts Historical Society, as a curiosity suitable to be preserved among their collections ; and the sword which belonged to my wife's grandfather, Captain Linzee, of the British Royal Navy, who commanded one of the enemy's ship's lying off Charlestown during the same battle, I give to my wife."

As Mrs. Prescott, and the other heirs of Captain Linzee, desired that the swords should not be separated, Mr. Gardiner, who was Mr. Prescott's executor, sent them both to the Historical Society, accompanied by an interesting letter addressed to the Hon. Robert C. Winthrop, its President, and to be found, dated April 19th, 1859, in the volume of the "Proceedings" of that Society published in 1860, pp. 258 – 264.

Resolutions offered by Mr. Winthrop were unanimously adopted, directing the swords to be arranged in a conspicuous place in the halls of the Society, crossing each other, as they had been crossed in Mr. Prescott's library, and with suitable inscriptions setting forth their history and the circumstances of their reception.

A tablet of black-walnut was, therefore, prepared, to which they now stand attached, crossed through a carved wreath of olive-leaves ; while over them are two shields, leaning against each other, and bearing respectively the Prescott and the Linzee arms.

On the right, next to the hilt of Colonel Prescott's sword, is the following inscription :—

The sword
of
COLONEL WILLIAM PRESCOTT,
worn by him
while in command of the
Provincial forces
at the
Battle of Bunker Hill,
17 June, 1775,
and
bequeathed to the
Massachusetts Historical Society
by his grandson
WILLIAM H. PRESCOTT.

On the left, next to the hilt of Captain Linzee's sword, is the following inscription :—

The sword
of
CAPTAIN JOHN LINZEE, R. N.,
who commanded the
British sloop-of-war " Falcon "
while acting against the Americans
during the Battle of Bunker Hill,
presented to the
Massachusetts Historical Society,
14 April, 1859,
by his grandchildren
THOMAS C. A. LINZEE
and
MRS. WILLIAM H. PRESCOTT.

On two separate scrolls is the following inscription :—

These swords
for many years were hung crossed
in the library
of the late eminent historian
WILLIAM HICKLING PRESCOTT,
in token of
international friendship
and
family alliance.

They
are now preserved
in a similar position
by the
MASS. HISTORICAL SOCIETY,
in memory
of the associations
with which they will be
inseparably connected.

On the evening of Thursday, April 28, 1859, at a meeting of the Society, held at the house of its President, the Hon. Robert C. Winthrop, the Rev. Dr. N. L. Frothingham — who, at the special meeting of the Society, called together by the death of the historian, had in apt and beautiful words offered an affectionate tribute to the character of his friend and parishioner — read the following lines, which, in words no less apt and touching, give the poetical interpretation of

THE CROSSED SWORDS.

Swords crossed, — but not in strife!
The chiefs who drew them, parted by the space
Of two proud countries' quarrel, face to face
Ne'er stood for death or life.

Swords crossed, that never met
While nerve was in the hands that wielded them;
Hands better destined a fair family stem
On these free shores to set.

Kept crossed by gentlest hands!
Emblems no more of battle, but of peace;
And proof how loves can grow and wars can cease,
Their once stern symbol stands.

It smiled first on the array
Of marshalled books and friendliest companies;
And here, a history among histories,
It still shall smile for aye.

See that thou memory keep,
Of him the firm commander; and that other,
The stainless judge; and him our peerless brother, —
All fallen now asleep.

Yet more; a lesson teach,
To cheer the patriot-soldier in his course,
That Right shall triumph still o'er insolent Force:
That be your silent speech.

Oh, be prophetic too!
And may those nations twain, as sign and seal
Of endless amity, hang up their steel,
As we these weapons do!

The archives of the Past,
So smeared with blots of hate and bloody wrong,
Pining for peace, and sick to wait so long,
Hail this meek cross at last.

And so was fitly closed up the history of this singular trophy, if trophy that can be called which was won from no enemy, and which is a memento at once of a defeat that was full of glory, and of triumphs in the field of letters more brilliant than those in the fields of war.

APPENDIX C.

EXTRACTS FROM A LETTER ADDRESSED BY MR. ED-
MUND B. OTIS, FORMERLY MR. PRESCOTT'S SECRE-
TARY, TO MR. TICKNOR.

(See p. 217, note.)

BOSTON, June 4th, 1859.

My DEAR SIR,

I well recollect the first interview I had with the author of "Ferdinand
and Isabella." I visited him at his library in his father's house in Bedford Street, where he resided in the summer of 1841. I had previously
read his History, and had copied, when a Sophomore, several of the closing
chapters of the work, by way of a voluntary rhetorical exercise, as I admired the purity and beauty of his style, little thinking, at the time, that
it would be my fate to copy several volumes of his subsequent compositions. I had heard that he was blind; and, from the nature and amount
of his historical lore, I had expected to see an old gentleman, somewhat
the worse for wear. My surprise was very great when I was greeted by
a tall, handsome man, in the prime of life, who did not appear to me over
thirty years of age, although at that time he must have been about forty-
five. He seemed amused at the surprise, which I did not probably entirely
conceal, and asked me if I had not expected to find him halt, lame, and
maimed, as well as blind.

He was more strongly attracted, he told me, to civil than to literary
history, as his audience would be so much larger; — the literary historian,
necessarily, in a great measure, addressing himself to scholars, who may
alone be supposed to be deeply interested in his subject, and who alone
are competent to decide upon his merit, while the civil historian has the
world for his audience, and may interest every man who has civil or religious rights and liberties to study and defend. This was the substance
of the first conversation I ever had with Mr. Prescott, though, at this distance of time, I do not attempt to report his exact language.

Although he enjoyed the variety of a sea-shore, country, and city life,
there was a uniformity, regularity, and order in his mode and habit of
living, that I have never seen equalled by any other man. One day was
very much the counterpart of another; and I sometimes thought that he
had reduced life to such a system, and regulated his every action so much
by rule, that there was danger of merging volition in a mechanical, clock-
work existence, and losing liberty in the race for knowledge and fame.

19   D D

This regularity and uniformity of life were undoubtedly necessary for the preservation of his health, and the performance of his self-imposed literary tasks.

Mr. Prescott has given some account, in the Preface to his "History of the Conquest of Peru," and, I believe, in the Prefaces to his other works, of the nature and degree of his impaired vision, of his use of a noctograph or writing-case for the blind, and of the general duties of his secretary, with all of which you must be familiar; but perhaps it may not be without interest, if I give from memory a brief sketch of his mode of writing a chapter of history.

It was the habit of Mr. Prescott, as you are aware, to study the grand outlines of his subject, and to plan the general arrangement and proportions of his work, — classifying the various topics he would have to treat, and dividing them into books and chapters, — before studying them closely in detail, when preparing to compose a chapter. When he had decided upon the subject to be discussed, or events to be related, in a particular chapter, he carefully read all that portion of his authorities, in print and manuscript, bearing on the subject of the chapter in hand, using tables of contents and indices, and taking copious notes of each authority as he read, marking the volume and page of each statement for future reference. These notes I copied in a large, legible hand, so that, at times, he could read them, though more frequently I read them aloud to him, until he had impressed them completely on his memory. After this had been accomplished, he would occupy several days in silently digesting this mental provender, balancing the conflicting testimony of authorities, arranging the details of his narrative, selecting his ornaments, rounding his periods, and moulding the whole chapter in his mind, as an orator might prepare his speech. Many of his best battle-scenes, he told me, he had composed while on horseback. His vivid imagination carried him back to the sixteenth century, and he almost felt himself a Castilian knight, charging with Cortés, Sandóval, and Alvarado on the Aztec foe.

When he had fully prepared his chapter in his mind, he began to dash it off with rapidity by the use of his writing-case. As he did not see his paper when he wrote, he sometimes wrote twice over the same lines, which did not have a tendency to render them more legible. His usual fluency of composition was sometimes interrupted, not by a dearth, but by too great copiousness of expression, several synonymous phrases or parallel forms of speech presenting themselves at once. All these he wrote down, one after the other, in duplicate, to be weighed and criticised at leisure, not waiting to settle the difficulty at the time, fearing that by delay he might lose the ease of style which usually accompanies rapidity of composition. When beginning to describe a battle, he would often, to rouse his military enthusiasm, as he said, hum to himself his favorite air, "O give me but my Arab steed," &c.

As the sheets were stricken off, I deciphered them, and was ready to read them to him when he had finished the chapter. He was as cautious in correction as he was rapid in writing. Each word and sentence was carefully weighed, and subjected to the closest analysis. If found wanting in strength or beauty, it was changed and turned until the exact expression required was found, when he dictated the correction, which was made by me on his manuscript. He allowed nothing to remain, however beautiful in itself, which he did not think added to the beauty and strength of the whole. He hated fine writing, merely as fine writing. I have known him mercilessly to strike out several pages of beautiful imagery, which he believed on reflection had a tendency rather to weaken than enhance the effect he desired to produce.

After the chapter had been thus carefully corrected, I copied it in a large, heavy, pike-staff hand, that those who run might read. I had to acquire the hand for the occasion, and my practice in that line may account for my present legible, but somewhat inelegant chirography. When the chapter was copied in this large hand, Mr. Prescott re-perused and re-corrected it. He then read again my copy of the original notes that he had taken from the authorities on which he founded his chapter, and from them prepared the remarks, quotations, and references found in his footnotes, which were also usually rapidly stricken off with his writing-case, and copied by me in the same large, legible hand with the text. This copy was again and again carefully scrutinized and corrected by himself.

Mr. Prescott believed that an historian could not be too careful in guarding against inaccuracies. I recollect that, when he had finished the "History of the Conquest of Mexico," the whole manuscript was submitted to yourself for critical suggestions and corrections, the value of which he acknowledges in his Preface. When the manuscript was sent to press, before the plates were stereotyped, the printed sheets were sent to the author, for his final corrections, besides being subjected to the careful inspection of Mr. Nichols, the corrector of the Cambridge press, and to the sharp eye of Mr. Charles Folsom, whose critical acumen Mr. Prescott fully appreciated.

Mr. Prescott loved his books almost as he loved his children; he liked to see them well dressed, in rich, substantial bindings; and if one, by any accident, was dropped, "it annoyed him," he said jestingly, "almost as much as if a baby fell."

APPENDIX D.

LITERARY HONORS.

(See p. 224, note.)

FROM the time when, in 1838, Mr. Prescott's reputation "burst out into sudden blaze," literary honors of all kinds awaited him in profusion, both at home and abroad. I will give here a list of the more considerable of them in the order of time.

1838. Massachusetts Historical Society, Boston.
American Philosophical Society, Philadelphia.
Rhode Island Historical Society, Providence.
1839. Royal Academy of History, Madrid.
Royal Academy of Sciences, Naples.
American Antiquarian Society, Worcester, Mass.
New York Historical Society, New York city.
Georgia Historical Society, Savannah.
New Hampshire Historical Society, Concord.
1840. American Academy of Arts and Sciences, Boston.
Literary and Historical Society of Quebec.
1841. Herculaneum Academy, Naples.
Doctor of Laws, Columbia College, South Carolina.
1842. Kentucky Historical Society, Louisville.
1843. Doctor of Laws, Harvard College, Massachusetts.
Indiana Historical Society, Indianapolis.
1844. Maryland Historical Society, Baltimore.
National Institute, Washington, D. C.
1845. French Institute, Academy of Moral Sciences, Paris.
Royal Society of Berlin.
1846. New Jersey Historical Society, Princeton.
1847. Royal Society of Literature, London.
Society of Antiquaries, London.
New England Historic-Genealogical Society, Boston.
1848. Doctor of Laws, Columbian College, Washington, D. C.
1850. Doctor of Civil Law, Oxford, England.
1851. Mexican Society of Geography and Statistics, Mexico.
1852. Royal Irish Academy, Dublin.
1854. Wisconsin Historical Society, Madison.
1856. Historical Society of Florida, St. Augustine.
Historical Society of Iowa, Burlington.
1857. Historical Society of Tennessee, Nashville.

He received the honors of membership from several societies of young men in different parts of the country, two or three of which, like a debating-society at Cambridge, a literary association at Philadelphia, and one at Marysville, Kentucky, took his name. He was not insensible to such marks of regard from those who, in the coming generation, are to be a part of the voice of posterity.

APPENDIX E.

TRANSLATIONS OF MR. PRESCOTT'S HISTORIES.

I. SPANISH.

HISTORIA del Reinado de los Reyes Católicos, D. Fernando y Dª. Isabel, escrita en Inglés por William H. Prescott, traducida del Original por D. Pedro Sabau y Larroya. 4 tom. 8vo. Madrid, Rivadeneyra, 1845, 1846.

Historia de la Conquista de Méjico con una Reseña preliminar de la Civilizacion antigua Mejicana y la Vida del Conquistador, Hernan Cortés, escrita en Inglés por William Prescott (sic), y traducida del Original por D. J. B. de Beratarrechea. 3 tom. 8vo. Madrid, Rivadeneyra, 1847.

Historia de la Conquista de México con una Ojeada preliminar sobre la antigua Civilizacion de los Mexicanos y con la Vida de su Conquistador, Fernando Cortés. Escrita en Inglés por W. Prescott (sic), y traducida al Español por Joaquin Navarro. 3 tom. 8vo. México, impreso por Ignacio Cumplido, editor de esta Obra, 1844—6.

The second volume contains one hundred and twenty-four pages of notes on the whole work, by D. José F. Ramirez, and the third consists of seventy-one lithographic prints of the antiquities of Mexico, portraits of persons who have figured in its history, &c., with explanations to illustrate them, by D. Isidro R. Gondra, head of the Mexican Museum.

Historia de la Conquista de Méjico con un Bosquejo preliminar de la Civilizacion de los antiguos Mejicanos y la Vida de su Conquistador, Hernando Cortés, escrita en Inglés por Guillermo H. Prescott, Autor de la "Historia de Fernando e Isabel," traducida al Castellano por D. José Maria Gonzalez de la Vega, Segundo Fiscal del Tribunal Superior del Departamento de Mejico, y anotada por D. Lucas Alaman. 2 tom. 8vo grande. Méjico, imprenta de V. G. Torres, 1844.

I have imperfect notices of the following translations into Spanish : —

Historia de los Reyes Católicos por Guillermo Prescot (sic), traducida por D. Atiliano Calvo. Edicion ilustrada con buenos grabados que representan diversos pasages, vistas y retratos de los mas célebres personages. 1 tomo. 4to.

Historia del Descubrimiento y Conquista del Perú, con Observaciones preliminares sobre la Civilizacion de los Incas. 2 tom. 8vo. Madrid.

There is also a translation of the "History of Philip the Second," but it is, perhaps, not yet all published.

II. French.

Histoire du Règne de Ferdinand et d'Isabelle, traduite de l'Anglais de Guillaume H. Prescott, par J. Renson et P. Ithier. 4 vol. 8vo. Paris et Bruxelles, Didot, 1860, 1861.

Histoire de la Conquête du Méxique, avec un tableau préliminaire de l'ancienne Civilisation Méxicaine, et la Vie de Fernand Cortés, par William H. Prescott, publiée en Français par Amédée Pichot. 3 vol. 8vo. Paris, F. Didot, 1846.

Histoire de la Conquête du Pérou, précédée d'un Tableau de la Civilisation des Incas, par W. H. Prescott, traduite de l'Anglais par H. Poret. 3 vol. 8vo. Paris, F. Didot, 1860.

Histoire du Règne de Philippe Second, par Guillaume H. Prescott, traduite de l'Anglais par G. Renson et P. Ithier. Tomes I. et II. Paris, F. Didot, 1860.

Don Carlos, sa Vie et sa Mort, par W. H. Prescott, traduite de l'Anglais par G. Renson. 8vo. Bruxelles, Van Meenen et Cie, 1860.

III. Italian.

Storia del Regno di Ferdinando e Isabella, Sovrani Cattolici di Spagna, di H. Prescott (sic), recato per prima volta in Italiano da Ascanio Tempestini. 3 tom. 8vo. Firenze, per V. Batelli e Compagni, 1847, 1848.

A notice of the original work by the Marquis Gino Capponi, who took much interest in having it translated, may be found in the "Archivio Storico Italiano," Tom. II., 1845 ; Appendice, p. 606.

A portion of the "History of the Conquest of Peru" was translated into Italian and published at Florence in 1855 and 1856, in two parts, but it was made from the Spanish version and not from the original English. The first is entitled, "Compendio dello Notizie generali sul Perù avanti la Conquista, ec., tratto dalla Storia di Guglielmo Prescott, e recato in Italiano da C[esare] M[agherini]." 8vo. Firenze, Tipografia Galileiana, 1855. The other part is entitled, "Scoperta e Conquista del Perù, Storia di Guglielmo Prescott, tradotta da C[esare] M[agherini]." 8vo. Firenze, Tipografia Galileiana, 1856. This last translation stops at the year 1551, the year of Gonzalvo Pizarro's death.

IV. German.

Geschichte der Regierung Ferdinand's und Isabella's der Katholischen von Spanien. Von William H. Prescott. Aus dem Englischen übersetzt [von H. Eberty]. 2 Bände. 8vo. Leipzig, Brockhaus, 1842.

Geschichte der Eroberung von Mexico, mit einer einleitenden Uebersicht des frühere mexicanischen Bildungszustandes und dem Leben des Eroberers, Hernando Cortez. Von William H. Prescott. Aus dem Englischen übersetzt [von H. Eberty]. 2 Bände. 8vo. Leipzig, Brockhaus, 1845.

Geschichte der Eroberung von Peru, mit einer einleitenden Uebersicht des Bildungszustandes unter den Inkas. Von William H. Prescott. Aus dem Englischen übersetzt [Von H. Eberty]. 2 Bände. 8vo. Leipzig, Brockhaus, 1848.

Geschichte Philipp's des Zweiten, von William H. Prescott. Deutsch von Joh. Scherr. 8vo. Theil I. – III. Leipzig, O. Wigand, 1855, sqq.

Das Klosterleben Carl's des Fünften, von W. H. Prescott. Aus dem Englischen von Julius Seybel. 8vo. Leipzig, Lorck, 1857.

.This last constitutes the twenty-third volume of Lorck's "Conversations- und Reise-Bibliothek."

V. Dutch.

Zeden, Gewoonten en Regeringsvorm in Peru vóór de Komst der Spanjaarden, geschetst door W. H. Prescott, uit het Engelsch vertaald door Mr. G. Mees, Az. 8vo. pp. 162. Amsterdam, P. Kraij, Junior, 1849.

This is a translation of the first book of the "History of the Conquest of Peru," omitting a considerable number of the notes.

All the historical works of Mr. Prescott, in the original English, have been reprinted both in Paris and in Leipzig; and, I believe, other translations have been made of some of them, notices of which I have failed to obtain. The "History of Ferdinand and Isabella" is said to have appeared in Dutch and Russian, but I have no distinct account of either.

APPENDIX F.

CONVERSATION OF MR. PRESCOTT SHORTLY BEFORE HIS DEATH.

THE last printed notice of Mr. Prescott and of his conversation is a very interesting one, by the Reverend William H. Milburn, of New York, the blind, or nearly blind, friend of whom Mr. Prescott speaks more than once in his letters. From their common misfortune they had a strong sympathy with each other; and Mr. Milburn, having chanced to visit the historian the evening but one before the day of his death, wrote an account of his interview immediately afterwards to the Messrs. Harpers for their " Weekly," February 12th, 1859.

" On the evening in question," says Mr. Milburn, " Wednesday, January 26th, Mr. Prescott entered the library with a slower and heavier step than when I had been in the habit of seeing him years before; but his manner had the same unaffected simplicity and cordial warmth. Whether a stranger would have perceived it, I cannot say; but my ear, sharpened by necessity, at once detected the work of paralysis in an occasional thickening of the speech, — I mean, a difficulty in perfect articulation now and then Among his very first inquiries was a particular one concerning the members of your own firm, — your health, the state and prospects of your business, &c., manifesting the deepest interest; adding the remark that, through all the years of his business and personal connection with your firm, he had never experienced anything but the greatest kindness and consideration at your hands; that his enjoyment of your success was undiminished; and that he felt particularly grateful for the kindly mention which had been made of his personal affliction last year in your paper, and for the handsome notice of the third volume of his ' Philip the Second' in the current number of your ' Magazine.'

" He then proceeded to a mention of various mutual friends that had passed away since our last meeting, especially of the Hon. Abbott Lawrence and Mr. Francis C. Gray, at whose dinner-tables we had often met; and then of some of his surviving friends, especially of Mr. Ticknor, who, he said, had shortened and brightened what, but for him, must have been many a sad and weary hour; and of Mr. Agassiz, concerning whose Museum he expressed the liveliest interest. He remarked that the eyes of the latter had suffered greatly from his work, and that he would be sadly balked in his prospects, but that he was able to find relief in manifold manipulating labors. This led him naturally to speak of his own and my infirmity, which were about equal in degree, and of the different lives we had led; — his, of retired study; mine, of travel and active toil.

" He added : ' I suppose that Ticknor will never write another book;

19 *

but he has been doing perhaps better for the community and posterity by devoting himself for several years to the interests of the Boston City Library, which may be taken in good part as his work, — and a more valuable contribution to the good of the people has seldom been made. It is a rare thing for such an institution to get a man so qualified by taste, knowledge, and accomplishment to look after its interests with such energy and patience.'

"Of Mr. Gray he observed : 'Poor Gray ! I think he was the most remarkable man I ever knew for variety and fulness of information, and a perfect command of it. He was a walking Encyclopædia. I have seen many men who had excellent memories, provided you would let them turn to their libraries to get the information you wanted ; but, no matter on what subject you spoke to him, his knowledge was at his fingers'-ends, and entirely at your service.'

"He then led the conversation to his English friends, to some of whom he had given me letters on my recent visit to that country. He first spoke of Lady Lyell, the wife of the celebrated geologist. 'She is one of the most charming people I have ever seen,' he said. 'When she married Sir Charles, she knew nothing of geology ; but, finding that her life was to be passed among stones, she set herself to work to make friends of them, and has done so to perfection. She is in thorough sympathy with all her husband's researches and works ; is the companion of his journeys ; oftentimes his amanuensis, for her hand has written several of his books ; and the delight and cheer of his whole life. Unaffected, genial, accomplished, and delightful to an almost unequalled extent, she is one of the rarest women you can meet. And,' he continued, 'you saw my friend Dean Milman. What an admirable person he is ! I had a letter from him only a day or two since, in which he gave an interesting account of the opening of his Cathedral, St. Paul's, to the popular Sunday-evening preachings, — a matter which has enlisted all the sympathies of the Bishop of London and of himself. He has been a prodigiously hard worker, and so has acquired a prematurely old look. Accomplished as historian, divine, poet, and man of letters, he is at the same time among the most agreeable and finished men of society I saw in England.'

"'Did you see Dean Trench ?' he proceeded. Upon my replying in the affirmative, he added : 'I am sorry never to have seen him ; I have heard such pleasant things concerning him. He did me the favor some time since to send me his "Calderon," which I enjoyed greatly.' Replying in the negative to my inquiry as to whether he had read the Dean's books on 'Words,' &c., he said, 'They shall be the very next books I read.'

"'England 's a glorious country,' he said, ' is n't it ? What a hearty and noble people they are, and how an American's heart warms toward them after he has been there once, and found them out in their hospitable homes !'

"I said : 'Mr. Prescott, are n't you coming to New York ? We should all be very glad to see you there.' 'No,' he replied, 'I suppose that the days of my long journeys are over. I must content myself, like Horace, with my three houses. You know I go at the commencement of summer to my cottage by the seaside at Lynn Beach, and in autumn to my patrimonial acres at Pepperell, which have been in our family for two hundred years, to sit under the old trees I sat under when a boy; and then, with winter, come to town to hibernate in this house.   This is the only travelling, I suppose, that I shall do until I go to my long home.   Do you remember the delightful summer you spent with us at Lynn, two or three years ago?   I wish you would come and repeat it next summer.'

"In another part of the conversation he said: 'Those men with eyes have us at a serious disadvantage, have n't they?   While they run, we can only limp.   But I have nothing to complain of, nor have you; Providence has singularly taken care of us both, and, by compensation, keeps the balance even.'

" He then spoke with entire calmness of the shock which his system had received from his first stroke of apoplexy last year; said that it had weakened him a good deal; but he was very grateful that he was able to take exercise, although confined to a spare diet, and not allowed to touch meat or anything of a stimulative kind; and managed, moreover, to keep up his literary labors.   'I have always made my literary pursuits,' he said, ' a pleasure rather than a toil; and hope to do so with the remainder of " Philip," as I am yet able to work two or three, and sometimes more, hours a day.'   He stated that his eye had suffered considerably from the blow, and, while we talked, he found it necessary to shade his face.   In the course of the conversation we were joined by the ladies of the family, Mrs. Prescott, her sister, his daughter, and daughter-in-law.   He then spoke in glowing and grateful terms, as I alluded to the interest taken in his health throughout the country, of the kindness which he had invariably experienced at the hands of his countrymen.   ' I can never,' he said, ' be sufficiently grateful for the tokens of esteem, regard, and affection, which I have had from them through all the years of my literary career.   True, it makes me feel like an old man to see my fifteen volumes upon the shelf, but my heart is as young as it ever was to enjoy the love which the country has ever shown me.'   When I said it was a cheering thing for a man to know he had given so much happiness as he had done by his books, he said that it was his own truest happiness to trust that he had been able to confer it.   He said he hoped to live to finish ' Philip,' which was now three fifths done.   As I bade him good by, I said, 'God bless you, Mr. Prescott; I know I breathe the prayer of the country when I say, May your life be spared for many years, to add volume after volume to the fifteen.'   He rejoined, ' My greatest delight is the love of my friends and their appreciation of my labors.'

" Little did I think that the hand which so warmly grasped mine as he led me down the stairs would, ere eight and forty hours were past, be cold and stiff in death.   Peace to the memory of one of the sweetest and noblest men that ever lived!

" Yours very truly,

" WILLIAM H. MILBURN."

APPENDIX G.

ON HIS DEATH.

SOON after Mr. Prescott's death I received many notes and letters, expressive of affection and admiration for him. From among them I select the following.

The first is by Mr. George Lunt, who was his secretary in 1825-6, and knew him well. See *ante*, p. 78.

ON A LATE LOSS.

IMITATION OF HORACE, LIB. I. OD. XXIV.

Quis desiderio sit pudor, &c.

What time can bring relief—
What blame reprove our grief?
    The well-beloved lies low!
The funeral strains prolong,
O Muse of tragic song,
    With liquid voice and harp attuned to woe!

Does, then, perpetual sleep
Hold him? and bid us weep
    In vain to seek through earth
For honor so unstained,
Such manly truth maintained,
    Such glory won and worn by modest worth?

By all the good deplored,
No tears sincerer poured,
    Than fell thine own, O friend!
Yet pious thou in vain,
Claiming for earth again
    Gifts, which kind Heaven on no such terms will lend.

No fond desires avail,
Friendship's deep want must fail,
    Even love's devout demand;
Inexorable Death,
Pledges of deathless faith,
    Keeps souls once gathered to the shadowy land.

And oftenest to that bourne
They pass, nor more return,—
    The best we miss the most;
Hard seems the stroke of fate,
But Heaven bids us wait,
    And there, at last, rejoin the loved, the lost.

Another short poem came anonymously to my door, but was afterwards ascertained to have been written by the Rev. George Richards, then a clergyman of Boston. It was founded upon some remarks made by me at the meeting of the Historical Society, February 1st, on the occasion of Mr. Prescott's death, concerning his wish, that, previous to their final deposit in the house appointed for all living, his remains might rest for a time in his library, under the shadow, as it were, of the books he had so much loved; the remarks being nearly the same with those about the same circumstance in the account given, at page 414, of his last days and burial.

Mr. Richards entitled his poem

THE HISTORIAN IN HIS LIBRARY.

His wish fulfilled! 'T is done, as he had said:
Borne sadly back, with slow and reverent tread; —
Now closeted, — the dead with kindred dead.

Ye need not listen, — no low-whispered word
From that hushed conclave will be overheard;
Nor start, — as if the shrouded sleeper stirred.

He rests, where he hath toiled: the busy pen
Misses the busier brain; nor plods, as when
It traced the lore of that far-searching ken.

He lies amid his peers; the storied great
Look down upon him, here reclined in state, —
As mute as they who speechless round him wait.

His task is done; his working-day is o'er;
The morning larum wakens him no more, —
Unheard its summons, on that silent shore.

The pomp of Kings, the Incas' faded pride,
The freighted bark, the lonely ocean wide,
Dread war, glad peace, no more his thoughts divide.

He lies, like warrior, after set of sun,
Stretched on the plain where his great deeds were done,
Where he the green, immortal garland won.

Round him the relics of the hard-fought field,
Helmet and lance and unavailing shield,
And well-proved blade he never more shall wield.

So leave him, for a while, in that still room,
His books among; — its sober, twilight gloom
Fit prelude to the stiller, darker tomb.

The last of these tokens that I shall cite is from one of the most faithful and valued of his English friends. It is

FROM DEAN MILMAN.

DEANERY, ST. PAUL'S, February 19th, [1859].

MY DEAR MR. TICKNOR,

I must unburden myself to some one of the profound sorrow which I (I should have written we) feel for our irreparable loss. I have had the happiness to form and retain the friendship of many excellent men; no one has ever, considering the short personal intercourse which I enjoyed with him, and our but occasional correspondence, wakened such strong and lasting attachment. He found his way at once to my heart, and has there remained, and ever will remain, during the brief period to which I can now look forward, as an object of the warmest esteem and affection. I think I should have loved the man if I had only known him as an author; his personal society only showed his cordial, liberal, gentle character in a more distinct and intimate form. That which was admiration became love. There is here but one feeling, among those who had not the good fortune to know him, as among those who knew him best, — deep regret for a man who did honor to the literature of our common language, and whose writings, from their intrinsic charm and excellence, were most popular, without any art or attempt to win popularity.

The suddenness of the blow aggravates its heaviness. I had written to him but a few weeks ago, (I doubt not that he received my letter,) expressing the common admiration with which his last volume was received here by all whose opinion he and his most discerning friends would think of the highest value. In one respect he has ended well, for he never surpassed passages in the last volume; but it is sad to think that he has ended, and left his work incomplete. I can hardly hope that much can be left finished by his hand; if anything is left, I trust it will pass into the hand of him best qualified to shape and mould it into form, *yourself.* As I feel that I can express our sorrows to no one so fitly as to you, so there is no one to whom the sacred memory of our friend can be intrusted with equal confidence. From all that I have heard, his end (premature as our affection cannot but think it) was painless and peaceful; and if — as surely we may trust — the possession and the devotion of such admirable gifts to their best uses, — the promotion of knowledge, humanity, charity, in its widest sense; if a life, I fully believe, perfectly blameless, the discharge of all domestic duties so as to secure the tenderest attachment of all around; if a calm, quiet, gentle, tolerant faith will justify — as no doubt they may — our earnest hopes; it is that better *peace* which has no end.

Both Mrs. Milman and I trust you will undertake the friendly office of communicating our common sorrow to those whose sorrow must be more pungent than ours, though, I venture to say, not more sincere. We shall always think with warm interest of all those who bear the honored name of Prescott, or were connected by ties of kindred or affection with him. And permit me to add to yourself our kindest condolence, our best wishes, and our hopes that we may see you again, and soon, in Europe.

Believe me, my dear Mr. Ticknor,

Ever your sincere friend,

H. H. MILMAN.

INDEX.

INDEX.

20

Cambridge : Stereotyped and Printed by Welch, Bigelow, & Co.

CPSIA information can be obtained
at www.ICGtesting.com
Printed in the USA
BVHW081556120819
555665BV00013B/1097/P